LORDS OF THE LAND

AF775477

OXFORD STUDIES IN MODERN LEGAL HISTORY

The series aims to publish monographs of high quality and originality on history covering the period 1750 onwards.

Lords of The Land

Indigenous Property Rights and The Jurisprudence of Empire

MARK HICKFORD DPhil (Oxon)
2008 New Zealand Law Foundation International Research Fellow

OXFORD
UNIVERSITY PRESS

OXFORD
UNIVERSITY PRESS

Great Clarendon Street, Oxford OX2 6DP

Oxford University Press is a department of the University of Oxford.
It furthers the University's objective of excellence in research, scholarship,
and education by publishing worldwide in

Oxford New York

Auckland Cape Town Dar es Salaam Hong Kong Karachi
Kuala Lumpur Madrid Melbourne Mexico City Nairobi
New Delhi Shanghai Taipei Toronto

With offices in

Argentina Austria Brazil Chile Czech Republic France Greece
Guatemala Hungary Italy Japan Poland Portugal Singapore
South Korea Switzerland Thailand Turkey Ukraine Vietnam

Oxford is a registered trade mark of Oxford University Press
in the UK and in certain other countries

Published in the United States
by Oxford University Press Inc., New York

© Mark Hickford, 2011

The moral rights of the author have been asserted
Database right Oxford University Press (maker)

Crown copyright material is reproduced under class Licence Number C01P0000148
with the permission of OPSI and the Queen's Printer for Scotland

Contains public sector information licensed under the Open Government Licence v1.0
(http://www.nationalarchives.gov.uk/doc/open-government-licence/open-government-licence.htm)

Crown Copyright material reproduced with the permission of the Controller, HMSO
(under the terms of the Click Use licence)

First published 2011

All rights reserved. No part of this publication may be reproduced,
stored in a retrieval system, or transmitted, in any form or by any means,
without the prior permission in writing of Oxford University Press,
or as expressly permitted by law, or under terms agreed with the appropriate
reprographics rights organization. Enquiries concerning reproduction
outside the scope of the above should be sent to the Rights Department,
Oxford University Press, at the address above

You must not circulate this book in any other binding or cover
and you must impose the same condition on any acquirer

British Library Cataloguing in Publication Data
Data available

Library of Congress Cataloging in Publication Data
Library of Congress Control Number: 2011939972

Typeset by Newgen Imaging Systems (P) Ltd, Chennai, India

ISBN 978–0–19–956865–9

10 9 8 7 6 5 4 3 2 1

For Victoria and Alexandra and
In memory of Tiffany Hickford (1972–1997) and Raymond Griffin (1930–1996)

Preface and Acknowledgements

This work would not have been possible without the generous support of the Trustees of the New Zealand Law Foundation in selecting me as the 2008 New Zealand Law Foundation International Research Fellow. Without that backing, I would not have had the opportunity to undertake additional research in the United Kingdom, Australia, and New Zealand or to obtain leave for sustained periods of writing. For this, I am indebted to the support of Sir Geoffrey Palmer and Dame Sian Elias, Dr David Collins QC, Dr Matthew Palmer, Professor Geoffrey McLay and Associate Professor Shaunnagh Dorsett, each of whom supported me in applying for the fellowship in the first place and have provided encouragement, support, and advice ever since. At the Foundation, Lynda Hagen and Dianne Gallagher supplied invaluable patience and guidance. I owe an enduring debt to three of my teachers at undergraduate level, Andrew Sharp, Keith Sorrenson, and David Williams, and their subsequent influence on my thinking ever since, as I have revisited their work with a new appreciation and for fresh insights. Their ongoing counsel has proved invaluable. Throughout the doctoral thesis period and since then, my Oxford dissertation supervisor, John Darwin, and Paul McHugh, Andrew Sharp, and JGA Pocock, have always supplied much appreciated wise counsel, collegial company and inspiration. Without the urging and encouragement of John Darwin and Bain Attwood through discussions and correspondence, I would never have considered writing this book let alone ventured it given the pressures of professional legal practice and civil service. My warmest thanks are owed to John Darwin both as the supervisor of my doctoral dissertation at Oxford, and for his persistent and generous support since then. I am also especially indebted to the warm support of the late AWB Simpson—justly characterized in the *Guardian* as 'one of the greatest academic lawyers of his generation in the fields of legal history, legal philosophy and—more recently—human rights', who welcomed this project to the *Oxford Studies in Modern Legal History* stable. His kind words in January 2008 set this project moving in earnest. Professor ATH Smith and Dean Knight have proved wonderful hosts at the Faculty of Law at Victoria University of Wellington during my periods of annual leave from the Crown Law Office. I am grateful for the visiting positions afforded me at Nuffield College at the University of Oxford (where I was hosted by John Darwin) and at the Centre for Public Law at Victoria University of Wellington in 2009 and 2010. These positions allowed me to focus on writing and researching major parts of the book.

Throughout the past decade, I have benefited greatly from the ongoing assistance and advice of Jon Wilson, Zoë Laidlaw, Damon Salesa, Simon Potter, Miranda Johnson, Bernard Cadogan, Bain Attwood, Michael Belgrave, Richard Boast, Andrew Fitzmaurice, Peter Mandler, Ian Hunter, Duncan Ivison, John Hutton, Damen Ward, Lisa Ford, Saliha Belmessous, Christopher Hilliard, Lindsey Te Ata o Tu MacDonald, Lyndsay Head, Geoffrey McLay, Edwin Fletcher, Duncan Bell, Henry Weston, Brent Parker, Jacinta Ruru, Andrew Sartori, Donald Loveridge, Ashley Gould, and Fergus Sinclair. From 1996 until 1999, I was especially privileged to have the company of excellent young Oxford students of history and the broader humanities Jon Wilson,

Zoë Laidlaw, Damon Salesa, Simon Potter, Melanie Newton, Jeremy Osborn, Eric Jabbari, James Onley, Yoav Alon, Troy Bickham, Helen Tilley, Ruth Watson, David Odo, and Andrew Fairweather-Tall: the inspiration and insights they offered through conversation, support, friendship, and their own work find their echoes in this manuscript. During that time, I benefited considerably from the lectures and seminars of Richard Drayton and the late John Burrow. I was also extraordinarily fortunate to be amongst those students attending the Modern British History seminars at St John's College from 1996 until 1999 and to benefit from listening to the insights of Ross McKibbin, Peter Ghosh, and the late Colin Matthew (1941–1999) who showed me much generosity. As a Crown counsel, I have been honoured to serve several Attorneys-General (Margaret Wilson, Dr. Michael Cullen, David Parker, and Christopher Finlayson), all of whom have contributed to my reflections on the subjects addressed in this study. Megan Simpson, a key member of the *Recovering New Zealand Lost Cases* Project at Victoria University of Wellington, supplied copies of archival materials on the occasions when I could not reach the archives on account of other commitments. Furthermore, I wish to express my profound gratitude to Sir David Baragwanath, Michael Taggart, James Belich, Richard Hill, Richard Ekins, and Justice Joseph Williams. Paul McHugh, Duncan Ivison, Ian Hunter, Richard Boast, and Bernard Cadogan were good enough to do me the honour of reviewing chapters or sections of chapters and providing comments. I also thank JP Ferguson, Matanuku Mahuika, Tack Daniel, and Anaru Mill for invaluable advice on sources and approaches. I gratefully acknowledge the assistance of the Liverpool Record Office and the gracious permission of the Earl of Derby to allow access to the papers of his ancestor, the fourteenth Earl of Derby. The research was eased through the immense skills of staff at a range of libraries and archival collections throughout the United Kingdom and New Zealand and in Australia (Adelaide, Sydney, and Canberra). The myriad kindnesses of staff at the Bodleian Library, the British Library, the Liverpool Record Office, the National Archives at Kew, the Palace Green section at the University of Durham library, the University of Cambridge library, the University of Nottingham library, the Faculty of Modern History library at Oxford, and the college libraries at St Antony's and Nuffield will always be remembered. I am grateful to the Sir George Grey Special Collections at Auckland City Libraries and to my cousin Donald Kerr for his guidance in the late 1990s and ever since on matters to do with Grey. I wish to express my heartfelt gratitude to Gwen Booth, Natasha Flemming (née Knight), Zoë Organ, and the team at Oxford University Press. This book is for all my extended family, and to my parents and grandparents, although the manuscript is but a small recompense for all that they have done over these many years. For longer than I care to remember, my immediate family, Victoria and Alexandra, have lived with this project; their support and encouragement have been unstinting and beyond repayment.

The views expressed in this book are personal to the author and do not represent the views of the Department of the Prime Minister and Cabinet, the Crown Law Office, or the New Zealand government as a whole.

Wellington, March 2011

Table of Contents

List of Maps

List of Abbreviations

AHS	*Australian Historical Studies*
AIM	Auckland Institute and Museum
AJHR	*Appendix to the Journals of the House of Representatives*
ANZ(W)	Archives New Zealand, Wellington
APL	Auckland Public Library (Auckland City Libraries)
ATL	Alexander Turnbull Library, Wellington
BL	British Library
CLJ	*Cambridge Law Journal*
CO	Colonial Office
CUL	Cambridge University Library
DUL	Palace Green section, Durham University Library
EHR	*English Historical Review*
ER	English Reports
FO	Foreign Office records, National Archives, Kew, London
GBPP	*Great Britain Parliamentary Papers*
HJ	*Historical Journal*
HlDu	Hocken Library, Dunedin
HPD	*Hansard's Parliamentary Debates*
HSANZ	*Historical Studies, Australia and New Zealand*
JBS	*Journal of British Studies*
JICH	*Journal of Imperial and Commonwealth History*
JLH	*Journal of Legal History*
JMH	*Journal of Modern History*
JPS	*Journal of the Polynesian Society*
LRO	Liverpool Record Office
ML	Mitchell Library, State Library of New South Wales
MP	Melbourne Papers, Royal Archives, Bodleian Library microfilm
nd	not dated
NLA	National Library of Australia, Canberra
NS	New Series
NZCA	New Zealand Court of Appeal
NZJH	*New Zealand Journal of History*
NZPCC	*New Zealand Privy Council Cases*
NZULR	*New Zealand Universities Law Review*
OLC	Old Land Claims
OLJS	*Oxford Journal of Legal Studies*
OS	Old Series
RH	Rhodes House Library, University of Oxford
T	Treasury records, National Archives, Kew, London
TNA	The National Archives, Kew, London
TRHS	*Transactions of the Royal Historical Society*
USSC	United States Supreme Court
VUWLR	*Victoria University of Wellington Law Review*

Key Māori Terms

Long vowels are not marked in quotations unless indicated in the original text.

hapū pregnant; clan or descent group associated with a distinct territory and settlement or settlements, and which may take collective action for certain purposes.

iwi bone; largest scale descent group, ordinarily defined by descent from a named ancestor.

kāinga (comprising *kā* or burn together with *inga*, meaning a place where fires have burnt) village, community or settlement.

Kīngitanga king movement.

mana power, prestige, authority, spiritual force, or power, charismatic authority or presence. For fuller discussions of the dimensions of this concept refer to Joan Metge, *Tuamaka: The Challenge of Difference in Aotearoa New Zealand* (Auckland, 2010), 69–70, 126.

pā a fortified settlement, fortress, typically presenting with palisades and earthworks (including trenches and raised ramparts).

rangatira chieftain, usually of a *hapū*; member of the senior aristocratic descent lines of a *hapū* or *iwi*.

whānau be born; familial group of descendants stemming from a recent named ancestor or ancestors.

Table of Cases

Table of Legislation and Bills

Acts of Provincial Councils

Acts of the Parliament of New Zealand

New South Wales

Bengal

1

Preliminaries

OVERTURE—FORGING NATIVE TITLE IN AN EMPIRE OF VARIATIONS, 1837 TO 1862

Herman Merivale saw it—saw a central conundrum of native title in the pretensions of empire, one that still perplexes: the relationships between indigenous property rights and political autonomy and authority. Speaking as permanent under-secretary to the Colonial Office before a Select Committee of the House of Commons in 1857, Merivale, a former Drummond professor of political economy at Oxford (1837–1842) and fellow of Balliol College, characterized Māori as regarding themselves as 'politically lords of the land as well as landlords'.[1] Merivale saw this as a policy problem looking for policy solutions. Others did not see it as an issue, seeing native title, for all the suppositions of jurists and Māori politicians to the contrary, simply as a species of private property right denuded of any political or constitutional significance. Merivale thought that it had to be cleared away before the labours of 'real colonisation' could begin.[2] Colonies were places of becoming after all—places of transplantation where novel communities were established. A thick-set man, familiar with his James Cowles Prichard on the natural history of man and Thomas Pownall's eighteenth-century work on *The Administration of the Colonies*, along with François Guizot on civilization and Michel de Montaigne's *Essays*, Merivale penned lectures on colonies and political economy, as well as articles in *The Edinburgh Review* on topics as varied as Mexico and the western prairies, and Connop Thirwell's *History of Greece*.[3] James Stephen, his illustrious predecessor as permanent under-secretary, knew him by reputation as 'the lecturer on colonisation'.[4] Having been an academic and senior civil servant, Merivale was no *parvenu* on the status of indigenous populations in the 'wide circuit of [Britain's] colonial enterprise'.[5] He did not resolve the conundrum. He was always, as it were, snared in a process of working

[1] Merivale, 7 July 1857, *GBPP1857*, sess. 2, ix (HC171), 10. For convenience, this thesis employs the term 'Māori' although the indigenous population within New Zealand was ordinarily referred to as 'natives', 'aborigines', or 'New Zealanders' until the mid-nineteenth century. After 1840, the terms 'maori', 'mauri', or '*tangata Maori*', denoting 'usual' or 'ordinary people', increasingly materialized in the sources. 'Tangata Maori' appeared in Dieffenbach, *Travels in New Zealand*, II, 7; Prichard, *Researches into the Physical History of Man*, V, 124; Hursthouse, *New Zealand, or Zealandia, the Britain of the South*, I, 154. Intrusive Europeans were eventually characterized as 'pakea' or *pakeha*, usually treated as meaning 'strange' or 'extraordinary'.

[2] Merivale, *Lectures on Colonization and Colonies*, 2nd edn, 62 (note).

[3] For example, Merivale, 'Mexico and the Great Western Prairies', 157–92; Merivale, 'Thirwall's *History of Greece*', 83–108.

[4] Stephen to Earl Grey, 12 October 1847, Parris, *Constitutional Bureaucracy*, 74.

[5] '[W]ide circuit of [Britain's] colonial enterprise': Merivale, *Lectures on Colonization and Colonies*, 2nd edn, 492.

through and finding out. In this, he was not alone. The tricks of historical light should not obscure the point that this puzzle persisted. The underlying conundrum continues to this day, as the cases of New Zealand (regarding the foreshore and seabed question, for example), Canada, Australia, and the United States of America attest to.[6]

There is, then, a broader purpose to this study. To see and to examine native title in the jurisprudence of empire—to pursue and recover a history of indigenous property rights in the jurisprudence of empire—requires seeing such rights as not encased within the walls of transposed courts and legalistic genres. The histories of native title exemplify the themes of an empire of variations and 'negotiated empire'.[7] They also illuminate the workings of an imperial historical constitution *predominantly* political albeit juristic in parts. In other words, therefore, we see a pre-eminently political constitution. As a term, 'political constitution' resonated and was undoubtedly familiar to writers such as George Dyer (1817) and the 'liberal Anglican' historian, Thomas Arnold (1830).[8] 'When we contemplate a political constitution, we should have in view, not a baseless fabric, floating only in the imagination of a poet, but a real structure to be brought into use and practice; imperfect, indeed, it may be, yet, in the main, durable; and, though ruinous in part, yet habitable by man'[9] As used in this study, political constitutionalism represents a flexible way of framing the distribution of political and legal authority within a polity, as well as a culture and ways of resolving disagreements about what is to be done (and sometimes but not necessarily why), which may be addressed through political or juridical contests or both.[10] To use John Griffith's aphorism, minted when analysing a different context, the constitutional setting was an ongoing process without end and a pre-eminently political one where '[e]verything that happens is constitutional [and] if nothing happened that would be constitutional also'.[11] Where governmental conduct was concerned, such constitutionalism did not require complete pre-act authorization in the form of posited law although, undoubtedly, areas of statute law and case law gave authority to certain acts.[12]

[6] See also Webber, 'Beyond Regret: *Mabo*'s Implications for Australian Constitutionalism', in Ivison, Patton, and Saunders (eds), *Political Theory and the Rights of Indigenous Peoples*, 63: Webber spoke of the recognition of indigenous title as necessarily involving the acceptance, if only provisional, of a measure of normative or political autonomy. For cautions expressed regarding Webber's approach in a contemporary context, see Rowse, 'The National Emergency and Indigenous Jurisdictions', in Altman and Hinkson (eds), *Coercive Reconciliation: Stabilise, Normalise, Exit Aboriginal Australia*, 50–4. On the foreshore and seabed question and issues of *mana* in New Zealand, see Ministerial Review of the Foreshore and Seabed Act 2004, *Pākia ki Uta, Pākia ki Tai*, I, 96–8. For a consideration of the interlocking complexities of autonomy and territory insofar as the Ngāi Tūhoe of Te Urewera were concerned, see Binney, *Encircled Lands*. For a recent presentation of some Māori opinion on constitutionalism in the twenty-first century, see Mulholland and Tawhai (eds), *Weeping Waters*.

[7] On 'negotiated empire', see Travers, *Ideology and Empire in Eighteenth-Century India*, 41; Marshall, *The Making and Unmaking of Empires*, 272; Daniels and Kennedy (eds), *Negotiated Empires*.

[8] Dyer, *Four Letters on the English Constitution*, 1, 3, 14, 31; Arnold, 'On the Social Progress of States', in *The Miscellaneous Works of Thomas Arnold DD*, 98, 100.

[9] Dyer, *Four Letters on the English Constitution*, 13.

[10] This discussion is developed further below.

[11] Griffith, 'The Political Constitution', 19.

[12] Here I am drawing a distinction between political constitutionalism and a particular interpretation of legal constitutionalism which holds that all governmental action must be (or *ought* to be) pre-authorized by positive law.

Here, in focusing on the dynamism of the practical life of constitutionalism, and what its histories illuminate, the notion of a 'historical constitution' is used differently from the sense in which JWF Allison deploys it.[13] It is a product of the often anonymous activity of many folk—sometimes creative, sometimes noisome, sometimes conducted in hushed quietude, often discordant and contested. As with Charles Darwin's 'myriads of tiny architects' crafting coral reefs and the monument of Lagoon Island, the jurisprudence of empire was worked out through the living practices of politics and the mustering and use of intellectual sources in these practices, including those sources deploying legalistic ways of seeing and speaking, more than the courts.[14] As Joshua Getzler warns, 'to dig deeply into the contemporary micro-text of *leading cases* risks allowing the litigation history, much of which is contingent or accidental, to determine which areas of fact are indeed relevant for historians later to examine'.[15] Like glacial moraines, the printed words of books shared on the law of nations between distant parts of empires, and the reports of cases in the courts, have tended to outlast the memories of the 'wordy warfare' of pamphlets, fraught political negotiations, and debates.[16] They confer an impression of broad, travelling uniformity.

Yet these juristic texts and reports of court decisions are entangled with a host of other sources in the inherently fluid processes of politics. As a result, the peculiar practices of politics in a particular colony and those of Britain touching on that colony yielded a much less uniform and much more parochial or provincial set of understandings. While New Zealand may be used as an illustrative pivot for this study, that is not to suggest that it is a mastering model or precedent.[17] One begins to see an empire of variations with regional or even more localized understandings marking the politics of trans-oceanic empire tying Britain to particular colonies in certain ways. We also see change over time. In this sense, South Australia, New South Wales, Upper Canada, British Columbia, and New Zealand gave rise to peculiar, parochial sets of problems and solutions at different points in time. The striking histories of colonial New Zealand allow us to examine and reflect on these larger themes. Through political and juristic contestation over time, we may discern a thickening appreciation of 'native title'—a building of detail and content—and its place within the jurisprudence of empire and imperial constitutionalism.

Colonial New Zealand may be seen as a series of enclave-like, cross-cultural meeting places between transposed peoples and voyaging intellectual sources (including legalistic genres) and Māori sources and ways of seeing. In complex inter-cultural negotiations, these intersecting and entwining sources were not completely communicable or translatable to the others not familiar with such exogenous sources. But practical ways of getting things done between and amongst indigenes and settlers allowed *modus vivendi* to emerge and local understandings and applications of imported sources to

[13] Allison, *The English Historical Constitution*.

[14] Charles Darwin, 12 April 1836: Keynes (ed), *Charles Darwin's Beagle Diary*, 418. For Darwin and constitutionalism as presented by William Stubbs, see Burrow, *A History of Histories*, 410.

[15] Getzler, review: 'Michael Taggart, *Private Property and Abuse of Rights in Victorian England*', 820–1 (emphasis added).

[16] The phrase 'wordy warfare' is Carleton's in 'New Zealand', 459.

[17] The term 'New Zealand', although deployed here for convenience, is itself a construction and is not an especially stable concept (as those engaged in Crown constitutional practice appreciate, the legal definition alone has proved ambulatory and contested over time, with differing legal consequences). See Ballantyne, 'On Place, Space and Mobility in Nineteenth-Century New Zealand', 55–7.

be inflected by practices on the ground. Evidently, other factors were at play, including fluid intra-Māori and intra-European politics, each playing to different constituencies and agendas, each exhibiting their own conditions and politics of interiority and exteriority—internal and external hinges or what, in other contexts, Pocock refers to as an *aussenpolitik* (histories of relations with others) as opposed to an *innenpolitik* (histories of self-formation).[18] It is in the mingling of these concrete phenomena of living disputes and political practices that we see the production of native title—native title in the making. Such an approach allows one to move beyond the 'pathologies of litigation'.[19] I argue that this approach allows us to see areas of doctrinal consensus much more clearly along with areas of doctrinal disquiet, discomfort, or disagreement. How juristic texts and legal-political conceptions of indigenous communities fared in often fraught conversation in distinct colonial off-shoots (such as New Zealand as opposed to its Australian neighbours or Upper Canada) and the metropolitan debate connected to them shows that the processes and answers given were not necessarily communicated or acted upon in other colonies. Charting any such trans-colonial connections must be undertaken with care and be sensitive to dynamism over time. Native title was lived and thought about in empire's intimate, local and regional circuits—their parochial peculiarities specific to time and space while informed by exogenous sources strained from Europe and larger trans-oceanic networks, including North America.

In what follows, 'native title'—a compendious phrase—is used to denote a range of relations of power and authority in relation to land and other natural resources that Māori were considered to have and which were referred to variously as 'title to the soil' (occurring in 1839, for instance), 'territorial rights of the natives' (1841), 'native title',[20] 'native rights to land', 'aboriginal title', 'native territorial title', and 'occupating [*sic*] title in commonage' (1844). In this book, acknowledging the cautions of Ballara and Salesa, 'Māori' is used for reasons of convenience as a term for the indigenous peoples of New Zealand.[21] As is better appreciated through the researches of Ballara and others, the principal political units of indigenous communities throughout the archipelago called New Zealand were *hapū*, translated loosely as clans or sub-tribes. When used here, 'Māori' is not intended as an unproblematic a-historical or a trans-historical concept. Following 1840 in particular, with Britain asserting sovereignty in New Zealand, the term 'Maori' as a name for the indigenous populations of those islands, increasingly appeared in a variety of official sources, notably from the 1850s.

[18] Pocock, *Political Thought and History*, 242.

[19] To adapt the phrase of Rawlings, 'Distinction and Diversity; Law and the LSE', in Rawlings (ed), *Law, Society and Economy*, 20–1.

[20] 'Native title' was used early on to describe the property rights in land of Māori *qua* indigenes. Illustrations include Colonial land and emigration, 'General report of the Colonial Land and Emigration Commissioners', 1842, *GBPP1842* (567), 10: 'Another association also in this country, who, before New Zealand became a colony, had bought land there under a *native title*, and having resold a portion of it, had engaged to the purchasers to expend a certain amount of the money received in sending out labourers' (emphasis added). We also find references to 'native title' in the context of the Cape Colony in correspondence of the third Earl Grey as Secretary of State for Colonies: Earl Grey to Sir Henry Smith, 21 June 1848, 'Cape of Good Hope. Correspondence with the Governor of the Cape of Good Hope, relative to the state of the Kafir tribes on the eastern frontier of the colony. (In continuation of the papers presented February 1847)', *GBPP1847–1848* [912] [969], 68.

[21] Ballara, *Iwi*, 42; Salesa, *Racial Crossings*, 21–5.

These references increased in volume at certain points especially in 1844 if one counts parliamentary papers within the United Kingdom alone.[22] More commonly, we find references to 'aborigines', 'natives', or 'New Zealanders'.[23]

Throughout this study New Zealand is treated as a convenient pivot and staging post for analysing the trans-oceanic politics of empire in the mid-nineteenth century because it also engages the metropolitan heart of empire, the United Kingdom. It provides a particular way for looking into at a certain time what John Darwin characterizes as a 'British world-system',[24] a system marked not only by shared themes but also by an untidy riot of regional variations. If comparative approaches to Britain's 'trans-marine empire' convey anything, they suggest a messily contingent, occasionally haphazard empire of variations throughout the mid-nineteenth century rather than generic models of uniformity.[25] New Zealand, as a place for peopling by means of British settlements, engaged questions concerning the occupation of territorial space by incremental settlement and indigenous communities and how pluralistic political and legal authority was configured relative to territorial space. It did so at a time when a number of territories were brought within the British world-system—South Australia in 1836; the Sind and Natal in 1843; and the Orange River Sovereignty in 1848. As a settlement colony, like South Australia—*colonia* in the proper sense[26]—New Zealand posed messy puzzles as to how to manage the pressures of ambulatory settlement and relations between the colonial occupation of space and pre-existing populations (if at all). The British world-system furnished neither easy nor identical answers. The period from 1837 until 1862 will be focused on. Concrete proposals to settle New Zealand from Britain in a systematic way emerged in 1837. It also coincides with the release of the report of the House of Commons Select Committee on aborigines.[27] The end date of 1862 is chosen because the first Native Lands Act was enacted in that year, setting out a statutory scheme for addressing customary territorial rights in New Zealand. Events beyond that year will be alighted on—for example, 1865, when the Native

[22] Although a crude form of illustrative accounting, periods of intensity in the official published record coincided with periods of parliamentary deliberation. For instance, there were 57 references in the evidence before the House of Commons Select Committee on New Zealand in 1844, including the following: Thomas McDonnell, 13 May 1844, 'Report from the Select Committee on New Zealand; together with the minutes of evidence, appendix, and index', *GBPP1844* (556), 8; Shortland to Stanley, 17 April 1843, ibid, 54. There were fewer references in other sets of papers up to the end of the decade. In 'New Zealand. Further papers relative to the affairs of New Zealand. (In continuation of papers presented 10th April 1854)', *GBPP1860* [2719], we see 209 references in 488 pages and in 'Papers relating to the recent disturbances in New Zealand', *GBPP1862* [2798], there were 505 references amongst 492 pages.

[23] Salesa, *Racial Crossings*, 21.

[24] Darwin, *The Empire Project*, 1–12.

[25] For 'trans-marine empire', see Merivale, 'The Colonial Question in 1870', 153. For this reason, amongst others (to be addressed in the following chapters), caution must be expressed about any overarching thesis of 'territorial sovereignty' as the shift in orientation that occurred throughout Britain's colonial empire, as if these 'models' were transposed effortlessly or seemingly converged in such a way (see Ford, *Settler Sovereignty*).

[26] Lewis, *An Essay on the Government of Dependencies*, 170: 'A *colony* properly denotes a body of persons belonging to one country and political community, which, having abandoned that country and political community, form a new and separate society, independent or dependent, in some district which is nearly or wholly uninhabited, or from which they expel the ancient inhabitants' (emphasis in original).

[27] 'Report from the Select Committee on Aborigines (British Settlements)', *GBPP1837* (425).

Rights Act was passed. That colonial legislation purported to confirm Māori as entitled to the rights and privileges of natural-born British subjects. It also directed that in 'any action in which the title to or any interest in [land clothed with native title]...any issue... whether they be issues of fact or of Maori Custom or Usage shall be tried in the Native Lands Court'.[28] But 1862 affords us a convenient point at which to terminate our narrative, as it was also the year when a commitment to leave New Zealand responsible for the conduct of its native affairs was embedded. This decision was rooted both in material concerns—money and military power—and in intellectual concerns—how to incentivize colonial responsibility for decisions and how to recalibrate constitutional patterns of authority within an empire.

CHAPTER OUTLINE

This book explores the history of native title as a phenomenon of the law and politics of trans-oceanic empire in and through time, and as a merchant of change in law and politics during a time of fraught anxieties and considerable transition, traversing what David Eastwood has suggestively characterized as an 'age of uncertainty'.[29] In doing so, it will serve to reveal three key interacting characteristics of native title in mid-nineteenth-century British legal and political histories, which are set out briefly below in this overture to the introductory section. Later in this introduction, I will raise points, to be explained in detail throughout the following chapters, relating to the way in which native title was treated as a contestable concept (gathered under the phrase of the 'politics of negotiability') and what native title seen in such a light may tell us about imperial constitutionalism and Māori autonomy. I propose to give a broad sweep of the range of issues to be traversed and to set out a number of the filters applied.[30]

Chapter Two will set out the political and intellectual milieu swirling through British policy debates regarding indigenous peoples' rights to property in the 1830s and early 1840s. It will explore the influences of *ius gentium* (the law of nations)[31] and the resilience of tropes of stadial history (a theory of history divided into stages) and how these fed into conceptions of indigenous property rights and claims together with their place in the narratives of civilization and progress (or regression). The transposition of the logics of stadialism to New Zealand settings inflected stadial themes in interesting ways. It is salutary to recall Pocock's observation that 'the stadial sequences shaped in Europe—were designed to meet European (including British) needs and dealt with European phenomena'.[32] As I have argued elsewhere, there was no simple translation of stadialism

[28] Native Rights Act, 26 September 1865, 29 Vict 11.

[29] Eastwood, 'The Age of Uncertainty', 91–114.

[30] The term 'filter' is taken from Bernard Porter, 'Giant Vegetables (review of Belich, *Replenishing the Earth*)', 8.

[31] On *ius gentium*, law shared by all peoples, and *ius inter gentes*, the norms governing the relations between one people and another, see Armitage, 'Hobbes and the Foundations of Modern International Thought', in Brett, Tully, and Hamilton-Bleakley (eds), *Rethinking the Foundations of Modern Political Thought*, 228–9; Stein, *Roman Law in European History*, 94–5. For recent, illuminating discussions, see Boucher, *The Limits of Ethics in International Relations*; Tuck, *The Rights of War and Peace*; Hunter, 'Global Justice and Regional Metaphysics' in Dorsett and Hunter (eds), *Law and Politics in British Colonial Thought*, 11–29.

[32] Pocock, *Barbarism and Religion*, 167.

from the later eighteenth century into the early nineteenth century—it mingled with Christianized forms of political economy and senses of historical change.[33] Nor was it a monist intellectual frame for native title. A mix of nineteenth-century adaptations of *ius gentium*, political economy, and histories of progress and decline (including what Duncan Forbes characterized as 'liberal Anglican' histories)[34] drew upon older strains of stadial theory. Identifying any lessons and insights of stadialism and these other scavenged discourses for legalistic genres on native title still requires searching analysis and mapping—in short, a focus on reception in concrete political disputes and programmes and not simply the composition of sources as abstract texts.[35] Chapter Two also focuses on an emerging 'New Zealand Association' in 1837, proposing to settle parts of New Zealand on the lines of 'systematic colonization' and responses to such proposals from varied configurations of interest, including the Colonial Office, factional elements within Viscount Melbourne's rather precarious ministry and missionary societies. In levering off that contestation, the chapter explores the rather vague and general content of the Association and the Colonial Office's views in 1837 on the rights of the indigenous persons inhabiting New Zealand—the 'question was not very much discussed'. But it argues that this ambience of generality gradually gave way to increased (albeit contestable) detail as the advocates of systematic settlement (including 'colonial reformers') encountered criticisms from the Colonial Office.

Chapters Three and Four consider the motif of 'discipline'—disciplining the spatial extent and pace of growth in settlements—together with the functionality of recognizing 'territorial rights of the natives' in select fields, such as New Zealand, but not necessarily others and not in identical ways. In an empire of variations, British North America, New South Wales, and South Australia provide different vignettes and angles of vision. As this study will demonstrate, the ambiguities of metropolitan liberalism in all its complexities ranging across Whig and philosophic radical sensibilities as well as strains of toryism did not dissolve in distant colonial theatres.[36] As well as generating their own parochial trajectories, colonial New Zealand and the making of native title became theatres for the conduct of Westminster politics by other means. Acknowledging pre-existing indigenous 'territorial rights' and asserting the centrality of the incoming Crown in supervising dealings with such rights permitted imperial and colonial administrators to exert disciplinary constraints on settlement expansion. In additional fields of policy, Whigs such as Lord John Russell were self-consciously aspiring to be 'busy in introducing system, method, science, economy, regularity and discipline'.[37]

These chapters also consider the resilience of the logics of early nineteenth-century adaptations of stadialism and the manner in which these adaptations mingled with what was at root a whiggish political trope of 'discipline'. These sorts of complicated,

[33] Hickford, '"Decidedly the Most Interesting Savages on the Globe"', 122–67; Mandler, *The English National Character*, 21–6.

[34] Forbes, *The Liberal Anglican Idea of History*.

[35] Cf Hunter, 'Vattel's Law of Nations', 108–40.

[36] On the ambiguities of early nineteenth-century metropolitan 'liberalism' in the United Kingdom, refer to the excellent discussion in Hilton, *A Mad, Bad, & Dangerous People?*, 518–24.

[37] Russell to Chadwick, 9 October 1836, in Donajgrodski, 'Sir James Graham at the Home Office', 103. On the state as a social disciplinarian in Whig politics, see also Harling, *The Modern British State*, 88–98.

untidy mingling ought not to be surprising. A number of participants and commentators on fraught conversations about indigenous property rights were not academic political theorists in earnest but politicians, officials, and what Stefan Collini names 'public moralists' (such as John Stuart Mill) in earnest—commentators and often activists who drew on strands of political thought and inhabited its idioms with assurance.[38] Thomas Babington Macaulay, as Burrow reminded us, comfortably deployed aspects of initially Scottish concepts of the progress of civil society in conjunction with a gradualist and pragmatic conception of politics supped from the *oeuvre* of Edmund Burke.[39] The principally whiggish political project of 'discipline' predicated upon unresolved, contestable questions as to the content of native title was perceived as allowing a crisis of stasis and inactivity in colonization. The New Zealand Company considered this project, inherited by Sir Robert Peel's Tory administration and administered under Viscount Stanley's auspices as Secretary of State for Colonies, to have resulted in such a crisis and the near financial and political failure of organized settlement. The promises of colonial settings in New Zealand, as envisioned in the exhortations of the Company and its sympathizers, would not be realized.

With the New Zealand colonial garden withering on the vine, the Company, and other critics of imperial and colonial administration, increasingly mustered sources extraneous to colonial New Zealand drawn from *ius gentium* (including northern American jurisprudence) and stadialism. But, in so doing, these diverse actors entered and fanned a debate about the persistence of native title, indigenous political authority, and custom. They also influenced debates about the nature of imperial and colonial constitutionalism, including where to locate pre-eminent interpretative political constitutional authorities within it; that is, whether a governor conducting diplomacy with Māori polities, or a governor assisted by responsible institutions in the form of an assembly. Still others pressed for unimpeded liberty to engage in transactions for acquiring territories from Māori neither mediated nor superintended by government. A renewed intellectual and financial commitment to putatively quieting native title and indigenous autonomy by means of purchasing Māori territorial claims via governmentally sanctioned negotiation emerged. As such, convergence on policy outcomes was sought in the later 1840s and early 1850s, and largely attained, although underlying motivations differed.

Chapters Five to Seven consider the persistent significance of native title to political constitutionalism, as the scattered colonies of New Zealand were supplied with a 'representative constitution' in the form of an imperial enactment. Through diversifying the pool of politically relevant actors, the New Zealand Constitution Act 1852[40] expanded a key role for political activists, as designers, proposers, and makers of law and policies—enabling them to enlist legislative resources for law-making (and time in the calendars of legislative business). It further multiplied the points for applying pressure *within* the nascent colonial polities: the 'six colonies of New Zealand'. Putatively voluntary compacts with Māori polities—deeds of purchase in particular—were treated as giving rise to serial forms of agreed moments of coexistence (*modus*

[38] Collini, *Public Moralists*, 1–4.
[39] Burrow, 'Introduction', in Macaulay, *History of England*, 8.
[40] 'An Act to grant a representative constitution to the colony of New Zealand', 30 June 1852, 15 & 16 Vict, c72 (Imp).

vivendi) across time and space. As I have argued elsewhere in the context of the twentieth century, the singular success of many Māori politicians (chiefs and others) was to present these moments not as final events unto themselves but punctuated moments in conversations without end.[41] This proved to be the most salient and enduring feature of political constitutionalism in colonial New Zealand. Whatever was done in their relationship with governments remained contestable—these relations could be revisited, refreshed, and perhaps adjusted as circumstances changed. In an allied vein, Richard Boast suggestively characterized these sequences of agreement announcing or recording the adjustments of relations over time as 'multi-textualism'.[42] These negotiated arrangements often agreed to scope the boundary lines of expanding *anglophone* jurisdictions where the Crown's preferred interpretations might be pre-eminent, with the inland boundaries adjusting, moving outwards, and occasionally shrinking, as in the Taranaki in 1844 or expanding, as with Wanganui in 1848. These patterns persisted in the subsequent decade. Deeds of purchase, therefore, were a principal legal 'technology' used to bring Māori gradually within the pale of the introduced normative orders of colonial settlement and to construct temporary *modus vivendi*, which were often revisited as the pressures of settlement on territorial space and natural resources altered. Ushering in English laws, the transformational effect of purchases was such that they were treated as constructing English tenure to land conveyed via subsequent Crown grants. These forms of negotiated empire became places for drawing in exogenous idioms which were used to characterize constitutional situations and change, whether in the forms of *ius gentium* or other intellectual genres, as well as for generating what eventually became endogenous ways of speaking and seeing. These experiments, some of which were expressed legislatively, resonated with whiggish constitutional tropes of adjusting forms of government and legal policy to societies in transition, as was the case with colonial and indigenous New Zealand. As Burrow remarked, the early-to-mid-nineteenth-century forms of whiggism were 'not assimilable to contractarianism and doctrines of natural rights' but rather tended to stress 'a conception of civilization as the spontaneous, unintended transformation and (for the most part) improvement of society and manners, which tended to make the relation of government to society one primarily of adjustment and mediation'.[43] Further, converting native title into Crown-derived titles in the wake of extinguishment was considered as a gateway for admitting Māori into the statutorily defined franchise under the Constitution Act. This issue in itself became a contested ground for intra-colonial politicking.[44] For certain settler activists, if the Constitution Act permitted the enfranchisement of Māori while native title prevailed, such communities, plied by Crown mediated diplomacy (and its gifting of financial and other resources), would only serve to encourage the despotism of governors.

Because empire in New Zealand, as in many areas of Britain's world-system, was partial, incomplete, and far from embedded, native title continued to represent a touchstone of indigenous strategic independence and political autonomy. Combined with the emerging Kīngitanga (and the choices Māori *hapū*, or factions within *hapū*, made

[41] Hickford, 'Strands from the Afterlife of Confiscation', in Boast and Hill (eds), *Raupatu*, 189.

[42] Boast, 'Recognising Multi-textualism', 547–82; Boast, 'Treaties and Agreements in Colonial New Zealand'.

[43] Burrow, *Whigs and Liberals*, 126.

[44] Herron, 'The Structure and Course of New Zealand Politics 1853–1858'.

as to whether or not to affiliate with the Kīngitanga), the Waitara purchase negotiated in 1859 and early 1860 ignited and intensified these arguments about native title and constitutionalism. Chapter Seven particularly focuses on the ways in which these arguments were mustered and finally settled on a statutory jurisdiction to address indigenous property rights. The book will then turn to its conclusions.

THREE KEY INGREDIENTS—NON-JUSTICIABILITY, CONCEPTUAL INCOMMENSURABILITY, OR JURISDICTIONAL INCOMMENSURABILITY: THE PRE-EMINENCE OF POLITICS AND POLITICAL CONSTITUTIONALISM IN THE MAKING OF NATIVE TITLE

One key ingredient in imperial and colonial treatments of 'native title' in New Zealand was that it was not viewed as necessarily justiciable in the ordinary courts. In this sense, native title need not have been the justiciable sort that jurists in Australia, Canada, New Zealand, and the United States recognize in the later twentieth and early twenty-first centuries and seemingly take for granted as the way in which native title was understood historically in the mid-nineteenth century. Unsurprisingly, current early twenty-first-century understandings familiar with *Te Weehi v Regional Fisheries Officer* (1986) or *Ahousaht v Attorney-General of Canada* (2009) do not necessarily echo or reflect anglophone historical mid-nineteenth-century understandings.[45] Thus, in the later 1840s, a judge of the Supreme Court of New Zealand, an early advocate for applying the jurisprudence of the Supreme Court of the United States on 'Indian title' to New Zealand, stated: 'The rights and dominion which native tribes exercise over land are not such as come within the cognizance of the Tribunals'.[46] This was even the case after the granting of representative institutions to colonial New Zealand from 1852, with the so-called New Zealand Constitution Act—an enactment of the imperial legislature in Westminster—in play. Years later, in 1863, William Martin, formerly the first chief justice of colonial New Zealand, remarked that the 'case stands thus no native can, in any way, enforce any right of ownership or occupation of land, held by the native tenure, in the courts of the colony'.[47] Martin, for one, saw this aspect of non-justiciability, even though it might be contested as a legal interpretation, as a vital limitation to the capacity of Māori to exercise the 'rights and privileges' of 'British subjects' supposedly guaranteed under the third article of the Treaty of Waitangi. The indeterminacy as to whether non-justiciability was a sustainable legal interpretation was enough, in Martin's view, to require a statutory response to clarify the legal situation.

Martin's account requires careful unpacking and contextualization (Chapter Seven). But it points to a major historical issue hobbling understandings of native title in colonial New Zealand and in the broader imperial constitution. Whether an event is amenable to judicial scrutiny and potential legal remedy has tended to be tied to concerns with the appropriate functions of the courts within broader constitutional

45 *Te Weehi v Regional Fisheries Officer* [1986] 1 NZLR 680; *Ahousaht v Attorney-General of Canada* 2009 BCSC 1706.

46 Chapman, legal notes, undated [1846], Ms-Papers-8670-0417, ATL.

47 Martin, 'Observations on the proposal to take Native Lands under an Act of the Assembly', CO209/178, fo.163, enclosed in Martin to Fox, 16 November 1863, CO209/178, fos.144–144a, TNA.

arrangements that are partly political and partly juridical, by which I mean subject to judicial oversight and remedy.[48] Incontestable and determinate juridification of native title had not occurred if 'juridification' is used in the sense of framing political conflict and rights in predominantly legal terms and considered to be subject to judicial resolution. Less starkly, and much more softly, some jurists, such as George Arney (third chief justice of New Zealand) and Alexander Johnston in the 1850s and early 1860s, saw customary notions underlying indigenous property rights—the relevant norms of the indigenous community about land, whatever those might be—as not able to be fully accommodated within or recognized by the transposed common law or *ius gentium*.[49] In this sense, we also see a form of jurisdictional incommensurability although expressed *sotto voce*, as these judges in May 1861, for instance, saw the procedure and constitution of the Supreme Court as not 'well adapted' for investigating and determining native title, nor did they recommend that it be so adapted.[50] Perceived non-justiciability or incommensurability during this time elevated the significance of these proprietary claims in political arenas rather than legal or juridically driven constitutionalism in the courts. It encouraged early Victorian policy-makers to consider how to craft windows of communicability between plural indigenous normative and legal orders and those of the European newcomers, especially in relation to territorial claims and rights of government and political authority regarding land and other natural resources. These imperfect designs—including expeditions to seek out indigenous customary views on authority over land, as well as deeds drawn up in the diplomacy of purchase and various legislative measures drawn up in London and in New Zealand—took on an experimental demeanour throughout the 1840s, 1850s, and 1860s. This sort of experimentalism in legal design or architecture was a chief theme in dealing with native title throughout the 1850s and 1860s in particular. Contemporaries, including judges (Martin), colonial politicians, and legally trained officials (Francis Fenton), certainly knew it.[51] In Britain, politicians, like the fifth Duke of Newcastle under Lyme (Henry Pelham Fiennes Pelham-Clinton) and Chichester Fortescue, as well as civil servants, such as Sir Frederic Rogers, Merivale, and James Stephen, knew it too.

Numbered among these experiments were many failures and missteps. Aspirations were thwarted, altered, or expired. Our beginnings never know our endings. One ambitious experiment—the Native Council Bill of 1860[52]—passed the House of Lords. Yet Viscount Palmerston withdrew it in the House of Commons for lack of political support. The General Assembly of New Zealand produced its own competitive version of a Native Council Bill in late 1860 at odds with the imperial version, igniting a rash of arguments about diverse constitutional orders, native title, and the legal and political autonomy of Māori communities. But these failures remain important. They allow the recovery of otherwise lost pathways. To adapt Quentin Skinner's words, they permit us to see how

[48] For a useful discussion on justiciability, see Harris, 'Judicial Review, Justiciability and the Prerogative of Mercy', 631–60. For a helpful way of framing legal rights as opposed to political rights (of which legal rights may be regarded as a subset), see Dworkin, *Justice for Hedgehogs*, 405–406.

[49] See Chapters Six and Seven.

[50] See Chapter Six.

[51] Fenton, *Observations on the State of the Aboriginal Inhabitants of New Zealand*, Appendix A, 43.

[52] The long title of the Bill was 'An Act for the better Government of the Native Inhabitants of New Zealand and for facilitating the purchase of Native Lands': *House of Commons Parliamentary Papers*, Bills, 1860, vol 35 (317).

conceptions of native title and their relationships with political autonomy and constitutionalism 'reflect[ed] a series of choices made at different times between different possible worlds'.[53] Such was the significance of the theory and practice of Crown-Maori constitutional relations, and how such relations were tied to native title, and to the reality of Maori pre-eminence over native land, that it attracted a number of European commentators, eager to propose solutions to the puzzle of these relations, some of whom wished to use the issue to gain influence or to become trusted advisors to rising men in government.

Secondly, and closely related to the first point, native title had a political and constitutional significance in other ways. The treatment of native title in the practices of imperial politics, as well as the comparative silences and subordination of legalism and litigation, suggests the pre-eminence of political constitutionalism rather than a form of common law or legal constitutionalism. This is not to deny the significance of legalistic genres or the fact that jurists participated in the non-curial politics of the colonies and imperial administration. But the place of native title and its debated relationship with the Treaty of Waitangi (1840) reminds us of the pre-eminently political nature of Britain's imperial constitution. The territorial claims of Europeans and Māori communities were made and construed in a variety of non-curial processes. These processes included the diplomacy of purchase transactions, commissions appointed to investigate putative acquisitions from Māori and to recommend actions to the colonial governor, and the efforts of colonial government to lure Māori into participating in the introduced legal orders of the colonial system through resident magistrates and statutory experiments of the imperial Parliament and the colonial legislature. This was not a simplistic process of categorizing, of exerting order, or fashioning legibility. One of the objectives was to lure Māori polities into operating within or inside the introduced colonial legal system—to be disciplined by it and to acknowledge its pre-eminent ranking—even if only gradually. Legislation became an important tool or technology, even if largely aspirational in terms of practical effect and enforcement, with a view to securing these points or places of intersection between diverse Māori communities and novel colonial institutions, particularly resident magistrates. Another important experiment was the effort to synopsize English law (in 1858 and 1860, for instance) and to present it as an attractive way of dealing with a variety of legal issues, including civil injuries and real property.[54] Both attempts used the term '*ture*' for 'law', a neologism that had its etymological roots in an adaptation of the word 'torah', but which appeared in the speeches of Māori chieftains (*rangatira*) from time to time.[55]

Unsurprisingly, Māori did not necessarily wish to make their lives within these introduced frameworks or to accept the interpretative pre-eminence of such frameworks in any *modus vivendi* sketched and worked through with settlers. Many did not recognize the interloping Crown as having an antecedent right to prescribe norms and enforceable rules.[56] Even if it were recognized as having such a right (authority),

[53] Skinner, 'Introduction: Seeing Things their Way', in *Visions of Politics*, I, 6.

[54] See Chapter Seven.

[55] For instance, Buddle, 'Notes of Native speeches delivered at Ngaruawahia 11th April 1860 on the arrival of a deputation sent from Taranaki to present the allegiance of the Ngatiruanui and Ngatiawa tribes to Potatau', CO209/153, fo.451, TNA.

[56] Cf Oakeshott on 'authority' in 'Talking Politics', *Rationalism in Politics and Other Essays*, 442 ('by the acknowledgement of authority I do not mean approval of what is prescribed or the recognition of power to enforce prescription; I mean the recognition of an antecedent right to prescribe').

it was notorious that it did not have power or, in other words, the 'ability to procure with certainty a wished-for response in the substantive conduct of another'[57]—neither empire nor its infantile jurisdictions were practically embedded so to speak. Indigenous economic, as well as political preponderance persisted in a variety of areas.[58] To determine when, why and how it was undermined, requires localized, time-sensitive histories. The fact that Māori chieftainship and politics, and indigenous local and regional loyalties and attachments were not tamed or brought within the pale of colonial governance was well appreciated. It is overly crude to suggest that totalizing 'myths of empire' or colonial jurisdiction were required or acted upon.[59] To talk about 'myths of empire', for instance, is to obscure rich debates within the histories of colonization. In the broadly conservative *Quarterly Review*, Travers Twiss, Merivale's successor as Drummond professor of political economy, contended in considering the Hapshurg empire in 1848 that 'It is evident that so many and such highly diversified elements can be combined in one political system, on no other condition than that the supreme government shall scrupulously respect the historical peculiarities of the different races'. Twiss adjudged this to be and 'always will be the secret of imperial sway; and the observance of this fundamental condition has contributed in a great degree to maintain the ascendancy of British rule in the East'.[60] Empire, as with Britain itself, was predicated on differential laws applying in different places and treating subjects differentially—it was by no means predetermined that dynamic and contested forms of an early-to-mid-nineteenth-century 'liberal constitutionalism' would insist on an 'empire of uniformity'.[61] It is partly for this reason that this study prefers to re-orient the angles of vision towards an empire of variations.

Britain's empires were dense with problematic customs and contestations. As officials such as Rogers in the Colonial Office well knew, the practices and conceptual technologies of governance and jurisdiction were sufficiently flexible to allow for pluralistic legal and political orders. Not for them, the soothing simplicities of Jupiter's calming words for Venus in *The Aeneid* on immortal or boundless 'empire without end', although Augustan Rome proved acutely aware of its imperial order of variable

[57] Ibid, 445.

[58] Monin, 'Maori Economies and Colonial Capitalism', in Byrnes (ed), *The New Oxford History of New Zealand*, 125–46; Monin, *Hauraki Contested, 1769–1875*. Monin's notion of 'dual agency' is presented rather starkly. The evidence does not suggest that '[a]fter 1840 Maori were forced to look to the [introduced colonial] courts for redress when business dealings with Europeans went awry' ('Maori Economies', 137). The picture is rather more nuanced and depended very much on the parties at issue case by case and their geographical locale.

[59] For 'myths of empire', see Belich, *Making Peoples*, 231–2; Belich, 'Riders of the Whirlwind', in Boast and Hill, *Raupatu*, 33–47, 36–8. For references to a 'British desire for substantive sovereignty', see Belich, *The New Zealand Wars and the Victorian Interpretation of Racial Conflict*, 78.

[60] Twiss, 'Austria and Germany', 186. On the broad conservatism of the *Quarterly Review*, see 'Wellesley Periodical Introductions Browse' for this journal, <http://wellesley.chadwyck.co.uk> (last accessed 20 September 2010): 'It defended the old order in Church, in State, and in Society, with varying degrees of vehemence or conciliation as party issues flared or smo[u]ldered. But its party bias has been over emphasized'.

[61] The term 'empire of uniformity' is Tully's: *Strange Multiplicity*. Ian Hunter's work on early modern political thought brings out the degree to which, even within Europe, forms of political rationality and rule were characterized not by uniformity but by radical variety and contestation, driven by rival cultural and political programmes: Hunter, *The Secularization of the Confessional State*.

regimes.[62] British South Asia was suffused with such variations, as Jon Wilson, Peter Marshall, and Robert Travers have demonstrated.[63] Predominantly focusing on the later eighteenth century, Richard Drayton and Eliga Gould have conceptualized the stretch of these incomplete legal geographies of empire.[64] At the technical levels of jurisprudence and legalism, Shaunnagh Dorsett has analysed the conceptual and practical flexibility of 'jurisdiction' subordinate to claims of overarching authority elsewhere: 'The common law had long recognised alternative autonomous jurisdictions as functioning under its "superintendence", for example ecclesiastical law or law merchant'.[65] William Blackstone's *Commentaries on the Laws of England* (1765–1769) acknowledged variegated jurisdictions.[66] These 'technologies' of jurisdiction, as Shaunnagh Dorsett and Shaun McVeigh have characterized them, could be related to space or to persons or moveable things.[67] Seeing jurisdiction as tied to proprietary interests within the normative and practical supervisory control of those purporting to govern others and space—territorial jurisdiction—was neither unusual nor unconventional. Locke spoke of it in these terms in the late seventeenth century.[68] Hugo Grotius also expressed such a view in *De Iure Belli ac Pacis* (1625).[69]

Conversely, Māori displayed their own understandings of superintendence and authority over the embryonic colonial settlements—understandings that were themselves subject to challenge and change. For Māori leaders, like so many Alfreds contemplating the settlement of the Danes and the Danelaw turning into something looking rather permanent, the settlements, and the normative assumptions brought with them, became troublesome—proving to be incapable of incorporating completely within indigenous frames of reference. Māori were increasingly confronted with a problem of indigenous governance over territorial spaces inhabited by newcomers. Considerable indigenous political autonomy continued, certainly in hinterland areas not directly contiguous with the still relatively fragile bridgehead settlements of colonists. In areas contiguous with those settlements, Māori abilities to determine the meaning of relations and transactions with the newcomers lived on in a number of dealings, but fixing tipping points with precision in time and space remains difficult and messy at the historical micro-level. The point is, however, that it is not enough to ascribe the loss of autonomy over time to the large-scale materialism of mounting demographic pressure as settlements expanded. To see where local indigenous communities lost the power to determine concrete outcomes or to influence how relationships were understood by others requires a micro-historical approach to particular localities at particular points in time. These ought to be seen as very much local or regional stories.

62 Virgil, *The Aeneid*, trans Fagles, I, ll.332–3: 'On them I set no limits, space or time; I have granted them power, empire without end'.

63 Wilson, *The Domination of Strangers*, 77–103, for instance (cf Wilson, 'A Thousand Countries to Go To', 81–109).

64 Drayton, 'Maritime Networks and the Making of Knowledge', in Cannadine (ed), *Empire, the Sea and Global History*, 80–1; Gould, 'Zones of Law, Zones of Violence', 489–500.

65 Dorsett, 'Sworn on the Dirt of Graves', 193.

66 Blackstone, *Commentaries on the Laws of Engliand*, III, 30–85.

67 On the technologies of jurisdiction, see Dorsett and McVeigh, 'Questions of Jurisdiction', in McVeigh (ed), *Jurisprudence of Jurisdiction*, 11–14.

68 Locke, *Two Treatises of Government*, Laslett (ed), II, §§120–1.

69 Grotius, *De Iure Belli ac Pacis*, II.3.4.

The absence of legally actionable rights did not, of course, preclude imperial or colonial arguments predicated on legalistic sources or characterizing interests in land and other natural resources, such as waterways and fisheries, as 'rights' from a normative if not legally enforceable perspective. As this book will show, there were many examples of such participation and these roles were politically salient and influential ones. Māori were treated as subjects and formulators of customary law—of 'customs' and 'usages'—albeit not uncontroversially.[70] The question of customary law and native title swirled around the edges of certain cases before the Supreme Court in New Zealand in the 1850s, such as *Meurant v Keir* (1854) and *Busby v White* (1859), but was either not touched upon directly or evaded.[71] Yet, if accepted to exist, this law relative to authority over land and other natural resources was not something that was necessarily thought of or treated as communicable in anglophone terms, with considerations turning to legislatively creating resident magistrates and specialist tribunals to address it.[72] For one thing, as Chapters Five to Seven will demonstrate, native title was not necessarily treated as a right of the common law or as recognizable in English common law transposed across the seas.[73] Coupled in certain cases with perceived non-justiciability, this view of incomparability reinforced the pre-eminence of politics and colonial governmentality as the manner in which relations between Māori and the Crown could be addressed concerning authority over land, as well as any indigenous claims to ongoing authority and any indigenous territorial claims. In this way the Treaty of Waitangi (1840) came to figure in accounts of the normative obligations of the imperial Crown and its colonial representatives. That is, the treaty was interpreted as a foundational document for working through the substance of what Māori signatories obtained regarding rights and musing on the normative (if not legally enforceable) obligations disciplining the conduct of the incoming Crown. We see this sort of thought emerging saliently at various points in discussions on indigenous property rights in the mid-to-late 1840s, for instance, as well as in the 1850s. In this way, the Treaty demonstrates a particular angle of Frederick Cooper's point that 'empire could also become a moral space, the unit in regard to which righteous political behavior was debated'.[74]

The histories of native title are also histories of how Europeans saw the Treaty of Waitangi in law and history. It did not have an unchallenged pre-eminence in such

[70] For an illustration of the controversies, refer to Hickford, 'Law and Politics in the Constitutional Delineation of Indigenous Property Rights in 1840s New Zealand', in Dorsett and Hunter (eds), *Law and Politics in British Colonial Thought*, 249–68. Compare the comments of Tim Rowse on Australian Aborigines: 'Britons, Settlers, and Aborigines', in Harris (ed), *Civil Society in British History*, 298.

[71] Both cases are unreported but are the subject of scrutiny and contextualization as part of the *New Zealand Lost Cases Project* (headed by Shaunnagh Dorsett, Richard Boast, Geoffrey McLay, and Megan Simpson of Victoria University of Wellington, and myself and my former colleague at the Crown Law Office in Wellington, Damen Ward).

[72] Hickford, 'Framing and Reframing the *Agōn*', in Belmessous (ed), *Native Claims*; Hickford, 'Law and Politics'.

[73] The intersection between common law and customary notions of law and tenure remains an issue, including the extent to which the common law is able or prepared to accommodate customary concepts. It is one of the central difficulties underlying the issue concerning the recognition of Māori customary title in the foreshore and seabed of New Zealand. Noel Pearson, for one, in his 'Land is Susceptible of Ownership', in *Up From the Mission*, 111, notes that native title is not a common law title but is a title recognised by the common law.

[74] Cooper, *Colonialism in Question*, 163.

anglophone discussions. It would be anachronistic to suggest otherwise.[75] But it did figure as an element in principally anglophone political discourse along with *ius gentium*, theories concerning histories of progress and regression in human societies through time, English common law, and political economy. Its significance within Māori discourses in the first two decades was rather more regional and localized, with a much more noticeable stress upon it in the far north of the North Island of New Zealand where it was initially signed. Many descent groups to the south continued to regard it as a peculiarly Ngā Puhi text.[76] Reflecting on the Treaty of Waitangi in 1864, the settler politician Hugh Carleton (1810–1890) argued that '[b]y adopting the *form* of treaty, meaning thereby a compact between two independent nations, we subjected ourselves to all the incidents of treaty, hampering ourselves with the dogmas of international law'. He concluded that it involved 'us in a strange dilemma; for the right of interpretation either belongs to the natives, equally with ourselves, or else to the Crown alone; the first conclusion rendering all government impossible; the second, endowing the Government with the powers of a despot'.[77] For the purposes of treaty-making, Māori were treated as subjects of *ius gentium*. But, in the period of this study, they never fully escaped its universe or the sources populating that universe, including those of Twiss and, particularly, Emerich de Vattel's *Le Droit des Gens*, as presented in English by Joseph Chitty the elder (1834).[78] 'It is evident to our historic sensibility', as Pocock says, 'that any such treaty was a compact between two discourses, two means of understanding and operating what it was, and the modern indigenous nation has access both to European means of interpreting a treaty and to the modernised form (whatever it may be) of the indigenous discourse by which the treaty may have been understood then.'[79] I would say that multitudinous discourses were admitted as to questions of government and property rights, not merely two. I would also suggest that various historical Māori communities had access to diverse anglophone discourses and may (or may not) have chosen to use pieces of them.

As we will see in Chapters Two and Three, others from 1840 thought that specifically United States legal texts on 'Indian title' and *ius gentium* or the law of nations ought to explain the metes and bounds of the rights of Māori—a particular early nineteenth-century adaptation of the concept 'in the beginning all the World was America'[80] transposed to New Zealand. Some, including the colonial judge Chapman, fond of United States sources on 'Indian title', argued that the Treaty of Waitangi was unnecessary, sowing nothing, except perhaps confusion. The works of two American jurists in particular, James Kent in various editions of his *Commentaries on American Law*[81] and Joseph Story in *Commentaries on the Constitution of the United States* (1833), proved to

[75] Hickford, 'Making "Territorial Rights of the Natives"'; Ballantyne, 'The State, Politics and Power, 1769–1893', in Byrnes (ed), *The New Oxford History of New Zealand*, 100.

[76] Refer to Chapter Seven.

[77] Carleton, 'New Zealand', 429 (emphasis in original). Carleton, educated at Eton and Trinity College, Cambridge, was a member of the House of Representatives for the electorate of the Bay of Islands from 1853.

[78] Vattel, *Le Droit des Gens, Ou Principes de la loi naturelle, appliqués à la conduit & aux affaires des nations & des souverains [The Law of Nations or the Principles of the Law of Nature applied to the Conduct and Affairs of Nations and Sovereigns]*, (ed) Joseph Chitty.

[79] Pocock, 'Law, Sovereignty and History in a Divided Culture', 487.

[80] Locke, *Two Treatises of Government*, Laslett (ed), II, §49.

[81] Kent, *Commentaries on American Law*, (3rd edn, 1836; 4th edn, 1840).

be serviceable carriers of information concerning the title and political autonomy of Native Americans. Each of these texts freighted interpretations of northern American jurisprudence to British colonies. Decisions of the Supreme Court of the United States on 'Indian title' under the chief justiceship of John Marshall (1801–1835)—*Johnson v M'Intosh* (1823), *Cherokee Nation v Georgia* (1831), *Worcester v Georgia* (1832)—were distilled in these works.[82] The Colonial Office in London resisted the application of American jurisprudence on 'Indian title' for much of the 1840s. Viewing United States jurisprudential texts as irrelevant or unhelpful and not wishing to be tied to *à priori* abstractions on native title, the Colonial Office preferred identifying and consulting Māori custom or customary law on the ground.[83] The historical and living practices of negotiated politics (and the negotiated agreements these practices produced) were seen as constitutive of the law of nations between colonizing interlopers and indigenous tribes. Locating and identifying indigenous law or norms on interests in land and the government of territorial space proved an indubitably difficult and long-winded process, filled with frustration and disappointment.[84] By the 1850s, officials and politicians in colonial New Zealand doubted whether the English common law on real property could accommodate indigenous notions of property rights at all. Māori politics could be viewed as inside or outside the colonial polity as it suited Māori or settlers. Māori elites certainly did not consider themselves as encapsulated or encased within transposed sources about law and histories of civilization or progress even though Europeans might have thought otherwise. Indeed, it is in the interesting practice of real politics and their interplay with languages or vocabularies of political thought (including legalistic genres) rather than abstract principles of law worked out *à priori* that the legal histories of native title in empire can be properly distilled and laid bare.

Proprietary interests speak to more questions than simply the tangibles of soil and extractable resources. Property itself is a relationship of power and articulates a political relationship between persons.[85] Multi-dimensional, it speaks to both time and space.[86] It can account for and describe a peculiarly dense or thick relation of power relative to a thing or resource. '[P]roperty can be regarded both as a method of conferring authority and as a counterpoise against such authority.'[87] The sinews of strategic, as well as intimate, localized power and politics suffuse questions about entitlements to natural

[82] *Johnson v M'Intosh* 8 Wheat 543 (1823); *Cherokee Nation v State of Georgia* 5 Pet 1, 8 L Ed 25 (1831); *Worcester v State of Georgia* 6 Pet 515, 31 US 350 (1832) (USSC). For an excellent account of the Marshall court decision in *Johnson v M'Intosh* 8 Wheat 543 (1823) (USSC), see Robertson, *Conquest by Law*. For historical contexts to the decisions of that court on 'Indian title' and the status of Native American nations, see Howe, *What Hath God Wrought*, 355, 412–14, 422, 423, 424; Wilentz, *The Rise of American Democracy*, 427–8.

[83] Hickford, 'Making "Territorial Rights"', chs 3 and 4; Hickford, '"Decidedly the Most Interesting Savages"'; Hickford, '"Vague Native Rights to Land"'187–9.

[84] Hickford, 'Law and Politics'; Hickford, '"Vague Native Rights to Land"'.

[85] Gray and Gray, *Elements of Land Law*, 102; Watson Hamilton and Bankes, 'Different Views of the Cathedral', in McHarg, Barton, Bradbrook, and Godden (eds), *Property and the Law in Energy and Natural Resources*, 29–30.

[86] For illustrative discussions of this concept, see Gray and Gray, *Elements of Land Law*, 14–27, 69–70. Conventionally, to use the illustration of a river*bed* for the spatial dimensions, a fee simple interest in or title to the surface of land entails proprietary authority to the space occupied by the water column, the superjacent air space to a reasonable height, and the space comprising the soils beneath the bed of the river. The doctrine of estates treated proprietors as holding interests for a slice of time, with the fee simple estate potentially being an estate of unlimited temporal duration.

[87] McLean, 'Property as Power and Resistance', in McLean (ed), *Property and the Constitution*, 1.

resources, such as land. Authority to speak for these resources—to determine who may use them and in what ways and to determine who was entitled to speak authoritatively for them—was invariably an issue of potential and actual contention. This brings us to the unsettled and unsettling cusp of the complicated divide between the public and the private—between public rights and private rights, between public law and private law. Questions of political authority and property rights could often go together—commingling. They often did so in New Zealand at a time when Māori opinion leaders and political elites still commanded significant asset bases in the form of land.[88] They were also able to exert a meaningful and, in some areas, determinative influence on the meaning of their relations with strangers. For this reason Merivale noted in 1857 that, 'it is alleged that the natives, from having this territorial right admitted, acquire a notion that it is connected with the right of dominion'.[89]

Native title came to be seen as a key component of ongoing Māori political authority where indigenous interpretations of relations with strangers or guests (whether pākehā settlers or other Māori) and their normative meanings held sway or were seen as preponderant. It was also a lever in political negotiations. In this sense, property rights were political boosters for indigenous communities—things they could trade on or refrain from trading. To extinguish native title by purchase—so the theory of colonial administration went—would be to nullify Māori political autonomy and jurisdiction or to reduce it considerably.[90] Thus, in clause 5(1) of the Native Council Bill proposed by the Duke of Newcastle in 1860, 'the native law shall not be maintained in any district or part thereof after the native title to the same shall have been extinguished'. 'Native title' was there defined as the 'rights of the [aboriginal] inhabitants to any "native lands"'. The relations between indigenous property rights and political authority became embroiled in unresolved discussions about the Māori concept of chiefly '*mana*' (crudely translated as 'prestige' or 'authority') and how it relates to natural resources, autonomy, rights of government, and property rights—a question that persists into the twenty-first century. We see examples of this occurring throughout the nineteenth century.[91]

Historiographically, connections between property rights and broader questions of political status are not startling.[92] Belich understood that property transactions did not necessarily extinguish the vending community's claims to political authority over the property in question, although the two might go hand in hand.[93] In later times, as land-holdings were fragmented through sale to others, including the Crown, these portfolios of land-holding proved to be diminishing bases for Māori elites from which to lever political power and standing. In the late twentieth century and early twenty-first century in particular, we begin to find claims to political authority and rights of government (often using terms such as *rangatiratanga* appearing in the Treaty of Waitangi or chieftainship, *kaitiaki* (guardian) status and *mana*) occurring in circumstances

88 Hickford, 'Framing and Reframing the *Agōn*'.

89 Merivale, 7 July 1857, *GBPP1857*, sess 2, ix (HC171), 10.

90 Hickford, '"Decidedly the Most Interesting Savages"', 163; Hickford, 'Law and Politics'.

91 See, for instance, 'The Effect of "Mana" on Native Tenure', 12 June 1888, *New Zealand Herald*; *AJHR*, 1890, G-1, 15–16. For the nuances of *mana* and its spiritual dimensions, see Metge, *Tuamaka*, 44, 63, 87, 88, 126.

92 Wilson, *The Domination of Strangers*, 32–3; Brewer and Staves (eds), *Early Modern Conceptions of Property*; Wilson, 'Governing Property, Making Law', 16–17; Hickford, 'Framing and Reframing the *Agōn*'; Hickford, 'Law and Politics', 249–51.

93 Belich, *The New Zealand Wars*, 78.

where the claims were not principally based on or tied to land-holdings but to political influence over people and places. The ability of long-standing or emerging leaders to bring communities with them or to build consensus, if only for a time, and to muster resources behind select issues, proved increasingly vital. Different, often contestable ways of establishing and demonstrating political pre-eminence or influence in Māori communities emerged as new leaders arose, forging new constituencies and relationships or recasting existing ones. By this time, the quantities of land in the possession of indigenous communities had fallen, often substantially.[94]

Native title as a concept subject to change in the politics and jurisprudence of empire was under-girded and suffused by complex histories. As a concept with such histories, it was '*not* closed by a frontier', to use the words of Ludwig Wittgenstein: the games played were 'not everywhere circumscribed by rules'.[95] It is mistaken to see the often heated debates about native title as evidence of some unproblematically extended historical chain of causation and influence—a golden thread of continuity—tying sixteenth-century sources of legal and political thought (the writings of Franciso de Vitoria, Bartolomé de Las Casas, and Domingo de Soto) with the nineteenth-century to the seventeenth and eighteenth centuries. Yet some contributions, such as that of Frederika Hackshaw (1989), the significant analyses of constitutional legitimacy by Frederic Brookfield (1989, 1999 and 2006), and the path-finding earlier works of Paul McHugh (1984, 1987, and 1991) prior to his important 'Pocockian turn' in the 1990s, have been wont to do just that.[96] In these accounts, the stories of native title, seen uncontroversially as a species of right recognized in British imperial common law, become a rather more reduced story of foundations in the sixteenth century or, say, the late eighteenth century (for Brookfield) and of recognition in instruments, such as the Royal Proclamation of October 1763, and leading early nineteenth-century cases, of loss and forgetfulness for a time and then re-discovery and remembering in the later twentieth century.[97] Owing to his Pocockian turn, McHugh has since distanced himself from these earlier tendencies in his scholarship, most dramatically in a magisterial work on aboriginal societies and the common law.[98] Mark Walters observes

[94] Although land proprietorship could still be seen as critical, if the issues were orientated and framed in a way that proprietorship of land could be presented as giving groups an *entrée* into political negotiations in certain statutory frameworks. A recent example may be seen in the mandatory requirement of 'continuous title to contiguous land' in s 32 of the Foreshore and Seabed Act 2004 (NZ). This provision reflected that negotiators from the *rūnanga* (councils) of two groups (Ngāti Porou and Te Whānau a Apanui, who had retained considerable amounts of coastal land adjacent to the foreshore and seabed) were already in negotiation concerning their interests in the foreshore and seabed with the then government.

[95] Wittgenstein, *Philosophical Investigations*, §68. See also, Tully on the broad concept of global citizenship, *Public Philosophy in a New Key—volume II*, 245.

[96] Hackshaw, 'Nineteenth Century Notions of Aboriginal Title and their Influence on Interpretations of the Treaty of Waitangi', in Kawharu (ed), *Waitangi*; Brookfield, 'The New Zealand Constitution', in Kawharu, *Waitangi*, 10–11; Brookfield, *Waitangi and Indigenous Rights* (1999, 2006), 52; McHugh, 'Aboriginal Rights of the New Zealand Maori at Common Law'; McHugh, *The Māori Magna Carta*. On *Vitoria, Las Casas*, and *de Soto* see Pagden, 'Dispossessing the Barbarian', in *Spanish Imperialism and the Political Imagination*, 13–36; Brett, 'Scholastic Political Thought and the Modern Concept of the State', in Brett, Tully, and Hamilton-Bleakley (eds), *Rethinking the Foundations of Modern Political Thought*, 130–48.

[97] Brookfield, *Waitangi and Indigenous Rights*, 52.

[98] McHugh, *Aboriginal Societies and the Common Law*; McHugh, 'Proving Aboriginal Title', 303–8. The beginnings of this turn were evident in 1995: McHugh, 'The historiography of New Zealand's constitutional history', in Joseph (ed), *Essays on the Constitution*, 344–67.

that 'McHugh challenges some key assumptions about Aboriginal legal history that his earlier legal scholarship helped to make respectable (perhaps even orthodox) for a generation of judges and lawyers—including the very idea that a general common law doctrine of Aboriginal rights existed historically'.[99]

There is no doubting the historical and contemporary attraction of the approaches that the later McHugh rightly challenges wherein otherwise distinct episodes, texts, and writers are picked up and teleologically linked across the vastnesses of human time. In 1888, for example, a fellow of the Royal Asiatic Society, GW Rusden, and an animated critic of those who permitted Charles Gordon to be vanquished on the 'ramparts of Khartoum', drew connections between himself commenting on the 'groans of the Maoris' and the 'philanthropist', Las Casas, for literary and political effect: 'to lift the voice of rebuke in the presence of Princes'.[100] Yet, to elevate such continuities and to accommodate their political thrust uncritically, obscures the variegated richness of how the sources of legalistic and political thought, including the works of John Locke and Emerich de Vattel, were transposed across the seas, deployed in new debates, and mingled with novel circumstances, 'escap[ing] [their] original context to take part in arguments of which [their authors would have been] wholly unaware'.[101] Use and therefore meaning of the notions of 'native title', 'native tenure', or 'territorial rights of the natives' was not the application of some transcendental theory of law. Twiss, for one, saw New Zealand in 1846, along with the United States, as historically distinctive places relative to indigenous populations and European empire-building from a legal perspective in the law of nations (*ius gentium*). Thus, he claimed that a 'further accessorial right of settlement has, *in modern times*, been recognised by the practice of civilised nations in both hemispheres, namely a right of pre-emption from the aborigines in favour of the nation which has actually settled in the country'.[102]

THE DYNAMISM OF NATIVE TITLE—THE POLITICS OF NEGOTIABILITY AND THE JURISPRUDENCE OF EMPIRE

Conceptions of native title were dynamic in two distinct senses. For one thing, how to conceive and explain indigenous property rights to anglophone and indigenous populations was subject to conversations without end and was often treated as negotiable and contestable, with these negotiations and contests occurring predominantly in political non-curial sites. These points of negotiability and contest arose in a number of contexts throughout the 1840s, 1850s, and early 1860s. Disputes concerning Māori property rights dramatized the convoluted relations within political processes, especially at Westminster and in colonial New Zealand, as well as between the Crown and Māori. The political marketplace in New Zealand and Britain, filled with dispersed clusters of political influence and authority—indigenous and British—encouraged contest and negotiability.

[99] Walters, 'Histories of Colonialism, Legality, and Aboriginality', 823.

[100] Rusden, *Aureretanga*, iv–v.

[101] Skinner, 'Afterword', in Armitage (ed), *British Political Thought in History, Literature and Theory, 1500–1800*, 284.

[102] Twiss, *The Oregon Question Examined, in respect to Facts and the Law of Nations*, 176 (emphasis added).

Indeed, debating native title involved the conduct of Westminster and colonial politics by other means. Informal clusters of politicians, traders, pamphleteers, and political economists coalesced, dispersed, re-grouped, and unravelled again on issues of colonization. Other, more formal groups crystallized. We see the New Zealand Land Company (or 'New Zealand Company'), incorporated in March 1839 looking to spearhead 'systematic colonization' in New Zealand, and the Canterbury Association, formed on 27 March 1848 for the purpose of establishing a Church of England settlement in New Zealand and active until 1852. The most active members of the Canterbury Association included John Robert Godley and George William Lyttelton, the fourth Baron Lyttelton, and brother-in-law to William Ewart Gladstone's wife. These forms of political entrepreneurship brought people of social and political ambition, shared sympathies and familial bonds together around issues, and contributed to building coalitions of interest.

The pressures exerted by events and the entrepreneurial politics of governmental and non-governmental groupings or networks in New Zealand and Britain, as they jockeyed for advantage, pressed policy-makers, jurists, and politicians, both in New Zealand and the United Kingdom, to elaborate the analytical content of native title or to refrain from doing so and to encourage ongoing analytical indeterminacy.[103] Not to commit to a particular definition of 'territorial rights of the natives'—to satisfice or attain a policy object while leaving the theoretical underpinnings unresolved or indeterminate—allowed flexible adjustments in approach, and the absence of intellectual and political closure.[104] Imperial governments were able to present the appearance of broad consensus on outcomes at certain points in time even if the consensus masked considerable debate as to the rationale for acting in a certain way. This proved to be the key to living with indeterminacy. Behaviourally, this tendency is unsurprising. It was seldom the case that officials or those with whom they dealt were willing to incur the transaction costs of minutely ascertaining the exact metes and bounds of a politically or legally actionable entitlement to tangibles, such as land. Often it was enough to treat the claims of either party as subject to any existing rights abstractly without specifying either what those rights were in substance or what they required practically.

Debate and negotiation flourished in these circumstances, with punctuated equilibriums emerging from time to time as issues settled, if only briefly, to be disrupted again. Indigenous polities also contributed to the situation of negotiability—to the thickening of conceptions about native title, relations between claims to territorial spaces, and the distribution of political authority to speak about the disposition of land and how it may be used. These contributions emerged in a number of arenas. They emerged through negotiations around deeds of purchase with colonial officials, in commissions investigating direct settler purchases of land from Māori in the early decades of the colony, in dealing with itinerant resident magistrates, such as Fenton in the Waikato, and in commercial transactions allowing European settlers to occupy land on Māori terms, as in the pastoral runs of the Wairarapa. A politics of negotiability emerged on the back of diplomacy with Māori polities around the occupation of space and authority over it, as well as the risks and actuality of warfare.

103 Hickford, 'Making "Territorial Rights"', 23, 49–51; Hickford, '"Decidedly the Most Interesting Savages"', 154–66; Hickford, '"Vague Native Rights to Land"', 187–96.

104 Hickford, 'Making "Territorial Rights"', 18. This particular use of the term 'satisfice' is not picked up by Bain Attwood in his reading of the thesis: see Attwood, *Possession*, 86.

The unstoppable stream of people through British immigration in the 1850s and 1860s—what James Belich refers to as 'settler booms'[105]—did not undermine the hard core of this negotiability. It persisted as an issue to be addressed in spite of what Belich terms 'explosive settlement'.[106] Elaborate processes were maintained (purchase) or engineered (the specialist Native Land Court in its various legislative incarnations from 1862) by colonial governments in the 1860s to address 'native land' on an ongoing basis.[107] Owing to the impression of apartness, 'native title' furnished a lever for anglophone settler and Māori communities to effectively contest the transposed forms of colonial administration—the pretensions of that government to use the legal resources at its disposal (through the legislature for example) to construct points of intersection and communicability with Māori politics regarding land and the control of territorial space. As Margalit has noted, 'negotiation is meant to bring about cooperation, so recognizing the other as a party for negotiation acknowledges that the other party is worthy of cooperation'.[108] Distinctions must be drawn between compromise on the frame or framing of negotiations and 'compromise *in the* negotiation, once the setup for the negotiations is agreed upon'.[109] The framing and reframing of the *agōn*, the politics of negotiability in empire, shows native title to be an agonistic concern.[110] That is, native title was not predicated on abstract consensus but on ineradicable conversation, disagreement, and contest. To focus in a de-contextualized manner on the place of native title in the case law of the courts, whether in *Regina v Symonds* before the Supreme Court of New Zealand in 1847 or on *Johnson v M'Intosh* in the United States Supreme Court in 1823, could give the impression that 'native title' was a subject of broad consensus in the jurisprudence of European settler empires rather than difference and disagreement.[111] It should not. The cases themselves—discrete exercises in dispute-resolution with their own contexts—were deployed as resources in raging political arguments in the 1840s, 1850s, and 1860s about native title, and the rights of government of indigenous polities retaining native title. It should not give rise to the view that such cases authoritatively pronounced and settled what the law was on the substance and meaning of native title in the jurisprudence of empire, let alone determined the meanings of native title and political approaches taken to it. Indeed, Kent McNeil's salutary caveat in his legal theoretical approach to aboriginal title at common law has been ignored such that much more doctrinal agreement and clarity has been introduced than is historically merited.[112]

[105] Belich, *Replenishing the Earth*, 361.

[106] The argument here differs from the generalities of that presented by Belich in 'Riders of the Whirlwind', in Boast and Hill, *Raupatu*, 39–41.

[107] On the persistence of purchase and its significance, see Boast, *Buying the Land, Selling the Land.*

[108] Margalit, *On Compromise and Rotten Compromises*, 42–3.

[109] Ibid, 43 (emphasis in original).

[110] On the concept of the *agōn*, see Muldoon, '"The Very Basis of Civility"', in Kymlicka and Bashir (eds), *The Politics of Reconciliation in Multicultural Societies*, 114–35. As applied to a New Zealand context: Hickford, 'Framing and Reframing the *Agōn*'.

[111] *R v Symonds* [1840–1932] (1847) NZPCC 387; *Johnson v M'Intosh* 8 Wheat 543 (1823).

[112] McNeil, *Common Law Aboriginal Title*, 2: '[Historically] a pot-pourri of irreconcilable approaches [were in evidence], often with a noticeable absence of sound legal principle behind them.... The approach to indigenous land rights taken in this book is therefore legal rather than historical'.

Politics is historically located, as Raymond Geuss suggests: 'it has to do with humans interacting in institutional contexts that change over time, and the study of politics [or law for that matter] must reflect this fact'.[113] Acting politically is historically situated in more ways than that of course. It also engages various ways of seeing or speaking, ways of framing and reframing questions and issues about what is to be done, as well as forming, reforming, and nourishing networks or configurations of people and interest through meetings, correspondence, clubs, societies, and social occasions. Different networks vied to present themselves as reliable and pre-eminent interpreters of the constitutional settings at the imperial and colonial levels. The relative indeterminacy of political constitutionalism as opposed to thoroughgoing codified legal constitutionalism lent itself to this sort of flexibility, dynamism, and ambiguity.[114] Political questions invariably involve decisions which require choices between conflicting alternatives in circumstances where some constituencies or audiences might be disappointed or aggrieved.[115] As Bernard Williams observed, political disagreements 'may involve many different kinds of understanding and political traditions; they can tap into various areas of... historical deposit'.[116] One may see a 'pluralism of values'[117] but also a multiplicity of histories in unending conversation, whether peaceable or not. '[C]ontexts are reconfigured and shape future possibilities and closures.'[118] Against this background, mapping and accounting for the concrete reception of intellectual sources transposed from across the seas in live disputes is vital to seeing native title in the jurisprudence and politics of trans-oceanic empire. This book supplies an account of the use (including the tactical deployment and distribution) and translation of various intellectual sources, whether those on *ius gentium* and the common law, from one context or particular period to another. In Mandler's words, such an approach permits us to assess the relative 'throw' or weight of such sources in practice.[119]

The texts constituting these sources comprised congeries of ideas and ways of seeing bundled together. In this vein, Anthony Pagden rightly cautioned that it is not enough to see these sources as political devices since to do so is to 'obscure their very real explanatory importance'.[120] Tying the use of sources drawn from the law of nations, political economy, or histories, for instance, to the activities of particular political debates and persons or groups of people over time also assists. The late Colin Matthew 'recognized that, since the immediate, external characteristic of almost any given historical world is its infinity, real and evidential, one of the most necessary and reliable ordering principles for the historian is precisely that offered by "ideas": the intellectual and conceptual structures erected by the historical subjects themselves'.[121] This sort of approach also allows us to see both change and constancy in meaning and attribution. Stability of meaning can often suggest stasis and a lack of testing. There can be interesting discordances between on-the-ground practices and understandings, which outwardly suggest

[113] Geuss, *Philosophy and Real Politics*, 13.
[114] Cf Barber, 'Against a Written Constitution', 17.
[115] Cf Mouffe, *On the Political*, 10.
[116] Williams, *In the Beginning was the Deed*, 77.
[117] Berlin, 'Two Concepts of Liberty', in Hardy (ed), *Liberty*, 217.
[118] Cooper, *Colonialism in Question*, 13.
[119] Mandler, 'The Problem with Cultural History', 96–7.
[120] Pagden, 'The American Indian as Barbarian', 3 (long abstract).
[121] Ghosh and Goldman, 'A Brief Word on "Politics" and "Culture"', in Ghosh and Goldman (eds), *Politics and Culture in Victorian Britain*, 5.

consensus but which conceal profound disagreements as to the underlying principles or intellectual approaches.[122] Thus, there may be ongoing indeterminacy in the sense that the concrete outcomes of particular disputes or particular decision-points are agreed in the absence of any agreed rationale or in the presence of intense disagreement as to what rationale or principles for action to prefer. This state of affairs potentially enhanced the indeterminacy of the politics of negotiability because the process of decision-making had not necessarily established an agreed pathway for what to do and why—whether the decision should be repeated and, if so, in what circumstances remains uncertain and contested.

Indeterminacy in itself encourages a diversity of views about what the constitutional frameworks do or do not require, as well as disagreement, contestation, and negotiation on what course of action to pursue—all of these being questions on which reasonable people can disagree. Ambiguity can be useful. It permits a measure of adaptation to the incalculability of life. A tacit agreement to disagree (or even an express agreement to that effect) may be as good as it gets. The physical words within texts scavenged for use on debating the meaning of indigenous property rights—whether in Vattel's work *The Law of Nations; or, Principles of the Law of Nature, applied to the conduct and affairs of nations and sovereigns* (as translated into English by Joseph Chitty the elder in 1834) or James Kent's *Commentaries on American Law* or the reports of court decisions—remained impervious to change in practical circumstances: the words persisted.[123] But *modus vivendi* worked out on the ground were under constant negotiation, whether that ground was in metropolitan or colonial settings. The landscape of native title, coupled with what it said about political relations in imperial contexts, was fluid. Each negotiated point of agreement or the reductionist output of a whole host of relationships and discussions committed to paper was not necessarily an accurate or complete reflection of all that transpired—a major and unavoidable limitation of any concrete text, whether a deed of purchase or a treaty (including the Treaty of Waitangi). Such moments fell to be reinterpreted in novel circumstances although the words on the page always suggesting discipline and constraint on possible interpretations.

Secondly, these politics contributed to the making of native title through contesting how territorial claims were framed and how they related to the distribution of political authority, whether colonial or indigenous. Native title revealed competing claims to pre-eminence in sorting out preferred policies and outcomes amongst and between imperial administration, the executive of the colonial government in New Zealand, the general legislature and the provincial legislatures, and Māori conurbations of power and authority. A long-standing critic of imperial pre-eminence in native title issues, Charles Adderley, rounded on the Duke of Newcastle's proposed Native Council Bill in the House of Commons in August 1860 on the following basis: 'The entire local executive must be responsible to the local legislature; and two legislatures, side by side, and independent of each other; a Native Council and representative assembly on the same ground would make hopeless confusion, and must end in referring every question back to England'.[124] Fortescue, parliamentary under-secretary to Newcastle at the Colonial

[122] Sunstein, 'Incompletely Theorized Agreements', 1733–72. See also Connolly, *The Terms of Political Discourse*, 1–41.

[123] Hickford, 'Law and Politics', 265. See also the illuminative account in Hunter, 'Natural Law, Historiography, and Aboriginal Sovereignty', 137–67.

[124] *HPD*, 3rd series, 21 August 1860, col 1648.

Office, countered that, 'Now, on the contrary,... this [Native Council] Bill—without going into the question of its expediency, or of whether the same object could be better attained by other means—was not a violation of the Constitution Act [1852], but rather framed in its spirit, and was no infringement of the rights of self-government conferred upon the colonists of New Zealand'.[125] As such, conceptions of native title in empire were dynamic in another way. For jurists, such as Henry Chapman and Martin, the first chief justice of New Zealand, as much as for imperial policy-makers, colonial New Zealand represented a mid-nineteenth-century puzzle of asserted but not necessarily effective 'internal dominion' over otherwise autonomous indigenous polities. Native title to land—'native land'—was seen as a lynchpin of indigenous independence and 'nationality'. Indeed, fixating on land because of the land market within New Zealand, particularly from the 1830s onward, elevated the significance of land and authority over it as a tactical and strategic lever in the ongoing politics of negotiability. A vibrant market for land drove the emphasis in the second article of what came to be called the 'Treaty of Waitangi'—'the chiefs of the united tribes and the individual chiefs, yield to Her Majesty the exclusive right of pre-emption over such lands as the proprietors thereof may be disposed to alienate at such prices as may be agreed upon between the respective proprietors and persons appointed by Her Majesty to treat with them'.

Native title may be seen as one way of making a landscape and the relationship of pre-existing indigenous populations and British colonial settlement to that landscape intelligible to colonial administration.[126] But, except in the broadest and conceptually thinnest of senses—identifying areas that were or may have been subject to native title—legibility was never truly achieved nor was analytical consensus on what such legibility might actually look at obtained (if it could ever be in a markedly fluid and pluralistic political environment).[127] At key points in time, judges, politicians, and officials disagreed amongst themselves on how to identify areas clothed with native title, what it looked like, and what it meant for legal and political behaviour. Politics and political constitutionalism was such that deep intelligibility was not a prerequisite for determining what was to be done on a case-by-case basis. Much indeterminacy remained, as befitted a pre-eminently political form of constitutionalism. For the participants, it was often convenient that this was so. Interacting interpretative communities—colonial and imperial, as well as Māori—lived with both practical and theoretical indeterminacy, as to what was to be done and why.

The broad, non-analysed functionality of native title aided colonial state formation at the outset in New Zealand and the embedding of colonial administration at various points centred on coastal settlements or enclaves. In particular, forging broad conceptions of native title helped this process in two ways. First, they assisted the incoming Crown to discipline the spatial extent of British settlement and the pace of its expansion out of beachheads through controlling the giving and withholding of legal recognition (security of tenure) to certain transactions with indigenous polities. Through recognizing pre-existing indigenous property rights and the then pre-eminence of the Crown in

[125] Ibid, cols 1643–1644.

[126] Scott, *Seeing like a State*, 2–3, 35–6, 38–45. On the cautions around state building in the mid-nineteenth century, see Bayly, *The Birth of the Modern World 1780–1914*, 252–4.

[127] In this sense, this account agrees with Frederick Cooper's cautions about Scott's notion of 'legibility' in Cooper, *Colonialism in Question*, 140–2.

legalizing transactions with the holders of such rights, colonial government was able to assert its political and legal authority inexpensively. In this way native title was a tool for policing and pacifying settlers.[128] Using aboriginal title represented an imperial administration asserting power within New Zealand.[129] Imperial administrators reluctantly recognized that unauthorized land-hunting could not be prevented but might be integrated into a series of disciplinary endeavours of monitoring or licensing activities and revenue collecting. A sense of managing anglo-settlers in motion was incorporated through a transactional media of price and territorial ordinance stipulations. As Sir George Gipps, governor for New South Wales, lamented in 1840, '[a]s well it might be attempted to confine the Arabs of the desert within a circle, traced upon their sands, as to confine the Graziers or Woolgrowers…within any bounds that can possibly be assigned to them'.[130] In this sense, these anxieties concerning managed settlements, proprietary acquisitions, and revenue collection proceeded into hinterlands beyond exotic beach-lines.

Imperial administration and its colonial representatives were able to use the presence of native title to discipline settlers. Vitally, the Crown subjected both itself and its subjects to this legal and normative discipline or constraint. It need not have done so but it did. Against this background, settlements—buildings and roadways, streetscapes occupying space—were platforms, places of legal density with local ordinances, and imperial laws applying to them, enforceable through local courts. Colonial New Zealand began on the beaches. These beachhead settlements or 'bridgeheads'[131] were staging posts for legal, political, and demographic lunges into the hinterlands and along the coasts. Yet the fiscal resources available to colonial administration were meagre at best throughout the 1840s, 1850s, and 1860s with occasional surges from imperial sources to arrest perceived trouble *ex post facto* in 1845–1846, for example.[132] What is striking about the colonial experiment in New Zealand is that the possibilities of expanding colonial settlement were cramped by needing to unravel the knot of native title and diverse Māori political authority. In circumstances where colonial administration did not yet have access to sufficient financial or military resources, the giving or withholding of legal recognition to certain land transactions was one of the few regulatory levers at its disposal. Of course, some settlers might risk the possibility of legal non-recognition, as John Weaver and Peter Karsten observe in important comparative works.[133] New Zealand was no exception. To some it might not have mattered in relation to security of tenure in land provided they could still access markets for any produce derived from their pastoral activities, benefitting commercially if only for a time.

Contests concerning the legal recognition of transactions with those in command of areas of 'native title' were also contests about *who* determined the thrust of colonial administration and the disposition of policy on the barriers towards Māori

[128] Hickford, '"Making Territorial Rights"', 3–4, 50, chs 2, 3, and 4.

[129] Foucault, 'Two lectures', in Dirks, Eley, and Ortner (eds), *Culture/Power/History*, 215. Other versions of this developing preoccupation with asserting discipline can be witnessed in policing histories within New Zealand: Hill, *Policing the Colonial Frontier*, I.

[130] Gipps to Russell, 19 December 1840, CO201/300, fo.246a, TNA.

[131] Darwin, 'Imperialism and the Victorians', 614–42.

[132] Hickford, '"Decidedly the Most Interesting Savages on the Globe"'.

[133] Weaver, *The Great Land Rush and the Making of the Modern World, 1650–1900*; Karsten, *Between Law and Custom*, 66–73.

participation in the colonial land market and commercial opportunities. In a picturesque metaphor, Peter Baldwin notes, '[s]tates may be lumpy', by which he meant, they may be 'interventionist in one aspect, insouciant and unconcerned to act in another': they may be one thing or another at different points across the board and not necessarily consistently.[134] In speaking of mid-nineteenth-century government within the imperial metropole and a 'political history of trust' in establishing the legitimacy of the British state in the 1840s and 1850s, Martin Daunton has argued that 'fiscal favouritism' was to be purged and the political elites to be protected through 'constraining state expenditure and, as far as possible, excluding the state from involvement with economic interests'.[135] This form of policy was strongly associated with that strain of political thought and programme described as 'liberal' and 'non-interventionist' by Boyd Hilton.[136] The financial parsimony of colonial administration, while a feature that assisted the legitimacy of the early Victorian state in the eyes of certain taxpayers in the United Kingdom and New Zealand,[137] also hurt its legitimacy in the eyes of certain Māori and settlers. Unable to project power or authority beyond the settlements effectively, it was seen as weak and powerless to exert a powerful influence on outcomes at key points in the two decades after 1840. A number of Māori saw themselves as more effective governors of territory and makers of governments than the British.

Secondly, native title was part of a sequenced means or technology of incorporating Māori within the introduced colonial body politic. It was sequenced in that it was seen as a prelude to complete incorporation of indigenous populations in settlement colonies. Extinguishing or quieting native title was tied to boosting the resources at the disposal of the infantile colonial state through yielding land to be put at its command—land that could place government in a pre-eminent position to allocate and distribute land to others through Crown grants. Recognizing native title reflected a temporary acknowledgement of legal and political plurality, the meanings of which would need to be translated and rendered intelligible in the introduced terminology or grammar of 'rights' and transformed incrementally into Crown land unburdened by the trace of 'territorial rights of the natives'. Thus, the presence of unextinguished title abutting colonial New Zealand was treated as emblematic of a several-headed creature made up of numerous Māori polities confined to a string of islands. Containment and absorption of these native title areas was a prelude to overcoming an otherwise anarchic or pluralistic situation of several competing powers—relics of multifarious pasts pre-dating the arrival of the Crown from across the seas. Yet this very aspiration would be discomforted and contested by the concrete practices of negotiability both on the ground in New Zealand and in the pressure politics of the imperial metropole, as will be seen in Chapters Six and Seven.

The title itself was not only tied to a particular form of communal social organization, which was to be modified or removed, but a sense of historicity, specifically the mist-ridden past. Thus, native title not only had a spatial quality—a coverage of areas not yet subject to English tenure. It also had a temporal quality. Areas clothed with

134 Baldwin, 'The Victorian State in Comparative Perspective', in Mandler (ed), *Liberty and Authority in Victorian Britain*, 66.

135 Daunton, *Trusting Leviathan*, 63.

136 Hilton, *A Mad, Bad, & Dangerous People?*, 518–24.

137 Daunton, *Trusting Leviathan*, 28, 63; Harling, 'The Powers of the Victorian State', in Mandler (ed), *Liberty and Authority in Victorian Britain*, 25–50, 28.

native title were places of the historical past. For imperial and colonial policy-makers and opinion leaders, when one was looking at 'territorial rights of the natives', one was looking into the pasts of Europe and the world. The title was intended to be effaced, extinguished, or rubbed out in order to modify and transmute the pluralism acknowledged to exist into something altogether more congenial to the asserted pre-eminence of colonial government. As a concept, native title domesticated and pacified indigenous communities philosophically, treating Māori and Native Americans as inside empire's broader claims to authority over space but as potentially outside embedded empire—empire embedded through institutions able to determine or to exert a tangible influence on concrete outcomes on the ground. In other contexts, Taiaiake Alfred and James Tully have identified the risks to indigenous communities of being subsumed through adopting these introduced ways of talking.[138] Native title was denuded of much of its political significance (rights of government) and treated as a private property right subordinate to colonial administration and able to be transmuted into legal interests dependent on an introduced tenurial system once extinguished. Also underscoring this approach was, to use Peter Mandler's term, an undoubtedly 'civilizational perspective'.[139] The nature and content of property as recognized through institutions of law and politics said much about the relative progress of societies (both indigenous and colonial) and their place, if at all, in a narrative of civilization. Civilization was rare and accordingly something arduous to obtain. Opinions profoundly differed as to the respective roles of missionaries or fully fledged colonization and colonial administration as agents of change. In his musings on political economy, John Stuart Mill advanced the view that colonization 'involve[d] the future and permanent interests of civilization itself, and far outstretch[ed] the comparatively narrow limits of purely economical considerations'.[140] With the granting of representative institutions to New Zealand settlements under the New Zealand Constitution Act 1852, the place of native title in the electoral franchise also required assessment and debate. The strains of late Georgian and early Victorian thought on the franchise and property rights were not simple, especially in circumstances where the franchise itself was seen as a form of property.[141] As John Burrow notes, Gladstone was thought to have made a misstep in speaking of the franchise as a 'right'.[142]

As will be demonstrated, the intellectual languages informing this perspective were drawn from a variety of ways of speaking and seeing—ecclesiological or theological perspectives, strains of *ius gentium* and *ius inter gentes*, early nineteenth-century versions of political economy, stadial and 'liberal Anglican' histories. By these means Māori were incorporated as 'natives' of Westminster metaphorically in the absence of their awareness of or consent to this incorporation. Nicholas Thomas uttered a similar view saying, '[t]he point to grasp about entanglement [involving strangers and

[138] Alfred, *Peace, Power, Righteousness*, 80–8, 150; Tully, *Public Philosophy in a New Key—volume I*, 259–60.

[139] Mandler, '"Race" and "Nation" in Mid-Victorian Thought', in Collini, Whatmore, and Young (eds), *History, Religion, and Culture*, 231.

[140] Mill, *Collected Works of John Stuart Mill*, JM Robson (ed), III, 963.

[141] Lieberman, 'The Mixed Constitution and the Common Law', in Goldie and Wokler (eds), *The Cambridge History of Eighteenth Century Political Thought*, 346.

[142] Burrow, *Whigs and Liberals*, 46.

indigenous persons] is that histories may be linked but not shared'.[143] From the 1830s, Māori—even eventually pākehā New Zealanders—were used in this fashion, perhaps most memorably by Thomas Macaulay. He imagined a future, when 'some traveller from New Zealand shall, in the midst of the vast solitude, take his stand on a broken arch of London Bridge to sketch the ruins of St Paul'.[144] The tools and logic of stadial analysis were undoubtedly influential in informing policies and practices on native title. Stadial theory, or a theory of historical development over time, predicated on stages in which a particular mode of subsistence predominated or prevailed—hunting and gathering, pasturage, agriculture, and commerce—has been largely associated with sophisticated Scottish and francophone analyses emerging in the eighteenth century.[145] Yet it persisted as a way of framing and seeing indigenous property rights well into the nineteenth century. As will be seen in Chapters Two and Three, debates persisted as to whether civilization, translated as progress in types of property, was best achieved through active external European agency or intervention or through the simple proximity or neighbourhood and example of European settlements. Property (and how one appropriated property) was central to understanding the place of a particular society in this theory through the lens of natural jurisprudence.[146] Māori were implicated in the stadial sequence, albeit not without early nineteenth-century innovations, as horticulturists given to agriculture—planters of crops, such as *kūmara*—in the absence of plough technology.[147] My intention in an earlier work in 1999, followed up in 2006, was to demonstrate how the techniques of analyses predicated on stadial history and *ius gentium* were actively deployed in debates and policy thought on 'territorial rights of the natives' during the mid-nineteenth century.[148] The use of some of the key tropes of, say, stadial logic—the emphasis on predominant modes of subsistence in a given society and tying that to proprietary interests and government—persisted into the 1850s and 1860s.

A number of influential figures able to traverse colonial and imperial politicking, George Grey or Henry Sewell, for instance, supplied different interpretative points of emphasis to this theme of incorporation or accommodation. Grey endeavoured to transform Māori from subjects of *ius gentium* into politically domesticated subjects, with selected chieftains collected as allies and presented to the rest of the world as British subjects.[149] The policy device of 'amalgamation', as understood by Grey and Merivale, had a clear racial undertone. For Merivale, 'amalgamation' meant the 'union of natives with settlers in the same community, as master and servant, as

[143] Thomas, *In Oceania*, 13; Thomas, *Entangled Objects*.

[144] Macaulay, 'Ranke's *History of the Popes*—revolutions of the Papacy', 228. See also, MLC [Trollope], *The New-Zealander on London Bridge*, 12, 18–20, 22–3, 25; *New Zealand, a poem*; Buller, 17 June 1845, *A corrected report of the debate in the House of Commons, on the 17th, 18th, and 19th of June on the state of New Zealand and the case of the New Zealand Company*, 6. Cf Dening, *Mr Bligh's Bad Language*, 262–76 ('Purea' of Tahiti); Smith, *European Vision and the South Pacific, 1768–1850*, 252–3.

[145] Stein, 'The Four Stage Theory of Development of Societies', in Stein, *The Character and Influence of the Roman Civil Law*, 395–409; Pocock, *Barbarism and Religion: Volume Four*, 168–71 (centrality of 'appropriation').

[146] Haakonssen, *The Science of the Legislator*.

[147] Hickford, '"Decidedly the Most Interesting Savages on the Globe"'.

[148] Hickford, 'Making "Territorial Rights"', 25–38.

[149] Hickford, 'Making "Territorial Rights"', 233, 299–300.

fellow-labourers, as fellow-citizens, and, if possible, as connected by intermarriage'.[150] He regarded 'amalgamation, by some means or other, [as] the only possible Euthanasia of savage communities'.[151] As Bernard Cadogan shows persuasively, Grey's lengthy career reveals an 'amalgamationist' strain, not only in respect of Māori and Xhosa in the Cape Colony, but also in producing 'neo-Harringtonian' settler communities predicated on freehold parcels of land.[152] In broad conceptual terms, incorporation was a trope familiar to Westminster politicians who had experienced debates concerning repeal of the Test Act and the Corporation Act, as well as the emancipation of Roman Catholics in 1828 and 1829.[153] Indeed, Canningites such as Charles Grant the younger (Baron Glenelg) in the discussions around Catholic emancipation actively deployed the theme rhetorically: if Roman Catholics were incorporated, 'the moderate party will then come forward, while the violent party will be constrained and kept within bounds'.[154] Throughout the 1830s, Ireland, that oft-vexing part of Britain's empire, continued to pose considerable challenges to policy-makers in London. Sewell, following Grey chronologically but becoming one of his political contemporaries on account of Grey's episodic returns to New Zealand, was a legally trained, second-generation incorporationist within New Zealand.

But politicians of different views could coalesce on the broad outcome or design without agreeing on ways and means or motives. As a colonial politico, Sewell wrestled with detailed experimental proposals, whether in the form of the design of the Native Reserves Act 1856, for which he expressed much affection, or the variety of experiments in 1858 aspiring to court Māori attentions and to supply statutory corridors for Māori to access the colonial body politic and economy on colonial terms. As a colonial law officer in 1862 (Attorney General), he again analysed the legal parameters of the 'territorial rights' of Māori.[155] Sewell, like others such as Francis Dart Fenton or William Martin, and imperial figures of influence, including Sir Frederic Rogers, was looking to craft windows or portals of communicability between indigenous and introduced colonial norms around property and political authority. Speaking to a House of Commons Select Committee, Sewell surmised that the 'extinction of their tribal right and the substitution of an individual title to land is the first step, and the most important step, towards, if possible, saving them'.[156]

Imperial policy-makers were acutely aware of the inherent pretence of asserting effective territorial jurisdiction and political authority over swathes of territory such as New Zealand. This is not the novel insight into empire that some have claimed. Alan Ward, in his classic and unsurpassed study *A Show of Justice*, observed this point from the localized colonial perspective almost 40 years ago.[157] As Lisa Ford has recently argued, this fluidity and tentativeness was as much a feature of colonial New South Wales as of colonial northern America and the early United States.[158] Many politicians

150 Merivale, *Lectures on Colonization and Colonies*, 2nd edn, 511.
151 Ibid.
152 Cadogan, 'Constituting the Settler Colony and Reconstituting the Indigene'.
153 Hilton, *A Mad, Bad, & Dangerous People?*, 379–97; Drescher, *Abolition*, 245–66.
154 *HPD*, 2nd series, 12 May 1828, xix, cols 598–600.
155 See Chapter Seven.
156 'Report from the Select Committee on New Zealand', *GBPP1857*, sess. 2, ix (HC171), 23.
157 Ward, *A Show of Justice*.
158 Ford, *Settler Sovereignty*, 51.

and officials in London expressed comfort with such a pluralistic situation, needing no 'myths of empire' to ease themselves psychologically. The motif of incorporating indigenous populations vied uneasily with that of alliance and diplomacy—what Merivale referred to as the 'policy of insulation'—of a sort that applied in the United States, leaving 'them, in their allotted reserves, subject to their own laws and usages, so far as our established morality may allow of these prevailing'.[159] Accustomed to the innate fragility and fluidity of empire's pretensions in New Zealand, a number of imperial officials, including Rogers, successor to James Stephen and Merivale as permanent under-secretary to the Colonial Office, nevertheless saw it as temporary. Others, like Merivale, who reflected on the New Zealand situation in the early 1860s as war erupted once more, saw the peculiar recognition of native title in New Zealand as a failure. Musing in 1861, Merivale claimed, '[i]f the doctrine that the natives were absolute owners of the soil, and not compellable to part with it, was to be maintained, British settlers should have been excluded and the North Island maintained as a native reserve'.[160] Better still, then, to have 'treated [Māori from the beginning] as clients for whom the British government was authorised to act—no fancied "right" of ownership acknowledged, but fair compensation always made them whenever land, over which a tribe was accustomed to range, was taken for the use of settlers'.[161] In this vein, the treaty initially entered into at Waitangi on 6 February 1840 was a precursor, a curtain-raiser to the Crown's formal admission to the politics of negotiability with pre-existing Māori polities.

'LORDS OF THE LAND'—MID-NINETEENTH-CENTURY NEW ZEALAND WAS NOT A PLACE FOR 'BANAL CONSTITUTIONALISM'

New Zealand is an interesting place in which to see indigenous property rights in the jurisprudence of settlement-empire. In the 1840s, 1850s, and early 1860s it was a place where several forms of settler-indigenous political relationship coexisted and vied for pre-eminence, irrespective of what the formalities of anglophone constitutionalism and the timbre of claims to overarching sovereignty, authority, or jurisdiction might suggest.[162] These relations were not static. We see a shifting mosaic of coexisting sources and practices of pākehā and Māori political and legal authority—sometimes competing, sometimes mingling, sometimes capable of being interpreted by each participating community in ways congenial to its preferred views of government and power in New Zealand, sometimes not. Crudely put, '[absolute pākehā settler or Māori self-rule or] sole control, limited control, and shared control' coexisted.[163] Marked by polyvalent authority, both amongst Māori and within Britain and its settler populations, one witnesses a variety of competing and changing interpretations of political authority and relations of power.[164] Recently, Lauren Benton has noted that, 'Even in

[159] Merivale, *Lectures on Colonization and Colonies*, 2nd edn, 522–3.
[160] Ibid, 498 (note). [161] Ibid.
[162] Belich, 'Governors and the Māori (1840–1872)', in Sinclair (ed), *The Oxford Illustrated History of New Zealand*, 75–6; Belich, 'Hobson's Choice', 203.
[163] Belich, 'Hobson's Choice', 203.
[164] Cf Hulsebosch, *Constituting Empire*, 5.

the most paradigmatic of cases, an empire's spaces were politically fragmented; legally differentiated; and encased in irregular, porous, and sometimes undefined borders'.[165] New Zealand was characterized by varying degrees of governance insofar as the infant colonial state was concerned. Concepts of what the Colonial Office in London called the 'territorial rights of the natives' proved to be a key lever in setting out and negotiating the relations of colonial administration to the entwined issues of Māori political authority and authority concerning the command of territorial space. Concrete practices on the ground informed the politics of negotiability at the intra-Māori level and within colonial settlements, as well as amongst and between imperial and colonial politics.

Exploring native title in these contexts informs us about the real life of both New Zealand's historical constitution and the imperial historical constitution.[166] Looking at native title and its relationship with the historical colonial and imperial constitution yields important insights as to how these constitutions operated in practice, as well as how common law ways of thinking and politics grappled with uncertainty and the territorial claims of indigenous communities. It is not enough to prefer factors on the ground in the colonies as driving concepts of native title. They certainly did not do so exclusively. As Darwin has said, localized pressures both in colonies and in the imperial metropole drove the political marketplace of empire: 'the chaotic pluralism of British interests at home and their agents and allies abroad'.[167] If it makes sense to see the empire as a network, web-work, or a series of web-works, then it also makes sense, as this study will show, to look at the trans-oceanic ties of imperial politics, law, and policy-making and how these affected or were inflected by entanglement with the messiness of indigenous and colonial politics.[168] In other words, such an approach allows one to explore the interactions between the metropolitan and colonial within a single 'analytic field', as methodologically challenging as that might be.[169] What follows is not only a history of part of Britain's 'empire project'[170] localized in time and place, but one that is trans-oceanic in scope. Darwin's important *Empire Project* approaches empire from this perspective as well.

Throughout this mid-nineteenth-century period, formulators of, and contributors to, imperial policy on colonial settlement and native title, missionaries, and settler politicians, wrestled with making portals or windows of communicability between Māori conceptions of power and authority over place (land, water) and introduced ways of seeing property rights and rights of government. Examples of such efforts multiplied in the 1850s and early 1860s. By 1858 the General Assembly in New Zealand had passed a Native Territorial Rights Act 1858, a Native Districts Act 1858, and a Native Circuit Courts Act 1858. Disputes regarding these experiments reverberated in London. They converged with various strands of the politics of Westminster, producing views and prompting reflections on imperial politics and constitutionalism. In doing so, they

165 Benton, *A Search for Sovereignty*, 3.

166 Andrew Sharp used the phrase 'real life of the constitution' in 'The Treaty in the Real Life of the Constitution', in Belgave, Kawharu, and Williams (eds), *Waitangi Revisited*, 308–29.

167 Darwin, *The Empire Project*, 3.

168 On 'networks', see Laidlaw, *Colonial Connections, 1815–45*, 13–16; Magee and Thompson, *Empire and Globalisation*.

169 Cooper and Stoler, 'Between Metropole and Colony', in *Tensions of Empire*, 15.

170 For the concept of 'empire project', see Darwin, *The Empire Project*, xi.

tell us about constitutionalism in mid-Victorian politics. For a Peelite Tory in 1852, such as William Gladstone, the place of native title afforded him opportunities to critique constitutional design for New Zealand. During the second reading of the New Zealand Constitution Bill in May of that year, Gladstone complained, '[i]nstead of suffering [colonial governments] to judge what are the measures best adapted to secure their peaceful relations with the aboriginal tribes, and endeavouring to secure their good conduct . . . a minister sitting in Downing Street must determine how the local relations between the inhabitants of the colony and the aboriginal tribes are to be settled, in every point down to the minutest detail'.[171] In 1861 Gladstone, in office as the Chancellor of the Exchequer in the Liberal Party ministry of Palmerston, cautioned the Secretary of State for Colonies, his long-standing Peelite confidante the fifth Duke of Newcastle, about the 'hopeless & incurable faults of our plan of attempting to manage such controversies whether on paper or in the field from the other end of the globe'.[172] For Gladstone, 'the doom of that system is written even if its hour be not yet come'.[173] Māori politicians (*rangatira* amongst them) and communities grappled likewise with new emphases and perspectives brought from across the seas, particularly the focus on the market in land. The failures of those involved tell us much about coping with these issues. They reveal a rich vein of talk and action about what to do with concepts of native title and how to understand it.

Constitutionalism within New Zealand was and remains pre-eminently political rather than juristic. The configurations and structures of settler politics gave rise to a politics of negotiability. Likewise, a politics of negotiability characterized the intersections amongst and between Māori communities, settler communities, and colonial administration. In the mid-nineteenth century, these were not places for what I call 'banal constitutionalism'. By 'banal constitutionalism' I mean a type of constitutional thought and practice, and a sense of relevant constitutional histories that is so dominant that it need not be demonstrated.[174] 'Banal constitutionalism' implies complacence and an absence of testing in politics—the forgetting of being because one's assumptions are never challenged. By contrast, constitutionalism in colonial New Zealand was not the sort that was unreflectively accepted as endemic and axiomatic.[175] Constitutional argument attracted the ardent and sophisticated attentions of pākehā New Zealanders.[176] It was to be found in the media of newspapers and pamphlets (published in New Zealand and the United Kingdom), as much as in a profusion of lectures and memoranda. Similarly, participants in disputes concerning New Zealand within metropolitan Britain in the 1840s, 1850s, or 1860s, whether in the Colonial Office or the imperial legislature, were inexorably drawn into New Zealand matters of constitutional moment. New Zealand was a place of contestation about indigenous property rights, claims to natural resources such as land, and the place of such rights and claims

171 Morley, *The Life of William Ewart Gladstone*, I, 645.

172 Gladstone to Newcastle, 30 January 1861, BL AddMss44531, fo.113.

173 Ibid.

174 I have adapted this concept from the suggestive idea of 'banal unionism' used by Colin Kidd in *Union and Unionisms*, 23. Kidd adapts the notion of 'banality' in this sense from the term 'banal nationalism' coined by the sociologist Michael Billig.

175 For a later period where this was arguably the case, at least insofar as anglophone forms of constitutionalism were concerned in New Zealand, see Hickford, 'Strands from the Afterlife of Confiscation'.

176 Cf Sharp, 'Constitutionalism', in Miller (ed), *New Zealand Government and Politics*, 108.

in larger debates about colonial constitutionalism. Māori and pākehā claimed the ability to challenge and shape those political and legalistic arrangements that claimed to act on them.[177] Not only did they claim such abilities but they acted upon them. They were also able to muster armed men in sufficient numbers. From the perspective of the Colonial Office in London, a multiplicity of constitutional positions amongst pākehā and Māori remained consistent with claims to overarching authority relative to non-British foreign powers—Britain's dominion in New Zealand as against the rest of the world.

Others might not have shared such a view. Irrespective of how European powers other than Britain may have interpreted such claims, various Māori disagreed with the view that Britain had acquired overarching authority in New Zealand. The negotiability and conditionality of Māori participation in Britain's empire or world-system was certainly appreciated. Indeed, it overstates the case to claim that British opinion leaders in the settlements or in the metropole insisted on what Belich has characterized as a 'myth of empire' without recognizing the underlying tentativeness and incompleteness of empire in New Zealand. Imperial and colonial policy-makers, as well as settler politicians, such as Sewell in 1857 or 1859, for example, were aware of Māori thinking and acting outside the introduced constitutional order and its norms and were interested in confronting, contesting, or negotiating with this observed practice. Irrespective of that awareness, however, some influential commentators, including the first chief justice of New Zealand, Martin, sought to characterize such indigenous politics as occurring within the remit of colonial governance.

In all of these different views, native title proved to be an important lever in these relationships on the ground and in imperial outlooks in London. Imbuing native title with the quality of a 'right' in the introduced parlance of European rights-talk admitted Māori into a place at the heart of colonial administration where they could effectively contest the introduced constitutional order and the ways in which rights to territory were conceived and functioned.[178] This is not to say that various Māori elites were not endeavouring to carve out a specific form of associative participation (if not subjecthood) within empire. In recent suggestive work, Lyndsay Head has argued for just such a view, particularly in relation to elements of Ngāti Kahungunu, although she has chosen the problematically anachronistic term 'citizenship'.[179] I would suggest the more neutral term of 'association' in the sense that Māori elites pursued a variety of ways to frame their association with the imperial constitution. But 'citizenship' and 'subjecthood' represent a sense of subordination to, or incorporation within, a larger political entity or conglomerate, which Māori may not have entertained. British constitutionalism was not a singular phenomenon but comprised a variety of historically articulated forms or voices. In its political guise, British imperial constitutionalism proved adept at accommodating a range of possible forms of association with the amorphous and multi-dimensional Crown.

Notions of native title were forged in these dynamic settings. The subject of indigenous property rights provided a fertile field for creative disorder and ingenuity in

[177] Cf Ivison, 'Consent or Contestation?', in Webber and McLeod (eds), *Between Consenting Peoples*, 189. I am grateful to Duncan Ivison for sharing early drafts of his paper with me.
[178] Cf Ivison, 'Consent or Contestation?'.
[179] Head, 'Land, Authority and the Forgetting of Being in Early Colonial Maori History'.

constitutional and political discourse in New Zealand and Britain. Conceptions of native title were both made and in the making still. In this state of flux, legal genres transposed from across the seas, whether the common law or the law shared by all peoples (*ius gentium*), did not have the tranquillizing effect on these debates. They fueled them. They did not yield abstractly 'correct' legalistic answers. They provided different, often discordant, angles of vision or ways of seeing. At most, they furnished interpretive fields. The history of native title tells us about questions of law and power, their historicity and their contingencies. In this setting, incoming colonial government was often merely one more party pulled into internal Māori disputes and politics. Native title to land was mired in this universe of politics and constitutionalism. Indigenous property rights were not as the jurisprudence of empire thought them to be. In the hands of some, legalistic genres were certainly influential in disciplining the framing parts of the political debate on the nature and extent of native title, but were not determinative. Native title was not reducible to the interpretation of a unitary legal text or an ensemble of texts. This study, like Matthew Palmer's on the place of the Treaty of Waitangi in New Zealand's law and constitution, examines native title at play in the parry and thrust of the practices of politics.[180] In looking at the spatially and temporally localized histories and negotiated practices of native title, this study seeks to undermine the perceived timelessness of aboriginal rights, which seems to pervade or underlie various common law-orientated accounts or even seemingly casual observations in recent histories. It is not enough to speak en passant in the twenty-first century about '*rights of* self-determination' unquestionably, as if the concept applied reflexively and non-analytically in the mid-nineteenth century.

Broad terms such as 'modernity', 'jurisdiction', or 'sovereignty' applied generically or retrospectively to nineteenth-century actors or phenomena ought not to be allowed to become controlling, deterministic factors in historical explanation with the result of obscuring the rich nuances of actual political and legal interplay in the 1840s and 1850s.[181] Importantly, legal-political conceptions of 'jurisdiction' and 'sovereignty' did not conform to tidy lines or analytical categories. They were not the stuff of a transcendental collage or a magpie's hoard of professional legal texts, authoritatively determining what 'jurisdiction' was or was not conceptually; something that would have been applied properly only if it had been understood as part of some sort of abstract professionalized science. Messiness abounded. Influential settler politicians—many, like Sewell and William Fox, trained as lawyers—used legalistic genres in political debates about native title. Native title was barely discussed in the introduced colonial courts and court-based litigation did not exercise the interpretative or generative influence on native title that certain accounts might imply. Belich cautions against the determinism of one's own legalistic expertise—seeing law as the central canvass across which arguments were brushed and drawn—and the 'retrospective Utopianism of reform by appeal to a mythical golden age [or a mythical golden legal concept, which would

180 Palmer, *The Treaty of Waitangi in New Zealand's Law and Constitution*.

181 As Frederick Cooper cautions in *Colonialism in Question*, 8–9, when using broad analytical or abstract categories: 'First, the usefulness of an analytic category doesn't follow from its salience as an indigenous one: such concepts must perform analytic work, distinguishing phenomena and calling attention to important questions. Second, the academic's endeavor to refine and sharpen analytic categories may obscure the ways in which historical actors deployed similar terms, thereby complicating the task of understanding forms of discourse in their own contexts'.

have applied if only the relevant law was understood correctly]'.[182] Elsewhere he warns against any determinism in historical analysis, 'defining determinism as the promotion of one of several major historical forces to a master variable'.[183]

In this vein, while the decision of the Supreme Court of New Zealand in *Regina v Symonds* (1847) has received considerable attention in threads of the historiographical literature, to focus on case law provides a misleading impression of the place of native title in imperial politics and histories and risks overly elevating the ritualistic play of the courtroom. Legalistic genres and sources on *ius gentium* and the common law were certainly developed within the New Zealand and imperial debates on native title. But it was a highly episodic development in terms of cases. We find a more persistent use of such sources and ways of speaking amongst participants in political life. It would be mistaken to draw stark and schematic distinctions between a pre-positivist legal order and a legal positivist one and to see this alleged change in the nineteenth century as the key driver in changing conceptions of native title or the legal status of indigenous societies in colonial politics.[184] Legal positivism did not underscore any such alleged shift, although legal scholars in the 1980s and since have contributed to the view that it mattered profoundly to the fate of indigenous property rights in introduced colonial legal systems.[185] Likewise, to simply speak of 'scientific racism' as influential in this sense, uncritically allowing polygenists such as Robert Knox (1791–1862) and 'evolutionists' active and principally influential at a later time, such as Herbert Spencer (1820–1903), Charles Darwin (1809–1892), and Alfred Wallace (1823–1913), to converge is not illuminative.[186] Nor is it correct to attribute the supposed shift in colonial approaches to indigenous communities to 'social Darwinism' (as McHugh does in *Aboriginal Societies*), which is far too early and anachronistic for the 1860s, as John Burrow pointed out some time ago.[187] Critically, the elements of policy and intellectual sources, including the 'civilizational perspective' identified by Mandler, that came to be associated with a statutory encasing of indigenous claims to territorial space were already evident in the decade preceding that of the 1860s and had obtained a purchase on developments regarding native title.

From an allied but different perspective, Damen Ward has entered the fray from the standpoint of the 'politics of jurisdiction'.[188] As Eliga Gould and Damen Ward have demonstrated through deep research, jurisdiction is a useful analytical tool with which to approach the ambivalent legal status of indigenous populations and questions of violence, as well as the susceptibility of indigenous people to criminal prosecution and the

[182] Belich, 'Hobson's Choice', 206.

[183] Belich, 'How Much Did Institutions Matter?, in Greene (ed), *Exclusionary Empire*, 250.

[184] McHugh, 'A History of the Modern Jurisprudence of Aboriginal Rights', in Dyzenhaus, Hunt, and Huscroft (eds), *A Simple Common Lawyer*, 225.

[185] Ibid.

[186] Belich, *The New Zealand Wars*, 323–4. Tony Ballantyne uses the broad term 'scientific racism' in discussing Belich's approach in 'Colonial Knowledge' in Stockwell (ed), *The British Empire*, 194. As Peter Mandler has noted, Knox's influence was limited: *The English National Character*, 74; Mandler, 'The Problem with Cultural History', 96–103.

[187] McHugh, *Aboriginal Societies*, 125–6; Burrow, *Evolution and Society*. See also Burrow, *The Crisis of Reason*, 92–6.

[188] Ward, 'The Politics of Jurisdiction' and Ward, 'A Means and Measure of Civilisation', 001–023.

enforcement of colonial criminal law.[189] Ward, for one, identifies the significance of jurisdiction to debating issues of constitutionalism in colonial New Zealand but in a way that has not valorized the explanatory power of claims to 'jurisdiction' (particularly those seen through court decisions) above all other historical explanations. He has seen it as an issue that occasionally converged with questions of indigenous property interests. But jurisdiction, too, posed its own spheres of political concern in settler politics. As with indigenous property rights, arguments concerning jurisdiction were also presented in a variety of sites and not simply curial ones. Ward thus agrees with the approach that the 'conflation and confusion of legal categories is best appreciated by explicating the differing views of legal principles and categories from within the policy debates'.[190] Elsewhere, Ward has unsurprisingly cautioned against any tendency to see any particular legal doctrine—whether 'jurisdiction', 'territory', 'property', or 'sovereignty'—as supplying a key to understanding any form of colonial government.[191]

UNRAVELLING AND REFRAMING MĀORI CONSTITUTIONAL AND POLITICAL THOUGHT ON TERRITORIAL RIGHTS

In worlds of contested, dispersed, and polyvalent sites of authority, Māori had their own senses of constitutionalism. Māori concepts of association with *anglophone* empire were not the same as absorption or submergence within empire. Relations to land reveal this quality. Various elites within Māori communities displayed ease in adjudging the conduct of the agents of the Crown from across the seas. Just as importantly, they felt able to present themselves as better interpreters of how the introduced forms of legal and political authority ought to be conducted. Literacy amongst Māori was increasingly widespread. It shaped set-piece rhetorical engagements with colonial government and imperial administration through the publication of letters and the presentation of petitions. This was not only a feature of parts of the Kīngitanga. Those who were comfortable with presenting themselves as allies of the incoming settlements, and the normative orders brought with them, were also confident in their abilities to judge and critique the pretensions of colonial governments. As scholars like Monty Soutar have argued, Māori choices favouring alliance with the Crown were as much strategies to do with creating and building spaces of political autonomy for Māori tribal groupings who opted for such alliances relative to other tribal groupings.[192] That is, where a tribal grouping preferred to expand its range of political choices through alliances with the Crown or its settlers, either the Crown or those settlers could be lured in to assist in boosting the commercial and political autonomies of the grouping relative to its erstwhile tribal competitors or any putative tribal hegemon. Ngāti Whare and Ngāti Manawa strategically determined that some of their constituent *hapū* would align

189 Gould, 'Zones of Law, Zones of Violence', 489–500.

190 Ward, 'Constructing British Authority in Australasia', 483–504.

191 Ward, 'Imperial Policy, Colonial Government and Indigenous Testimony in South Australia and New Zealand in the 1840s', in Dorsett and Hunter, *Law and Politics in British Colonial Thought*, 229–47. See also Ward, 'Legislation, Repugnancy and the Disallowance of Colonial Laws', 381–402.

192 Soutar, 'Ngāti Porou leadership'.

with the colonial administration while others would assist those associated with the Kīngitanga.[193] To package these choices unproblematically as histories of resistance or alliance with an incoming Crown is to obscure the richness and many of the complexities of Māori politics and political thought.

What the presence of the inextricably complicated Crown (its officers, and its official and informal cultures) was generally prized for was not the legalistic norms introduced by its settlers.[194] Rather, what was prized was access to such norms and to the mobile, fluid trans-oceanic world-system that the constitutional position of the Crown appeared to represent, preferably on Māori terms.[195] Ongoing negotiated associations with parts of (and possibly within) a wider 'British world' were in the offing. The impression is one of a politics of negotiability without end—a willingness to preserve spaces for ongoing negotiation and re-negotiation. Māori politicians were also able to engage in forms of intellectual arbitrage, selecting some introduced resources, such as legalistic vocabularies or legal standards, as appealing or useful, and refraining from using others. A number of Māori chiefs, such as Wīremu Tāmihana, engaged in frequent letter writing. In the words of one historian, the intention of Tāmihana, a key theorist of the Kīngitanga, was to retain his community's 'political autonomy and pluralist structure'.[196] Of course, it would be a mistake to see policies, practices, and discussions concerning indigenous territorial claims or property rights as unremittingly secular. Ecclesiology was undoubtedly important. Māori adapted and used ecclesiological tropes to judge and criticize the incoming colonial interpretations of territorial claims and entitlements to territorial space, as well as constitutional orders. Hence, figures such as Rēnata Tama-ki-Hikurangi Kawepō of Ngāti Kahungunu or the so-called 'king-maker', Wīremu Tāmihana Tarapīpipi Te Waharoa of Ngāti Hauā, combined various legalistic and ecclesiological vocabularies to produce both set piece and *ad libitum* criticisms of colonial constitutionalism, whilst artfully constructing novel forms of indigenous constitutional behaviours and order.

In doing so, many also asserted rights and expressed views on constitutional order and government with a sense of entitlement independent of the introduced constitutional law as conventionally interpreted by pākehā jurists and politicians. Prominent Māori figures like Tāmihana did not accept the newcomers' claimed ascendancy in the districts beyond littoral settlements at New Plymouth or Auckland. They claimed an ability to negotiate and, ultimately, to determine the legal and political meaning of relationships with land and natural resources generally. Recognizing such practices also begins to blur the boundaries casually assumed to exist between the activities and discourses of British politics and those of indigenous Māori politics.[197] Communication

[193] Personal communication with John Hutton. See also Binney, 'Te Upokokohua: The Curse of Confiscation on Te Urewera', in Boast and Hill, *Raupatu*, 222–32, 223–4.

[194] On the complexities and problematic of '*the Crown*' (noting that the convenient shorthand of the definite pronoun '*the*' obscures those complexities) (as well as the ways in which Māori actors could claim an interest in it as participants and exerters of influence), see Hickford, 'John Salmond and Native Title in New Zealand', 853–924; Hickford, 'Strands from the Afterlife of Confiscation'.

[195] Judith Binney, for example, evocatively captured the nascent glimmerings of these networked relationships in 'Tuki's Universe', in Sinclair (ed), *Tasman Relations*.

[196] Head, 'Wiremu Tamihana and the *Mana* of Christianity', in Stenhouse and Wood (eds), *Christianity, Modernity and Culture*, 60.

[197] Cf Travers, *Ideology and Empire in Eighteenth-Century India*, 250–1.

is always risky to those who do not wish to be interpreted by others as accepting the legitimacy or determinative force of the politics they are criticizing or using to interact with strangers or settlers because it is useful for them to do so, episodically or on an ongoing basis. Pākehā jurists, politicians, officials, and media had sufficient conceptual and linguistic repertoire to characterize Māori practices and thought as having been brought *within* transposed or introduced *anglophone* conceptions of constitutionalism. Indeed, a risk for Māori elites was that where they chose to interact with settlers in transactions for the sale and purchase of land or in inviting resident magistrates to visit their communities, such behaviours could be interpreted as suggesting complacent allegiance on their part to the incoming Crown, acceptance of its pre-eminent authority or its preferred interpretations. In 1963, MPK Sorrenson noted: 'Contemporary European observers... adopted their own political and constitutional terminology to describe the movement and generally regarded it, for differing reasons, as an attempt to emulate European forms of government'.[198] Many Māori might disagree with such a view, acting as if outside of the colonial body politic.

In these circumstances, it is erroneous, this study argues, to see the myriad interactions between Māori polities, colonial and imperial politics through the binary lenses of coercion and resistance. New interpretative networks and communities were being formed, and dissolved and reconfigured, or simply reshaped in the to-ing and froing over questions as to who or what had meaningful authority to speak for territorial spaces and the ability to exert an influence on practical outcomes affecting those spaces. This pattern would not die. Evidence of it persisted with Māori communities adapting and appropriating texts, such as the Treaty of Waitangi or the scriptures, to criticize the perceived failings of colonial government. Legalistic interpretative genres were framed and deployed to criticize the normative shortcomings and inconsistencies of introduced government. In 1881, *The Northern Luminary* reported elite Māori attendees at a meeting in Waitangi on 24 March raising the 'question of right to the foreshores and fisheries, it being alleged that the Treaty never surrendered the sovereignty of the foreshores, and expressly reserved the right to the fisheries'.[199] The preceding observation, in looking to an episode in 1881, demonstrates that posing 1862 as a terminal date for this inquiry is largely deployed as a convenient time-bound boundary marker, as with so many endeavours to set out chronological boundaries to a study of a nuanced subject. Indeed, as I have intimated elsewhere, the politics of negotiability gave rise to conversations without end—there can be no permanent closure, and why should there be?[200]

[198] Sorrenson, 'The Maori King Movement, 1858–1885', in Chapman and Sinclair (eds), *Studies of a Small Democracy*, 33.

[199] 'Waitangi Meeting', *The Northern Luminary, Kawakawa, Bay of Islands*, 2 April 1881, r2.

[200] Hickford, 'Strands from the Afterlife of Confiscation', 189.

2

An Empire of Variations: Problems of Settlement and the Property Rights of Indigenous Populations

SEEING NATIVE TITLE THROUGH STADIALISM AND *IUS GENTIUM* ENTWINED

Juristic sources were not engaged alone in assessing native title or in constructing what may be characterized as a jurisprudence of indigenous property rights. While certainly drawn upon, they intermingled and contested with other sources in a larger pooling of influences at Westminister, throughout the United Kingdom, and in the colonial settlements themselves—reportage on ways of seeing colonies and the status of pre-existing populations. In approaching relations between incoming colonial settlements and these extant indigenous communities, Whigs such as Lord John Russell and Viscount Howick exhibited an attachment to stadial (or conjectural) history.[1] Russell (born in 1792) was Secretary of State for War and Colonies from 2 September 1839 until 2 September 1841. Much implicated in the initial phase of a developing appreciation of indigenous proprietary rights for Māori, he was a student of Dugald Stewart's in Scotland from 1809 to 1812. Stewart was the main transmitter of learning on Scottish interpretations of stadial history.[2] Russell acknowledged 'New Zealanders' as:

> not mere wanderers over an extended surface, in search of a precarious subsistence; nor tribes of hunters or of herdsmen; but a people among whom the arts of government have made some progress; who have established by their own customs a division and appropriation of the soil; who are not without some measure of agricultural skill, and a certain subordination of ranks: with usages having the character and authority of law.[3]

Similarly, he announced on 13 February 1841 that Māori were 'aboriginal inhabitants... not in that low and mean state of capacity and cultivation in which the natives of some regions have been found'.[4] Such constructions were no rarity. Commentators with

[1] Hilton, *A Mad, Bad & Dangerous People?*, 475.

[2] Stewart, *Elements of the Philosophy of the Human Mind*, I, ch 4, §8. This treatment of Stewart is influenced by Collini, Winch, and Burrow, *That Noble Science of Politics*, 32–44; Stewart, 'Account of the Life and Writings of Adam Smith, LLD', in *Essays on Philosophical Subjects*, 293.

[3] Russell to Hobson, 9 December 1840, CO380/122, fo.73a, TNA; cf draft, Stephen, 29 October 1840, CO209/8, fo.491: 'On the part of the natives themselves, we shall have to contend with all the bad habits of an indolent predatory and wandering life'; Russell to Hobson, 28 January 1841, CO209/8, fos.454–6a, TNA.

[4] 'Lord John Russell and the New Zealanders', *Journal of Civilization*, 16.

various objects became fond of construing Māori as 'agriculturists' of a sort (or rather horticulturists planting *kūmara* or destroying the margins of forests, using a destructive train of fire to yield fern roots that could then be gathered for sustenance).[5] For some authors, these analyses contained spatially constrained implications for proprietary entitlements. Hence, writing anonymously in the *Dublin Review* (1840), Henry Chapman surmised: 'The New Zealanders do not require an enormous breadth of land, for they are, and always have been, cultivators—not hunters like the American Indians'.[6] A key point of distinction was environmental: 'America abounds with animals which either serve as food for the natives, or furnish them with the means of procuring by barter such objects as are suited to their wants—New Zealand on the contrary, has no aboriginal animals'. On this particular approach, '[a]mong hunters, such as the American Indians are at this day, no circumstance could give value to a small quantity of land, so as to make it provide for the subsistence of the natives; but with a race of cultivators, a great breadth of land is valueless'.[7] Versions of stadial history, as an overall form of analysis and speaking, still touched and suffused the intellectual repertoire of many influential persons in the early nineteenth century. Henry Temple, Secretary of State for Foreign Affairs as Viscount Palmerston for a period of ten out of the seventeen years from 1830, was yet another Stewart pupil.[8] Moreover, he had boarded at Stewart's home when attending Edinburgh University. Further, the instruction of William Lamb, the second Viscount Melbourne, was profoundly imbued with a peculiarly stadial appreciation of moving history whilst under the tutelage of the influential John Millar at Glasgow from 1799 until May 1801. His extant notes revealed the permeation of these influences, with the future premier referring to '1.—Hunters and Fishers—Natives of America—Little or no property—small societies—2. Shepherds—Tartars—Arabs—Ancient Germans—Property in Herds and Flocks—Society enlarged by greater facility of subsistence'.[9] This whiggish attachment to stadialism proved particularly resonant in the way it appraised indigenous populations and their normative relations with landscapes or natural resources, such as land, throughout an empire of variations.

Stadial history, derived from predominantly Scottish scholarship, habitually invoked a theory of history divided sequentially into three or four stages. Each stage was predicated upon a distinctive mode of subsistence, such as the pursuit of game and the collecting of fruits, or the husbandry of flocks.[10] Adam Smith expressed this view most succinctly, when commenting on four sequential aeons of human pathway—'1st, the age of hunters; 2nd, the age of shepherds; 3rd, the age of agriculture; and 4th, the age of commerce'.[11] Elsewhere, Smith referred to societies of 'hunters' and 'shepherds' (the 'second period of society'), 'nations of husbandmen', and when considering developments in preparations

5 See discussion below and Memorandum, New Zealand Company, undated, CO209/18, fos.331a–2, enclosed in Somes to Stanley, 11 November 1842, 317–22a; Wakefield to Ward, 30 May 1842, CO209/18, fo.260, TNA, referring to 'the agricultural habits of the aborigines'.

6 Chapman, 'New Zealand', 188.

7 Chapman, 'Zealand, New', *The Encyclopaedia Britannica*, XXI, 979.

8 Brown, *Palmerston*, 30–6.

9 Lecture notes, December 1799, Melbourne Mss, box 120/1-11, MP; cf Mitchell, *Lord Melbourne, 1779–1848*, 48–9.

10 For analyses, see Meek, *Social Science and the Ignoble Savage*, 2, 5–36; Pocock, *Barbarism and Religion: Volume Four*, 167–80. Generally, see Hont and Ignatieff (eds), *Wealth and Virtue*.

11 Smith, *Lectures on Jurisprudence*, Meek, Raphael, and Stein (eds), I, 25.

for war and justice.[12] In Smith's account, as in that of David Hume's preceding and less-elaborated perspectives on this point, property was treated as a mother lode and weathervane of civilization.[13] By 1803, John Millar presented the distribution of proprietorship and the manner of property's inception and recognition as vital components in assessing a society's place in historical time but also the nature of its governmental institutions.[14] Furthermore, the role and status of women relative to men within a given community was often a focal point in stadial theory. Tacitus had noted in his *Germania* how the 'care of house, home and fields' was left to womenfolk, the elderly and weaklings while the hale men despised peace but were indolent when not warring.[15]

Antiquity supplied insights as to the significance of those communities who, having become conversant with agricultural techniques (the plough especially), became relatively *sedentarized* through occupying territorial space in a somewhat stable fashion, generating transactional relations with strangers—trading commodities, for instance—from a spatially secure base. In 1767, Adam Ferguson wrote that, '[T]he inhabitants of Britain, at the time of the first Roman invasions, resembled, in many things, the present natives of north America: they were ignorant of agriculture; they painted their bodies; and used for cloathing [*sic*], the skins of beasts'.[16] Non-Scottish scholars, such as Antoines-Yves Goguet and Thomas Carte, driving historical narratives from biblical or Celticist sources, also broadly concurred in the perspective that, '[i]t was sedentary living and the appropriation of lands which created the social space necessary to state, market and culture, to the movement of laws, goods and ideas'.[17] Pocock has reminded us of the peculiarities of European historical narratives in which the histories of the European peninsula were presented as the outcome of periodic incursions of 'shepherding' peoples and their subsequent 'civilization'.[18] This stadial or conjectural theory of history conveyed expectations as to the nature and substance of proprietary interests at different moments in time. William Robertson contemplated the introduction of commerce, explaining, '[m]en are, indeed, far advanced in improvement before commerce becomes an object of great importance to them', adding:

> They must even have made some considerable progress towards civilization, before they acquire the idea of property, and ascertain it so perfectly as to be acquainted with the most simple of all contracts, that of exchanging by barter one rude commodity for another.[19]

Echoes of these assumptions lingered into a subsequent century, were manipulated, and translated into varying contexts by numerous writers. Thus, the early nineteenth-century adaptations, although various, its principal theoretical sources, lying in the eighteenth century and Millar's tome on the distinction of ranks, were not necessarily the most proximate historical sources for these adaptations. Alexis de Tocqueville's *Democracy in America* (1831), well read by philosophic Whig, philosophic radical, and tory audiences alike for

[12] Smith, *An Inquiry into the Nature and Causes of the Wealth of Nations*, Skinner (ed), II, 279–89, 297–305.

[13] Phillipson, *Adam Smith*, 108.

[14] Mandler, *The English National Character*, 24.

[15] Tacitus, *The Agricola and The Germania*, trans H Mattingly, 114.

[16] Ferguson, *An Essay on the History of Civil Society*, 75.

[17] Pocock, *Barbarism and Religion: Volume Four*, 77.

[18] Ibid, 2.

[19] Robertson, *The History of America*, I, 3.

diverse reasons and agendas,[20] contended how civilization failed to germinate amongst Native Americans despite earnest efforts of the 'Jesuits' in Canada and the 'Puritans in New England'.[21] Sedentarization again emerged as a vital ingredient in encouraging the formation of complex, settled civil societies. 'It is among hunting peoples', Tocqueville wrote, 'that civilization has the greatest difficulty managing to establish its dominion.' Indeed, the 'great failing of these legislators of the Indians was not to understand that, to succeed in civilizing a people, it is necessary above all to get them to settle down, and they can only do so by cultivating the soil; so it was first a matter of making the Indians farmers'.[22] Tocqueville proclaimed how it 'is in the forests of the New World, and not among the Europeans who populate its shores, that the ancient prejudices of Europe are found today'. What were these prejudices? They were the prejudices of the hunter and the warrior against the industry of farmers and other labourers. 'Hunting and war [having become "national customs"] seem to him the only cares worthy of a man'. The difficulty, according to Tocqueville, was that '[m]en who have once given themselves over to the idle and adventurous life of hunters feel an almost insurmountable distaste for the constant and regular work required by farming'.[23] '[I]n all that we call Teutonic institutions [or 'the customs recounted by Tacitus']', he contended, 'I am tempted to see only the habits of barbarians, and the opinions of savages in what we call feudal ideas.'[24] The significance of what Salesa analyses as 'racial crossings' in his pioneering study on nineteenth-century approaches to 'race mixing', attracted Tocqueville's attentions as primary agents of change. 'Wherever half-breeds have multiplied', argued Tocqueville, 'savages are seen to modify little by little their social state and change their mores.'[25] Much to the American jurist Joseph Story's chagrin, it appeared to him that Tocqueville had in successive editions borrowed much from his own text of *Commentaries on the Constitution of the United States* (1833) without any attribution.[26]

This is not to say, however, that other authors were not inclined to present interpretations of historical change predicated on predominant modes of subsistence. There was no shortage of writers to whom literate political elites could resort to frame past and present as well as the dynamics of change in particular communities, including indigenous populations in southern Africa, northern America, or Australasia. The evangelical cleric John Bird Sumner deployed stadial tropes in musing upon the origins of the human species: 'Adam and his posterity would have been hunters, supported by the produce of the chase, till their increase in numbers forced them first to the more regular occupation of shepherds, and afterwards still farther, to the higher improvements of agriculture'.[27] Sumner, appointed bishop for Chester in 1828 and Archbishop of Canterbury by Lord John Russell in 1848, was no stranger to elite political life. Furthermore, various scholarly descendants of Dugald Stewart's literary enterprises, such as Thomas Chalmers, the holder of the chair in moral philosophy at St Andrews from 1825, continued Stewart's themes on philosophic history and political economy

[20] Crook, *American Democracy in English Politics 1815–50*, 175–98.

[21] de Tocqueville, *Democracy in America (De La Démocratie en Amérique)*, Eduardo Nolla (ed), II, 530.

[22] Ibid, 530–1. [23] Ibid, 531. [24] Ibid, 532. [25] Ibid, 534.

[26] Story to Lieber, 9 May 1840, in Story, *Life and Letters of Joseph Story, Associate Justice of the Supreme Court of the United States, and Dane Professor of Law at Harvard University, edited by his son William W. Story*, II, 380.

[27] Sumner, *A Treatise on the Records of Creation, and on the Moral attributes of the Creator*, I, 48.

in diverse ways. Apparently, Chalmers did evangelicize it overall in a trope concerning political economy.[28] Nevertheless, this account of Chalmers is a narrative beyond the concerns of this study. Further, this is not the entire story. Many disparate intellectual sources influenced both Russell and Palmerston. For one thing, the former contributed to an early nineteenth-century anglocentric whiggish literature on the interpretation of English constitutional history and was not, for a time (apparently until the 1830s), particularly enamoured of Stewart's political economy.[29] This attachment to English constitutional history in the Foxite sense was as much a reason for Russell's appearance as a so-called liberal Anglican Whig with a faith in managed constitutional development than Stewart's instruction per se. Early nineteenth-century adaptations of the logics of stadialism lurked within so-called 'liberal Anglican' histories associated with scholars such as Thomas Arnold—the past was seen to live in the present and vice versa. Arnold was one of a group of scholars, other Noetics such as Henry Milman and Renn Dickson Hampden, based at one time or another at Oriel College in Oxford University.[30] Duncan Forbes and Richard Brent characterized Richard Whately along with Arnold as 'liberal Anglicans', with Arnold arguing for an identity of an Erastian church and the state in the United Kingdom supportive of Christianity.[31] Arnold, for one, thought Barthold Niebuhr to have poured too much scorn on the methods of eighteenth-century stadialism. Troubled by the social conditions of England, Arnold displayed a profound sense of anxiety as to what he perceived to be underlying the economic and intellectual conditions of the British population.[32] To narrowly prefer one's own kin to strangers could be presented as signs of a lack of improvement. As long ago as 1830, in an essay appended to the first volume of his work on Thucydides, Arnold viewed the narrow confines of tribal affiliation or clannishness as problematic—as signs of unimproved states of mind.[33] The testing ground for any individual or state, whether or not one centred on a multi-dimensional Crown (as in the United Kingdom and its empires through time), was to enlarge the circle of their concerns. This had a normative or moral significance too tied to Christianity—the spirit of revelation:

> As men in proportion to their moral advancement learn to enlarge the circle of their regards; as an exclusive affection for our relations, our clan, or our country is a sure mark of an unimproved mind, so is that narrow and unchristian feeling to be condemned, which regards with jealousy the progress of foreign nations, and cares for no portion of the human race but that to which itself belongs.[34]

As for individuals, so it was for states. A 'natural period in history, marking the transition of every country from what I may call a state of childhood to manhood',

[28] Hilton, *The Age of Atonement*, 39, 55–63; Chalmers, *On Political Economy in connexion with the moral state and moral prospects of society*; Chalmers, 'Political economy of a famine', 252. Cf Gambles, 'Rethinking the politics of protection', 929–31, for Tory concepts.

[29] Russell, *Essay on the History of the English government and constitution from the reign of Henry VII to the present time*; Hilton, *The Age of Atonement*, 38, n 8; Francis and Morrow, *English Political Thought in the Nineteenth Century*, 77–82.

[30] Hilton, *A Mad, Bad & Dangerous People?*, 465.

[31] Forbes, *The Liberal Anglican Idea of History*, 1, 2, 71, 121, 139, 147; Brent, *Liberal Anglican Politics*, 178–82; Arnold, *Fragments on Church and State*, 28, 58, 65.

[32] Forbes, *The Liberal Anglican Idea of History*, 4.

[33] Arnold, 'On the Social Progress of States' [1830], in *The Miscellaneous Works of Thomas Arnold, D.D.*, 111.

[34] Ibid.

Arnold surmised, was that captured by Thucydides in the transition from 'hereditary monarchy with established rights and limitations' to 'tyrannies established in nearly all the cities', increased revenues, flourishing shipbuilding, and 'ambition [turning] towards sea-power'.[35] Cycles of dawn, halcyon noon-time, and twilight decay suffused Arnold's liberal Anglican commentaries. Ancient histories of Greece and Rome continued to supply both admonitory and inspiring parallels to Britain's varied predicaments and challenges in the nineteenth century. Such uses of historical analogy, it is to be recalled, remained persistent.[36] In 1870 Herman Merivale saw comparisons between Britain's imperial fields and Athenian seaborne influence across sea routes and islands as opposed to the landed power of Sparta.[37]

Constitutional and governmental design was closely tied to the historically assumed conditions of proprietorship and civil society within a given community. 'Should any one propose', warned James Mill in *The History of British India* (1817), 'for a band of roving Tartars, the regulations adapted to the happiness of a regular and polished society, he would meet with neglect or derision.'[38] This broad political-economic approach towards understanding proprietorship and forms of governance combined an intermingling of two elements—first, an *initially* Lockean sense of tying appropriation to labour or exertion and, secondly, a developing but still contestable understanding as to the limits of *de facto* and *de jure* possession of an exclusive sort regarding seemingly open, unfenced spaces in mercantile or commercial societies. In 1833 George Poulett Scrope (1797–1876), an influential Whig parliamentarian, discussed a 'simple rule' that 'appears to have been universally adopted by every fraction of the human race', specifically, 'what a man obtains from nature *by his own exertions* becomes *his property*'. Here, the 'ideas of *meum* and *tuum*, founded on the natural law of appropriation by labour, are as old as the union of any two or three human beings in society'.[39] Scrope, himself an exponent of Edward Gibbon Wakefield's colonization schemes and a brother to Charles Edward Poulett Thomson (1799–1841), promulgated a robust view of law and legal sovereignty: the law itself is merely 'the *will* of the sovereign'.[40]

Jurisprudence, specifically *ius gentium*, also figured importantly. Within the Colonial Office, there was a predisposition—particularly on Stephen's part (as one instructed in the nuances of legal usage)—to approach issues with a form of legalism.[41] Stephen resorted to *ius gentium* in order to manage negotiations with the United States consular functionaries regarding the status of commercial fisheries in New Zealand during 1840—thus, recourse to discursive frameworks with consequences for

[35] Thucydides, *History of the Peloponnesian War*, trans Warner, I, 13.

[36] Collini, Winch, and Burrow, *That Noble Science of Politics*, 189–90.

[37] Merivale, 'The Colonial Question in 1870', 152–75.

[38] Mill, *The History of British India*, I, 429. On Mill generally, see the important account in Wilson, *The Domination of Strangers*, 135–44, and Stokes, *The English Utilitarians and India*, 53–4, 60–1, 70, 77, 78, 90.

[39] Poulett Scrope, *Principles of Political Economy*, 164–9.

[40] For discussion of 'will of the sovereign', see ibid, 103–6. On Scrope and Wakefield, see Semmel, *The Rise of Free Trade Imperialism*, 75, n 4, 97–8, 117–18.

[41] For example Robinson and Gallagher, *Africa and the Victorians*, 20: 'Whether a man entered the ruling circle through patronage, which was still usual, or through examination, which was becoming less rare, aristocratic traditions of duty to the whole nation and disdain for its parts persisted, as did the *legalism* with which they approached their problems' (emphasis added); Stephen to Hope, minute, 14 November 1842, CO209/18, fo.324a, TNA.

imperial practices.[42] More particularly, a jurisprudential account of relations with the indigenous inhabitants of a tract of territory courses through much of the narrative of imperial entanglements. It characterized a conception of certain Māori as possessing a capacity for treaty relations. Non-English, especially civilian Roman, sources of legal perspective were also used, particularly in relation to the interconnected regimes of *ius gentium* and *ius naturale*, natural law (often where novel or contentious issues or disputes were raised).[43]

Non-municipal, imperial issues involving a legalistic response often encouraged a resort to non-English texts. Crucially, these sources tended to be regarded, nonetheless, as sufficiently indigenized or 'English', furnishing idioms for conducting or presenting politicized conversations amongst anglophone participants themselves if not aboriginal inhabitants in New Zealand.[44] As such, a diverse series of sources could be referred to in the attempt to attain an opinion on an emerging political issue. This constituted a legitimate convention at this time. Certainly, in particular quarters, there was juridical evidence of a treatment of *ius naturale* or *ius gentium* as having been relevantly incorporated into municipal legal perspectives. In consequence, indigenized expressions of *ius gentium* were present in *dicta* attributed to Lord Mansfield in a series of decisions, including *Triquet v Bath* or *Heathfield v Chilton*.[45] In the former decision, Mansfield, presiding in the court of King's Bench, opined that the law of nations applied to England. This 'law' was to be collected from the practice of varied (European) nations and writers such as Hugo Grotius ('there being no English writer of eminence, upon the subject'). This conception of a 'law of nations' (*ius gentium*, for convenience) was inherently discursive in its shaping of political deliberations within the Colonial Office and in its relations with diverse persons or corporate assemblies beyond. It was, as James Mill aptly suggested, partly analogous to a 'ceremonial of a court, or the established forms of polished society'.[46]

In addition, early nineteenth-century evidence suggests that certain jurists remained comfortable with deploying forms of stadialism and mingling these with assessments of aboriginal populations in the light of *ius gentium* or natural law. Hence, the Supreme Court of New South Wales displayed such a tendency in regarding the legal status of aboriginal violence *inter se*. It described aborigines as 'harmless inoffensive savages' possessing 'natural rights' in the state of 'wandering about the country'.[47] In jurisprudential terms, this language of assessing the modes of subsistence supposedly pursued

[42] Stephen to Vernon Smith, 27 November 1840, CO209/6, fos.204–5; Vernon Smith to Gipps, 8 December 1840, CO209/6, fo.207a, TNA.

[43] Nassau Senior, 'Law of nations', 310–12; Lobban, *The Common Law and English Jurisprudence*, 19–26; Stein, *Legal Evolution*, 74–5.

[44] 'And the important point to remember is this, that the New Zealanders will not stop to ask us to define territorial rights for them, nor will they defer to the authority of writers on the *Jus Gentium*': 5 July 1847, *The Colonial Intelligencer; or the Aborigines' Friend*, 10 (1847), 152.

[45] *Triquet v Bath* (1764) 3 Burr 1478, 1481; 97 ER 936, 938; and *Heathfield v Chilton* (1767) 4 Burr 2015, 2016; 98 ER 50, 50.

[46] Mill, *Essays on Government, Jurisprudence, Liberty of the Press and Law of Nations, written for the supplement to the Encyclopædia Britannica*, 5 ('The article Law of Nations'); Mill, 'The law of nations', in *Encyclopædia Britannica*, Macvey Napier (ed), XIV, 134; see also Nassau Senior, 'Law of nations', 306–12.

[47] *Rex v Ballard or Barrett*, 13 June 1829, Supreme Court of New South Wales (Chief Justice Forbes and Justice Dowling presiding); see also, arguments of Dr Wardell and William Wentworth in *Rex v Lowe*, 18 May 1827, Supreme Court of New South Wales (Chief Justice Forbes and Justice

by indigenous populations represented a versatile approach to legal analysis. Indeed, certain courts used it comfortably and often meshed it with conclusions on *ius gentium* and appraisals of the political and legal significance of such modes of subsistence.

Trails of transmission to a particular colony and the relevance of empire

New Zealand Māori and their relations with landscapes were certainly analysed through a mingling of the logics of stadialism and *ius gentium*, a law of nations. Overall, however, we see an assembling of diverse sources—expressing, reflecting, and adjusting theological, jurisprudential, historical, and political economic genres—rather than tidily insulated capsules of thought. Technical aspects of these fluid genres or registers were deployed concretely in institutional configurations and relations, as well as policy disputes. Inextricably untidy human affairs could be distilled and rendered legible through sources drawn from *ius gentium* and stadial theory. The testing grounds often formed around whose preferred sources or preferred interpretations of sources would prevail on a particular question of what to do and why. Senior politicians, including aristocratic dynasts Lord John Russell and Viscount Howick, as well as Colonial Office functionaries, such as James Stephen, permanent under-secretary at the Colonial Office from 4 February 1836 until May 1848, inhabited a constellation of intellectual sources that they comfortably deployed in argument and in support of policy outcomes. These sources did not constitute a static corpus of learning or doctrine, nor were they irrelevant to their ways of perceiving political processes or distant locations. They used these sources self-confidently, contentiously, and argumentatively and approached political issues with an historical and legal frame of mind. These idioms or genres also configured and disciplined how these figures conceptualized or framed questions. These inhabited vocabularies were dynamic and mutable, as scholars such as John Burrow have noted in relation to political theory. As Burrow suggested in a broadly analogous situation, 'It is often more helpful, in writing the history of political thought [or of political process one could say], to think of political theories as vocabularies we inhabit, with their various claims, opportunities, and constraints, than as doctrines to which we subscribe'.[48] We are particularly fortunate with New Zealand exhibiting a rich profusion of often fraught conversations contesting sources explicitly, oft-times in ways affording opportunities to appraise the varying weight given to certain analyses of relations between settling newcomers and indigenous communities. Texts purporting to analyse these sorts of relations juristically were certainly available in the 1830s, a critical decade for the settlement of South Australia and the mooting of proposals for systematically settling New Zealand.

Yet, as will be seen in Chapters Three and Four, these sources were not necessarily gathered up and deployed. Much turned on localized contingencies—accessibility to certain texts or the inclinations of particular individuals, such as Henry Chapman in the United Kingdom and New Zealand or Sir George Gipps and John Walpole Willis in New South Wales. The Colonial Office often preferred its own sense of applicable precedents, mining its own narrative of practices. Thus, several possibilities for applying

Stephen presiding): B Kercher, Division of Law, Macquarie University, Australia, *Decisions of the Superior Courts of New South Wales, 1788–1899*, available at <http://www.law.mq.edu.au/scnsw>.

48 Burrow, *Whigs and Liberals*, 5.

United States jurisprudential approaches to native title to indigenous New Zealand emerged at distinct points in the 1830s and early 1840s. One set of contingent possibilities materialized in Australia. Another arose in Britain. In May 1840 Willis, a puisne judge in New South Wales to whom Gipps resorted to as a source of counsel, prepared an extensive paper marked 'private' concerning the 'acquisition of New Zealand as a dependency of New South Wales with reference to lands obtained by British Subjects from the Aborigines [of New Zealand]'.[49] Willis, in turning to the law of nations to discuss this topic, cited Vattel, praising the 'moderation of the English Puritans who first settled in New England; who notwithstanding their being furnished with a Charter from their Sovereign purchased from the Indians the lands they resolved to cultivate'. William Penn followed this 'laudable example'.[50] Willis remarked on the compatibilities of British experience in northern America with the early nineteenth-century British experience in New Zealand, seeing the similarities between the puritans in the former and the English missionaries in New Zealand. In his paper, the trove of sources drawn on attested to a favoured stock of high-level texts covering colonies and native title. Willis' notes traversed Kent's *Commentaries on American Law*, Clark's *A Summary of Colonial Law* (1834), and, apparently, Robert Montgomery Martin's *History of Austral-Asia* (1836).[51] Willis in Sydney discerned, as did Stephen in London, that in demonstrating the 'fallacy of the pretended Rights of British Subjects to Lands which have heretofore been obtained in the Dependency of New Zealand' would 'inevitably' prompt 'much raucous abuse'.[52] Willis remarked how the 'assertion of... Principles, however just, opposed as they are to individual interests of much magnitude' tended to lead to such disputes. As Zoë Laidlaw explores, Willis endeavoured to forge networks with Viscount Stanley and Robert Hay, the permanent under-secretary of the Colonial Office from 6 July 1825 until Stephen's appointment in February 1836.[53]

Chapman (1803–1881) was a correspondent of John Stuart Mill when in Britain or New Zealand, sending over a 'beautiful set of ferns' from New Zealand to Mill, as well as news of New Zealand affairs.[54] He assumed the role of first puisne judge of the Supreme Court of New Zealand on 26 December 1843 during that court's infancy under the chief justiceship of William Martin. Chapman first turned to journalism in 1833, 10 years after migrating to Canada, when he founded with Samuel Revans the *Daily Advertiser* in Montreal, the first daily paper published in Canada. He continued with a journalistic career upon returning to Britain in 1835. As a journalist, he was closely connected with the *London and Westminster Review* and there was talk in 1836

[49] Willis, 'Notes on the acquisition of New Zealand as a Dependency of New South Wales with reference to lands obtained by British Subjects from the Aborigines', May 1840, Mitchell Library, Sydney, Pamphlets collected by Mr Justice Wise, ML A857, 11-68 (microfilm CY746).

[50] Ibid, fos.19–20.

[51] Clark, *A Summary of Colonial Law*; Kent, *Commentaries on American Law* 1st edn; *Commentaries on American Law*, 3rd edn; *Commentaries on American Law*, 4th edn; Martin, *History of Austral-Asia*. Robert Montgomery Martin (1803?–1868), a statistician and a prolific historical writer was most well-known for authoring several books on the British colonies, including *The British Colonial Library*.

[52] Willis, fo.2.

[53] Laidlaw, *Colonial Connections, 1815–45*, 34, 112, 117.

[54] For instance, Mill to Chapman [November 1835], in Mineka (ed), *The Earlier Letters of John Stuart Mill 1812–1848*, XII, 284–5; Mill to Chapman, 29 February 1848, in Mineka (ibid), XIII, 731–3.

of Chapman establishing a radical paper with William Molesworth, JT Leader, and John Roebuck. In Roebuck's Benthamite *Pamphlets for the People* in 1835, Chapman contributed a number of articles promulgating the pre-eminence of the ballot box in a constitution and asserting a Jacksonian democratic position.[55] Associated with the liberal-radical politics of Roebuck and Mill in the United Kingdom,[56] Chapman eventually gravitated towards Wakefieldian proposals for the systematic colonization of New Zealand (as did Samuel Revans). His friend Revans voyaged first to New Zealand, arriving in the New Zealand Company settlement at Port Nicholson and establishing its first newspaper, the *New Zealand Gazette*. In February 1841 Chapman was appointed an agent for the sale of putative New Zealand Company lands acquired in New Zealand.[57] In that capacity, he travelled into northern England at the request of the directorate of the New Zealand Company 'for the purpose of disseminating information respecting the colony and the objects of the Company'.[58] He was not simply a colonial judge in New Zealand. He also presented as an investor, claiming properties in Nelson through the New Zealand Company, as well as owing £150 that remained unpaid for over a year.[59] Chapman identified the salience of United States jurisprudence on 'Indian title' in the fifth issue of *The New Zealand Journal* published in London in April 1840 under the auspices of the New Zealand Company. In that forum he concluded that the Marshall court decisions of *Johnson v M'Intosh* (1823), *Cherokee Nation v Georgia* (1831), and *Worcester v Georgia* (1832) were authorities for the position that '[p]rior discovery... in contemplation of international law gives to the discovering nation a right of sovereignty, as against all other civilised nations without any regard to the relation which the discovering nation might choose to establish with the native tribes'.[60] He also echoed these views elsewhere. In *The Comparative Prospects of Our New Colonies* (1841) he surmised the 'course which ought to have been pursued, in conformity with well-established principles of international law, was simple enough', specifically, 'Her Majesty's sovereignty ought to have been asserted throughout New Zealand, by virtue of prior discovery and occupation'. He added, 'This right of sovereignty should be understood to have force only against European powers, but the rights of the chiefs should be in all cases guaranteed'.[61] Leaving the substance of indigenous territorial rights relatively moot in *The New Zealand Journal*, Chapman stated that it 'must be clear that the rights reserved to the native tribes could only be of a modified character, but whether those rights were abridged or extensive—whether they were confined to a mere right of occupation, or amounted to something deserving the name of sovereignty, was a question which did not affect the relation between the discovering nation and other civilised powers'.[62] Here, in 1840, Chapman alluded to the ties between political authority over space and proprietary rights but refrained from exploring these linkages, opting to focus on the rights accruing to a 'discovering'

55 Chapman, 'The American Ballot-Box', in Roebuck (ed), *Pamphlets for the People*.

56 Thomas, *Philosophic Radicals*, 229, 297, 326.

57 Ward to Chapman, 18 February 1841, CO208/149, fo.350, TNA.

58 Minutes, Court of Directors, 22 July 1841, CO208/182, fo.111, TNA.

59 Minutes, Court of Directors, 22 June 1843, CO208/182, fo.21, TNA.

60 *Johnson v M'Intosh* 8 Wheat 543 (1823) (USSC); *Cherokee Nation v State of Georgia* 5 Pet 1, 8 L Ed 25 (1831); *Worcester v State of Georgia* 6 Pet 515, 31 US 350 (1832); see Chapman, 'The English, the French, and the New Zealanders', 1.

61 Henry Chapman, *The Comparative Prospects of Our New Colonies*, 174.

62 Chapman, 'The English, the French, and the New Zealanders', 1.

European polity relative to others.[63] As will be seen in Chapter Four, Chapman considered these ties more directly in 1846–1847, but those reflections were a consequence of his reflections on his time as a puisne judge in New Zealand.

The attractiveness and utility of the multi-volume collections of James Kent (*Commentaries on American Law*) and Joseph Story (*Commentaries on the Constitution of the United States*)[64] was that each relatively portable text conveyed a cargo of decisions distilled in summary, able to be transposed across the seas, and presented both a persuasive *ex post facto* account of the histories of relations between Native American communities and European settlements together with updated footnotes across editions. Gipps cited Story in relation to Māori in 1840. At one level, these texts formulated generic assessments of these Native American communities. 'There is no doubt', said Story, 'that the Indian tribes, inhabiting this continent at the time of its discovery, maintained a claim to the exclusive possession and occupancy of the territory within their respective limits, as sovereigns and absolute proprietors of the soil.'[65] Yet the casual albeit understandable temptation to see a developing American jurisprudence on Native Americans as something that would have applied inexorably or ought to have applied to New Zealand must be avoided. Instead, considering its precise uses in argument on indigenous property rights, one sees contested claims for its relevance. In this sense, it is important to chart exact uses and moments when these sources were actively called upon, and whether and how their claims to meaningful relevance were debated. As I have discussed elsewhere, a vital conveyor or carrier source proved to be Joseph Chitty the elder's 1834 English edition of *The Law of Nations or the Principles of the Law of Nature applied to the Conduct and Affairs of Nations and Sovereigns* by Emerich de Vattel.[66] According to the Stationery Office archive at this time, it enjoyed a life in use for colonial governors.[67] Furthermore, this English translation of Vattel's tome on *ius gentium* often materialized in political disputes in Westminster departments or Parliament, an observation that will be demonstrated in this book.[68] Vattel was even

[63] Hickford, '"Decidedly the most interesting savages on the globe"', 182; Hickford, '"Vague Native Rights to Land"', 175–206; Hickford, 'Settling some very important principles of colonial law', 15.

[64] Kent, *Commentaries on American Law*; Story, *Commentaries on the Constitution of the United States*.

[65] Story, *Commentaries on the Constitution of the United States*, I, 5.

[66] Hickford, '"Decidedly the Most Interesting Savages on the Globe"', 131–2, and Hickford, '"Vague Native Rights to Land"', 180–1. The full citation for Vattel's work is *Le Droit des Gens, Ou Principes de la loi naturelle, appliqués à la conduit & aux affaires des nations & des souverains [The Law of Nations or the Principles of the Law of Nature applied to the Conduct and Affairs of Nations and Sovereigns]*, Chitty (ed).

[67] For instance, J Church, comptroller (Stationery Office) to Spearman, 28 December 1837, CO18/21, fo.91, referring to 'Chitty on the Law of Nations' [either Chitty, *A Practical Treatise on the Law of Nations, relative to the legal effect of war on the commerce of belligerents and neutrals; and on orders in council and licences* (London, 1812) or (but more probably due to its generalist qualities) Chitty's 1834 edition of Vattel's text]' at a cost of 10*s*.6; William Spain, a New Zealand land claims commissioner, possessed Chitty's edition of Vattel's text: Spain to FitzRoy, 13 April 1844, CO209/33, fos.102–4a, TNA.

[68] Vattel, *The Law of Nations or the Principles of the Law of Nature applied to the conduct and affairs of Nations and Sovereigns*; English translation Chitty (ed). References to Vattel include: Stephen, minute, on Gipps to Russell, 19 February 1840, CO209/6, fo.33a, TNA; 'Report of the select committee of the House of Lords appointed to inquire into the present state of the islands of New Zealand', *GBPP1837–1838*, xxi (680), 460 (Samuel Hinds testimony).

used baldly in imperial discussions with Māori. The Whig sympathizer, William Spain, as a commissioner investigating the territorial claims of the New Zealand Company, entertained the possibility of explaining to Ngāti Toa *rangatira* Te Rauparaha how indulgent Britain had been in not seizing aboriginal territories under a Vattelian (pre) text.[69] He informed Te Rauparaha:

> The Government has treated the natives well throughout the whole of the colonization of these islands. What is the law which regulates all Nations in Europe in taking possession of a Country like this? Here is a vast country whose scanty population is incapable of occupying the whole. In such a case it is a law with the natives of Europe that the inhabitants of such a country have no right to appropriate to themselves more land than they have occasion for, or more than they are able to settle or cultivate. Their unsettled habitation in these regions cannot be held a true and legal possession—and the natives of Europe too closely pent up at home... are lawfully entitled to take possession of it... But how have the Natives of this Country been treated?... they have been paid largely and liberally for their land. England adopts the mild and generous course, and treats fairly and protects the Natives.[70]

Te Rauparaha was not impressed.[71] Spain would additionally refer to Vattel in his final report on disputed purchases in Taranaki.[72] Significantly, major works of English authors, such as George Cornewall Lewis' *An Essay on the Government of Dependencies* (1841), Charles Clark's *A Summary of Colonial Law* (1834), or William Burge's *Commentaries on Colonial and Foreign Laws generally and their Conflict with each other and the Law of England* (1838), while setting out broad precepts, did not commend legal-policy solutions to the distinct problems of indigenous property rights, if any, in places like New Zealand, upper Canada, South Australia, Natal, or New South Wales.[73] Not for Stephen or his successor as permanent under-secretary in the Colonial Office, Herman Merivale, the episodic engagement of a self-dramatizing legalist politician-scholar, like Cornewall Lewis (1806–1863), or barrister, such as Burge, who had been Attorney General in Jamaica. Stephen and Merivale not only lived the experience of legal-policy formulation and design but also reflected on it, framing it intellectually. For all the attractions of reifying a single text from the distant standpoint of the early twenty-first century, Lewis' political engagement with the practical and intellectual messiness of colonial governance was limited, and such involvement as he did have owed much to his political influence as a senior member of particular ministries.[74] A jurisprudentially minded politician, he attended John Austin's otherwise poorly

[69] Spain to FitzRoy, 13 April 1844, CO209/33, fos.102–4a, TNA; private secretary to Viscount Palmerston and central Whig secretary for Hampshire. See Oliver (ed), *The New Zealand Dictionary of Biography: volume I, 1769–1869*, 402.

[70] Spain to Te Rauparaha, March 1844, CO209/37, fos.152a–4, TNA. To Robert FitzRoy, the governor, Spain expressly revealed his reliance upon 'Chitty's New Edition of The Law of Nations from the French of de Vattel—published in 1834 page 100': Spain to FitzRoy, 13 April 1844, CO209/33, fo.102a, TNA.

[71] Te Rauparaha to Spain, 27 March 1844, CO209/37, fos.157–8a, TNA.

[72] Spain to FitzRoy, 31 March 1845, CO209/37, fo.219a, TNA.

[73] Cornewall Lewis, *An Essay on the Government of Dependencies*; Clark, *A Summary of Colonial Law*; Burge, *Commentaries on Colonial and Foreign Laws generally and their Conflict with each other and the Law of England.*

[74] See Chapter Six.

attended lectures in jurisprudence at London University in 1829 and 1830.[75] There was an underlying sense in which the real life of imperial law and practice was experienced inside the ministerial department and barely or episodically in the worlds of courts, academia, or elite political or jurisprudential texts.[76] In advising and counselling on imperial matters, Stephen, Merivale, and Rogers supped both the nourishment and frustrations of lived practice. So too did Viscount Howick, having fashioned himself as an expert through practice as an intellectually orientated and activist parliamentary under-secretary for colonies (November 1830 until April 1833) as well as Secretary of State for Colonies (as the third Earl Grey) from July 1846 until 27 February 1852. He authored an extensive reflection drawing upon his experiences and readings, with prognoses offered to those sympathetic to a whiggish perspective on imperial policy.[77]

Stadial histories and *ius gentium* mediated the influences of early nineteenth-century receptions of monogenism as well. Monogenism, a common predilection within early nineteenth-century evangelical texts, considered humanity, in spite of its physical diversities, to be derived from a single origin.[78] As such, Prichard concluded, 'all human races are of one species and one family'.[79] This perception was chiefly premised upon assumptions of ancient diffusionary migratory trails, as illustrated by comparative physiognomy and linguistic affinities. Robert Latham would persist in stressing these evidential features in 1850 and 1851.[80] An American observer, Horatio Hale, engaged in similar theorizing.[81] Researches of a naturalist in New Zealand, Ernest Dieffenbach, affirmed this orientation regarding Māori with the comment, 'history leads us to conclude the races are not different in their origin, and forbid the idea of inferiority, and of the necessity of one race being superseded by another'. In addition, he elaborated that, 'different races are the radii from the common centre; and that the differences which we observe are due to peculiar circumstances [hereditarian or environmental factors] which have developed certain qualities of body and mind'.[82] Dieffenbach's observations cannot be disregarded as isolated from the literary enterprises associated with either Latham or Prichard since both of these individuals appreciatively referred to his endeavours, confirming networks or circuits of monogenist tendencies and readerships. This monogenism has been acknowledged as possessing *an* intellectual presence—admittedly challenged by polygenism—by recent chroniclers whilst this study accepts that evidential assumption in a general sense (with sustenance from both primary and

[75] Smith, 'Lewis, Sir George Cornewall, second baronet (1806–1863)', in *Oxford Dictionary of National Biography*; online edn, May 2009 at <http://www.oxforddnb.com/view/article/16585>, accessed 30 April 2010.

[76] Hickford, 'Making "Territorial Rights".

[77] Earl Grey, *The Colonial Policy of Lord John Russell's*, a work subjected to searching political critique in Rt Hon CB Adderley MP, *Review of 'The Colonial Policy of Lord J. Russell's Administration'—by Earl Grey, 1853; and of Subsequent Colonial History, Part I.*

[78] Ellis, *Polynesian Researches*, II, 49–52; Sumner, *A Treatise on the records of creation*, I, 45–50, II, 34–5, 44, 407.

[79] Prichard, *The Natural History of Man*, 546.

[80] Latham, *The Ethnology of the British Colonies and Dependencies*, 203–4, 214; Latham, *The Natural History of the Varieties of Man*, 562; see also MacGillivray, *Narrative of the Voyage of HMS Rattlesnake*, I, 80–4 ('Australian' and 'Papuan race'); Burrow, 'The uses of philology in Victorian England', in Robson (ed), *Ideas and Institutions of Victorian Britain*, 180–204.

[81] Hale, *United States exploring expedition*; Wilkes, *Narrative of the United States exploring expedition*, 172.

[82] Dieffenbach, *Travels in New Zealand*, II, 137.

secondary literature, including Niel Gunson's exemplary account of missionary activities in the Pacific).[83] Importantly, advocates of monogenism predominated in the ethnological subsection of the British Association for the Advancement of Science and in its literary output.[84] Monogenism intersected with 'humane' sympathies towards aborigines, as witnessed in a *Christian Observer* segment on New Zealand:

> Some infidel physiologists have accounted for the melting away of savages before civilized intruders, upon the principle of inferior races yielding to superior; and have told us, that however much philanthropy may mourn over it, the 'dark varieties of man' have not the high cerebral configurations of the caucasian standard, which includes all the white nations, and are therefore destined to give way before them, as monkeys and lions are driven out before Hottentots and Caffers.[85]

Yet, it expounded that 'negroes, North American Indians, Otaheitans, New Zealanders . . . were created by one common Father with ourselves, and redeemed by the one blood, and need to be regenerated by the same Spirit'.[86] It is difficult to discern any profound dissension from this sympathetic monogenist quality in discussions addressing aboriginal proprietary rights-status at this time. In 1842, an anonymous contributor to *The Encyclopædia Britannica* musing upon 'man', confidently asserted that the observed variations within humanity (whether described as 'tribes', 'races', 'divisions', or 'varieties') did not preclude a unified source for the genus *homo* consistent with scriptural tenets or philosophical and scientific deductions.[87] In this article, Māori were consigned to Johann Blumenbach's fifth variety or division, the *'Malay'*.[88] Yet, through the variations in human life and physiologies, arenas of intellectual and political contentiousness persisted regarding policy overseas or the import of Amerindians, Marquesans, or Māori to proprietorship issues, in spite of monogenism. Accordingly, monogenism did not instruct imperial policy-makers on what ought to be done. By the 1840s, there was much scholarly literature concerning human migration in many separate contexts. This literature remained diverse, but its extensive reach was revealed in the oft-read ethnographic tomes of Prichard, and in the assumptions of a variety of 'liberal Anglican' historical texts written by Whately and Thomas Arnold.[89] Historical analysis remained important to appraising ethnographic presents. The influential Prichard surveyed the ancient dispersion of human groupings such as *Belgae* and Caledonians.[90] He noted the tenuous quality of a term such as *'aboriginal inhabitants'*, *'autochthones'*, or

[83] For example Chambers, *Vestiges of the Natural History of Creation*, 263–4, 279, 281; Samson, *Imperial Benevolence*, 9–10; Stepan, *The Idea of Race in Science*, 1–2, 7, 9, 35–44; Stocking Jnr, *Victorian Anthropology*, 33–4, 49–53; Gunson, *Messengers of Grace*, 206–7; Young, *Colonial Desire*, 10 *et seq*. One polygenist source was Knox, *The Races of Men*. Salesa, *Racial Crossings*, explores the prevailing force of monogenism generally but also acknowledges the challenges posed by polygenist thought.

[84] For example *British Association for the Advancement of Science; seventeenth meeting*, 'journal of sectional proceedings' (1847); Prichard was vice-president of its ethnology subsection by 1847.

[85] *The Christian Observer*, 70. See also Harris, *The Great Commission*, 362–5.

[86] Ibid.

[87] 'Man', in *Encyclopædia Britannica*, XIV, 199, 201–3.

[88] Ibid, 200; Blumenbach, *De Generis humani varietate nativa*.

[89] Arnold, *The Effects of Distant Colonization on the Parent State*, 29–31; Arnold, *An Inaugural Lecture on the Study of Modern History*, 39; Forbes, *The Liberal Anglican Idea of History*, 70–1.

[90] Prichard, *The Eastern origin of the Celtic nations proved by a comparison of their dialects with the Sanskrit, Greek, Latin and Teutonic languages*, 1–5. Prichard's literature on the 'natural history' of the human species was cited in Anonymous, 'Man', in *Encyclopædia Britannica*, XIV, 194.

'*indigenæ*' in describing populations where histories of peoples in motion were increasingly recognized through a dispersion of species or shared linguistic roots, as discovered in philological research.[91] Arnold, for one, occasionally used Prichard as a source on 'races' or 'peoples'.[92]

Other authors, such as Robert Wilmot-Horton and Malthus, contributed to this field concerning a migratory diffusion of humankind and the pertinence of this mobility to policy measures in early nineteenth-century Britain. Inconsistent, uncertain definitions of 'races', often equated with 'varieties', 'tribes', 'peoples', or 'nations', permeated certain of these accounts along with an appreciation of these 'peoples' as having been persistently in motion throughout historical time, pursuing sustenance.[93] To certain contemporary commentators such an historical viewpoint entailed a pessimistic prognosis. Hence David Buchanan, a political economist, considered the 'earth being in a manner filled with people, and no more vacant space remaining for new emigrations, the great check to population, from the want of subsistence, must now be felt in all its force'.[94] There were differing slants on this tableau of history, with prominent authors, such as Richard Whately, focusing upon a degeneration towards 'savagery', recalling the earlier anxieties of Adam Smith and Adam Ferguson that histories were not simply progressive.[95] Additional authors like Robert Chambers contested this formulation with a naturalizing or organic thesis on improvement or 'civilization', as against Whately's stresses upon periodic divine revelation. Chambers asserted, '[t]o have civilization, it is necessary that a people should be numerous and closely placed; that they should be fixed in their habitations, and safe from violent external and internal disturbance'.[96]

Stadial history was increasingly treated in the early nineteenth century as prima facie applicable to supposedly 'cruder' forms of non-European community.[97] Far from falling into disuse, it was cast as a *provisional* way of understanding alien communities. In 1826, Malthus himself, above all preoccupied with populations and subsistence, remarked upon 'checks in the islands of the South Sea', including those obstacles experienced by the 'different tribes' in New Zealand on the basis of James Cook's voyaging reportage.[98] In referring to stadial conditions of subsistence—Amerindians 'hunting and fishing'—he developed the spatially constrained, pessimistic metaphor of an 'island'. He argued that, 'a savage tribe in America surrounded by enemies, or a civilized and populous nation hemmed in by others in the same state, is, in many respects,

[91] Prichard, ibid, 1, 3.
[92] Arnold, *The History of Rome*, I, 529.
[93] Buchanan, 'Emigration', in *Encyclopædia Britannica*, VIII, 684. See also Brown, 'Britain', in *Encyclopædia Britannica*, V, 295; Brown, 'Celtæ', in *Encyclopædia Britannica*, VI, 274.
[94] Buchanan, 'Emigration', in *Encyclopædia Britannica*, VIII, 684. Cf Malthus, *An essay on the principle of population*, I, 8: 'In Europe there is the fairest chance that human industry may receive its best direction. The science of agriculture has been much studied in England and Scotland; and there is still a great portion of uncultivated land in these countries'.
[95] Whately, *Introductory Lectures on Political Economy*, 3rd edn, 101–2. Richard Whately (1787–1863), professor of political economy, Oxford University; Archbishop of Dublin (1831–1863).
[96] Chambers, *Vestiges of the Natural History of Creation*, 285.
[97] Bayly, *Imperial Meridian*, 152; Bayly, 'The British and Indigenous Peoples, 1760–1860', in Daunton and Halpern (eds), *Empire and Others*, 34–5; Collini, Winch, and Burrow, *That Noble Science of Politics*, 60; Burrow, *Evolution and Society*, 48; Stocking, *Victorian Anthropology*, 32–3. O'Brien, *Narratives of Enlightenment*.
[98] Malthus, *An Essay on the Principle of Population*, 6th edn, I, 68–72.

circumstanced like the islanders'.[99] Malthus cautioned that, 'the emigrant, impatient of the distresses which he feels in his own country, is by no means secure of finding relief in another'.[100]

This history was used to assist 'knowing' about aboriginal property. Combined with partial intelligence received from oceanic and landed voyagers such as James Cook, Augustus Earle, or James Busby, it assisted policy formulators (including Stephen) in characterizing Māori legally, economically, and geopolitically as limited 'agriculturists' cultivating vegetables and self-consciously appropriating territories for resources—nourishment, shelter.[101] Recent archaeological evidence suggests that Māori were indeed gardeners, and were oceanic voyagers and extensive coastal traders with a sense of the shape of the islands they inhabited.[102] Pointedly, representations of Māori, even of northern Māori as opposed to their South Island-dwelling counterparts, were mutable rather than stable or uniform, including the apparently *core* view of Māori as agriculturists or at least horticulturists. Different writers stressed different attributes of this view. In 1830 the Colonial Office had not adverted to the subject of aboriginal proprietorship in New Zealand. It was content with general statements predicated upon its sparse information and existing intellectual sources concerning the archipelago, as with Stephen's bald comment that Māori were 'owners & sovereigns of the soil'.[103] This study launches with this generality.

Certainly, stadial history's assumptions were no longer necessarily oriented towards a linear progression of human communities through stages. Some early nineteenth-century accounts viewed communities as having degenerated into 'savagery' from a scriptural Eden.[104] 'Many of the savage tribes which are now found in different parts of the earth appear, as has been remarked, to be descendants of nations which had previously attained a certain degree of civilization.'[105] An important change occurred in seeing the possibility that some communities existing in 'savagery' or 'barbarism' were ensnared and might not effectively transform themselves in the absence of external British intervention. '[S]o the savage himself, though he may be...a soil capable of receiving the seeds of civilization, can never, in the first instance, produce it, as of spontaneous growth.'[106] Still, the form of such assistance was increasingly disputed—whether geographically proximate European settlers offering lessons in 'civilization'

[99] Ibid, 66. For references to Native Americans, see ibid, 26, 35–6. On the significance of Malthusian moments and efforts in countering these moments, see Eastwood, 'The Age of Uncertainty', 107–10; Winch, *Riches and Poverty*.

[100] Malthus, *An Essay on the Principle of Population*, 6th edn, I, 67.

[101] For example Hawkesworth, *An Account of the Voyages undertaken by the order of his present Majesty for making discoveries in the southern hemisphere*; Beaglehole, *The Journals of Captain James Cook on his voyages of discovery*; Savage, *Some Account of New Zealand*; Earle, *A Narrative of a Nine Months' Residence in New Zealand in 1827.* On early oceanic wandering and information, see Williams and Marshall, *The Great Map of Mankind*, 272, 279–80, 285–6, 293–4; Williams, 'The Pacific', in Marshall (ed), *The Oxford History of the British Empire*, 552–75.

[102] Binney, 'Tuki's universe', in Sinclair (ed), *Tasman Relations*, 15–33, 16; Belich, *Making Peoples*, 44–50, 72–5; Irwin, 'Against, across, and down the wind', 167–206; Tuki's chart, 1793, MPG532/5, TNA.

[103] Stephen, minute, 25 May 1830, CO201/215, fos.696–7, TNA.

[104] Whately, *Introductory Lectures on Political Economy*, 121–3.

[105] Library of Entertaining Knowledge(Craik), *The New Zealanders*, 9.

[106] Whately, *Introductory Lectures on Political Economy*, 3rd edn, 112; Forbes, *The Liberal Anglican Idea of History*, 70–1.

both osmotically and directly or whether assumed 'savages' ought to be separated, isolated with a limited collection of European instructors, such as missionaries.[107]

As this chapter and subsequent chapters argue, however, a crucial point of instability in the assessment of Māori as cultivators of fertile soils arose by virtue of their lacking plough technology, a feature that might be associated with savagery in spite of their consumption of gathered vegetables. In 1830, it was noted, 'their agriculture [is] imperfect, they have no knowledge of metals, writing is unknown to them'.[108] Substantive material and civil improvement were associated with increasingly mechanical or technologically assisted forms of agriculture (such as water mills or steel hand mills) accompanied by pākehā interspersions. In 1852, Martin Russell conveyed this vulnerability of Māori 'agriculturist' status in saying:

> Justly it is remarked by Mr Yate, that a prospect more pleasing could not meet the eye of a philanthropist than the sight of the British plough breaking up the deserts of New Zealand, under the direction of indigenous labourers. The introduction of ploughs and harrows, all of which were made at Waimate [mission station], did, without doubt, constitute a momentous era in the history of that country.[109]

In 1859, Arthur Thomson continued this theme with references to, 'tattooed natives... seen between the plough handles'.[110] The *core* representation and assumption of Māori as 'cultivators' remained, underlying discussions regarding New Zealand. John Hawkesworth's presentation of Cook's voyaging journals remarked upon their consumption of 'fern root, yams, clams, and potatoes'; their non-use of metals, such as iron.[111] To a Select Committee in 1844, Māori 'were neither a pastoral people, nor one living, like the North American Indians, by the chase, and therefore requiring a great extent of country for their support'. Indeed, 'they derived their chief subsistence from the produce of the soil and agriculture, rude as it was'.[112] In commenting on 'Polynesians' overall, Herman Merivale, professor in political economy at Oxford, stated that, 'on the whole, [they] appear to be a race of less concentrated energy, perhaps an inferior mental organization to the Americans;... cultivators of the soil, and living associated in more numerous communities'.[113] Hursthouse stated, '[t]he *Maori* was a stationary, man-eating, fisher-farmer—not a hunter living by the chase'.[114] In 1855, Whately, as archbishop of Dublin, explained that, 'these [New Zealanders] were very far from being in as low a state as the New Hollanders, for they cultivated the ground, raising crops of the cumera (a sweet potato), and clothed themselves, not with skins, but with mats woven by themselves'.[115] Tying the indigenous inhabitants of Australia

[107] Ross, *John Philip (1775–1851)*, 141; Stocking, *Victorian Anthropology*, 33–4.

[108] Library of Entertaining Knowledge (Craik), *The New Zealanders*, 14.

[109] Russell, *Polynesia*, 354; Yate, *An Account of New Zealand*, 2nd edn, 198. FitzRoy, *Remarks on New Zealand in February 1846*, 58–9.

[110] *The Story of New Zealand*, II, 298–9; Arthur Saunders Thomson, 1817? (baptized 2 January 1817)–1860, military surgeon, medical scientist and historian; graduated MD, 1837, from Edinburgh University; appointed surgeon to 58th (Rutlandshire) regiment of foot, 1847, for service in New Zealand; died in China; Ellis, *Polynesian Researches*, I, 37.

[111] Hawkesworth, *An account of the voyages*, III, 43; II, 410; Thomas, *In Oceania*, 83.

[112] Report from the Select Committee appointed to inquire into the state of New Zealand, and into the proceedings of the New Zealand Company, *GBPP1844*, xiii (556), vii.

[113] Merivale, *Lectures on Colonization and Colonies*, 1st edn, II, 157.

[114] Hursthouse, *New Zealand, or Zealandia*, I, 157.

[115] Whately, *On the Origin of Civilisation*, 12.

to a form of base savagery was a trope of relative long-standing. Edward Gibbon, in his magisterial account of *The History of the Decline and Fall of the Roman Empire* first published from 1776, referred to William Dampier (1651–1715) as his source in comparing the 'natives of New Holland' to the 'Icthyophagi [fish-eating people] who, in the time of Diodorus Siculus, wandered along the shores of the Red Sea'.[116] As Secretary of State for Colonies and War from July 1846, Henry George, the third Earl Grey (Viscount Howick until 1845), considered Māori 'agriculturist' attainments in a despatch of 23 December 1846. He suggested, 'they lived in a great measure at least upon the produce of the soil (chiefly perhaps its spontaneous produce [*fructus naturales*]), practised to a certain extent a rude sort of agriculture'.[117] As an extensively propertied whiggish aristocrat, Grey perceived the notional advantages of incorporating certain, admittedly unspecified, Māori into a hierarchy of proprietary or tenurial interests.[118] These observers, policy formulators, or participants in political processes were not necessarily earnest theorists however. An oft-cited text warned against mere theoretical mimicry but still employed features of stadial history:

> Theoretical writers are fond of talking of the natural progress of the species to the agricultural state, from and through the pastoral; as if the one were a condition at which it was nothing less than impossible for a people to arrive, except by first undergoing the other. In countries circumstanced like New Zealand, at least, the course of things must have been somewhat different; inasmuch as here we find the agricultural state begun, where the pastoral never could have been known, there being no flocks to tend.[119]

From the early nineteenth century, such forms of historical analysis began to cohabit with those variegated threads of information derived from New Zealand itself.[120] Stadial historical analysis touched ethnographic assessments of alien populations, demonstrating that a stadial theory of history was readily used when considering the political and proprietary conditions of populations in exotic locations, such as New Zealand or other Pacific islands. James Cowles Prichard's nascent ethnographic literature exhibited this general tendency as early as 1813.[121] Prichard imbibed Dugald Stewart's instruction on

116 Gibbon, *The History of the Decline and Fall of the Roman Empire*, IV, 167, n 10. Of New Zealand, however, Gibbon chanced the imagined view that much more might be expected if the rumoured presence of an ancient, barely remembered 'race of cannibals' near the 'commercial and literary town of Glasgow' was correct: 'New Zealand may produce in same future age, the [David] Hume of the Southern Hemisphere' (Gibbon, *The History of the Decline and Fall*, David Womersley (ed), I, 1001).

117 Earl Grey to Grey, 23 December 1846, CO209/47, fo.273, TNA.

118 Ibid, fo.278. See also *HPD*, 3rd series, Howick, 29 January 1840, vol 40, col 778: 'all that the best laws and best government can accomplish is by assuring to exertion its true reward, by providing for the security of person and property'. Cf Kriegel, 'A convergence of ethics', 440–1, 445, 447–50; Pocock, 'The varieties of whiggism from Exclusion to Reform', in Pocock, *Virtue, Commerce, and History*, 308.

119 Library of Entertaining Knowledge, *The New Zealanders*, 172. For citation of this text with approval, see Fox, *The Six Colonies of New Zealand*, 70–1. Cf Prichard, 'On the extinction of human races', 169. A similar observation is issued in Bayly, *Empire and Information*, 167–8.

120 This type of cohabitation was not novel as Donald Winch demonstrated in 'The cause of good government', in Collini, Winch, and Burrow, *That Noble Science of Politics*, 95–6, 114–15. J Burrow initially defended a subtly distinctive view, suggesting the declining pertinence of a Scottish stadial historical approach in the early nineteenth century: *Evolution and Society*, 58–62, also referring to Mill, *The History of British India*.

121 Prichard, *Researches into the Physical History of Man*, G Stocking (ed); Stocking, *Victorian Anthropology*, 48–53; cf Anonymous, 'Senior on political economy', 87–8: assessing Senior, *An Outline of the Science of Political Economy*; Merivale, *Lectures on colonization and colonies*, 1st edn, II,

philosophic history at Edinburgh University from 1805 until 1808. The alleged historical progression or, alternatively, regression, of Pacific *insula* dwellers was stressed. Initially, he noted little or no advance, relegating these populations to, 'that rude unimproved state, which precedes all division of professions and employments'. Thus, 'their political condition is that of perfect equality without any difference of ranks'.[122] Yet, a concern with physical or 'racial' human characteristics (such as physiognomy, hair texture, or complexion) also permeated Prichard's *oeuvre*. Thus, of Māori, '[w]e are informed that their complexion varies from black, which appears to be the original hue of the race, and is still the colour of those tribes which are in the most natural state, to a yellowish or olive tinge'.[123] Even then, however, there was a mingling of Scottish historical influences, construing certain stages as characteristic of Pacific 'nations': 'miserable destitute savages, who lead a wandering life in pursuit of... scanty sustenance', and those who 'have become pastoral or agricultural'.[124] Such a perception concerning a selective use of historical perspective was succinctly captured with, '[w]henever the testimony of historians affords any information, we shall avail ourselves of this resource'.[125] Prichard manipulated history in 1839 in his commentaries on extinct 'races'. He noted that where 'the simple pastoral tribes come into relations with the more civilized agricultural nations, the allotted time of their destruction is at hand'.[126] Hence, Prichard's approaches were conducive to accommodating a Scottish philosophy of stadial history as a provisional instrument of analysis.

Suggestions of this history's casual, even unconscious uses were evident in Charles Darwin's thoughts on the 'natives' of Tierra del Fuego—physiognomy merging with observations on wandering modes of subsistence: 'The cause of their warfare appears to be the means of subsistence [and]... in search of food they are compelled unceasingly to wander'.[127] Māori did not evidently or unqualifiedly impress the whiggish Darwin, however. Not unusually, he compared these aborigines unfavourably with Tahitian inhabitants, a factor suggestive of the possible tensions or contradictions in any reception of encountered indigenous persons. Thus, 'the natives of Otaheite, who, when first discovered, were governed by hereditary kings, had arrived at a far higher grade than another branch of the same people, the New Zealanders,—who, although benefited by being compelled to turn their attention to agriculture, were republicans in the most

156: 'They [southern Africans] are a pastoral people, rich in flocks and herds, to whom the notion of property appears familiar'. Pointedly, Merivale cited expressly from Prichard's *oeuvre* (specifically, an 1831 edition of Prichard, *Researches into the Physical History of Man*) concerning emergent issues such as racial hybridity or miscegenation in ibid, II, 219–20.

[122] Ibid, 244.

[123] Ibid, 284–5. Anonymous, 'The black races of Polynesia'; Ellis, *Polynesian Researches*, 2nd edn, I, 78–84; Library of Entertaining Knowledge, *The New Zealanders*, 160–1; Latham, *The Ethnology of the British Colonies and Dependencies*, 214.

[124] Ibid, 245–6.

[125] Ibid, 243. Theological history and comparative philology could be incorporated within this reference to historical method: Prichard, 'On the various methods of research which contribute to the advancement of ethnology, and of the relations of that science to other branches of knowledge', in *Report of the seventeenth meeting of the British Association for the Advancement of Science*, 236; Stocking, *Victorian Anthropology*, 49–50.

[126] Prichard, 'On the Extinction of Human Races', 169. Cf Bannister, 'An account of the changes and present condition of the population of New Zealand', 362–76.

[127] Darwin, *Journal of Researches into the Natural History and Geology of the Countries visited during the voyage of HMS 'Beagle' round the world*, 215–16, 25 February 1834; Keynes, *Charles Darwin's Beagle Diary*, 222–4.

absolute sense'.[128] Equality, as opposed to 'artificial' government, retarded 'civilization' on this account, condemning humans to an indolent and bestial existence. Submission to securing goal-oriented advantages or excitements to ambitious enterprises would not occur in the absence of a hierarchical procedure: 'As we see those animals, whose instinct compels them to live in society and obey a chief, are most capable of improvement, so is it with the races of mankind'.[129] In applying these views to Māori, Darwin's perceptions were contrary to Johann Reinhold Forster's earlier perspectives that in a temperate climate, allegedly populous communities supposedly rendered Māori dynamic, 'jealous of their liberty and independence', and prone to competitive improvement rather than degeneracy.[130] Robert FitzRoy would linger upon an assessment of the physiological characteristics of 'New Zealanders' together with their respective communities' apparent political features.[131] As Thomas suggests in analogous circumstances, 'this comparative anthropology was thus political before it was physical'.[132] It was also historical. Polynesians inhabited other earlier times from Europeans within Britain. Using 'temporal devices implied affirmation of difference as *distance*'.[133] John Martin referred to historical insights on the 'infancy of human society' collected from researching Polynesian inhabitants.[134] Indeed, Chapters Two to Four display these conventionally provisional uses of a modified stadial history. This constellation of intellectual resources promulgated a paradigm of history with spaces for Māori within it. For a time, Native American experiences in northern America were especially pertinent to imperial comprehensions of an inhabited Pacific, and of Māori particularly. But, as this chapter, together with Chapters Three and Four will contend, the advocates of New Zealand's 'systematic colonization' were the most persistent users of these American examples. Thus, broadly shared 'evangelical' opinions did not supply or nourish details for imperial policies on aboriginal proprietorship in the period from 1830 to 1847. Figures ordinarily glossed as 'evangelical' and 'humane' persistently resorted to stadial historical analyses in policy formulation. James Stephen, the permanent under-secretary at the Colonial Office, was of a moderate evangelical Anglican ancestry. His father, also named James Stephen, and a House of Commons parliamentarian, was a foundation member of what came to be known as the Clapham sect. Furthermore, this elder Stephen married the sister of William Wilberforce in 1800, thus establishing helpful familial connections. His first spouse, Anne Stent, the mother to the younger James Stephen, had died in 1796. The younger James Stephen professed privately to a Colonial Office clerk, Henry Taylor: 'the religion of Jesus Christ affords the only plausible solution of the great mystery of human life, and the only solid foundation for any lofty or consolatory thoughts'.[135] Stephen

128 Darwin, *Journal of Researches into the Natural History and Geology of the Countries visited during the voyage of HMS 'Beagle' round the world*, 229. Cf Thomas, 'On the varieties of the human species', in Thomas, Guest, and Dettelbach (eds), *Observations made during a voyage round the world*, xxxii–xxxiii. On Darwin's whiggish sympathies, see Desmond and Moore, *Darwin*, 104–5.

129 Darwin, *Journal of Researches into the Natural History and Geology of the Countries visited during the voyage of HMS 'Beagle' round the world*, 229.

130 Forster, in Thomas, Guest, and Dettelbach, *Observations made during a voyage round the world*, 207–8. Glacken, *Traces on the Rhodian Shore*, 610–20.

131 FitzRoy, *Narrative of the surveying voyages of his Majesty's ships 'Adventure' and* ', II, 567–70.

132 Thomas, *In Oceania*, 82.

133 Fabian, *Time and the Other*, 16 (emphasis in original).

134 Martin, *An account of the Tonga islands*, I, xviii.

135 *Correspondence of Henry Taylor*, Dowden (ed), 49: Stephen to Taylor, 3 November 1833.

was instructed both in academia and in profession as a legal practitioner (initially based at Lincoln's Inn as a barrister), becoming counsel to the Colonial Office in 1813, and remaining so until 1836. Significantly, this younger Stephen characterized the Clapham sect membership to an editor of the *Edinburgh Review* (and once a pupil of Dugald Stewart), Macvey Napier, as follows:

> They were the Founders of those great Religious Societies which form so remarkable an element in our Political and Moral conditions at the present day.... They were the real secret Society for the abolition of the Slave Trade & of Slavery. It was their great object to give to the Evangelical Party a more Philosophical and liberal spirit; & they lived and died in the straightest intimacy.[136]

This, however, may very well describe an underlying sentiment but of itself does not furnish any detail respecting proposed policies towards an aboriginal community. Presumably, the permanent under-secretary was also very much aware in his policy advice—an issue of practice—of an initially Scottish theory of history, divided sequentially into distinct stages. He tellingly described Māori in 1840 as 'after their rude fashion, agricultur[a]lists' rather than 'huntsmen'.[137] Likewise, Charles Grant the younger, becoming the first Baron Glenelg in 1835, acted as Secretary of State for Colonial Affairs from 18 April 1835 until 20 February 1839, in a whiggish administration during a crucial period in the development of imperial policy towards the question of New Zealand. During this time, the decision, on principle, to include parts of New Zealand within Britain's empire occurred on 20 December 1837.

Glenelg's personal history was convoluted. He served briefly as a Canningite Tory in the administrations of Viscount Goderich and the Duke of Wellington until his resignation in May 1828 (from the position of president of the Board of Trade and treasurer to the Royal Navy). However, this study is concerned with his cabinet role as principal Secretary of State for Colonies during Melbourne's second Whig ministry in the late 1830s. He can be described as an 'evangelical', and, like Stephen, was a son of an active Clapham philanthropist. In addition, he was a lay governor of the Church Missionary Society, and editor of the *Christian Observer* periodical from 1850 until 1858.[138] Yet he would construe Māori on 15 December 1837 as 'not Savages living by the Chase, but Tribes who have apportioned the country between them, having fixed Abodes, with an acknowledged Property in the Soil, and with some rude approaches to a regular System of internal Government'.[139] Here, he clearly resorted to the analytical lessons of stadial history in appraising an emergent imperial issue.

The 'colonization commissioners' for southern Australia in 1835 also deployed this provisional, conceptual framework in exchanges with Glenelg's office. It represented a convention of disputing and discussing. One of these commissioners, Robert Torrens, saw Australian aborigines as 'unlocated tribes [having] not [yet] arrived at that stage

[136] Stephen to Napier, 5 February 1844, BL AddMss34624, Napier papers; see also Stephen to Napier, 25 June 1838, BL AddMss34619, fo.178.

[137] Stephen to Vernon Smith, 28 July 1840, CO209/4, fo.343a, TNA; for his ancestry, see Knaplund, *James Stephen and the British Colonial System, 1813–1847*, 8, 9.

[138] Charles Grant, 1778–1866, was the son of Charles Grant, 1746–1823, author of *Observations on the state of society among the Asiatic subjects of Great Britain* (1792); see Bradley, *The Call to Seriousness*, 81; Hilton, *The Age of Atonement*, 226; Brent, *Liberal Anglican Politics*, 107, 108 (table), 123, 129, 282–4; Rosman, *Evangelicals and Culture*, 19.

[139] Glenelg, memorandum, 15 December 1837, CO209/2, fo.409, TNA.

of social improvement, in which a proprietary right to the soil exists'.[140] Importantly, these excerpts represented early nineteenth-century traces of a view concerning the historical placement of so-called 'cruder' communities. Pointedly, these persons were not thoroughgoing theorists but individuals implicated in pragmatic, political processes of government and administration, appropriating, sharing, and manipulating a series of intellectual and analytical vocabularies. Thus, it is inaccurate to treat these persons as either acolytes or adherents of a doctrine, whether settled, predictable, or determinative. This qualification remains important. This observation regarding an intermingling of intellectual heritages will be returned to in the body of the argument, but it suffices as a brief introductory signpost.

A NEW ZEALAND ASSOCIATION ADVOCATING 'SYSTEMATIC COLONIZATION'

> I have set on foot a new measure of colonization on principles which have worked so well for South Australia. The country is New Zealand; . . . A New Zealand Association is now in the course of formation: it will comprise a more influential body than which formed South Australia.[141]

This section commences with the emergence in 1837 of an unincorporated association, named the 'New Zealand Association'. This Association advocated the 'systematic colonization' of New Zealand. This chapter makes two central arguments that foreshadow the subsequent chapters. First, that in 1837, an initially terse conception of Māori proprietary rights-status was undermined through Colonial Office attempts to respond to emerging proposals for the 'systematic' or 'scientific' settlement of parts of New Zealand. This conception of what would be characterized in 1841 in a bald, formulaic fashion as 'territorial rights of the natives',[142] materialized haphazardly within the broader context of several intellectual strands. The New Zealand Association dramatized this process, using a concoction of two principal intellectual languages—stadial history and *ius gentium*. There was no determinative doctrinal specificity in either of these languages or any requirement that they apply to indigenous property rights within colonial settlements conceived in the 1830s. Indeed, until 1837, 'the question [had] not been very much discussed'.

First, the Association tersely accepted indigenous rights to territory. In doing so, it adapted to the observable practices of paper deeds on the ground within New Zealand.[143] Secondly, this acceptance was connected to the Association's proposal of 'improving' Māori through osmotic exposure to British commercial activities and *mores*. It advocated an incorporative theme of amalgamating Māori, not a policy of insulating Māori. It postulated a notion of intensive, systematic settlement for parts of New Zealand along the lines detailed by Edward Gibbon Wakefield. The New Zealand Association committee emerged on 22 May 1837. It appeared in London and encompassed a number of interpersonal networks that linked it to Parliament and executive

140 Torrens to Grey (nd) December 1835 (received 23 December), CO13/3, fos.168a–9, TNA.
141 Wakefield to Charles Torlesse, 12 May 1837, BL AddMss35261, fo.9.
142 Russell to Hobson, 28 January 1841, CO209/8, fo.454, TNA.
143 Hickford, '"Vague Native Rights to Land"'.

departments within Westminster. Politically, it was well connected. Its chairman was Francis Baring, an evangelical, a Whig member of the Baring financial family, and a first cousin to Sir George Grey, then Colonial Office parliamentary under-secretary.[144] In addition, he was a Whig parliamentarian for Portsmouth. In 1837 he was joint secretary of the treasury and was admitted to cabinet as Chancellor of the Exchequer in August 1839. Other than Baring, the Association boasted several other parliamentarians including William Hutt, together with the radical 'colonial reformers', Sir William Molesworth and Henry George Ward. Benjamin Hawes and the Scottish Free Church evangelical George Sinclair were also Whig parliamentarians and members of the Association. It had influential theological sympathizers such as Richard Whately, an advisor to the premier, Melbourne, and Whately's confidante, Samuel Hinds, who was also a member of the Association. Whately observed the Association's operations with favourable interest.[145] Those who supported its proposals tended to be Whigs or radical 'colonial reformers', such as Buller, Molesworth, and Ward, with whiggish connections of patronage. This cluster of individuals included some of those, such as Ward and Molesworth, who Thomas has carefully identified as parliamentary 'philosophic radicals'.[146] John Stuart Mill was also a supporter.[147] A moderate species of Anglican evangelicalism, together with a whiggish political and familial predilection, was shared by certain influential persons, both within the Colonial Office and amongst Association proponents of 'systematic colonization' (Baring and Sir George Grey). Charles Buller and scholars, such as Merivale, classified these proponents as 'colonial reformers', although these so-named 'reformers' were themselves hostage to internecine disputes or instabilities in membership.[148]

The Association's philosopher was the political economist and former convict, Wakefield, who, with fellow political economist Robert Torrens, lay behind proposals for settling South Australia. Morrell described Wakefield as 'the prophet of the new imperialism, the imperialism of great migration'.[149] With Torrens, he had established a Colonization Society in 1830, charged with the promotion of the principles of 'systematic colonization'.[150] His convict past tarnished his political respectability if not his capacity to influence contemporaries. Wakefield would resort to collecting influential political personalities to compensate for this past. Melbourne conveyed these qualms concerning Wakefield's personality to the Earl of Durham in 1838:

[144] The second baronet (1799–1882), not to be confused with the colonial governor (1812–1898).

[145] *Life and Correspondence of Richard Whately, D.D., late archbishop of Dublin*, EJ Whately (ed), I, 391–4: Whately to Senior, 8 November 1837. See also ibid, 414, Whately to Senior, 25 January 1838: 'I learn from Hinds that you have seen the little publication about New Zealand, and are disposed to think favourably of the plan. Considering its proximity to New Holland, and its manifold superiority, I think a colony there might deserve to be called New Byzantium, as being (according to the ancient oracle) placed "opposite to the city of blindmen"'.

[146] Thomas, *The Philosophic Radicals*, 13.

[147] Mill, *Principles of Political Economy with Some of their Application to Social Philosophy* , lib 5, 958–9 (in Robson (ed), *Collected Works of John Stuart Mill*, vol II). See also Winch, *Wealth and Life*, 54, 56.

[148] Buller, *Responsible Government for the Colonies*, 20; Merivale, *Lectures on colonization and colonies*, 2nd edn, vi–vii.

[149] Morrell, *British Colonial Policy in the Age of Peel and Russell*, 5.

[150] Marais, *The Colonisation of New Zealand*, 3–7.

> If this report of the appointment of Mr Wakefield were to be confirmed no power on earth could prevent an address to remove both him and Mr Turton from being moved & carried in the House of Lords and I believe the House of Commons. It is incredible that a man of common sense should show such ignorance or such disregard of public feeling & opinion as you have done in the selection of these gentlemen. If their abilities & powers were superhuman they would not counterbalance the discredit of their characters. They will materially weaken you; they will materially weaken us; they will cause every act of your Government to be viewed with a jealousy & suspicion to which they would not otherwise have been exposed.... I rely therefore upon your assurance that you will not give Mr Wakefield any public appointment whatever, that his name will not appear on any public document.[151]

Wakefield's theorem, albeit well trodden within the historiography, requires an introduction as it established a localized field for New Zealand in those intellectual contexts permeated by a largely historical, political, economic, and nascent ethnographic—chiefly Prichardian—literature. These contextual fields were relevant to anglophone perceptions of aboriginal proprietary rights-status within indigenous New Zealand. New Zealand was increasingly portrayed as a field for emigration. Wakefield had recently presented his 'systematic' notions in extensive testimony before a House of Commons Select Committee on the disposal of 'colonial lands'—specifically, those territories regarded as 'waste lands' available for distribution.[152] By 1837, Wakefield had authored several theoretical works on this systematized conception of 'colonization'.[153] His system was premised on the arithmetic of a 'sufficient price' or, in other words, an unstated threshold consideration paid for lands transferred from a foundation purchaser to subsequent settler or investor purchasers. Underlying the calculation of a 'sufficient price' was an intention to restrict the process by which wage earners could be transformed into proprietors. Settlement distribution would become relatively sedentarized.

The two central features of Wakefield's 'principles of colonization' were 'that the disposal of waste or public land should be by sale only [not grant], and at a sufficient price for the objects in view, and that the purchase-money should be employed as an emigration fund'.[154] Wakefield argued that, in the past, Britain had readily transferred extensive swathes of waste land at inexpensive prices or as outright grants, enabling immigrants to become instant proprietors.[155] This process had occurred in New South Wales, at Swan River in western Australia, and in Van Diemen's land in the early nineteenth century. One assumed consequence was that grave shortages of labour were incurred unless constrained labour was imported in the form of slaves or convicts. To a certain extent, even colonists would become their own labourers due to the relatively unrestrained proliferation of individuated proprietorship. A degenerate colony would result, with little leisure to expend on manners, arts, or literature. As Olssen expressed it: 'one found the pathology of the frontier, characterized by violence, crime, prostitution and debauchery'.[156]

[151] Melbourne to Durham, 18 July 1838, MP, Melbourne Mss, box 4/42.

[152] See Report, Select Committee on the disposal of colonial lands, GBPP1836, xi (512), 499–765.

[153] For example Wakefield, *A letter from Sydney*; Wakefield, *England and America*; Wakefield and Ward, *The British Colonization of New Zealand*; Wakefield, *The new British province of South Australia*; Wakefield, 'Mr Dandeson Coates and the New Zealand Association'.

[154] Wakefield and Ward, *The British Colonization of New Zealand*, 17.

[155] On land policies in New South Wales, see Van Diemen's land and western Australia: Kociumbas, *The Oxford History of Australia*, II, 120–49.

[156] Olssen, 'Mr Wakefield and New Zealand as an experiment in post-enlightenment experimental practice', 205. Cf Edmond, *Representing the South Pacific*, 133, 135; Constrained labour,

Systematic colonization would ensure both wealth *and* 'civil-ization'. Wakefield's theory was effectively summarized in outline by the New Zealand Company directorate on 14 May 1840 as an actuating maxim:

> It will be observed that the principle of colonization thus adopted by the Company is the sale of its lands at an uniform and sufficient price, and the employment of the greater portion of the purchase-money as an emigration fund.[157]

This was, moreover, a system with a precedent. A version of it had been employed in southern Australia, in a settled establishment centred on Adelaide and initially pursued by a promotional association—the South Australian Association instituted in 1833 (although the South Australian Colonization Commission, created with parliamentary sanction, eventually superseded this).[158] By 1839, this 'South-Australian' system was to be followed in New Zealand insofar as the diversity of circumstances permitted.

References to this 'South-Australian' enterprise as a precedent abounded in the Association's publicized literature in 1837. On 22 May 1837, the Association issued a 'statement of objects'. It contained a summation of its proposals for the systematic colonization of New Zealand's littoral. Particulars concerning the relative geographical position, 'extent, soil and climate, harbours, rivers, and natural productions' of the islands were appended to this 'statement'.[159] South Australia was treated as supplying a model for its subsequent objectives overseas. Nonetheless, the statement drew two distinctions between the New Zealand situation and southern Australia. First, 'the amount paid for land *to* the native tribes' in New Zealand would be deducted from the fund arising through the sale of territory to settlers and investors, adding, however, that, '[t]his deduction ... would probably be compensated by the facility of obtaining native labour for hire'.[160] The initial acquisition of territories from aboriginal persons was not explicitly provided for in the legislation sanctioning a southern Australian settlement; the prescribed region had been characterized as 'waste and unoccupied' in the lengthy statutory preamble. It began with: 'Whereas that part of Australia which lies between the meridians of the one hundred and thirty-second and one hundred and forty-first degrees of east longitude, and between the southern ocean and twenty-six degrees of south latitude ... consists of waste and unoccupied lands which are supposed to be fit for the purposes of colonization'.[161] This phraseology alone prompted lengthy delays in the execution of the enactment's purposes, with Glenelg's administration in the Colonial Office belatedly and intermittently insisting upon a formalized provision for

Wakefield, evidence, 22 June 1836, *GBPP1836*, xi (512), 559. Cf James Stephen's comments on planter society in the West Indies (1831), in Bell and Morrell, *Select Documents on British Colonial Policy, 1830–1860*, 373.

157 *The First report of the directors of the New-Zealand Company presented to the first general meeting of the shareholders on the 14th May 1840*, 12.

158 4 & 5 William IV, c95 (15 August 1834) (Imp), CO13/3, fos.291–4a, TNA; Burns, *Fatal Success*, 39–41; Pike, *Paradise of Dissent*, 52–119; Knaplund, *James Stephen and the British Colonial System, 1813–1847*, 76–82. For a contemporary scepticism regarding the 'self-supporting' quality of the southern Australian proposals, see Sir Charles Napier, *Colonization, particularly in southern Australia*, xix–xx.

159 For example Wakefield, *A Statement of the Objects of the New Zealand Association*.

160 Ibid, 6 (emphasis added); South Australia, ibid, 5–6.

161 4 & 5 William IV, c95 (15 August 1834) (Imp), preamble, CO13/3, fo.291, TNA.

aboriginal proprietary interests, if any.[162] The Office remained uncertain as to whether South Australian aborigines possessed any entitlements to property and, in any event, the Act required the sale of £35,000 worth of so-called 'Crown land' in South Australia before any settlement was established.[163] The political endeavours of the Association ought to be considered in conjunction with this southern Australian context. Torrens and Wakefield were certainly in contact with one another.[164] Secondly, the minimal purchases secured from the indigenous populace were conceived as constraining the spatial extent of any settlement, rendering a 'provincial machinery of government' unnecessary 'for some years'.[165]

The Association's 'statement' of objectives viewed Māori as vendors in property transactions and assumed aboriginal entitlements to territory. This viewpoint was premised on *ius gentium* and the historical progression of Māori beyond mere savagery. Māori were construed as 'an intelligent people, who have so far advanced beyond the savage state as to recognise property in land, *and* whose national independence has been virtually, not to say formally acknowledged by the British Government'.[166] Here, the 'statement' referred to the appointment of a British resident, James Busby, to the Bay of Islands (in the far northern Te Tai Tokerau region) and the recognition of a 'New Zealand flag' by the Tory Earl of Aberdeen in late 1834. That is, a rudimentary polity (rather than several, multi-faceted polities) enjoying relations with Britain was envisaged. This use of *ius gentium* was demonstrated through emphasizing James Cook's relatively accurate charting of a New Zealand archipelago, in 1769 and 1770, and his footfall upon its varied beaches. He was 'the first European that visited the country, and took... possession of it in the name of his sovereign'.[167] In the Association's eyes, this reduced indigenous New Zealanders reductively (and passively) to a theatre of *ius gentium*. As yet, there was no appreciation of fluidly layered Māori polities or localized perceptions of Ngā Puhi or Ngāti Toa descent-groupings as to authority over territorial space.

In what would act as a consistent theme in the Association's literature, Māori not only had a capacity to 'recognise property in land', but to transfer it and to become civilized in transferring it. In this viewpoint, the Association relied on a variety of intellectual sources such as the 1830 text *The New Zealanders*: 'The known history of mankind will not allow us to entertain a doubt that *even* the New Zealanders are perfectly capable of being civilized'.[168] For the Association, 'civilization' meant incorporation into proposed settlements through their spatially interspersed amalgamation with Māori situated

162 Grey to Torrens, 15 December 1835, CO13/3, fos.114a–15a; Stephen, memorandum, 10 December 1835, ibid, fos.122a–3; Torrens to Grey, (nd) December 1835, CO13/3, fo.166a; 'treatment of aborigines' in Torrens to Glenelg, 22 June 1836, enclosing colonization commissioners of South Australia to Glenelg, 14 June 1836, CO13/3, fos.367–8; 'First annual report of the colonization commissioners of South Australia', CO13/4, fos.527a–33, TNA.

163 On Colonial Office uncertainty, see n 162 above. On the sale of these lands, see Kociumbas, *The Oxford History of Australia*, II, 188–9.

164 Hindmarsh to Angas, 2 January 1836, A461, PR6 174, GF Angas papers, State library of South Australia.

165 Wakefield, *A Statement of the Objects*, 7.

166 Ibid, 3 (emphasis added).

167 Ibid, 1; cf 2 (appendix).

168 Library of Entertaining Knowledge, *The New Zealanders*, 401 (emphasis added) ('Ferocious as they are, they are probably not more so than our own ancestors in this very island were at one time': ibid).

within defined reserves amongst anglo-settlers. Ongoing commercial and social interaction with genteel Europeans would 'civilize' Māori. Reserves were not novel but what was novel was the intention to place Māori on constrained plots of land *within* anglo-settlements. Wakefield recounted this objective in 1840, saying that the reserve policy intended 'to make a native aristocracy, a native gentry, and for that purpose to reserve lands as valuable property [spread throughout the midst of anglo-settlements]':[169]

> Evidence has been collected, from which it may be inferred that the New-Zealanders possess a natural capacity for civilization—that instead of being gradually exterminated by intercourse with civilized men, this people may be brought to adopt the language, usages, laws, religion, and social ties of a superior race. This is an end to which the Association attach the highest importance.[170]

Placing Māori in history was crucial. Māori were appraised through observing their modes of subsistence and their eagerness to interact with European visitors. Commodifying goods for exchange presupposed the historical emergence of a conception of property. Historically, Māori were placed towards the 'savage' end of this sense of commerce and property. Yet, diversity characterized 'savagery'. On one account, 'New Hollanders' were unfavourably compared to 'New Zealanders' such that the former were construed as less eager or curious to engage in commerce with Europeans. They were characterized as 'sylvan satyrs' insensible to benefitting from the acquisition of European wares.[171] Surprisingly diverse sources noted this view of Māori. Samuel Marsden remarked on the eagerness for trafficking in chattels as early as 1814 and 1815 when he sought to establish a Church Missionary Society station at Rangihoua in the far northern districts of New Zealand. In 1819, he thought northern Māori 'like the Jews [have] a great natural turn for traffic; they will buy and sell anything they have got'.[172] Henry Chapman, a radical and Association publicist, uttered similar views when writing for the *Dublin Review* in 1840.[173] For New Zealand in 1837, the Association proposed external assistance in the form of 'systematic', regularized intervention beyond the scope of mission stations. Overall, this intensive approach to improving 'savagery' was derived from an intellectual appreciation of British interventions that was evident by 1837 in the literature of 'liberal Anglican' theologians like Whately and Arnold.[174] Intellectual expectations concerning the nature of property and proprietorship accompanied this historical perspective.

[169] Wakefield, evidence, 16 July 1840, *GBPP1840*, vii (582), 35.

[170] Wakefield, *A Statement of the Objects*, 4.

[171] For example, Barrow, 'Australasia', in *Encyclopædia Britannica*, IV, 208.

[172] *The letters and journals of Samuel Marsden 1765–1838: senior chaplain in the colony of New South Wales and superintendent of the mission of the Church Missionary Society in New Zealand*, John Elder (ed) (Dunedin, 1932), 219: Marsden to Pratt, 'Marsden's second New Zealand journal [29 July 1819–9 November 1819]'.

[173] Henry Chapman, 'New Zealand', 198.

[174] Whately, *Introductory Lectures on Political Economy*, [1831], 121–3.For Whately's observations on colonization and criticisms of penal colonies, see Whately, *Thoughts on secondary punishments in a letter to Earl Grey*, 190–4: 'We severed the humble from the nobles of our land, and formed the embryo of a plebeian nation': ibid, 195. See also Porter, 'Trusteeship, anti-slavery, and humanitarianism', in Porter (ed), *The Oxford History of the British Empire*, 200–1; Stocking, *Victorian Anthropology*, 33. Porter, 'North American experience and British missionary encounters in Africa and the Pacific, c1800–50', in Daunton and Halpern (eds), *Empire and Others*, 345–7.

The Association's intellectual commitment to transforming Māori was confirmed in the personal correspondence of Wakefield. In a letter to his brother-in-law, the reverend Charles Torlesse, in May 1837, he said, '[t]he New Zealanders are not savages properly speaking, but a people capable of civilization'. He continued with the comment that, '[a] main object will be to do all that can be done for inducing them to embrace the language, customs, religion and social ties of the superior race'.[175] This lexicon of improving or 'civilizing' was founded upon incorporating Māori into British settlements. This transitive syntax of 'improvement' would operate by degrees upon those Māori engaging in commercial interaction with European communities. Māori potential would be realized through exposure to Association settlers. A form of osmosis was involved. The Association's abiding conception of Māori proprietary rights-status was inextricably linked to its comprehension of transplanting and enlarging 'civilization' through organized anglophone settlement. Those Māori identified as comprising chiefly elites would be transformed into propertied gentry occupying reserves.[176]

Much information was devoted to a discussion of the 'native inhabitants'; establishing grounds for a Māori capacity for assumed 'civilization' and connected notions of proprietorship. Sources derived from James Cook's journals of oceanic voyaging and circumnavigation, together with accessible missionary accounts (William Yate, for instance), supplied the principal intelligence.[177] Certainly, Cook's account and initial cartography predominated. Māori potential for civil advancement was supposedly revealed by numerous illustrations, including their physical attributes, their 'sonorous' language reminiscent 'of the Greeks of Homer' and replete with 'metaphysical distinctions', their lyrical poetry, and their mastery in sculpting timber.[178] Similarly, they were alleged in this 'statement' to have acquired a monotheist predisposition, focusing upon a single deity, '*Atua*'. Christianity and commerce would act as the principal instruments for improving Māori.

The initial acquisition of territory from its aboriginal users was posed throughout this 'statement' as the central, regularizing mechanism in the Association's proposals. Māori were treated as having a capacity to vend property, presumably resting upon an acknowledgement of an aboriginal proprietary interest. This underlying premise was expressed elliptically as a Māori 'recognition' of property. Paradoxically, however, the particulars appended to the 'statement' did not unqualifiedly merit such a presupposition since there are several references to the minimal acreage of terrain that had been cultivated or appropriated by Māori. Similarly, stress was placed upon the primordial geographical characteristics or features of the archipelago, allegedly unmolested by human industry: 'The quantity of land brought under cultivation is a mere nothing, in comparison with the boundless primeval forests...—a fact most important with a view to colonization'.[179]

175 Wakefield to Torlesse, 12 May 1837, BL AddMss35261 (Wakefield papers), fo.9; cf Olssen, 'Mr Wakefield and New Zealand as an experiment in post-enlightenment experimental practice' (n 152 above), 213; Sorrenson, 'How to civilize savages', 103.

176 Wakefield and Ward, *The British Colonization of New Zealand*, 55–6.

177 Wakefield, *A Statement of the Objects*, 2–3, 5–6, 23 on Cook (appendix). Cf Yates, 'Images of "heathen" and Christian in the early CMS mission to New Zealand', 7–9; Salmond, *Two Worlds*, 87–296 (Cook).

178 Wakefield, *A Statement of the Objects*, 16 (appendix); Library of Entertaining Knowledge, *The New Zealanders*, 401.

179 Wakefield, *A Statement of the Objects*, 13 (appendix).

The commentary on 'native inhabitants' in the 'statement' portrayed distinctions between observed aboriginal subsistence practices in the North and South Islands. After considering Cook and other authors, it concluded that there was 'no agriculture or appropriation of lands to interfere with colonization' in the South Island.[180] Throughout the islands, the 'aborigines [were]...no charge upon the soil', thereby restricting the amount of territory that might require 'purchase'.[181] Thus, in spite of the visible presence of Māori inhabitants, it was presumed that, in spatial terms, they would not hinder the planting of systematic settlement—Māori would not require much territory. Finally, the Association was also mindful of the well-known House of Commons Select Committee on aborigines. This Committee released its main, second report on 26 June 1837. The Association's use of these sources was particularly evident by late 1837.[182] Certainly, the Association had access to parliamentary papers printing Colonial Office correspondence on the condition of aboriginal New Zealand. This explained its reference to the 'New Zealand flag' of 1834.

The Association's view of Māori 'civilizing' potential was muddied in its subsequent pamphlets and literature. This distortion was due to an inherent ambiguity in its use of 'savage' to describe Māori. Indeed, the Association's use of this term requires unpacking. Despite the supposed Māori proclivity for improvement, there were somewhat contradictory features to their condition that could be treated as undermining this potential. Māori were perceived paradoxically as savages—'a thoroughly savage people'[183]—and yet not savages. In one sense, they were characterized as profoundly imbued with savagery, partly on the basis that they were understood to participate in relatively ceaseless warfare. Moreover, '[e]xcepting some few tribes, who, through their intercourse with Europeans, have advanced considerably in the acquisition of new wants, they scarcely cultivate the earth, and are often exposed to famine'. Conversely, Māori were not construed as irredeemably savage in substance since they evidenced 'a remarkable capacity for becoming civilized—a peculiar aptitude for being improved by intercourse with civilization'.[184] This very ambiguity widened the possible range of Association policies towards Māori, a feature that would be realized in the years beyond 1839.[185]

Information transmitted from English-speaking sources within New Zealand was also included in this ambivalent image. Māori were portrayed as markedly threatened by the incremental and disordered (read 'unsystematic') settling of Europeans on the New Zealand littoral. This assertion permeated that literature associated with advocates of 'systematic colonization' or their sympathizers.[186] These Europeans would allegedly compromise Māori potentiality. Evidently, an acceptance of the possibilities of Māori agency and confidence in managing spasmodic or minor pākehā occupations of territorial sites was conspicuously absent. The Association referred to a deleterious situation supposedly pervading in New Zealand, claiming that it was due to rapacious European visitors or residents. Wakefield referred to this as the 'dark side' of the narrative. 'The crimes against the natives committed by some captains of English vessels, are so atrocious as to be hardly credible'.[187] Englishmen arrived with 'gunpowder, brandy, and

[180] Ibid. [181] Ibid.

[182] Wakefield and Ward, *The British Colonization of New Zealand*, 32–40, 401 (appendix).

[183] Ibid, 28. [184] Ibid, 28–9.

[185] See Chapters Three and Four.

[186] For example, Chapman, 'Zealand, New', in *Encyclopædia Britannica*, 976.

[187] Wakefield and Ward, *The British Colonization of New Zealand*, 31, 70–1.

debauchery'.[188] An inchoate quarrelsome 'colony' was assumed to have materialized intermittently; unauthorized settling was considered as having appeared in districts of New Zealand.

This treatment of New Zealand's condition swallowed missionary testimony before the Select Committee on aborigines. Sparse mission sources conveyed tales of entanglements with Māori descent-groupings in the slender northern peninsula of the northernmost major island. That is, these were localized island narratives not archipelagic stories. This limited geographical orbit is important since missiology has long embellished the import and geographical reach of this missionary presence.[189] Hence, the distribution of reported relations with disparate Māori favoured far northern New Zealand.

It was not through the Association but via missionary and itinerant trading sources that territorial 'purchase' entered the vocabulary of European relations with Māori. Yet, they were not discussed as a subject of policy concern until the Association's formation in 1837. From February 1815, paper deeds claiming territories through 'purchase' were increasingly procured. Samuel Marsden was an early progenitor of these deeds, supervising an 'acquisition' encompassing the construction of his mission *entrepôt* at Rangihoua in 1815.[190] Traders and mission representatives, such as Thomas Kendall and Richard Davis, conveyed indications of how European engagements with Māori were conducted formalistically. After 1830 especially, instances of these putative 'deeds' proliferated.[191] Often these deeds reflected relationships beyond the ken of European observers—relations not of vendor and acquirer but of insecure European visitors paying forms of tribute to certain paramount Māori.[192] Self-descriptions and titles of various 'native' descent-groupings were increasingly appreciated in these sources, but these clusters of persons were indiscriminately referred to as 'tribes'—with variant names of '*Nga-poui* [Ngā Puhi]' or '*Moury-wenoua* [Muriwhenua]' materializing.[193]

'Liberal Anglicanism' implied a political predisposition to construct a Whig-led coalition, encompassing, for instance, various dissenting Irish Roman Catholic and moderate evangelical elements in a broader than hitherto notion of governance and the political nation. This proclivity was a particular view of political incorporation[194] and,

[188] Wakefield, *A Statement of the Objects*, 19 (appendix).

[189] On the general background to mission stations, see Orange, 'The Maori people and the British Crown (1769–1840)', in Sinclair (ed), *The Oxford Illustrated History of New Zealand*, 29–35; Belich, *Making Peoples*, 134–7. See also Davidson and Lineham (eds), *Transplanted Christianity*.

[190] *The letters and journals of Samuel Marsden 1765–1838*, 122–3: Marsden to secretary, Church Missionary Society, 10 June 1815, 'Before my final departure from New Zealand I wished to obtain and secure as far as possible a legal settlement for the Europeans I had left upon the island'. Eugene Stock did not address Marsden's transaction at Rangihoua: see Stock, *The history of the Church Missionary Society*, I, 208–9.

[191] For example OLC1/734–736: James Kemp, deed, 8 October 1831; Richard Davis, deed, 20 December 1831, ANZ(W).

[192] Around which there is considerable debate: see *Muriwhenua Land Report—Wai-45*, ch 2, 'The people and the land', 11–52; Oliver, *Looking for the Phoenix*, 161–3; Mutu, '*Tuku whenua* and land sale in New Zealand in the nineteenth century', in Calder, Lamb, and Orr (eds), *Voyages and Beaches*, 316–28.

[193] These versions of 'Ngapuhi' and 'Muriwhenua' are derived from James Wyld, *The islands of New Zealand from the admiralty surveys of the English and French marine*. See also Ballara, *Iwi*, 58–60.

[194] Harvie, 'Revolution and the rule of law', in Morgan (ed), *The Oxford History of Britain*, 514–17.

interestingly, both committees were implicated in it. That is, the membership of each was symptomatic of this tendency. The members reflected the varied, occasionally imperially oriented interests to be found in the Commons, including moderate Anglican evangelicals such as Thomas Fowell Buxton, Sir George Grey, and Francis Baring, and the Roman Catholic Daniel O'Connell. In construing these elements as 'imperially oriented'—a problematic adjective to clasp and analyse—one is referring to a variety of potential or possible imperial (issue-sensitive) preoccupations on the part of, say, parliamentary or partially non-parliamentary clusters (such as the Association).[195] Such individuals could coalesce or converge around distinct issues of mutual interest only to diverge on other occasions. 'Liberal Anglican' Whigs, including Howick, courted these networks on issues such as the abolition of slavery throughout the empire.[196] Buxton, for one, was regarded as a parliamentary paramount within the evangelical anti-slavery interest. He had acquired a general reputation on trans-oceanic colonial issues. Indeed, he was described in a letter received from George Stephen as 'the parliamentary advocate—the acknowledged leader—the conventional referee on all colonial questions on the liberal side'.[197] In early 1837, Edward Stanley, the chief whip for the Whigs in the Commons, would occasionally approach both Buxton and his brother-in-law, Andrew Johnston, if Stanley anticipated a marginal division on a legislative measure. Thus, on 22 February 1837, Stanley informed each that 'there will certainly be a division in the House of Commons on Friday next, another Irish Corporation bill, when it is of the *utmost importance* that there should be as full an attendance of our friends as possible'.[198]

Indeed, this whiggish 'liberal Anglican' trend towards political incorporation was especially evident in the Select Committee on aborigines. Upon its appointment on 9 February 1836, its membership comprised thirteen persons, namely Buxton, Grey, Hardy, Bagshaw, Sir Rufane Donkin, Holland, Charles Lushington, Pease (a Quaker), Baines, Andrew Johnston, Plumptre, Wilson, and Colonel Thompson. This Committee had, nonetheless, been hearing evidence from some eleven witnesses in the two-month period from 31 July 1835, almost eight months before it recommenced its examination of witnesses on 12 February in the subsequent parliamentary session. Gladstone appeared in substitution for Hardy, both from 16 February 1836 and in the reconvened Select Committee, from 20 February 1837. In the historiography, this Select Committee is invariably referred to as an example of the usual features of parliamentary agitation addressing the political possibilities of 'humanitarianism' in the 1830s.[199] Yet its relevance to southern Pacific locations and aboriginal title was limited.[200]

195 Darwin, 'Imperialism and the Victorians', 641.

196 Brent, *Liberal Anglican Politics*, 252–98; Gross, 'The Abolition of Negro Slavery and British Parliamentary Politics', 66–7, 69, 70, 73, 77 (Howick).

197 Stephen to Buxton, 25 December 1835, RH, Mss Brit Emp s444, Buxton papers, xiv, fo.274. Cf Brent, *Liberal Anglican Politics*, 269–70; Parry, *The Rise and Fall of Liberal Government in Victorian Britain*, 102.

198 Stanley to Buxton and Johnston, 22 February 1837, RH, Mss Brit Emp s444, Buxton papers, xv, fo.189j (emphasis in original); also xv, fos.269a–d: Stanley to Johnston, 27 April 1837.

199 Elbourne, '"To colonize the mind"', 309, 313–14; Orange, *The Treaty of Waitangi*, 2. For recent nuanced accounts, see Elbourne, 'Imperial Politics in the Family Way', in Bain Attwood, and Griffiths,(eds), *Frontier, Race, Nation*, 111–35; Laidlaw, '"Aunt Anna's Report"', 1–28.

200 This Committee's object was to 'consider what measures ought to be adopted with regard to the native inhabitants of countries where British Settlements are made, and to the neighbouring

Three themes predominated in this Select Committee's collation of evidence and testimony. First, the Committee's report encompassed a variety of regions and histories within Britain's empire. The report's authors were principally concerned with dramatizing recent events in southern Africa, rather than aboriginal New Zealand, Australia, or Canada, although each of these areas featured in the Committee's evidence. The relatively limited treatment and visualization of New Zealand ought to be borne in mind. Substantial testimony dealt with the Cape-Xhosa contretemps and the subsequent annexation of Queen Adelaide province in May 1835 by Sir Benjamin D'Urban. John Philip, among others, such as Andries Stockenström, acted as a critical Select Committee informant on this subject.[201] On 26 June 1837, the select committee report published general principles on relations with indigenous populations.

Secondly, this report was noticeable for its preoccupation with methods of disciplining non-mission European transactional activity with indigenous populations beyond British establishments, including the supposed acquisition of proprietary interests. This imparted a preference for the use of undeniably extra-jurisdictional instruments—in the form of statutory measures—in regulating the behaviour of alien (typically, non-missionary) encounters with aboriginal communities. This jurisdictional emphasis was analogous in conception to features of imperial activity such as statute, sponsored by Glenelg, for addressing assumed misconduct in territories adjacent to the Cape colony.[202] This statute was praised by the select committee report. Thirdly, the Committee was staffed with moderate evangelical sympathizers, such as its chairman, Buxton, Buxton's brother-in-law, Andrew Johnston, and Grey. These persons, together with Buxton's familial relations, were influential in the drafting of the final report, indicating a coalescence of a Glenelgian department's disciplining anxieties with certain complementary intersections throughout a legislative arena.

In spite of focusing upon southern Africa, the veritable range of regions included within the Committee's purview is noticeable. Extensive missionary intelligence was provided throughout the course of the hearings. It concerned a multitude of territories, from Essequibo to Pacific islands. The London-based secretaries of three significant missionary agencies testified, specifically Dandeson Coates, lay-secretary for the Church Missionary Society, William Ellis for the London Missionary Society, and John Beecham of the Wesleyan Missionary Society. In its treatment of aboriginal proprietary interests, the Committee's proceedings extended a theme that Andrew Porter has connected with John Philip's missions in southern Africa at Philipolis or Griquatown, or those in the

tribes, in order to secure to them the due observance of justice and the protection of their rights; to promote the spread of civilization among them, and to lead them to the peaceful and voluntary reception of the Christian religion': report from the Select Committee on aborigines (British settlements), House of Commons, *GBPP1837*, vii (425), 3.

201 RH, Mss Brit Emp s444 (Buxton papers), xv, fos.311b–c: Johnston to Gurney, 9 June 1837; xv, fos.123e–h: Philip to Hannah Buxton, 13 December 1836; xv, fos.171–3: Buxton to Edward Buxton, 17 January 1837; xvi, fos.136–9: Johnston to Priscilla Johnston and Gurney, 8 June 1837, xv, ff.309a–h; xv, fos.311e–h: Johnston to Gurney, 10 June 1837. See also Galbraith, *Reluctant Empire*, 126–7; Macmillan, *Bantu, Boer, and Briton*, 187–90.

202 'An Act for the prevention and punishment of offences committed by His Majesty's subjects within certain territories adjacent to the colony of the Cape of Good Hope', 13 August 1836, 6 & 7 William IV, c57 (Imp), CO209/2, fos.22–2a; referred to in CO209/2, fos.20a–1: Glenelg to Bourke, 26 August 1836, TNA.

Pacific.[203] That is, aborigines would be sedentarized, occupying settled territory in or near mission stations or mission-sponsored hamlets. Sedentarizing aborigines involved an ongoing cultivation of the soil on the part of its users or occupiers. This would serve to expose aboriginal inhabitants to mission-station *mores* and commercial trading, as overseen by mission representatives. Philip's strategies of sedentarization and isolation of southern African aborigines in mission-centred communities coincided with views of the evangelical John Harris.[204] But these perspectives blossomed most coherently during the course of evidence presented before Buxton's select committee. Mission representatives within New Zealand were received as 'instrumental in preserving peace in the country... in abolishing the custom of *tapuing*, or rendering sacred and unapproachable a particular place or person; a superstition which posed the greatest obstacles to improvement and civilization'.[205] This alleged amelioration of a savage condition was, according to a rendition of 'improvements' composed by Coates, supposedly evident in regions throughout New Zealand. Similarly, a section from William Yates's evidence was summarily replicated in the report:

> What have been the effects of the exertions of the missionaries in a general manner?—Abolishing their superstitious observances, establishing the Sabbath, rendering the natives more industrious, bringing a large proportion of their land into a state of cultivation, preventing war, ameliorating the condition of the slaves, and making the language a written one.[206]

Significantly, Coates, Ellis, and Beecham released a book reproducing their Committee evidence.[207] In essence, their purpose was almost indistinguishable from the Association's objectives. Indeed, under their varied evidential narratives before the Select Committee, Māori were also treated as subjects of transformative 'improving' and conversion. Yet, their several accounts certainly differed from that of the Association in their choice of agency overseeing the expected transition of indigenous persons from a condition of 'savagery' to one of 'civilization'. Whereas the Association's frame of reference was premised upon intensive settlement, the proposals of the witnesses before Buxton's Committee suggested the restriction or denial of such settlement. According to Coates, Ellis, and Beecham, and the 22 June 1837 report itself, colonial establishments prompted aboriginal extermination in case after case, whether Canada, Van Diemen's land, or southern Africa. Concerning the 'South Sea' islands, the report stated that 'various governments of Christendom have respected the rights of the native chieftains'.[208]

[203] Porter, '"Commerce and Christianity": the rise and fall of a nineteenth-century missionary slogan', 610.

[204] Ross, *John Philip (1775–1851)*, 141; Porter, 'North American experience and British missionary encounters in Africa and the Pacific, c1800–50', in Daunton and Halpern, *Empire and Others*, 353–4; Harris, *The Great Commission*, 196. Gunson, *Messengers of Grace*, 270–1.

[205] Report, House of Commons, aborigines, *GBPP1837*, vii (425), 53.

[206] Minutes of evidence, House of Commons, aborigines, *GBPP1836*, vii (538), 200, cited in report, House of Commons, aborigines, *GBPP1837*, vii (425), 54.

[207] Coates, Ellis, and Beecham *Christianity, the means of civilization shown in the evidence given before a committee of the House of Commons on aborigines*; cf report, House of Commons, aborigines, *GBPP1837*, vii (425), 50–1 (William Ellis), 54 (Coates). See *Christian Observer*, 70, recommending a reading of Coates' testimony.

[208] Report, House of Commons, aborigines, *GBPP1837*, vii (425), 85.

There was no embellishment on 'rights of the native chieftains', suggesting the potential connotative fluidity of these 'rights', which they could encompass a variety of states or interests. Nefarious British merchants and seafarers were reputedly able to commit unspecified crimes with impunity in the southern seas. According to Buxton's Committee, '[a] new race of buccaneers will appear in the Southern Ocean, under whose oppressions the natives will sink'.[209] On these islands (including New Zealand), the report recommended appointing consular agents, 'armed with powers similar to those of British Consuls in the Barbary States'.[210] In short, they would possess 'a judicial authority to arrest, commit for trial, and try all British subjects committing offences within the limits of the Consul's commission'. Periodic visits by naval vessels were advocated. The internal affairs of these Polynesian islands would remain undisturbed.

A Buxtonian vocabulary on aboriginal property favoured vaguely expressed propositions since it principally addressed, in its own terms, 'exclusively pacific and benevolent' objects.[211] Buxton's personal correspondence did not refer to discussions of aboriginal proprietorship but to the amelioration and improvement of aboriginal conditions. Such vagueness was politically convenient for an Office remaining uncertain as to what the detailed policy repercussions of aboriginal proprietary interests might be. Thus, there was an undeniable generality regarding indigenous proprietary interests throughout the Committee's final report and findings. Nine principal 'suggestions' were advanced by the report with relative brevity.[212] In this context, the report's fourth principal 'suggestion', concerning the regulation of aboriginal property, was telling. It advised that any attempted acquisition by British subjects of indigenous lands, either within the Crown's dominions or beyond, ought to be 'declared illegal and void'.[213] Significantly, the language deployed was prescriptive rather than mandatory. Further, this restriction '*might* also be extended to lands situate within territories which, though not forming a part of the [monarch's] dominions, are yet in immediate contiguity to them'.[214] This was tentative. The 'impracticable' nature of applying such a maxim as an imperial principle of practice was admitted. Nonetheless, 'it should be distinctly understood, that all persons who embark on [the alleged assumption of native estates] must do so at their own peril, and have no claim on her Majesty for support in vindicating the titles which they may so acquire'. Interestingly, the tone of that statement was undeniably definite. It is this stylistic combination of the definitive with the diffident that, in retrospect, appears somewhat puzzling.

What is also striking is that the source of the fourth 'suggestion' cannot be explicitly located in the evidence presented before the Select Committee. There was an apparent

[209] Ibid. [210] Ibid.

[211] 'Prospectus of the Society for the extinction of the slave trade and for the civilization of Africa, instituted June, 1839 [14th February 1840]', in Buxton, *The Remedy; being a sequel to the African slave trade*, 6.

[212] Report, House of Commons, aborigines, *GBPP1837*, vii (425), 77–81. Each 'suggestion' was entitled with what could be loosely referred to as a synoptic heading, specifically, 'protection of natives to devolve on executive', 'contracts for service to be limited', 'sale of ardent spirits to be prevented', 'regulations as to lands within British dominions', 'new territories not to be acquired without sanction of home government', 'religious instruction and education to be provided', 'punishment of crimes', 'treaties with natives inexpedient', and 'missionaries to be encouraged'.

[213] Ibid, 78. John Philip's correspondence might have influenced this principle: see Ross, *John Philip (1775–1851)*, 141. Chapter Three will argue that it usefully converged with procedural principles of Whig imperial land management from 1831.

[214] Ibid (emphasis added).

formulaic acceptance of aboriginal property, but also a tentative working-out of how to restrain or minimize entanglements between Europeans and indigenous communities. A Buxtonian vocabulary was conveniently vague and Grey recited this vocabulary in the Office. It was this terse characteristic that conditioned an emergent political approach to aboriginal proprietary interests from 1837. What is noticeable is the largely diffident expression used by the Committee. The underlying bases for this quality cannot be recovered with ease. Buxton's correspondence concerning the authorship of the report fails to reveal any intelligence in this vein.

Thus, a measure of political convergence occurred between the Colonial Office's participation in this Select Committee's hearings and the views of persons such as Buxton concerning appropriate policies towards aboriginal populations. At the general level of sentiment, Buxton's terminology converged with a Glenelgian (and Greyesque) language on aboriginal proprietary rights, something that was evident from 1835 in the instance of southern Australia.[215] Grey referred to the possibility that the statutory limits of South Australia 'extend very far into the interior of New Holland, and *might* embrace in its range numerous Tribes of People, whose proprietary title to the soil, we have not the slightest ground for disputing'.[216] In that regional arena, Buxton's rhetoric in the House of Commons was cited as indicative of concerns animating imperial approaches overseas.[217] Torrens and his fellow commissioners provided '*reasonable* assurances' that 'injustice towards the Aboriginal Natives of that part of the globe' would be averted.[218] This suggested the possibility of a degree of subtle management, or at least negotiation with Buxton, on the part of Colonial Office representatives, particularly Grey. Indeed, Grey served as an active Office liaison within Buxton's Committee. He provided Buxton with access to various departmental documents during the process of drafting the report in early 1837. This included information on the recent situation in southern Africa before Stockenström was despatched as lieutenant-governor.[219] From Buxton's perspective, this indicated Grey's significance to the proceedings of the Select Committee at the outset and to Buxton's ongoing role as chairman. Earlier evidence readily demonstrates an established contact between the two individuals.[220]

Buxton's Select Committee was managed through Grey's presence.[221] Grey was influential in fashioning the ultimate report. In mid-1837, he evidently suggested the deletion of many excerpts from the then draft report regarding the frontier conflagration in southern Africa that commenced in December 1834.[222] Certainly, the report, together with the related testimony, represented an endeavour on the part of certain evangelical elements within the House of Commons to pronounce upon an issue with imperial implications, as in the instances of slavery and post-emancipation apprenticeship. In

215 Grey to Torrens, 17 July 1835, CO396/1, fos.21–3, TNA; Grey to Torrens, 15 December 1835, CO13/3, fos.114a–15a; Torrens to Grey, December 1835, CO13/3, fo.166a, TNA.

216 Grey to Torrens, 15 December 1835, CO13/3, fo.115, TNA (emphasis added).

217 Reynolds, *The Law of the Land*, 105–6.

218 Grey to Torrens, 15 December 1835, CO13/3, fos.115–15a, TNA (emphasis added); ibid, fos.1-61–9a: Torrens to Grey, December 1835 (received 23 December 1835), CO13/4, fos.169–70a: Torrens to Grey, 8 January 1836 and fos.173–4: Torrens to Glenelg, 7 January 1836.

219 RH, Mss Brit Emp s444, xv, fo.14: Buxton to Hannah Buxton, 10 February 1836.

220 RH, Mss Brit Emp s444, xiv, fos.100–1: Grey to Buxton, 20 September 1835.

221 RH, Mss Brit Emp s444, xv, fos.12–13: Priscilla Johnston to Sarah Buxton and Gurney, 6 February 1836; ibid, xv, fo.9: Buxton to Hannah Buxton, 5 February 1836.

222 RH, Mss Brit Emp s444, xv, fos.319a–h: Buxton to Gurney and Sarah Buxton, 17 June 1837.

this process of collecting and structuring *viva voce* evidence, Buxton undoubtedly predominated, along with his daughter, Sarah Buxton, and a first cousin through marriage, Anna Gurney.[223] The Colonial Office managed a principal archive of information represented as intelligence while Grey and the Office's librarian furnished materials.[224]

Yet Grey participated actively in the final revisions of the report, assuming an influential role in ensuring a version amenable to the Colonial Office, much to Buxton's concern. At points, Buxton lamented Grey's influence on the drafting of the report with the words, 'Such gashes and ghastly wounds as he had the heart to make!... While I am writing, down comes a packet... containing Grey's alterations—tho' dreadful, they are bearable, even if we have to submit to them all'.[225] Buxton pursued tactical approaches, overly aware of the persistent necessity of parliamentary negotiation with, say, executive elements, such as the Office. In any event, Buxton ultimately expressed a measure of satisfaction with the report. Indeed, in June 1837, he privately and prematurely fancied that its release had effectively forestalled any proposed settlement in New Zealand.[226] However, the Association's objectives were considered within the intimate counsels of the Melbourne administration in later 1837, as opposed to parliamentary spheres. Buxton's report was a contextual source for the Association and Office but, importantly, reflected the relative vagueness that existed concerning the substance of aboriginal title.

Clearly, the Association's comprehension of aboriginal New Zealand also introduced a relevance for *ius gentium*, as witnessed by Wakefield's literary tomes in 1837—*The British Colonization of New Zealand* particularly. The Association viewed New Zealand as subject to a claim of British sovereignty as opposed to other European states. Cook's footfall on New Zealand shores in 1769 and 1770 was considered a sufficient basis for this claim (discovery).[227] Māori independence was accepted within this notional limitation. Coates's literature agreed with this position: 'The possession too, taken of the islands by Captain Cook in the name of this country, would, it is presumed, form a good title against other Nations, though none at all against the rights and sovereignty of the Natives'.[228] *Ius gentium* was invoked again. Opinions diverged on what this meant for property in New Zealand. Glenelg's office, however, was committed to a line of precedents within its own records. Stephen himself was professionally influenced by a series of policy minutes and letters premised on Māori 'independence' and non-British status.[229] It remained uncertain as to what this implied for transactional behaviour involving property within New Zealand. This uncertainty established a basis for dispute between the Association and Colonial Office personnel in that their respective notions of *ius gentium* entailed a divergence in opinion.

223 RH, Mss Brit Emp s444, xv, fo.227: Buxton to Gurney and Sarah Buxton, 18 March 1837.

224 RH, Mss Brit Emp s444, xv, fos.311b–c: Johnston to Gurney, 9 June 1837.

225 RH, Mss Brit Emp s444, xv, fos.319a—h: Buxton to Gurney, 17 June 1837.

226 RH, Mss Brit Emp s444, ii, fos.131–8: Buxton to Joseph John Gurney, 25 June 1837.

227 Wakefield, *A Statement of the Objects*, 3; Wakefield *The British Colonization of New Zealand*, 53.

228 Coates to Stephen, 5 January 1838, CO209/3, fo.131, enclosing 'notes for the information of those members of the deputation to Lord Glenelg respecting the New Zealand Association, who have not attended the meetings of the committee on the subject', confidential, 28 December 1837, fos.133–44a, 143a, TNA.

229 See Owens, 'New Zealand before Annexation' in Rice (ed), *The Oxford History of New Zealand*, 43.

Evidently, Church Missionary Society representatives viewed themselves as able to acquire property from Māori. However, they seem to have assumed that no implications for Māori sovereignty flowed from these transactions. Property transactions had clearly occurred within New Zealand in the recent past, with plentiful examples of parchment deeds of purchase in the 1830s or even as early as, say, 1815 or 1821.[230] In 1838, for instance, the Association was already involved in the nascent stages of negotiating private purchases from Europeans in New Zealand, particularly Thomas McDonnell.[231] This transactional practice in the field, as it were, was synthesized and reified through its incorporation into the annals of Colonial Office intelligence. The supposed alienation of land occupied or used by Māori was treated as a cogent issue for both the Association and the varied missionary agencies. In both rhetorical and policy terms, Māori were evidently admitted as vendors of territory in 1837 and 1838. Engagement in property transfers (interpreted in the Office as land 'sales'[232]) was translated through the conceptual prisms of stadial history and 'law'. That is, Māori were not roaming hunters and collectors; they acted diplomatically and participated in trade and commercial activity.

From 1837 the Association's conventional assumption appeared to be that a single transaction of land 'purchase' was sufficient to acquire both proprietary title and an entitlement to govern, by extinguishing indigenous sovereignty: 'The natives would part with land which they scarcely know how to cultivate, and with a dominion which they are incapable of exercising beneficially: and in return they would obtain, besides the *price in money or goods actually paid for the land ceded*, all the rights of British subjects'.[233] Purchase was treated as equivalent to cession. 'Sovereignty' consisted of the 'sovereign rights of chiefs'.[234] This approach was premised on a received understanding of Māori custom. On this account, political command of, or pre-eminent influence over, territorial space underpinned the substance of Māori chiefly sovereignty. Once transferred, sovereignty was eclipsed. This notion of 'purchase', in one form of expression or another, would prove to be an attitude that would persist in materializing at times, not only in the deliberations of the Association's successor entities but even within the Colonial Office's literature.[235] A much more nuanced Association view of Māori sovereignty and land tenure was aired in April and May 1838 by Baring, its chief witness before a House of Lords

230 See, eg Richard Davis, deed of purchase, 20 December 1830, OLC1/736, ANZ(W); John Butler, deed of purchase, March 1821, Ms0823, ATL; J Polack, deed of purchase (Bay of Islands), 30 August 1833.

231 Minutes, New Zealand Association Committee, 4 January 1838, CO208/185, fo.112a (Polack land); ibid, fo.88: 10 October 1838; ibid, 88a: 17 October 1838 (McDonnell, Hokianga land), TNA.

232 These putative 'sales' ought to be historically analysed as rather more nuanced forms of transactional conduct: see Head, 'Land, Authority and the Forgetting of Being in Early Colonial Maori History', 147–68; Parsonson, 'The Challenge to Mana Maori', in Rice, *The Oxford History of New Zealand*, 178–9; Parsonson, 'He Whenua te Utu ("the payment will be land")'; Ballara, 'The Pursuit of Mana?, 523–5, 526–8; Lian, 'Interpreting Maori history', 456–61 (Māori land transactions); Mutu, '*Tuku whenua* and land sale in New Zealand in the nineteenth century', in Calder, Lamb, and Orr, *Voyages and Beaches*, 321–6.

233 Wakefield and Ward, *The British Colonization of New Zealand*, 54 (emphasis added).

234 Ibid, 53.

235 Stephen, draft instructions to Hobson, 24 January 1839, CO209/4, fos.214, 216, TNA (marginal note at fo.215 in Hobson's handwriting).

Select Committee investigating New Zealand.[236] Wakefield, however, was not present, having opted for a relatively concealed role in Durham's mission in the two Canadas. Baring said that 'sub-chiefs' and the 'different heads of families' rather than 'chiefs' per se were entitled to enter proprietary transactions.[237] Concerning Māori tenure, Baring was not always particularly clear in response to examination, whilst the identity of Baring's sources on this subject was not especially apparent:

> [*Duke of Richmond*] What is your opinion as to the present tenure of land by natives in that country? [*Baring*] As far as we can make out, they had always been extremely tenacious of their Land tenure, and [still] are, I believe: of course that can only rest on testimony. They have had no documents of any kind, but most of their wars are on account of land disputes.
>
> Can the head of a family, who is a proprietor, sell without the consent of a chief? [*Baring*] It is very difficult to say whether, when the Chiefs have sold Land, they get the concurrence of their sub-chiefs; that is an inquiry which we have not gone into, for it would not suit us to take too many small detached Portions of Land; we should be purchasers of a few Hundred Acres here and there if we bought from sub-chiefs.[238]

Baring's commentary differed markedly in its tone from the relative certainty which attended the observer John Nicholas' earlier remarks on Māori proprietary concerns in 1814 and 1815, these comments appearing in the Association's 22 May 1837 'statement of objects': 'Landed property is accurately defined in New Zealand, there being among the chiefs a mutual recognition of their respective territories, and an understanding that no encroachment is to be made on any without the general consent'.[239] Non-Association testimony, such as that of Robert FitzRoy, contributed to this increased sense of temerity and uncertainty. They indicated that, in spite of so-called deeds of purchase, Europeans merely occupied discrete areas on Māori sufferance with indigenous paramountcy persisting. FitzRoy said, 'they consider that when a European purchases their land, he is taken from that moment under the protection of their tribe', and '[i]t is a conditional sale, such as 'We sell them to you to hold as long as we shall permit you"'.[240] Consequently, there was confusion rather than clarity within the Committee, resulting in a tame report merely favouring the status quo and Colonial Office predominance in policy creation.[241] Despite this increased uncertainty, there was an ongoing reification of the 'gentleman' or chieftain (*rangatira*) as a central reference point and arbiter of property transactions. This important observation has been broadly noted in recent literature.[242] In any event, property transactions were continuing apace in 1838 regardless

[236] *GBPP1837–1838*, 'Report from the select committee of the House of Lords appointed to inquire into the present state of the islands of New Zealand and the expediency of regulating the settlement of British subjects there', 327–682. Cf Adams, *Fatal Necessity*, 118–19.

[237] *GBPP1837–1838*, xxi (680), Baring, evidence, 1 May 1838, 'Report from the select committee of the House of Lords appointed to inquire into the present state of the islands of New Zealand and the expediency of regulating the settlement of British subjects there', 327–682, 478–9.

[238] Ibid, 478–9. The sources for Baring's opinion are not evident from Association records although the earlier testimony of Association member, Hinds, and possible sympathizers, such as Joel Polack, may have contributed. Polack appears to be an improbable source, however, in view of his notions regarding territorial transactions with Māori: Polack, *New Zealand*, II, 201–2, 205–6.

[239] John Liddiard Nicholas cited in Wakefield, *A Statement of the Objects*, 27 (appendix); Nicholas, *Narrative of a Voyage to New Zealand*.

[240] 'Report from the select committee of the House of Lords appointed to inquire into the present state of the islands of New Zealand', *GBPP1837–1838*, xxi (680), 327–682, 501, 504.

[241] Ibid, 329.

[242] *Muriwhenua Land Report—Wai-45*, 29.

of the House of Lords Select Committee and its collection of witnesses, including those who were members of the Association, such as Baring.

Yet, in this parliamentary arena, Baring defended legislation as the appropriate method for regulating land acquisition in New Zealand. The House of Lords Select Committee's membership included the Duke of Wellington, the Duke of Richmond, Glenelg, the Earl of Devon, Lord Aberdeen, Viscount Canning, Durham (who departed for Canada on 24 April, however), the Earl of Ripon (formerly Goderich), Lord Brougham and Vaux, and the Bishop of London. It had emerged at the instigation of the Earl of Devon by virtue of a motion dated 30 March 1838 and proved to be a useful theatre for the mission secretariats and Association representatives.[243] It was instituted to consider the earlier Charles Enderby petition and was arguably unopposed by Glenelg, chiefly as a means of broadening processes of political facilitation (already complicated by the opposing pamphlet strategies of the missionary agencies and Association).[244] Possibly, these processes could be accomplished with the assistance of prominent peers of either a tory or whiggish persuasion, such as Wellington, Glenelg, Richmond, and Aberdeen. On the concept of an anticipated Association bill, Baring emphasized that both aboriginal tenure and sovereignty could be purchased in a single transaction:

> The Queen merely authorises us, Her Subjects, [pursuant to a statute] to purchase this Sovereignty of the Natives, and to make it over to Her.
>
> [*Duke of Richmond*] You may now purchase and may make it over to Her without the Bill?
>
> I do not believe we can purchase without the Bill. I hold that she is the sovereign, but I am afraid public opinion would not allow me to maintain that'.[245]

Association member Samuel Hinds, an Anglican reverend (from 1849, Bishop of Norwich), provided an intriguing account of aborigines as rights-bearers. Hinds was a 'liberal Anglican' theologian and a close follower of Whately. His view was both revealingly personal and indicative of a profound strand of Association thought on that issue, one that would eventually become associated with certain members of its successor entity, the New Zealand (Land) Company.[246] He did not accept the existence of 'sovereignty' or 'rights' for Māori but considered it tactically astute for the Association to act as if Māori

[243] Earl of Devon, *HPD*, 3rd series, 30 March 1838, vol xlii, 152–5. Cf Adams, *Fatal Necessity*, 118–19; Burns, *Fatal Success*, 61–2.

[244] Enderby to Melbourne, 16 December 1837, CO209/2, fos, 445–446; minutes, New Zealand Association committee, 14 December 1837, CO28/185, fo. 116, TNA. Charles Enderby forwarded the petition of 16 December 1837 to Melbourne. It was signed by a number of individuals with interests in the sea-borne and whaling commerce around New Zealand or in eastern Asia, including George Young and George Lyall. Enderby was the son of Samuel Enderby and had succeeded to the Enderby shipping firm, one that remained extensively interested in the whaling fisheries throughout the Australasian seas. He was also a member of the Association, whilst the petition was strategically engineered with Association awareness and complicity.

[245] 'Report from the select committee of the House of Lords appointed to inquire into the present state of the islands of New Zealand', *GBPP1837–1838*, xxi (680), 327–682, 484.

[246] On Hinds' intellectual background, see Brent, *Liberal Anglican Politics*, 145–6; for subsequent comparable sentiments or assumptions of New Zealand Land Company representatives, *vide*, see Somes to Palmerston, 7 November 1839, CO208/147, fo.167, TNA; Somes to Palmerston, 7 November 1839, FO58/1, fos.182a–3. 'Discovery' was treated as an appropriate foundational (if only prima facie or provisional) argument for claimed 'sovereignty' in other circumstances such as the Oregon boundary negotiation: *GBPP1846*, lii (695), Pakenham to Earl of Aberdeen, 12 September 1844, enclosing 'statement of the American plenipotentiary, containing the claims of the United States to the Oregon territory', 3 September 1844, 125–31, esp 125–7; 'statement

did possess rights per se in that it would placate an unspecified opinion within Britain. He also indicated the freshness of discussions concerning aboriginal 'sovereignty':

> Within the last few years, however, the justice of this claim [settling sovereignty claims by permitting first European discoverers the right of sovereignty to alien territory] has been questioned; and it has been asserted that savages as well as civilized Men have Sovereign rights. I do not myself think that they have; but it has been the wish of the Association not to offend any scruples, and therefore they have carefully in this [proposed] Bill waived the Question, and allowed the claim to a sovereign right of some kind to exist in those savages.[247]

In this reference, he envisaged a vaguely outlined parliamentary (possibly, 'moderate evangelical') opinion and its varied networks of non-parliamentary connections. As such, Hinds' testimony illustrated the relevance of a strategically adopted discourse or a pragmatic, tactical use of sources. This discussion, together with its accompanying intellectual language (*ius gentium*), exercised the Select Committee, as it mused upon the political repercussions of the Association's proposals. Hinds explicitly cited his sources:

> We suppose the New Zealanders, and not Great Britain, to be in Possession of the Right of Sovereignty, and we propose, accordingly, that a Purchase should be made of the Sovereignty as well as of the Fee Simple of the Land. We have some precedents for this.... Sir Stratford Canning took possession in 1815 of Singapore, it was at that time in the Possession of the Malays, the Subjects of the Sultan of Jahore. In 1825, he found, I think, some Inconvenience arising from the Sultan's Claims, and the English bought the Domain of the Sultan for a Sum of Money;... When Penn purchased Pennsylvania he no doubt understood that he purchased the Sovereignty as well as the Fee Simple of the Land, for I can conceive no one mad enough to found a Colony in the midst of Barbarians without securing the Colonists against their Interference as Sovereigns. Vattel certainly speaks of Penn's Treaty as if he understood him to have purchased the Sovereign Rights as well as the Fee Simple.... The Question has not been very much discussed; it has been taken for granted, and I think with Reason, that the Savage is in a State of Pupillage, and must be treated as we treat Children.[248]

Hinds used legalist sources in exhorting 'purchase' as sufficient to extinguish indigenous 'sovereignty'. His testimony also revealed the significance of selectively resuscitating episodes in imperial policy regarding alien polities as well as a recently re-translated literary text on *ius gentium* by an eighteenth-century jurist, Vattel. Yet, the Select Committee's noticeably terse report advocated executive (Colonial Office) rather than legislative determination of the New Zealand issue. Secondly, it illustrated support for the gradualist 'improvement' allegedly inherent in the ongoing mission approach to introducing affected Māori inexorably to anglophone 'civilization'.[249] However,

of the British plenipotentiary, containing the claims of Great Britain to the Oregon territory', 12 September 1844, ibid, 131–5.

247 *GBPP1837–1838*, xxi (680), 459. See also Hinds, *The latest official documents relating to New Zealand*, 12–13. Cf Beecham, *Remarks upon the latest official documents relating to New Zealand.*

248 *GBPP1837–1838*, xxi (680), 460; and Hinds' Vattelian 'cultivation' argument against aboriginal sovereignty: 'I conceive that civilized people have a right, an inherent right, over countries that have not been subject to Civilization, whether those Countries are uninhabited, or partially inhabited by Savages, who are never likely themselves to cultivate the country': ibid, 459. See also Vattel, *The Law of Nations or the Principles of the Law of Nature applied to the conduct and affairs of Nations and Sovereigns*, lib I, cap xviii, §209 (Pennsylvania).

249 *GBPP1837–1838*, xxi (680), 329.

the missionaries were not unanimous. Beecham, of the Wesleyan Missionary Society, acknowledged that a settlement community might be sensibly permitted beyond the influences of mission stations.

What transformed the situation in early 1838, however, was the Association's insistence on securing a parliamentary statute authorizing a settlement in accordance with the southern Australian precedent.[250] The Association consistently refused to accept the Office's demand that it incorporate under a charter as a joint-stock corporation. Thus, two evangelical Association members, Baring and Sinclair, introduced a bill into the Commons on 1 June 1838.[251] This proposed bill reflected the preoccupations of the Association. As in Hinds' testimony before the House of Lords Select Committee, it sought to assuage possible missionary suspicions. Russell signified ministerial assent to the introduction of a bill, ostensibly for reasons of discussion and due parliamentary process.[252] Yet, Glenelg also warned Durham against any undue confidence, as Melbourne's ministry did not 'in any degree pledge themselves to the future support of [the bill], but that they hold themselves at liberty to take any course they may think fit with regard to it at any of the subsequent stages'.[253] In this context, the Association laboured earnestly to ensure continuing interest in its New Zealand proposals. The somewhat hectic pace of political activity at the Colonial Office from December 1837 failed to assist the Association. Stephen privately catalogued the range of imperial pressing issues in a communiqué to Macvey Napier. He remarked: 'I have contrary to my expectations had on my hands the business arising out of two revolts in Canada,—a new struggle with the West Indies,—and an impeachment, or something very like an impeachment of Lord Glenelg'.[254] Nevertheless, Stephen also displayed a continuing interest in the concept of a corporate entity managing the organized settlement of New Zealand. In this, he revealed an intriguing scepticism concerning the political influence of missionary interests, in spite of his moderate evangelical credentials.[255] Notably, Grey—the second baronet—was possibly also implicated in this attitude as parliamentary under-secretary.[256] It is interesting, therefore, to note that his sister, Jane Grey, was the evangelical and Association chairperson Francis Baring's spouse.[257] Grey himself was a devoted Anglican evangelical committed to a sense of personal atonement, as was Stephen. Stephen's activities coalesced with those of Grey and the Grey family network generally (including Howick) rather than entirely with Glenelg. Stephen's relations with Howick had been forged during the first Grey administration from November 1830, especially on the slavery question. Howick, Grey, Labouchere, Durham, and Baring were all related. Whiggish grandees retained

[250] Durham to Glenelg, 30 December 1837, CO209/2, fos.434–9a, TNA; Baring to Glenelg, 28 May 1838, CO209/3, fos.284–5a, TNA; Glenelg to Baring, 1 June 1838, ibid, 286–7; Evans to Glenelg, 25 June 1838, ibid, fos.290–1.

[251] 'A bill for the provisional government of British settlements in the islands of New Zealand', ordered to be printed by the Commons, 1 June 1838, CO209/3, fo.549, TNA; *HPD*, 3rd series, vol 42, col 541.

[252] Glenelg to Durham, 5 February 1838, CO209/4, fos.296–6a, TNA.

[253] Ibid.

[254] Stephen to Macvey Napier, 7 March 1838, BL AddMss34618, fo.611; Newbould, *Whiggery and Reform, 1830–41*, 215–23.

[255] Stephen to Labouchere, 15 March 1839, CO209/4, fos.327a-328.

[256] Stephen to Howick, 5 February 1845, Add 7888/II/338, CUL: 'If his [Grey's] advice and mine had been taken, New Zealand would have been colonised before this [New Zealand] Company came into being. Lord Glenelg hesitated'. (Stephen papers.)

[257] Brent, *Liberal Anglican Politics*, 123-129.

primacy.[258] Howick conveyed this sense in correspondence with Melbourne concerning the revolt in the Canadian provinces. Stephen was within his orbit of interpersonal connections, often deferring to Howick for advice and occasionally for protection from political criticism.[259] Howick reported that, 'I met Stephen this morning in the park', adding, 'I wish you would send for him and hear what he has to say yourself'. He expanded with the comment that, 'I know this w[oul]d be rather a severe trial of your patience for he has not a good manner of communicating his opinion but they are those of a very able man & well worth listening to tedious though he may be'.[260] Perhaps, Stephen's implication in this network also reflected Grey's intensely active role in the Colonial Office during his lengthy tenure as parliamentary liaison. Stephen regularly engaged with him professionally. On 26 December 1837, Russell hinted at Grey's energy compared to Glenelg in stating:

> It is my duty to state to you, however disagreeable it may be to do so, that I do not expect the affairs of our colonies to prosper in the hands of Glenelg. He is a man of abilities and integrity, with great powers of speaking, and of the most kind and amenable disposition. [Yet] from indolence or irresolution, he so delays and hesitates that complaints keep me from [my labours]; politicians, merchants, governors, officers.... *Sir G Grey is worn to shreds*. I know not what should be done, but if it would make matters easier to Glenelg, I would give up for him my office, and take his.[261]

Ultimately, the bill was ambiguously drafted in that it conflated the terms 'treaty' and 'contract' in the specialized senses of acquiring 'sovereignty' and property in territory. In clause 10, for instance, it stated: 'That it shall be lawful for the said Commissioners to make and enter into such treaties or contracts as they shall deem expedient...for the cession...of any sovereign rights, territories, lands or hereditaments, within the said Islands'.[262] Thus, the Association's earlier accounts of an aboriginal capacity to alienate both territory and sovereignty to European persons appeared in its political strategizing—in the form of a bill and Select Committee testimony. Property, after all, was *the* integral part of its proposals for concentrated settlement in New Zealand (on a South Australian model). Exclusive management of the transfer of title was essential to the generation of sufficient revenue, as demonstrated by the crucial clause 33 in the bill. The 'commissioners for settlements in New Zealand' were to include Durham, Lord Petre, Enderby, Hinds, Ward, Molesworth, and William Bingham Baring. There was a noticeable slant on whiggish, moderate 'radicals' such as Durham, Molesworth, and Ward. Nonetheless, Baring's role in introducing the bill indicated some sympathy from an evangelical compass. Consequently, it remains difficult to disentangle the bewildering array of interpersonal connections operating on the New Zealand issue within

[258] On whiggish hierarchical concerns see Kriegel, 'A convergence of ethics', 449-450; Mandler, *Aristocratic Government in the Age of Reform*, 2-3, 19. On Stephen's earlier connections with Howick, see, Bod Mss Eng Lett d7, (Taylor papers), fos.206 *et seq*: Taylor to Miss Fenwick, 12 May 1833; ibid, fo.213: Stephen to Taylor, 11 September 1833.

[259] Stephen to Howick, 5 February 1845, Add 7888/II/337-341, CUL; Add 7888/II, fos. 342-343: Howick to Stephen, 25 February 1845, (Stephen papers); Stephen to Grey, 1 July 1837, Gre/B126/11, DUL; Gre/B126/13: 'draft of a bill for the prevention and punishment of offences committed by His Majesty's subjects within the territories of certain barbarous and uncivilized tribes'.

[260] Howick to Melbourne, 27 December 1837, Melbourne Mss, box 7/76, MP.

[261] Russell to Melbourne, 26 December 1837, Melbourne Mss, box 13/54, MP (emphasis added).

[262] 'A bill for the provisional government of British settlements in the islands of New Zealand' CO209/3, fo.551, TNA; Edward Betts Hopper diary, 10 May 1838, Ms1033, ATL.

either the Commons or House of Lords. Ward, for one, was a cousin to the then Home Secretary, the first Marquess of Normanby.[263] The personal correspondence fails to supply indications about the effects of these connections on policy formulation, obliging one to resort to reasonable probabilities to account for activity. The Church Missionary Society, however, rigorously opposed the bill through a petition and an intensive lobbying campaign.[264] Yet there was no easy disjunction between evangelical sympathizers within Melbourne's ministry and those inclined towards 'systematic colonization'.

Ultimately, the bill was resoundingly rejected in the Commons on its second reading on 20 June, having been defeated by a division of ninety-two against thirty-two votes. Dissatisfaction among the measure's opponents was due to the Association's sponsorship of a bill in the absence of ministerial sanction rather than the blithely assumed concerns with aboriginal protection.[265] Such a measure, requiring possible sustenance from Treasury revenue sources, was construed as repugnant to ministerial primacy. Howick's initial interest in 1837, for instance, had waned to such an extent that by June 1838 he approved the defeat of the measure in the Commons. He considered the bill provocatively non-ministerial as it had not yet been approved by ministers.[266] The Association had fatally attempted to bypass the government. An incorporative or facilitative political process that had commenced in June 1837 had faltered. This emergent discord in opinion ultimately implied policy ramifications for Māori polities in 1839, 1840, and thereafter.

FROM ASSOCIATION TO COMPANY

The Association was initially quiescent after its ignominious defeat in the Commons on 20 June 1838. The influential support it had gathered in the persons of Charles Poulett Thomson and Durham was withered by distractions elsewhere, such as Canada. Indeed, Melbourne's ministry finessed the irritations posed by whiggish 'radicals' like Henry Ward and Durham. This was pursued in a fraught parliamentary theatre, partly by despatching the latter to a complicated Canada, partly by its tacit byzantine use of tory factional support—and vice versa (with Sir Robert Peel and Wellington pursuing their personal stratagem here).[267] This was an undeniably precarious tactic, but it managed to sustain a stressed and beleaguered ministry, although its principal leaders experienced much strain. Russell eagerly anticipated the parliamentary session's termination in 1838 with a profoundly exhausted tone. In essence, the ministry's strategy involved retaining whiggish control under continuing challenge and was broadly one of managing and enervating 'radical' influence on policy directions. Even Wakefield

[263] Newbould, *Whiggery and Reform*, 250.

[264] Coates to Stephen, 20 June 1838, CO209/3, fo.160, enclosing petition, fos.161–2, TNA.

[265] *HPD*, 3rd series, 20 June 1838, vol 43, cols 876–80 (Howick's opposition); 872 (W Gladstone's opposition); refer to debate generally, 871–82. This position disagrees with Adams, *Fatal Necessity*, 120.

[266] Howick, journal, 20 June 1838, Gre/V/C3/3, DUL: 'we in the end threw out the most monstrous proposal I ever knew made to the House'. On the Colonial Office's retrospective view, see Grey to Normanby, memorandum, 28 February 1839, CO209/4, fos.316a–22a, TNA. Cf Glenelg to Durham, 5 February 1838, CO209/4, fo.296, TNA.

[267] Newbould, *Whiggery and Reform*, 218–19, 222, 224; Newbould, 'Sir Robert Peel and the conservative party, 1832–1841', 543–5. Cf Gambles, 'The boundaries of political economy', 313, 316.

sympathizer Daniel O'Connell's signal of support for the Association's proposed legislation received relative indifference from the Colonial Office.[268] Apparently, from early 1838, the Melbourne administration considered a potentially disruptive revolt on the part of fractured 'radicals' in the Commons increasingly improbable.[269] Nonetheless, another persuasive source implied that confidence in such an expectation could not have been readily assumed at the time.[270] Thus, Melbourne's ministry stressfully strategized in the Commons, occasionally with Tories under Peel. It deftly marginalized so-called 'radical' activities on imperial issues such as Durham's policies in Canada, or municipal subjects, including the Irish poor relief, corporation, and tithes legislation.[271]

Yet, although the New Zealand question was momentarily removed from dramatic Westminster parliamentary politics, it imposed an indelible imprint upon policy processes at the Colonial Office. This was illustrated in the preceding section. If anything, Glenelg received a second wind with the Association's parliamentary defeat and the sheer onrush of other political issues buffeting the ministry. After the defeat of their bill on its second reading, a truncated Association committee membership remained. Ward, Molesworth, and Benjamin Hawes became officially absent, although Ward and Molesworth (with Buller) remained as Wakefield's foremost theoretical sympathizers in the Commons.[272] Durham and Wakefield had departed for Canada, although Durham nominally continued as Association governor for a time prior to its constitutional demise—he was absent from Britain from 24 April, returning to Portsmouth by 28 November. Baring lingered influentially during this time, retaining responsibility for various Association resolutions as chairperson. In August 1838, the Association resolved beneath his auspices:

> That notwithstanding the temporary failure of their application to Parliament this association are determined to persevere in their efforts for assuring to the inhabitants of New Zealand the blessings of Christianity & Civilization & to this Country the advantages of a well organised system of Colonization.[273]

On 29 August 1838, the Association transformed itself into a commercialized joint-stock corporation named the New Zealand Colonization Association. It thus sought to regain ministerial patronage by belatedly announcing its satisfaction of a ministerial provision stipulated by Glenelg. It attempted to re-invite a Colonial Office charter offer by becoming a joint-stock corporation, after having refused this offer in early 1838.[274] Durham, Ward, and Molesworth were not ostensibly involved at this stage, with Durham in Canada. Non-parliamentary members predominated, specifically persons with established commercial interests, such as Joseph Somes, a shipping magnate. The new Association continued with transactions for territory in New Zealand,

[268] O'Connell to Glenelg, 18 May 1838, CO209/3, fo.502; Grey to O'Connell, 30 May 1838, CO209/3, fos.504–4a, TNA.

[269] Newbould, 'Lord Durham, the Whigs and Canada, 1838', 369. But its margins were slight in the Commons nonetheless: Lord Broughton (JC Hobhouse), *Recollections of a Long Life, with additional extracts from his private diaries*, Lady Dorchester (ed), VI, 59–60.

[270] Thomas, *The Philosophic Radicals*, 390–3.

[271] *Early Correspondence of Lord John Russell 1805–1840*, Russell (ed), II, 238: Russell to Melbourne, 12 December 1838; Newbould, *Whiggery and Reform*, 222.

[272] Gross, 'Commons and empire, 1833–1841, 253.

[273] Enclosed in Evans to Glenelg, 31 August 1838, CO209/3, fo.294, TNA.

[274] Baring had recognized the necessity for a 'joint-stock' formation on Glenelg's view: Baring to Glenelg, 28 May 1838, CO209/3, fo.284, TNA.

negotiating with Thomas McDonnell, a resident at Hokianga. Accordingly, as this successor Association unsuccessfully endeavoured to elicit ministerial support, it continued with the possibility of territorial transactions. As early as 31 October 1838, proposals were mooted for mounting an expedition to institute settlement within New Zealand irrespective of the satisfactory conclusion of negotiations with McDonnell.[275] This process of attempted acquisition was commercially motivated both in order to sustain financial interest in its corporate activity and, circuitously, to nourish such activity. It was speculative, both commercially and politically, in unsuccessfully courting ministerial attention (exhibiting few parliamentarian members in later 1838). This symbiotic process continued apace, particularly from 2 May 1839 with the advent of a further—and substituted—incorporation styled the 'New Zealand Land Company', accompanied by a prospectus no less.[276] According to this prospectus, its principal object was commercial speculation on lands within New Zealand, although a subsequent critique of this corporation admitted: 'It is very possible—nay more, it is probable, from the character of members of the Direction, that, in joining this association, they were actuated by philanthropic considerations'.[277] These 'considerations' constituted engaging in territorial transactions with Māori vendors and in the re-granting of reserves to Māori.

Durham was recruited as its governor, with Somes acting as deputy-governor. Within its directorate as at 2 May were Lord Petre (a Roman Catholic peer), Russell Ellice (a merchant involved in eastern Asian commerce), another shipping magnate, George Lyall, William Hutt, Torrens, George Young, Sir Henry Webb, John Buckle, Sir George Sinclair, and John Ward as secretary. Members of its erstwhile competitors—like the New Zealand Colonization Society in late 1838—such as Buckle, Torrens, and Lyall were included.[278] This Company endeavoured to nourish networks with those persons who have been characterized as 'moderate radicals' for reasons of analytical convenience; that is, persons favouring a Wakefield model of 'systematic colonization' as opposed to an outright distrust of imperial entanglements.[279] Sir William Molesworth later became a director, as did Baring.[280] Two prominent evangelicals—namely, Sinclair and Baring—remained influential.[281] Moreover, this corporation afforded commercial patronage opportunities or destinations for Baring's brother, Thomas Baring, or for Molesworth's younger sibling, Francis Molesworth, in a transplanted or even a trans-*provincial* (New Zealand) locale.[282] Nonetheless, whereas the New Zealand Association was an inherently parliamentary body in terms of its membership, the Company was conspicuously less so.

[275] Minute, 31 October 1838, CO208/185, fos.91–1a; minute, 28 November 1838, CO208/185, fos.92a–3, TNA; Burns, *Fatal Success*, 72–3.

[276] For example prospectus, 2 May 1839, New Zealand Land Company, CO209/4, fo.558; see also prospectus, 1 June 1839, New Zealand Land Company, CO208/1, fos.242–3a, TNA.

[277] Anonymous, *The New Zealand Company*, 5.

[278] Torrens to Stephen, 6 November 1838, CO209/3, fos.297–7a; Lyall to Glenelg, 14 December 1838, CO209/3, fos.313–14; Lyall to Grey, 28 December 1838, CO209/3, fos.317–26; Grey to Lyall, 6 February 1839, CO209/3, fos.322–3, TNA; Burns, *Fatal Success*, 73–6.

[279] Newbould, *Whiggery and Reform*, 218; Thomas, *The Philosophic Radicals*, 379.

[280] Ward to Molesworth, 8 July 1839, CO208/147, fo.50; Ward to Baring, 18 June 1839, CO208/147, fo.30, TNA.

[281] Hilton, 'The Role of Providence in Evangelical Social Thought', in Beales and Best (eds), *History, Society and the Churches*, 228–9: Sinclair was a Free Church evangelical of Scottish ancestry.

[282] For example Mulgan, *The City of the Strait*, 79; CO208/185, fos.230–1a: minutes, 13 April 1840; Spedding, 'New theory of colonization', 517–18.

Still, despite discomfort with its inherently commercial nature, Wakefield, as its conceptualist and as a political tactician, eventually renewed his interest in New Zealand as a field for transplanted systematic settlement. But he did not apparently perceive the requisite *necessity*, as in 1837, of a ministerially licensed venture, advising his dining colleagues on 20 March 1839 to 'possess [them]selves of the soil' irrespective of Office policy.[283] This defining strategy was selected when Hutt reported Labouchere's unwillingness in March 1839 to introduce legislation licensing systematic colonization in New Zealand. Hutt stated 'that from conversations he had with Mr Labouchere [14 March] he felt quite satisfied no bill would be introduced this session—as Mr L. told him that the great pressure of business on important questions such as Canada &c would preclude the probability of their being able to give any attention to [New Zealand]'.[284] Hutt continued with the caveat 'that even if gov[ernmen]t should bring in a bill at once it would have more than an injurious tendency than otherwise because they would introduce a clause to the following effect "That no land should be purchased in the colony... after the passing of the bill—except from the gov[ernmen]t" '. As such, he reportedly continued, 'the Comp[an]y would then have to pay the government's price, instead of the natives' which would in all probability amount at least to 500 per cent more than what they can purchase for now'.[285] Yet, these same persons misleadingly informed a gathering of share subscribers to the corporation on 21 March that an interview with Normanby had proved 'satisfactory'.[286]

Company projects were pursued in a relatively concealed manner through the formation of a committee consisting of five directors: Lord Petre, Somes, Wakefield, Gordon, and Hutt. This committee conducted negotiations with the New Zealand Colonization Association's (or Company's) competitors for governmental favour—Durham's moribund 'New Zealand Company of 1825 and 1826' and Lyall and Torrens' New Zealand Colonization Society. The former 'New Zealand Company' of 1825 and 1826 persisted as a shade. It did not operate commercially on a sustained basis but claimed to have acquired territories within the Hokianga. A memorial to William Huskisson, the president of the Board of Trade, possibly dating from 1825, and signed by John George Lambton (Durham), Robert Torrens, Edward Ellice, and George Lyall, among others, suggested the possibility of the government giving a 'British Company a privilege for opening a Commercial intercourse with these islands ["New Zealand"], and of purchasing from the Natives the lands on which the Flax plant is produced'.[287] If such privileges were not accorded, the memorialists averred, 'the French or the Russians may charter a Company for these important objects'. The principal records of the 'New Zealand Company' of 1825 and 1826 dated from 1839, however, and these were insubstantial, containing a list of members and an assertion of its prior purchase. It might have been a speculative invention with Torrens and its members realizing that their 'interests' would have to be 'bought out' by others. Torrens and Lyall revitalized it as a 'New Zealand Colonization Society' in later

[283] Edward Hopper, diary, 20 March 1839, Ms1033, ATL; Wakefield, *Adventure in New Zealand from 1839 to 1844*, I, 16: 'The new Company was thus forced into the adoption of what has been termed land-sharking, as far as acquiring lands by assignment from savages'.

[284] Ibid; cf Adams, *Fatal Necessity*, 139–40.

[285] Ibid.

[286] Minutes, 21 March 1839, CO208/185, fo.97, TNA.

[287] Memorial, nd [1825], BL AddMss38, 763, fo.100 (Huskisson papers).

1838, proposing a chartered corporation's administration in New Zealand.[288] The direction committee of Wakefield, Somes, Petre, Gordon, and Hutt negotiated for the assignment of the claimed interests of these conflated entities. These negotiations resulted in the enlarged 'New Zealand Land Company' (2 May). The committee also induced financial interest on the part of 40 share subscribers (at £500 per share) as opposed to the initial 20 resolved on as at 17 December 1838. It was in this context that Wakefield's brother, William Wakefield, was swiftly selected as 'principal agent' for the Company's purchasing (territorial acquisition from Māori) and surveying expedition on a vessel acquired from Somes' fleet for £5,250—the *Tory*. This expedition departed Plymouth for New Zealand on 12 May 1839. William Wakefield's instructions reflected the essentially commercial orientation of the Company, specifically in relation to its principal object—territorial acquisition in aboriginal New Zealand for the corporation:

> In the pursuit of the first object, you will constantly bear in mind that the profits of the Company must, in a great measure, depend on the judgment which you may exercise in selecting places of future location. As the world is free to purchase lands in New Zealand upon the same terms as the Company, it should be your especial business to acquire spots which enjoy some peculiar natural advantage.[289]

If anything, the incorporation in May 1839 represented a watershed. The Company revitalized Association objects. This corporation's initial prospectus was issued on 2 May 1839 with a recitation of Association precepts on systematic settlement but also with an evident interest in securing commercial sustenance through a share subscription programme or acceptance of deposits on alleged territorial purchases. It stated: 'This Company has been formed for the purpose of employing capital in the purchase and re-sale of lands in New Zealand, and the promotion of emigration to that country'.[290] A second prospectus followed on 10 June. Such literature, in its invitation for share subscriptions, was publicized and commercially penetrative. It also presented past relations with the Colonial Office throughout 1837 and 1838 in a provocative fashion. It blithely claimed that the formation of the Company represented the satisfaction of Glenelg's condition of a joint-stock entity. Networks of Company agents were formed or advertised extensively in the printed media in places like Birmingham, London, Glasgow, Edinburgh, Thorverton in Devonshire, Portsmouth, Falmouth, and Maidstone.[291] By later 1839, an extensive array of gen-

[288] Torrens to Stephen, 6 November 1838, CO209/3, fos.297–7a, TNA; CO209/3, fos.299–312; 'Outline of a plan for establishing under the protection of the British Crown an independent native government in the islands of New Zealand': ibid, fos.313–14: Lyall to Glenelg, 14 December 1838; Grey to Lyall, 6 February 1839, ibid, fos.322–3.

[289] New Zealand Company, 'Instructions from the New Zealand Land Company to Colonel Wakefield, principal agent of the company', 3–4; CO209/4, fos.535–5a, TNA; Ward, *Information relative to New Zealand, compiled for the use of colonists*, 116.

[290] Prospectus, 2 May 1839, CO209/4, fo.558; minute, committee of five directors (Wakefield, Lord Petre, Hutt or Heath, Gordon, Joseph Somes), 15 April 1839, CO208/185, fos.130a–31; minute, committee of five directors, 17 April 1839, CO208/185, fo.131; minutes, 'at a general meeting of the subscribers to the New Zealand Colonization Company', 2 May 1839, CO208/185, fo.100; also prospectus, 10 June 1839, CO208/1, fos.242–3a, TNA; Ward, *Information relative to New Zealand*, 2nd edn, 115.

[291] Mouteils to Ward, 24 May 1839, CO208/1, fos.71–1a; Millar to Evans, 30 May 1839, CO208/1, fo.73; Finlayson to Wood, 1 April 1839, CO208/1, fo.75; Hall to Ward, 3 April 1839, CO208/1, fo.85; Chatfield to Ward, 3 April 1839, CO208/1, fo.93; Ward to agents for the vending of lands—John Crawford (Glasgow), Kettle (Elham), H. Hughlings (Halifax), James Bridges (Edinburgh),

teel connections had been secured in provincial committees concerned with emigration to New Zealand, including the Duke of Argyll in Glasgow not to mention Whately, now archbishop in Dublin.[292] On 22 May 1839, Durham forwarded a copy of the initial prospectus to Normanby. He informed the principal Secretary of State that 'large tracts in the [antipodean] islands' had been 'purchased' and the Company had 'dispatched an expedition thither for the purpose of making preparations for a settlement'.[293] Wakefield's *Tory* expedition was thus presented as a fait accompli. The Colonial Office could not scornfully deny Durham's influence, despite his politically gruelling experiences with the Canadian mission. Labouchere minuted: 'It appears to me that you can hardly refuse to grant an interview to Lord Durham and his associates'. He concluded, however, that 'I would ... in doing so state distinctly that you do not pledge yourself in any manner to recognize or cooperate with the association'.[294] Receipts from the Company's balloted land order purchasers—acquiring a derivative corporate title—amounted to £68,861–12 (2 August) with a total credit balance of £81,119, an increase from its 24 June balance level of £4,920.[295] Many of these ballotees were absentee 'purchasers' remaining in Britain.

Against this persistent lobbying pressure, the process of drafting Hobson's instructions proceeded. Labouchere, Stephen, and Normanby repeatedly insisted to various individuals that neither the Company nor its assumed titles acquired from indigenous persons could be acknowledged.[296] Yet, Labouchere's parliamentary statements on this subject on 25 June 1839 were ambiguous, with a slant upon the non-recognition of 'fraudulent' or 'excessive' purchases as opposed to any purchases per se. John Ward, the company secretary and a former *Edinburgh Review* essayist,[297] stressed this feature in his correspondence with Company agents or its prospective purchasers under a balloted selection process for urban or rural lots within anticipated New Zealand settlements. He dissembled and informed the Company's Glasgow agent that '[s]everal of our directors were in their places in the house, and they all concur in approving the speech in so far as it announced ... all purchases made bôna fide would be confirmed'.[298] Ward's manipulation of ambiguous Office statements was not restricted to personal correspondence.

R.B. Stone (Eastbourne, Sussex), 13 June 1839, CO208/147, fo.28; also Ward to George Whiting (Maidstone), 15 June 1839, CO208/147, fos.28–8a, TNA; Ward, *Information relative to New Zealand*, list of provincial age nts for the Company, 150–1.

292 Russell to Stephen, 7 November 1839, CO209/4, fo.580, TNA.

293 Durham to Normanby, 22 May 1839, CO209/4, fo.553, TNA.

294 Labouchere to Normanby, 27 May 1839, CO209/4, fo.557a, TNA; cf ibid, Stephen, minute.

295 Finance committee, 24 June 1839, CO208/185, fos.161–75; finance committee, 2 August 1839, CO208/185, fos.188–9a, TNA.

296 J Barton Gooch and W Batts to Normanby, 18 June 1839, CO209/5, fo.216a; Colonial Office to J Barton Gooch and W Batts, 26 June 1839, CO209/5, fos.217–17a; Green to Normanby, 15 July 1839, CO209/5, fo.229; Dent to Russell, 8 October 1839, CO209/5, fo.204; Colonial Office to Greenwood, 16 September 1839, CO209/5, fos.232–2a, TNA.

297 Ward, 'Prison discipline', 316–56; Ward, 'Police of the metropolis', , 358–95.

298 Ward to Crawford, 5 July 1839, CO208/147, fo.48; Crawford to Ward, 3 July 1839, CO208/1, fos.942–2a, TNA. Ward had also been a commissioner for the inspection of certain prisons from 6 January 1837 and a secretary to the 'Colonial [Colonization] Society': ATL, Ms1009-2/23, 'copies of letters &c relating to Mr Ward, 1836–1838' (Webster papers); Poulett Thomson to Ward, 6 April 1836; Poulett Thomson to Ward, 24 April 1838; Hutt to Ward, 6 May 1838; Benjamin Hawes to committee of 'Colonial Society', 30 December 1837; Dr Thomas Arnold to Ward, 1 January 1838.

In a preface dated 9 June 1839 that accompanied publicized corporate literature, Ward asserted:

> Early in the present session, notice was given by a member of parliament connected with the Company [Hutt], of a motion for leave to introduce a bill to effect [a permanent establishment of law in settlements in New Zealand]. At the request of the secretary of state for the colonies the motion was withdrawn, upon a distinct understanding that some measure tending to the accomplishment of the same desirable end, should be adopted on the part of the Crown, with the least practicable delay. The Government has thus expressly recognised ... the duty ... of affording the protection of English laws and institutions to the intended colony.[299]

Similarly, two corporate members, Hutt and barrister Standish Motte, had defended unrestricted purchase from Māori in March 1839, founded upon Colonial Office perceptions concerning an allegedly independent New Zealand included within a realm of *ius gentium*.[300] The manipulation of a historically acknowledged 'independence' (a 'declaration of independence' in 1835) haunted the Colonial Office in this respect. Indeed, the Office's focus upon asserting executive management of transactional activities with indigenous persons implicitly constrained the competence of Māori to engage in such hitherto unconstrained encounters. In 1839 this consequence was not adverted to. Glenelg had, however, countenanced such a restrictive outcome in 1836 on the part of Bourke, the then governor for New South Wales, in constraining certain Australian aborigines via a proscribing executive proclamation issued against Europeans. Those aborigines affected dwelt within the Port Phillip district and were prevented under Bourke's proclamation from effecting earlier land-alienating 'treaties' with an association of putative purchasers (the 'Port Phillip Association' from Van Diemen's land).[301] Perhaps unwittingly—there is no archival evidence either way—Motte and Hutt's assertive correspondence resonated with a distinctly past rhetoric of non-governmental ventures in various northern American hinterlands.[302] In its proposals to acquire territory for commercial return, the Company probably also recalled earlier criticism levelled indirectly against so-called 'moderate' radicals—specifically, Durham affiliates, such as Ward—aligned with certain Whigs (Edward Ellice, connected with Grey family interests) on Durham's Canadian mission.[303] Clearly, the corporation engaged in subtly and expediently shifting arguments if one compares the statements of either Baring or Hinds in 1838. Thematically, there was a persistent emphasis, in 1839, upon an unhindered corporate capacity to enter into territorial transactions with Māori,

[299] Ward, *Information relative to New Zealand*, v–vi.

[300] Motte to Normanby, 4 March 1839, CO209/4, fo.519a; Labouchere to Motte, 11 March 1839, CO209/4, fos.525–7a, TNA.

[301] Glenelg to Bourke, 13 April 1836, *GBPP1836*, xi (512), 740: Glenelg stated that Australian aborigines could not be recognised as having 'any right to alienate to private adventurers the land of the colony'. If so, 'such a concession would subvert the foundation on which all proprietary rights in New South Wales at present rest'. Bourke, proclamation, 26 August 1835, *GBPP1836*, xi (512), 738.

[302] See Pagden, 'The struggle for legitimacy and the image of empire in the Atlantic to c1700', in Canny (ed), *The Oxford History of the British Empire*, 47–8; Richter, 'Native peoples of north America and the eighteenth-century British empire', in Marshall, *The Oxford History of the British Empire*, 347–71; Tully, 'Rediscovering America', in *An Approach to Political Philosophy*, 137–76.

[303] Thomas, *The Philosophic Radicals*, 382–3. Edward Ellice was an intimate friend and companion to Durham and was Howick's uncle by marriage, ibid, 380.

whilst treaty relations were marginalized as a specifically Crown-centred activity. Accordingly, on 23 December 1839, Ward stated:

> According to the treasury minute [dated 19 July 1839 of the then New Zealand Company director, Francis Baring, in his capacity as Chancellor of the Exchequer], the territories of the Company will, upon cession of sovereignty by the native chiefs, become a part of the colony of New South Wales. The necessity of such a cession, however, is understood to be applicable only to the relation between the Crown and the Natives, and not as in any way waiving the rights of Great Britain as against foreign powers. For the Queen of England has, by the *law of nations*, an indisputable title to the sovereignty of New Zealand, founded upon the possession taken in the name of George III by the discoverer of those islands in 1769, and upon the exercise of numerous acts of sovereignty in them at subsequent periods.[304]

Ward's opinion was presaged by what would prove an undeniably useful corporate textual resource from mid-1839 into 1840 concerning *ius gentium*, namely a source authored by John Dunmore Lang in London.[305] An overarching 'sovereignty' in New Zealand had been obtained by virtue of Cook's prior discovery. In addressing himself to Durham, Lang, a politically active presbyterian minister based in Sydney, importantly transmitted a northern American source as a basis for characterizing normative relations with Māori (Lang used the terms 'New Zealander', 'native', and 'aborigine'). This source was a decision of the Marshall court in *Cherokee Nation v State of Georgia*.[306] Lang used it to critically characterize the governmentally unlicensed Port Phillip association that had endeavoured to acquire territories through purchasing 'treaties' in the so-named Dutigalla and Geelong districts of Port Phillip. That court held, said Lang, that 'if the new country... discovered is inhabited, and under a government of any kind, the mere discovery of it by a civilized nation, (while it still gives such a nation a right to colonize it...) confers on that nation no right of sovereignty over it—no right of property to a single inch of its territory'.[307] This usage revealed a circuitous path of intelligence—Australia (Port Phillip), and a viewing of New Zealand from London. Histories in motion indeed.

Ward specifically used Lang's text in collaboration with that arch rhetorical tactician Wakefield. Ward's citations of, *inter alia*, Lang indicated not only what he read but also what he neglected or omitted from, say, Lang's texts and how he refigured what he deployed. In the Company literature—much influenced by Wakefield's earlier *The British Colonization of New Zealand* (in which Ward had collaborated)—there were implicit references to the literature of Lang on comparative philology (linking 'Malay', 'Polynesian', and 'Rarotongan' according to Lang), racially defined migratory trails,

[304] Ward, *Information relative to New Zealand*, 2nd edn, viii (emphasis added). This was subsequently adapted in 1840 with an explicit introduction of the term 'pre-emption' and northern American juristic literature: Wakefield, testimony, 17 July 1840, select committee appointed to inquire into the statements contained in the petition of the merchants, bankers, and shipowners of the city of London (presented 22 May 1840), respecting the colonization of New Zealand, *PP1840*, vii (582), 511 (53); *The First Report of the directors of the New Zealand Company, presented to the first general meeting of the shareholders; on the 14th May 1840*, 27–8 ('international law'). See also Chapman, *Comparative prospects of our new colonies*, 186.

[305] Lang, *New Zealand in 1839*, 'letter iv, on the principles on which a British colony in New Zealand ought to be established and conducted, London, June 1839', 78.

[306] 5 Pet 1 (1831) (USSC); Lang, *New Zealand in 1839*, 75.

[307] Ibid, 74–5.

and *ius gentium*.[308] Māori were located and inscribed into a globalist history, one that defended them as credible vendors of property, at least to respectably 'honest' purchasers as opposed to dissolute others (whaling crews, for instance). Lang characterized the 'New Zealanders' generally 'as mere children, incapable of managing their own property except through the agency of some liberal, enlightened, Christian government, acting as their trustees'.[309] Lang and Ward supplied a literary cargo that the Company could scavenge politically. The Company claimed the mantle of a 'humane' policy of transactional engagements with aborigines. But from its viewpoint, the Company legitimized increasingly intensive levels of engagement and entanglement with Māori. Commercial objects were also invariably within view. The 'intentions of Her Majesty's government render[ed] it highly important in order to prevent the best situations in New Zealand from being bought up by other speculators to the prejudice of the Company,—that steps should be immediately taken to extend the Company's purchases'.[310] The *Dublin Review* in 1838 saw the method adumbrated in *The British Colonization of New Zealand* as one of obtaining a 'right of property and a right of sovereignty over a sufficient quantity of land' for colonization purposes. A 'right of sovereignty' was not to be obtained 'over the whole territory'.[311]

Territorial 'purchase' from aborigines was acknowledged politically after the southern African and southern Australian episodes of the 1830s, although the management of these transactions was disputed. Paper deeds produced by Europeans in New Zealand were to be managed in an effort to secure revenue and imperial control—the whiggish ambition of self-financing settlements and managed settlement dispersion was present here. Procedurally speaking, Stephen and Labouchere could and did begin to claim that adventurers without law or ministerial sanction could not claim an efficacious or recognized title. This development was an integral part of an essentially whiggish imperial discourse formulated with increasing detail since 1831, with Goderich's directives, and after 15 December 1835 with southern Australia. It also reflected an admixture of Glenelgian and Greyesque elements—from whence derived a formalized procedure of transacting with rude aborigines—and a veneer of convergent Buxtonian vocabularies. In this, a principal suggestion advanced in the 1837 Select Committee report on aborigines was specifically useful in a convergent sense. There, the relevant suggestion stipulated not recognizing purported acquisitions of territory unmediated by the Crown.[312] At most, then, a general, non-analysed appreciation of indigenous persons as proprietors of territory was revealed as a foundational premise in haphazardly formulating imperial policies towards New Zealand. An administrative impulse towards accommodating such transactions succeeded a period of expensive (and imper-

[308] Ibid, 60–70 (note); Lang, *View of the origin and migrations of the Polynesian Nation*; William and Robert Chambers (eds), *Chambers's Information for the People*, II, 5.

[309] Lang, *New Zealand in 1839*, 12–13.

[310] Minutes, court of directors, 14 June 1839, CO208/180, fo.23, TNA. See also, ibid, 'deputation to Colonial Office', 13 June 1839, fos.21–2: 'Lord Normanby added that an examination would take place of purchases made from the natives by British subjects so as to ascertain whether they had been made bonâ fide or for an adequate consideration.... [H]e considered it desirable to encourage the investment of British capital in New Zealand'.

[311] 'Principles of Colonization—New Zealand', 91.

[312] Report, House of Commons, aborigines, *GBPP1837*, vii (425), 78; Kreigel, 'A convergence of ethics: Saints and Whigs in British antislavery', 449–50.

fectly comprehended) hostilities in southern Africa, a broad theme noticeable in other earlier imperial moments.[313]

Yet the general sympathies and policy anxieties underlying these concerns did not assist an imperial notion of what would occur territorially in any detail within New Zealand. If combined with a protective sentiment of sorts lurking within the rhetoric, such a premise appeared to bolster Office strategies of ensuring executive management and discipline. In essence, then, only it could assert that centrally located supervision over a formalized procedure of obtaining revenue from territories not yet conveyed to anglo-settlers. As such, a formulaic process of monitoring purchases from aborigines—as stipulated for southern Australia from 15 December 1835—confirmed this ministerial assertion. Intelligence from New Zealand filtered into these mingling portraits, triggering an enlistment of familiar intellectual and policy tools such as *ius gentium* and, perhaps less so, stadial history. Dysfunctional, impulsive territorial settlement was to be surveyed and disciplined—revenue would be secured from managing land sales. Broadly speaking, we can observe a convergence of 'radical' (chiefly Wakefieldian) viewpoints with whiggish concepts of managing territories enthusiastically supported by Howick.[314]

Indeed, the Association's proposals reflected this attitude in the 1830s, as did those foundational policies exhorted for Australia and Canada during Goderich's period as colonial secretary (1831). This became an aspect of Colonial Office practice with the writing of largely identical directions to representatives in New South Wales, Van Diemen's land, along with Upper Canada.[315] Collectively, these directions represented a whiggish ministerial-level concern—Goderich, and the then parliamentary under-secretary, Howick—albeit one with possibly prior administrative echoes in Australasia.[316] In spite of these older echoes, it cannot be doubted that Howick and Goderich opted for centralization in a freshly concerted manner with relevant directions issued to imperial representatives. The tenor of these directions can be briefly illustrated. In a despatch dated 28 January 1831 addressed to George Arthur, the lieutenant-governor for Van Diemen's land, Goderich opined that variable systems obtaining before 1831 did not, 'have . . . the intended effect of preventing large tracts of land from being appropriated by persons unable to improve [and] cultivate them'.[317] Uniform adherence to a process of territorial transfer mediated by public purchase at auction was suggested at a fixed price of 5*s* per acre. An emigration of 'unemployed' labourers rather than persons of substantial capital was also tentatively recommended as affording a means of obtaining

[313] Lenman, 'Colonial wars and imperial instability, 1688–1793', in Marshall, *The Oxford History of the British Empire*, 163; Richter, 'Native peoples of north America and the eighteenth-century British empire', 364. Marshall, 'Parliament and property rights in the late eighteenth-century British empire', in Brewer and Staves (eds), *Early Modern Conceptions of Property*, 532–3.

[314] Perhaps we can provocatively suggest connections with other features of policy during the 1830s and 1840s: Eastwood, 'Making public policy in 19th century Britain', 13–14 ('poor law' policy for instance).

[315] Goderich to Darling, 9 January 1831, CO202/25, fos.177–82 and Goderich to Darling, 14 February 1831 (New South Wales), fos.216a–21a; Van Diemen's land: Goderich to Arthur, 28 January 1831, CO408/7, fos.129a–35; Goderich to Colborne, 21 November 1831, CO43/43, fos.95–105: Upper Canada; Spedding, 'New theory of colonization', 528.

[316] Philipp, 'Wakefieldian influence and New South Wales 1830–1832', 173–6.

[317] Goderich to Arthur, 28 January 1831, CO408/7, fos.130, 132a–4; see also Goderich to Arthur, 29 January 1831, CO408/7, fos.135–41a; Goderich to Darling, 9 January 1831, CO202/25, fos.177, 179a–81; Burroughs, *Britain and Australia*, 35–58.

the symbiotic objectives of relieving distress in the United Kingdom and in allegedly labour-starved colonial environments. Indeed, the absence of an accessible supply of labour was considered a perennial difficulty in the case of New South Wales.

Importantly, this series of Goderich despatches constituted a literary cargo accessible to Colonial Office personnel, as did the Select Committee report of August 1836 concerning the disposal of 'unoccupied' or 'waste' colonial territories. These well-springs of information would have been familiar to operatives within the colonial department. It ought to be recalled, that both Howick and his first cousin, Sir George Grey, attended that Committee. In essence, the opinions expressed in Goderich's directives readily mingled with Association counsels and, perhaps crucially, coalesced with the Grey interest in the person of Howick. After all, it appears that Howick was intimately involved in the design of the policy embedded in these directions, not to mention the format of the directions themselves. He remained consistently interested in the question of the disposal of Crown territory, with a decided preference for sale (except where grants were favoured for reasons of infrastructural development). This was illustrated both in parliamentary speeches and in Howick's book on imperial administration. In that tome he stated, '[t]he system which was adopted has effectually answered its purpose of ensuring a just and fair distribution of the Crown lands, to those most capable of turning them to account; and at the same time it has afforded the means of meeting, in some degree, the greatest want of the colonies, by providing a fund to meet the sending out [of] a large number of free labourers'.[318] He issued memoranda concerning the minimum upset price for crown acreage, advising on one occasion at least £1 initially and a subsequent price of £5 for western Australia on 11 May 1838.[319]

Howick celebrated the systemic features of a policy predilection introduced in 1831—he would continue to do so as Secretary of State for War. Yet, acute inconsistencies bedevilled the treatments of territorial transfer throughout imperial regions, including the 19 districts of New South Wales, Port Phillip in 1836, Swan River, and Van Diemen's land. Even the foundational Goderich directives from 1831, intended as an initial trial formula, faltered with occasional concessions when confronted with undisciplined European purchasing enterprises throughout the latter half of the decade (these aspects were adequately considered by Burroughs[320]). Goderich's terminology is of interest since it formed a backdrop to aboriginal proprietary interests from an imperial viewpoint, both discursively and policy-wise. It asserted a preoccupation in 1831 that implicitly exercised Office considerations of aboriginal New Zealand as a place for 'purchase':

> With respect to the price which has been fixed upon land, it will, I doubt not, be thought extravagant by those, who have been accustomed to obtain it, practically speaking, for nothing; were the price not higher than which it has hitherto been attempted to realize, it would not effect one of the chief objects in view—a great restriction of the extreme facility of acquiring land, which now exists. This is absolutely essential for the purpose of checking the dispersion of settlers...[321]

318 Grey, *The Colonial Policy of Lord John Russell's Administration*, I, 310 and 305–13 generally; Howick, *HPD*, 3rd series, 14 October 1831, viii, 1832, 771; Howick, *HPD*, 3rd series, 25 June 1839, 48, 898–9, 904, 907; Winch, *Classical Political Economy and Colonies*, 107–8.

319 Howick, 11 May 1838, memorandum, Gre/B146/B11, DUL.

320 Burroughs, *Britain and Australia*, 203, 208–10.

321 Goderich to Darling, 14 February 1831, CO202/25, fo.220, TNA.

A connected concern regarding the spatial dispersal of settlement was vital.[322] This concern permeated Office correspondence from 1838 once the incorporation of New Zealand into empire was admitted in principle. That is, the unsanctioned flourishing of trading centres in the islands (at Kororāreka, for instance) triggered an anxiety that had long irritated and smouldered in New South Wales and the Cape colony. If anything, the Cape's abortive territorial extensions in 1835 had exacerbated these sensitivities.[323] Wakefield had likewise advocated concentrated settlement. As seen, the Association extensively exploited such a concern in its promotional literature: the spectre of 'irregular' settlement and expensive confrontations between European villainy and indigenous inhabitants. It was an ongoing concern congenial to a report on New Zealand's political condition by William Hobson, received belatedly from New South Wales on 1 February 1838.[324] This report was significant to Hobson's career in introducing him to favourable notice within Glenelg's Office. Hobson eventually accepted the Office's offer (ventured in December 1838) to become the first consul and lieutenant-governor to New Zealand on 14 February 1839; his appointment as consul was confirmed on 13 August 1839.[325] His 1837 report advocated constrained jurisdictional and proprietary spaces—'factories' on an East Indies model—at sites of existing European habitation, in the Hokianga, Cloudy Bay, and Bay of Islands. Hobson suggested that 'if factories were established [in these localities] and other places as the occupation by British subjects proceeds; a sufficient restraint could be constitutionally imposed on the licentious whites, without exciting the jealousy of the New Zealanders or of any other power'.[326] With the political resistance of the Association on the New Zealand settlements bill question—its evident reluctance to accept ministerial oversight—Hobson's report proved an attractive conceptual alternative. It conveniently coincided with the Office's assumptions concerning Māori as participating in transactions (vending flax or land, for instance). It also tallied with its historical (expenditure-conscious) treatment of aboriginal New Zealand as possessing an inchoate independent diplomatic character. The Office's view on *ius gentium* triumphed—for a time. After all, Hobson endorsed the use of treaties to secure Māori recognition of a factor's jurisdiction within New Zealand. In addition, these factors, advised Hobson, ought to act as 'magistrates' and 'be accredited to the United Chiefs of New Zealand as a political agent and consul'.[327]

322 RD Hanson, evidence, 16 June 1836, *GBPP1836*, xi (512), 533–46 ('injurious dispersion', 534); Philipp, 'Wakefieldian influence and New South Wales 1830–1832', 176–7; Weaver, 'Beyond the fatal shore', 1002 (Swan river), 1003–4 (southern Australia), 1004–5 (New South Wales); Duly, *British Land Policy at the Cape*, 163: 'greater unity in land alienation order within the Empire'.

323 Keegan, *Colonial South Africa and the origins of the racial order*, 148–50; Macmillan, 'The frontier and the kaffir wars 1792–1836', in Walker (ed), *The Cambridge History of the British Empire*, VIII, 314–22. For the relevance of these concerns in New South Wales to New Zealand, see Tapp, *Early New Zealand*, 135–44.

324 Bourke to Glenelg, 9 September 1837, CO209/2, fos.24–9a, enclosing Hobson to Bourke, 8 August 1837, fos.30–7a, TNA.

325 Hobson to Grey, 14 February 1839, CO209/4, fos.100–3; Stephen to Backhouse, 12 December 1838, CO209/5, fos.28–34a; Stephen to Backhouse, 3 July 1839, ibid, fos.40–1; Palmerston to Hobson, 13 August 1839, CO209/5, fos.44–6 (number one); Strangways to Labouchere, 14 August 1839, CO209/5, fo.42, TNA; *The Dictionary of New Zealand Biography; volume I: 1769–1869*, William Hobson, 1792–1842, 197 (KA Simpson entry).

326 Hobson to Bourke, 8 August 1837, CO209/2, fo.35a, TNA.

327 Ibid, fo.36.

Several important observations ought to be made here. Portentously, Hobson stressed the prominence of certain 'chieftains' residing in the distant northern peninsular Te Tai Tokerau region of New Zealand's North Island. These chieftains, presented as 'united' or confederated, were reified as potential sources of indigenous consent to a formalized British presence, chiefly due to the preponderance of both European settlement and mission stations in that region (particularly Hokianga and Bay of Islands). Even in this instance, however, there were doubts, on Hobson's part, about the constitutional quality of the 'united' chieftains: 'They have not . . . any government whatsoever nor could a meeting of the Chiefs who profess to be the heads of the United Tribes take place at any time without danger of bloodshed'.[328] He suggested that they lacked the political maturity to enact legislation. However, these points undermined the quality of Māori 'independence' in imperial policy. Here, again, was Busby's reference to an interminable risk of warfare; the paradox of 'united' chieftains and lurking savagery.

Secondly, Hobson's report permitted elements within the Office to deflect Church Missionary Society pressures, thus proving Hobson's report a useful instrument indeed. Coates, heartened by the Association's legislative failure, pressed the Office with Church Missionary Society proposals. These propositions advocated the substantive isolation of the southern archipelago from concentrated settlement. A periodical circuit of an assize court based in Sydney was advised, together with 'an efficient consular agent' and the institution of a chiefly code of laws.[329] As with Stephen, Grey evidently considered Hobson's proposals of factories and courts more palatable than Coates' essentially mission-focussed views. Stephen regarded Church Missionary Society proposals as 'impracticable'.[330] On 21 January 1839, Stephen still favoured chartering a commercial organization to finance the construction of public works, as Howick had favoured in 1837. Thus, he recommended 'a Charter of Incorporation be granted to persons now applying for it, who should be called 'the New Zealand Company'.[331] Disciplining settlement was anticipated via a 'well regulated land system'. Yet, given 'unauthorized acquisitions', Stephen advised, 'it *may* be necessary to declare the invalidity of any title to land not acquired through the Crown—a declaration which might be safely made when the preponderating numerical interest is in favour of it but not afterwards'.[332] After all, imperial intervention in New Zealand had been sanctioned in principle, and the Office accepted the tales of a deleterious European impact on Māori.[333]

Moreover, the Company itself participated in this process as successor to the Association. It released promotional literature in 1839 attuned to those investors and consumers obtaining a derivative Company title.[334] The audience for this *oeuvre*

[328] Ibid, fo.34a.

[329] Coates to Glenelg, 23 July 1838, CO209/3, fos.163–4a; petition of the committee of the Church Missionary Society for Africa and the East, 22 June 1838, CO209/3, fo.162; Stephen to Grey, minute, 26 July 1838, CO209/3, fo.170a, TNA: 'As for the proposal to establish a "court of assize" in New Zealand by the royal authority in pursuance of the N[ew] S[outh] Wales Act it is almost needless to observe that it is impracticable'.

[330] Grey to Glenelg, 27 August 1838, CO209/3, fo.172; Stephen to Grey, minute, 26 July 1838, ibid, fos.161–2, TNA.

[331] Stephen, 21 January 1839, CO209/4, fo.197, TNA.

[332] Ibid, fos.200a–1a (emphasis added).

[333] I consider this background more fully than possible here in Hickford, 'Making "Territorial Rights"', ch 2.

[334] Ward, *Information relative to New Zealand.*

remains difficult to identify, but it included potential purchasers of putative corporate titles to lands, some of whom referred to published Company material; this constituted the Company's public opinion.[335] Such literature was conceptually accommodationist towards Māori insofar as it envisaged incorporating chiefly Māori proprietors, albeit in a fashion subordinate to corporate suzerainty. *Rangatira* or chieftains were compared with distinguishable 'gentlemen'. Lang had referred to *rangatira* as innumerable propertied 'freemen', suggesting that superior chiefly 'authority... like that of the chiefs amongst the ancient Germans [according to Tacitus]' was recognized in times of war.[336] These Māori would be located within discrete reserves, responsive to the several 'social' gradations the Company identified as characterizing Māori polities—*ariki*, *rangatira*, and *taurekareka*.[337] Thus, whilst initially they were 'independent' subjects of *ius gentium* without an anglicized municipal law, they would subsequently be re-granted portions of their former lands. This observation regarding a measure of 'incorporation' was grounded in a sense of 'proprietorship' and a connected social gradation analogous to that obtaining in the peculiarly ministerialist image of whiggish governance in Britain, as embodied by Whig chiefs such as Howick.[338] Indeed, various corporate members—such as Molesworth or Baring—perceived their peculiar propulsion of enterprises into spacious antipodean locations as coinciding with a hierarchical *weltanschauung* they readily expressed in London. It would also resonate as a theme vented by persons other than a company (what Belich has referred to as 'reproductive colonisation'[339]). These were aspirational objects in that they figured in an optimistic, publicized, reprinted literature (two editions of Ward's text were published).[340]

Again, a predominant theme in this promotional literature was an ambivalent perception of Māori as 'savages'. Thus, Māori were not treated as exhibiting traits of desolate, irretrievable savagery in certain respects—a notorious potential for commerce was envisaged. Alternatively, however, they were explicitly received as having not sufficiently cultivated the soils; they had not furrowed the earthen soils with plough technology. Hence, there was a focus on the mediating mode of subsistence. Collecting 'vegetables', such as *kūmara*, was a prominent feature, recalling Ward's selected references to Edward Gibbon's eighteenth-century narrative on Rome: the introduction to southern seas islands of 'the vegetables and animals most useful to human life' by oceanic navigators.[341] As noted by Donald Winch, '[a] philosophy of history is required to

[335] George Buck to Ward, 30 June 1839, CO208/1, fos.359–61a, TNA; Stephen had received a second edition copy by January 1840: ibid, fos.212–13: Ward to Stephen, 22 January 1840.

[336] Lang, *New Zealand in 1839*, 12.

[337] New Zealand Company, 'Instructions from the New Zealand Land Company to Colonel Wakefield, principal agent of the Company', 9–13; Ward, *Information relative to New Zealand*, 2nd edn, 68, referring to 'Areekees, or chieftains; the Rangatiras, being the gentry, or middle class; and the Cookees [*taurekareka*], or slaves'; Ward, *A Show of Justice*, 35–6. Fox, *Colonization and New Zealand*, 15.

[338] Bannister, *British Colonization and Coloured Tribes*, 277, 278–9; eg Lorimer, *Colour, Class and the Victorians*, 45–53, 58–9, 106–7; Stoler, *Race and the education of desire*, 124–7; Mandler, *Aristocratic Government*, 44–84 ('grand whiggery', Holland House).

[339] Belich, *Replenishing the Earth*, 178; Belich, 'Neo-Britains: an overview/underview', *The British World: diaspora, culture and identity since c1880*, conference, 26 June 1998, Institute of Commonwealth Studies; Wake, 'George Clarke and the government of the Maoris: 1840–45', 353.

[340] Cf Canny, 'England's New World and the Old, 1480s–1630s', in Canny, *The Oxford History of the British Empire: volume i*, 152–5.

[341] On Gibbon, see *The History of the Decline and Fall of the Roman Empire*, IV, 169 (note).

establish the stage of civilisation'.[342] This was a translation of (initially Scottish) stadial historical usages in a specifically southern Polynesian context. Indeed, the emblematic signals were undeniably present, namely references to an absence of coinage, letters, the cultivation of vegetables without employing ploughs, not to mention the presence of irrepressible warfare. Here, then, was a profoundly disquieting 'savage', namely those otherwise communal, sociable persons who consumed other humans (anthropophagy). This sense of unease flourished in an already lengthy series of spasmodic narratives, resonating with incidents such as the beach slaying of Cook at Kealakekua Bay.[343] These stadial historical influences also pervaded Prichard's ethnology in 1813 with his references to the 'primitive manners and character' of New Zealanders. Whilst they had 'made more progress in the arts of life', than the inhabitants of Papua, they were, 'perpetually carrying on war with each other, to which they were stimulated... by the desire of eating the flesh of their antagonists'.[344] In this bewildering textual theatre of partial reportage, presumptive characterization, and tactical objectives, Ward's corporate literature conversed directly with Glenelg's prior assessment of Māori as 'not savages living by the chase' in his prominent memorandum of 15 December 1837.[345] Thus, this Company text asserted:

> They are both physically and intellectually superior to the New Hollanders, but, although their capabilities of cultivation are great, they are yet essentially a savage people. We will not attempt to disguise the black side of the picture. They are dirty in their persons, and sometimes overrun with vermin. They have hitherto scarcely known the meaning of arts, trades, industry, or coin; they have no roads, beyond footpaths, from place to place. Their liberty depends upon the protection which each individual can give himself; consequently, although the territory is divided among various independent tribes, there is no regular system of law, or government in any. Their most conspicuous passion is war, and they kill and sometimes eat their vanquished enemies, scalping and exhibiting their heads as trophies. This latter practice may remind us that the head of Oliver Cromwell was exhibited for several years over the doors of Westminster Hall, and that it is not a century since the heads of the rebel lords of 1745 were exposed to the public gaze on Temple Bar.[346]

[342] 'The cause of good government: Philosophic Whigs versus Philosophic Radicals', in Collini, Winch, and Burrow, *That Noble Science of Politics*, 118; Pocock, *Virtue, Commerce, and History*, 152–3.

[343] Pocock, 'Tangata whenua and enlightenment anthropology', 36–7;Williams, 'The Pacific: exploration and exploitation' in Marshall (ed) *The Oxford History of the British Empire*, 552–75, 562–3; Sorrenson, *Maori Origins and Migrations*, 60–8; Belich, *Making Peoples*, 122, 125 ('red' and 'brown' savages); cf Belich, 'Myth, Race and Identity in New Zealand', in Hiery and McKenzie (eds), *European Impact and Pacific Influence*, 44–64, 46; Langford, *A Polite and Commercial People, England 1727–1783*, 513–15.

[344] Prichard, *Researches into the Physical History of Man*, 1st edn, 282–3, 245–8, 250 (Scottish stadial influences); Merivale, *Lectures on colonization and colonies*, 1st edn, II, 219–20.

[345] Glenelg, memorandum, 15 December 1837, CO209/2, fos.409–9a, TNA; Pocock, 'Nature and history, self and other', in Calder, Lamb, and Orr, *Voyages and Beaches*, 37–8 ('The shepherd is not decisively removed from the "savage", the *selvaggio* or forest food-gatherer—we recall that Polyphemus was shepherd and cave-dweller at the same time—and the agrarian engaging in trade had not reached the point where his land is exchangeable for cash. This could be called the Waitangian moment, at which Glenelg... could declare that the Maori were, "not New Zealand [*sic*] savages living by the chase", but had the capacity to apportion lands among themselves').

[346] Ward, *Information relative to New Zealand*, 2nd edn, 62; cf Pocock, 'Tangata whenua and enlightenment anthropology', 37 on the pertinence of ploughing to cultivation status.

When not participating in warfare, these aborigines attended to the 'cultivation of their vegetables, or getting in the harvest, or in fishing, or in making distant excursions, or in the social festivities and amusements with which the tribes frequently entertain each other'.[347] Arguably, in describing the 'native inhabitants' of these remote islands, no resort was had to theological texts concerning immediate postdiluvian occurrences—possible descendants of Shem, Ham, or Japheth—although perhaps there were *indirect resonances* (*via* citation *en passant*) with an inchoate, theologically inspired monogenist ethnography (linked to persons such as Prichard). There was, illustratively, a bibliographical reference to Lang's work which demonstrated access to, and use of, such an ethnography: a focus upon comparative philology, as well as the assumption of a single source for humanity in spite of racial diversity.[348] Moreover, there were additional signals. Those darker aborigines from Australia were construed as inherently hapless. As such, there were positive comparative references in Ward to Māori as deriving from an uncertain 'Asiatic' migratory fount or as displaying a range of hues in complexion varying from a 'dark chestnut' to the 'light agreeable tinge of an English brunette'.[349] This is a point to revive the earlier cautions regarding nomenclature. In 1839, the term '*maori*'—denoting 'usual' (or 'indigenæ aborigines' as Prichard preferred in 1847)[350] as in *tangata Māori* or 'usual people'—was neither used by the Colonial Office authors, nor their correspondents, whether or not domiciled in New Zealand for a time. Terms such as 'New Zealander' or, more generically, 'aborigine' or 'native' were employed, reflecting the broadly ranging locations into which imperial entanglements could be inscribed—southern Africa, Australia, and Canada. Hence, on 5 November 1840, then parliamentary under-secretary, Vernon Smith, said, 'we are told that we have in N. Zealand a finer race of aborigines *than elsewhere*, more capable of mental & moral improvement', with 'elsewhere' describing a vast extent indeed.[351] As witnessed, various Company or former Association sympathizers occasionally used 'savage' as a descriptor, whilst 'barbarous' appeared spasmodically in certain Colonial Office literature, expressly suggesting 'uncivilized'.[352] Such diversity in titling or characterization indicates the sheer difficulties of responding to imperial occurrences as an analytical exemplar of 'two worlds' (*te ao Māori* and *te ao pākehā*) or even experiences shifting 'between worlds' (*pae*) in 1837 to 1839 (anachronistic *pākehā*—'stranger' or 'extraordinary'—and *maori*).[353] In distant anticipation, one might suggest that by 1847, these varied sources also clearly referred to indigenous persons within New Zealand in a telescoped fashion as *Māori*, or in Prichard's instance, as 'Maorians or New Zealanders', and as participants in diverse descent-based or familial entities with now systematically

347 Ibid, 66.

348 Lang, *New Zealand in 1839*, 70 (monogenism); Prichard, *Researches into the Physical History of Man*, 1st edn, iii (preface: monogenism), 244–7 (linguistics); Stocking, 'From chronology to ethnology', in ibid, lxxxiii; Prichard, 'Remarks on the application of philological and physical researches to the history of the human species', in *Report of the British Association*, 530 *et seq*.

349 Ward, *Information relative to New Zealand*, 2nd edn, 62 (Dr John Dunmore Lang), 64–5 (John Savage); cf Ward, *The Natural History of Mankind*, 60 ('their physiognomy is intermediate between the Malay and European, in many instances approaching more nearly to the latter'); Sorrenson, *Maori origins and Migrations*, 11, 14.

350 Prichard, *Researches into the Physical History of Man*, V, 124.

351 Minute, 5 November 1840, CO380/122, fo.151, TNA (emphasis added).

352 Russell to Hobson, royal instructions, 9 December 1840, CO380/122, fo.73a, TNA.

353 'Maori'—defined as 'native'—appears in Dieffenbach, *Travels in New Zealand*, I, 29, II, 7.

investigated aboriginal titles ('tribes' expressed as 'Nga-pui' or 'Nga-te-toa').[354] Yet, indigenous self-description also obtained and was evidently transmitted spasmodically—such as 'moodoo whenua' (*muriwhenua*) in 1793—but imparted an uncertain, ephemeral tracery in both internal and external Colonial Office correspondence; often transmissions without echoes.[355]

Importantly, however, this Company-Office correspondence constituted a privileged intra-European discussion, albeit one partly informed through its own filtering of beach-line and hinterland relations (at and near mission stations, including Waimate) with certain Māori. Māori agency was partially operating within the midst of these diverse sources (insofar as it was communicated or transmitted), engendering a sensation of ambiguity, provided its auditors hearkened. Aboriginal terms and names, at least, appeared spasmodically, were conducted, and were translated in formats and contents meaningful to anglophone recipients: deeds of purchase, fungible conceptions such as dominion, and sovereignty.[356] The Office's notion of disciplining transactional conduct was responding to unlicensed, unknown Europeans engaging with 'natives' or 'aborigines', producing emblematic materials of these engagements—a tracery of acquisitive deeds, fossilized for posterity. Generically comprehended aborigines, whether in Natal, New Holland, or New Zealand, were addressed procedurally as a segment encapsulated within this developing Office notion—a process of disciplining settlements. Certain Māori—those who had encountered reporting Europeans—had effectively projected a partial image into these recordings of themselves as historical occupiers of geopolitical locations, as warriors. Thus, Māori had influenced their discursive and pragmatic treatment within a distant Colonial Office. They might have partially 'possessed' (after Dening) portions of European representations of themselves experienced in shore-line or hinterland entanglements, but these 'possessions', as Dening has reminded us, might not have been mutually comprehensible—a constrained appreciation of agency.[357] Such 'possessing' might have generated a bewildering disquiet, mingled with incomprehension, and introduced intellectual assumptions (*ius gentium*, for instance). As yet, there was little literary transmission of unfiltered Māori correspondence or perceptions into the privileged offices of the colonial secretary, as would occur signally from 1840.[358] Conceptually, however (and on balance), aborigines merely represented conceptual cyphers or persons of straw in Office deliberations from 1837 until 1840.

In the Company, the Colonial Office perceived indiscipline and an unnerving political independence. Ironically, the Company's predecessor—the Association—had imparted a view of irregular anglophone settlement and the possible extinction of aborigines in a distant archipelago. A Glenelgian office acceded to this view and was pressured

[354] Prichard, *Researches into the Physical History of Man*, 3rd edn, V, 122. Cf 'Report to the New Zealand Company, by Ernst Dieffenbach M.D., the Company's naturalist', *Twelfth Report of the directors of the New Zealand Company: 26th April 1844*, 89F–90F, referring to 'Nyatiawa', 'Ngatinhatuigh', and 'Cafia'.

[355] Philip King to Joseph Banks, 10 November 1793, Ms9/95, fo.2, NLA.

[356] Dening, *Mr Bligh's Bad Language*, 201: 'the strangers were the observers, catching the symbols but not the signs, translating the outward formalities of the other's signals but not their meanings'.

[357] Ibid, 161, 169–70, 207–8, 253–7; Dening, *Islands and Beaches*, 20–1; Sahlins, *How 'Natives' Think; about Captain Cook, for example.*

[358] For example Hone Heke to Mair, 16 October 1844, NZMs724, APL; FitzRoy to Stanley, 15 April 1844, CO209/27, fo.265, TNA: 'the natives are now frequent letter writers'.

into responsively recognizing the necessity to formulate proposals on aboriginal New Zealand. Yet, both the Association (eventually) and the Company proffered a competing, non-ministerial proposal for planting settlement in aboriginal New Zealand. Their proposals were largely responsive to domestic Westminster politics, not to ministers alone necessarily, but to chiefly 'moderate' radical and commercial elements affiliated with certain whiggish figures such as the Earl of Durham or the Baring connection. These domestic politics, then, occasionally intersected or coalesced with imperially orientated constituencies of interest located in London and elsewhere—what John Darwin has characterized as 'domestic' or metropolitan bridgeheads'.[359] Emigration was entwined with 'sufficient prices' for territories and expectations of consequent revenues funding the export of labourers. In relation to the New Zealand archipelago, an imperial conception of aboriginal proprietary rights initially emerged in the jostling spaces of negotiation and discord between the Company and the Colonial Office. That is, contestable political relations generated the construct and substance of aboriginal property-rights discourse, not philanthropic humanity or evangelicalism, allegedly moderate or otherwise. These categories constituted important features insofar as they provided an influential field of sentiment or conceptual background in the 1820s and 1830s. But neither was determinative, nor do they adequately explain the shifting aspects of imperial practice.

A CORPORATION ACQUIRING TERRITORIES

Wakefield's *Tory* expedition was instructed to produce deeds of purchase with Māori markings of assent on them, thereby securing territory for the Company settlers and investors. Such was the aspiration. Ironically, after 1839, the Company became part of the Office's problem of undisciplined European settlement. This use of paper deeds was important as illustrated in subsequent recollections of negotiation participants in 1844. A Taranaki individual, 'E Kaka', in referring to a corporate deed executed on 15 February 1840 for Taranaki district, stated that 'he thought it was a deed to go to England that the gentlemen there might know his name in case he was killed by Waikato'.[360] In October 1839, for instance, several chieftains, including two senior *rangatira* of Ngāti Toa, Te Rauparaha and his nephew, Te Rangihaeata, executed a deed of purchase with Wakefield. Under this deed, the northern third of the south island (to 43 degrees south latitude), was 'acquired' by the Company's expedition. Thus, parallels of latitude were used in the deed to inscribe the extent of acquisition. To Te Rauparaha, however, this parchment and the relations established thereby with Wakefield were possibly emblematic of his contested territorial claims to northern Ngāi Tahu land in the north of the south island. As Wakefield commented in his journal: 'An immense portion on the Southern Island is uninhabited; but having been conquered by the Kafia [Kāwhia; that is, Ngāti Toa], is acknowledged to be theirs'.[361]

359 Darwin, 'Imperialism and the Victorians'; see also the discussion in Darwin, *The Empire Project*, 3.

360 Spain to FitzRoy, 31 March 1845, CO209/37, fo.249, TNA.

361 'Colonel Wakefield's third despatch to the New Zealand Company', 24 October 1839, *Supplementary Information relative to New-Zealand*, 111–59, 126. Te Rangihaeata ('Rangiata') signed the deed on 28 October, ibid, 134; Deed of purchase, 25 October 1839, *AJHR* 1888, appendix, I-8, 58–9.

William Wakefield thus accepted Ngāti Toa claims of 'conquest' and proceeded accordingly.[362] Moreover, Te Rauparaha was furnished with items of usefulness to a warring chieftain, including muskets and powder. Wakefield was unaware that his deed was potentially a rhetorical tool, useful to Māori in the midst of a set of contentious territorial claims. Prominent Ngāti Toa were asserting a centrality in negotiating with pākehā. Te Rauparaha would not treat or translate the deed as an absolute transfer of properties: 'I heard the names mentioned [in negotiation] as places Rauparaha had conquered', reported one witness.[363] There is evidence to suggest a Ngāti Toa comprehension of Wakefield's deed as conferring circumscribed territorial interests—possibly analagous to a licence to occupy and use tribal territory and resources.[364] Subsequent accounts collected by William Spain suggested sites referred to as 'W[h]akatu' and 'Taitapu' as discrete sites for anglophone settlement. Wakefield was merely a recent arrival on the scene bearing pieces of paper.[365] If anything, these Ngāti Toa claims to territory formed part of what could be described as a confederacy of conflicting histories (warfare, rivalry, competitive commerce) involving several Māori *hapū* (predominantly descent-based groups) over time.[366] 'Rauparaha then told... Wakefield that the people [divisions of Te Ātiawa] who sold Port Nicholson had no right to it, they were only there on sufferance.'[367] There was no reason to suppose that Wakefield foreshadowed anything to the contrary. Indeed, Wakefield conceivably became their pākehā, an unwittingly co-opted client or ally, inserted into the fluidities of inter-*hapū* politics.[368] This assumption of 'unoccupied' territory rested upon assumptions of the Company's unincorporated predecessors. Māori were regarded as minor cultivators of the soil, occupying little in spatial terms in spite of their notoriously extensive trading networks.[369] Accepting Te Rauparaha's claims to discrete parts of *Te Waipounamu*, Wakefield satisfactorily concluded that he had purchased Ngāti Toa and Te Ātiawa lands.

362 Parsonson, 'He Whenua te Utu ("the payment will be land")', ch 6; 'Instructions from the New Zealand Company to Colonel Wakefield, principal agent of the Company', CO209/4, fo.536a, TNA: 'It will be necessary for you to touch at Entry Island [Kapiti], the seat of the tribe to which... both sides of Cook's strait belong'.

363 Spain to FitzRoy, 31 March 1845, 'Porirua', CO209/37, fo.450a, TNA.

364 McKay, *A Compendium of Official Documents relative to Native Affairs in the South Island*, II, 54–5. Cf ATL, 85-173-5/6, 'Opinions of various authorities on native tenure, 1890' 1890, *AJHR*, G-1, 6 (Board of Inquiry).

365 Cf 'minutes of the proceedings at Waikanae (Cook's straits district) on 12th February 1844', CO209/27, fo.327a; Fox to Wakefield, 11 May 1846, CO209/51, fos.138a–9a, TNA.

366 Wiremu Naera Te Kanae, 'The history of the tribes Ngati-toa-rangatira, Ngati-awa-o-rungao-te-rangi, and Ngati-raukawa, having special references to the doings of Te Rauparaha', trans G Graham, Ms874b, 17, HlDu; Tamihana Te Rauparaha, 'Narrative of the origin and progress of the wars of Ngatitoa and others with Ngaitahu', trans Edward Shortland, Ms96c, HlDu; H Evison, *Te Wai Pounamu*, 114–15; Parsonson, 'The challenge to mana Maori', 174–5. On the prominence of genealogy, see Shortland, *The Southern Districts of New Zealand*, 92–104.

367 Spain to FitzRoy, 31 March 1845, 'Porirua', CO209/37, fos.448–8a, TNA; also regarding Heretaunga (Hutt), Clarke junior to Clarke, 16 August 1843, CO209/23, fo.273, TNA.

368 Parsonson, 'He Whenua te Utu ("the payment will be land")', 191–7.

369 Ward and Wakefield, *The British Colonization of New Zealand*, 28–9; Wakefield, *A Statement of the Objects*, 13 (appendix).

Several proclamations and a treaty

Two forms of imperial document reflected procedural acts intended to bypass or undermine unauthorized claims to territory by the Company and less ambitious acquirers of territory—proclamations and a treaty with certain Māori. Importantly, each documentary form was publicized and spoke to anglophone audiences in New Zealand, New South Wales, and Britain, as well as Māori listeners and participants. Hobson's instructions from Normanby envisaged these documents as bolstering assertions of executive centrality in negotiating territorial purchases throughout New Zealand. These assertions would secure management of a revenue base in treating acquired territories as sources of revenue in accordance with whiggish policies favoured since 1831. Hobson's immediate superior, Gipps, as governor for New South Wales, issued a proclamation at Sydney to this effect in January 1840. It indicated that the United Kingdom would 'not acknowledge as valid any title to land which either has been or shall be hereafter acquired... which is either not derived from or confirmed by a [government] grant'.[370]

In this context, Port Phillip lessons from 1835 and 1836 travelled and were applied pre-emptively to New Zealand locations. Proliferating paper deeds required improvised pincering or bypassing tactics to secure the possibilities of disciplining bridgehead settlements and constructing a revenue base. New Zealand constituted an experiment in land management and land revenue. Hobson proclaimed a similarly termed version to Gipps's proclamation at Kororāreka in the Bay of Islands in New Zealand on 30 January 1840. It stipulated that the Crown 'does not deem it expedient to recognize any titles to land in New Zealand which are not derived from or confirmed by Her Majesty'.[371] A commission was to be instituted to investigate European claims to territory in the period preceding January 1840. These documents proclaimed imperial territorial discipline with aboriginal title merely featuring as a scarcely analysed, accessorial quality that was implicit in the acts of land-hunting that Hobson's infant administration would endeavour to manage. Thus, a concept of pre-emption began to figure in the publicized rhetoric, but substantive discussions of aboriginal title were absent.

Yet, Hobson's proclamation was merely an initial act expressing anxieties over imperial territorial discipline in a New Zealand field. A subsequent diplomatic act appeared in the form of a Māori language treaty document (the Treaty of Waitangi), first marked by attending Māori at Waitangi on 5 and 6 February 1840. Sections of Māori were therefore treated as subjects of *ius gentium*. The diverse histories experienced by this Māori treaty text at a number of sites throughout New Zealand as various Māori markings were collected have been well documented elsewhere. It remains unnecessary to explore these narratives.[372] However, there were several treaties rather than two texts, with one expressed in a missionary-Ngā Puhi dialect; another versed in English. At each of these sites oratory and orally conducted negotiations were layered upon the treaty texts such that each site possesses an historical treaty glossed upon the text

[370] Enclosed in Gipps to Normanby, 9 February 1840, CO209/6, fo.11, TNA.

[371] 'Copies or extracts of despatches from the Governor of New South Wales, bearing the date the 9th and 19th days of February 1840, containing the reports of Captain Hobson, RN, of his proceedings on his arrival in New Zealand; together with a copy of the reply of the secretary of state thereto', *GBPP1840*, xxxiii (582), 575–85, 582. See also Mathew, *The Founding of New Zealand*, Rutherford (ed), 28; Colenso, *The Authentic and Genuine History of the Signing of the Treaty of Waitangi, New Zealand, February 5 and 6, 1840*, 12–13.

[372] For example Orange, *The Treaty of Waitangi*, 32–59; Adams, *Fatal Necessity*, 159–64.

through oral negotiations, remaining beyond the compass of anglophone records.[373] In its English expressions, the Treaty included a specific clause that referred to 'pre-emption', thus attaching a specialist term of art to a conception of territorial management already favoured by prominent Whigs such as Howick (especially), Russell, and Normanby.[374]

Before this moment, such a meaning of 'pre-emption' appeared only in United States court opinions. This term materialized in a treaty that bore Gipps's influence at Sydney since subsequent events indicated his familiarity with relevant United States jurisprudential material.[375] Indeed, Gipps appears to have been the proximate source, whether of his own accord, through advice from Willis, or through Richard Bourke's prior experience with the Port Phillip episode in 1835 and the legal opinions relating to that incident published in the *Parliamentary Papers*, or even a combination of these factors. Gipps was an extensive collector of tomes concerning European histories and *ius gentium*, and he deployed these sources in defending the entitlement of imperial administrations to manage anglophone settlers and territories in alien locations.[376] The Treaty's second article also formulaically referred to the 'chiefs and tribes of New Zealand, and to the respective families and individuals thereof', retaining the 'undisturbed possession' of their 'lands and estates forests and other properties' in the absence of any embellishment.[377] An English version of this Treaty initially presented at Waitangi remained politically useful. It represented a textual basis for pre-emption in New Zealand, for the pre-eminence of the Colonial Office's visualization of disciplined territorial acquisition throughout that archipelago. In substance, these were intra-European conversations, with the Office endeavouring to re-order disarrangements represented by a multiplicity of unlicensed deeds of acquisition. These discussions or exchanges were not yet noticeably discomfited by anxieties regarding any Māori responses to these attempts at managing Europeans. Territorial management was a principal preoccupation for Hobson, as evident in his instructions. These instructions mentioned 'extensive acquisitions' of territory having been executed and the probability of a 'great addition' to such 'purchases' before Hobson's arrival in New Zealand: 'The embarrassments occasioned by such claims will demand your earliest and most careful attention'.[378] The ambition of

[373] Cf McKenzie, *Oral Culture, Literacy and Print in early New Zealand*; Binney, 'The Maori and the signing of the Treaty of Waitangi', in *Towards 1990*, 20–31, 27–9.

[374] Hobson to Gipps, 5–6 February 1840, CO209/6, fos.53–3a, TNA: 'The Chiefs of the United Tribes, and the individual Chiefs, yield to Her Majesty the exclusive right of preemption over... such lands as the proprietors thereof may be disposed to alienate, at such prices as may be agreed upon between the respective proprietors and persons appointed by Her Majesty to treat with them in that behalf'.

[375] Gipps' draft (unsigned) treaty, 'memorandum of agreement' (14 February 1840, deleted), Nar/3, miscellaneous New South Wales estrays on New Zealand affairs, microfilm, NLA; and Willis, 'Notes on the acquisition of New Zealand as a Dependency of New South Wales with reference to lands obtained by British Subjects from the Aborigines', May 1840, Mitchell Library, Sydney, Pamphlets collected by Mr Justice Wise, ML A857, 11–68 (microfilm CY746).

[376] On aspects of Gipps' collection, *vide*, ML018.2 Pal, 193–7, State library of New South Wales: *Two days sale by auction at Government House; a catalogue of plate, books, household furniture, piano-forte, horses, carriages, cows, &c, &c, the properties of his Excellency Sir George Gipps* (Sydney, 1846).

[377] Hobson to Gipps, 5–6 February 1840, CO209/6, fos.53–3a, TNA; *Facsimiles of the Declaration of Independence and the Treaty of Waitangi*, no folio reference (University of Auckland, New Zealand and Pacific collection).

[378] Normanby to Hobson, 14 August 1839, *GBPP1840*, xxxiii (238), 625.

self-financing settlement enclaves was to be realized through the management of 'territorial rights of the natives' and 'waste lands' rather than presumed 'waste lands' per se. New Zealand was to comprise fields of purchase as opposed to conquest or seizure: 'To the natives or their chiefs much of the land of the country is of no actual use, and, in their hands, it possesses scarcely any exchangeable value'.[379] Normanby continued, '[m]uch of it must long remain useless, even in the hands of the British government also, but its value in exchange will be first created, and then progressively increased, by the introduction of capital and of settlers from this country'.[380] In 1840, a pre-emptive privilege intruded into imperial relations with Māori in a distinctly memorialized manner: an article within a treaty.

In 1839 and 1840, the Company's rhetoric in Westminster argued for its right to acquire territories within New Zealand in an unmolested fashion. It required a surfeit of territories for its own revenue sources. This commercial requirement was exacerbated by the necessity to protect dividends for its shareholders. By February 1840 nine vessels bearing emigrants had been sent. The Company argued that the interposition of the Crown through a treaty document was strictly unnecessary. Tactically, it pursued this issue not with a recalcitrant or obstructive Colonial Office but with Palmerston's Foreign Office in an extensive letter from the Company's deputy-governor, Somes.[381] A complete list of the corporate directorate was strategically appended. It included the names of the governor for the Company, Durham, and a shipping magnate, George Young. The Company was trying to solicit the assistance of another executive department relevant to Westminster assessments of New Zealand since Hobson was also a consul. Normanby's successor, Russell, advised Stephen on 16 November that the Company's letter was being discussed with Palmerston and ought to be considered in cabinet.[382]

Somes expressed confusion on the Company's behalf concerning Normanby and Russell's refusal to negotiate with, or extend any recognition to, the Company. He considered the much-fêted 'declaration of independence' (28 October 1835), together with the supposed northern Māori confederacy it mentioned, as merely chimerical. The diplomacy, concentrating on a treaty instrument, was seen as spurious. The directorate was characterizing historical interaction with Māori polities under *ius gentium*. British sovereignty had obtained in New Zealand since 1769 with Cook's proclamations at Mercury Bay on 15 November of that year and later in Queen Charlotte Sound on 31 January 1770. Pre-existing 'sovereignty' provided cover for Wakefield's *Tory* venture. It alleged that this 'discovery' and footfall on New Zealand's littoral constituted 'sovereignty by possession':

> The law of nations we believe recognises no other mode of assuming dominion in a country, of which the inhabitants are so barbarous as to be ignorant of the word sovereignty, and therefore incapable of ceding sovereign rights. This was the case with the New-Zealanders

379 Ibid.

380 Ibid. A tax was proposed for uncultivated lands.

381 Somes to Palmerston, 7 November 1839, FO58/1, fos.177–92, TNA.

382 Russell, minute, 16 November 1839, CO209/4, fo.53a, TNA: 'I have heard from Lord Palmerston on this subject. The cabinet must consider the question, & an abstract of the present state & of all that has been done since 1831 would be very useful. It should be presented at the F. Office'.

> from whom it would have been impossible for Captain Cook to have obtained, except in mockery of the truth, British Sovereignty by possession.[383]

Implicitly, enterprising individuals could proceed to the archipelago, acquire terrain, and establish settlements. Moreover, the directorate, in its 14 May 1840 shareholders' report, confirmed this Company position. These sentiments reflected the publicized version of the Company's rhetoric. But it did not lie overly comfortably with Henry Petre's later defensive references to the Port Nicholson settlement as requiring a provisional constitutional structure while it existed in a 'foreign country'.[384] This emphasized the plasticity of argument in the literature which, on the one hand, principally functioned as an advertisement for Company establishments within New Zealand (Petre)—in other words, literature responding to a need to attract settlers. On the other hand, it functioned as a political weapon against the Colonial Office (the official and private correspondence of directors). Notably, however, Foreign Office recipients of the Somes' letter treated it as sufficiently persuasive to merit a despatch to Stephen. This correspondence of Somes was accordingly forwarded by Stephen's counterpart, the permanent under-secretary for the Foreign Office, John Backhouse, to the Colonial Office on 15 November 1839.[385] Yet, in response, the colonial department employed indifference, prompting Backhouse to issue an additional Foreign Office request for a reply on 11 March 1840.[386]

Ultimately, the concerns of the Foreign Office were defeated by a combination of delay, Stephen's assured memorandum in reply, and the reports received in July of Hobson's narrative of events. Stephen accorded priority to the Office's prior practice (in which he was personally implicated). He asserted a series of early nineteenth-century precedents recognizing New Zealand as beyond existing Victorian dominions.[387] These incidents included a reliance on a triad of extra-jurisdictional statutes, as well as the supposed recognition of the archipelago's independence by William IV in 1835. This received a partial embellishment on Stephen's part with a reference to the acknowledgement in that year of a so-called New Zealand ensign by the then colonial secretary, the Tory Earl of Aberdeen.

The importance of native title to controlling Europeans was revealed in Gipps' defence of imperial territorial control. Under Normanby's instructions, Gipps introduced legislation at Sydney for establishing a commission to investigate unauthorized territorial acquisitions in New Zealand. Opposition expressed through William Wentworth, a prominent New South Wales personality, accentuated his anxieties. Wentworth had purported to acquire extensive swathes of the South Island *via* a deed marked by Ngāi Tahu *rangatira* visiting Sydney.[388] Gipps' Legislative Council address on 9 July was notable for its clear use of *ius gentium*. Portentously, this incident

[383] Somes to Palmerston, 7 November 1839, FO58/1, fos.182a–3, TNA; Vattel, *The Law of Nations*.

[384] Petre, *An Account of the settlements of the New Zealand Company, from personal observation during a residence there*, 34–5.

[385] Backhouse to Stephen, 15 November 1839, FO58/2, fos.19a–20, TNA.

[386] Backhouse to Stephen, 11 March 1840, CO209/8, fo.66a, TNA; Stephen, 11 and 12 March 1840, CO209/8, fo.68a, TNA.

[387] Stephen to Backhouse, 18 March 1840, 'papers relative to New Zealand; printed solely for the use of Cabinet', FO58/2, fos.21–1a, TNA; Stephen, memorandum, 21 November 1839, CO209/4, fos.332–41a, TNA.

[388] Deed of purchase, 15 February 1840, Mitchell Ms Aw51 (Wentworth papers), State library of New South Wales. See also Evison, *Te Wai Pounamu*, 123.

incorporated Māori into an anglicized reception of Amerindian narratives. Here, the act of cultivating was imbued with a juridical significance: to competently transfer proprietary interests to alien visitors, one ought to 'cultivate' territories as agriculturists. This was clearly evocative of a Vattelian perspective; that is, of viewpoints associated with the jurist Vattel, cited by both Wentworth and Gipps. Vattelian perceptions concerning *ius naturale* dictated that each human community was obliged to cultivate the soils of the earth in order to feed this planet's inhabitants—cultivating territory was an obligation '*imposée à l'homme par la nature*'.[389] However, earthly soils failed to provide sufficient sustenance if they remained uncultivated by idle humanity ranging erratically hither and thither. Hence, Vattel referred to those individuals 'who, to avoid labour, choose to live only by hunting and their flocks'; in other words, persons who both pursue game or gather fruits and shepherd animal flocks. A notion of natural jurisprudence (*ius naturale*) intruded. There was an assumption that:

> Those who still pursue this idle mode of life, usurp more extensive territories than, with a reasonable share of labour, they would have occasion for, and have, therefore, no reason to complain, if other nations, more industrious and too closely confined, come to take possession of a part of those lands.[390]

Ius naturale, entwined with concepts of the historical progression of human communities, was informing *ius gentium*, the normative relations between bodies of humans in exotic encounters. Gipps baldly stated, '[t]o be independent in the full sense of the word, there must be a form of government, there must be cultivation of the soil, and there must be individual rights to property'.[391] The detail furnished was undeniably historical, enmeshed with a jurisprudential idiom. A history of practice was emerging—gubernatorial instructions emanating from a distant Colonial Office, legislation, treaties, and proclamations—complete with discursive strategies cast in attending roles. Gipps was unquestionably required by Hobson's instructions to ensure the passage of a bill. Yet, stringent opposition was evident with this opposition requiring, in its turn, an addition of detail.

Wentworth assailed Gipps' bill in June and July 1840. He claimed that no credible equivalence could be claimed for Māori in relation to Amerindian populations. Māori polities had allegedly attained a more civilized character than the latter.[392] Wentworth was defending one version of New Zealand's recent past; a past predicated on 'squatting' and largely unfettered entry into commercial-exchange relations with Māori. Gipps was assailing this version, at least concerning territorial transactions. Wentworth averred that independent Amerindian tribes had, on various occasions, exercised, without any interruption or supervision, the unqualified right of disposing of land which the governor intended to deprive Māori. Anterior practice, therefore, was considered inconsistent. Wentworth referred, *inter alia*, to an enactment in 1662 of an assembly in Virginia. Under this enactment, no Amerindian 'monarch' was to convey nor any English subject to purchase an indigenous estate within the limits of the settlement.

389 Vattel, *The Law of Nations*, lib I, cap vii, §81; cf Pagden, *Lords of all the World*, 78–9.

390 Ibid. For a discussion of this view in relation to contemporaries of Vattel, see Pocock, 'Tangata whenua and enlightenment anthropology', 36–40.

391 Gipps, address to the Legislative Council, 9 July 1840, in Sweetman, *The Unsigned New Zealand Treaty*, 107–32, 127–8; transcript in *The Sydney Herald*, 13 July 1840, x, 1013, 2, 5–6.

392 Sweetman, *The Unsigned New Zealand Treaty*, 83–4. A detailed coverage of Wentworth's position is presented in ibid, chs 4 and 6.

For Wentworth, a poignant feature of this measure was that it did not doubt the validity of previous transactions. He lamented the paucity of juristic sources discussing the direct purchase of native title by a subject. He suggested, in a minor passage, that had the point arisen it would have been determined in 'provincial courts' and not in the courts at Westminster (whose decisions were reported).[393]

Responding to Wentworth on 9 July, Gipps constructed three general principles that he describes as 'fully admitted, and indeed received... political axioms'.[394] Whilst there was no direct reference to 'common law' here, the tenor of his address repeatedly conflated the supposedly observed anterior practice of 'England' with 'English law', an anglicized notion of *ius gentium*.[395] His initial principle was that 'the uncivilized inhabitants of any country have but a qualified dominion over it, or a right of occupancy only'. Indigenous property rights to territory were constrained by this expression. Gipps suggested that a given population must obtain a 'form of government, and subjugate the ground to their own uses, by the cultivation of it' before they can grant territory to alien individuals.[396] His second principle recited the maxim of 'pre-emption'; that is, indigenous title is reputedly inalienable to persons or entities other than the Crown or those it permits to obtain estates from 'natives'. Further, Gipps commented, '[s]econdly, that if a settlement be made in any such country by a civilized foreign power, the right of pre-emption of the soil, or in other words, the right of extinguishing the native title, is exclusively in the government of that power, and cannot be enjoyed by individuals without the consent of their government'. Gipps' ultimate point in this passage stated that colonies could only be established with the consent of the Crown. In these passages, Gipps introduced coherence such that he characterized his earlier proclamation as a 'notice' or 'warning' of what the 'law' *was*.

Gipps also commented that, to a certain extent, 'all savages are independent, and according to the description of [William] Robertson, they lose their independence in proportion as they become civilised [whilst] [w]hat gives the right of a country is not independence, but civilization'.[397] This reference to Robertson invoked a peculiarly conjectural conception of history, divisible into stages of development based on modes of subsistence. Significantly, Gipps' reliance on Robertson was clarified in the form that his address took when forwarded to Russell via despatch (16 August 1840). In that format, he specifically mentioned one of Robertson's histories, citing extensively from it.[398] The unpolished crudeness of hunting and pasturage was assumed. Incidentally, Gipps could elicit support from Normanby for this account. Certain passages within Hobson's instructions suggested that many of the territories throughout the three major islands of New Zealand could not be of actual use to Māori. Instead, these territories could be characterized as 'waste land'.[399] In this vein, then, a notion of aboriginal

[393] Ibid, 75–6, 82, 83–4.

[394] Gipps to Russell, number two, 16 August 1840, 'copies or extracts of correspondence relative to New Zealand', *GBPP1841*, xvii (311), 559–60.

[395] Ibid, 560–2. [396] Ibid, 560.

[397] Sweetman, *The Unsigned New Zealand Treaty*, 127–8; cf *GBPP1841*, xvii (311), for the printed form of Gipps' address, 9 July 1840, 559–74, 571.

[398] Robertson, *The History of America*, lib IV, §§3–4; cited by Gipps in *GBPP1841*, xvii (311), 572. For a discussion of William Robertson, see Meek, *Social Science and the Ignoble Savage*, 136–45; Brown (ed), *William Robertson and the Expansion of Europe*. Also see Pocock, *Barbarism and Religion: Volume Four*, 189–90.

[399] Normanby to Hobson, 14 August 1839, *GBPP1840*, xxxiii (238), 623–8, 625.

rights to territory (characterized as 'occupancy') was ensnared in the process of delimitation. Despite the strident contest, the Legislative Council consented to the bill on Tuesday, 4 August 1840, although not without criticism. The colonial chief justice supported the bill, reminding his colleagues that '[i]t was enough for this Council and all Her Majesty's subjects' that *de jure* 'sovereignty' had been asserted over the islands of New Zealand 'on behalf of Her Majesty' (alluding to Hobson's proclamations on 21 May).[400] Yet, the Colonial Office advised disallowance of the measure (without prejudice) due, in the main, to the eventual separation of the New Zealand dependency from New South Wales towards the end of 1840.[401]

CONCLUSION: CONVERSING WITH A CORPORATION

Māori might as well have inhabited a mist-ridden darkling plain.[402] Neither the Company nor the Office critically interrogated diverse precepts of Māori proprietary tenure or the organization of their polities. This feature remained a cogent characteristic of their relationship until later 1840 and gave correspondingly extensive rein to anglophone intellectual sources, applied to Pacific sites comprising a *theatrum mundi*.[403] Māori were received and subsumed by *ius gentium*, conceptions of progressing history, and voyaging intelligence. Possible complexities or nuances in aboriginal relations were dimly grasped. Importantly, the details of imperial discourse were not, as the earlier historiography of 'humane' trusteeship or moderate evangelicalism would encourage, conversing with Māori in a generously protective fashion. It was not even 'talking past' Māori at this juncture.[404] There was no conversational engagement with Māori *as* aborigines at all. Concerns regarding aboriginal proprietary rights emerged tangentially and haltingly in relation to formalizing principal procedural issues such as the management of territory or the collection of sustainable revenues. 'Purchase' was separated from 'sovereignty' in the drafting of Hobson's instructions. These administrative concerns were primarily those of policy technicians and facilitators, including Stephen, Grey, and Glenelg. As such, it becomes increasingly difficult to confidently (and conventionally) assert that 'the Colonial Office was still opposed [to the Company] on the

[400] Sweetman, *The Unsigned New Zealand Treaty*, 73. See ibid, 72–3 where the deliberations of the Legislative Council are recounted. The text of this legislation (4 Vic number 7 of New South Wales) is printed in the 'copies or extracts of correspondence relative to New Zealand', *GBPP1841*, xvii (311), 493, 549–51.

[401] For the version passed as an ordinance, number two, see CO209/9, fos.154–6a, TNA, enclosed in Hobson to principal secretary of state, 27 July 1841, ibid, fos.150–1a; Stephen to Hope, 20 January 1842, CO209/9, fos.144a–5, TNA.

[402] Thomas, *Colonialism's Culture*, 57–8: 'This underlines again, the limitations of the assumption that "colonial discourse" is automatically apparent to the colonized in the first place. Given that much of what we refer to by that term was addressed not at colonized populations, but at public opinion within colonizing nations, it needs to be acknowledged that the discourse may not have impinged upon indigenous consciousness at all'.

[403] Dening, *Mr Bligh's Bad Language*, 373: 'It was a period when the nations of Europe and the Americas saw themselves acting out their scientific, humanistic selves.... The theatre of the Pacific was about making that unreal metaphor ['the expansion of Europe'] real at home and abroad'.

[404] Metge, *Talking Past Each Other*; Waitangi Tribunal, *Muriwhenua Land Report—Wai-45*, 55–6.

grounds that it was necessary to protect the Maoris from predatory settlers'.[405] Rather, we may discern periods of convergence or coalescence, as well as divergence (to be witnessed in Chapters Three and Four). As seen, a *conception* of what would ultimately be construed as 'pre-emption'—signifying those claims on the part of the Office or its representatives to exclusively supervise territorial transactions with aborigines—was anticipated. The Company was perceived as undisciplined in terms of its proposals to acquire territories and establish settlements without Office sanction. Indeed, the transformation of the non-commercial Association into the Company introduced these issues of territorial 'discipline' to the fore.

Yet, the use of the specialized term 'pre-emption' with an accompanying cast of American juristic sources was not evident until 1840. This emergent development will be addressed in Chapter Three. In 1839, only the Company referred to 'pre-emption', but in its broadly understood literary sense as entailing a right of first offer or refusal.[406] Stephen himself used such a *concept* if not the term of art: 'application may be made to Parliament to declare that all title to land acquired in New Zealand by British subjects shall be held subject to be repurchased by the Crown on the repayment of the price given for such lands'.[407] This is not to say that the particular northern American literary cargo of pre-emption was not present in the 1830s, merely that it enjoyed a spasmodic, localized usage. Others, such as Bannister, a barrister, former New South Wales attorney-general and Aborigines' Protection Society member (in 1839), would not use it at all.[408] The Office had not yet incorporated it as a defining feature of imperial discourse and practice towards Māori proprietary status. As Chapters Three and Four argue, it would only do so under massed political pressure from the Company. At the outset of this chapter, all this ground might have seemed familiar and well-trodden. Adams recognized the revenue-sourcing role of a focus upon managing land purchases.[409] But he did not fully integrate this appreciation with re-narrated tales of relations between the Office and projectors for 'systematic' settlement in New Zealand or the pedigree of imperial themes (discourse and practice) expressed by the Office. Nor was its improvised quality appreciated. These intertwined features—of Westminster politics and administration—are too readily ignored in English, New Zealand, and even imperial histories.[410] Aboriginal policies for New Zealand became embroiled in

[405] Winch, *Classical Political Economy and Colonies*, 112.

[406] Strang to Labouchere, 15 August 1839, CO209/5, fos.351–1a, TNA, government exercising 'her right of pre-emption to the exclusion or prejudice of those deriving right from the Company [as opposed to the aborigines]'; Labouchere to Strang, 20 August 1839 (no reference to the term 'pre-emption'), CO209/5, fos.352–2a, TNA.

[407] Stephen, 30 April 1839, CO209/4, fo.533a, TNA.

[408] See, eg Bannister, *Memoir respecting the Colonization of Natal in South-eastern Africa presented by the Cape of Good Hope Trade Society to the secretary of state for the colonies*, vii, ix, xii–xiii; *British Colonization and Coloured Tribes*, 263–4; Motte, *Outline of a system of legislation for securing protection to the aboriginal inhabitants of all countries colonized by Great Britain*; received December 1840 at Colonial Office (CO209/8, fos.426–41a, TNA) with 'memorial of the Aborigines Protection Society to Lord John Russell'. By 1848, as discussed in Chapter Four, this absence of juristic sources drawn from United States literature in at least one Aborigines' Protection Society would have dissipated: Chamerovzow, *The New Zealand Question and the Rights of Aborigines*; William Burge, the barrister, did use these US 'pre-emption' sources however: 16 January 1836, legal opinion, Bonwick, *Port Phillip Settlement*, 376–80.

[409] Adams, *Fatal Necessity*, 14, 194–7.

[410] For example Hoppen, *The Mid-Victorian Generation, 1846–1886*, 156–8.

imperial trajectories or extensions of Westminster parliamentary and departmental politics—Canada predominated dangerously. In a sense, then, Māori were 'natives' of Westminster. At times, a whiggish ministry endeavoured to accommodate or facilitate the legislative interests represented by projectors for 'systematic' settlement abroad (as in 1837). Parliament represented a cynosure of pressures and interests with diverse imperial intersections. At other moments—from mid-1838 until 1839—the ministry tended to opt for resistance or curtailment sensing divergences and disorganization within such interests.

3

Incredulity from a Distance: Disputing the Content of Indigenous Proprietary Entitlements, 1840 to 1844

This chapter demonstrates how imperial policies used the recognition of pre-existing native title to 'discipline' or manage New Zealand Company-established settlements at Port Nicholson and elsewhere from 1840. In doing so, native title enjoyed a functionality in colonial state-formation or building. Nevertheless, after 1842, collecting privileged (governmental) intelligence on Māori proprietary interests, together with processes of disciplining land transactions involving Europeans within New Zealand, unsettled relations between settlers, the Company, and the Colonial Office. Policies and ideas on native title were 'made' in these circumstances. It is simplistic to suggest that disputes concerning a treaty at Waitangi per se were central or that its meanings were static. This Treaty was inherently contestable, as its second article was emblematic of a sympathetic yet formulaic, procedurally oriented vocabulary of indigenous proprietary rights vesting in Māori. Formulaic and non-analysed, it merely recited a view of Māori as possessing 'lands and estates forests and other properties' in the absence of any clarity as to what such terms signified. As a Colonial Office sanctioned document, enjoying diverse responses and experiences throughout New Zealand, its terminology represented a point for commencing arguments as to proprietary interests, but not an answer or series of answers. The Colonial Office and anglophone audiences did not receive it as a range of treaties with experiences specific to each site where Māori signings occurred, but as a single, material document. It was used in conjunction with additional Colonial Office documents referring to 'territorial rights of the natives'. The second article in the *English* Treaty version guaranteed 'to the Chiefs and Tribes of New Zealand and to the respective families and individuals thereof the full exclusive and undisturbed possession of their Lands and Estates Forests Fisheries and other properties'.[1] Yet its formulaic phraseology belied the potential to contest what its terms signified to its audiences at Westminster or within New Zealand as the haphazard gathering of information on Māori proprietary notions proceeded after Hobson's advent in 1840. This phraseology could not be comprehended with any exactitude as it was uncertain what Māori 'possessed' or what such 'possession' substantially

[1] Hobson to Gipps, 5–6 February 1840, CO209/6, fos.53–53a, TNA; *Facsimiles of the Declaration of Independence and the Treaty of Waitangi*, no folio reference (University of Auckland, New Zealand and Pacific collection).

entailed. What it denoted was potentially controversial and certainly malleable, not coherently appreciated.

Other documentation issued by the Colonial Office in 1840, such as Hobson's royal instructions, invoked an analogous phraseology regarding the 'territorial rights of the natives'.[2] But, in the absence of either analysis or detail, this terminology merely invited political debates and misapprehensions as the Colonial Office dealt with the Company. At most, it ephemerally obscured the confusion and incoherence characterizing policy tendencies. What remains paramount is to acknowledge the destabilizing impact of intelligence collection on European theoretical expectations regarding indigenous proprietary interests. In the unsettling of these Office relations, particularly at Westminster, the content and extent of proprietary entitlements for Māori were profoundly disputed, with political consequences. From 1839, the Office remained preoccupied with disciplining the expansion of anglophone settlement in New Zealand by investigating territorial purchases undertaken without its sanction. It enjoined the collecting of intelligence of unexpectedly confusing and diverse conceptions of proprietary entitlements within New Zealand so as to render its acquisitions of territory from Māori politically efficacious and procedurally unimpeachable.

Adams misleadingly courts anachronism in mentioning a 'correct' interpretation of articles within a treaty, in swiftly proceeding through his account on 'land and colonization'.[3] This chapter might concur in aspects of Adams' thesis as a commencement for discussion, but differs from his contention that 'politicians from Lord John Russell to Earl Grey *misunderstood* the [treaty] land guarantee for so long'. This remains overly simplistic, as is the conception of a 'truth' in views upon Māori proprietary concerns.[4] It is to suggest that there was always a predetermined and statically correct legal interpretation of native title, one that would not be hostage to Eurocentric (or at least anglocentric) theoretical presumptions or to behaviours that would generate future grievances. There was much more conceptual and political contestability existing at Westminster and in colonial New Zealand than Adams' rapid analyses permit. Conceptions within indigenous communities also adapted to changing forms of relationship as settlement niches appeared in coastal places such as Whanganui, Port Nicholson, New Plymouth, and Auckland. What Adams barely referred to as a 'Eurocentric view of "waste" lands' is examined here in a more nuanced fashion; with reference to the discursive features of a vocabulary on native title and the tactical deployment of sources concerning the location of Māori within mediating idioms such as *ius gentium* and stadial histories.[5] In this fashion too, this study argues for an increasingly detailed, critical consideration of 'aboriginal title' as a contestable concept. This can be revealed by delving into the terrain beyond the hints and blanket suggestions about the Company becoming 'one of the vociferous opponents of the recognition of Maori tenure' in the researches of Belgrave and Tonk.[6]

[2] Russell to Hobson, 28 January 1841, CO209/8, fo.454, TNA.

[3] Adams, *Fatal Necessity* 188 ('what the treaty actually meant').

[4] Ibid, 190 (emphasis added). See Adams, 'British intervention in New Zealand, 1830–1846', 253.

[5] Adams, *Fatal Necessity* 190.

[6] Belgrave, 'Pre-emption, the Treaty of Waitangi and the politics of Crown purchase', 27; Tonk, '"A difficult and complicated question"', in Hamer and Nicholls (eds), *The Making of Wellington, 1800–1914*, 39: 'The establishment of Crown pre-emption in this way was intended to provide the new government with a substantial income through the resale and use of cheaply acquired demesne lands'.

Notions of indigenous property rights can be seen as developing in a series of contested processes, punctuated by points of broad concurrence on approach between Company and Colonial Office. Processes involving the dispute of intellectual sources concerning *ius gentium* or historical perceptions, intelligence on indigenous relations with landscapes and investigating Company territorial claims, together with the Company's political relations with the Office, were critical to this development of a discourse. An imperial inclination towards disciplining anglophone settlements was also critical and indigenous property rights discourse contributed to such disciplinary ventures. A comprehension of indigenous territorial interests as possessed by Māori was constructed through these processes such that it remains problematic to unqualifiedly discuss the Colonial Office as eventually approaching 'the sense in which the Maori chiefs and Hobson had understood [the land guarantee in a treaty]'.[7]

This chapter also continues to engage with the uses of United States jurisprudence, arguing that it did not supply a readily acceptable doctrine at common law or *ius gentium* concerning indigenous property in antipodean arenas. Conceptually, the Office under Glenelg, Normanby, and Russell asserted imperial control of British settlements and transactional engagements with 'natives'. However, these assertions occurred haltingly in the context of relations with supporters of 'systematic' settlements within New Zealand. This chapter disputes the notion that a United States literature would have applied *ipso facto* to relations with Māori (or, implicitly, to aborigines within Australia), suggesting that this jurisprudence potentially converged with certain concepts and tendencies underlying imperial practices but did not inform policies.[8] This potential convergence invited the use of these intellectual sources on the part of New Zealand Company partisans, yet was not readily endorsed within Russell's department, as will be explored in this chapter.

After 1839, political relations between the Colonial Office and the New Zealand Company were increasingly entangled with Māori: 'There they were, native and stranger, each making plays about themselves that the other could not see, but bound together by an environment that now for each included the other'.[9] Yet Office and Company were observing and participating in New Zealand from a distance, each preoccupied with their own organizational objects, enterprises, and senses of internal practices; with concerns as much internal to their relations at Westminster as meaningful to antipodean contexts. This pattern of occluded observing continued throughout the 1840s, characterizing the generation of an indigenous proprietary rights discourse. It entwined itself with increasing layers of detail in imperial practices. Its arenas for discussion were not only the Colonial Office and the Company but also colonial settlements, parliamentary *fora*, in debates within the House of Commons and select committees. Twice in 1845 alone, the number of attending parliamentarians

[7] Adams, *Fatal Necessity*, 187.

[8] Thus, it departs from the suggestions of the earlier literature of McHugh in *The Maori Magna Carta: New Zealand Law and the Treaty of Waitangi*, 105–12; Reynolds, *The Law of the Land*; Belgrave, 'Pre-emption, the Treaty of Waitangi and the politics of Crown purchase', 24, 27: 'As McHugh has argued, there was no need to include these issues in the Treaty; the *doctrine* would have applied anyway' (emphasis added). But compare these earlier references with McHugh's different stance on this issue in McHugh, 'Law, history and the Treaty of Waitangi', 43; McHugh, *Aboriginal Societies and the Common Law*, 125.

[9] Dening, *Mr Bligh's Bad Language*, 254. See also, Thomas, *Oceania*, 13.

in New Zealand debates exceeded two-hundred (including Russell, with Peel and Sir James Graham for the Tories), with one of these debates attracting 369 members in the ayes and noes columns.[10]

As argued in Chapter Two, these discussions intersected with familial and political web-works of the Company, and with mediating idioms, chiefly formulations of stadial histories and *ius gentium*. These idioms were infused with histories and a nascent ethnography of the early nineteenth century about human origins, competitions for nourishment, voyaging, and dispersions.[11] These were the themes of Malthusian demographic anxieties of a 'perpetual struggle for room and food', conflicting and mingling with those counter-themes of improving (perhaps preserving) aborigines through mission stations, mission-administered hamlets, or optimistic proposals for 'systematic' emigration.[12] As Eastwood suggests, these last involved 'dispersing... Malthusian fears', whilst trafficking with discourses and apprehensions still thoroughly imbued with Thomas Malthus' views on varying conditions of subsistence relative to population.[13] Charles Buller, a New Zealand Company director (since 16 December 1841) and 'radical' parliamentarian allied with the Whig grandee, Howick, cautioned the Commons in this vein on 6 April 1843: 'It is the constant swelling of population and capital up to the very brim of the cup that is the permanent cause of uneasiness and danger in the country; and this that makes the ordinary vicissitudes of commerce fraught with such intense misery to our population'.[14] He exclaimed, '[w]hen I ask you to colonize, what do I ask you to do but to carry the superfluity of one part of our country to repair the deficiency of the other [a colony]: to cultivate the desert by applying the means that lie idle here'.[15] Moreover, Thomas Carlyle was sensitive to such strategies in his 1840 account of chartist agitation and the 'condition-of-England question'. He stated: 'to the overcrowded little western nook of Europe, our Terrestrial Planet, nine-tenths of it yet vacant or tenanted by nomades [*sic*], is still crying, Come and till me, come and reap me!'.[16] According to certain sources inhabiting this *oeuvre*, these inexorable (naturalized) historical processes of subsistence-seeking and populations in motion might yet extinguish aborigines, if not carefully managed. Malthus warned: 'If the United States of America continue increasing, which they certainly will do, though not with the same rapidity as formerly, the Indians will be driven further and further

[10] See Chapter Four.

[11] For example Prichard, *The eastern origin of the Celtic nations*, 1–4; Prichard, *Researches into the Physical History of Mankind*, 2nd edn, II, 105–78; Wheaton, *History of the Northmen, or Danes and Normans, from the earliest times to the conquest*.

[12] Malthus, *An essay on the principle of population*, 6th edn, I, 95. Cf Merivale, *Lectures on colonization and colonies*, 2nd edn, 551 (Sandwich Islands and Tahiti); Barrow, 'Polynesia', in *Encyclopædia Britannica* vol 18, 321 (Sandwich Islands); Buxton, *The Remedy; being a sequel to the African slave trade*, 8 ('prospectus of the Society for the extinction of the slave trade and the civilization of Africa'); Matthew, *Emigration Fields*, 126–8; Eastwood, 'The Age of Uncertainty', 109.

[13] Ibid, 109; Stocking, *Victorian Anthropology*, 34–5. See, eg Buller, *Systematic colonization*, 4–18. Cf Semmel, 'The Philosophic Radicals and Colonialism', in Shaw (ed), *Great Britain and her Colonies 1815–1865*, 77–92, 84–6; Pike, *Paradise of Dissent: South Australia 1829–1857*, 41–6.

[14] Buller, *Systematic colonization*, 14. Buller's election as director: minutes, court of directors, 16 December 1841, CO208/181, fo.193, TNA.

[15] Buller, *Systematic colonization*, 24. Buller had been a pupil of Thomas Carlyle: see Reid, *Life and letters of the first earl of Durham*, II, 156–7.

[16] Carlyle, *Chartism*, 112. See also *The debate upon Mr. Ward's resolutions on colonization, in the House of Commons, 27 June 1839*, Ward, 2–11 (chartism and migration).

back into the country, till the whole race is ultimately exterminated'.[17] These were the instructions of a modified stadial historical literature suffused with Malthusian tales of diffusionary migrations in pursuit of cherished subsistence sites (and more besides).

Several examples demonstrate this tendency amongst varied authors. To George Cornewall Lewis in 1841, these heritages of peopling territorial tracts accompanied by the occasional expulsion of prior populations were implicit in ancient and recent definitions of a 'colony':[18] 'A colony properly denotes a body of persons belonging to one country and political community, who, having abandoned that country and community form a new and separate society, independent or dependent, in some district which is wholly or nearly uninhabited, or from which they expel the ancient inhabitants'.[19] Durham in 1839 would mention 'colonization' as an instrument for swelling English numbers to an irresistible majority within the Canadian provinces where he allegedly 'found a struggle, not of principles, but of races'.[20] In 1848, Stephen blithely referred to 'territorial settlements' (explicitly including 'Australian colonies') as a distinct category, 'the main purpose of which is the extension of the British race over unoccupied territories', as if prior inhabitants did not exist or were readily obviated.[21] As David Buchanan stated in 1842, '[b]ut though the civilized communities of the world never violently emigrate into each others [*sic*] territories, they frequently invade the domain of the savage, by obtruding new settlers on his uncultivated territories'.[22] He added that 'all the efforts of the original proprietors to dislodge them are found unavailing'. In 1839, the enormity of these potentially extirpating consequences for aborigines vexed the whiggish Merivale as a fellow of Balliol College and occupant of the Drummond political economy chair at the University of Oxford 'To modern European settlers... whose desire it is to spread themselves as so many individual lords over the soil, the unfortunate beings whom they displace serve as constant incitements to savage cruelty, or to still worse avarice'.[23] Yet, Merivale, in a fashion redolent of Carlyle in 1840, would conclude his introductory lecture with a note of optimism, relating to the United Kingdom's providentially granted maritime reach along oceanic thoroughfares. He proclaimed, '[o]ur position and our power, the unrivalled capacity of our people, and the gigantic means at our disposal by the progress of events, were given us not to extend a barren empire, but to sow the seed of future nations'.[24]

Unsurprisingly, Hilton has observed a 'persistent oscillation between optimism and pessimism' in relation to political economic approaches in the earlier nineteenth

[17] Malthus, *Essay on Population*, 6th edn, I, 8: 'These observations are, in a degree, applicable to all parts of the earth, where the soil is imperfectly cultivated'.

[18] Lewis, *An Essay on the Government of Dependencies*, 170.

[19] Ibid.

[20] Durham, 'Report on the affairs of British North America, from the earl of Durham, Her Majesty's high commissioner', in Lucas (ed), *Lord Durham's Report on the affairs of British North America*, II, 16; Tully, *Strange Multiplicity*, 158–62; Ajzenstat, *The Political Thought of Lord Durham*, 73–100.

[21] Stephen, 'colonies and colonial policy', nd [1848?], CO325/47, fos.1, 4, TNA.

[22] 'Emigration', *Encyclopædia Britannica*, VIII, 684.

[23] Merivale, *Introduction to a course of lectures on colonization and colonies begun in March, 1839*, 27. On Merivale as a Whig sympathizer, see BL AddMss34618, (Macvey Napier papers), fos.8–10, 146–7; Merivale to Napier, 16 January 1837 and June 1838; Hilton, *The Age of Atonement*, 47–8.

[24] Merivale, *Introduction to a course of lectures on colonization and colonies*, 39–40; Carlyle, *Chartism*, 112–13; Arnold, *The effects of distant colonization on the parent state*, 29–31.

century.[25] This comment applies equally to the subsets of 'emigration' and 'colonization'. As such, New Zealand was not merely a terrestrial fragment, but a segment of integrated approaches to anxieties both imperial and localized within Britain. In an array of some accounts, disciplining anglophone settlements might speculatively preserve Māori—as imperfect agriculturists rather than mere pursuers of '*feræ naturæ*'—from historical tendencies towards extirpation, as in the musings of William Fox, Patrick Matthew, a Chartist,[26] and Henry Chapman, legal advocate to the Company in 1840.[27] Indeed, for Matthew, this perceived Māori status was the '*philanthropic reason*' for introducing regularized settlements—'There is no alternative—either the New Zealanders must be civilized, or they will be destroyed'.[28] Indeed, 'preservation, amelioration, and study of the feeble races of mankind' was of interest to the Aborigines' Protection Society, to sections of the British Association for the Advancement of Science, and to various authors, including Matthew, but was not necessarily of concern to imperial policy-formulation.[29] It represented a possibly welcome sideline but was not central to Office policy anxieties. To Chapman, New Zealand represented an 'interesting' archipelagic theatre in his 1842 article on 'Zealand, New' in *The Encyclopædia Britannica*: 'But within the last two years the New Zealand group has been made the theatre of so extraordinary a movement in colonization, that we are induced to devote to the subject a greater space than would otherwise have been justifiable'.[30] Matthew, amongst others, treated indigenous New Zealand as a distinctive arena with its cultivating inhabitants, in that its settling would not be 'as simple an affair' as southern Australia:

> Colonization is comparatively a simple matter, when few aborigines are in the way, or when they are swept down without compunction, as the incumbering trees of the forest, or reduced to slavery, and made subservient to the progress of the settlement.[31]

[25] Hilton, *The Age of Atonement*, 35.

[26] Wells, 'The historical context of natural selection', 241; Desmond, *The Politics of Evolution*, 75–6, 425 (bibliographical note).

[27] Fox, *Colonization and New Zealand*, 15; Chapman, *The comparative prospects of our colonies*, 176–7 ('The natives of New Zealand evince a much greater aptitude for civilization than any other aboriginal people known, except the South Sea Islanders of the same race. They never were hunters, as the North American Indians are'). Fox, William, 1812? (baptized on 2 September 1812)–1893; educated Wadham college, Oxford, 1828; graduated BA, 1832, and Master of Arts, 1839; influenced at Oxford by Richard Whately; succeeded Arthur Wakefield as resident agent in Nelson for the New Zealand Company, September 1843; accepted offer of Sir George Grey to become Attorney General for New Munster province (February 1848).

[28] Matthew, *Emigration Fields*, 145; see also ibid, 126–8. New Zealand Company support for the re-publication of this tome was declined: minutes, court of directors, 22 February 1844, CO208/182, fo.118, TNA.

[29] Hodgkin, 'On inquiries into the races of man', in *Report of the eleventh meeting of the British Association for the Advancement of Science*, 54 (Hodgkin noted that the 'extinction of a variety of man', unlike the loss of the dodo, might be avoided: ibid).

[30] Chapman, 'Zealand, New', in *Encyclopædia Britannica*, XXI, 975. Chapman acted as editor of the Company-sponsored publication *The New Zealand Journal* until 1842. In July 1841, he travelled throughout northern England, 'for the purpose of disseminating information respecting the colony and the objects of the Company': minutes, court of directors, 22 July 1841, CO208/181, fo.111, TNA.

[31] Matthew, *Emigration Fields*, 137.

DISCIPLINING 'ADVENTURERS WITHOUT LAW': THE USES OF *IUS GENTIUM*, 1840 TO 1844[32]

From 24 October 1842, a plethora of disputes tangled Colonial Office discussions with New Zealand Company advocates. These arguments concerned the contents and parameters of Māori territorial entitlements.[33] Initially, this discord remained chiefly internal to relations between these British interests but also seared through parliamentary and ministerial theatres. Disputatiousness emerged with the Company's irritation expressed at investigations in New Zealand of its 1839 (and 1840) deeds of territorial purchase from certain Māori descent-groupings.[34] Its financial position suffered with the credibility of its titles upon which its settlement enclaves rested, as these were reviewed through this investigative process commencing in May 1842. As argued in Chapter Two, the Company's foundational purchases, entered into with elements of Ngāti Toa, Ngāti Raukawa, and Te Ātiawa, were sources of commercial security; of derivative territorial purchases from investors chiefly located in Britain.

Importantly, a consensual moment between Office and Company (dating specifically from 18 November 1840) preceded these Office and Company contests.[35] A *concordat* emerged later in 1840 during Russell's tenure as Secretary of State once the Company effectively dramatized and enlisted a substance of Whig-affiliated parliamentary support, principally *via* a select committee in the House of Commons. This process of demonstration commenced with a contrived campaign in London. The campaign began on 16 March 1840 with the concealed deliberations of a committee of the Company's directorate, named a 'secret political committee'.[36] This committee included Gibbon Wakefield, Somes (Company deputy governor), Baring (at this time also Chancellor of the Exchequer), Hutt (parliamentarian for Hull from 13 December 1832 until 23 June 1841), and Russell Ellice. It resolved at its initial gathering that 'it is desirable that petitions should be presented to parliament stating the circumstances in which New Zealand is now placed with reference to the sovereignty, and praying the immediate establishment of British law and government'.[37] As such, a petition concerning the allegedly insecure and anarchic state of European settlements was swiftly prepared. By 6 April the committee had secured London mayoral sanction for a publicized meeting in Mansion House and, ultimately, Guildhall (13 April), concerning the condition of New Zealand. Resolutions for the meeting were agreed upon within the committee and the meeting presenters were selected, including Baring's brother, Thomas Baring—an avowed Tory. Thus, a petition was carefully crafted for

[32] For mention of the phrase 'adventurers without law', see Edward Betts Hopper, diary, 14 May 1838, Ms-1033, ATL: 'His lordship [the Earl of Devon] also suggested the policy of shewing the disposition now manifested by bold adventurers to go out under any circumstances—adventurers without law'.

[33] Somes to Stanley, 24 October 1842, CO209/18, fos.250–6, TNA.

[34] See 141-162 below.

[35] Somes to Russell, 22 October 1840, CO209/8, fos.242–3a, TNA; Somes to Russell, 19 November 1840, CO209/8, fos.257–8a, TNA; arrangement, 18 November 1840: McKay (ed), *A Compendium of Official Documents relative to Native Affairs in the South Island*, I, 38–40.

[36] Political committee, New Zealand Company, 16 March 1840 ('secret, not reported'), CO208/185, fo.218, TNA.

[37] Ibid.

presentation to the Commons, not as a parochial Company document but as a generalized petition expressing anxieties concerning New Zealand affairs. This petition, entitled a 'petition of Merchants, Bankers, and Shipowners of *London*', was signed by commercial interests connected with or sympathetic to directors of the New Zealand Company or the corporation itself—Arthur Willis, Sons and Company, Desborough, and Young.[38] It lamented the absence of legal coverage for their commercial practices within New Zealand. But it also advanced a view of that archipelago as included within tales of an anglicized *ius gentium*, consisting, in part, of European maritime voyaging—exploratory tendencies concluding in acts of 'discovery'. Hence, this petition, as a concealed corporation document, claimed:

> That, in consequence of the want of a regular authority in New Zealand, emigrants to that country have had no means of acquiring land for settlement except by effecting purchases from the barbarous natives of the country, a practice which is forbidden by every other civilized government having relations with savages, and which is calculated not only to produce great uncertainty and endless litigation with respect to titles of land, but also to render impossible the adoption of any judicious system in the disposal of waste land by competent authority, for the purposes of colonization.[39]

Importantly, however, the Company in 1840 demonstrated the breadth of its relatively non-partisan support out-of-doors amongst London-centred commercial interests as well as intersections between its directorate and parliamentary factions, particularly whiggish and radical elements (Baring, Durham, Buller). It purported to reflect a constituency of political-commercial interests that required attentive negotiation from ministries—as later in 1837—rather than relative indifference—as in 1838 and 1839. These interests were shown as elements of substance with a potentiality for exerting political pressure upon an imperial administration. One director, an alderman and parliamentarian named Thompson, was requested on 5 May to approach 'Lord Eliot to appoint a time to receive a [corporate] deputation on the subject of parliamentary proceedings'.[40] Eliot had been named as a 'tory' in view of his securing appointments during Peel's ministry from later 1841, as chief secretary for Ireland and postmaster-general respectively.[41] In February 1840, however, he was a member of the provisional committee in Buxton's 'society for the extinction of the slave trade and for the civilization of Africa', instituted in June 1839.[42] He was also a confidante of Wakefield.[43] Thus, in courting imperially oriented Tory sympathizers such as Eliot, a practised diplomatist, the Company exhibited its broad parliamentary connections. Indeed, the Company had received sustenance from prominent scholarly 'liberal Anglicans', such as Whately, a confidante of Melbourne, an intimate colleague of Hinds (the Company's agent in

[38] 'New Zealand:—petition of merchants, bankers, and shipowners of *London*', *GBPP1840*, vii (582), appendix one.

[39] Ibid, 136.

[40] Minutes, board of directors, 5 May 1840, CO208/180, fo.143, TNA. Thompson was possibly 'William Thompson', a director of the Bank of England from 1827 until 1851, and Lord Mayor for London in 1829.

[41] *The Dictionary of National Biography*, Stephen and Lee (eds), VI, 603–4: Eliot, Edward Granville, third Earl of St Germans, 29 August 1798–1877, diplomatist; parliamentary member for East Cornwall from 1838 until 1845.

[42] Buxton, *The Remedy*, 11–14.

[43] Stanley to Peel, 26 December 1842, BL AddMss40467 (Peel papers), fos.343–4; Martin, *Edward Gibbon Wakefield*, 37.

Yardley in 1839 for vending the corporation's supposed territories in New Zealand), and Archbishop in Dublin.[44] Durham remained its governor whilst Baring, Chancellor of the Exchequer since August 1839, was a prominent director. In this sense, then, the Company was displaying the tendrils of its political and commercial connections to an executive department discharged with monitoring imperial locations and occasionally facilitative of imperially oriented interests.

By July, the Company's advocates were prepared to establish a Commons Select Committee to review the petition. On 7 July 1840, Eliot, in seeking the institution of such a Select Committee, harassed Russell's administration at the Commons with a cargo of literature addressing *ius gentium*, including that of Vattel and the commentaries of the American jurisprudent, James Kent. He suggested that a Vattelian view upon indigenous property rights was peculiarly apt for New Zealand. In its turn, this suggestion indicated an indifference to the Colonial Office's investiture of Māori with an inchoate agriculturist status premised upon observed subsistence patterns: 'Vattel did not place much value on the territorial rights of erratic races of people, who sparely inhabited immense regions and allowed them to remain a wilderness, because their occupation was war, and who drew their subsistence chiefly from the forest'.[45] In using *ius gentium* tactically in this fashion, there was little engagement with intelligence received from New Zealand insofar as it did not traffic with notions of Māori as cultivators of the soil—that is, whether they were ephemeral or substantive agriculturists. He seemed to assume that Māori were occupiers of scant territory as they thinly populated New Zealand, thereby defending his conflation of Amerindians and Māori. Additionally, Eliot recited lengthy excerpts from Kent's discussions on Supreme Court opinions in the United States, including *Worcester v Georgia*:[46] 'The natives were admitted to be the rightful occupants of the soil, with a legal as well as just claim to retain possession of it, and to use it according to their own direction, though not to dispose of the soil at their own will, except to the government claiming the right of pre-emption'.[47] Transplanting migrating Europeans was crucial as to 'leave the Indians in possession of the country was to leave the country a wilderness'.[48] Russell opted for not opposing Eliot's motion for a select committee: 'If the noble lord persists in his motion, I shall not now oppose it'.[49] Russell referred to Eliot's use of Vattel not Kent, proclaiming that he and Normanby had acted in compliance with what Vattel had considered laudable in the alleged conduct of William Penn in seeking 'an agreement with the

[44] Minutes, board of directors, 7 November 1839, CO208/180, fo.99, TNA: 'Resolved, that the best thanks be offered to the Lord Archbishop of Dublin, for the aid afforded by his Grace in promoting the public meeting lately held in Dublin'. See also Whately to Senior, 25 January 1838 and Whately to Hinds, 28 January 1840, *Life and Correspondence of Richard Whately*, Whately (ed), I, 414–15, 445–6.

[45] *HPD*, 3rd series, 1840, vol 60, col 528.

[46] Ibid, cols 527–8; *Worcester v Georgia* 6 Pet 515; 31 US 350 (1832).

[47] Ibid, col 527.

[48] Ibid, 527–8, citing from *Johnson v M'Intosh* 8 Wheat 543, 590 per Chief Justice Marshall (1823).

[49] Ibid, 545. '[Russell] did not dispute the principle of the passage quoted by the noble lord from Vattel. On the contrary, he thought the conduct of the British government had been in entire accordance with the principle so laid down' (ibid, 532).

natives to purchase their land and territory'.[50] Russell refrained from engaging with Eliot's use of northern American analogies.

Select Committee members included Eliot (as chairperson), Labouchere, George Hope, Gladstone, Henry Tufnell, a lord of the Treasury, Vernon Smith, Baring, Hutt, and Robert Stewart. On 13 July, Howick and Benjamin Hawes were admitted to the Select Committee whilst Hutt was discharged (as he was to supply evidence). Hawes was a parliamentary acolyte of Howick and, as noted previously, a member of the New Zealand Association of 1837. Those examined before this Select Committee included Edward Gibbon Wakefield, Saxe Bannister, John Ward, Coates, Beecham, Samuel Hinds, Enderby, and Hutt, at least five of whom were Company sympathizers or members. Wakefield had been elected as a director on 9 April 1840.[51] Russell's department was out-manoeuvred by the Company's deployment of witnesses and intellectual sources. Eliot sought to draw policy connections between New Zealand and Port Phillip ('Australia felix'), where John Batman had tried to acquire territories—approximately 600,000 acres—on behalf of a 'Port Phillip Association' through 'treaties' with local Dutigalla clan aborigines as 'possessors' in June 1835. As such, Eliot requested Colonial Office materials on 'the disallowance of certain purchases of land made from the natives' at Port Phillip, but such a request was resisted.[52] Gairdner, a senior clerk at the Colonial Office, informed Stephen and Vernon Smith that it was arranged that such evidence was already included in Henry Ward's Select Committee 'report on waste lands [and] therefore not to be given again'.[53] Still, these prior events at Port Phillip would now be generalized and used in Eliot's forthcoming report on New Zealand as indicative of a peculiarly northern American literature on *ius gentium* that criticized non-governmental 'acquisitions' of territory from aboriginal populations by Europeans.

Crucially, the Company's ability to pressure ministry representatives was revealed in its preparation of a petition, a Guildhall gathering, and a Select Committee in the Commons. Its supporters—Lang, Chapman, and Wakefield—exhibited a familiarity with northern American sources on *ius gentium* (specifically, Marshall court opinions), as well as Vattel, perhaps regarding these sources as sufficiently anglicized or indigenized to comprehend and order imperial entanglements with pre-existing inhabitants in distant locations.[54] Indeed, later in 1847, Chapman, as puisne judge in the Supreme Court at Auckland, demonstrated his intimacy with this American material, as did William Martin, the chief justice, in assisting the then governor George Grey's efforts to reassert imperial management over territorial transactions following

[50] Ibid, 534.

[51] Minutes, board of directors, 9 April 1840, CO208/180, fo.136, TNA.

[52] Eliot to Russell, 20 July 1840, CO209/8, fos.8–8a, TNA; Stephen to Vernon Smith, 21 July 1840, ibid, fo.9a. On Port Phillip, see McNeil, *Common Law Aboriginal Title*, 224–5; Shaw, 'British Policy towards the Australian aborigines, 1830–1850', 270; Bonwick, *Port Phillip Settlement*, 333–4. Shaw, *A History of the Port Phillip District*, .47–9.

[53] Gairdner, minute, 21 July 1840, CO209/8, fo.9a, TNA; Gordon Gairdner, senior clerk, 30 April 1837–1 January 1860, *Officeholders in modern Britain: vi. Colonial Office officials*, compiled J Sainty, 40.

[54] This northern American material comprised *Fletcher v Peck* 6 Cranch 87 (1810); *Johnson v M'Intosh* 8 Wheat 543 (1823); *Cherokee Nation v State of Georgia* 5 Pet 1; 8 L Ed 25 (1831); *Worcester v State of Georgia* 6 Pet 515; 31 US 350 (1832); *Mitchel v United States* 9 Pet 711; 9 L Ed 283 (1835), all decisions issued during John Marshall's tenure as chief justice of the United States Supreme Court.

FitzRoy's recall and departure as governor.[55] The third Earl Grey would celebrate the *Symonds* opinion as 'a valuable record of the principles of law applicable to cases of this nature'.[56] Significantly, however, on 28 August 1845, the law officers of the Crown did not mention this northern American material at all in considering an identical issue—the legality of FitzRoy's executive waiver of pre-emption in 1844. These officers even stated an opposite conclusion to that of Chapman and Martin, namely that such a limited waiver would not conflict with imperial legislation requiring Crown management of land transfers and the price of 'waste lands'.[57] The *Symonds* opinion, on the contrary, held that FitzRoy's proclamations of 26 March and 10 October 1844 were evasions of that 1842 statute. Certainly, the United States material selected by Lang, Wakefield, and Eliot was not referred to in any printed collections of law officers' opinions or in the barrister William Burge's commentaries upon colonial laws.[58] These American sources deployed by the Company supplied a legal coverage legitimizing its purported acquisitions in New Zealand, on the basis of Britain's alleged entitlements to 'sovereignty' there due to Cook's prior 'discovery'.[59] Yet, this was accomplished through privileging the corporation's particular activities ('systematic' or 'scientific' settling) as against other alleged 'purchasers'—or 'speculators'—in New Zealand, characterizing these others as irregular hunters of land. On 17 July 1840, Wakefield introduced a United States jurisprudential treatment of imperial relations with indigenous territories in the form of John Marshall's 1823 opinion in *Johnson v M'Intosh*.[60] He informed Eliot's Select Committee, 'I have brought with me a book, being the eighth volume of the report of cases argued and adjudged in the supreme court of the United States, by

[55] *Regina v Symonds* [1840–1932] (1847) NZPCC 387 (reported at PRO, CO209/53, fos.45–6, per Justice Chapman); Martin, *England and the New Zealanders*, 19–25. As noted in Chapter Two Chapman was intimately connected with Company objects. In 1841 he was appointed as an agent for the sale of putative Company lands (Ward to Chapman, 18 February 1841, CO208/149, fo.350, TNA) whilst he also acted as editor for a periodical it sponsored, *The New Zealand Journal*.

[56] Earl Grey to Grey, 3 December 1847, CO209/53, fo.42a, TNA.

[57] Thesiger *et al* to Stanley, 28 August 1845, CO209/39, fos.155–6, TNA; referring to 5 & 6 Vict, c36 (Imp): 'In obedience to your Lordship's request we have the honor to report that in our opinion the effect of the Proclamation being merely to waive the right of pre-emption which the Crown acquired under the Treaty of Waitangi it will not be inconsistent with the provisions of the 5 & 6 Vict c 36 although in order to perfect the Title a grant to which the Crown is to be a party is essential; but to obviate any doubt which might arise whether the land might not be considered to vest in the Crown though for an instant and for the purpose of the Transfer and so be brought within the definition of the Act, we think it advisable that in the Grants to be made in these cases the Crown should not be a granting party but merely a ratifying and confirming party' (ibid, fos.155a-156). See also CO209/40, fos.385–6a: memorandum [received 12 August 1845]; Frederick Thesiger, 1794–1878; first Baron Chelmsford; created DCL by Oxford University, 8 June 1842; elected a fellow of the Royal Society, 19 June 1845; 15 April 1844 appointed solicitor-general in succession to Sir William Follett; Attorney General from 29 June 1845.

[58] Chalmers, *Opinions of Eminent Lawyers on Various Points of English jurisprudence*; Burge, *Commentaries on colonial and foreign laws generally*.

[59] For example Lang, *New Zealand in 1839*, 74–5; Chapman, *The comparative prospects of our colonies*, 174: 'The course which ought to have been pursued, in conformity with well-established principles of international law, was simple enough. Her Majesty's sovereignty ought to have been asserted throughout New Zealand, by virtue of prior discovery and occupation. This right of sovereignty should be understood to have force only against European powers, but the rights of the chiefs should be in all cases guaranteed'.

[60] 8 Wheat 543 (1823) (USSC); John Marshall was chief justice of the United States Supreme Court from 1801 until 1835. See Berman, 'The concept of aboriginal rights in the early legal history of the United States', 637–67; Wheaton, *Elements of International Law*.

Henry Wheaton, counsellor-at-law, in which is reported a case before [that court]'.[61] He continued, privileging it as a source of 'ancient law':

> The title of the case is Johnstone *v* Mackintosh [*sic*]; and that report seems to contain a very full statement of the ancient law upon the subject of the exclusive right of the supreme authority to the waste lands of a country inhabited by savage people. Several questions were put to me on former occasions, which I was unable to answer, from my ignorance of legal matters, but I find that this report contains an answer to those questions.[62]

Wakefield and his examiners recognized *Johnson* as American literature with a potential for transmission into exotic non-northern American locations such as New Zealand. Accordingly, its application remained contestable. One illustration suffices. Hope inquired of Wakefield: 'With reference to the doctrine asserted by the American jurists on the rights of discovery over savage tribes, is it inconsistent with that claim that acts should be performed recognizing their independence on all points except the making of treaties and the disposal of lands to other nations or individuals?' Wakefield responded that there appeared to be no inconsistency, stating, 'that is the doctrine of the established law of the United States'.[63] Again, much uncertainty or neglect attended legalistic discussions of indigenous property rights. Henry Wheaton himself did not mention the Marshall court decisions when dealing with 'rights of property' in his international law text in 1836, suggesting that 'native Indians' were consistently treated as mere cyphers by interloping European polities.[64] Nevertheless, Wheaton would traverse these topics in subsequent editions, as in 1846.[65]

Eliot issued a report dated 30 July 1840, transferring this jurisprudential cargo to an antipodean context, encompassing not only New Zealand but also Port Phillip in what became Victoria—an *ex post facto* characterization of events. In this vein, it was critical of the procedures adopted by the Colonial Office for permitting, *ipso facto*, British 'adventurers without law' to proceed to New Zealand shorelines and enter into unhindered proprietary deals with Māori. Its foundational observation was that New Zealand had 'attracted British emigrants, in large numbers to its shores'.[66] Imperial discipline ought to have been swiftly asserted in circumstances 'where Englishmen have been residing for years past in a condition of society which can only be described as one of positive anarchy'.[67] The Office's assumed indolence in normatively guiding (disciplining) these developments was supposed to have resulted in severe implications for anglo-settling: 'Disputes about the boundaries of land purchased [from Māori] have arisen, and conflicting claims have been set up'.[68] It was supposed, as Merivale had lectured in 1839, that a European emigrant's 'first impulse, if a man of spirit and energy, is to separate from his brethren, to plunge into the wilderness, to erect his own domestic monarchy

[61] Wakefield, evidence, 17 July 1840, *GBPP1840*, vii (582), 511.

[62] Ibid. [63] Ibid, 514.

[64] Wheaton, *Elements of International Law*, I, 210: 'In the various wars, treaties, and negotiations, to which the conflicting pretensions of the different states of Christendom to territory on the American continent have given rise, the primitive title of the Indians has been entirely overlooked, or left to be disposed of by the states within whose limits they happened to fall'.

[65] Wheaton, *Elements of International Law*, 3rd edn, 73–4; Hickford, '"Vague Native Rights to Land"', 182–3.

[66] *GBPP1840*, vii (582), vi. [67] Ibid, vii.

[68] Ibid. Cf ibid, John Blackett (described as a mate in the service of the Royal Navy), evidence, 17 July 1840, 519.

apart from all others'.[69] Coates' own communications with the Colonial Office suggested a decrease in commodious behaviour both amongst and between Māori and Europeans at sites like Kaikohe when Māori transferred identical or contiguous tracts to various European visitors.[70]

Thematically, Eliot's Select Committee report was attuned to restraining or managing transactions involving European settlements and Māori, interposing a vigorous imperial administration in the liminal spaces of political-diplomatic negotiations and proprietary transactions. It also focussed upon acreage pricing of territories transferred from the Crown to anglo-settlers, with the Select Committee advising a Wakefieldian uniform price at not less than 20 shillings per acre.[71] In essence, this accorded with Russell's recent instructions to a land and emigration commission, consisting of Thomas Elliot, Edward Villiers, and Torrens. Russell suggested rather disingenuously, in view of its various applications, that, since 1831, a principle had been 'most distinctly acknowledged and inflexibly observed' such that 'waste lands' could not be transferred *via* a 'gratuitous donation'.[72] For Russell, the status of allegedly 'unoccupied lands' was relatively unproblematic in that such territories would be vested in right of the Crown: 'every private title must rest upon a Royal grant as its basis';[73] 'New Holland and probably New Zealand contain districts which it is not possible to exhaust by any rational scheme of colonization for a long course of years'.[74]

What introduced issues of indigenous proprietary rights into focus—thence requiring integration into the disciplining and revenue-collecting orientations of whiggish imperial administration—was the presence of prior inhabitants together with the production of 'purchase' deeds with Māori by 'adventurers'. This remained the essence of 'humane' impulses in imperial policy formulation (clearly not simply missionary predilections operating upon Stephen). In this sense, there was a conjunction or convergence between the Committee and the Office as to the mechanics of administering and disposing of imperial territories. Similarly, at this broadly thematic level, the Aborigines' Protection Society committee under Buxton, Thomas Hodgkin, another Quaker, and others, favoured disciplining the presence of European migrants in distant fields in their commercial engagements with indigenous populations: 'Instead of opposing colonization, [the committee] only desired to see the system on which it is now extensively carried on, so improved as to render the spread of British colonies beneficial, not ruinous, to the Aborigines'.[75]

[69] Merivale, *Introduction to a course of lectures on colonization*, 24.

[70] Coates to Stephen, private, 11 June 1840, CO209/8, fos.163–3a, TNA, enclosing 'extract of a letter from Mr. R. Davis to D. Coates, *Esq*, dated Waimate, Nov 18/39', fos.164–5.

[71] *GBPP1840*, vii (582), ix: 'the lands to be vested in the Crown shall be disposed of, by sale only, at a uniform price, and not by auction, such price not being less than 20*s*. per acre. In preferring the South Australian principle to any other mode of disposal of public lands, Your Committee are glad to express their concurrence in the instructions given on this head by [Russell] to the Colonial Land and Emigration Commissioners, which *expressly recommend the adoption of this principle in the future colony of New Zealand*' (emphasis added); Russell to Elliot, Villiers, Torrens, 14 January 1840, CO385/19, fo.252, TNA.

[72] Russell to Elliot, Villiers, Torrens, 14 January 1840, CO385/19, fo.243, TNA.

[73] Ibid, 242.

[74] Ibid, 251. In indices of correspondence, Australia and New Zealand were often clustered together: see, eg CO326/315 and CO326/316.

[75] *The second annual report of the Aborigines' Protection Society*, 21. See also, *The third annual report of the Aborigines' Protection Society*, 36, 40–1; Stocking, *Victorian Anthropology*, 242–3; Rose, *Curator of the Dead*, 105–9, 111–13.

Eliot's report introduced a literature that was distinctly American. This was novel, as it was a literature that explicitly located aborigines in an imperial disposal of proprietary interests. It specifically referred to Kent's legal commentaries and *Johnson*, and responded to Wakefield's citation of the latter in his evidence on 17 July. The Company was endeavouring to preserve a territorial status quo in which it was already embedded with its own purchase deeds and settlers. Its deeds were the bases of its titles, as were its emigrants already placed upon New Zealand coasts. It sought to characterize other purchasers as rapacious land-hunters, not as agents of systematic settlements. Eliot's report favoured Company views on the alleged irregularity of land purchasing within New Zealand. Thus, the jurisprudential sources raised in the Committee hearings supplied a fount for critiquing Colonial Office policies towards indigenous New Zealand whilst privileging Company (Wakefieldian) precepts on territorial transfer. On this account 'the acknowledgment of the independent nationality of the natives has given a sanction to the acquirement of land by individual purchasers'. Eliot's report alleged that '[w]hen the right of the natives to sell to all the world was admitted by the British Government, it followed that all persons, whether British subjects or others, had a right to buy without its sanction'. Hence, the Committee urged, there was no curative for this situation but the swift enactment of legislation to arrest the ill consequences of 'unrestricted colonization', an unsanctioned process that might undermine the preservation of 'that interesting race'— Māori.[76] Imperial legislation would be required to confirm the 'possessory rights of the natives', but that 'the Crown should have the exclusive right of pre-emption over all such lands as they may be disposed to alienate'.[77] This critique of recognizing a diplomatic independence in at least certain Māori and in the subsequently swift speculative pursuit of territories was also evident in the Company directorate's report of 14 May 1840 to its shareholders: 'Upon mature reflection your directors see no other effectual remedy for these evils, than for the government to take upon itself the duty of a trustee for the public, and to become the sole proprietor of all the lands in New Zealand, on the principle of equitable compensation to those who have *bonâ fide* obtained possessions there'.[78] Two months subsequently, Eliot's report stated that a remedial imperial enactment would have proved unnecessary had:

> the British Government... from the year 1769 downwards, never lost sight of the principle which was formerly acted upon by this country, and by all other European powers, with regard to their North American possessions, and had refused to recognise any titles to land founded on purchases made by private persons from savages. This principle has been adopted by the United States, and it has constantly guided their government in its dealings with its Indian tribes inhabiting the North American continent, and it has been solemnly declared by the Supreme Court of Judicature in the United States to be a principle of international law. According to this principle, the nation by whose subjects a new country is discovered, acquires thereby a title to its possessions as against all foreign powers. That title, when completed by occupation, gives to the discovering nation the sole right to purchase the soil from the natives, to establish settlements within its territory, and to regulate its relations with foreign powers.[79]

[76] *GBPP1840*, vii (582), vii. [77] Ibid, ix.

[78] *The first report of the directors of the New Zealand Company*, 32.

[79] *GBPP1840*, vii (582), vii and note: '*See* particularly the case Johnson *v* Macintosh, 8 Wheaton's Rep. 543. *See* also Kent's Commentaries, vol. 3, p.376'.

Furthermore, it was assumed that Glenelg and Bourke, the then New South Wales governor, had used this American principle in Port Phillip. In Eliot's Select Committee of 1840, any Māori historical agency was formalistically eliminated with the recitation of an introduced northern American jurisprudence to fill out the Office's hitherto satisficing[80] policies represented by asserting a non-theorized pre-emptive entitlement. Māori were subsumed into a jurisprudential account of imperial encounters with indigenous inhabitants in northern America. Amerindians were introduced into tales of New Zealand with Wakefield inviting the uses of jurisprudential sources for prescribing imperial practices. The prior occupation of land by indigenous communities was explained as a rhetorical adjunct to the central issue of an imperial administration managing proprietary transactions. Māori were treated as part of a policy landscape—part of a multifarious procedural terrain involving the managing of settlement and revenue. Certainly, in later 1840, interest was expressed in obtaining statistical returns from imperial governors regarding receipts from the sale of 'waste lands' since 1 January 1831.[81]

Indigenous 'possessory rights' merely performed a secondary conceptual function, underpinning substantive discussions concerning anglophone elements enlisting *ius gentium*. Imprecision persisted regarding the understanding of such entitlements. The Company's strategy had shifted to characterizing itself as assisting Russell's Colonial Office in the tactics of pre-emption—suggesting that it had acted on behalf of an indolent Crown in acquiring territories for settling. It indicated the transmission of a literature on *ius gentium*, previously localized to United States scenes but applicable to situations in the southern Pacific. Intriguingly, however, there were contra-indications in the musings of Wakefield and the directorate as late as 24 July 1840, thus suggesting the tactical concerns of the Company in using intellectual sources. In July, the directorate asserted that Gipps' 14 January 1840 proclamation of an impending investigation into non-sanctioned acquisitions of land from Māori was unlawful at 'international law'. What was objectionable was the Crown's claim 'to interfere with private rights of property in a country which the Crown itself declares to be a foreign, independent, sovereign state (and which rights were previously acquired by purchase and cession from chiefs or others having equally valid powers with those whom the Crown has since acquired sovereign rights)'.[82] Similarly, in its negotiations with Thomas Woollcombe of the affiliated 'Plymouth Company' (based in Devon and Cornwall) throughout 1840, the Company used a definition of pre-emption predicated on a party merely possessing a first option to acquire territory from a vendor.[83] Perhaps these distinct approaches also reflected sheer confusion and ambiguity in legalistic approaches to relations with aborigines overseas.

In treating the sympathetic disposition of the Select Committee as partisan, Stephen rejected Eliot's deployment of United States jurisprudence as imparting no insights for imperial policies towards indigenous New Zealand and, politically, as a tool for Company sympathizers within parliamentary spheres. Stephen was sensitive to the

[80] 'Satisficing' is used to signify deciding upon or pursuing a course of action that would meet the minimum requirements necessary to satisfy a specific objective.

[81] Circular, 21 December 1840, CO854/2, fo.423, TNA.

[82] Minutes, court of directors, 24 July 1840, CO208/180, fo.172, TNA.

[83] Minutes, court of directors, 25 June 1840, CO208/180, fo.159, TNA; minutes, court of directors, 16 July 1840 CO208/180, fo.163, TNA..

tactical nature of these proceedings. This jurisprudence had not emerged in Office musings on indigenous New Zealand in the past (whether overseen by Glenelg, Normanby, or Russell). It would not resurface in Colonial Office records again until 1844.[84] Gipps exhibited an intimacy with it in Sydney, New South Wales (August 1840). He invoked the relevant literature, citing that of Kent. Yet, there was not the predictability of its thoroughgoing doctrinal accessibility or application as McHugh, Reynolds, or Hackshaw might suggest.[85] Once Wakefield raised *Johnson v M'Intosh* as an intellectual source on 17 July 1840, Stephen disputed any pertinence for that Marshall court opinion concerning questions of imperial policy towards indigenous communities.[86] He expressed these viewpoints in a memorandum of 28 July to Vernon Smith, the latter acting not only in his capacity as parliamentary under-secretary but also as an Eliot Select Committee member. This memorandum's provenance is not clear as it is embedded amongst unrelated correspondence. Yet one might imagine Vernon Smith requesting Stephen for an opinion on the case following its production by Wakefield before the Commons Committee.[87] Stephen distanced himself with an appraisal of the *Johnson* decision: 'The case of *Johnson and MacIntosh* [*sic*] proves that a grant from an Indian Tribe of lands in the state of [Ohio] would confer on the practice no valid title in defezance of a Title derived under a grant from the United States'.[88] Continuing with that passage, Stephen commented: 'It shows that the whole Territory over which those tribes wandered was to be regarded as the property of the British Crown in right of discovery and of conquest—and that the Indians were mere proprietors on sufferance. Such is American law'.[89] In contrast to Gipps in New South Wales, he distinguished opinions from a United States Supreme Court as irrelevant: 'British law in Canada is far more humane, for there, the Crown purchases of the Indians, before it grants to its own subjects'. He refrained from supplying evidence of this assumed distinction, whilst variations in the territorial practices of Canadian provinces, such as Prince Edward Island, were all too evident, as Russell noted in January 1840.[90] Yet the answer lies in Stephen's understanding of what Marshall observed in *Johnson v M'Intosh*: discovering European jurisdictions 'claimed and exercised, as a consequence

[84] Motte to Hope, opinion, 'land claims in New Zealand', 31 May 1844, CO209/32, fos.288–305, TNA. The speculative nature of this jurisprudence applying to New Zealand is revealed in Elliot, memorandum, June 1843, CO209/24, fo.137: 'This stipulation in the Treaty [on pre-emption] is ***believed*** to be in consonance with the mode of dealing with the aboriginal owners or claimants of Lands in analogous cases in other parts of the world: to fall into a broad current of precedent' (emphasis added).

[85] McHugh, *The Maori Magna Carta*; Reynolds, *The Law of the Land*, 46–8; Reynolds, *Frontier*, 134–5, 137–8; Hackshaw, 'Nineteenth century notions of aboriginal title and their influence on the interpretation of the Treaty of Waitangi', in Kawharu (ed), *Waitangi*, 92–120.

[86] 8 Wheat 543 (1823).

[87] Hickford, '"Decidedly the Most Interesting Savages"', 151.

[88] Stephen to Vernon Smith, 28 July [1840], CO209/4, fo.343, TNA. In the manuscript source, this minute was misdated with a pencilled inscription '1839' (when Vernon Smith was not in the Colonial Office until September). Unfortunately, this incorrect notation has been followed by McHugh and Mellor: McHugh, 'Aboriginal title in New Zealand courts', 240, n 21;Mellor, *British Imperial Trusteeship*, 355–6. Note that the term '[Ohio]' was inserted in the original in substitution for a misspelling whereas the misguided '[not]' was added to the original by an editorial flourish (perhaps either Stephen or Vernon Smith), creating a double negative. This extract reads correctly if the reference to '[not]' is expunged.

[89] Stephen to Vernon Smith, 28 July [1840], CO209/4, fo.343, TNA..

[90] Russell to Elliot, Villiers, Torrens, 14 January 1840, CO385/19, fos.248–9, TNA.

of [the] ultimate dominion [asserted on the basis of prior discovery], a power to grant the soil, while yet in possession of the natives'.[91] Marshall concluded: 'Thus has our whole country been granted to the crown while in the occupation of the Indians'. Such 'grants purport to convey the soil as well as the right of dominion to the grantees'. In referring to the conveyance of the proprietorship of Virginia, Marshall opined: 'It has never been objected to this, or any other similar grant, that the title as well as possession was in the Indians when it was made, and that it passed nothing on that account'.[92] The jurist Story in his *Commentaries on the Constitution of the United States* (1833) echoed these sentiments.[93] Moreover, the innards or contents of Native American title were as sparingly appreciated in Canadian contexts as indigenous property was understood in New Zealand or Australia. Evidence abounds of this indifference about the substance of these rights in the investigation of the Canadian Indian Department's operations during the late 1830s and throughout the 1840s.[94] This evidence also indicates that concerns were expressed in certain quarters as to how Amerindian interests in Upper Canada had been undermined through a diverse range of British territorial policies since the beginning of the nineteenth century. Vast blocks had been acquired from 1818 in Upper Canada to furnish spaces for future settlements. Annuities were paid rather than a single 'purchase' sum. Some territories had been leased by Iroquois bands for 999 years with the encouragement of the imperial administration in the early nineteenth century and succeeded by patent grants from the Crown.

In treating the Select Committee sympathies towards the Company as partisan and politicized, Stephen rejected the report's use of this *ius gentium* literature in New Zealand or neighbouring Australia. The report attempted to integrate this American literature with Wakefieldian premises and the Goderich directives since 1831, mantling these practices with non-English textual sources. Stephen and Vernon Smith favoured policy rather than being riveted to any pre-set legal discourse.[95] Significantly, Duly and Burroughs have demonstrated that there were significant variations in imperial territorial policies even following 1831, indicating an empire of variations even as assorted 'systematizing' tendencies were observed in a Colonial Office haphazardly orienting towards a distantly imposed 'empire of uniformity' throughout settlement colonies.[96] *Ius gentium* intermeshed with northern American sources might supply the literary foundations for 'regularity' in alienating 'waste lands'. Yet, Stephen thought such jurisprudence self-serving, commenting warily, '[w]hatever may be the ground occupied by international jurists they never forget the policy and interests of their own country'. Further, 'Vattel, in the interest of Holland, laid down the principle of open fisheries. Mr. Marshall, great as he was, was still an American, and adjudicated against the rights of the Indians'.[97] Again, a sense of stadial histories emerged, echoing Glenelg's prior assessment

[91] 8 Wheat 543, 574. [92] Ibid, 579–80.

[93] Story, *Commentaries on the Constitution of the United States*, I, 8, 135.

[94] Jarvis to Macaulay, 7 March 1839, CO42/516, fos.165–72, TNA; Jarvis to commissioners of Indian affairs, 30 January 1843, CO42/516, fos.118–55a, TNA; 'report of committee no. 4, on Indian Department [1st February 1840]', ibid, fos.7–18a.

[95] Hickford, '"Vague Native Rights to Land", 185; Hickford, '"Decidedly the Most Interesting Savages"', 151–5.

[96] Duly, *British Land Policy at the Cape*, 185. Burroughs, *Britain and Australia*, 202–51 ('theoretical considerations' in imperial territorial policy). For the phrase 'empire of uniformity', see Tully, *Strange Multiplicity*, 58–98.

[97] Stephen to Vernon Smith, 28 July [1840], CO209/4, fos.343–3a, TNA.

of Māori attainments in December 1837 ('not Savages living by the Chase')—personnel in Westminster pursuing familiarity in intellectual appraisals of distant Māori. In suggesting that *Johnson v M'Intosh* was inapplicable, Stephen opined:

> the New Zealand[er]s are not wandering tribes; but bodies of men, till lately, very populous, who have a settled form of Government, and who have divided and appropriated the whole territory amongst them. They are not huntsmen, but after their rude fashion, Agricultur[a]lists.[98]

Mission representatives within New Zealand, such as Thomas Kendall, Richard Davis, and George Clarke, Kororāreka beachcombers or traders, had secured their location upon territorial tracts amongst Māori via deeds of 'purchase', as both the Colonial Office and Company well knew.[99] The first such recorded deed was entered into by Church Missionary Society agents with one 'Ahoodee o Gunna [*Te Uri-o-Kanae*] king of Rangee Hoo [*Rangihoua*]' on 24 February 1815.[100] Whatever the intentions of Samuel Marsden or the Māori parties—difficult to divine in both cases—this relationship at Rangihoua was acknowledged as having been mediated by a document that claimed to be a deed of 'purchase'. Yet, from 1839, the Office tried to discipline such entanglements, having opted in later 1837 and early 1838 for facilitating interests that favoured an allegedly 'systematic' settlement of New Zealand. Ironically, the conduct of these disparate pathfinders in New Zealand, including mission-station catechists and traders, had, in purchasing territories, paved a way for the Company's subsequent use of paper deeds as purportedly reflecting acquisitions within New Zealand and the Office's belated efforts to discipline unsanctioned anglophone-settling. Significantly, then, Durham had informed Wakefield of the soundness of this approach as early as 3 September 1837. He stated: 'In South Australia there was no appropriated land—in New Zealand there is—acquired by purchase from the native proprietors'.[101] Despite what Belgrave argues, the Company's recognition of Māori title was not 'largely a piece of window dressing, designed to appease influential public opinion moulded by the [Church Missionary Society] and the Aboriginal Protection Society'.[102] It was recognized in earnest for mounting a politically and commercially persuasive basis for its proprietary, settling, and commercial operations, an insight that administrators within the Office well appreciated.[103] There was, unsurprisingly, an element of propaganda. But 'native title' was principally functional.

Moreover, this Office, under Russell and Stanley, haltingly constructed notions of indigenous proprietorship in contests with the Company from 1840 as it asserted its

[98] Ibid, 343a. Cf Glenelg, memorandum, 15 December 1837, CO209/2, fo.409, TNA.

[99] For example Richard Davis and 'Tohu', deed of purchase, 20 December 1831, OLC1/736, ANZ(W); 'list of lands held in trust for the natives by the Church Missionary Society, at Port Nicholson or in the neighbourhood of the New Zealand Co[mpany]'s settlement', OLC1/658–9; *Muriwhenua Land Report—Wai-45*, ch 3, 'Pre-Treaty transactions'. The first deed of purchase in New Zealand was signed under Marsden's auspices at Rangihoua, 24 February 1815: Salmond, *Between Worlds*, 505–6.

[100] Nicholas, *Narrative of a Voyage to New Zealand*, II, 194–5. See also 'Nayti [Ngaiti]', evidence, 10 April 1838, *GBPP1837–1838*, xxi (680), 117 (copy of deed produced).

[101] Durham to Wakefield, 3 September 1837, Ms140/5:2, ATL.

[102] Belgrave, 'Pre-emption, the Treaty of Waitangi and the politics of Crown purchase', 28.

[103] Sorrenson has hinted at this interpretation in 'Treaties in British colonial policy: precedents for Waitangi', in Renwick (ed), *Sovereignty and indigenous rights*, 23, 27–8. See also Shaw, *A History of the Port Phillip District*, 47–9, 61–2, 112.

management of territories in New Zealand. Thus, a Colonial Office could attempt to bypass the practice of producing paper deeds of 'purchase' representing the unauthorized placement or dispersal of Europeans within *Australasian* aboriginal territories—New Zealand, Port Phillip—by inserting itself into this process. This might be accomplished by disciplining the transactional engagements of 'adventurers without law' through investigating, managing, and perhaps vitiating these deeds; by managing future territorial transactions (recognizing certain titles albeit not others, acreage pricing, surveying); and by collecting sales revenues. This was a process localized in space and time albeit perhaps with ramifications for regions beyond such as Port Natal. Territorial claims were putative imperial assets. Gipps' activities in Sydney and Hobson's at Kororāreka—in two proclamations purporting to prohibit non-governmental territorial transactions with Māori—were predicated upon this predisposition in policy.[104] Glenelg's department approached unlicensed 'purchases' at Port Phillip in this fashion, wishing to bypass paper deeds of land purchase drafted by a 'Port Phillip association'. It denied the legitimacy of these transactions. Were such transactional engagements with aborigines recognized, 'such a concession would subvert the foundation on which all proprietary rights in New South Wales at present rest'.[105] As Stephen noted in October 1836, 'the case of Port Philip [*sic*]' illustrated a 'prevailing triumph of popular feelings over positive law [since] a large body of persons appeared in that vicinity, & having formed themselves into an organised association, took possession of considerable tracts of land under grants from the neighbouring chiefs'.[106] He continued by stating, '*with this semblance of title*... Port Philip [*sic*] assumed the appearance of an established settlement, with extensive & valuable flocks & herds'—paper deeds providing cover for ovine accumulation and pastoral enterprises.[107] The Company opted for an identical strategy to this 'Port Phillip association', using paper deeds with aborigines. These imperial disciplinary preoccupations mingled, in their turn, with Wakefieldian precepts on funding emigration, sufficient acreage prices, and revenue from transferring 'waste lands', as recognized in Chapter Two. As Glenelg cautioned Bourke:

> It is wholly vain to expect that any positive laws will be energetic enough to repress the spirit and enterprize and speculation in which the unauthorized settlement of Port Philip [*sic*]... has originated.... To engage in such a struggle would be wholly irrational. All that remains for the Government is to assume the *guidance* of enterprizes, which it may conduct to happy results, though it cannot prevent or retard them.[108]

Somes, elected as governor of the New Zealand Company on 3 September 1840 after the incapacitation and eventual death of Durham (28 July 1840), suggested a cordial adjustment of relations between Company and Office in October 1840: 'The scene of the

[104] Gipps to Russell, 9 February 1840, CO209/6, fo.6, TNA: 'The third proclamation [14 January 1840] was issued, in order to put an end, as far as possible, to the speculations in New Zealand lands, which were then being carried on in Sydney'.

[105] Glenelg to Bourke, 13 April 1836, *GBPP1836*, xi (512), 740.

[106] Stephen to 'colonisation commissioners' (South Australia), 27 October 1836, CO396/1, fo.232, TNA.

[107] Ibid (emphasis added). Cf Saxe Bannister, evidence, 17 July 1840, *GBPP1840*, vii (582), 516–17, referring to 'case[s] of private individuals setting about this sort of [settlement] enterprise without infringing the prerogative of the Crown [Port Natal, Honduras]'.

[108] Cited in Bannister, *Memoir respecting the colonization of Natal, in south-eastern Africa*, 4 (emphasis in original). See also 'regulation of our migrations, not their prohibition': Bannister, *British enterprise beyond sea, from the earliest original sources to the present times*, I, lxxx.

Company's operations is now part of Her Majesty's Dominions: its property is now under the protection of her Majesty and of the laws of England'.[109] Somes continued: 'It has also become of great importance to the Company that we should without delay know in what light the government intends to regard the rights which have been acquired by the Company as well as by other persons who have purchased land and expended money in the settlement of New Zealand'.[110] On 5 October 1840, the court of directors had established a secret committee consisting of Somes, Petre, Willis, Gowen, and Wakefield.[111] Company members, Petre and Baring, together with a parliamentary supporter, Buller, managed negotiations with Vernon Smith, Stephen, and Russell throughout October 1840. Buller appears to have been responsible for representing the Company in advising amendments to the suggested arrangement during the negotiation process.[112]

Russell was preoccupied with managing revenue collection (acreage pricing) and anglo-settlement dispersion in distant locations through disciplining transactional procedures, namely those of proprietary purchase. He advised Vernon Smith in October 1840 that a corporation could be included within 'the intentions of government respecting past and future sales of land'.[113] He suggested that '[w]here persons have acquired land at a very low rate, and have incurred expence [*sic*] in improvement & settlement, land to be granted at the rate of an acre for every five shillings so expended'.[114] This concession materialized in an agreement between Office and Company, in the fourth clause of the agreement's first part (18 November). Thus, 'the Company' would be issued with 'a grant from the Crown to them, . . . of as many acres of land as shall be equal to four times the number of pounds sterling [that is, five shillings per acre] which they shall be found to have expended', on, *inter alia*, 'the purchase of lands in New Zealand from the native chiefs and others', transmitting emigrants, executing constructions for settlement sites.[115] Aboriginal proprietorship was incorporated as a procedural feature of disciplining anglo-settlements. The Office and its procedures in Britain and New Zealand would determine what was bought and what was not. Recognizing and discussing aboriginal property was inextricably procedural. Making 'territorial rights of the natives' through a Colonial Office constrained European interlopers and assured revenue sources via the management of land sales.[116] This was crucial. Such an approach coalesced with imperial legislation enacted in 1842 for the management of a category of territory named 'waste lands' in 'Australian provinces', including 'adjacent islands' such as New Zealand.[117] No 'waste

[109] Somes to Russell, 22 October 1840, CO209/8, fo.241a, TNA.

[110] Ibid, 242.

[111] Minutes, court of directors, 5 October 1840, CO208/180, fo.198, TNA; Secret committee, 5 October 1840, CO208/186, fo.20; ibid, 13 October 1840, fos.21–2; ibid, 21 October 1840, fos.23–4, TNA.

[112] Stephen, minute, 23 October 1840, CO209/8, fo.247, TNA; Russell, minute, 24 October 1840, CO209/8, fos.247a–8, TNA.

[113] Russell, minute, October 1840, CO209/8, fo.297a, TNA; cf Vernon Smith to Russell, 14 October 1840, CO209/8, fo.296a, TNA; Stephen, minute, 30 October 1840, CO209/8, fos.299a–300.

[114] Ibid, fo.298.

[115] Clauses four and one (part one), arrangement, 18 November 1840: McKay, *A Compendium of Official Documents*, I, 38–9.

[116] Russell to Hobson, 28 January 1841, CO209/8, fo.454, TNA: 'territorial rights of the natives'.

[117] Stanley to Hobson, 15 September 1842, CO537/121, fo.3–3a, TNA; 'An Act for regulating the sale of waste land belonging to the Crown in the *Australian* Colonies', 5 & 6 Vict, c36 (22 June 1842)

land of the Crown' was to be 'sold at less than 20 shillings an acre'.[118] Thus, Russell's successor, the Whig-turned-Tory affiliate Viscount Stanley, persevered with this revenue-oriented and settlement-disciplining strategy from late 1841. Stanley acted to legislate this policy through promoting what became 'An Act for regulating the sale of waste land belonging to the Crown in the Australian colonies' in 1842.[119] Stanley's private papers contain an extensive memorandum dated October 1841 from Thomas Frederick Elliot on 'letters bearing on the intention' of the imperial government to use a fixed and uniform price of land throughout New Zealand. In May 1841, Justice Willis of New South Wales provided Stanley with extensive notes on the alienation of Crown lands in the Port Phillip district ('Australia Felix') of New South Wales according to the recent instructions and regulations of 31 May 1840, 5 December 1840, and 21 January 1841.[120] In 1840, the Company's territorial theatre in New Zealand, albeit privileged by the *concordat*, was accordingly constrained:

> The lands so to be assigned to the Company shall be taken by them in that part of the Colony of New Zealand at which their settlement has been formed, and to which they have laid claim in virtue of contracts made by them with the Natives or others, antecedently to the arrival of Captain Hobson, as Her Majesty's Lieutenant-Governor at New Zealand.[121]

In addition, its ultimate grant in *each* of Port Nicholson and New Plymouth was not to exceed a specified acreage (160,000 acres). Russell's office appointed the Treasury's James Pennington to calculate the Company's acreage entitlements under the agreement's criteria. These concessions were characterized as 'the adjustment retrospectively of the claims which the Company has established to favourable consideration for themselves and for the emigrants whom they have sent to New Zealand'.[122] Given subsequent events, this agreement was bedevilled with inconsistencies, with the text defying those acts executed under it, rendering it a veritable shape-changer. By 31 May 1841, Pennington had already produced two reports indicating that the Company was entitled to receive a Crown grant comprising 531,929 acres.[123] A court of directors' minute construed this as 'land which the Company is entitled to receive *immediately*', a position they would persistently exhort from 1840.[124] This amount increased to at least 712,593 acres by 6 July 1845.[125] Viscount Stanley, then Secretary of State for Colonies, stated, 'you will perceive that the total amount proved to the satisfaction of [Pennington] to have been expended by the Company under the agreement of November 1840 amounts

(Imp), s 2: 'by the Words "*Australian* Colonies", as employed in this Act, are intended and described the Colonies of New South Wales, Van Diemen's Land, South Australia, and Western Australia, and New Zealand'.

118 Stanley to Hobson, 15 September 1842, CO537/121, 11, TNA. 5 & 6 Vict, c36 (Imp), ss 8, 5, and 11.

119 'An Act for regulating the sale of waste land belonging to the Crown in the Australian colonies', 5 & 6 Vict c36 (22 June 1842).

120 Willis, May 1841, 920 Der(14), 24/2, Liverpool Record Office (LRO).

121 McKay, *A Compendium of Official Documents*, I, 39 (cl five, pt one).

122 Stephen to Vernon Smith, 14 October 1840, CO209/8, fos.281a–2, TNA.

123 Vernon Smith to colonial land and emigration commissioners, 31 May 1841, CO209/11, fos.1-37–8a, TNA.

124 Minutes, court of directors, 3 June 1841, CO208/181, fo.72, TNA (emphasis added).

125 Stanley to Grey, secret, 6 July 1845, CO209/40, fos.346a–7, TNA; Hope to Grey, 27 November 1845, CO209/39, fos.468–9a (1,300,000 acres). The agreement of 18 November 1840 became embroiled with William Spain's investigation of the Company's alleged purchases of land: see 141-154 below.

to £178,148-4-2'.[126] By 1845, these acres were scattered throughout several enclaves: Company settlements at Nelson, Wellington, New Plymouth, 'New Edinburgh', Otago (*Otākou*), Whanganui, and Manawatu. The territorial constraints in the arrangement shifted imperceptibly. Thus, it was a profoundly political and procedural arrangement, with the procedures arising in the staged disciplining of proprietary transactions, acreage amounts, and hence settlement-dispersion. As Henry Ward warned Labouchere in the Commons on 27 June 1839, 'the Government cannot check the tide of emigration [to New Zealand]'.[127]

Yet, the Office could try to control the pace and geographical extent of settlement. As Stephen appreciated, premature settlement-dispersion was to be disciplined. Should the Crown encourage 'settlements anywhere and everywhere, [it becomes] bound to follow the settlers with protection, police, the administration of justice and so on—thus multiplying indefinitely the expenses of governing the country and promoting the premature dispersion of the inhabitants'.[128] Caution was observed in finessing and finalizing the arrangement, with Russell noting, '[a]s we have to deal with Mr. Wakefield, who is behind the curtain, it will be desirable . . . to have the Agreement looked over by the Solicitor General or if the Attorney General is in town, by him'.[129] This cautionary review would impart no paper trails, however: 'I do not mean a formal reference but that we should see how the agreement would be construed by the Lords, the Judges, or the Court of Chancery'.[130] It did not emerge in Russell's personal papers.[131] A charter for the Company followed on 12 February 1841.[132] This charter secured the Company's coveted ambition of securing governmental sanction of its commercial and territorial objects within New Zealand. These impending events excited Wakefield. On 26 October 1840, he informed his fellow director, William Molesworth, '[t]he main parts are in Lord Elliot's [*sic*] report with this addition, that our Company is really to be the agent of the state for colonising [New Zealand]'.[133] He continued, 'Lord John has behaved very well and Stephen excellently', noting that, 'I am very glad to think that your spec[ulation] in New Zealand shares must now turn out very profitable'.[134] Yet, the Company delayed declaring its substantial dividend of ten per cent until 1 May 1841, once assured of its concordat with Russell's department.[135] Thus, these tales of a corporation and Colonial Office were complex.

126 Stanley to Grey, secret, 6 July 1845, CO209/40, 346a. 'Minutes of communications between Lord Stanley and a deputation from the directors of the New Zealand Company consisting of the Hon[oura]ble Francis Baring, Viscount Ingestre, Sir Isaac Lyon Goldsmid Bart & George Frederick Young Esq', 27 June and 1 July 1845, CO209/39, fos.338–8a, TNA.

127 *The Debate upon Mr. Ward's Resolutions on Colonization, in the House of Commons, 27 June 1839*, Ward, 'New Zealand is colonizing itself', 28.

128 Stephen to Vernon Smith, 1 February 1841, CO209/11, fo.40a, TNA; Vernon Smith to Russell, 1 February 1841 and Russell, 2 February 1841, CO209/11, fo.40a.

129 Russell, minute, 24 October 1840, CO209/8, fo.248, TNA.

130 Ibid.

131 *Vide*, PRO30/22/3E (Russell papers, PRO).

132 McKay, *A Compendium of Official Documents*, I, 42–7.

133 Fawcett, *Life of the Right Hon Sir William Molesworth, Bart, MP, FRS*, 179. Molesworth resigned as a director in February 1843: minutes, court of directors, 9 February 1843, CO208/181, fos.301–2, TNA; ibid, fos.302–4.

134 Fawcett, *Life of the Right Hon Sir William Molesworth*, 180.

135 Minutes, court of directors, 23 April 1841, CO208/181, fo.37, TNA; Anonymous, *The New Zealand Company*, 8.

The Company was not solely speculative in its enterprises. It behaved as an earnest agency of systematic colonization. In 1839, before it released its initial prospectus of 2 May, a committee of its provisional directors (Wakefield, Petre, Hutt, Somes, and Gordon) oversaw Ernst Dieffenbach's appointment as a naturalist to accompany the *Tory* expedition.[136] It supervised or arranged for the introduction of various British flora and fauna, including bees (in May 1842), into New Zealand settlements. Hence, 'the Court [of directors] has taken steps through Mr. Gowen, one of the directors, and also a member of the Council of the Horticultural Society of London to procure and send out by the first vessel a supply of the seeds of all the best fruits &*c* cultivated in Great Britain'.[137] As such, the Company's directorate earnestly assumed an obligation not only for transplanting anglophone settlers to New Zealand shorelines but also flora in keeping with aspects of later eighteenth-century explorations.[138]

These consensual moments in 1840 and 1841 coincided with Office attempts to deal with indigenous New Zealand. Importantly, both the November 1840 agreement and 1841 charter were bequeathed to Peel's Tory ministry in late 1841, specifically to Stanley, Secretary of State for Colonies from 3 September 1841 until 23 December 1845, and his parliamentary under-secretary, George Hope. Each document possessed an ongoing trajectory that accompanied the relations between Company and Colonial Office as ministries and personnel were altered. The 18 November arrangement substantially repeated provisions of a draft prepared by Stephen for Vernon Smith and Russell on 14 October 1840, after the outlined terms were initially submitted by a Company deputation consisting of parliamentarians Petre, Baring, and Buller at their 13 October interview with Russell.[139] The Company's paper included references to issues of administering indigenous New Zealand beyond its commercial relations with the Colonial Office. One term said, '[a]ll lands in [New Zealand], except those held by natives, to vest in the Crown according to the instructions of Captain Hobson'.[140] But these references were expelled from the *concordat* as Russell was overseeing the preparation of royal instructions for Hobson in anticipation of his elevation to a full governorship and New Zealand's jurisdictional separation from New South Wales (accomplished in 1841).[141] Aboriginal proprietorship was considered in the development of Hobson's royal instructions (5 December 1840), a general paper on governing in New Zealand (9 December 1840), and in a specific paper on aborigines on 28 January 1841. These papers were collegially created with Vernon Smith, Stephen, and Russell participating in the preparation and guiding of text-

[136] Minutes, committee of directors, 19 April 1839, CO208/185, fo.131a, TNA; minutes, committee of directors, 22 April 1839, CO208/185, fo.132.

[137] Minutes, committee of management, 26 September 1843, CO208/188, fo.103, TNA. Pheasants and bees: see Wakefield, *Adventure in New Zealand from 1839 to 1844*, II, 197. See also minutes, special committee on expenditure, 21 December 1842, CO208/186, fo.183.

[138] Cf Rigby, 'The politics and pragmatics of seaborne plant transplantation, 1769–1805', in Lincoln (ed), *Science and Exploration in the Pacific*, 81–100.

[139] Stephen to Vernon Smith, 14 October 1840, CO209/8, fos.279, 282–2a (first clause, first part), fos.283a–4 (fourth clause, first part), TNA; Petre, Baring, Buller, New Zealand Company paper (nd), CO209/8, fos.291–6, TNA.

[140] Petre, Baring, Buller, New Zealand Company paper (nd), fo.291, TNA.

[141] Williams, 'The foundation of colonial rule in New Zealand', 57–8. Cf Russell, *HPD*, 3rd series, 7 July 1840, 60, col 535: 'He admitted that, if New Zealand should be formed into a colony, it would be right hereafter to separate it from New South Wales, and that it ought not permanently to be a dependent of that colony'.

ual contents. The assumptions of stadial histories clearly surfaced. Textual or tactical processes are rarely confined within the binding of books. Russell echoed earlier and concurrent political *and* literary characterizations of Māori as historical 'cultivators' and 'appropriators' of territories. These characterizations cannot be regarded as mere tokens of a discourse on proprietorship but as consistently illustrative of an approach to construing Māori from a distance, in the relative absences of privileged (gubernatorial or consular) intelligence networks in New Zealand. Hence, Russell noted in a 9 December 1840 paper addressing 'general rules' for administering New Zealand, that: 'They are not mere wanderers over an extended surface, in search of a precarious subsistence, nor tribes of hunters or of herdsmen'. Māori were 'a people among whom the arts of government have made some progress; who have established by their *own customs* a division and appropriation of the soil'.[142] Here, Māori were characterized as 'barbarous tribes', perhaps redolent of ancient Germanic groupings as described by Tacitus, although this is not certain in the Colonial Office's instance.[143]

There was much confusion on the subject of nomenclature. Merivale commented in 1839 that '[i]t has been observed, that classical antiquity was acquainted only with barbarians, not with savages'.[144] In any event, 'barbarism', absences of 'civilization', and 'savagery', were temporal markers of persistent pasts.[145] This impression of Māori as belonging to an historical yet paradoxically still operational past affected perceptions of their politics, their ways of life, and their relations with strangers and land—as possessors of 'customs' and as agriculturists included within stadialism. In 1839, FitzRoy pointedly reminded the audience of his *Beagle* voyaging narratives that one ought not to 'entirely forget the painted savages who opposed Caesar—or the sacrifices of the druids!'.[146] The allegedly inchoate senses of property possessed by Māori were temporally transformed into a paramount title of the Crown once 'purchased' by its imperial representatives. An historical transformation occurred through 'purchase' in that supposedly 'civilized' British conceptions of proprietorship succeeded to areas where crude 'customs' had initially operated. Territorial acquisition was profoundly transformative in this sense, both intellectually and in policy terms. Against this background, Russell's preoccupations with regularly settling New Zealand were undeniably evident—'the sale and settlement of waste lands' was a headline within this paper:

> The Marquis of Normanby has anticipated and provided for the great and peculiar difficulty by which the regular colonization of New Zealand was impeded. I refer, of course, to the large claims advanced by persons in virtue of contracts or grants said to have been

[142] Russell to Hobson, 9 December 1840, CO380/122, fo.74, TNA (emphasis added).

[143] Ibid, fo.73a. Cf Whately, *Introductory lectures on political economy, delivered at Oxford in Easter term, [1831]*, p., 106 (note): 'For the New Zealanders, for instance, who may be regarded as savages as far as my present purpose . . . '.

[144] Merivale, *Introduction to a course of lectures on colonization*, 29: 'No state of life like that of the American Indians, or the Hottentot, is described by ancient writers, except in the traditions of the Laestrygons and the Cyclops. They were spared, therefore, the greatest moral difficulty of colonization'.

[145] Fabian, *Time and the Other*, 75.

[146] FitzRoy, *Narrative of the surveying voyages of His Majesty's ships 'Adventure' and 'Beagle'*, II, 609. This comparative sentiment was echoed by Hadfield to Grey, memorandum, 1846, GNZ Mss17, 112, 114, APL. See Millar, *The Origin of the Distinction of Ranks*, 4th edn, 156, referring to the 'natives of the island of Borneo' and the '*Suevi*' commented upon by Caesar.

made by the native Chiefs. In my present want of information as to the measures which may have been taken to give effect to his instructions, I can state merely that Her Majesty's Government perceive no reason for receding from them.[147]

Here, Russell invoked two policy priorities. First, 'a commission should ascertain, and... the law should determine, what lands are private and what are public property'. Secondly, 'all lands held by private persons, and not actually in cultivation, should be subjected to an annual tax, the non-payment of which should be followed by the confiscation and seizure of land'.[148] Stephen had prepared the initial draft of this paper as early as 29 October, and claimed authorship of it and its flaws, if any. Russell mused upon it carefully, making additions and omissions, recognizing its generally meandering quality but adjudging it 'the fruit of much experience and reflexion'.[149] But this 9 December *communiqué* was preceded by a sparsely termed, formulaic section concerning the 'civilization' and 'protection of aborigines' in the 5 December 1840 royal instructions to Hobson. It responded to concerns in George Grey's self-publicized report upon instructing and improving aborigines within Australia, a report that represented the denouement of his expeditions throughout western Australia.[150] This report was received at the Office in September 1840.[151] In the 9 December 1840 paper, Russell had advised Hobson to refer to Grey's annexed report: 'As an illustration of the manner in which men far more ignorant of the arts of civilized life than the New Zealanders may be won over by gentleness and skill to execute laborious works, (such, for example, as opening roads,) I would refer you to the accompanying report, lately addressed to me by Captain Grey'.[152] The 5 December section merely addressed issues of religious and general instruction of Māori but not their assumed proprietary entitlements. Vernon Smith expressed discomfort with its terseness; its swift references to instructing distant aborigines. He described the section as 'meagre'. Here, he said, '[w]e are told that we have in N. Zealand a finer race of Aborigines than elsewhere, more capable of mental and moral improvement... now is the time for a new treatment'.[153] He spoke of Grey and southern Asia:

> If the experiment of their elevation should be attempted, tho the alteration should not be forcible or immediate, the necessary object must be to make them British. Nor have we the difficulties of religion that India has presented to us. The prudence of the Brahmins there had raised a rampart of religious terror in another world and the deepest humiliation in this to defend their strange mixture of idolatory and philosophy. We have heard no such [view?] in the mind of the N. Zealanders... I am happy to find that Capt Grey is not far from agreeing in his able paper on the treatment of the natives.[154]

[147] Russell to Hobson, 9 December 1840, CO380/122, fo.75, TNA.

[148] Ibid.

[149] Stephen to Vernon Smith, 29 October 1840, CO209/8, fo.460a, TNA; Russell, 20 November 1840, ibid, fo.461.

[150] Grey, *Journals of Two Expeditions of Discovery in North-west and Western Australia*, II, 372–88.

[151] Grey to Russell, 4 June 1840, CO201/304, fos.245–6a, enclosing 'report upon the best means of promoting the civilization of the aboriginal inhabitants of Australia', fos.247–63a, TNA.

[152] Russell to Hobson, 9 December 1840, CO380/122, fo.74a, TNA. See also Russell, minute, 31 December 1840, CO209/8, fos.452–3, TNA.

[153] Vernon Smith, 5 November 1840, CO380/122, fo.151, TNA.

[154] Ibid, fos.150–1a.

Russell responded, '[t]his subject is more fully treated in the further instructions which I have yet under consideration', here anticipating the paper of 9 December and the additional instructions on aborigines dated 28 January 1841.[155] Neither analytical clarity nor consensus was particularly evident within Russell's department, as it sought to mask confusion and grasp a modicum of certainty. Drawing analogies with aborigines elsewhere whilst also acknowledging diversities amongst such populations occurred within Office processes. Yet, assessments of aboriginal proprietary entitlements certainly mingled with viewpoints concerning the historical placement of assumed 'savagery' and Māori. These assessments were markedly premised upon observed modes of subsistence, reified in Westminster politics—that recurring, core assumption of Māori as rudimentary 'agriculturists', planting *kūmara*. As early as 1823, John Bigge's report on the condition of New Zealand alerted Office recipients to the settled quality of cultivating Māori: 'The cultivation of their land is very neat and careful and the necessity of giving them protection against the ravages of the pigs has taught them the art of making substantial fences'.[156] Vernon Smith tellingly commented, 'I take it for granted that in dividing public from private land, the lands now occupied & *cultivated* by the Aborigines will be left in their possession'.[157] Russell concurred in stating that '[w]hat appears to be necessary is, 1 That according to the... instructions the lands occupied by the natives & not sold by them, should be recognized as their property'.[158] Such references to a notion of aboriginal inhabitants 'occupying' and 'cultivating' territorial spaces recalled phraseology appearing elsewhere in documents prepared for Hobson's instruction. A proviso in the letters patent for erecting New Zealand as a colony separate from New South Wales stated:

> nothing in these our letters patent contained shall affect or be construed to affect the rights of any Aboriginal natives of the said colony of New Zealand to the *actual occupation & enjoyment* in their own persons or in the persons of their descendants of any lands... now *actually occupied or enjoyed* by such natives.[159]

These references to 'occupation' or 'occupied' in conjunction with a terminology invoking patterns of 'cultivating' were reminiscent of intellectual sources concerning the proprietary rights-status of 'savages' or those termed 'uncivilized'. These influences upon policy formulation remain complex, the connections notoriously difficult to establish. But 'occupancy' possessed a currency in stadial histories. An 1842 article on 'property', for instance, in *The Encyclopædia Britannica*, considered the ambiguity of the term 'occupancy' as it historically (and by *ius naturale*) 'gave the right to the temporary *use* of the soil', but eventually, with the 'art of agriculture', 'gave also the original right to the permanent property in the *substance* of the earth itself'.[160] It began with musings upon the sources of historical proprietorship as transient possession that temporarily individuated items from a commonage—'the general property of mankind'. Hence, 'it is reasonable to suppose that all was in common amongst them, and that every one took from the public stock to his own use such things as his

155 Russell, minute, ibid, fo.151a.
156 *Historical Records of New Zealand*, McNab (ed) I, 590: Bigge to Bathurst, 27 February 1823.
157 Vernon Smith to Stephen, 24 December 1840, CO209/8, fo.442, TNA (emphasis in original).
158 Russell, minute, 31 December 1840, CO209/8, fos.452–2a, TNA.
159 Letters patent, 10 November 1840, CO381/57, fo.6a, TNA (emphasis added).
160 'Property', in *Encyclopædia Britannica* vol 18, 661 (emphasis in original).

immediate necessities required'.[161] Similarly, *Johnson v M'Intosh*, that source deployed by Wakefield and Eliot, referred to Amerindians as possessing a 'title' or 'right of occupancy'.[162] This entitlement did not constitute 'an absolute and complete title in the Indians'.[163] Where Māori were precisely located in this schema remained uncertain. In conjunction with 'cultivating', a phrase such as 'actual occupation' certainly conveyed a sense of limitation as to proprietorship—perhaps limited to physically inhabited or cultivated tracts, exhibiting fortified locations (*pā*) or residential communities (*kainga*). Without analysing the significance of his phraseology, Matthew mentioned 'cultivation-labour' as constituting the soundest 'property right', whilst the 'pasturing of flocks' followed sequentially in significance for establishing territorial interests.[164] Much confusion suffused these sources, indicating that it remains crucial to be aware that theoretical niceties were neither earnestly observed nor complied with. Russell's department responded to varied textual source materials, including prior appraisals of Māori within its records. Satisficing was critical, however, in the formulation of policies addressing aboriginal title in the sense that its despatches seldom performed more than a functional role of requiring, chastising, enjoining, or approving administrative conduct. There was minimal theoretical engagement with notions of aboriginal proprietorship beyond the convoluted, albeit sparse, intelligence received from New Zealand. There was no casual assumption, as Millar proposed, that a linear progression from hunting and collecting, through shepherding and non-peripatetic agricultural pursuits, occurred in the absence of external agencies.[165] There was, perhaps, a perspective reminiscent of the viewpoints of Sumner, Lang, and Whately regarding the post-diluvian stadial degeneracy into 'savagery' of certain aboriginal populations, requiring, in its turn, managed European agency to arrest such a decline. In this context, laudatory references to Grey's report implied such a perspective within Russell's office in 1840 since Grey, a protégé of Whately, clearly anticipated the imposition of European agency to salvage 'aborigines' from inexorable decline and perhaps extinction.[166] But comprehensions of Māori territorial interests were clearly premised upon observing their assumed patterns of subsistence and ways of life.

Turning to theoretical assumptions, however, there was a diversity of opinion rather than consensus upon the possibilities of Māori extinction. On this subject, the views of Stephen and Vernon Smith were clearly distinguishable. In 1840, Stephen was certain that Māori would be extinguished: 'Believing as I do that nothing can save the New Zealand Race from extermination, and yet fully perceiving that the [government] must act on the opposite assumption, and must strive with all their power to avoid this

[161] Ibid, 660: 'For, by the law of nature and reason, he who first began to use it acquired thereon a kind of transient property, that lasted as long as he was using it, and no longer; or, to speak with greater precision, the *right* of possession continued for the same time only that the *act* of possession lasted' (emphasis in original)'.

[162] *Johnson v M'Intosh* 8 Wheat 543 (1823), 587 ('title of occupancy'), 588 ('right of occupancy').

[163] Ibid, 588.

[164] Matthew, *Emigration Fields*, 222 ('noted *land-property right*' (emphasis in original)).

[165] Millar, *The Origin of the Distinction of Ranks*, 3–9. Cf Lang, *View of the Origin and Migrations of the Polynesian nation*, 89–90.

[166] On Grey's relations with Whately family, see Whately to Grey, 30 October 1840, GL W16(1), 130–1; Whately to Grey, 10 November 1840, GL W16(2), 132–3; Whately to Grey, 29 October 1847, GL W17(1), 134–6, APL, introducing 'a son of my dear & lamented friend Dr. [Thomas] Arnold': Grey's conceptions of 'improvement'. Stocking, *Victorian Anthropology*, 81–7.

calamity'.[167] Vernon Smith doubted this view, expressing a noticeable scepticism: 'If the difference of races is such that everyone can foresee the extinction of the inferior by the abler (rather this judgment is generally doubtful when the invader is the judge) all that humanity can dictate is that the end of these unfortunate beings should be accompanied by as little terror of cruelty as possible'.[168] Similarly, there were distinctions in such viewpoints beyond the Office, such as with Merivale and Darwin. Merivale specifically argued against that 'philosophical traveller', Darwin, suggesting that the 'ameliorative' impact of managing European interactions with aborigines (insulating them from internecine warring or famine) and instructing them in sedentary or settled agricultural pursuits was undeniable. In his nineteenth lecture on 'native' or 'savage tribes', Merivale did not accept that an inexorable, 'universal operation' of extinction was in process, thereby doubting 'a noxious influence of [an allegedly 'stronger'] race upon [a 'weaker'] race'.[169] In 1845, Buller appeared to accept the inexorable tendencies towards a degrading and eventual annihilation of aboriginal populations dwelling in proximity to Europeans, as would William Fox at Nelson.[170] Unsurprisingly, in view of these disparate sources in later 1840, Stephen's preparation of the 9 December despatch depicted a muted perception on the eventual fate of Māori, a view that seemed uncertain as to the consequences of 'systematic' settling in New Zealand.

Russell referred to the subject of supposed Māori 'customs' concerning proprietary rights in his 28 January 1841 instructions to Hobson on aboriginal New Zealand: 'It would appear to be the custom or understanding of the natives', he wrote, 'that the lands of each tribe are a species of common property, which can be alienated on behalf of the tribe at large, only by the concurrent acts of its various chiefs'.[171] Such a perception of proprietorship in common coincided with certain expectations concerning those proprietary interests possessed by persons participating in supposedly cruder levels of subsistence-seeking, including the pursuit of game or temporary cultivations through planting a sufficiency for the subsistence requirements of a given community.[172] Here, commonage was deemed to be a signal, a temporal marker, and a policy expectation, of what 'savage' or 'barbaric' practices conformed to historically. There was a supposition from an intellectual distance, therefore, informed by filtered versions of intelligence amongst Office records, which tended to portray Māori as 'tribal', rudimentary cultivators or planters, and also as conceivers of proprietorship as a species of shared entitlements. This expectation represented a commencement point (but not an ending) for musing upon Māori conceptions of territorial claims in imperial-colonial practices. Russell's commentary

[167] Stephen to Vernon Smith, 28 December 1840, CO209/8, fo.446, TNA.

[168] Vernon Smith to Russell, 5 November 1840, CO380/122, fo.151, TNA.

[169] Merivale, *Lectures on colonization and colonies*, 2nd edn, 545; see also ibid, 542–52; and 'philosophical traveller', ibid, 541. Cf Reynolds, *Frontier*, 122, where Reynolds misreads Merivale's argument here.

[170] Buller to Stanley, confidential, 26 April 1845, CO209/39, fo.297, TNA; Edward Wakefield to Earl Grey, 5 December 1845, Gre/B130/2A, enclosing W. Fox to Wakefield, 22 April 1845, DUL. See also Evidence of depopulation: Dandeson Coates and J. Beecham, evidence, 11 May 1838, *GBPP1837–1838*, xxi (680), 181–3.

[171] Russell to Hobson, 28 January 1841, CO209/8, fos.454a–5, TNA. See also Gipps to Hobson, 6 March 1841, CO209/9, fo.8, TNA: aborigines as participating in and using a commonage. Cf Blackett, evidence, 17 July 1840, *GBPP1840*, vii (582), 518–20, 524–6 ('*Mr. E Buller*: Then a tribe hold their lands in common; there is no such thing as private property in the hands of an individual?—I can hardly answer that question').

[172] Millar, *The Origin of the Distinction of Ranks*, 156.

concluded with a cautionary phrase exemplifying imperial uncertainties concerning the contents of such assumed 'customary' practices: 'But this statement of so obscure a fact may be inaccurate, and it may possibly be the prevalent opinion amongst some of the tribes, that an individual has a valid title to a particular tract, or, at least, has the power of disposing of it for his own benefit'.[173] Russell's engagements with this issue demonstrated the persistent paucity of information accessible to an executive department in spite of two recent parliamentary select committees in 1838 and 1840. Moreover, there were such a variety of viewpoints expressed in these committees, combined with tentative or qualified tones, that they supplied inadequate administrative guidance.

More disturbingly for the Office, immersed in this intelligence it received, were suggestions of a confusing complexity in reported Māori concepts of territory. In 1840, Robert Maunsell, a Church Missionary Society representative, introduced the term '*take*' in relation to aboriginal title, denoting a 'root' or foundation to an assertion of interest in a territorial tract.[174] In this assessment, the difficulties of negotiating territorial transfers with Māori were evident: 'The land does not, generally speaking, belong to one individual, but chiefly to the tribe'.[175] Maunsell personalized his conception of '*take*' in stating, '[o]ften there will be only one main proprietor or *take* (root) as they denominate him; but if he be not a chief of rank the head man will take upon him[self] to dispose of the spot'.[176] This observation was additionally complicated with Maunsell admitting that a *take* might be embodied in a multiplicity of persons, stressing the significance of intra-Māori political relations and diplomacy. Using the terminology of '*take*' represented a portentous development. It introduced a reputedly indigenous conception albeit in a manner that still conveyed a distorted penetration of Māori agency—*via* European narratives—in the transmissions and retellings of indigenous terms by pākehā. It reflected a substantially layered version of indigenous property rights within New Zealand in that it addressed the diverse possibilities of Māori relations with territorial locations. Such a version or perception would become associated with figures such as FitzRoy (perhaps), and certainly Edward Shortland—as an assistant protector for aborigines, initially responsible for the Bay of Plenty region, Octavius Hadfield (chiefly at Ōtaki near Wellington), and William Martin.[177] Yet, in 1840, it was not specifically noted insofar as any intelligence received in the absence of information supplied by Hobson's nascent administration was treated as merely indicative of sheer complexity and uncertainty. A *rangatira* using *tapu* to distinguish, appropriate, or preserve intact any item (such as a chattel) or tract of territory was acknowledged as possible on the basis of

[173] Russell to Hobson, 28 January 1841, CO209/8, fo.455, TNA.

[174] ATL, 85-173-5/6 [*AJHR* 1890, G-1]: McKay, 'Opinions of various authorities on native tenure, 1890', 6; Robert Maunsell, 24 October 1810?–1894; Church Missionary Society member ordained as a priest in 1834; arrived in New Zealand on 26 November 1835; from June 1839, based at Maraetai at the Waikato heads: see *The New Zealand Dictionary of Biography: volume I, 1769–1869*, 285.

[175] ATL, 85-173-5/6 [*AJHR* 1890, G-1]: McKay, 'Opinions of various authorities on native tenure, 1890', 6.

[176] Ibid.

[177] FitzRoy, *Remarks on New Zealand*, 39: '*take*' denoting 'root' as a '*casus belli*'. Shortland, journal,'N[orth] Island', 12 October 1842, NZMs15/3, APL; Shortland, *The Southern Districts of New Zealand*, '*taki*', 96; Shortland to Clarke, 15 August 1843, NZMs998/4, APL; Shortland to Clarke, 'notes for information of Mr. J.J. Symonds by direction of Governor FitzRoy', 14 March 1844, NZMs998/4, APL; Shortland to Martin (nd), HlDu, Ms86B [1852/1853]; Shortland to Hawes, 25 February 1847, HlDu, Ms86B; Hadfield to Grey, memorandum, 1846, GNZ Mss17, APL.

pre-existing missionary and non-mission sources of intelligence.[178] Here, '*rangatira*' status was particularly bemusing as Māori chieftainship was considered by several sources of intelligence to be non-hereditary or obtained through the demonstration of exceptional personal characteristics. In 1834, Lang observed, 'every man is either a Rangatira, [that is] *a gentleman* who knows no superior and who knows no authority; or a miserable slave [*taurekareka*]'.[179] FitzRoy commented, '[e]very New Zealander now styles himself *rangatira*'.[180] This imparted substantial difficulties in identifying those Māori with whom negotiations for the acquisition of settlement territories ought to be conducted. Searching for chieftains with whom to converse stressed the identity and assumed role of paramount warriors within a descent grouping (even if descent clusters, such as *iwi* or *hapū*—often vaguely referred to as 'tribes'—could themselves be located). As such, information was to be requested each half-year by 'the protector of aborigines... embracing with the utmost possible exactness, every topic connected with the increase or decrease of the numbers, the social and political condition, the education, and the intellectual, moral and religious improvement of the objects of his case'.[181] Concerns with the collection of intelligence were partly motivated by these uncertainties—a prudential wish to harden categories of 'learning' on Māori—and tactical reasons—nourishing governmental management of relations with both pākehā settlers and aborigines, including territorial transfers. Efficacious, untrammelled territorial transfers to the Crown were required to regularize settlement dispersion. In this vein, Stephen accepted managing transactional engagements with Māori for settlement territories as procedurally paramount, such that imperial practices ought to acknowledge that:

> the lands are not ours, but theirs—that we have no title to them, except such as we derive from purchase—and that their future claims upon us in respect of such lands, are the claims not of paupers for alms, but of vendors for the fulfillment of a binding contract.[182]

UNSETTLING INTELLIGENCE, 'DISCIPLINING MOMENTS', AND THE EXTENT OF NATIVE TITLE

> A *picture* held us captive. And we could not get outside of it, for it lay in our language and language seemed to repeat it to us inexorably.[183]

Disputing the extent of aboriginal territorial rights-status directly emerged as a feature of the political relations between the Colonial Office and the Company, and, in

[178] Craik, *The New Zealanders*, 150–1; Stephen to Vernon Smith, 28 December 1840, CO209/8, fo.446a, TNA; Lang, *View of the Origin and Migrations of the Polynesian Nation*, 9–10 (ceremonial of '*taboo*' or '*tapu*'). See also Shortland to Clarke, 14 March 1844, NZMs998/4, APL, enclosing 'notes written for information of Mr. J.J. Symonds by direction of Governor FitzRoy': 'For whereas several may have a joint right to those parts, wh[ich] have never been resided on or *tapued* to any particular person'.

[179] Lang, *View of the Origin and Migrations of the Polynesian Nation*, 7 and note: 'Chieftainship is acquired in New Zealand, as among the ancient Germans, only through the influence of personal character'.

[180] FitzRoy, *Narrative of the Surveying Voyages of His Majesty's ships 'Adventure' and 'Beagle'*, II, 608.

[181] Russell to Hobson, 28 January 1841, CO209/8, fos.456–6a, TNA.

[182] Stephen to Vernon Smith, 28 December 1840, CO209/8, fos.445a–6, TNA.

[183] Wittgenstein, *Philosophical Investigations*, para 115.

a formalistic sense, from constructing clauses in the 18 November 1840 arrangement between them. This was a cornerstone of 'making' native title from 1840. Interpretative difficulties were unexpected. Russell's office was eager to ensure collections of revenue through land disposal, to survey hardened boundaries, and to project 'colonization' plantations. Russell and Stephen's subsequent recollections were of an Office prepared to oversee, through a charter relationship, a subordinate company organizing settlements in districts abutting Cook Strait. Nevertheless, from 1842, imperial procedures established to 'discipline' colonial settlements, such as commissioners reviewing the validity of Company deeds of conveyance, began to unsettle the Company as it failed to secure effective titles within its settlements. The Company brought political pressure to bear upon the Office in a series of negotiations between its directors and the colonial secretary, as the Company endeavoured to enforce its interpretation of native title. It contended for a constrained interpretation of such title on the basis of intellectual sources obtained from stadial history and *ius gentium*. This pressure increased as the financial position of the Company worsened due to its ongoing failure to procure sound grants of title from the imperial administration within New Zealand. Thus, discussions between the Company and Office turned to the content or substance of aboriginal proprietorship in New Zealand.

In 1840, Stephen acknowledged that consensual arrangements with the Company ought to 'be brought, if possible, to a speedy close, for until they are settled, nothing can be done towards the colonization and settlement of the country'.[184] In a memorandum to Hope in 1841 he stated, '[t]he welfare of the colony is deeply involved in their prosperity', whilst he assumed on 2 July 1841 that this corporation would possess 'one million acres' of territory.[185] For Russell, a corporation could direct and expedite the procedures of surveying contiguous sections for anglo-settlement, inscribing parallelograms onto unmarked New Zealand hinterlands. On 19 June 1845, before the House of Commons, Russell averred that 'commercial companies formed in this country are highly useful for the purpose of colonisation'.[186] He claimed, 'There are many things the government cannot do for themselves; as, for instance, the collecting of emigrants, placing them together in companies, and providing for their location within a colony'. He did not anticipate complications: 'I recollect that the difficulty that occurred to me was as to making a survey of the islands, and in having surveys made'.[187] Moreover, 'I must own that I had not the foresight to perceive that there would be numberless disputes with respect to all the Waste Lands of New Zealand'.[188] In addition, his personal correspondence indicated such a perspective. He advised Somes, 'I did not suppose that any claim could be set up on the part of the natives to the millions of acres of land which are to be found in New Zealand, neither occupied nor cultivated, nor in any fair sense, owned by an individual'.[189]

[184] Stephen, minute, 23 October 1840, CO209/8, fo.247a, TNA; Stephen to Howick, 5 February 1845, Add/7888/II (Stephen papers), 338, CUL.

[185] Stephen to Hope, memorandum (nd) [September 1841], CO209/11, fo.295a, TNA; Stephen to Vernon Smith, minute, 2 July 1841, CO209/11, fo.239a.

[186] Russell, 19 June 1845, *A Corrected Report of the Debate in the House of Commons*, 223.

[187] Ibid.

[188] Ibid.

[189] Russell to Somes, 29 June 1844, PRO30/22/4C (Russell papers), fo.194a, TNA.

Russell's preoccupations in negotiating with the Company in October 1840 indicated his interest in the placement of settlers and surveying. Surveying envisaged creating detailed sections upon maps and assisting the efficient deployment of settlers. Regularizing the dispersion of settlement involved controlled surveying patterns, as with the concurrent operations of the Tithe Commission office within Britain.[190] Accordingly, '[t]he square or rectangle [was] admitted to be the figure best suited to the subdivision of lands'.[191] A marginal note to Stephen's 14 October draft of the *concordat* with the Company even suggested that each block granted to it of no less than 50,000 acres be 'a solid square or a solid equilateral triangle'.[192] Ultimately, the configuration of a 'solid parallelogram' was favoured: 'As far as such natural landmarks may admit, each block shall be nearly as possible a solid parallelogram, of which no one side shall be more than twice the length of any other side'.[193] As yet, there was little suspicion of the nominality of a negotiated empire—of the inaccessibility of New Zealand hinterlands. This latter point (implying the former) would be reported to Westminster in 1845 and 1846 with tales of warring in the northern Te Tai Tokerau between Heke (and Kawiti) and regular European military together with other factions of Ngapuhi.[194] In later 1840, such apprehensions were absent in the Colonial Office. It was preoccupied with the regularity or otherwise of anglophone settlements; not perceiving the superficiality of its empires. Yet its relations with the Company were far from untroubled.

Practices of imperial land discipline (focussing upon proclaimed 'pre-emption') required reviewing the substance of the Company's deeds of purchase with, say, Ngāti Toa or Te Ātiawa *hapū*, in accordance with Hobson's proclamation (29 January 1840). There was now a New South Wales ordinance for New Zealand and a swiftly established New Zealand legislative council would eventually substitute it with its own from 9 June 1841.[195] As Stephen advised Russell, '[t]he proposed ordinance for reclaiming lands acquired from the native chiefs in New Zealand was suggested by Lord Normanby, and in obedience to that suggestion was proposed to the local legislature by... Gipps'.[196] Gipps appointed persons as land commissioners from New South Wales to investigate pre-proclamation territorial claims, namely Edward Godfrey, Francis Fisher, and Mathew Richmond.[197] This investigative process triggered further issues about the interpretation of clauses within the 18 November arrangement and

190 Moore, 'Wallace's Malthusian moment: the common context revisited', in Lightman (ed), *Victorian Science in Context*, 301–3. On New Zealand, see Byrnes, 'Surveying—the Maori and the land', 88–90.

191 Robert Kearsley Dawson (Tithe Commission office) to Russell, 22 December 1840, CO209/7, fo.379, TNA; surveying was addressed in Russell to Hobson, 5 December 1840, CO381/57, fos.31a–2, 32a–3, 34a–5a, and 36–7.

192 Stephen to Vernon Smith, 14 October 1840, CO209/8, fo.285, TNA.

193 McKay, *A Compendium of Official Documents*, I, 39. See also 5 & 6 Vict, c36 (Imp), s 15.

194 Grey to Stanley, 19 January 1846, CO209/42, fos.65–6, enclosing, Grey, 'memorandum upon the mode in which military operations can be most advantageously conducted in New Zealand', 6 December 1845, CO209/42, fos.71a–2, TNA.

195 CO209/9, fo.154, 4 Vict, number two (9 June 1841), TNA.

196 Stephen to Russell, 30 October 1840, CO209/8, fo.299a, TNA.

197 Gipps to Russell, 16 August 1840 (received 5 January 1841), CO209/6, fos.233–5a, TNA; Gipps to Russell, 9 October 1840, reporting appointments of Francis Fisher, Mathew Richmond and Edward Godfrey, to enquire, 'into claims to grants of land', CO209/6, fos.407–7a, TNA. See, eg John Jones and William Wentworth claims, OLC1/734–6, ANZ(W); James Kemp on behalf of the Church Missionary Society, OLC1/497–9, ANZ(W).

Māori proprietary rights. Belgrave has indicated that Gipps' and Hobson's proclaimed pre-emption was effective in preventing the 'runaway speculation in Maori land'.[198] Instituting the procedure for reviewing New Zealand Company paper deeds fell to William Spain, a Whig appointee (of Russell himself), who commenced his tasks as commissioner at Wellington (Port Nicholson) on 16 May 1842.[199] Hobson retained Godfrey and Richmond for reviewing non-corporation territorial claims. Importantly, as Spain's investigations proceeded, the Company's early optimism at the appointment of Stanley as Secretary of State for Colonies in September 1841 foundered. William Wakefield warned the corporate secretary, Ward, of the territorial and rhetorical repercussions of Spain's activities, stating that this commissioner's swift enforcement of the 18 November 1840 *concordat* would be hindered by his examination of the Company's alleged deeds of purchase.[200] Eventually, Wakefield produced selected anglophone-settler views sympathetic to those of the Company. These would become conveniently available for consumption in parliamentary papers at Westminster. One disgruntled observer stated:

> I believe [Spain] is just, and well-disposed; but who would not nurse a commission of 1,000*l*. a-year? And the method of writing down the examination in two languages, and hearing all the stuff that all the natives in the island may have to say, after they have been crammed by missionaries, protectors, land-sharks, &c, is so prolix, that it may last longer than the Trojan War and cost more than the impeachment of Warren Hastings.[201]

Rhetorically, the Company was obliged to argue about the extent and substance of the proprietary interests of Māori as 'aborigines' or 'natives' nominally included within a Promethean trans-oceanic empire. William Wakefield stated, '[n]o similitude exists between these natives and those of North America and New Holland', explaining, '[i]n those countries, a reserve of a million acres in a block would not be sufficient to maintain a small hunting tribe'.[202] In New Zealand, 'from the agricultural habits of the aborigines, the portions allotted to the natives will, shortly, not only secure to them ample means of subsistence, but a large fund for the amelioration of their moral and physical condition'.[203] Chapman echoed this attitude in 1842 in stating that Māori 'do not require an enormous breadth of land, for they are, and always have been, cultivators, not hunters like the American Indians'.[204]

Somes followed this intelligence with a lengthy campaign of Company correspondence directed at Stanley, attempting to harass and persuade him to embrace the Company's view on Māori as possessors of property. Evidently, an investigative process

[198] Belgrave, 'Pre-emption, the Treaty of Waitangi and the politics of Crown purchase', 29 (and note).

[199] 'Journal of proceedings in Commissioner's court', May 1842, CO209/18, fos.270–0a, TNA. In Port Nicholson district itself, there had been delays to surveying the urban and rural sections for Company immigrants due, in part, to administrative differences of opinion between its surveyor-general until 1842, William Mein Smith, and the principal agent, William Wakefield: see Patterson, '"A queer cantankerous lot"', in Hamer and Nicholls (eds), *The Making of Wellington, 1800–1914*, 61–87, 67–81.

[200] Ward to Wakefield, 30 May 1842, CO209/18, fo.260, TNA; *The twelfth report of the directors of the New Zealand Company*: Wakefield to Ward, 30 May 1842, 21k.

[201] 'Extracts from private letters', [no name], 9 March 1844, *GBPP1844*, xiii (556), 713.

[202] Ward to Wakefield, 30 May 1842, CO209/18, fo.260, TNA.

[203] Ibid.

[204] 'Zealand, New', in *Encyclopædia Britannica*, vol XXI, 979.

started in distant New Zealand, albeit sanctioned by the Office, might have deleterious pragmatic consequences for a corporation such as the Company. Somes accentuated these mischievous results in letters to Stanley. Spain's 'misconception' of the 18 November 1840 *rapprochement* was 'in relation to lands'. This misapprehension was 'productive of so much mischief to the Company and the settlers, by shaking all confidence in titles, by the stoppage of all sales of land, by the "postponement" (in the words of Colonel Wakefield) "of numberless undertakings proposed by means of loans on land" '.[205] Unconditional grants of territory were sought in pursuance of Pennington's calculations of the Company's entitlements. 'It is difficult to imagine', Somes insisted, 'how the commissioners could have imagined that the title of the New Zealand Company, thus derived from an agreement with the Crown, could, in any respect, be regarded as coming within the scope of an inquiry into the validity of titles *derived from the aboriginal inhabitants*.'[206] Stanley remained preoccupied with due process, with the treatment of aboriginal title as conducive to securing and managing revenue sources and the patterns of colonial settling. In searching for responses to Company assertions, he said that 'the Crown cannot give away what does not belong to it—question of what belongs [to] it must be decided on the spot by the proper authority?'.[207]

There was confusion as to the substance of Māori titles with Stanley openly wondering whether the Company's interpretation and its expectations might be accurate, thus demonstrating the tensions between the Office's references to 'occupation and enjoyment' and procedures for investigating titles in New Zealand. Stanley asked Hope, '[h]ave you looked at the passages to wh[ich] they refer in the charter & royal instructions. They seem to me to bear the interpretation put upon them [by the Company] of *indicating* the limit of native rights?'.[208] Westminster and localities in New Zealand were producing potentialities for realizing the confusion and uncertainties subsumed beneath a 'land question'. Indeed, these uncertainties were beginning to spin beyond the strictures of anglophone theoretical expectations on Māori proprietary rights and perhaps even casual assumptions of its management in contexts of 'systematic' settling. On 21 December 1842, Somes insisted, 'the only interests which our law has ever recognised as possessed by savages, is that of "actual occupation or enjoyment" '. He asserted, 'this would obviously be a peculiarly fitting measure for the rights of an agricultural population like that of New Zealand, requiring no extent of territory for hunting or pasture, but confining itself to the small areas which it could cultivate'.[209] A memorandum delivered by the Company clearly indicated its stance: 'If an interest in land, never yet recognized by any Christian nation, as possessed by savages, is to be attributed to the natives of New Zealand; if the aborigines are to be regarded as being... proprietors of the whole surface of New Zealand, ninety-nine hundredths of which are probably

[205] Somes to Stanley, 24 October 1842, *GBPP1844*, xiii (556), 296.

[206] Somes to Stanley, 24 October 1842, CO209/18, fos.254a–5, TNA (emphasis in original). See also Somes to Stanley, 2 November 1842, CO209/18, fos.335–6; Hope to Mangles, 7 December 1842, CO209/18, fos.288–92; Mangles to Hope, 15 December 1842, CO209/18, fos.339–40; Stanley to Hope, December 1842, CO209/18, fos.346–7a; Hope to Somes, 10 January 1843, CO209/18, fos.388–400.

[207] Stanley to Hope, minute, December 1842, CO209/18, fos.346a–7, TNA.

[208] Ibid, fos.347–7a (emphasis in original).

[209] Somes to Stanley, 21 December 1842, CO209/18, fos.383a–4, TNA.

covered with primeval forest,—then, doubtless, the claims of the natives would be co-extensive with those of the Company'.[210]

Somes stressed pre-existent 'knowing' on indigenous property rights in a lengthy missive to Stanley on 24 January 1843, distinguishing 'vast regions, which the early discoverers found occupied by scanty tribes of savages', from Ottoman dominions or princely demesnes throughout southern Asia.[211] For Somes, practices of *ius gentium*, infused with comparative political and historical observations of relative modes of subsistence or governmental systems—'an obvious difference of circumstances necessarily led to a different practice'—ought to inform sensible policies in alien locations: 'Whatever degree of power over property the refinement of the civil law or the peculiar institutions of feudality might give, however complicated and intangible the rights which the various laws of inheritance, bequest, trust, or tenancy might have created, we have always respected and enforced them'.[212] On this account, such practices of recognition were 'extended to Turkey, to India, and even to countries enjoying less of regular government and civilization, provided that the laws in force have reached such a degree of perfection as to give individuals a property in land'.[213] This was not a dispute of waging accurate against inaccurate constructions of treaty articles as Adams might suggest. Rather, these discussions concerned an assumed certainty or clarity in appreciating the substance of indigenous proprietorship from afar (*ipso facto* 'knowing') evidently disturbed by Spain's procedures or intelligence gradually transmitted from New Zealand through a Colonial Office. It was claiming to get to the meanings underneath the bare words. In these contexts, the Company was irritated by what it perceived as inconsistencies in the formulaic expressions on aboriginal proprietary interests appearing in Office-sanctioned documents: 'Lord Normanby's plan [in 1839] appears to us to have been founded on a strange medley of the two principles applied by our law to the two different kinds of countries acquired by the Crown', that is, by recognizing 'the rights of native proprietors', yet 'suddenly viewing them as savages in the eyes of the law' through asserting a pre-emptive entitlement for a Crown travelling to New Zealand *via* 'cession'.[214] The Company claimed privileged access to authentic 'law' (a discursive cul de sac or closure to discussions), to the significance of spaces underneath formulaic references to 'actual occupation and enjoyment', and to 'full exclusive and undisturbed possession of their lands and estates forests fisheries and other properties'. On 15 February 1843, Somes said, '[t]he only question is, whether your Lordship asserts any other native titles than that of occupancy'.[215] Responding to Somes, however, the Office resorted to these *formulae*, as it were, in its documents, preferring not to engage with the substantive implications of these bare references to proprietary interests. Neither Stanley nor Hope were prepared 'to join with the Company' in discarding 'the Treaty of Waitangi, after obtaining the advantages guaranteed by it,

210 Memorandum, New Zealand Company, undated [December 1842], CO209/18, fos.331–1a, TNA. See also ibid, Somes to Stanley, 21 December 1842, CO209/18, fos.383–3a; Hope to Mangles, 7 December 1842, CO209/18, fo.335a ('That conclusion [of Stanley] is that with every disposition to assist the Company, he cannot go further than to direct the governor to make to them a grant of the specific lands claimed subject to *all* claims of prior title, such claims to be investigated, as by law provided, before the Commissioner' (emphasis in original)).

211 Somes to Stanley, 24 January 1843, CO209/26, fos.74a–5, TNA.

212 Ibid, fo.74a. 213 Ibid, fos.74a–5. 214 Ibid, fos.76–6a.

215 Somes to Stanley, 15 February 1843, CO209/26, fo.290a, TNA.

even though it may be made "with naked savages" or though it might "be treated by lawyers as a praiseworthy device for amusing and pacifying savages for the moment" '.[216] Hope concluded that Stanley's 'final answer must be that as long as he has the honor of serving the crown he will not admit that any person... can curtail a legal, moral, or honorary obligation to dispoil [*sic*] others of their lawful and equitable rights'.[217] Such 'rights' remained undefined and malleable but predicated upon a process of an investigative commission under Spain. As Stephen minuted, 'his Lordship will not hazard a definition of what may constitute an actual possession or enjoyment of land by the New Zealanders'.[218] Here was the crux of Stanley's stance since 1841, specifically a commitment to a formulaic, functional comprehension of aboriginal title. Privately, in mid-1843, Stanley seemed to support the 'actual occupation' of 'natives' as reflecting their substantial rights.[219]

Crucially, Somes and the Company's advocates responded to intelligence reports and retellings of detailed Māori conceptions of territorial rights with incredulity from a distance: 'It requires little discernment to conceive what a mass of perjuries the boundless mendacity of savages will produce, under the direction of white advisers;... what strange notions of right will be advanced on the strength of unknown and incomprehensible customs of a savage state'.[220] Māori in the vicinities of Company settlements were characterized as prone to myopic capriciousness or to mendacity insofar as the complexities of their varied or discordant notions of proprietorship prolonged Spain's investigations and confounded Company expectations of the substance of native title. Behavioural aspects of 'savagery', prefigured in various influential texts (including Whately or Malthus), were again intellectually conflated with Māori. Thus, Māori were distanced historically (temporally) as belonging to 'savagery' but were regarded, nonetheless, as sufficiently 'known' *as* 'savages' such that little substantive interrogation of Māori was required according to Company sources.[221]

A complicated morass of information furnished through supposedly indigenous sources (Te Ātiawa, Ngāti Toa, Ngāti Tama) was deemed to coincide with cupidity or an imprudent desire to pursue ephemeral pecuniary advantages. This impression of

[216] Hope to Somes, 1 February 1843, CO209/26, fo.119a, TNA; Hope to Somes, draft, 29 January 1843, CO209/26, fo.95a.

[217] Ibid, fos.119a–20.

[218] Stephen to Hope, 16 February 1843, CO209/26, fo.304, TNA; Hope to Somes, 1 March 1843, CO209/26, fo.306a: '[Stanley refers] the decision of those rights, to the Commr. of Land Claims'. See also Elliot and Villiers to Stephen, 30 April 1842, *The Twelfth report of the directors of the New Zealand Company [26th April 1844]*, 72g, where the commissioners preferred obtaining information from the governor guided by those 'general rules, founded upon long experience in other countries of the savage nature, which have been laid down by the Secretary of State'.

[219] Stanley, memorandum, (nd) June 1843, CO209/24, fos.136–6a, TNA.

[220] Somes to Stanley, 24 January 1843, CO209/26, fos.85–5a, TNA. See also 'New Zealand', *Fisher's Colonial Magazine and journal of trade, commerce and banking* I, 204–5: '[The proposition that] the whole land of the island[s] was appropriated, and the property of either tribes or individuals [could be contradicted]... The fact is, that the country is most thinly populated, and the few there are living on the sea-coasts; whilst the interior of the country is the undivided unappropriated domain of nature, and clearly the waste lands of the crown, over which the rights of sovereignty should be exercised when wanted'.

[221] Malthus, *An Essay on the Principle of Population*, 6th edn, 12–16; Whately, *Introductory lectures on political economy*, 106–13. Cf Fox, *The Six Colonies of New Zealand*, 70, note ('Whately, Polit. Econ., Lect. v. See some sensible remarks on savage character there; and also in his Rhetoric, pp.50 and 71').

cupidity was exacerbated in Company eyes by the imperially sanctioned payment of compensation to placate disaffected elements of such Māori on account of criticized Company paper deeds.[222] Māori deemed to have been insufficiently consulted in the negotiation of these deeds of acquisition, such as Te Ātiawa at Kumutoto, Te Aro, or Pipitea *pā*, or those considered to require additional inducement, were identified as recipients of compensation. Complex processes of competition, collusion, and alliance were involved amongst Māori descent-groupings. The payment of sums of compensation agreed upon by a Company representative (Wakefield) and an assistant protector of aborigines, George Clarke junior, was opted for as a procedurally convenient means of assuaging unsatisfied expectations on the part of certain Māori. This process was briefly marred in 1843 by the temporary unwillingness of the Company to abet the negotiation of compensation levels pending the outcome of its correspondence campaign with Stanley and Hope.[223] In January 1844 this compensation process was resumed in earnest upon Governor FitzRoy's progress through the Company settlements. Ultimately, a sum of £1,500 was agreed upon to assuage diverse Te Atiawa claimants in Port Nicholson's environs, with portions of this figure apportioned amongst various *pā* sites, a process replete with difficulties—£200 at Kumutoto and £200 at Pipitea for instance. Te Rauparaha and Te Rangihaeata of Ngāti Toa were dissatisfied with the £300 offered for their claims in Heretaunga (the Hutt). Clarke junior complained of anonymous Europeans supposedly telling Māori that 'the sum I awarded them would not purchase an ordinary house at Port Nicholson'.[224]

The use of Māori, translations, and myriad interpreters frustrated certain onlooking settlers, whereupon these recorded frustrations could be used by the Company to harass imperial administration. To some emigrants these procedures of 'compensation' and of using Māori sources and language exacerbated not only capriciousness but also 'savagery', and retarded 'improvement': 'What is the use of perpetuating such a miserable jargon of fourteen letters. The sooner it is consigned to the tomb of the Capulets the better'.[225] Collecting information within New Zealand was not a simple process. It remained difficult to identify what discriminatory perspectives local pākehā employed to assist in locating privileged Māori individuals, if these persons did not volunteer themselves. It was not always clear who they were searching for or what a 'chieftain' was, whether classified as *rangatira*—ordinarily denoting a chiefly person—or *upoko ariki*, a paramount. At this stage, there was little engagement with varieties of chiefly lineage within Māori descent-groups (*kahui ariki*, or aristocratic lines), including, for instance, male primogeniture procedures, or *tuakana* (senior) and *teina* (junior)

[222] See Clarke to Shortland, 28 October 1843, CO209/27, fo.142a, TNA.

[223] Spain to Wakefield, 22 May 1843, CO209/22, fos.323–3a, TNA; Spain to Shortland, private and confidential, 31 May 1843, enclosing Spain to Wakefield, 3 April 1843, CO209/22, fos.314–17. See also Freeman to Spain, 16 January 1843, CO209/20, fos.202–2a, TNA; Freeman to Wakefield, 16 January 1843, CO209/20, fo.202a; Freeman to Clarke junior, 27 January 1843, CO209/20, fos.202a–3; Tonk, '"A difficult and complicated question"' in Hamer and Nicholls (eds), *The Making of Wellington 1800–1914*, 55–9.

[224] Clarke junior to Clarke, 1 April 1844, qMs-0469, fo.384, ATL; see also Clarke junior to Hamilton (private secretary to FitzRoy), private, 11 November 1844, qMs-0468. On 'compensation', see Spain to FitzRoy, 13 April 1844, CO209/33, fos.89–116a, TNA; Spain to Shortland, 'report of Commissioner Spain', 12 September 1843, CO209/23, fos.219–24a, TNA; 'Schedule of compensation', 11 April 1844, CO209/37, fos.104a–5, TNA.

[225] 'H' to [anonymous], 10 May 1844, *Letters from Wanganui. New Zealand.*

progeny of elite families.[226] There was considerable uncertainty regarding whether a *rangatira* entailed a propertied 'freeman' or a veritable chieftain with political advantages. Edward Shortland, as a sub-protector for aborigines from 1843, did exhibit an increasing familiarity with the relevance of recited genealogies to aboriginal proprietorship, particularly during his sojourn to the South Island.[227] He recollected that '[w]ith the New Zealander, genealogical questions are inseparable from investigations of claims to land'.[228] Ancestries or *whakapapa* ('*wakamoi*') connected with territorial spaces formed the commencement of arguing a '*taki* [*take*]' or 'root of the [claim to] land', that was linked to the locations and usages of one's ancestral lines.

Often, however, efforts made to identify chiefly status or sources of political hierarchy within Māori communities were frustrated and perplexed by shifting or complicated information concerning proprietorship. Occasionally, this information was supplied and *manipulated* by certain Māori, such as Te Rauparaha of Ngāti Toa. In 1844, there was a distinct impression of foiled European attempts to identify the principal chiefly proprietor and political authority in the Heretaunga district near Wellington; that is, whether it was Te Rauparaha, Te Kaeaea ('*Taringakuri*' or '*Turinga Kuri*') of Ngāti Tama or an unnamed child.[229] There was a persistent delusion that intelligence and Māori communities could be rendered relatively sedentary and fossilized with their territories accurately and swiftly surveyed. There was a palpable disquiet at being toyed with, as in circumstances where Te Kaeaea enquired, rhetorically (or not), 'why do you follow us from place to place to take away our land?'.[230] Here, there was also an accompanying image for many encountered Māori, such as Ngāti Toa, that myriad pākehā incursions had not yet ceased to be manageable, such that those intrusions could be manipulated and integrated into the operations of local indigenous communities.[231] As Belich has reminded us, early pākehā numbers, certainly in terms of armed individuals, were reminiscent of a relatively sizeable incoming *hapū* (roughly a 'sub-tribe').[232]

A paucity of information did not prompt a discursive resort to swift characterization (a typing of 'savagery') but to an increasing and confusing array of intelligence details emerging from New Zealand. Nor was this characterization necessarily a disingenuous perception on the part of Company representatives or sympathizers. It was a typing of sorts. Irrespective of collected intelligence, Māori *qua* aborigines would remain located and explicable within *ius gentium* or stadialism (observing means of subsistence) with ramifications for discussions on a generic aboriginal character (whether 'savage' or 'barbaric'). It was not premised upon what Bayly refers to as 'information gaps'.[233]

[226] Thomson referred to *ariki* and *tana* ('or, next in succession, corresponding to the royal family') in 1859, *The Story of New Zealand*, I, 94. For an explanation of these features, see Parsonson, 'He Whenua te Utu ("the payment will be land")', ch 2.

[227] Shortland, *The Southern Districts of New Zealand*, 92–104, 309 ('*kotore*' and '*teina*').

[228] Ibid, 96.

[229] 'Taupo, near Paramatta, Porirua', notes, 9 March 1844, CO209/37, fos.136–6a; Forsaith to superintendent (southern district) [Richmond], 21 March 1844, CO209/37, fos.140–7a, TNA. See Maning, *Old New Zealand*, intro. Hocken, 75.

[230] Forsaith to Richmond, 21 March 1844, CO209/37, fo.142a, TNA.

[231] Edward Meurant, diary, 1 July 1843, NZMs234, APL; see also 'Motuhia', deposition, trans Edward Meurant, 3 July 1843, CO209/22, fo.389; 'Rapana', deposition, trans Edward Meurant, 3 July 1843, CO209/22, fo.392, TNA.

[232] Belich, 'The Governors and the Maori (1840–1872)', in Sinclair (ed), *The Oxford Illustrated History of New Zealand*, 76.

[233] This study thereby contrasts with Bayly's account in *Empire and Information*, 171, 173, 370.

Here lay the central contests in appraising the extent of indigenous proprietary interests vested in Māori. Advocates of the Company in locations such as Nelson produced accounts allegedly illustrating the absurdities of relying upon Māori sources of intelligence concerning indigenous territorial rights: 'To expect a correct knowledge of rights to landed property and clear division of it from savages, seems in itself perhaps somewhat preposterous'.[234] Again, these localities became places for arguments about the extent of indigenous property rights rubbing up against colonial settlings. The editor of the *New Zealand Colonist and Port Nicholson Advertiser* espoused some definite ideas about land law, who had what estate, and the rights of the natives: 'As the foundation of the assertion of British sovereignty in this island is the recognition of the Native titles to land, it is obvious that the Government cannot interfere summarily to dispossess the natives, or to enable the European settlers to take possession of land nominally conceded to them'. 'If', wrote the editor, 'the title of the native be valid, he must, we would submit, be required to assert it in a court of law, through the instrumentality of the Protector of the Aborigines; or, if this should be deemed inexpedient, as we imagine would be the case, his title must be extinguished by purchase, either by the individual claimant of land, or by the Agent of the New Zealand Company.'[235] This paper ran for a year between August 1842 and August 1843. What makes his comments a little more interesting is that the editor was one Richard Hanson—an English barrister, one of the first admitted to the New Zealand Supreme Court. He was also crown prosecutor for Wellington at the time and later became chief justice of South Australia.

Such were the anxieties of the Company's directorate that it approached Russell, pursuing his favour in June 1844, anticipating that his statements would clarify those intentions underlying the 18 November 1840 *concordat* in a manner conducive to Company interests.[236] Yet, from 1842, Stanley assumed a procedural attitude to the assessment and conveyance of Māori and alleged Company titles. He preferred the acquisition of intelligence in New Zealand locations, the disciplinary investigation of titles putatively acquired from Māori, or the mediation of an authorized government agent (as in the instance, in 1844, of *Otākou*—'Otago'—as an eventual site for 'New Edinburgh' or Dunedin). He evaded defining the substance of native title, as it performed a disciplinary, procedural function. This accorded with patterns of imperial practices formulated during the times of Normanby and Russell.

A violent episode at a rivulet, Tuamarina, in the fertile Wairau vale on 17 June 1843, was also treated as a 'disciplinary moment' concerning proprietary interests by the imperial administration at Auckland and Westminster. In essence, it revealed the potential of elements in the loose Ngāti Toa hegemony to deflect and circumscribe the distribution of colonial settlement or at least proposed pastoral activities unsanctioned by Māori or imperial representatives. It was preceded by localized Ngāti Toa and Ngāti

[234] Alfred Domett, 'Narrative of the Wairao [*sic*] massacre, and proceedings connected therewith', enclosed in Fox to W Wakefield, 19 January 1844, *The thirteenth report of the directors of the New Zealand Company*, 173. See also Dillon to Stanley, 15 June 1844, CO209/32, fos.71–2, TNA, enclosing 'narrative of the Wairau massacre, and proceedings connected therewith', *The Nelson Examiner and New Zealand Chronicle*, 28 December 1843, 11, fos.80–5a.

[235] *New Zealand Colonist and Port Nicholson Advertiser*, I, issue 6, 19 August 1842, 2.

[236] Somes to Russell, 26 June 1844, PRO30/22/4C, fos.190–1; Russell to Somes, 29 June 1844, PRO30/22/4C, fos.192–5, TNA. Company representatives would use this correspondence to their advantage in subsequent negotiations with the Colonial Office: Harington to Earl Grey, 24 December 1846, 'statement The New Zealand Company', Gre/B147/43; 'Replies', Gre/B147/46, DUL.

Tama resistance in areas like Porirua (early 1842) and the Hutt to Company-introduced settlers endeavouring to secure the occupation of their claimed rural sections (acquired from the Company).[237] Yet, Spain, Stanley, FitzRoy, and Shortland used the Wairau 'moment' to criticize and discipline Company settlements on the basis of aboriginal proprietary rights, although their understandings of these rights varied. They did not interpret Māori agency as a threat to empire but as an aid to imperial control. Indeed, the formulaic utility of aboriginal territorial rights was illustrated, if not a consensus as to their substances. Infiltrating Company surveying parties irritated Ngāti Toa elements, resulting in the destruction of surveyors' huts constructed with locally sourced *raupō* (bulrush). The principal Māori participants were male and female elements of Ngāti Toa *hapū* under Te Rauparaha and Te Rangihaeata engaged in (probably strategic) seasonal plantings in the vicinity in order to demonstrate an interest in the territory. A Company settlement deputation from Nelson ventured out to the contested site in the Wairau to detain Te Rauparaha on a charge of arson. In the subsequent *mêlée*, twenty-two pākehā were slain, including eleven captives who were 'tomahawked' by Te Rangihaeata and members of his party in the presence of Te Rauparaha.[238] Arthur Wakefield, the Company's Nelson agent, and brother to William and Edward Gibbon Wakefield, was among those slain.

Politically, the presence of Ngāti Toa and certain of their allies at the Wairau collision reconfirmed suspicions of imperial representatives and certain Company sympathizers concerning Māori entitlements to Wairau territory (in short, those Māori one ought to converse with). The vale disputed by Ngāti Toa with pre-existing South Island descent-groupings was associated with Ngāti Toa claimants affiliated with Te Rauparaha (of a *teina* or junior lineage) and his *mana* as opposed to other Māori or even Ngāti Toa connected with, say, Puaha, a relative of Te Rauparaha but of a *tuakana* (senior aristocratic) line (Te Maunu).[239] Te Rauparaha had warned Spain's court that he denied having transferred any of his interests at Wairau to the Company. He stated, 'Wairau I wanted to keep to myself. You are still pursuing me'.[240] He thus personalized connections between his alleged claims, including those of Ngāti Toa most intimately connected with him, and the fertile vale itself. Willoughby Shortland, interim

[237] For example, Swainson to Murphy (police magistrate, Wellington), 12 September 1842, CO209/20, fo.204, TNA ('They ['a party of natives'] have taken possession of nearly the whole of the section upon the River Hutt, where I am located, leaving me but seven acres out of one hundred. They have forcibly driven off my tenants, threatened my life if I presumed to clear any more land, and they have destroyed the whole of my timber'); Swainson to Murphy, 19 November 1842, CO209/20, fos.204–4a; Murphy to Swainson, 29 November 1842, CO209/20, fo.204a. See also Shortland to Spain, 30 September 1843, CO209/33, Spain to Shortland, 14 November 1843, fo.141a, fos.141a–3; Clarke to Shortland, 28 October 1843, CO209/27, fos.149–50, TNA; *William Swainson FRS, FLS: naturalist and artist; family letters and diaries 1809–1855, final destiny New Zealand*, Swainson (ed), 105: Swainson to Parkes, 2 February 1844.

[238] Shortland to Stanley, 13 July 1843, CO209/22, fos.45–56a; Stephen to Hope, 28 December 1843, CO209/22, fos.247–54, TNA; CO209/27, fos.323–43a: 'minutes of proceedings at Waikanae (Cook's straits district) on February 12th 1844'; Clarke junior to Clarke, 16 August 1843, CO209/23, fos.260–70; Ironside, deposition, 24 June 1843, *GBPP1844*, xiii (556), 155–7, 155–6. For general accounts, see Evison, *The Long Dispute: Maori land rights and European colonisation in southern New Zealand*, 121–3. For an excellent account see Parsonson, 'He Whenua te Utu ("the payment will be land")', 220–5.

[239] Genealogical information: Shortland, *The Southern Districts of New Zealand*, appendix; Clarke junior to Clarke, 16 August 1843, CO209/23, fo.264a, TNA; Ballara, *Iwi*, 141.

[240] Edward Meurant, diary, 1 July 1843, NZMs234, APL.

administrator in New Zealand after Hobson's death in September 1842, issued a 'disciplinary' proclamation prohibiting any further encroachments onto lands disputed with Māori. It was issued as a caveat to pākehā but was unsurprisingly formulaic in its citation of 'native owners of the soil', 'their territorial rights', and that it was awaiting the procedural determinations of claims to territory by Spain.[241] Auckland followed Westminster's appreciation of the uses of aboriginal property. Complexities were still only dimly perceived but aboriginal title was deemed useful nonetheless in restraining the settling activities of the Company.

As a moment of such 'discipline', Wairau enjoyed a lengthy trajectory. Shortland's successor, Robert FitzRoy, studiously used its 'lessons' didactically as a study in the discipline of otherwise unruly colonial settlers as late as February 1844. FitzRoy, an evangelically inclined tory sympathizer, was appointed by Stanley to replace Hobson as governor and arrived in New Zealand in December 1843.[242] FitzRoy was a grandson of Augustus Henry, the third Duke of Grafton and nephew by marriage of Viscount Castlereagh (the second Marquess of Londonderry) and once a failed Tory parliamentary candidate for Ipswich. In 1841, as a Tory candidate for Durham (offered to him by his consanguineous maternal uncle, Charles Stewart, the third Marquess of Londonderry), he won the seat and was later responsible for a bill in July 1842 'for requiring and regulating examination of Masters and Chief Mates of Merchant Vessels'. FitzRoy proved to be a didactic individual prepared to hector anglophone settlement, and to manipulate it to the disciplines of normative empire by regularized territorial transactions and stable revenue collections. Along with Stanley he proposed to attain a self-financing empire embracing those settlement enclaves precariously lurking along a New Zealand littoral. Thus, he wanted to constrain and control the dispersion of settling through discipline and revenue-collecting transactions, trusting that his measures would also contribute to New Zealand's ability to be self-financing and not a drain upon a distant Treasury.[243] At a conference convened at Waikanae on 23 February 1844, FitzRoy stated, with Te Rauparaha attending, that 'the pakehas [at Wairau] were wrong;—they had no right to build houses upon land to which they had not established their claim,—upon land the sale of which you disputed, and on which Mr. Spain had not decided'.[244] 'My present opinion', he said in Sydney on 9 December 1843, 'is that the English are to blame and that the consequences of their conduct, however fatal, were brought upon themselves.'[245] This construction of what an affray at Wairau signified received the endorsement of Stanley's department, which treated it procedurally and legalistically. Stanley wrote '[t]hat the natives were and had ever been the actual occupants of the soil is not disputed', concluding that 'the attempted dispossession of them by the methods already mentioned [signals of surveying], without any process of

[241] Shortland, proclamation, 12 July 1843, *GBPP1844*, xiii (556), 140–1.

[242] See Desmond and Moore, *Darwin*, 104; Francis, *Governors and Settlers*, 214–15.

[243] FitzRoy to Stanley, 16 May 1843, CO209/24, fos.122–5a, TNA; Stanley to FitzRoy, 26 June 1843, CO209/24, fos.140–2.

[244] 'Minutes of proceedings at Waikanae (Cook's straits district) on February 12th 1844', CO209/27, fo.340, TNA: 'When I first heard of the death of ... the pakehas who fell at Wairau, I was very angry, and thought of hastening here with many ships of war, with many soldiers and several fire–moved ships (steamers)', ibid, 325.

[245] FitzRoy to Stanley, 9 December 1843, CO209/24, fos.197a–8, TNA.

law, was a lawless act, and the resistance was justifiable'.[246] In a particular sense, one of Howick's preoccupations in 1838, regarding the control of 'unauthorized occupat[io]n of land' beyond the surveyed exterior boundaries of permissible settlement in New South Wales, was realized at Wairau. Howick had suggested a 'small moveable corps of natives... to patrol the whole frontier', whereas, at Wairau, what could be conceptually seen as a version of this 'native corps' (albeit not commanded by pākehā officers) crystallized in the Māori slaying of unlicensed Company adventurers.[247] Māori were instruments of territorial discipline in a sanguine display of acting upon native title, through slaying 22 unwelcome pākehā.

More to the point, Māori activities at Wairau were translated into a legalistic framework comprehensible to anglophone observers—a perspective predicated upon impressions of tortious legal nuisances and trespasses. Stephen remarked that Māori 'set to work to abate a nuisance, or to repel an encroachment by burning the hut itself'.[248] At the affray itself, on 17 June, Te Rangihaeata allegedly said, 'I do not go to England and Port Jackson to burn grass [*raupō*] growing there; I burn the grass growing on my own land; you are certainly a set of fools. What a set of fools you are'. He reportedly added, 'I have given you Waikato, Motuaka, and Port Nicholson [*Te Whanganui-o-tara*] and I am keeping Wairau for myself, and still you are wanting to take it from me'.[249] And again: 'What do you want with Rangiaiata that you should come here to bind him? Do I go to Port Jackson or to Europe to steal your lands, have I burned your house, have I destroyed your tents or anything belonging to you?'[250]

The Wairau affray possessed a didactic quality—lecturing Europeans on the usefulness of aboriginal property rights in constraining settlers. The making of aboriginal proprietary rights was performing its intra-European role of marking the spatial extent of anglo-settlement, of regularizing the surveying and settlement process and hence the collection of territorial revenue. In February 1844, FitzRoy chastised the magistrates in Nelson, less the slain police magistrate, Henry Thompson, who had issued the fatal warrant for Te Rauperaha's arrest on 12 June 1843. One of the magistrates, Constantine Dillon, resented this extraction of a didactive quality from what he referred to as 'the Wairau massacre'.[251] For FitzRoy, the incident at Wairau was about 'breeding' and discipline, in the sense of expected anglo-settler behavioural compliance. In other words, compliance with norms on aboriginal territorial rights and revenue, as stipulated by the Colonial Office and its assistants in distant places, was expected. Constantine Dillon noted, '[FitzRoy] says, which I was much pleased to hear him say, for it will shew what a fool he is at home, that Raupohara [*sic*] was justified in killing Mr. Thompson

[246] Stanley to FitzRoy, 10 February 1844, CO209/22, fo.258a, TNA; Stephen to Hope, 2 March 1844, CO209/22, fo.386a.

[247] Howick, 11 May 1838, Gre/B146/B11, DUL.

[248] Stephen to Hope, 28 December 1843, CO209/22, fo.248, TNA.

[249] Ibid, 'Rapana', deposition, 3 July 1843, trans E Meurant, fos.392–2a; see also 'Motuhia', deposition, 3 July 1843, trans Meurant, fo.389: 'Then Rangiaiata said, and rose, "What adds if I have burned those things. I have burned my own, that grows on my own land. I am not foolish, by going to Europe and burning what grows there—but you are foolish in coming here"'.

[250] Clarke junior to Clarke, 16 August 1843, CO209/23, fo.269a, TNA.

[251] *The Dillon Letters: the letters of the hon. Constantine Dillon, 1842–1853*, Sharp (ed), 31: Dillon to Lady Dillon, 11 February 1844.

and the others, for that Mr. Thompson was acting illegally'.[252] Dillon also remarked that FitzRoy was dubbed 'king of the Cannibal Islands'. Alfred Domett, a Nelson inhabitant and friend of Dillon, addressed a poetic 'petition' or 'recantation' to FitzRoy as 'King Fizgig the First, one of the kings of the Cannibal Islands'. Brimming with sarcastic resentment at imperial land discipline, Domett's verse assailed a situation in which, '[b]efore us the savage's tomahawk glitters—yourself [FitzRoy] and the gallows stand frowning behind us'.[253] The Wairau incident revealed the political instabilities that tangled conceptions of aboriginal proprietary rights-status.

Armed with translated depositions, FitzRoy approached the events at Wairau didactically, as productive of territorial disciplining. He would also do so at Taranaki later in 1844 when overturning Spain's recommended award of territory to the Company in the vicinity of New Plymouth. This decision involved severe conflict of opinion between Spain and FitzRoy as to the authenticity of relevant Māori 'customary' ideas, thereby revealing the local political instability wrought by endeavouring to collect such varied information. In ignoring Spain, FitzRoy privileged the intelligence and opinions derived from Clarke, the chief protector for aborigines, and his son, George Clarke junior, responsible as assistant protector of aborigines in the Port Nicholson district (embracing Ōtaki, Waikanae, Nelson, and Wellington) since 1841 for liaising with Company interests (particularly William Wakefield). Clarke junior was the initial source of anxiety as to the commissioner's proposed award of a Crown grant to the Company.[254] Released (chiefly Te Ātiawa) captives of Waikato were returning to the Taranaki vicinities at issue, beginning to cultivate plots and to revive historical claims to territories formerly associated with their decent-groupings. This was merely one facet of a morass of complexities. Clarke junior demonstrated an uncritical but perhaps politically useful awareness of orally recited Te Ātiawa histories, displaying the possible ranges of interests implicated in the Taranaki issue. He identified four parties with interests to be considered in any political negotiation, three of which were 'opposed to each other'. He specified those of Te Ātiawa *hapū* who were now returning from their *heke*, or southward 'migration' in conjunction with Ngāti Toa and others towards Kapiti and its environs. He mentioned vestiges of '*Ngatiawa* [Te Ātiawa]' captured by Waikato at Pukerangiora and those groupings who had remained in the northern Taranaki district after this defeat. On Clarke junior's evidence, Waikato had 'exercised no acts of ownership [planting cultivations for instance] upon the land [especially near the coveted fertile Waitara region] which in maori [*sic*] as well as English law would have constituted a right to the land'.[255] The sources of these views on Māori 'law' were

[252] Ibid., 31–2; FitzRoy to Stanley, 15 April 1844, CO209/27, fos.266–9a; 'Minutes of the proceedings at Waikanae (Cook's straits district) on February 12th 1844', CO209/27, fos.341a–3; cf Shortland to Stanley, 13 July 1843, CO209/22, fos.52, 54a; Stephen to Hope, 28 December 1843, CO209/22, fos.247a–50, TNA; FitzRoy to 'chiefs of Wanganui', 23 November 1844, qMs-0793, ATL.

[253] Domett, 'Recantation or an humble petition from the gentlemen & inhabitants of Nelson to the high & mighty prince Fizgig the First, one of the kings of the Cannibal Islands', qMs-0617, ATL.

[254] Clarke junior to Clarke, 'private', 27 June 1844, qMs-0469, 403–8, ATL. On 'Port Nicholson district' covered by Clarke junior, see Clarke junior to Clarke, 6 October 1841, qMs-0469, 403–8, ATL. On the Company's alleged acquisitions in Taranaki and on the narrative of FitzRoy's policies, see Waitangi Tribunal, *The Taranaki Report: Kaupapa Tuatahi—Wai-143*, 17–44.

[255] Ibid, 404.

not disclosed. Fault-lines among pākehā, as between Spain and Clarke junior (merely twenty-one years of age in 1844) contributed to the telling of discordant tales concerning indigenous property rights. Clarke, the chief protector for aborigines, supported his son's opinion, as did FitzRoy, on his affiliate Clarke's advice. FitzRoy unsurprisingly listened to protectors of aborigines based at Auckland, who were discharged with addressing aboriginal issues. Clarke was a trusted adviser, of which we have evidence elsewhere.[256] Clarke junior grandiosely claimed on 11 November 1844 in a communication to FitzRoy's private secretary, Hamilton, 'I have settled the question of the Hutt with Te Rauparaha and Rangihaeata and will pay over the money [£300] this evening'.[257] Versions of intra-Māori politics, a form of agency, penetrated intra-pākehā relations through the retelling of indigenous political narratives. Spain, a whiggish appointee, primarily associated with Russell and Palmerston, was marginalized, much to Spain's chagrin as his personal relationship with FitzRoy deteriorated on issues of salary and tenure of appointment. His relative jurisdictional status and independence as a counsellor of moment was eclipsed. Moreover, he did not appear to have been directly informed of FitzRoy's decision to ignore the commissioner's recommendations as to allegedly 'authentic' customary notions of property.[258]

Here, then, was a conflict as to authenticities with political implications for pākehā fully within the terrain of indigenous proprietary interests. The governor advised Wakefield that a 'large number of natives would be set aside by Mr. Spain (namely those who were absent, or in captivity, at the time their lands were said to have been sold) whose claims I am bound to recognize and maintain'.[259] Spain, throughout his review of Company deeds of acquisition, tended to prioritize Māori claimants who demonstrably cultivated the soils in question or had erected sites for fortification or residence—questions of 'occupancy' informed by filtered selections of intelligence. He persisted in his view of the Taranaki subject in his final report dated 31 March 1845.[260] FitzRoy informed Company immigrants at New Plymouth that 'it was absurd to suppose because these natives had been taken away from their country that they had lost all claim to the land on which they were bred and born'.[261] Thus, he endorsed a view of Māori residence or domicility in certain locations as not having been disturbed by absences of claimant populations deemed indigenous ('native'), warring inroads, or claims of conquest where not exercised at a thorough proprietary level. He continued with this speech, stating that 'people talked about them being slaves but he denied that he was like the poor negro who was carried away from his country and educated in slavery'. He analogized their predicament to that of English mariners captured during

[256] For example Clarke to FitzRoy, confidential, 24 February 1845, qMs-0468, 75–8, ATL.

[257] Clarke to Hamilton, private, 11 November 1844, qMs-0468, 66, ATL.

[258] Wakefield to Spain, 23 August 1844, CO209/33, fo.163, enclosing FitzRoy to Wakefield, 8 August 1844, fos.164–4a, TNA; Spain to FitzRoy, 31 March 1845, CO209/37, fos.273a–6, 280, TNA.

[259] FitzRoy to Wakefield, 8 August 1844, CO209/33, fos.164–4a, TNA; FitzRoy, *Remarks on New Zealand*, 29–31: 'But even the New Zealand usages, which in this case are more to the purpose do NOT prevent a man who has been captured (or a slave) from owning and retaining land', ibid, 30. R Montgomery Martin endorsed FitzRoy's view, *The British Colonies*, V, 170, relying upon *Remarks on New Zealand*.

[260] Spain to FitzRoy, 31 March 1845, CO209/37, fos.273a–6, TNA.

[261] 'Governor FitzRoy's visit to Taranaki—notes of proceedings', 2 August 1844, qMs-0795, fo.5, ATL.

conflicts with France. In reducing Spain's suggested award to the Company of 60,000 acres to a mere 3,300 to 3,500—there was confusion as to the precise figure—he did not listen to Spain's versions of aboriginal title. Outlying settlers were removed to sites within the constrained block.[262] FitzRoy agreed to financially massage the territorially reduced settlement enclave at New Plymouth with funding assistance (£1,500).[263]

From a Company viewpoint, there was no security in titles. No Crown grants had been issued to the Company in any of its settlements at Wellington, Nelson, or New Plymouth under the 18 November 1840 agreement. In addition, FitzRoy was caustic in his denunciation of European territorial ambitions in the Whanganui district. On 23 November 1844 he informed chieftains at Whanganui that '[the pākehā] are vexed at having been disappointed about the land which they were told by ignorant men belonged to them. They will soon leave you'.[264] Paradoxically, FitzRoy regarded Māori as 'unrestrained beings of impulse', as 'fickle' in their pursuits of novel items but invariably complicated, such that he reported Selwyn, the Bishop for New Zealand, remarking that '[t]hey (the natives) are a rope of sand; you cannot hold them'.[265] FitzRoy exemplified tensions in attitudes towards Māori territorial claims. In Wellington in early 1844 he operated on the basis of notions of a constrained 'occupancy' when discussing the payment of compensation to disaffected Māori in return for unchallenged titles. But he also hearkened to Māori land-claiming beyond this limited sense of 'occupancy', when constraining the blurred boundaries of settlements in southern areas dominated by the Company.

FitzRoy clearly thought of Māori in early 1844 as claiming territories beyond those that they used for residence and plantings: '[The Māori] are not free to roam, as the Aboriginal Natives of some other countries,—every acre of land is claimed—and no encroachments on it tolerated'.[266] Yet, against this, he was also aware of the relevance of physical occupation of a territorial space to understandings of native title. He defined areas of 'occupancy' as inalienable by Māori in the hearing of land claims brought by the Company. These areas were restricted to *pā*, cultivations and villages—areas physically occupied and used by Māori. On 29 January 1844, he said, '[u]nquestionably what ground is in actual use and cultivation of the Natives must be considered as theirs'. He defined 'cultivation grounds' as 'those tracts of country which are now used by the Natives for vegetable productions, or which have been so used by the Aboriginal Natives of New Zealand since the establishment of the Colony'.[267] Wakefield had hoped to restrict Māori to 'cultivation grounds' established at the formation of the settlement

[262] FitzRoy to Wicksteed, resident agent for the Company, New Plymouth, 22 November 1844, CO209/33, fo.171a, TNA.

[263] FitzRoy to Wicksteed, 22 November 1844, CO209/33, fos.171–4, TNA; Wicksteed to FitzRoy, 23 November 1844, CO209/33, fo.183a; FitzRoy to King, 25 November 1844, CO209/33, fo.188–8a, enclosing FitzRoy, memorandum, 25 November 1844.

[264] FitzRoy to 'chiefs of Wanganui', 23 November 1844, qMs-0793, ATL: 'The Pakehas who really have ill will towards you are a *very* few bad or foolish men. You should not mind them.... *No land shall be taken from you against your consent*' (emphasis in original). Cf Anonymous, *Letters from Wanganui, New Zealand*, 'Alpha' to Anon., March 1844, 4, 6–7.

[265] FitzRoy to Stanley, 24 February 1845, CO209/33, fos.218a–19, TNA.

[266] FitzRoy, memorandum, CO209/27, fo.374, TNA, enclosed in FitzRoy to Stanley, 15 April 1844, 261–94.

[267] 'Minutes of the conference held at major Richmond's on Monday 29th January 1844 [present FitzRoy, Spain, Wakefield, Hamilton, Clarke, Forsaith, Dr Evans, Richmond]', CO209/37, fos.84–94a, TNA. See also Spain to Shortland, 12 September 1843, CO209/23, fo.219a.

but not beyond. Spain's suggested awards to the Company invariably excepted *pā*, cultivation sites, and villages.[268] A curious intermingling of conceptions occurred as to indigenous property rights—both 'occupancy' and 'claiming' territories—as imperial administrators chased the centrifugal implications of policies settled at Westminster and negotiated at varying locations in New Zealand. Where 'waste lands' or spaces for settling existed amidst such intellectual and pragmatic tensions remained difficult to determine.

Ultimately, for the Office, in his despatches and policies, FitzRoy envisaged too much agency on the part of Māori; too much capacity to deflect settlement enterprises such that his rigid application of territorial discipline threatened confidence in the economic prosperity of New Zealand's fledgling anglophone enclaves. That is, imperial discipline through native title had proved to be overly effective, to the point of undermining the settling of New Zealand itself. By November 1844, Hope was critical of FitzRoy's implications that there was no 'waste land' available for distribution in New Zealand: 'I cannot but think that he pushes the doctrine of property in natives . . . too far—& my main obj[ectio]n . . . is that . . . he assumes apparently that there is no land which the Crown can claim as waste'.[269] FitzRoy's financial strategies crumbled, as in the circumstances where he attempted to boost land sales through his so-called 'waiving' of pre-emption upon payment of a fee (initially ten shillings, eventually one penny).[270] Despite initially optimistic reports (April 1844), his fiscal experiments failed to increase transactional activity such that revenue from Crown grants of land was disappointing relative to expenditure. His successor, Grey, would campaign from 1846 to discredit FitzRoy's attempts at a panacea.

The limits of FitzRoy's and Stanley's versions of territorial discipline were displayed in this economic miasma, in the persistent political pressures exerted by Company sympathizers at Westminster, and in a series of events that could not be classified as 'disciplinary moments'. Away from the Company's regions, the disaffection of Ngā Puhi leader Hōne Wiremu Heke Pōkai was treated as warring and 'rebellion' once it was received as challenging the signals of an imperial presence (repeatedly felling a British ensign near Kororāreka).[271] These events were treated as personally embarrassing to FitzRoy and as a slight against governorship, rather than any potential for exploitation as a source of 'discipline'. His control of the situation developing with Heke in Te Tai Tokerau, as opposed to anglophone-settling in southern reaches, was demonstrably chimerical, his sensibilities irritated by Heke's ironic correspondence: 'Believe me I have no desire that we should be subdued—To this I think you are ready to consent—We

[268] For example Spain to FitzRoy, 31 March 1845, 'Port Nicholson district', CO209/37, fos.77a–8, TNA; Attwell, 'NZ Co. land claims in the 1840s: the Spain commission & the McCleverty awards' (September 1992, Historical Branch, Department of Internal Affairs), 2.

[269] Hope, minute, 22 November 1844, CO209/40, fo.259a, TNA.

[270] Proclamation, 26 March 1844, CO209/27, fos.446a–7, TNA. The right of pre-emption would be waived over limited portions of land upon the satisfaction of certain conditions. For instance, fees were payable in ready money as a contribution to the government's land fund, 'at a rate of four shillings per care for nine-tenths of the aggregate quantity of land over which it might be requested', to waive pre-emption. On the issuing of a Crown grant, a further six shillings were payable. No Crown grant would be issued for any 'pah, or native burying ground, or land about either' (ibid).

[271] Belich, *The New Zealand Wars and the Victorian interpretation of racial conflict*, 36–44; Belich, *Making Peoples*, 206–11; Sorrenson, 'Maori and Pakeha', in Rice (ed), *The Oxford History of New Zealand*, 151–2.

say that you are in error. You[r] reply to us is the same. Then both are wrong—If you are right so are we. To another subject listen . . . '.[272] In any event, FitzRoy had effected the legacies of Hobsons' administration and a formulaic or non-analysed appreciation of 'territorial rights of the natives' as deployed by the Colonial Office since 1839. He illustrated this in the Company settlement areas through his treatment of incidents at Wairau, Taranaki, and Whanganui, where he constrained Company settlement activities and expansion through stringently observing the due process of hearing claims and interests of diverse Māori groupings as 'territorial rights of the natives'. Native title, although still unanalysed as to its legal substance, was imperially functional nonetheless. In this process, FitzRoy privileged certain information sources (like the Clarke family interest and protectors generally) over others with deleterious consequences for his relations with Company settlements such as Wellington, New Plymouth, and Nelson. Thus, the Office, in using *formulae* on indigenous 'territorial rights' without committing itself politically to definitions of aboriginal proprietorship, left a space for collecting intelligence on Māori proprietary interests within New Zealand.

Commercially the Company was aware of its precarious position once the initial onrush of interest in its shares and land-balloting subsided in Britain. Ross Mangles, a parliamentarian in the Commons and a directorate member from 22 April 1841, issued a report for its court of directors on 3 June 1841, seeking to address strategies for reviving such pecuniary interest. He warned that 'a stagnation has taken place in the interest with which, at an earlier period the public regarded that colony'.[273] At this moment, a mere thirty-four persons signalled a possible intention to proceed to the Company's proposed 'second colony', eventually named Nelson, although, of these, a number remained uncertain.[274] Mangles advised re-establishing agents for the Company's vending of those titles that it claimed in New Zealand. However, he recommended instituting agencies in 'principal cities and emporiums of trade throughout the United Kingdom for the sale of its lands' rather than opting for minor urban centres such as Thorverton in Devon as in 1839.[275] In late 1842, elements within a special committee on expenditure, such as Wakefield, retained a confidence in the Company's ability to manage '*its* property' in New Zealand with a view to the pecuniary interests of its shareholders, if Stanley displayed no interest in using it as an instrument of 'colonization'.[276]

Still, the issue of the security of its titles emerged dramatically at this time. A 'special committee' was appointed to manage negotiations with Stanley and Hope on

[272] Heke to FitzRoy, 21 May 1845 (trans HT Kemp), CO209/35, fos.84–4a, TNA; see also trans T Forsaith, CO209/35, fos.93–8a; Clarke to FitzRoy, 1 July 1845, CO209/35, fo.48a ('now assumed the character of an open insurrection'). Cf FitzRoy to Heke, 6 August 1845, NZMss227, APL, fos.41–3; FitzRoy to Heke, 29 September 1845, NZMss227, fos.14–16, APL.

[273] Minutes, court of directors, 3 June 1841, CO208/181, fo.64, TNA; Ross Mangles, 1801–1877; appointed as secretary to the government of Bengal in the judicial and revenue departments, 13 May 1835; elected as parliamentarian for Guildford in 1841, retaining this seat until 1858; elected director of the East India Company, 14 April 1847; chairman, 1857–1858.

[274] Ibid, fo.62. For an example of publicized Company literature on 'Nelson', see Ward, *New Zealand. Nelson, the latest settlement of the New Zealand Company*. Cf Jennings, *New Zealand colonization*, 8–9.

[275] Ibid, fos.64–5, suggesting 'Glasgow, Liverpool, Birmingham, Manchester, Leeds, Sheffield, and Belfast'.

[276] Minutes, special committee on expenditure, 21 December 1842, CO208/186, fo.184 (emphasis added).

22 December 1842, comprising, at various moments, individuals such as Buller, Wakefield, Mangles, Petre, Hutt, Henry Aglionby, and Sir Isaac Lyon Goldsmid. It confidently and misleadingly reported in May 1843 that its 'property' constituted 'no less than 959,827 acres of land,—the greater part already, and the remainder to be very soon, at its absolute disposal, in a fertile and beautiful country'.[277] But it also acknowledged its increasing liquidity difficulties in that the realization of its receivables was considered doubtful. Thus, the Company's severe liquidity predicament was evident by 1843 in its seeking specific permission for borrowing in a supplemental charter (through instruments such as debentures and mortgages) and loan funds to £100,000 secured upon 'a certain quantity of land' and the unpaid instalments on its shares as collateral.[278] Ultimately, Goldsmid, for one, a Company director and prominent financier, provided ten debentures at £1,000 each to the Company in November 1843.[279] In addition, Goldsmid advanced £25,000 in September 1845 at an interest rate of 'three and a half per cent per annum'.[280] The Company tried to attract new substantial levels of investment interest with the publicized establishment of additional settlement enclaves at Nelson, New Plymouth, and 'New Edinburgh'. Yet, crucially, it lacked a 'marketable title to [its] lands', a situation exacerbated by Spain's investigations and the irritation of putative 'purchasers' of Company-derived titles within New Zealand.[281] In view of these worsening issues of liquidity, any payment of compensation to Māori *via* imperial representatives in connection with ineffective or criticized Company deeds from 1839 was rendered problematic. Indeed, William Wakefield chiefly drew on funds for compensation and general finances through the presentation of bills in the Company's name at lending institutions such as the Union Bank of Australia.[282] In July 1845, a special credit of £2,000 was applied for via the Union Bank of Australia for the benefit of Wakefield in New Zealand, secured by a personal guarantee from Goldsmid.[283] As seen, these events involved arguments over the extent of aboriginal territorial interests vesting in Māori.

With a gubernatorial administration centred at Auckland (founded in 1840), intelligence was haltingly collected about diverse and nuanced Māori proprietary precepts. This information eventually inflected intellectual and policy expectations at Westminster concerning aboriginal property. As Office, colonial administration, and

[277] Report of the special committee, 22 May 1843, CO208/186, fos.313, 318–19, TNA.

[278] Minutes, court of directors, 6 July 1843, CO208/182, fo.25, TNA; minutes, court of directors, 13 July 1843, CO208/182, fo.28; minutes, court of directors, 27 July 1843, CO208/182, fo.32 (supplemental charter).

[279] Minutes, court of directors, 9 November 1843, CO208/182, fo.68, TNA; Sir Isaac Lyon Goldsmid, 1778–1859, Jewish financier; entered his father's firm of Mocatta and Goldsmid, bullion brokers to the Bank of England and East India Company.

[280] Minutes, court of directors, 4 September 1845, CO208/182, fo.401, TNA; Hope to (Attorney General), 22 July 1843, CO209/26, fos.466 *et seq.*

[281] Minutes, court of directors, 28 March 1844, CO208/182, fo.135, TNA; Evans to Harington, 7 August 1845 (criticizing 'long delay of the New Zealand Company's contract with us'), CO209/39, fos.457–8, TNA; Ingestre to Stanley, 5 August 1845, CO209/39, fos.417–7a. Cf Belgrave, 'Pre-emption, the Treaty of Waitangi and the politics of Crown purchase', 28: 'Economic interest correlated substantially with attitude to native tenure, not just in 1840, but in the years which followed'.

[282] Minutes, court of directors, 22 August 1844, concerning the presentation of a bill for £1,546.7.10 in compensatory payment to various Māori, CO208/182, fo.229, TNA.

[283] Minutes, court of directors, 15 July 1845, CO208/182, fo.369, TNA; 24 July 1845, CO208/182, fo.380; 31 July 1845, CO208/182, fo.387.

Company discovered, specifics could be unsettling for policy assumptions. Initially, with the commencement of Hobson's period at Auckland, and the establishment of an aborigines protectorate department, Hobson was instructed to collect materials (perhaps qualifying as 'knowing' or 'learning') on Māori proprietorship. From 1842 particularly, this information travelled to a Colonial Office at Westminster, and was occasionally published and mused upon in parliamentary papers. Spain's investigative procedures contributed to this process of collecting intelligence concerning various Māori notions of proprietorship. Both principal sources of information were potentially disturbing at Westminster to the extent that the materials were not necessarily reconcilable with pre-existing sources or intellectual assumptions on indigenous territorial rights.

On 15 December 1842, Clarke and his sub-protectors were requested to furnish reports 'on the nature of the holding of landed property among the aborigines of New Zealand, settling the more particularly whether they have an individual right or a common right or interest in the soil and what is the right or interest of the chief'.[284] Pursuing efficacious property transactions with Māori underlay the Auckland administration's instruction to the protectorate department to obtain 'more definite information' on native title. That is, *theoretically*, such engagements would be politically secure in that possible sources of dissent would be anticipated and sufficiently assuaged or placated. Moreover, efficacy in this sense would enhance the centrality of imperial administration in territorial transfers, thereby abetting its disciplining of pākehā. Instructions were issued to the itinerant sub-protectors to gather information. Willoughby Shortland forwarded these reports to Stanley on 30 October 1843, with Clarke summarizing what he perceived as 'the most prominent parts of information'.[285] Clarke spoke of '*particular* claims' to title and to generalized forms of title claimed by '"hapus" and families' to 'what may be very properly termed their waste lands'.[286] 'Even here', he advised, 'they must be able to substantiate some sort of title, which is considered equitable, such as having been the first discoverers, having kindled their ovens, built their canoes, or exercised some other such act of ownership which gives *them* the preference upon those lands.'[287] Clarke's object was to advise upon procedures for unlocking Māori proprietary interests to acquirers acting for the Crown.

Edward Shortland's precise, localized treatment of intelligence on Māori descent-groupings and indigenous property rights in the Bay of Plenty and South Island conveyed tales of complexity to an administration at Auckland. Shortland attempted to record Māori narratives on these subjects with extensive precision, as in his notes prepared for John Jermyn Symonds' procedural use in an expedition to Te Waipounamu for the acquisition from Māori of a 'New Edinburgh' site, initially in the Banks Peninsula area. These notes outlined 'the precautions to be taken by persons engaged in purchasing

[284] Colonial secretary's office to Clarke, 15 December 1842, IA4/271, fos.90–1, ANZ(W): 'more definite information' on aboriginal tenure was sought, ibid, fo.90.

[285] W Shortland to Stanley, 30 October 1843, enclosing Clarke to [Shortland], 17 October 1843, 647, *GBPP1844*, xiii (556), 628–9; also enclosing, *inter alia*, E Shortland to Clarke, 14 August 1843, ibid, 640–1; Shortland to Clarke, 15 August 1843, ibid, 643–4; Clarke junior to Clarke, 14 June 1843, ibid, 638–40.

[286] Clarke to [Shortland], 17 October 1843, *GBPP1844*, xiii (556), 645.

[287] Ibid, 645 (emphasis in original).

land from New Zealanders'—subjects of procedure.[288] Shortland regaled Symonds and FitzRoy with tales of frequent conquests, warring '*Kaitahu* [Ngāi Tahu]' disrupting '*Ngatimamoe* [described as 'a branch of Waitaha']' and then mingling together through marriage alliances even though still beset by quarrelling *inter se*. He layered his views of indigenous proprietary interests at Banks Peninsula, predicating these perceptions on classes of Māori claims possessing ranked priorities. These priorities ranged from '*i a ratou te tururuturu o te kaika*' or 'those [claims] of persons who have especially a right to the place' to '*nga piringa*' or 'those persons allied to the former'. He advised that it was necessary to obtain the names of individuals entitled to an individual right or '*i a ratou te tururuturu o te kaika*' before completing any purchase of land. In discussing lands, Clarke and Shortland began to use terms such as '*waka* [canoe]' as denoting a 'primary division' of Māori, '*iwi* [bone]', '*hapu* ['smaller communities' according to Shortland's account]' in describing Māori interests at a communal level, stressing the prominence of shared ancestors to aboriginal title. Shortland realized that genealogical trails were linked to claims to territories and resources. Such a conclusion accentuated the significance of identifying, if at all possible, the complicated intersections of historical, familial, and political relations amongst and between Māori descent-groupings. He stressed unclear, shifting boundaries and '*kainga tautohe*' as denoting 'debatable lands', 'a never failing cause of war till one party has lost all its principal men'.[289] Shortland was attuned to the contestable narratives of these ancestral relations, particularly in the contexts of Ngāti Whakaue and Ngāi Tahu, having travelled through their localities and listened to their chroniclers.[290] Shortland attempted to convey localized Māori names for different types of proprietorship, carefully charting the political relations signified by these types of interest in land or resources (including eel weirs, for instance).

This approach represented a valorization of contested Māori claims *inter se* to a proprietary interest sufficient to deflect anglo-settlement incursions. Clarke and Shortland reified territorial claims on the part of Māori groupings such that proprietary interests encompassed both 'cultivated' and 'non-cultivated' tracts. This style of interrogating varied notions of territorial claims throughout the islands—of being alive to fractured Māori politics, albeit sporadic and incomplete (as if there could ever be completeness)—and began to permeate the approaches of other persons such as Donald McLean.[291] Clearly, this information was neither a static nor particularly an embodied corpus of

[288] Shortland to Clarke, 14 March 1844, NZMs998/4, APL. See also Shortland to Clarke, 18 March 1844, ibid; Edward Shortland, 1812?–1893 (baptised, 19 May 1812); brother of Willoughby Shortland; educated at Exeter Grammar school, Harrow and Pembroke college, Cambridge, where he graduated Bachelor of Arts in 1835 and Master of Arts in 1839; studied medicine and admitted as an extra-licentiate of the Royal College of Physicians in 1839; private secretary to Hobson from 1840; appointed protector of aborigines, 3 August 1842 (Colonial Secretary's Office to Clarke, 3 August 1842, IA4/271, fos.64–5, ANZ(W)).

[289] Shortland to Clarke, 15 August 1843, 'enclosure b', NZMs998/4, APL.

[290] Shortland to Clarke, 23 December 1842, NZMs998/4, fos.1–6, APL; Shortland to Clarke, 14 August 1843, NZMs998/4, fos.1–5, APL..

[291] For example McLean to Clarke, 17 December 1844, CO209/33, fos.196–211, TNA. On McLean generally, see Belich, *Making Peoples*, 191, 196, 198, 214, 216, 225 ('Grey and his master land buyer Donald McLean'); Donald McLean, 1820–1877; appointed to the protectorate of aborigines in March 1844, as a sub-protector in the Taranaki district, through the favour of the Colonial Secretary, Andrew Sinclair;, appointed police inspector in Taranaki when Grey abolished the protectorate department in 1846; appointed chief land purchaser in 1852: *Dictionary of New Zealand Biography; volume I—1769–1869*, 255–8 (Alan Ward entry).

'knowing' or 'learning' as Clarke and his associates acquired localized forms of intelligence from diverse Māori with varied interests and histories through their filtered retellings of Māori narratives. By 1847, Shortland's appreciation of the aspects of Māori concepts concerning interests in land expanded, becoming rather more nuanced.[292] They were filtered accounts in that they addressed imperial territorial concerns. But this intelligence permitted a partial penetration of Māori agency in these narratives, particularly when considered in conjunction with a demonstrable willingness on the part of Ngāti Toa and others forcibly to resist pākehā infiltration. Native title was potentially less formulaic (and accordingly more detailed) but also potentially exploitable for an imperial administration. This reportage was portentous. FitzRoy's successor, George Grey, would prove especially adept at exploiting these collected forms of intelligence in a manipulative fashion so as to obtain territorial spaces for settlement-dispersion.[293] Such intelligence would assist land alienation, as will be explored in Chapter Four. Stanley (particularly) and Hope proved to be responsive to the contents and policy implications of these information sources. By 1845, Hope was particularly prepared to reject corporation attitudes or sources that restricted Māori proprietary entitlements to physical 'occupancy' represented merely by residential, fortified, and cultivated sites. Other than respecting governmental founts of intelligence (such as these were), Hope's attitudes were exacerbated by his irritation at Company political strategies in Westminster, including the enlistment from 1844 of whiggish paramounts such as Howick and Russell in assailing Tory departmental management. Increasingly, however, the suspicions of certain Māori were aroused as these processes of collecting information on possible proprietary interests persisted. Frederick Tuckett, a Quaker and the agent for the Company in selecting a site for a proposed 'New Edinburgh', commented on this wariness in April 1844 whilst expressing irritation with John Symonds: 'Mr. [Symonds] made an abrupt and extraordinary remark to me, as I conclude, intending to convey his disapprobation of my having gone on shore, informing me that the Maories were very jealous, and did not like or understand the spying out of the land'.[294] McLean also noted Māori unwillingness to furnish information on respective territorial interests in Taranaki: '[Katatori] will not allow of, or consent to any information being given as to land, or individual portions pointed out, fearing it might prejudice his assumed influence'.[295]

Yet the Company possessed its own competing sources of intelligence, particularly in the forms of Edward Jerningham Wakefield's literature concerning adventures within New Zealand and that of its naturalist until 1841, Ernst Dieffenbach. The

[292] Shortland to Martin (nd) [1852/1853?], NZMs998/4, APL; Shortland to Hawes, 25 February 1847.

[293] See Chapter Four. On Grey's general cynicism in his conduct of territorial and political relations with indigenous populations, see Peires, *The Dead will Arise*, 51–2, 53–5. This view is endorsed by Keegan, *Colonial South Africa and the origins of the racial order*, 288 (but Grey cannot be readily characterized as a 'utilitarian liberal' as Keegan suggests. His patronage connections with Whately and conceptions of 'amalgamation' and 'improvement' would imply a 'liberal Anglican' attachment).

[294] Hocken (ed), *Contributions to the Early History of New Zealand [settlement of Otago]*, 203: Tuckett, diary, 5 April 1844.

[295] McLean to Clarke, 17 December 1844, CO209/33, fo.197a, TNA.

latter's reportage was periodically printed in *The New Zealand Journal*.[296] Wakefield demonstrated an appreciation of the unsettled complexities of Māori territorial claims due to expeditionary warring and migratory tendencies of various *hapū*. He drew a distinction between an occupying 'aboriginal tribe' in Taranaki—the '*Ngatiawa*' (Te Ātiawa)—and interloping '*Waikato*'.[297] Similarly, he spoke of '*Kawia* [Ngāti Toa]' disrupting '*Ngatimutunga*'. Intriguingly, these accounts echoed Malthusian narratives of diffusionary migrations in human histories, such that Māori might be treated as having fallen into this literature's insights. Indeed, Polynesians were broadly considered to be extensive voyagers (whether deliberate or accidental), deriving from Malaysian migratory sources.[298] Edmund Halswell was instructed as a Company appointee to the office of commissioner for the management of Company territories reserved for Māori, to collect information on ranging subjects, including detail on population, age, and gender-distribution, relative political rankings, and agricultural industries. He was to bear 'in mind that there is a wide distinction between those savages, who have become versed, to some limited extent, in useful arts, and those, who more barbarous, have never risen beyond the occupations of hunting and fishing and having no fixed abodes'.[299] This last instruction revealed the extent to which Company expectations of Māori were influenced by existing prognostications on 'savagery', modes of subsistence, and property. These intellectual expectations travelled as much as those persons uttering or hearkening to them. However, Company information sources did not dislodge sources ordinarily favoured by the Colonial Office, particularly gubernatorial despatches and the communications of officers responsible to the governor, provided that gubernatorial despatches were regularly forwarded to London.

Nonetheless, the Company was a persistent source of information. Wakefield's brother, William, the Company's principal agent, was assembling information for the directorate on Māori orthography—'*Ngatiracowa* [Ngāti Raukawa]'—and 'customary' practices upon arriving in New Zealand with the *Tory* in 1839. He acknowledged that he was at the mercy of Māori informants—to the complexities and varieties of information supplied—but managed to identify what he referred to as 'tribes' and the 'special names of tribes' (perhaps *hapū* in certain circumstances). He admitted his continuing reliance on two texts published in Britain as reflecting the state of what he construed as the 'science of ethnography' on New Zealand.[300] To varying extents, both Dieffenbach and the younger Wakefield collected or hearkened to Māori orthographies, narratives of histories and peoples in motion, disrupting or despoiling alien populations. Clearly, however, these observers were more familiar with Māori groupings in the proximity of Company settlements. Texts containing their views were not broadly accessible

[296] 'The valley of the Hutt: Dr. Dieffenbach's narrative, addressed to the editor of the New Zealand Gazette [18 August 1840]', *The New Zealand Journal*, II, 27 February 1841, 50–2; 'Report to the directors of the New Zealand Company, respecting the natural productions and present state of New Zealand', *The New Zealand Journal*, II, 13 March 1841, 61–3.

[297] Wakefield, *Adventure in New Zealand*, I, 35–6; Ballara, *Iwi*, 66–7.

[298] Lang, *View of the origin and migrations of the Polynesian nation*, 16–17, 20–1 (La Perouse), 48, 63–5; Barrow, 'Polynesia', in *Encyclopædia Britannica*, XVIII, 315.

[299] Ward to Halswell, 13 October 1840, CO208/149, fo.155, TNA.

[300] Wakefield, journal, 22 November 1839, CO208/307, fos.88a–90a, TNA. The two texts were Library of Entertaining Knowledge, *The New Zealanders* and Ward, *A Statement of the objects of the New Zealand Association*.

until 1843 and 1845. Buller forwarded Dieffenbach's *Travels* to Peel in 1845.[301] He used aspects of this text, such as calculations of Māori populations, in his negotiations with Stanley for resolving, without delay, the Company's predicaments in relation to finance and land.[302] Copies of Wakefield's tome were issued, at the request of the court of directors, to an unspecified list of parliamentarians.[303]

Personal correspondence and the forwarding of texts assisted in nourishing political relations and in keeping an issue alive for occasionally inattentive political figures. Edward Jerningham Wakefield in his *Adventure* insisted that Māori descent groups in the Port Nicholson district merely asserted contestable 'claims' to territories against each other; that these 'claims' were what the Company acquired in its deeds.[304] William, his brother, had acquired a similar appreciation in later 1839, whilst travelling through Hokianga district. Edward Jerningham Wakefield argued that in Māori terms, '[t]he first clearer became the acknowledged owner of a tract of hitherto intact land: the first axeman in a primæval forest laid claim to the surrounding trees'. He added that 'a claim to waste land beyond this natural one of seizure and occupancy was unknown to them at this time [before the advent of Company-sponsored settlements]'.[305] From a Company perspective, Pennington's awards were supposed to convert these claims into Crown-approved titles to the extent of his calculations of acreage. Spain's investigations from 1842 unsettled and overthrew this supposition. Corporate intelligence was shunted aside by networks of intelligence-provision privileged by a Colonial Office, specifically those bearing the imprimatur of its imperial representatives—a governor and his personnel. In essence, the Company was competing with unexpected, commercially unsettling views concerning its deeds of purchase and indigenous property rights.

CONCLUSION

Contested politics at Westminster, and pre-existing paper deeds in New Zealand, gave rise to formulaic renditions of aboriginal territorial interests as both conceptual and pragmatic assistants to managing British settlements in New Zealand. These *formulae* were embedded with confusion and uncertainty, principally due to administrative inadvertence on the part of a harassed Colonial Office, to an understandable willingness to 'satisfice', and to focus upon the process-oriented tasks of negotiating with a pressuring, politicized Company. Discussions on the extent of aboriginal proprietary interests emerged as unsettling intelligence penetrated relations between an Office and the Company, undermining their confidence in any concurrence *inter se* as

[301] Buller to Peel, 1 May 1845, BL AddMss40516, fo.4: 'It is not I fear worth much: the author being a painstaking but not very acute or sensible man. Such as it is however it contains more of an account of NZ than any work I know of': Dieffenbach, *Travels in New Zealand*. See also Gibbons, 'Non-fiction', in Sturm (ed), *The Oxford History of New Zealand literature in English*, 37–8.

[302] Buller to Stanley, confidential, 26 April 1845, CO209/39, fos.295a–6; see also '[S]uggestions for the consideration of Lord Stanley submitted on behalf of the New Zealand Company', 5 May 1845, CO209/39, fo.313a, TNA.

[303] Minutes, court of directors, 24 April 1845, CO208/182, fo.327, TNA.

[304] Wakefield, *Adventure in New Zealand*, I, 87: 'Colonel Wakefield was accordingly obliged to buy of the natives, not certain lands within certain boundaries, but the rights, claims, and interests of the contracting chieftains, whatsoever they might be'.

[305] Ibid, 86.

to the substance of aboriginal titles. These intelligence sources suggested that diverse Māori claims to territory or assertions of political interest in negotiations concerning the transfer of certain tracts to pākehā were sufficient to constitute a cognizable proprietary right beyond what was physically 'occupied' or 'cultivated'.

Investigative procedures instituted in New Zealand from 1840, reviewing the deeds of territorial acquisition relied upon by the Company and other alleged 'purchasers' from diverse Māori throughout the archipelago, contributed to this unsettling situation as it also stressed imperial exertions of territorial discipline over anglophone settlements. These sources of information were privileged by a Colonial Office by virtue of their derivation from personnel answerable to a gubernatorial administration at Auckland. Yet, formulaic, non-analysed conceptions of aboriginal title assisted in disciplining the dispersion and patterns of anglophone-settling from 1840. Formalizing governmental conduits for collecting intelligence concerning Māori proprietary interests also abetted imperial administrators' claims to manage territorial relations with aborigines. But, by 1844, signals were multiplying that these processes of imperial practice were beginning to profoundly undermine the 'systematic' settling of New Zealand itself. This archipelago and its tortuous 'land question' were transformed into a tactical and persistent pressure-point on imperial policies bequeathed to Stanley and Hope by Melbourne's ministry. This pressure even reached Peel and his Home Secretary, Sir James Graham, who would refer to New Zealand as 'our Algeria'.[306] Significant discussions on the substance of indigenous proprietary rights occurred in these contexts, as will be explored in Chapter Four. Clearly, a discourse of such rights arose tendentiously in these circumstances, a process not analysed by either Belgrave or Adams in his seminal work on New Zealand's annexation, such that the idiomatic nuances and relational politics affecting this discourse were ignored.

[306] Graham to Peel, 15 October 1845, BL AddMss40451, fos.386–7.

4

'Vague Native Rights to Land': Constitutionalism, Native Title, and Pursuing Settling Spaces, 1844–1853

In the mid-nineteenth century, we find particular New Zealand adaptations of United States jurisprudence concerning 'Indian title' emerging from the Supreme Court during John Marshall's tenure as chief justice from 1801 until 1835. In this way, New Zealand exhibits patterns of difference. In May 1844, Standish Motte, a barrister, and once a chairman of the New Zealand Colonization Association (1838), an old shareholder in the Company and, initially at least, a sympathizer of its objectives in New Zealand, re-entered Colonial Office correspondence.[1] Motte had promised an opinion for Hope concerning the land question in New Zealand. He was explicit in his resulting 31 May 1844 opinion entitled 'Land claims in New Zealand' that a resort to United States and European continental sources on *ius gentium* was required to characterize aboriginal territorial relations. Motte produced a narrative of these relations in northern America that the Colonial Office was not especially interested in (certainly, Stephen rejected it in July 1840). He also cited European continental authors (Vattel especially), treating their insights as seamlessly shifting across time and space, from northern America to New Zealand. In 1840, Motte had not used these sources at all in a treatise on legislating for aborigines.[2] Yet, by 1844, they possessed a currency concerning questions of aboriginal land. After all, they surfaced in Eliot's Select Committee report of 1840, publicized in parliamentary papers for a readership expressing an interest in New Zealand's condition. Motte stated, '[t]he English jurists & writers on colonial law scarcely approached the question [of disputed aboriginal territorial claims]'. Thus, '[i]n Mr Burge's admirable book [*Commentaries on Colonial and Foreign Laws* (1838)] it is not mentioned, and it is principally to the American & continental writers we must refer to for information'.[3] Significantly, these founts of information constituted translations construing legalistic entanglements with Amerindians in northern America, filtered through relatively recent judicial pronouncements and legal texts, emerging especially from 1823.[4]

[1] Burns, *Fatal Success*, 89, 99.

[2] Motte, *Outline of a System of Legislation, for securing protection to the aboriginal inhabitants of all countries colonized by Great Britain*. Rose, *Curator of the Dead*, 110–12.

[3] Motte to Hope, 31 May 1844, 'Land claims in New Zealand', CO209/32, fos.295–5a, TNA. Burge, *Commentaries on Colonial and Foreign Laws.*

[4] Howe, *What Hath God Wrought*, 422 and 355.

Within Colonial Office records there was no trace of older colonial northern American sources as instructors for conducting imperial entanglements in aboriginal New Zealand. Few printed sources after the late eighteenth century discussed legalistic relations with Amerindians or the proprietary rights-status of indigenous populations, certainly not at any length.[5] The second edition of Thomas Pownall's book on the administration of Atlantic colonies represented a rare contemplative exception in that it referred to the economic modes of subsistence pursued by Amerindians, their sense of attunement to sylvan warring, and voluntary 'cession' as an advisable arbiter of settlement relations with Amerindians.[6] In addition, tales of prolonged Mohegan (Mohican or Mahican) litigation against Connecticut, dating from a 1703 petition of Oweneco, son of Uncas, a Mohegan *sachem*, and addressing territorial entitlements, purchased no echoes either in Motte's or in Office musings upon distant New Zealand.[7] Significantly, there is no evidence of the transmission of these sources into New Zealand contexts of imperial management. Improvization was an abiding theme in approaching local imperial fields such as New Zealand in the 1830s and 1840s. Importantly, his detailed assessment of those 'dwelling' ('where their castles are') and 'hunting' rights possessed by Oneida or Mohawk populations in 1765 bore scant resemblance to those expressions pervading Motte's opinion or the Marshall court decision in *Johnson v M'Intosh*.[8] Similarities arose in the observation of modes of subsistence, in the singular appraisal of Amerindians as acquiring sustenance from the chase and in associating a distinctive 'law of nations' relevant to that historical stage: 'An exact and strict observance of the laws of sporting, the protection of the game, and the most rigid sanction of the *hunt*...become the *laws of nations* to an *hunting nation*'.[9] George Chalmers, a collector of English legal opinions, commented that Amerindian territories, '[were] only considered as waste, because [they] was uncultivated, and therefore open to the occupancy and use of other nations'.[10] Motte introduced the maxims of *Johnson v M'Intosh* through Kent's recently published commentaries on United States law. Hence, '[t]his assumed but qualified dominion of the Indian Tribes, regarding them as enjoying no higher Title to the soil than that founded on simple occupancy and to be incompetent to transfer their Title to any other power than the Government which claims the jurisdiction of their Territory by right of discovery arose in a great degree from the necessity of the case'.[11] In 1846, Travers Twiss recognized the localized application of this so-called axiom—restricted to New Zealand and the United States—when contemplating an international legal subject as Merivale's successor in the Drummond

[5] Smith, *Appeals to the Privy Council from the American plantations*, 417.

[6] Pownall, *The Administration of the Colonies*, 159–81; cf Pownall, *The Administration of the Colonies*, 65–6 where he declined to address 'Indian affairs', deeming it advisable to impart such matters to those, 'men best versed thro' experience and success in those matters'. See also Young, *Political Essays concerning the Present State of the British Empire.*

[7] Smith, *Appeals to the Privy Council from the American plantations*, 424 *et seq*; Pagden, *Lords of All the World*, 85; Walters, '*Mohegan Indians* v. *Connecticut* (1705–1773) and the legal status of aboriginal customary laws and government in British North America', 803–29. Yirush *Settlers, Liberty, and Empire*, 133–141.

[8] 8 Wheat 543 (1823) (USSC).

[9] Pownall, *The Administration of the Colonies*, 160–1 (emphasis in original).

[10] Chalmers, *Political Annals of the present united colonies, from their settlement to the peace of 1763, book I*, 28.

[11] Motte to Hope, 31 May 1844, CO209/32, fo.298a, TNA (emphasis in original); Kent, *Commentaries on American law.*

chair of political economy at Oxford. Twiss associated it with 'the more humane spirit of the modern code of nations' in the 1840s (certainly after 1817 and 1818 according to his text).[12] This 'code', an idiom of supposedly humane impulses, clearly remained contestable in that this intrusive legalist vocabulary could generate profound policy disputes. Yet, in 1846, Twiss regarded its distinctiveness as resting on the emphasis placed upon territorial 'purchase' as opposed to mere 'conquest' or seizure. He saw it as a geographically localized approach, as well as one localized in time.

Motte continued, chiefly mimicking Marshall in his *Johnson* opinion through Kent's citations, 'To leave the Indians in possession of the country, was to *leave the Country a Wilderness*, and to govern them as a distinct people or to mix with them and admit them to an inter community of privileges was impossible under the circumstances of their relative condition'. Accordingly, 'the peculiar character & habits of the Indian nations rendered them incapable of sustaining any other relation with the whites than that of dependance [*sic*] and pupillage'.[13] He conflated the condition of Amerindians with Māori following a disquisition on what he thought was the admitted 'knowing' of Māori practices from a distance—their modes of sustenance and their histories of warring: 'The great difference appears to be that the Indians are *hunting tribes* wandering over a wide tract of country in search of game, while the New Zealander is more confined to the locality of his tribe and cultivates the earth, living on faunaceous food'.[14] Motte was granted access to the Office librarian, George Mayer, and the 'printed records', but not to manuscript sources 'without a special order from Lord Stanley'.[15] The Office controlled access to intelligence sources whilst collecting diverse opinions upon imperial questions. Hope thought that '[h]is argument is much that used by Sir G. Gipps on bringing in the Land Ord[inance] [in 1840]'.[16] As such, it prepared Hope as a member of an upcoming Select Committee sponsored by Company sympathizers for possible legalist arguments used to criticize Office policies. Indeed, Motte's opinion concerning 'land claims' was submitted as evidence to that Select Committee in June 1844 with Hope's authorization.[17] Again, Westminster strategies intruded into questions of

[12] Twiss, *The Oregon Question examined, in respect to facts and the law of nations*, 176.

[13] Motte to Hope, 31 May 1844, CO209/32, fo.298a, TNA (emphasis in original). Cf *Johnson v M'Intosh* 8 Wheat 543, 590 (1823) per Chief Justice Marshall: 'But the tribes of Indians inhabiting this country were fierce savages, whose occupation was war, and whose subsistence was drawn chiefly from the forest. To leave them in possession of their country was to leave the country a wilderness; to govern them as a distinct people was impossible, because they were fierce, and were ready to repel by arms every attempt on their independence'. For treatments of *Johnson v M'Intosh* and Marshall court jurisprudence concerning Native Americans generally, compare Tully, *An Approach to Political Philosophy*, 173, where he suggests that Marshall rejects the 'agricultural argument for dispossession based explicitly on the *Two Treatises* [of Locke]'; Tully, 'Placing the *Two Treatises*', in Phillipson and Skinner (eds), *Political Discourse in Early Modern Britain*, 277–8; Williams junior, *The American Indian in Western Legal Thought*, 308–17. See also Lindsay Robertson's excellent account in *Conquest by Law*; Banner, *How the Indians Lost their Land*, 178–90.

[14] Motte to Hope, 31 May 1844, CO209/32, fo.300a, TNA (emphasis in original): 'Many of the Indians however cultivated the Earth previous to the early colonization of America, altho' they were not confined to vegetable food'.

[15] Stephen, minute, 22 May 1844, CO209/32, fo.287a, TNA; Hope, minute, 24 May 1844, CO209/32, fo.287a.

[16] Hope to Stanley, 9 June 1844, CO209/32, fo.308a, TNA. See Chapter Two for Gipps's address to the legislative council of New South Wales.

[17] Hope to Motte, 8 June 1844, CO209/32, fos.306–6a, TNA; Motte to Hope, 4 June 1844 CO209/32, fos.307–8.

aboriginal title. Two moments of political significance materialized in 1844 and 1845: first, Select Committee proceedings sympathetic to Company anxieties regarding its putative antipodean titles; and, secondly, extensive debates within the Commons that marshalled Whig and Tory paramounts. In early 1844, the Company endeavoured to bypass Stanley and Hope through its favoured instrument of a parliamentary Select Committee. Frustrated with Stanley and Hope's resistance to Company proposals on instructing the immediate issuance of Crown grants to territories in the Port Nicholson district and elsewhere, its directorate essentially resorted to bypassing Colonial Office dealings with due processes and aboriginal title. On 21 December 1843, the directorate resolved 'that all irritating questions of relative rights should be promptly and conclusively settled on just, comprehensive principles, delay in such settlement being to the last degree dangerous to the public peace, and all chance of cordiality between the races'.[18] A sense of anxiety pervaded its musings upon a worsening financial predicament and its continuing inability to secure the amity of either Stanley or Hope. There was much confusion as to the failure of deputations to Stanley in February 1844 to obtain Company objects that were expressed by propaganda. The Company was convinced of the 'necessity of some public statement [by Stanley] as to the existing condition of the question relating to the Company's land claims'. In addition, it expected 'measures to be adopted for the protection of life, and property in New Zealand in order to restore public confidence and enable the Company to effect sales of its land'.[19] In this atmosphere of mutual irritation the Company mounted a campaign of political attrition against Stanley's administration. It courted the affiliation of a sympathetic Whig aristocrat, Howick, to whom Buller and Hawes were allied as advocates of 'systematic' emigration. Palmerston informed Russell that, for Buller, Howick, 'was the god of his idolatry'.[20] Political tendrils connecting Buller and this prominent whiggish chieftain were gently nourished through correspondence.[21] Similarly, Russell was approached for the purpose of acquiring his opinion on the significance of the 18 November 1840 *concordat* between the Company and the Office.[22]

A Company director and Tory parliamentarian, Henry Aglionby, moved the creation of a Select Committee in the Commons in April 1844. This Committee was instituted in an unscheduled fashion with sparse parliamentary resistance in the late evening of 30 April 1844. Vernon Smith denounced Aglionby's tactics: 'Now, at one o'clock in the morning, the same honourable member [Aglionby], without saying a word as to the enquiries which the Committee were to institute, proposed to nominate fifteen members to act upon it, ten of whom were supporters of the government, whilst one (Mr Roebuck) was the supporter of he did not know who'.[23] Stanley recollected his suspicions in subsequent correspondence to Peel: 'They prepared a list of names, studiously selected from *our* side of the House, but previously thoroughly imbued by

[18] Minutes, court of directors, 21 December 1843, CO208/182, fo.92, TNA.

[19] William Hutt, minutes of deputation to Colonial Office, 17 February 1844, CO208/182, TNA.

[20] Palmerston to Russell, 20 December 1844, PRO30/22/4D, fo.41, Russell papers, TNA.

[21] Minutes, court of directors, 29 March 1844, CO208/182, fos.140–1, TNA.

[22] Russell to Somes, 29 June 1844, PRO30/22/4C, fos.192–5, Russell papers, TNA; minutes, 'special political committee', New Zealand Company, 27 June 1844, CO208/188, fo.272, TNA.

[23] *The thirteenth report of the directors of the New Zealand Company*, 53. Martin, *The British Colonies*, VI, 214–15. See also *HPD*, 3rd series, vol 74, cols 516–17; Morrell, *British Colonial Policy in the Age of Peel and Russell*, 113–15.

Charles Buller with the views of the Company'.[24] The eventual membership of the Select Committee included Howick, Hope, Roebuck, Aglionby, Hawes, Sir Robert Inglis, Viscount Ebrington, and, from 3 May 1844, a lord of the Treasury, Edward Cardwell (as a specific nominee of Stanley on 30 April). Edward Cardwell (1813–1886) entered the House of Commons on petition as a member for Clitheroe in 1843 becoming a secretary to the Treasury by 1845. Howick, selected as Committee chairperson, was, by 1844, the senior, politically active parliamentary representative of the Grey family interest and faction. In conjunction with this Committee in the Commons, a 'special political committee' of the Company's directorate was formed, consisting of Aglionby, Wakefield, Hutt, Mangles, and Marjoribanks, in an attempt to present Company opinions before Howick's Committee. But, according to its minutes, it seldom convened.[25] Indeed, it remains difficult to assess the influence of Company strategies upon this Select Committee, as opposed to Eliot's committee, a factor exacerbated further by Howick's evident primacy in the drafting of the ultimate report dated 23 July 1844. Indeed, Howick's journal entries indicated the personalized quality of the report and the noticeable absence of interventions from elsewhere.[26] If anything, Howick's intellectual and political sympathies with Company objects, together with his personal predominance during the Committee hearings, were critical to the eventual report.

Howick's Select Committee coincidentally accepted Motte's legal sources regarding aboriginal property. Marshall court jurisprudence was indirectly admitted via Gipps as supplying an accurate portrait of aboriginal title in New Zealand. This use of Gipps and of Marshall court opinions was augured by the position assumed in Eliot's Select Committee on New Zealand. There is little sense of the processes by which this admission of sources occurred in Howick's journal, although he evidently devoted much time to its drafting. Indeed, when Howick finalized his report, he expressed relief that 'this very troublesome business is over'.[27] His report clearly depended upon his reading of previously printed parliamentary papers, along with evidence submitted before his Select Committee, indicating his probable source for Gipps' views on Māori in 1840 before the New South Wales legislative council. Certain personal papers, however, probably date from his musings on this report and its drafting or, alternatively, his eventual participation in Commons' debates on the New Zealand situation in mid-1845. In an intriguing series of notes extracted from his reading of parliamentary papers he acknowledged possible tensions within imperial ideas of aboriginal title. Hence, he mused:

> [Russell] to Captn. H. Jany 28/41—royal instructions have established principle of respe: [respecting] territorial rights of natives as owners of soil. Lands of aborigines to be defined—... Reference to customs of natives as to property in land being obscure—No European to purchase native land.[28]

24 Stanley to Peel, 17 December 1844, cited by Morrell, *British Colonial Policy in the age of Peel and Russell*, 113–14 (note) (emphasis in original).

25 Minutes, 'special political committee', 19 June 1844, CO208/188, fos.266–7, TNA; 21 June 1844, fos.267–8; 24 June 1844, fos.268–9.

26 Howick, journal, 2 July 1844: 'NZ[d] committee in the morning'; 4 July 1844, 5 July 1844, 9 July 1844, 10 July 1844, 12 July 1844: 'I have not made much progress with my report'; 13 July 1844: 'I staid the whole afternoon at home working hard at my NZ[d] report'; 23 July 1844, Gre/V/C3/10, DUL.

27 Howick, journal, 23 July 1844, Gre/V/C3/10, DUL. See also ibid, 2 July 1844: 'devoted the evening to reading the interminable NZ[d] papers'; 10 July 1844: 'working hard at my NZ[d] report [whilst remaining home in the evening]'.

28 DUL, Gre/B161/87: entitled in catalogue, 'memoranda on New Zealand 1845'.

He concluded this section with a comment: '*nb* how far this despatch qualifies instruct[io]ns very hard to understand—it almost seems to imply yet does not distinctly make an admission of *vague native rights to land* not "in their actual occupat[io]n or enjoyment"'.[29] Howick thus crystallized the essence of these discomfiting tensions, already identified in Chapter Three. Policy-makers in London, such as Stephen and Russell, did not anticipate the complexities of Māori territorial rights; whilst this proved especially disturbing as Office functionaries encountered persistent Company pressure from later 1842. Stephen could use this impression of surprise to evade complicity in the shortcomings of an imperial policy that, in 1840, had not foreseen these complications, by observing that investigations conducted under the auspices of the Auckland administration suggested that immediate Crown grants could not be issued to the Company. Stephen mentioned that problems with 'waste lands' were not expected. In a substantial minute dated 20 June 1843, he advised Hope that '[w]hen Lord John Russell made his agreement with the New Zealand Company his Lordship did not know whether or not there was a single acre of wild land in the country, of which the Queen was proprietor in right of her Crown'. In addition, Russell 'had dealt with them as meritorious emigrants or settlers who, on the Australian or (if you will) on the Wakefield principle, were to have as many acres as they had expended crowns on colonization'.

A distinction was drawn between Australia and New Zealand: 'In New Holland that principle is readily applied[,] for there the whole country is vacant excepting so far as the Crown has granted it'. Stephen continued: 'But in New Zealand it [could] be applied only by giving the Company confirmatory grants of the requisite number of acres to be taken from the land purchased by themselves'.[30] Where a deficiency of territory prevented the capacity of the Company to obtain an appropriate extent of land under Pennington's decisions, those 'waste' or 'wild lands' within the Crown's demesne ought to become accessible. Accordingly, 'the deficiency must be made good from any *wild* lands or *unsettled* lands belonging to the Crown in any other part of New Zealand'.[31] Stephen endeavoured to define these territorial categories on the basis of prior imperial practices, stating, '[t]he words "wild", "unsettled", "waste" and so on have been invariably used in all Public Acts, in all correspondence and negociations [*sic*] to designate the species of land to which emigrants or settlers acquire a title by the expenditure of money on colonization'. Stephen insisted that this principle was implicit in imperial legislation concerning the acquisition of 'waste lands' enacted on 22 June 1842, whilst he also referred to 'the prevalent doctrine about colonization' associated with those variants adhered to by Wakefield and Howick.[32] This 'doctrine' assumed that 'waste land is a thing utterly worthless both in exchange and in use, until labour and capital, are applied

[29] Ibid (emphasis added). Consider the 'charter for erecting the colony of New Zealand and for creating and establishing a legislature and executive therein', 10 November 1840: 'the rights of any Aboriginal natives of the said colony of New Zealand to the actual occupation & enjoyment in their own persons or in the persons of their descendants of any lands in the said colony now actually occupied or enjoyed by such natives', CO381/57, fo.6a, TNA.

[30] Stephen to Hope, minute, 20 June 1843, CO209/24, fos.178a–9, TNA. On Australia as 'vacant', see Richter, 'The Strange Colonial North American Career of *Terra Nullius*', in Attwood and Griffiths (eds), *Frontier, Race, Nation*, 160–70; Reynolds, *Aboriginal Sovereignty*, 1–15, 92–3; King, '*Terra nullius* and *terra aboriginum*', 75–91; Sorrenson, 'Treaties in British colonial policy' in Renwick (ed), *Sovereignty and Indigenous Rights*, 24–7.

[31] Stephen to Hope, minute, 20 June 1843, CO209/24, fo.179a (emphasis in original).

[32] Ibid: 'An Act for regulating the sale of waste land belonging to the Crown in the *Australian* Colonies', 5 & 6 Vict, c36 (Imp). See LRO, 920Der(14), 24/2 (Stanley papers): memoranda [1842], 'Land Sale Act', 'heads of a bill for sale of Crown lands in Australia and New Zealand'.

to it: & that they who introduce labour and capital thereby acquire the highest possible claim to have a proportionate amount of land assigned to them'.[33] Yet, Stanley advised, 'proof of title' ought to be imparted to FitzRoy, thereby favouring localized processes of imperial territorial discipline in accordance with preceding practices authorized during Russell's tenure.[34]

As with other Select Committee reports, Howick's report clearly embraced those opinions cherished by its chairperson albeit with apparent support from fellow Committee members, such as Aglionby and Roebuck.[35] Howick's report reflected his self-confidence in 'knowing' the substance of New Zealand territorial issues from a distance. But it also revealed his ability to craft a form of leverage (a report) against which imperial administration could be critiqued at Westminster and in colonial New Zealand. Both *ius gentium* and stadial histories were swirling together in this account. As contended in Chapters One to Three, they exemplified significant vocabularies for analysing indigenous populations in and through time. The boundaries of native title would be constrained to those territories physically occupied. Howick's report materialized as a discursive nodal point through which influential intellectual assumptions streamed concerning 'savagery' and 'proprietorship', supported by whiggish and tory sympathizers of 'systematic' settling. It was the Company's trawling for literature on this issue in its correspondence with Stanley from 1842 that furnished disputes with the Office together with the intermittent detailing of indigenous property rights. In its treatment of proprietorship, the report and Company directorate 'promoted a scheme in terms of which not only past cultures, but all living societies were irrevocably placed on a temporal slope, a stream of Time—some upstream, others downstream'.[36] It was naturalized in that it was inexorably applicable (and 'known') and ordered fragmentary, diverse records or pieces of information into a pattern that was permanently inscribed into observed earthly histories. In such an account, there was an elision of Māori political and historical agency. Additionally, they were still construed as vulnerable to historical tendencies of degeneracy or retrogression into abject 'savagery' or 'barbarism'—a theme generally shared in both controversial and non-controversial literature on natural histories and political economy, although the stimuli for these tendencies incited differing opinions amongst authors.[37]

These themes were swallowed within an animated, often internally inconsistent field of varying racial assessments about Māori, as embraced within unstable categories, including 'Malay' or 'Polynesian' divisions, and as ethnographically, physically,

[33] Stephen to Hope, minute, 20 June 1843, CO209/24, fos.179a–80 'To me, therefore, it appears that the N. Zealand Company having rendered to N. Zealand the required service of introducing settlers and capital are entitled to an acre of waste land for every crown of their expenditure': Hope to Stanley, minute, 20 June 1843, ibid, fos.181–1a, TNA.

[34] Stanley, minute, 22 June 1843, CO209/24, fo.181a, TNA.

[35] On Select Committees, chairpersons, and information-collection, see Eastwood, '"Amplifying the province of the legislature"', 285. Aglionby and Roebuck subsequently corresponded with Howick on New Zealand issues: eg Aglionby to Howick, 30 September 1844, Gre/B75/2/16, DUL.

[36] Fabian, *Time and the Other*, 17.

[37] For instance, see Twiss, *On Certain Tests of a Thriving Population*, 82, for a relatively orthodox, non-controversial opinion; Chambers, *Vestiges of the Natural History of Creation*, 285–7; and Chambers, *Explanations*, 3 for a controversial source; Stocking, *Victorian Anthropology*, 41–5; Bowler, *Evolution*, 141–8. Consider also a physician and well-versed New Zealand source: Martin, *New Zealand; in a series of letters*, 290–2, emphasizing 'a law of change' comprising two sub-laws, one tending to improvement and perfectibility, the other to deterioration and, finally, destruction.

historically, and politically different.[38] Non-referenced aspects of this field were scavenged or selected, occasionally emerging in Office records. Stephen, for one, exhibited an appreciation of observed racial distinctions in a 12 September 1843 minute concerning immigration and settlement strategies in Australia. He commented that there was 'not on the globe a social interest more momentous... than that of reserving the continent of New Holland as a place where the English race shall be spread from sea to sea unmixed with any lower caste'.[39] Although there was an appreciation of racial distinction, Māori were inconsistently characterized racially when mentioned at this level of generality in Colonial Office records. On occasion, Stephen baldly referred to 'black races'.[40] It remains critical to recall that versions of stadial history, premised upon assumed modes of subsistence, operated more particularly within these circumstances of observing distinctions.

Significantly, indigenous proprietary rights performed effectively as a policy feature disciplining anglo-settlement in New Zealand since the inception, in 1839, of Hobson's instructions. Yet, by 1844, Howick stressed the prosperity or otherwise of fledgling British settlements. Stanley's policy, a legacy of procedures established under Normanby and Russell, had not only disciplined settlement-dispersion, but also effectively stultified a corporation, sanctioned by Russell in an 18 November 1840 *concordat* to act as a potential agency of organized, 'systematic' settlements. Office functionaries had not foreseen this stultification, as Russell had insisted in correspondence to Somes (29 June 1844).[41] For Howick, as with Stanley's department, native title was chiefly *performative*: it could be integrated into a deliberative series of purchase transactions monitored by the Crown, resulting in a more secure revenue base and relatively controlled settlements. Indeed, Howick embodied this view of integrated imperial approaches to 'systematic' settling in temperate New Zealand climes—an antipodean '*Austral Britain*'[42]—and extinguishing indigenous property rights as a procedural mechanism for the Crown's management of a spectrum of transactions, which concluded in the controlled placement of settlers. This was apparent from his assessment and defence of those principles exemplified in the Goderich directives of 1831 regarding the centralized management of 'waste lands' and the uses of revenues from their sale.[43]

[38] For example Barrow, 'Australasia', in *Encyclopædia Britannica*, IV, 215–16; Barrow, 'Polynesia', in ibid, XVIII, 315; 'Man', in ibid, XIV, 200; Latham, *The Ethnology of the British colonies and dependencies*, 203–4; Prichard, 'On inquiries into the races of man', in *Report of the British Association for the advancement of science*, 52–5; Angas, *Savage life and scenes in Australia and New Zealand*, I, 303–7; Marjoribanks, *Travels in New Zealand*, 71: 'Their colour is of a light clear brown, varying much in shade, and sometimes even lighter than a native of the south of France'; Lorimer, 'Science and the secularization of Victorian images of race', in Lightman (ed), *Victorian Science in Context*, 212–17; Stoler, *Race and the Education of Desire*, 124–7 (race and class as fluid semantic fields).

[39] Stephen, minute, 12 September 1843, cited in Morrell, *British Colonial Policy in the Age of Peel and Russell*, 90.

[40] For example Stephen to Lyttelton, minute, 26 February 1846, CO209/35, fo.47, TNA.

[41] Russell to Somes, 29 June 1844, PRO30/22/4C, fos.192–5, TNA.

[42] 'Principles of colonization—New Zealand', , 67–96; Earl Grey, 'memorandum on colonial policy drawn up by me in 1849', confidential, 8 February 1849, Gre/B143/B3, fo.9, DUL, referring optimistically to Australia and New Zealand: 'Such is the actual state of things and the prospects for the future in the more important of those British colonies which possess temperate climates, and which are fitted for the residence of large European populations'.

[43] Howick, memorandum, 11 May 1838 (New South Wales), Gre/B146/B11, DUL; Howick, 3 December 1831, 'memorandum on Col[onel] Arthur's despatch on land granting & emigration', Gre/B144/2, DUL.

Hence, notions of indigenous property rights-status formed part of a calculus for collection of revenue and disciplining intra-European activities. In this sense, New Zealand represented a thematic development on imperial land-management experiences in New South Wales, Port Phillip, and southern Australia, with the added slant of a lengthy history—since 1815—of using purchase deeds in transactions with Māori. Evidently, this disposition was not merely personal to Howick. The predispositions of such a policy had resulted during Russell's tenure in a commission on colonial land and emigration presided over by Thomas Elliot, and Stanley's legislation enacted in 1842 concerning the transfer of antipodean 'waste lands'.[44] Importantly, many issues arising within the context of Pennington's decisions as to the Company's entitlements to acreage or FitzRoy's territorial and revenue policies within New Zealand were procedurally referred to Elliot and his colleagues for a deliberative opinion. Stanley and Hope adopted this approach on several occasions.[45]

New Zealand was envisaged as a settlement site—as a field for emigration. Critically, conspicuous warring and forcible disruption—*occuli usupare*—or seizures of territories alighted upon by a visiting and avaricious eye, while perceived to characterize narratives within southern Africa, were thought not to be signifiers of these antipodean imperial practices of deliberative European settlement mediated by purchase.[46] New Zealand was not to be a place for wars and conquests. A combined juristic vocabulary of property rights and 'purchase' represented mechanisms that might prevent the possibilities of the decline and extinction of aborigines in New Zealand. Company rhetoric suggested a substantial degree of convergence on the broad parameters of approach to aborigines and territory, if not on the detailed means of securing the confirmation of Company titles and the placement of its settlers. Accordingly, Somes informed Stanley on 25 January 1843 that as the 'heir of a patrimony so large [in the territories reserved within Company settlements for aboriginal uses] the native chief, instead of contemplating European neighbours with jealous apprehension, as a race destined to degrade and oust them, would learn to view with delight [their] presence'.[47]

Still, Howick saw native title as an accessorial feature of his cherished government-funded emigration and 'free trade' responses to the 'condition-of-England' question.[48] He thought that these responses might capture substantial electoral support for Whig candidates, as illustrated in correspondence with Russell and his personal musings. Mandler identifies Howick as a Whig who keenly assisted Russell's political strategies

[44] Burroughs, *Britain and Australia*, 216–28; Haines, *Emigration and the Labouring Poor*; Russell to Elliot, Villiers, Torrens, 14 January 1840, CO385/19, fo.236, TNA.

[45] Elliot, Villers to Stephen, 8 April 1843, CO209/40, fos.46–6a, TNA; Shaw Lefevre and Charles Wood, memorandum, 19 November 1844, CO209/40, fos.230–59.

[46] Keegan, *Colonial South Africa and the Origins of the Racial order*, 120, 121, 136, 140–50; Pretorius, 'The British Humanitarians and the Cape Eastern Frontier', in *Archives Yearbook for South African History*, I, 18–19, 21. See also Guyana in Menezes, *British Policy towards the Amerindians in British Guiana, 1803–1873*, 205–6. By 1838, Guyana was conceived of as a place of granting 'Crown lands' rather than regularized 'purchases' from Amerindians.

[47] Somes to Stanley, 25 January 1843, CO209/26, fos.99–113a, TNA; Jellicoe, *The New Zealand Company's Native Reserves*, 26–32.

[48] Howick, journal, [loose notes entitled 'state of the country', facing entries for 9 March 1845 to 11 March 1845]: 'Emigrat[io]n greatly extended & systematic', Gre/V/C3/10, DUL; Howick to Russell, January 1845, PRO30/22/4D, fos.87–94, TNA; Carlyle, *Chartism*, 5: 'condition-of-England question'; Mandler, *Aristocratic Government in the Age of Reform*, 227–8 (Howick and 'condition of England politics, 1845–1846').

to align the Whig chieftains with programmes for relieving the so-called 'condition-of-England'.[49] Howick encouraged any predilection to address the 'condition of the labouring classes', suggesting that the main policy ought to be the 'sweeping away of all restrictions upon the freedom of trade except those duties which we impose simply and exclusively with a view to revenue'.[50] Systematically organized emigration would represent an additional measure. Howick did not personally express substantial direct interest in indigenous New Zealand or in the Company per se except insofar as it coincided with his Whig factional strategies—as heir to the second Earl Grey—in hectoring Peel's ministry on a favoured series of subjects, especially the 'condition-of-England' issue, or 'present state of things', as he gently characterized it. Howick perceived 'emigration' along with 'free trade' as a means for relieving economic hardships in Britain. Moreover, his preoccupations with whiggish hierarchy, legal control, and proprietary discipline were readily apparent. Howick combined this strategy with his continuing interests in imperial issues—evident in Chapters Two and Three. Certainly, Howick's emphasis on ordered settlements was evident in his report: 'Additional means of enforcing obedience to lawful authority are required, not merely against the natives, but against the lower class of emigrants'.[51] In spite of these preoccupations shared with the Colonial Office, varied distinctions occurred in opinions as to the substance or contents of indigenous tenure, specifically in relation to the Company's procedural capacity to receive confirmed territorial titles. Against this context, effectively settling perturbed pākehā remained Howick's predominant anxiety. He emphasized that Māori were crude agriculturists who did not extensively occupy the soils in industry.

> The unoccupied land, previously to European settlement, was of no value to them, they were neither a pastoral people, nor one living, like the North American Indians, by the chase, and therefore requiring a great extent of country for their support; they derived their chief subsistence from the produce of the soil and agriculture, rude as it was.[52]

Howick's report stressed that 'the natives of New Zealand, till they learnt to do so from Europeans, attached no idea of value to unoccupied land'. Incorrect policies on aboriginal title—an 'erroneous view of this question'—had stifled the prosperity of the settlements, constituting a 'serious check to the progress of improvement'.[53] Clearly, indigenous proprietary rights assumed a central place in assessing imperial policies *towards* and *in* New Zealand. New Zealand as a successful experiment in settlement was imperilled. The principal difficulty was assumed to lie in the observation that since 1840 (in spite of Eliot's Select Committee), 'those rules as to the mode in which colonization ought to be conducted, which have been drawn from reason and from experience, have not been sufficiently attended to'.[54] Howick praised Gipps' address to the legislative council of New South Wales in August 1840 concerning his

[49] Mandler, *Aristocratic Government in the Age of Reform*, 228.
[50] Howick to Russell, January 1845, PRO30/22/4D, fo.88, TNA.
[51] Report, 'select committee appointed to inquire into the state of the colony of New Zealand; and into the proceedings of the New Zealand Company', *GBPP1844*, xiii (556), 11.
[52] Ibid, 7; Belgrave, 'Pre-emption, the Treaty of Waitangi and the politics of Crown purchase', 30.
[53] Report, 'select committee appointed to inquire into the state of the colony of New Zealand; and into the proceedings of the New Zealand Company', *GBPP1844*, xiii (556), 11, 7–8.
[54] Ibid, 3.

proposed ordinance for reviewing putative titles acquired from indigenous populations before the date of his January 1840 proclamation declaring the invalidity of any direct purchases from Māori. Gipps' three 'political axioms' were cited with approbation as 'rules' animating an appropriate 'mode of colonization'. For Howick, Gipps' first maxim was foundational. Thus, 'the uncivilized inhabitants of any country have but a qualified dominion over it, or a right of occupancy only'. Gipps explained this reference. He argued that 'cultivation' or 'subjugat[ion of the] ground to their own uses' was a basis for individuated aboriginal proprietorship. Otherwise, their property was mere commonage and could not be transferred to foreign subjects as the whole indigenous community had an interest in it which could not be easily unravelled.[55] In part, this treatment of aboriginal tenure revived what Pagden has referred to as a 'agriculturist argument' restricting aboriginal tenure to land visited with the application of labour, such as plantings of vegetables (*fructus industriales*), a perspective in which Vattel and Locke exemplified variants.[56] Yet, Howick's proximate source was Gipps' speech, as reported in a despatch printed within an extended collection of parliamentary papers with which Howick was familiar.[57] In 1849, the Hudson's Bay Company would try to use Howick's report to limit the property of aborigines in what became British Columbia.[58]

Using Gipps, Howick signalled that Māori as limited agriculturists, as planters of vegetables, were advanced in his assessment of indigenous proprietorship. Māori were circled within this meshing of history and law by parliamentary sympathizers of 'systematic colonization' in New Zealand. Howick's report resonated with these assumptions. Indeed, the reliability or relative authenticity of *viva voce* evidence presented to the Committee was determined by its degree of convergence with a stadial historical appreciation of Māori and what Howick privileged as 'the ancient and acknowledged principles of colonial law as laid down by Sir George Gipps'.[59] An apostasy from these maxims was deemed to have arisen within Stanley's department, as reflected in its allegedly erroneous perception of native title. Thus, this report referred to 'the manifest absurdity of attempting to apply the notions of English law, with respect to landed property, to such a state of society, and the utter fruitlessness of an endeavour to disentangle the complicated and conflicting claims set up by different tribes to wild land'.[60] There was a distrust of such material as overly relativizing and as unhelpful to policy formulation.

[55] Ibid, 3.

[56] For example, Locke, *Two Treatises of Government,* II, cap V, §§27 *et seq* ('The *Labour* of his Body, and the *Work* of his Hands, we may say, are properly his. Whatsoever then he removes out of the State of that Nature hath provided, and left it in, he hath mixed his *Labour* with, and joyned to it something that is his own, and thereby makes it his *Property*' (emphasis in original)). Pagden, *Lords of all the World*, 78–9; Pocock, 'A Discourse on Sovereignty', in Phillipson and Skinner (eds), *Political Discourse in Early Modern Britain*, 377–428, 419; Pocock, 'Tangata whenua and enlightenment anthropology', 36–40; Pocock, 'Removal from the wings [review article]', 12–13.

[57] Howick, notes on New Zealand parliamentary papers, Gre/B161/87, DUL; Gre/V/C3/10: journal, 2 July 1844.

[58] Fisher, *Contact and Conflict*, 66–7.

[59] Report, 'select committee appointed to inquire into the state of the colony of New Zealand; and into the proceedings of the New Zealand Company', *GBPP1844*, xiii (556), 6–7.

[60] Ibid, 7.

INTERROGATING CUSTOMS AND SOURCES OF UNEASE

Evidently, the localized review of Māori tenurial conceptions in New Zealand irritated critics of imperial policies on native title. Clarke and his assistant protectors of aborigines, such as Shortland, were conduits of these irritations. The latter warned: 'It is from purchasing lands, the right to which is contested by two hostile parties, either of whom is glad to avail himself of an opportunity to sell independantly [*sic*] of the other, that Europeans have unwarily fallen into so many difficulties'.[61] Aspects of Shortland's reportage even suggested that certain Europeans might have merely attained a status in Māori perceptions akin to licensees or squatters—'*he noho noa iho*'.[62] Inconvenient surprises awaited imperial policies on New Zealand shores. Ironically, pursuing Māori tenurial 'customs' was embedded in expectations of what norms regulated 'barbarians', 'natives', and 'uncivilized tribes'—customary practices rather than enacted laws were expected. Within localized investigations of assumed 'customs', therefore, was an instability that spun centrifugally to undermine European confidence in 'knowing' Māori. Through the collection of supposedly customary notions, Māori narratives concerning claims to territory penetrated intra-European conversations. Importantly, the habitual custom of 'tribal peoples' vis-à-vis 'real property' was considered as already 'known' in the theoretical expectations of certain members of the Company or Parliament, like Howick. Company representatives averred that descent-groupings, such as Ngāti Toa and Te Ātiawa, acquired inflated notions of proprietorship beyond mere physical 'occupancy' through the coincidental presence of pākehā. On this account, then, there were no reliable indigenous narratives of proprietorship prior to the advent of European visitors. Irritation was exacerbated by an increasingly intrusive Māori correspondence that occasionally conveyed limited views upon proprietorship.[63] Divergent, discomfiting sources, such as that of Dieffenbach, whose chronicled *Travels* alleged in 1843 that '[t]here exists a very distinct notion of the rights of landed property amongst the natives and every inch of land in New Zealand has its proprietor', were marginalized.[64]

Similarly, Hope, arguing in November 1844 that assumptions that no 'waste' or 'unoccupied' territories existed in New Zealand were erroneous, would also marginalize this perspective, associating it with FitzRoy's disappointing political performance.[65] This 'knowing' obviated local intelligence-gathering to a certain extent or limited it to

[61] Shortland to Clarke, 15 August 1843, NZMs998/4, APL.

[62] Shortland, *The Southern Districts of New Zealand*, 86.

[63] FitzRoy to Stanley, 14 April 1844, CO209/27, fo.265, TNA: 'the natives are now frequent letter writers'; Tamihana te Rauparaha to FitzRoy, 2 August 1845, CO209/35, fos.418–18a, TNA (translation, fo.419): 'I am pleased because Heretaunga has been given up to the Europeans—Rauparaha was greatly displeased with those people living at Heretaunga and if they had continued regardless of his word he Rauparaha would have taken up arms and fought against them'.

[64] Dieffenbach, *Travels in New Zealand*, II, 114. Nonetheless, Company proponents or sympathizers scavenged useful information from this literature, particularly details concerning Māori population density and distribution: Marjoribanks, *Travels in New Zealand* 70; Buller to Stanley, confidential, 26 April 1845, CO209/39, fos.295a–6, TNA; Buller to Stanley, 26 April 1845, CO208/188, fo.298, TNA.

[65] Hope, minute, 22 November 1844, CO209/29, fo.295a, TNA: '[FitzRoy's] plan of waiving the Crown's right of preemption is undoubtedly at [odds] with the views of [Howick's select] committee—but as these views were founded on the assumption that the native rights of property are of the most limited extent whereas the [governor] holds the distinctly opposite opinion it was impossible to object that his proceedings would coincide with their recommendations'. See Chapter Three.

identifying chiefly negotiators or those who were proprietors in common—an assumed signal of 'primitive' or 'tribal peoples'. This treatment conflicts with Adams' view of the Treaty of Waitangi as necessarily requiring the investigation of Māori 'customs' since Russell evidently expected the institution of such a process independently of this Treaty document in royal instructions to Hobson dated 28 January 1841.[66] Investigating 'custom' was impelled by regulating the dispersion of settlements and finding procedures for unlocking aboriginal tenure through purchase in a deliberate, ordered way.[67] This investigative approach undermined the Office's resort to the process of administrative satisficing in the conduct of imperial policies towards indigenous New Zealand. Formulaic expressions such as 'territorial rights of the natives' or 'occupation and enjoyment' in Colonial Office-sanctioned documents invited debate and diversity in opinions regarding property, not coherent categorizations, as well as a thickening of evidential and abstract content.[68] In his polemical report, Howick considered the position evident:

> In [the] charter and instructions, 'actual occupation and enjoyment' are clearly pointed out as alone establishing a right of property in land in the natives; and the rule is laid down that all other lands must be considered as vested in the Crown, in virtue of the sovereignty that had been assumed, and that they must be dealt with accordingly.[69]

Howick, as a Whig paramount, an advocate of ministerial oversight of settlement ventures, and a patron of individuals as diverse as Stephen and Buller,[70] criticized the Company for its precipitate despatch of expeditions and emigrants in 1839. This action had 'the unfortunate effect of placing those settlers and the agents of the [Company], from the very outset, on unfriendly terms with the officer whom Her Majesty's government found it necessary immediately to despatch from England for the purpose of establishing the authority of the Crown in the islands of New Zealand'.[71] Crucially, Howick's report argued that misunderstanding aboriginal property had undermined anglophone-settling within New Zealand. Inauspiciously, Howick's Committee was neither a ministerially responsive nor managed Committee. In this sense, it differed markedly from Buxton's Select Committee report upon aborigines in 1837. Howick's eventual report ought to be treated as essentially partisan and polemical. The report was characterized by ontestation and divisions over resolutions from 8 July until 23 July. This perplexed

[66] Adams, *Fatal Necessity*, 189–90; Russell to Hobson, 28 January 1841, CO209/8, fos.454a–5, TNA. See Chapter Three.

[67] See also Hadfield to Grey, memorandum, 1846, 'system of government among the New Zealand tribes', referring to political and territorial 'customs', GNZMss17, APL; 'Custom': 'a comprehensive term, denoting the manners, ceremonies and fashions of a people, which having turned into habit, and passed into general use, obtain the force of laws [*lex non scripta*]', in *Encyclopædia Britannica*, VII, 558.

[68] For example Coates, *The New Zealanders and their lands*, 9, 20–1, 25. Compare 'New Zealand', in *Fisher's Colonial Magazine and journal of trade, commerce, and banking*, I, 204 and Stammers, 'On the Rights of Aborigines in Cases of Colonial Settlement', in ibid, 290–5; Anonymous, 'The New Zealand question', 250–60.

[69] *GBPP1844*, xiii (556), 6.

[70] See Chapters One and Two. Earl Grey to Buller, private, 3 August 1846, Gre/B70/11/36, DUL; Grey to Buller, 23 February 1847, Gre/B70/11/55; Buller to Grey, 15 March 1847, Gre/B70/11/61; Stephen to Grey, 16 October 1847, Gre/B126/12, DUL; Stephen to Howick, 5 February 1845, Add/7888/II, fos.337–41, CUL; Howick to Stephen, 25 February 1845, fos.342–3; Stephen, diary, 12 July 1846, Add/7511, CUL.

[71] *GBPP1844*, xiii (556), 4.

Howick to a certain extent, as he indicated on 8 July 1844: 'I went straight to the railway stat[io]n to the [House of Commons] for the NZ^{d} comm[itt]ee where rather to my surprise Cardwell produced a set of counter resolutions to mine'.[72] Howick's positions were sufficiently supported, however. These resolutions were 'discussed at great length & upon a division it was determined by a majority that mine not his sh[oul]d be taken as the basis for consideration'.[73]

Hope submitted an opposing draft report on 23 July 1844 to that prepared by Howick. Hope's contrary report treated the Waitangi Treaty as significant to understanding Māori land rights, although no effort was made to explain these rights.[74] Perhaps the attitudes of Stanley and Hope were clearly expressed when Hope's draft noted that '[the Committee] are far from being of opinion that rights can be established by natives to the whole wild lands in the islands, but they are by no means prepared to assert that they cannot show such rights to parts of them'.[75] The mechanisms through which the substance of these rights could be understood were those created for localized collection of intelligence by itinerant protectors of aborigines and commissioners reviewing deeds of acquisition: 'Nor do your Committee think it would be prudent or right to give any decisive opinion on their extent, without a much fuller investigation, not only than that instituted by themselves, but than it would be possible to institute anywhere except in New Zealand itself'.[76] Here was the kernel of Hope's viewpoint as a formulator of imperial practices in conjunction with Stanley and Colonial Office conceptions of due processes established in New Zealand that derived, in their turn, from the Normanby and Russell periods. Hope was committed to procedures inherited from Russell, and this personal and political commitment was entrenched during FitzRoy's administration, not least because FitzRoy had been appointed by Stanley.

Again, there was an assertion of appropriate procedures for gathering governmental information in continuation of activities noted in Chapter Three. Stanley defended such a stance in the House of Lords on 10 July 1845: '*These laws—these customs—and the right arising from them on the part of the Crown—we have guaranteed when we accepted the sovereignty of the islands;...so far as native title is proved*—be the land waste or occupied—barren or enjoyed, those rights and titles the Crown of England is bound in honour to maintain'.[77] Hope delicately prepared avenues for political extrication, however. Accordingly, in Hope's suggested report FitzRoy was a potential scapegoat for matters awry in Company settlements. Stanley and Hope were implicitly prepared to jettison their gubernatorial appointee: 'Captain Fitzroy was, by those

[72] Howick, journal, 8 July 1844, Gre/V/C3/10, DUL.

[73] Ibid; Morrell, *British Colonial Policy in the Age of Peel and Russell*, 114.

[74] *GBPP1844*, xiii (556), 26: 'Your Committee, therefore, consider that the question of the extent to which the rights of Natives in land in New Zealand are to be recognised, is no longer one to be determined by reference to the general prerogative of the Crown, or to sound principles of colonization, but that it must be tried and decided upon the true construction of the Treaty only; and in considering the question, is to that point that they have directed their attention'.

[75] Ibid, 27. [76] Ibid, 27–8.

[77] *HPD*, 3rd series, 82, 319 (emphasis added) ('a large portion of the district in question [New Zealand Company settlements district] is distributed among various tribes, all of whom have as perfect a knowledge of the boundaries and limits of their possessions—boundaries and limits in some places natural, in others artificial—as satisfactory and well defined as were, one hundred years ago, the bounds... of districts occupied by great proprietors and their clans in the Highlands of Scotland' (ibid, 318–19)).

instructions [of 19 May and 26 June 1843] and a reference to previous correspondence, directed to make good at once, as far as the title of the Crown would enable him to do so, within the limits claimed by the Company, the titles of the settlers claiming under them'.[78] Again, the position of the Colonial Office was stated: 'Your Committee do not consider it to have been contemplated that the Crown could assert a right to no land by its own prerogative'. Hope's draft continued, 'on the contrary, whatever shall prove on inquiry to be affected by no proprietary rights, your Committee consider to have vested at once in the Crown'.[79] Both perceptions were pursuing settlement of land untrammelled by reported narratives of Māori claims to territory. However, Hope's option was narrowly dismissed upon a division,[80] and Howick's version was accepted.

Yet Stanley ignored Howick's report, irritating Somes, a Tory parliamentarian himself from 1844.[81] Stanley forwarded the report to FitzRoy on 30 July 1844 without comment, having not yet considered its several recommendations.[82] He ultimately advised FitzRoy on the Office's treatment of this report on 13 August. Stanley averred that there were a variety of 'uncivilized' or 'savage' populations, such that it was possible to distinguish certain populations from others. As there were varieties in humanity, so there was a diversity of 'savages', chiefly perceived through their relations to sources of sustenance—a Malthusian and stadial historical viewpoint. Stanley was unsure, even 'were the question one of mere theory', that he could 'subscribe unhesitatingly, and without reserve, to the fundamental assumption' of Howick's Select Committee concerning the propriety of Gipps' view on 'cultivation' as imparting constrained territorial rights:[83] 'There are many gradations of "uncivilized inhabitants", and practically, according to their state of civilization, must be the extent of their rights which they can be allowed to claim, whenever the territory on which they reside is occupied by civilized communities'.[84] This admission of diversity amongst the 'uncivilized' was unexceptional. Russell enunciated a similar viewpoint in August 1840 when instructing Gipps on varying strategies for transforming aboriginal inhabitants.[85] Stanley insisted that Māori were undoubtedly 'far above the inhabitants of the other Australian colonies'. Thus, he commented, the 'aborigines of New Holland generally are broken into feeble and perfectly savage migratory tribes'. In addition, he stated that these inhabitants were prone to 'roaming over boundless extents of

[78] *GBPP1844*, xiii (556) 29; Stanley to FitzRoy, 26 June 1843, PRO, CO209/24, fo.166.

[79] *GBPP1844*, xiii (556) 29 (emphasis added).

[80] Morrell, *British colonial policy in the Age of Peel and Russell*, 114.

[81] Somes was member for Dartmouth from 1844, and confirmed in the seat after an attempt to disqualify him as a government contractor. He died on 25 June 1845: *A Dictionary of New Zealand Biography*, Scholefield (ed), 315–16.

[82] Stanley to FitzRoy, 30 July 1844, CO209/27, fos.124–30a, TNA.

[83] Stanley to FitzRoy, 13 August 1844, 'Papers relative to New Zealand', *GBPP1845*, xxxiii (1), 145.

[84] Ibid.

[85] Russell to Gipps, 25 August 1840, *Historical Records of Australia, series I*, 774: 'We should run a risk of entire failure if we should confound in one abstract description of Aborigines the various races of people, some half-civilized, some little raised above the brutes, some hunting over vast tracts of country, others with scarcely any means or habits of destroying wild animals at all, who have encountered the discovering or invading nations of Europe over the face of the globe.... [T]he manner, in which [our duty] is to be performed, must vary with the varying materials upon which we are to work. No workman would attempt to saw a plank of fir, and cut a block of granite with the same instrument'.

country, subsisting from day to day on the precarious produce of the chase, wholly ignorant of or averse to the cultivation of the soil, with no principles of civil government, or recognition of private property'.[86] With these aspects noted, Stanley insisted, 'It is impossible to admit, on the part of a population thus situated, any rights in the soil which should be permitted to interfere with the subjugation by Europeans of the vast wilderness over which they are scattered'.[87] As such, all vague notions of 'justice' or 'humanity' required in policy was to 'endeavour, as civilization and cultivation expand, to embrace the aborigines within their pale, . . . to induce them, if possible, to adopt more settled modes of providing for their subsistence, and to afford them the means of doing so [through establishing reserves]'.[88]

Māori were distinctive by virtue of their status as practitioners of an 'agriculture, rude, indeed, but continuous'. Moreover, 'rights of property, as between tribe and tribe, and of individuals of each tribe *inter se*, were recognized and well understood'.[89] According to Stanley, these varying sources of sustenance entailed ramifications for imperial policies: 'I cannot think it would be either just or practicable to apply the same rule, with regard to the occupation of land, to classes of aborigines so widely differing from each other'.[90] In settlements managed by layered procedures emanating from a gubernatorial administration, Stanley stressed the observance of due processes as fulfilling policy requirements on aboriginal title. In these circumstances, it was predominantly the Company, 'colonial reformers' or 'radicals', such as Buller, and certain Whigs like Russell and Howick, who remained committed to those intellectual sources connected to northern American jurisprudence and Vattelian reasoning on *ius gentium*. Stanley resisted these increasingly partisan sources, considering 'theory' or intellectual assumptions as inapplicable even where these might have animated the policies to which he was attached (as in Russell's surprise in 1844 at the difficulty with locating unoccupied 'waste' land).[91] As such, the deployment of these intellectual resources was undeniably partisan and contestable, as was their rejection. Stanley's stance was not illustrative of a rigorous theoretical application of viewpoints upon aboriginal title that required, *ipso facto*, references to 'Maori customary law'.[92] Stanley assumed the poverty of provisional theory or modes of analysis in supplying policy guidance: 'What you and I have to do is to administer the affairs of the colony in reference to a state of things which we find, but did not create'.[93] *Ius gentium* was founded on the acts of Britain towards aboriginal New Zealand—on a treaty; on the prior recognition of 'independence' in a confederacy of chieftains principally dwelling in the far north of the North Island of New Zealand.

[86] Stanley to FitzRoy, 13 August 1844, *GBPP1845*, xxxiii (1), 145.

[87] Ibid. [88] Ibid, 145–6.

[89] Ibid, 146 (an inchoate agriculture was admitted as their 'main, though not their sole subsistence').

[90] Ibid: 'But whatever may be the right theory, it is indisputable that in practice a distinction has been drawn by the Acts of the British Government'; Hope to Peel, 5 February 1845, BL AddMss40559, fos.29a–30a: 'Now in truth the only essential point in which the com[mittee] differ from Ld. S. is whether or not the rights of the natives in land, ought to be, or can be, confined to what they "occupy and enjoy"' (ibid, fos.29a–30).

[91] Russell to Somes, 29 June 1844, PRO30/22/4C, fo.194a, TNA.

[92] Cf McHugh, *The Maori Magna Carta*, 132–3.

[93] Stanley to FitzRoy, 13 August 1844, 'Papers relative to New Zealand', *GBPP1845*, xxxiii (1), 146–7.

CUSTOM AND ITS DISCONTENTS, PART I—BULLER, STANLEY, HOPE, AND HOWICK

By 1844 and 1845, Stanley was insisting that Māori tenurial interests could only be comprehended through interrogating 'native law and custom', a position that was personal to him in Westminster given Hope's suspicions concerning the extent of aboriginal title. He stated that 'feeling the information necessary for the purpose [of determining the extent to which aboriginal title might be admitted] not to be within my reach in this country, I constantly refused to the New Zealand Company to define authoritatively here so difficult and important a question'.[94] Stanley was uncomfortable with any restriction of such title to those tracts actually in cultivation, on the basis of his comprehension of Māori practice. Thus, 'it appeared to me inconsistent with the practice of these tribes, who, after cultivating, and of course exhausting, a given spot for a series of years, desert it for another within the limits of the recognized property of the tribe'.[95] His own position harboured tensions, however. He assumed that Māori territorial rights could not extensively penetrate uncultivated locations in forested or mountainous terrain. Policy was beset by such tensions. In a revealing passage, he averred:

> On the other hand, I had no doubt that on your arrival in New Zealand, you would find that there were considerable tracts of country to which no tribe could establish a *bonâ fide* title: and still more extensive districts, to which, by personal communication with the chiefs, you would obtain a title on easy terms and by amicable arrangements.[96]

As seen in Chapter Three, Hope considered FitzRoy to have exaggerated the spatial extent of aboriginal territories through his uncritical reception via Clarke of tales derived from Māori themselves. For Hope, FitzRoy had proceeded too far on his substantive and procedural interpretations of aboriginal tenure, unforgivably rendering Stanley's administration vulnerable to assault within Parliament. In drafting a segment on this perplexing 'land question' for the use of FitzRoy's successor, George Grey, Hope's opinion was apparent: 'I consider it not only consistent with the observance of that guarantee [concerning aboriginal proprietary rights in the Treaty's second article], but in fact essential to rendering it effective that measures should be adopted for defining what these rights are'.[97] He concluded that 'such a step must, I feel convinced... place large districts at the disposal of the Crown as land to which no valid title can be shewn [*sic*] on the part of any one else'. In registering titles, Hope anticipated 'a large increase in the extent of land at the disposal of the Crown, without resort being had to purchase from the natives'.[98]

Against these perspectives, FitzRoy's intellectual assumptions were revealed in the seams of a despatch to Stanley defending his performance as governor. He endorsed the view that Māori had degenerated from a 'half-civilized' condition in mist-ridden pasts such that all that remained were 'the numerous and well-armed descendants,—the formidable "fragments" [or, as FitzRoy noted, '*toenga*']'. To these traces of halcyon periods, Māori still adhered with 'pertinacity'. Hence, 'the "ritenga Maori" ['*tikanga*

[94] Ibid, 147. [95] Ibid. [96] Ibid.

[97] Hope, memorandum, 'land question', 10 May 1845, CO209/38, fos.324–4a, TNA.

[98] Ibid, fos.324a, 326.

Maori'], or native "common law" cannot be set aside by force, or hastily'.[99] Although these aborigines had degenerated, they possessed an agency to resist or deflect colonial settlements or the attempted management of how to define relations between pākehā and Māori. The vulnerability of bridgehead colonial settlements to destruction was acknowledged with an analogous reference to events in Chile.[100] FitzRoy failed to address the fundamental delays in the resolution of a tortuous 'land question'.

Stanley's office, in pledging itself to FitzRoy's recall from the New Zealand governorship, was unwilling to indulge FitzRoy's defences.[101] In part, the recall was meant to placate the Company. Stanley brought the proposal to recall FitzRoy to Peel's cabinet.[102] Evidently, additional complications occurred in connection with unauthorized pastoral activities but such was the difficulty with the principal settlements at Whanganui, Wellington and New Plymouth that they seldom emerged into Office discourses, certainly not until 1847. A haphazard infiltration of pākehā into hinterlands beyond surveyed enclaves of settlements ('squatting') in pursuit of pasturage occurred, as in New South Wales and southern Africa. In such regions negotiating one's presence with Māori descent-groupings proved necessary (as in the Wairarapa for instance). However, disciplinary techniques, such as pursuing these persons with licensing, would not be attempted until George Grey's period as governor (from 18 November 1845) even though pasture licences had been permitted under the imperial legislation addressing the transfer of interests in Australasian 'waste lands'.[103] That legislation no longer applied to New Zealand after 1846.[104] Native title and its associated intellectual

[99] FitzRoy to Stanley, 10 November 1845, CO209/36, fos.420–20a, TNA. William Cotton, a companion of George Augustus Selwyn, noted another recorded instance of using *toenga* in this fashion, observing that Te Heuheu Tukino II used it in 1843: Hogan, *Renata's Journey*, 89.

[100] FitzRoy to Stanley, 10 November 1845, CO209/36, fos.425a–6: 'I looked at the totally exposed, and defenceless state of all the settlements, without walls, stockades, or any kind of sufficient protection: without even a place of refuge for women and children. I remembered the destruction in Chile of seven Spanish towns, in one night, by Aboriginal Natives far inferior to the New Zealanders in arms and warlike qualities'.

[101] Stanley to FitzRoy, 30 April 1845 (recall of FitzRoy), CO209/39, fos.20–2, TNA. For the revocation of FitzRoy's commission as governor, see Stanley to FitzRoy, 14 May 1845, BL AddMss40571, fos.53–5. A commitment to not indulging FitzRoy's defences of his performance continued under Stanley's successor, Gladstone: Gairdner, minute, 20 June 1846, PRO, CO209/36, fos.454a–5a; Stephen to Lyttelton, 22 June 1846, CO209/36, fo.429.

[102] 'Captain FitzRoy's conduct in New Zealand', 920Der(14), 29/1: 'New Zealand, 1844–1845'; 'Charles Buller and the New Zealand Company' (cabinet memoranda, 1845), 920Der(14), 27/5, LRO.

[103] See 'an ordinance to regulate the occupation of waste lands of the Crown in the province of New Ulster', 22 August 1849, 'further papers relative to the affairs of New Zealand', *GBPP1850*, xxxvii [1250], 61–6: cl 11, 'No person shall depasture cattle on, or otherwise occupy any waste lands of the Crown without a licence for that purpose, in such form and subject to such conditions as the Governor for the time being shall from time to time prescribe by notice in the New Zealand Government Gazette'. Cf 'An Act for regulating the sale of waste land belonging to the Crown in the *Australian* colonies', 5 & 6 Vict, c36 (Imp), s 17. On pastoral licensing in New South Wales, see Goodall, *Invasion to Embassy*, 48–9. On Grey's assumption of office as governor, see Grey to Stanley, 15 November 1845, CO209/38, fos.8–9, TNA; Grey to Stanley, 21 November 1845, CO209/38, fos.10–14a.

[104] The precise date at which the imperial legislation ceased to apply in New Zealand is difficult to identify. It appears that the waste lands legislation remained in force within New Zealand from 23 November 1842 (*Supplement to the New Zealand Government Gazette*, 2, number 48, 23 November 1842, proclamation of Willoughby Shortland) until at least 1847 (see 9 & 10 Vict, c104 (28 August 1846) (Imp) s 11: 'And be it enacted, that from after the passing of this Act the said recited Act shall not

resources became embroiled in partisan contests, demonstrating the instability of this concept's substance. The Company commenced a complicated campaign directed in the Commons and at Peel, endeavouring to harass the government in the former and to court the latter's favour. Eventually, this strategy proved effective, particularly once the Company had demonstrated the extent of its parliamentary support in the Commons during a prolonged debate from 17 June until 19 June 1845. A second period of conciliation or rapprochement between Office and Company glimmered towards the end of Stanley's tenure as Secretary of State for Colonies in 1845. This relative conciliation was noticeably expressed during the tenure of his two successors, Gladstone and Howick, the latter inheriting his father's title as the third Earl Grey from July 1845. Peel's Home Secretary and close advisor, Sir James Graham, was enlisted in this contest, indicating the profound significance of these disputes to Peel's ministry at least for a time. Not only did he participate in the eventual parliamentary debates but he also attended interviews with Company representatives, such as Buller, along with Stanley.[105] Furthermore, Graham was increasingly preoccupied with the vulnerability of Peel's ministry within and outside the Commons, commenting how the ministerialists had 'laboured hard, and not in vain to restore the prosperity of the country, and to give increased security to the aristocracy by improving the condition and diminishing the discontent of the great masses of the people'. Yet, he lamented, although these objects had been pursued 'without afflicting any real injury on the landed proprietors . . . we are scouted as traitors and denounced as if we were time-serving traders in politics seeking to retain place by the sacrifice of the interests of our friends'.[106] Subsequently, in April, he observed how the Maynooth measure could not 'fail to make an impression on the Roman Catholics, but the no-Popery feeling is strong throughout England and Scotland, and we must prepare to [e]ncounter a serious storm'. In saying so, Graham 'did not much like the division of last night', as '[i]n the minority the proportion of our friends was too large; in the majority we were left too much in dangerous dependence on our enemies'.[107]

The Company eventually outmanoeuvred Stanley in June and July 1845 into conceding its objectives to an extent, although he attempted to conceal these concessions nonetheless. Stanley's move to sacrifice FitzRoy in April 1845 proved insufficient. By that stage in any event, the imprint of native title was perceived as a feature to avoid in settling New Zealand locations. Thus, the introduction of constructs of native title and Māori claims to cultivated and non-cultivated territory were now seen as inconvenient. Buller earnestly appealed for Peel's intervention on 14 December 1844, whilst Peel

apply to Land situate in the Colony of New Zealand: Provided nevertheless, that nothing herein contained shall extend to invalidate any Act done in the said Colony in pursuance of the said recited Act before or within One Month after the passing of this Act shall have been made known by Proclamation by the Governor of the said Colony to the Inhabitants thereof'). See the application of 9 & 10 Vict, c104 (28 August 1846) (Imp), s 11, as announced in Earl Grey to Grey, 23 December 1846, CO209/47, fos.261–85a, TNA. See also CO208/129, fo.203a: 'Colonization circular, issued by Her Majesty's colonial land and emigration commissioners', 26 August 1848 ('sale of waste lands in the colonies').

105 Minutes, 'secret committee', 1 May 1845, CO208/188, fo.294, TNA; *A Corrected Report of the Debate in the House of Commons, on the 17th, 18th, and 19th of June 1845 on the State of New Zealand and the case of the New Zealand Company*, 19 June 1845, 213.

106 Graham to Croker, private and confidential, 22 March 1845, bundle 88, Mss Film 120, Graham Mss, Bodleian Library, Oxford.

107 Graham to Heytesbury, 4 April 1845, bundle 88, Mss Film 120, Graham Mss, Bodleian Library, Oxford.

relented, granting an interview.[108] Peel was initially indifferent, preferring to impart matters to Stanley. But Peel began to intervene in early 1845. By February 1845, Peel was treating the New Zealand issue delicately, sensing the potential vulnerability of the 'land question' to be gathered up by harassing Whig strategists. He advised his strategist, the Earl of Ellenborough (Edward Law), 'to remain quiet—not to presume defence is necessary—to wait until he is attacked', a suggestion Hope swiftly acceded to.[109] Perhaps Peel was aware of Buller's proximity to Howick. Interpersonal connections were again operating in favour of the Company. There was a sense on Peel's part that an assault would be commenced in the parliamentary sphere, probably with Whig assistance. The 'rights of natives to land' was the key issue. Indeed, Hope explained to Peel that 'the main question at issue with the Company [was] the extent to which the rights of natives to land in New Zealand [were] to be recognised'.[110]

Importantly, Buller presented the Company's expectations to Peel via correspondence on 15 February 1845, while these expectations would characterize subsequent negotiations with Peel's ministry into 1846. A confidential memorandum was included, indicating that the Company was 'interested on two accounts in the amicable settlement of the questions relating to the colony'.[111] These two reasons comprised the security of those settlers it had encouraged to emigrate and, secondly, those pecuniary concerns arising from its unsatisfactory claiming of territory in New Zealand since 1839. Buller clearly expected the Company to be granted forthwith a 'prima facie title, a right to possession', whilst the imperial administration at Auckland ought to 'extinguish native titles, where necessary' to achieve this objective.[112] Moreover, the Company would geographically circumscribe the ambit of its operations, restricting them to a southern portion of the North Island and to the entire South Island. This was opted for on account of separating its settlements 'from Auckland, from the missionaries [principally based in Te Tai Tokerau], [and] from the bulk of the natives', a theme that pervaded Company proposals into 1846.[113] A pattern of perceiving native title as procedurally and politically inconvenient to the flourishing of settlers was emerging. Māori claims to territory were to be avoided if possible. There was a financial element to these proposals, requesting that the government furnish the Company with a loan for £100,000, permitting the Company to 'exist merely for the purpose of realizing our present property', unless the ministry was prepared to acquire all Company 'property' outright for £300,000.

Buller's memorandum was issued with a provocative petition draft, having been prepared for the Company and delivered to Peel, undoubtedly as a caveat, hinting at the possibilities of upcoming parliamentary embarrassment. A subsequent version clearly assailed Colonial Office interpretations of Russell's *concordat* with the Company and

[108] Buller to Peel, 14 December 1844, BL AddMss40555 (Peel papers), fos.330–5; Peel to Buller, 23 December 1844, fos.336–7.

[109] Peel to Hope, 5 February 1845, BL AddMss40559, fo.33; Hope to Peel, 5 February 1845, BL AddMss40559, fos.35–6a.

[110] Hope to Peel, 5 February 1845, BL AddMss40559, fo.29.

[111] Buller to Peel, 15 February 1845, BL AddMss40559, fos.42–3a, enclosing 'confidential memorandum', fo.44.

[112] Ibid, fos.44a, 48a.

[113] Ibid, fo.49. See also Aglionby, report of Special Committee, 1 April 1846, CO208/188, fo.397, TNA.

presented the views of the Company.[114] Peel did not respond favourably, opting for returning the petition that eventually surfaced at the commencement of the bruising Commons debates on New Zealand in July 1845. On 1 May 1845 the Company instituted a 'secret committee' comprising Somes, Aglionby, Buller, Goldsmid, Ingestre, Lyall, and Wakefield with complete authority not only to conduct negotiations but to conclude any expedient arrangement with Peel's ministry.[115] It swiftly engaged in preparing reports reassessing the Company's stance on its settlements and claimed titles in New Zealand. It also sought concessions from Peel, Graham, and Stanley. It reaffirmed Buller's propositions canvassed with Peel on 15 February 1845 for relieving the Company's financial predicament and managing territories in New Zealand. In conversation at the Commons, Graham informed Buller that Peel's ministry could not proceed to negotiate with the Company 'under an appearance of pressure, or of a wish to shrink from discussion'. As such, any Company-sponsored motion ought to be withdrawn or disposed of before negotiations continued.[116] Peel was certainly intent on not being perceived to have conceded to Company pressure. On 1 May 1845, the 'secret committee' resolved to withdraw Buller's parliamentary motion, a moment that ushered in an episode of frantic conversations and exchanged confidential memoranda. These negotiations were punctuated by moments of mutual frustration, and they eventually collapsed by July 1845. Indigenous proprietary rights remained functional at the detailed level of policy-formulation. Buller identified the reification of Māori claims to territory that had arisen in the production of intelligence from New Zealand. He informed Peel, 'I am not for abrogating or disregarding that Treaty: but if no effectual means can be taken to obviate the interpretation put upon the 2nd article, it is utterly hopeless to attempt any arrangement of past disputes, or even to colonize [New Zealand]'. He added that the second article had 'been interpreted to include all the territory from which each tribe *claim* a right of excluding others'.[117] In April 1845, Buller stated on behalf of the Company that their:

> system . . . was to treat the soil as unappropriated wherever it was not in some way occupied; to vindicate to the Crown the ownership of all the unoccupied expanse; to encourage the settlement of European colonists; and to turn to account those peculiar facilities which the Aboriginal race of New Zealand appear to possess, for intermixture and amalgamation with the European population.[118]

By mid-1845, the financial predicament not only of New Zealand but also the Company was embarrassing and politically vexatious to Stanley, Peel, and Graham. Warring Māori associated with Heke's Ngā Puhi affiliates in Te Tai Tokerau did not assist distant perceptions, such activities being defined by FitzRoy's administration as an insurrection requiring regular military interventions rather than a potential 'disciplinary' moment for anglophone settlement. Heke effectively assaulted Kororāreka,

[114] Petition, 10 April 1845, CO325/43, fos.81–114, TNA.

[115] Minutes, 'extract from minutes of court of directors of the New Zealand Company', CO208/188, fo.293, TNA.

[116] Minutes, 'secret committee', 1 May 1845, CO208/188, fo.294, TNA.

[117] Buller to Peel, 10 May 1845, BL AddMss40556, fo.7 (emphasis in original). On the reification of Māori claims to territory in intelligence reportage, see Chapter Three, pp 141–162.

[118] Buller to Stanley, 'confidential', memorandum, 14/15 April 1845, CO208/188, fo.296, TNA; Buller, 'suggestions for the consideration of Lord Stanley submitted on behalf of the New Zealand Company', 5 May 1845, CO209/39, fos.308–20, TNA.

and Europeans evacuated the settlement.[119] In October 1845, Graham anxiously referred to New Zealand as 'our Algeria'.[120] Similarly, the Company's directorate created an identical trans-oceanic analogy, stating that 'the honor of our country . . . is tarnished by the resemblance of the condition of New Zealand to that of Algeria, or the great expense to this country of a war of extermination'.[121] In addition, imperial New Zealand was scarcely operational, with only £2,500 revenue being generated from land titles and Crown grants in the financial year commencing 1 April 1845.[122] FitzRoy recognized the fiscal and general economic difficulties: 'Colonization has already been stopped in New Zealand; and while land remains at a high price, nobody in this part of the world will buy'.[123] Stephen sensed these difficulties in May 1845, commenting that it 'is perfectly clear that the Australian Land Sales Act and all other ordinary general rules about lands in vacant colonies are utterly inapplicable to the case of New Zealand complicated as it is by the ingredient of an armed aboriginal population who lay claim to the whole soil of the country'.[124] Curiously, then, this had not been 'perfectly clear' in 1839, 1840, 1841, or 1842.

Yet, in the confusion of pressing politics, Peel oscillated between deferring to Stanley's opinion as departmental head, and episodic interventions in the conceptually complicated negotiations with the Company on native title. The Company persisted in desiring 'at the worst', or in accordance with Stanley's construction of the Treaty at Waitangi, 'an unconditional grant of any lands as to which the Court of Claims had made final awards in their favour'.[125] Stanley's stipulation at an interview that Māori 'accept' any such grants (through their acceptance of compensation) clearly rankled the Company. Stanley insisted to Peel that he was anxious to issue the Company with an 'unconditional grant' to the largest practicable extent of territory. Stanley endeavoured to concentrate Peel's attention on the procedural nature of native title, or, in other words, its capacity to be used in an ordered series of procedures to discipline the opening of territories for anglophone settlement through episodic, deliberative Crown-supervised purchase.[126] The substantive implications of law and stadialism had given way to the precedence of process or procedure in Stanley's account, as was evident from the mutually agreed minutes of interviews convened between Company representatives and Stanley on 27 June and 1 July 1845. Stanley anticipated that Crown grants could be readily issued at Wellington, Nelson, and Otākou to the extent of 370,000 acres. He commented it, 'appeared that at Otago a purchase had been effected under the mediation of the government officer [John Symonds], and that at Wellington and

119 FitzRoy to Stanley, 26 March 1845, CO209/33, fos.325–33a, TNA.

120 Graham to Peel, 15 October 1845, BL AddMss40451 (Peel papers), fos.386–7 (this private *communiqué* also discussed the potato famine in Ireland).

121 *The twentieth report of the court of directors of the New Zealand Company presented to the annual general court of proprietors: 29th May 1846*, 5.

122 CO209/34, fos.82–7: 'estimate of the probable expenditure [and revenue] of the government of New Zealand for the financial year 1845–1846, commencing 1st April 1845 and ending 31st March 1846', 1 April 1846. See also FitzRoy to Stanley, 20 August 1844, CO209/28, fos.118–18a, TNA.

123 FitzRoy, memorandum, 14 October 1844, CO209/29, fo.36, TNA.

124 Stephen to Hope, minute, 29 May 1845, CO209/29, fo.14a, TNA, referring to FitzRoy to Stanley, 14 October 1844, CO209/29, fos.9–13.

125 Ingestre to Peel, 18 July 1845, CO325/43, fo.57, TNA.

126 Stanley to Peel, memorandum, 21 July 1845, CO325/43, fos.79–80, TNA (memorandum referring to Ingestre to Peel, 18 July 1845, ibid).

Nelson a compensation had been agreed on to make up for the invalidity of previous titles, and accepted by the natives'.[127] He continued that it 'was thought necessary to attach to an unconditional grant, to be issued under positive orders, from so great a distance, and in the absence of communication with the local authorities, the record that the grant was made on the assurance of the applicants that the compensation money had been paid & accepted'.[128]

Native title was part of the procedural and political landscape— a feature to be unlocked for the release of settlement spaces. This emphasis on native title not as a disciplining constraint but as something to be evaded or unlocked emerged within Stanley's department during 1845. It was an element incorporated into those instructions prepared for FitzRoy's successor, George Grey, then serving as governor in southern Australia.[129] The instructions acknowledged that difficulties arising from disposing of territories had 'arisen chiefly or exclusively, in determining how the territory is to be divided between the Crown, the natives and the settlers claiming title through them'.[130] In a 'secret' despatch, an initial credit of £10,000 was provided to Grey, 'that you should employ in the purchase of lands from the natives, in such districts suitable in your judgement for the purposes of settlement'.[131] No parliamentary application was sought for this credit. Stanley commented, '[y]ou will, however, fully understand the motive for making this the subject of a secret instruction, and will of course be careful so to consider it'.[132] Stanley recognized the political complexity attending the territorial question. He encouraged 'the final adjustment of all questions arising out of the agreement of 1840, which, as long as they remain unsettled, cannot fail to be highly injurious to the prospects of the colony, and a source of embarrassment to yourself and to the government'.[133] Stanley wished to safeguard his personal prestige by concealing such a material concession to Company concerns. Westminster's anxieties, whether or not concealed, weighed heavily on Grey's shoulders. Grey's instructions were not sighted by Company deputations. But these deputations attained a distinct impression that the most advantageous stance they could expect from Stanley would be grants of Crown titles once relevant Māori accepted politically driven compensation awards.

Clearly, Stanley was sensing the political pressure on the question of indigenous proprietorship. In 1846, Peel informed Gladstone that 'he did not think Stanley had been happy in his management of the New Zealand question'. In continuing, Peel also contributed his own assessment in stating, 'I can hardly tell you, for instance, what trouble the New Zealand question gave me'.[134] Notably, as Stanley's successor, Gladstone favoured 'systematic colonization' as an effective means of transplanting

[127] Stanley to Peel, 'remarks [on Ingestre to Peel, 18 July 1845]', CO325/43, fo.58, TNA. Cf 'minutes of communications between Lord Stanley and a deputation from the directors of the New Zealand Company consisting of the Hon[oura]ble Francis Baring, Viscount Ingestre, Sir Isaac Lyon Goldsmid Bart & George Frederick Young Esq', CO209/39, fos.338–9, 27 June and 1 July 1845.

[128] Ibid, fos.58–8a.

[129] Stanley to Grey, 6 July 1845, CO209/40, fos.350–50a, TNA; Stephen, draft instructions [Stanley to Grey], 13 June 1845, CO209/38, fos.335a–6a, TNA.

[130] Stephen, draft instructions [Stanley to Grey], 13 June 1845, CO209/38, fo.336, TNA; Hope, memorandum, 'land question', 10 May 1845, CO209/38, fos.324–4a.

[131] Stanley to Grey, 'secret', 28 June 1845, CO209/40, fos.299–9a, TNA.

[132] Ibid, 301a–2 (emphasis in original).

[133] Ibid, 301–1a.

[134] Morley, *The Life of William Ewart Gladstone*, I, 298.

tractarianism and race, and was profoundly influenced by Wakefield and Lewis's *Essay on the Government of Dependencies*.[135] The conceptual complicity of the Whigs under Normanby and Russell in a policy since 1839 of enacted procedures disciplining settlement-dispersion could not be ignored, although Russell and Howick tactically stressed the erroneous conception of native title allegedly enunciated by Stanley and Hope.[136]

Yet the Company tired of Peel's strategies, opting for a parliamentary audience in a ranging debate from 17 June 1845. It determined by late May 1845 that negotiations had proved fruitless, reviving its petition and Buller's parliamentary motion.[137] Indeed, an imperial issue concerning native title and its uses reverberated at Westminster and dramatically unsettled Peel's ministry to the satisfaction of Whig tacticians such as Howick. Buller's motion was marginally defeated. As Howick stated, 'we then divided 172 [173] to 223 this considering their usual majority was a very bad division for the Gov[ernmen]t'.[138] Amongst those voting in favour of Buller's motion to institute a Select Committee to consider the 'state of the colony of New Zealand and the case of the New Zealand Company', were Lord Charles FitzRoy (the father of FitzRoy in Auckland), Baring, Cobden, Aglionby, Disraeli, Russell, Charles Wood, Labouchere, and Roebuck.[139] This parliamentary moment was crucial in that it prompted a revision in policies on native title, such that the disciplinary features initially accentuated under Russell and Stanley were increasingly downplayed.

Curiously, then, a Tory administration, buffeted by the apparent bankruptcy of an initially whiggish legacy of imperially exerted territorial discipline, paved the way for a revisionist policy, one oriented towards facilitating systematic settling. This would be attained by extinguishing Māori histories of claims to territory through a vigorous policy of government acquisition. In areas affected by Company claims to land, it was intended to restrict Māori to reserves for ambulatory cultivation. Alternatively, in sites where such claims could be avoided, settlement locations would be pursued in such regions, as in the South Island. This was evident on the receipt of an additional copy of Shortland's 18 March 1844 report on Māori political relations within the South Island, reciting tales of 'Kaitahu' (a southern indigenous dialectal variant of the name Ngāi Tahu) migrations and warring expeditions.[140] Stephen advised Lyttelton, parliamentary under-secretary to Gladstone at the Colonial Office, that Shortland's 'report [was] not I think of much value or interest but if reliance can be placed on the account here given of the numbers of people there will be little or no embarrassment about native claims to land in the Middle island'.[141] Moreover, having returned to Britain, Edmund Halswell, the former Company commissioner for managing its 'native reserves', contributed charts of New Zealand illustrating the assumed density of Māori population distribution throughout the archipelago. These

135 Matthew, *Gladstone, 1809–1874*, 74.

136 *A Corrected Report of the Debate in the House of Commons*, Howick, 18 June 1845, 134–5; Russell, 19 June 1845, 220–2. See also 'New Zealand. Draft instructions to Governor Grey', confidential, November 1846, Gre/B147/37, 9, DUL.

137 PRO, Ingestre to Stanley, 26 May 1845, CO209/39, fo.323; Buller to Stanley, 2 June 1845, CO209/39, fos.327–7a.

138 Howick, journal, 19 June 1845, Gre/V/C3/10, DUL; *A Corrected Report of the Debate in the House of Commons*, 285 (note).

139 See ibid, 285–7, for 'ayes' and 'noes' columns in the division.

140 Shortland to Clarke, 18 March 1844, CO209/36, fos.312–24a, enclosed in FitzRoy to Stanley, 1 November 1845, fos.310–10a, TNA. This report is referred to in Chapter Three.

141 Stephen to Lyttelton, minute, 22 May 1846, CO209/36, fo.311a, TNA.

charts, admitted into Office records, demonstrated a relative absence of Māori and, concomitantly, perhaps of aboriginal title claims in the South Island.[142] Indeed, Halswell supported his relatively crude census observations with a report received during Gladstone's tenure as Secretary of State for Colonies. Referring to the South Island, Halswell advised that 'on no part of the coasts is the population stationary; they wander from one place to another without fixed habitations though they frequently return to the same place'.[143] This passage within the report was duly emphasized with pencilled lining abutting its margin on the part of Colonial Office recipients. Halswell also misleadingly but interestingly stated that in 'the whole island, so far as I could learn there is not a single tribe properly so called, but the entire population consists of scattered families and remnants of tribes which were nearly exterminated about [20] years ago by the inroads of [Te] Rauparaha and the Kaw[h]ia tribes'.[144] Such a viewpoint succinctly demonstrated the sensitivities of Company sources and observations to Ngāti Toa historical narratives, as well as the ready merging of such narratives with coexisting assumptions amongst certain pākehā as to possible historical tendencies towards the extinction of entire aboriginal populations. Both perspectives could abet the vigorous extinguishment of inconvenient aboriginal title (chiefly limited to non-static cultivated sites) and the inexpensive location of areas allegedly unaffected by Māori 'occupancy' for settlement.

By 1846 and 1847, conceptions of native title conveyed through intelligence were not rejected outright but accepted as expedient preliminaries to extinguishing a range of potential Māori political interests or claimants asserting a negotiating interest in a territorial tract. The practices haltingly developed in New Zealand from 1842 became a central aspect to this procedural comprehension of aboriginal tenure.[145] This language intruded into Howick's (as the third Earl Grey) advice to Grey on the conduct of purchases from Māori. The identification of the potential range of Māori territorial claimants was counselled in order to ease processes of acquisition.[146] Theoretically, Māori could then be constrained within restricted areas, particularly 'reserves' for purposes of sustenance. Contrary to Morrell, this process commenced with Stanley and was pursued by his successor, Gladstone.[147] Moreover, it resulted in momentous consequences for New Zealand in the vigorous pursuit of a territorial-acquisition policy from 1846. Belgrave and Rutherford have addressed the extent of these acquisitions involving an estimated 33 million acres until 1853.[148] In any event, this revision seemed to have attained its apogee with Howick's appointment as Secretary of State for Colonies in 1846, and with Buller assisting the Colonial Office in the drafting

[142] Halswell to Gladstone, 2 April 1846, CO209/48, fos.193–5a, TNA; maps, MPG213 and MPG214, TNA (the base charts were those used for Wakefield's *Adventure in New Zealand*).

[143] Halswell, report, 2 April 1846, CO209/48, fos.193–5a, 195, TNA.

[144] Ibid, fo.195.

[145] For example, office of the Secretary of State for Colonies to Clarke, 21 April 1843, IA4/271, 116–17, ANZ(W).

[146] Earl Grey to Grey, 10 February 1847, CO209/44, fo.343a, TNA; Grey to Gladstone, 24 June 1846, CO209/44, fos.380a–2; Symonds to Grey, 19 June 1846 (Whanganui), CO209/44, fos.84–390a.

[147] Morrell, *British colonial policy in the age of Peel and Russell*, 127.

[148] Belgrave, 'Pre-emption, the Treaty of Waitangi and the politics of Crown purchase', 32–7; Rutherford, *Sir George Grey KCB, 1812–1898*, 163–87 (especially 'principal land purchases 1846–1853', table, 187 and 'South Island land purchase 1839–1853', map, 174).

of additional instructions to Grey in November and December of that year.[149] This intimacy of a Company representative in the preparation of such documents has not been recognized in the preceding historiography. Indigenous property rights were seen as sufficiently malleable and were subtly altered to adjust—it was functional after all. It could be conceived of indicating spaces for settlement where Māori claims to territory were absent, silent, or considered minimal, as in the South Island, Te Waipounamu.[150] This represented a coalescence of Company and Office perceptions. Intelligence on aboriginal proprietorship would be used to search for settling spaces and to placate the Company, although, financially, this revision would prove to be overly late, with the Company failing in 1850. In December 1845, Stanley announced the appointment of William McCleverty to assist the Company 'in their selection of land'.[151] Stanley assisted New Zealand with a pledge of financial aid to the extent of £100,000 for seven years at the rate of three per cent, which received parliamentary sanction.[152] Thus, the contested relations between Company and Colonial Office since 1839 obtained a form of political closure although, in the process, the Peel ministry's imperial management had been profoundly embarrassed.

Yet, the intellectual languages employed throughout these relations remained subject to contention. Indeed, in an interlude fraught with political tensions, the 1845 debates in the Commons recited a range of Company perspectives concerning the proprietary rights-status of Māori. Stanley would forward copies of reports concerning 'discussions' in the Commons to Grey such that the latter possessed a context of Westminster politics in discharging his instructions.[153] An unqualified introduction of Marshall court jurisprudence contrasted with the reification of 'claiming' or 'claims' to the emergence of territory within intelligence sources derived from New Zealand and the uncomfortable acknowledgment of these views in Britain by persons such as Stanley. These potential intersections of an imported *ius gentium* and investigations of Māori territorial rights were seriously contested. Buller construed investigation as futile when observing that convoluted Māori conceptions of 'custom' were sufficiently appreciated through their status as 'savages': 'As you recognise in savages no right but that of occupancy, it would be absurd to acknowledge any other right as derived from them by Europeans with respect to primeval forest or waste, which the hand of man has never touched to improve or render available to man'.[154] Buller reflected that incredulity from a distance often expressed regarding the value of efforts to collect diverse Māori points of view on questions of territorial rights. In Buller's view, given the indigenous awareness of the market in land in areas where European settlements were located, such attempts risked an absence of indigenous authenticity while merely inducing capriciousness and invented complexities. Inconvenient and confused Māori evidence

149 'New Zealand. Draft instructions to Governor Grey', confidential, November 1846, Gre/B147/37, DUL. See also Buller to Earl Grey, 'private', 3 August 1846, Gre/B70/11/36–38, DUL; Earl Grey to Buller, 'private', 23 February 1847, Gre/B70/11/55; Buller to Earl Grey, 'private', 15 March 1847, Gre/B70/11/61, DUL.

150 Hope to Ingestre, 7 August 1845, CO209/39, fos.400–400a, TNA.

151 Stanley to Grey, 18 December 1845, CO209/39, fo.475a, TNA; Stanley to Grey, 15 August 1845, CO209/39, fo.431, TNA; Attwell, 'NZ Co. Land claims in the 1840s", 2–3; Jellicoe, *The New Zealand Company's Native Reserves*, 51–6; Tonk, '"A difficult and complicated question"', 59.

152 9 & 10 Vict, c42, c82 (Imp).

153 Stanley to Grey, 15 August 1845, CO209/39, fo.432a, TNA.

154 *A Corrected Report of the Debate in the House of Commons*, Buller, 17 June 1845, 36.

produced before Spain was deemed to prove 'the utter absence of all definite notions of right to the soil, and of the utter precariousness even of occupancy in that horrible state of barbarism . . . Yet you have called these "rights", and spun a New Zealand law of real property out of savage customs, which common sense and ordinary care for improving the morality of the Native race should have made you wholly repudiate'.[155] Clarke was vilified as one principal conduit of these inconvenient approaches: 'Mr Clarke was a gunsmith, who had passed ten years in New Zealand in the mixed occupation of converting the natives and jobbing in land'.[156] Stanley remained steadfastly attached to the 'honour' of the Crown, to the need to consult indigenous narratives as to how they interacted with a given landscape, and to accord 'custom' primacy in explaining the content of native title:

> These laws—these customs—and the right arising from them on the part of the Crown—we have guaranteed when we accepted the sovereignty of the islands; and be the amount at stake smaller or larger; so far as native title is proved—be the land waste or occupied—barren or enjoyed, those rights and titles the Crown of England is bound in honour to maintain; and the interpretation of the Treaty of Waitangi, with regard to these rights, is, that, except in the case of the intelligent consent of the natives, the Crown has no right to take possession of land, and having no right to take possession of land itself, it has no right—and so long as I am a Minister of the Crown, I shall not advise it to exercise the power—of making over to another party that which it does not itself possess.[157]

Those members supporting Stanley resisted the introduction of American jurisprudential sources, insisting that they were of scant relevance to New Zealand. Rous, a member for Westminster, stated that '[Gipps] had also quoted some of the most celebrated lawyers of the United States—Chief-Justice Marshall, Judge Story, and Chancellor Kent—as they gave him some information as to what had taken place with reference to the Americans and the aborigines of that country, the Indians'.[158] Rouse acknowledged that both Gipps and Howick's Select Committee used sources that hitherto had enjoyed a localized pertinence, relevant to 'American Indians or to New Holland natives, whose independence we had never recognised'.[159] Certain sources within northern New Zealand, such as Samuel Martin, also criticized this attempted intrusion of American jurisprudence. Martin, president of the New Zealand chapter of the Aborigines' Protection Society, publicized and broached this critique in an Auckland pamphlet version of a 19 September 1842 letter to Stanley requesting representative institutions in pākehā settlements.[160] He castigated those arguments raised by Company parliamentary advocates.[161] Māori were 'natives' of Westminster. In the

[155] Ibid, 41.

[156] Ibid, 9 ('If a French gunsmith were to turn friar, and, after passing a similar period in a similar manner in this country, should offer his theory of the social condition of Great Britain from the period of Heptarchy to the present time, I should certainly pay no attention to his speculations').

[157] Stanley, House of Lords, *HPD*, 3rd series, 10 July 1845, vol 82, col 319.

[158] *A Corrected Report of the Debate in the House of Commons*, 18 June 1845, 90.

[159] Ibid.

[160] Martin, *New Zealand in 1842*, 10; Samuel McDonald Martin, 1805–10?–1848, editor of the *Southern Cross* from April 1843; appointed a magistrate, 3 May 1841, and reappointed November 1841: see *The Dictionary of New Zealand Biography; volume I—1769–1869*, 276–7.

[161] *New Zealand, in a series of letters*, 348: 'What an example to set before the other nations of Europe, especially France, which is now rioting and intoxicated with the blood of the victims of Africa and the innocent inhabitants of Tahiti!! Let the aristocracy of England, however, beware how they enlighten the people on the rights of property'.

Commons, Sir Howard Douglas (1776–1861), a member of Parliament for Liverpool, proclaimed:

> [Howick's select committee stated that a 'new fundamental principle of colonial law has...been discovered'] It is this,—'That the uncivilised inhabitants of any country have but a qualified dominion over it, or a right of occupancy only;...'. I should like to ask where this principle of colonial law, is to be found? I find it not in Vattel, nor in Vaughan's Reports, nor in Stokes, nor in Blackstone.... I suspect I know the origin of this new fundamental principle of colonial law. It comes, I think, from the land in which the Black Man is a slave, and the Red Men of the forest are driven and hunted from their lands, as the Seminole and other Indians have been, according to certain adjudications that Indians have no property to the soil or their respective territories than that of mere occupancy.[162]

In these parliamentary disputes, perceptions of historical processes remained crucial to understanding imperial aborigines. Stadial history, predicated on observing modes of subsistence in alien communities, was still used by 'liberal Anglican' historians, like Thomas Arnold and Whately, or literary figures such as Howick.[163] Stadialism was a pervasive analytical tool and both Whately and Arnold's literature represented a useful corollary to early nineteenth-century notions of stadial theory. Such theory was vigorously deployed in Westminster disputes about aboriginal proprietorship (and 'savagery') within New Zealand, especially from 1842, reaching a crescendo by 1845, with political consequences. It subsumed Māori from a distance. In these contexts, its most ardent purveyors were 'colonial reformers' (after Merivale and Buller) or advocates of Wakefieldian 'systematic' anglophone settlements—sympathizers of the New Zealand Company (its constituency), including Buller, Roebuck, and Henry Ward.[164] Prominent Whigs, like Russell, Labouchere, and Howick, also supported its historical insights in policy-formulation and the Commons. This support was, in certain respects, tactical (particularly on Russell's part, if not necessarily Howick's)—part of harassing a Tory ministry. Palmerston was sensitive to the tactics and politics of Whig parliamentary factions. He referred to Buller and Hawes as intimate supporters of Howick and his 'ultra free trade [and 'emigration'] doctrines' as a curative for the 'pressure of population upon subsistence & employment':[165] 'Of course Charles Buller & other persons who have engaged in land speculations in our colonies [New Zealand] preach up Emigration upon a large scale as a cure for all our domestic Evils, because at all events it would probably help them to turn their lands to good account'.[166] Buller had indeed been well rewarded for his advocacy of Company objects. In later 1843, he received £500 from the Company 'as a mark of acknowledgement for the importance of the professional services which he [had] rendered' in presenting its perspectives to Stanley and Hope.[167] He received a fee of £525 'for his professional services relative to the charter' in 1841, whilst Wakefield was awarded £1,000, 'in gratitude for services

[162] *A Corrected Report of the Debate in the House of Commons*, 18 June 1845, 124.

[163] Earl Grey to Grey, 23 December 1846, CO209/47, fos.271–1a, TNA; Arnold, 'The labourers of England', in Arnold, *Miscellaneous Works of Thomas Arnold, D.D.*, 155–9, 157; Forbes, *The Liberal Anglican Idea of History*, 70–1.

[164] Buller, *Responsible Government for Colonies*, 20; Merivale, *Lectures on colonization and colonies*, 2nd edn, vi–vii: 'colonial reformers'; Roebuck, *HPD*, 3rd series, 21 July 1845, vol 82, cols 848–50.

[165] Palmerston to Russell, 20 December 1844, PRO30/22/4D, fos.41–2, TNA.

[166] Ibid, fo.43.

[167] Minutes, court of directors, 24 August 1843 and 31 August 1843, CO208/182, fos.44, 46, TNA.

rendered'.[168] Buller also possessed shares to the value of £500.[169] Native title discussions occurred at the cusp of political, intellectual, and commercial preoccupations.

During the Commons debate on 23 July 1845, Russell, the senior Whig representative within the Commons, complimented Gipps' use of stadial histories and Vattel in August 1840. Hence, 'you must treat the people of that country as Sir George Gipps did... and must apply the principle of Vattel, who alleged that savages could only hold the land they occupied, and beyond that they should have no favour'.[170] Even then, however, there were often subtle inconsistencies in its treatment by such politicized individuals, with some orators stressing certain points in these viewpoints on histories and *ius gentium*. John Roebuck, for example, was scathingly sceptical of Māori attainments in developing proprietary notions, expressing scant confidence that merely reporting Māori narratives concerning interests in land could constitute meaningful intelligence or 'knowing'. He recounted how one witness's testimony before Howick's Select Committee relayed what Roebuck received as improbable. This witness 'drew such a picture of [a] description of the descent of land and its appanages, until [Roebuck] almost thought that they were getting to the history of a German barony'.[171] Their means of procuring subsistence from earthly soils were disdainfully compared with Amerindians: 'It had been proved over and over again before the [Select Committee in 1844] that the natives of New Zealand only occupied small pieces of land, which they kept till the soil was exhausted, and no longer'.[172] He was explicit in his expectations of an historically inexorable decline and extirpation of Māori: 'It was an undoubted fact, that all uncivilized races of savages ultimately perished wherever civilized man came', adding, that whilst this circumstance was regrettable, it uniformly and inexorably occurred as a historical process.[173] He preferred ignorance of aborigines rather than tales of empirical complexity drawn from local sources of intelligence.[174]

Unsurprisingly, these characterizations of Māori mingled with attitudes to the histories and potential of emigrations—movements of peoples and their peopling of relatively uninhabited territories with fertile environments.[175] These attitudes were further informed and sustained by diverse sources, including 'liberal Anglican' historical assumptions, associated with Whately, Julius Hare and Arnold. Their perceptions appealed to cyclic histories—Arnold's 'social progress of states'—comprising the seasons of a nation's progressions and regressions, through its dawn, noon-time, dusk, degeneration, and regeneration; the revitalizing movements and transplantations of, say, Germanic hordes within *imperium Romanum*.[176] That favoured motif of

168 Minutes, court of directors, 4 February 1841, CO208/181, fo.10 (Buller), TNA; 21 January 1841, fo.7 (Wakefield).

169 'List of shareholders of the New Zealand Company, 15th November 1845', in Harington to Earl Grey, 18 November 1845, Gre/B147/8, DUL.

170 *HPD*, 3rd series, 23 July 1845, vol 82, col 1019. For Gipps, see Chapter Two.

171 *HPD*, 3rd series, 21 July 1845, vol 82, col 849.

172 Ibid, col 848: 'The tribes were constantly wandering from place to place—they were here today, and there to-morrow, and there was, to use a legal expression, no assignable individual to be found as resident or proprietor.... They had no notion of boundaries, and they could not trace the land they claimed from river to river, or from mountain to mountain, in New Zealand, as this country could in India or elsewhere, or as the hon[ourable] gentleman could trace out his patrimonial acres'.

173 Ibid, cols 849–50.

174 Roebuck, *The Colonies of England*, 7–18.

175 Buchanan, 'Emigration', in *The Encyclopædia Britannica*, VIII, 684; Mill, 'Colony', in ibid, VII, 115.

176 Arnold, *The effects of distant colonization on the parent state, a prize essay*, 29–31; Arnold, *History of Rome*.

Whately, namely transformative 'civilizing' attending the disciplined introduction of anglophone settlements, would prove efficacious in arresting and improving the degenerative state of 'savagery'. This use of intellectual sources did not suggest histories consisting of stasis or stable categorizations but of motion and profound change. Māori were circled within the comprehension of these histories and represented certain of its motifs, especially that of migratory diffusion in pursuit of sustenance. Thus, a mode of subsistence analysis was meshed with an idea of mobile populations.[177] Once Māori ceased to be oceanic Polynesian voyagers and became predominantly land-dwelling 'New Zealanders', they were perceived as having conformed to the broad historical life-patterns of other land-dwelling populations. They warred, contested resources, and travelled in pursuit of sustenance. To this outline, 'liberal Anglican' cyclical histories contributed a dimension of populations increasing and receding tidally, perhaps even becoming extinct or submerged through subsequent incursions. Within these general intellectual contexts, discussion in Westminster regarding aboriginal title cannot be marginalized as unduly 'academic' and irrelevant since they clearly entailed consequences for Grey's activities and his areas of emphasis throughout his governorship from November 1845. The colonial and imperial metropolitan fields must be reintegrated and examined as much as the localized engagements between an increasingly resourced colonial presence and Māori polities.[178] 'Occupancy' was not buried beneath the refuse of these disputes but glimmered through procedures of negotiating with Māori.

DENOUEMENT: TWO GREYS AND THE SURVIVAL OF 'OCCUPANCY', 1845 TO 1853

This section argues that Grey's appointment and instructions—both confidential and open—represented a major concession to the Company's outlook on native title coupled with a renewed intellectual and material commitment to expanding anglo-settlement within New Zealand. Yet Grey also revealed all the ambiguities and confusion endemic in developing conceptions of indigenous property rights. Grey collected persons and, as a bibliophile, often forged and nourished interpersonal web-works through exchanging books.[179] Hadfield was a prime informant and advisor principally based at Wellington and Ōtaki.[180] He advised Grey on the condition of relations with

[177] Pocock, 'Nature and History, Self and Other'', in Calder, Lamb and Orr (eds), *Voyages and Beaches*, 25–44.

[178] Hickford, 'Framing and Reframing the *Agōn*'.

[179] On Grey as a bibliophile, see Kerr, *Amassing Treasures for All Times*; Kerr, *Old Books: an essay by Sir George Grey*, and 'Introduction', by Kerr (September 1998). See also Kerr, 'Sir George Grey, K.C.B. (14 April 1812–19 September 1898)', in *Dictionary of Literary Biography*, vol 184, 184–92, 187; *Address of Sir George Grey, K.C.B., to the members of the New Zealand Society, as their first president, 26 September 1851* (Wellington, 1851): 'It therefore is, I apprehend, our duty sedulously to collect and record facts and information in each department of science and human learning'.

[180] For example, Hadfield to Coates, 8 March 1847, qMs-0895, fo.57, ATL; Octavius Hadfield, 1814?–1904; educated at Pembroke College, Oxford from 1832; resident at Ōtaki and Waikanae from November 1839, but by 1844 was essentially based at Otaki. Grey visited Hadfield almost daily when in Wellington to which Hadfield had repaired during an almost five-year period of illness. Hadfield returned to the mission at Ōtaki in October 1849. Hadfield was a firm intimate of Selwyn, that other ally of Grey: *The Dictionary of New Zealand Biography; volume I—1769–1869*, 169–70; Rutherford, *Sir George Grey*, 206.

Māori in the Port Nicholson district: 'The natives in this part of the country appear quite quiet'.[181] He borrowed texts from Grey, including a tome concerning Hawaiian and Marquesan linguistics in an effort to assist his philology.[182] Grey also collected his own information directly from Māori sources. He lamented the losses occasioned to this reservoir of material through fire at his Auckland residence in 1848.[183] In view of FitzRoy's experiences and the castigation of Clarke in the Commons during June 1845, Grey did not listen to the Clarke family and disbanded the protectorate department in 1846, dismissing Clarke in June of that year. Instead, he forged and cultivated a direct line of reportage through a 'native secretary' expressly responsible to the governor. John Symonds was appointed to this office and was incorporated into Grey's interpersonal networks mediated by correspondence: 'Formerly the protector of each out-station corresponded directly with the chief protector at Auckland—the chief executive officer at each out-station was not acquainted with the contents of this correspondence, nor did it pass through him'.[184] Prior to this restructuring appointment, Grey exhibited his confidence in Symonds by selecting him to discharge specific transactional negotiations with Māori in pursuance of Stanley's instructions. Symonds was instructed to proceed to Whanganui and rapidly to resolve difficulties with the Company's entitlements there. Symonds was provided with £1,000 as an inducement to obtain Māori signatures for transferring a section of 40,000 acres, as stipulated under Stanley's 27 June 1845 instructions to Grey.[185] Grey was reaffirming the procedural expectations of his imperial instructions. He advocated the drawing of 'accurate plans' of all 'pahs, burying places and cultivations, . . . and their boundaries must be carefully marked out, so that in as far as possible all future misunderstandings on this subject may be avoided'.[186]

Ultimately, Grey was more comfortable in negotiating with Māori descent-groupings from whence intelligence sources were volunteered and tolerably reliable in the proximity of Company settlements rather than, say, Waikato. Unsurprisingly, from late 1845, he particularly relied on information conveyed via persons within his orbit, such as Hadfield. Hence, the Ngāti Toa histories and narratives of territorial occupation which implicitly asserted the right of Ngāti Toa *rangatira* to be consulted concerning 'purchase' transactions are readily found in Grey's personal records.[187] Grey's tendency to listen to persons in the vicinity of Company settlements, such as Hadfield or Richard Taylor, a missionary at Whanganui, understandably hardened this emphasis on localized sources of Māori intelligence in the area of Cook's Strait. Taylor, for one, expressed dissatisfaction with FitzRoy's supposed indifference and discourtesy towards Company settlers at Whanganui but was gratified at Grey's

[181] Hadfield to Grey, 6 May 1848, GL NZ H1(5), APL.

[182] Hadfield to Grey, 10 September 1847, GL NZ H1(3), APL.

[183] Grey to Gairdner, 14 July 1848, Gre/B99/6B/11, DUL: 'I also lost a large collection of songs & religious chants. . . . Such an opportunity of collecting these songs will probably never again present itself, & I fear the former mystical worship of the New Zealanders will become one of the forgotten things of the world'.

[184] Grey to Earl Grey, 4 February 1847, CO209/51, fos.199–9a, TNA.

[185] Grey to Symonds, 17 April 1846, NZMss227, fos.104–7, TNA.

[186] Ibid, fo.105.

[187] '"History of the conquest of the middle island by Ngati Toa", compiled by the chiefs of that tribe', enclosed in Hohoia Otane te Pokaitaia to Grey, 11 December 1851, GNZ MMss103, APL; see also Pūaha *et al* to Grey, 29 September 1852, GNZ MMss104, 'this is a narrative of the might of my tribe'.

apparent interest.[188] Significantly, Taylor dwelt within a district affected by disputes over the entitlements of Company emigrants to territories, whilst Grey was eager to resolve these difficulties. In a sense, he oriented his government towards Wellington, its environs, and its peculiar problems. His reputation was that of a 'rescuer' of colonies such as South Australia, and salvaging New Zealand was his next task.[189]

His relations with clergy, such as Taylor and Hadfield, in Company settlement regions, contrasted dramatically with his relatively unsympathetic attitudes towards missionaries in Te Tai Tokerau, like Henry Williams.[190] He even mounted lengthy litigation against Clarke—culminating in a hearing of the judicial committee of the Privy Council—on account of Clarke's land purchases and his role as 'land agent' for the Church Missionary Society in New Zealand.[191] Historically, he was implicated as a witness or signatory in several mission deeds of putative purchase in the slender uppermost peninsula of the North Island.[192] Grey notoriously denounced the lack of 'energy of character' and 'industry' allegedly exhibited by Clarke and his sons in their conduct of offices within the protectorate department.[193] Clearly, Church Missionary Society functionaries in New Zealand, like Clarke, Williams, and Taylor, accepted the capacity of Māori to transfer property in an unhindered fashion, and, unusually for the southern Pacific, aspired to acquire extensive domains.[194] Variations on or replications of missionary practices in negotiating with Māori for territory before 1840, such as a publicized gathering of interested Māori and a *korero* (or discussions), were occasionally deployed in government negotiations. In substance, however, these tactics of consultation were as much politically required in Russell's instructions to Hobson as dictated causally by mission practices in distant Te Tai Tokerau in the far north of the North Island. This was noted in Chapter Three. In any event, doubts have been properly expressed as to whether mission transactions were indeed conducted uniformly in this fashion.[195] Significantly, despite Clarke's position as chief protector for aborigines,

188 Taylor to FitzRoy, 14 April 1845, GNZ Mss297/1, 3–4, APL; Taylor to Coates, 20 May 1845, GNZ Mss297/1, 4–8; Taylor to Sadlier, 18 August 1845, GNZ Mss297/1, 14–18; Taylor to Coates, 28 February 1846, GNZ Mss297/4, 116, APL.

189 Hope to Stephen, 19 May 1845, CO209/38, fos.247a–8, TNA; Stephen, draft instructions [Stanley to Grey], 13 June 1845, fo.327; Hall, 'Imperial man' in Schwarz (ed), *The Expansion of England*, 147.

190 Williams defended the conduct of missionaries in the distant north of the North Island: Williams to Grey, 1 December 1847, NZMs478, 3/2, fos.1–25, APL; Williams, *Plain facts relative to the late war in the northern district of New Zealand.* Francis, *Governors and Settlers*, 223–4, makes a similar point on Grey's relations with Williams but my observation also stresses the principal contextual features of the location of Hadfield and Taylor as well as Grey's clear instructions to ease Company settlements.

191 Clarke to Colonial Secretary, 4 June 1847, Ms1009, ATL; Clarke to Coates, 9 November 1847, qMs-0464, fos.297–308, ATL; Merriman to Clarke, 10 July 1848, qMs-0464, fo.326, ATL: 'The court having given judgment in your favour in this suit, the Attorney-General has served us with a notice of appeal to the Privy Council.... I must fear that his Exc[ellency] allows his personal feelings to blind his judgment'; *Regina v Clarke* (1849–1851) NZPCC 516 (judicial committee advice issued 15th May 1851). The reasoning of the Supreme Court at Auckland is summarized at 519–20 (for further detail see also Hickford, '"Settling Some Very Important Principles of Colonial Law"').

192 For instance, James Kemp, deed of purchase, 8 October 1831; Richard Davis, deed of purchase, 20 December 1831, OLC1/734–36, ANZ(W), ATL; Clarke to Coates, 9 November 1847, qMs-0464, fos.297–307; George Clarke and Waka Nene *et al*, deed of purchase, 4 March 1836, fos.324–5.

193 Grey to Earl Grey, 4 February 1847, CO209/51, fos.198a–9, TNA.

194 Belgrave, 'Pre-emption, the Treaty of Waitangi and the politics of Crown purchase', 27–35; Gunson, *Messengers of Grace*.

195 Waitangi Tribunal, *Muriwhenua Land Report—Wai-45*, 65–6.

his views in that office cannot be linked to a stable Church Missionary Society body of opinion in New Zealand. It is misleading to regard his missionary approaches as peculiarly shaping the outlook of his department. What he shared with other members of the protectorate department, including those with no missionary attachments (such as Edward Shortland) was an approach to investigating 'customs' compelled by Russell's instructions to Hobson in 1840 and 1841. This point deserves emphasis. Grey's officers—Henry Tacy Kemp, Donald McLean, Symonds—and advisors (including Hadfield), irrespective of their personal histories, stressed this investigative and procedurally oriented method themselves. Grey was not inimical to it, having adopted a similarly inchoate, observation-based, 'ethnographic' approach in his travelogue of landed and maritime peregrinations throughout western Australia. After all, in 1840 Russell publicly approved Grey's views on observing and improving 'aborigines'.

Observations on 'customs' were structured to satisfy the requirements of the Colonial Office in Westminster. A confidence in disciplining anglophone settlement by privileging the governmental collection and control of information concerning procedures of negotiating with Māori could be used to unlock locations for settlement. Allegedly Māori 'customs' were carriers or conductors of an incomplete 'knowing'—albeit misleadingly claiming increasing completeness and exactitude—that addressed those procedural features implicit in negotiating with Māori on territorial subjects, an aspect neither pursued nor identified by Adams. Adams considered that from 1845 imperial policies now hearkened to Māori interpretations of the *Treaty* initially marked at Waitangi. However, the evidence does not sustain this stance, as will be explored in subsequent passages. It is possible to write histories of New Zealand that are not exclusively Treaty-centred. Furthermore, as will be demonstrated in subsequent chapters, the Treaty was still seen as very much a document of its place and time by various Māori leaders more interested in refashioning and renegotiating relations with the newcomers from across the seas in new bargains and arrangements.[196]

Securing Company titles was rendered crucial due to difficulties experienced with Crown deeds of grant issued by FitzRoy on 29 July 1845 for Port Nicholson and Nelson districts in accordance with Spain's reports on Company land claiming.[197] The Company contested aspects of these grants, refraining from taking them up in order to increase its negotiating leverage with imperial administration. Some aspects were litigated by other pākehā land claimants as in *Scott v Grace* in 1848.[198] Moreover, references to tracts exempted from the deeds of grant such as 'grounds actually in cultivation by the natives' were considered as intolerably vague by Company representatives, and by Grey also. Company strategies at Westminster throughout 1845 assisted the projection of its perceptions into Colonial Office records, with Gladstone responding sympathetically. Harington, secretary to the Company from 1844, advised Gladstone that FitzRoy's January 1844 definition of aboriginal 'cultivations' was injurious to flourishing settlements. Defined as 'those tracts of land which are now used by the natives for vegetable productions or which have been so used by any aboriginal natives

[196] Explored in subsequent chapters and in the section within this chapter entitled '*Modus vivendi* and proprietary rights—the politics of negotiability and living with indeterminacy'.

[197] Deed of grant, Port Nicholson, 29 July 1845, CO209/35, fos.7–10; deed of grant, Nelson, 29 July 1845, CO209/35, fos.11–14, enclosed in FitzRoy to Stanley, 1 August 1845, fos.3–4, TNA.

[198] *Scott v Grace* (13 May 1848) in Hickford, '"Settling Some Very Important Principles of Colonial Law"', 1–71.

of New Zealand since the establishment of the colony', Māori cultivated sections were treated by Harington as encompassing two classes of property.[199] These were areas that had either been in vegetable cultivation at Port Nicholson's inception but were subsequently 'improved' by settlers with assorted clearances or constructions and, secondly, 'lands which were in a state of waste'. This final category embraced discrete sections that were 'cultivated' sparingly as a politically motivated strategy for Māori claims to territory and entitlements in order to induce pākehā negotiators to consult with certain Māori as opposed to competing *hapū* (as with Ngāti Toa in Wairau).[200] Moreover, Grey noted that Māori in the proximity or in the midst of settlements such as Wellington tended to relocate to other cultivation sites once they had exhausted the soil's fertility. Grey was not acting out of generous motives. That is, cultivations per se could not effectively limit Māori title in such circumstances, as they had proved overly mobile since the commencement of settlement. Cultivating Māori were useful in some situations to anglo-settlers as they cleared wooded areas in advance of settlement, a point eagerly noted by Swainson in the Hutt (Heretaunga) district.[201] But Grey pointed out that such clearances did not effectively compensate emigrants claiming sections for several years where the land remained unavailable to them.[202] These difficulties with supposed vagueness required a withdrawal of the grants and their eventual replacement with the awards determined by McCleverty in favour of the Company in 1847.[203] Māori in certain sections of Wellington were encouraged to forgo cultivation areas within sections putatively belonging to pākehā in return for other acres granted them under deeds. Thus, in a 28 December 1846 despatch to McCleverty, Grey instructed him to attempt 'to make the necessary arrangements for acquiring from the natives of Port Nicholson those native cultivations which are situated in the sections of European settlers'.[204]

Clearly, the received notion of Māori as cultivators of *kūmara* influenced policy on native title. It continued to appear in literature concerning Māori ways of life, including that of George Angas' illustrated treatise regarding impressions of New Zealand.[205] Subscribers to this tome included Earl Grey, Grey, FitzRoy, Edmund Halswell, Stanley, Robert Owen, Wakefield, William Molesworth, and Selwyn. Angas stated that '[u]nlike the wandering savages of New Holland, the New Zealanders are a people having social communities; they dwell in fortified towns and villages, and are cultivators of the ground to a large extent'.[206] Grey's opinion did not undermine the importance of cultivations but introduced a more mobile, migratory notion of Māori groupings consistent with his observations of Māori practices together with his own and Hadfield's ideas on a global history animated by peoples, linguistics, and customary practices in motion. There was a convergence of these early nineteenth-century concepts of human history with stadial theory and a policy of investigating Māori voices on the possibilities of transferring proprietorship. Grey's opinions were neatly expressed in his instructions

199 Harington to Gladstone, 17 March 1846, CO209/48, fos.94–4a, TNA.
200 Ibid, fo.94a; Gladstone to Grey, (nd) March 1846, BL AddMss44363, fos.328–37.
201 *William Swainson, FRS, FLS: naturalist and artist*, 105: Swainson to Parkes, 2 February 1844.
202 Grey to McCleverty, 21 April 1847, NZMss227, fo.240, APL.
203 Jellicoe, *The New Zealand Company's Native Reserves*, 54–5.
204 Grey to McCleverty, 28 December 1846, NZMss227, fo.204, APL.
205 Angas, *The New Zealanders Illustrated*, 'preface', 1 July 1846 (no pagination).
206 Ibid.

to Symonds on the Whanganui transaction, although additional illustrations can be produced:

> I think it right to observe that the Natives of the District about to be disposed of have selected for themselves large reserves in the spots they considered most convenient and advantageous; and it would therefore be desirable in this the final settlement of the question, to induce them whenever practicable to abandon such cultivations as may not really be requisite for their own purposes and yet may interfere with the pursuits and prosperity of the settlers from being situated in sections owned by Europeans or from other courses.[207]

After 1845, local intelligence on aboriginal tenure and a revised imperial outlook on the subject of aboriginal title remained critical. As such, it is too swift to say, as Adams argues, that Grey's application of pre-emption was central to the process of substantial indigenous territorial alienation following 1845.[208] Pre-emption was only part of the narrative underlying Grey's policies. In any event, it had been an abiding theme in New Zealand's imperial experiences from 1840 with a relatively marginal interruption during FitzRoy's tenure as governor when pre-emption could be waived in limited circumstances under his 26 March and 10 October 1844 proclamations.[209] These FitzRoy initiatives were unquestionably minimal in their impact given that a minor extent of territorial purchases were confirmed via certificates issued under the governor and Colonial Secretary at Auckland's authority—90,016 acres acquired at one penny per acre as at 13 June 1846.[210] Prominent safeguards attended the consideration of granting any 'waiver' certificate, including the preservation from alienation of Māori *pā* or cultivated sites. Further, this acreage was principally granted in the vicinity of Auckland. Grey exaggerated the extent of the affected land, informing Gladstone that many purchasers of 'extensive tracts of land, over which the Crown right of preemption has never been waived [in a certificate], have been made in the most careless manner in many parts of this island'.[211] For Grey, FitzRoy's initiatives had encouraged a lack of discipline in territorial acquisition, thereby undermining the authority of imperial administration, although he could produce no evidence to this effect.[212] A reassertion of pre-emption was central to Grey's advent as governor, but his use of intelligence on aboriginal tenure in vigorously pursuing negotiations with Māori in territorial 'purchase' transactions was even more crucial. After all, pre-emption merely indicated who could negotiate on behalf of Europeans for settlement space. It did not assist in the discharge of an aggressive purchasing policy as set out in Stanley's instructions to Grey

[207] Grey to Symonds, 17 April 1846, NZMss227, fo.105, APL; Grey to Earl Grey, 9 April 1847, 'papers relative to the affairs of New Zealand', *GBPP1847–1848*, xliii [892], 19.

[208] Adams, *Fatal Necessity*, 193–209; Belgrave, 'Pre-emption, the Treaty of Waitangi and the politics of Crown purchase', 33, also supports Adams' argument.

[209] Proclamation, 26 March 1844, CO209/27, fos.446a–7, TNA; Proclamation, 10 October 1844, CO209/29, fos.21a–2. Belgrave, 'Pre-emption, the Treaty of Waitangi and the politics of Crown purchase', 33–4 is correct to state that these so-called 'waiver' of pre-emption certificates were attended with 'considerable safeguards' (see Chapter Three above).

[210] Grey to Stanley, 9 June 1846, CO209/44, fos.56–68, enclosing a schedule of acres acquired under the FitzRoy proclamations (13 June 1846), fos.70–70a, TNA; Belgrave, 'Pre-emption, the Treaty of Waitangi and the politics of Crown purchase', 33–4.

[211] Grey to Gladstone, 21 June 1846, CO209/44, fos.245a–6, TNA.

[212] Grey to Gladstone, 18 December 1846, CO209/46, fos.521–2a, enclosing 'an ordinance to authorise compensation in colonial debentures, to be made to certain claimants to land in the colony of New Zealand', 18 November 1846, fos.530–1a, TNA.

for salvaging imperial New Zealand from political and financial collapse. More was required than 'pre-emption' in a treaty.

From 1846, Grey and his officers vigorously and aggressively deployed received intelligence on the complexities of intra-Māori tenure and political relations. Intense negotiations with certain Māori were involved. Empire was pursued through negotiation, intimidation, and cajoling. The acquisitions at Porirua and the Wairau in March 1847 were illustrative, as these were de novo transactions for Grey and did not finalize negotiations that had faltered under FitzRoy. In his report to Earl Grey, Grey celebrated the purchase of Porirua on strategic grounds, arguing that it secured Wellington's hinterland:[213] 'The land claims which appeared in the circumstances of the colony, to require immediate adjustment were those advanced by the New Zealand Company:—1stly to the district of country including Porirua and lying between that place and Wainui—2ndly to the district of Wairau in the Middle island, and the country lying immediately to the southward of that district'.[214] In the former instance, Grey established a paper claim, substituting any of those associated with the Company, to approximately 25,000 acres, whereas an estimated three million acres were secured throughout the Wairau. These negotiations were pursued during Grey's detention of Te Rauparaha from 23 July 1846 and in the absence of the warring Te Rangihaeata. Each transaction revealed Grey's access to increased imperial Treasury funding; admissions that FitzRoy's attempted projects at rendering New Zealand self-financing were interrupted. He drew on this Treasury authorization of up to £25,000 in Sydney. A sum of £10,000 in specie was transferred from Sydney in early 1846.[215] He also enjoyed access to that confidential sum of £10,000 supplied on Stanley's authority. Significant sums were involved to placate and induce Ngāti Toa to adhere to these deeds, but were paid in instalments. For Wairau, Grey paid £3,000 with it being transferred to Māori in five annual instalments of £600 each. He regarded this district as containing '80,000 acres of the finest agricultural land, and about 240,000 acres of the finest pastural [*sic*] land'.[216] In addition, the acquired tract extended for approximately 100 miles southward of the Wairau vale, comprising territories 'I understand admirably adapted to European settlers, and... likely to be almost immediately occupied by sheep and cattle'.[217]

In preparing for his acquisition of the Wairau, Grey stressed the procedural aspect of conducting negotiations with Pūaha of Ngāti Toa and of obtaining political advantages with Ngāti Toa factions by placating Te Rauparaha's son, the restive Tāmihana Te Rauparaha, and Tamihana's cousin, Matene Te Whiwhi. 'I think those natives would not be indisposed to accompanying you with "*Puaha*" in the government brig to the "Wairau" for the purpose of inspecting the district and of selecting the native reserves'.[218] He concluded, 'I do not think that whilst they are with you the Ngāti Toa tribe would venture to attempt to commit any outrages, upon the whole I do not know

213 Grey to Earl Grey, 26 March 1847, CO209/51, fos.309a–10, TNA.

214 Ibid, fos.309–9a.

215 Grey to Gipps, 19 December 1845, NZMss227, fos.84–5, APL; Grey to Gipps, 14 May 1846, NZMss227, fo.117.

216 Grey to Earl Grey, 26 March 1847, CO209/51, fo.313a, TNA.

217 Ibid. Concerning the details of this transaction, see Phillipson, *Rangahaua Whanui District 13*,.83–95.

218 Grey to McCleverty, 20 November 1846, NZMss227, fos.175–6, APL (emphasis in original).

anything which would tend more to the settlement of the country than your adopting this course at once'.[219] Yet, in negotiating with Ngāti Toa representatives, Grey presented governmental claims to these districts as those of an additional *iwi* or significantly sized *hapū* descent-grouping jostling with indigenous polities. That is, local evidence suggests that imperial negotiations might have been conducted through the medium of supposed 'customs', as reported by Hadfield in an important memorandum for Grey in 1846.[220] Grey evidently read this memorandum as it bears the markings of his marginalia. Hadfield said that a 'victorious tribe... will occasionally abandon its claim to a portion of its own territory, in which opposing chiefs have fallen, for the sake of restoring peace, without in any degree tarnishing its honour, or impairing its reputation for courage & warlike conduct'.[221] Certainly, Wīremu Naera Te Kanae, an *ariki* and relative of Te Rauparaha, appeared to understand the Wairau transaction in this fashion: 'In 1847 Sir George Grey asked Rawiri Pūaha and his people to give over Wairau, the place where Wakefield and his comrades died—to the Queen in compensation for her dead'. According to Te Kanae, Grey could be represented as stating, 'Give me the land where my dead died'.[222] Ballara and Evison seem to concur in this assessment of how the transaction was negotiated. However, neither enters into the further implications of an imperial use of intelligence about the supposed tenurial notions of Port Nicholson district Māori—Ngāti Toa *et al*—posing as *generic* 'Maori' concepts in Hadfield's memorandum.[223] In 1890 Alexander McKay recognized that it 'is almost impossible to lay down any fixed rules for fully defining the law of Maori land tenure, as the customs vary in different locations'.[224] Hadfield, predominantly resident in Ōtaki and Wellington, would have been familiar with precepts on property associated with an environment of competitive relations existing amongst Ngāti Toa, Ngāti Raukawa, Te Ātiawa, Ngāti Apa, and others. These arenas of activity would have constituted his principal sources for observation.[225] He produced an account of migratory *iwi* and *hapū* competing territorially and in pursuit of resources. Pūaha possessed his own agenda having written to Grey in a placatory tone concerning the military support that his Ngāti Toa might afford in harassing disaffected and warring Māori associated with Te Rangihaeata.[226] Pūaha also warned Grey that Māori politics were complicated: 'do not suppose we are one people', he advised, adding, 'they are a different people—we are a different people—we devoured them, they devoured us'.[227] Shortland had also suggested that 'the tribe that had suffered least [in war]', would supply land 'to compensate the greater losses in war of the other party'.[228]

[219] Ibid, fo.176.

[220] Hadfield to Grey, memorandum, 1846, 'system of government among the New Zealand tribes', GNZMss17, fos.73–96, APL.

[221] Ibid, fo.80.

[222] 'The history of the tribes Ngati-toa-rangatira, Ngati-awa-o-rungao- te-rangi and Ngati-Raukawa having special reference to the doings of Te Rau-paraha', 28 August 1888 [trans George Graham, 20 April 1928], Ms874B, 19, HlDu.

[223] Ballara, *Iwi*, 71–2; Evison, *The Long Dispute*, 166–9. Cf Morrell, *British Colonial Policy in the Age of Peel and Russell*, 330.

[224] McKay, 17 March 1890, 85-173-5/6: 'opinions of various authorities on native tenure', ATL [*AJHR-1890*, G-1].

[225] For example Hadfield to Coates, 22 July 1840, qMs-0895, fo.7, ATL.

[226] Pūaha to Grey, 3 March 1846, CO209/42, fos.305–6, TNA.

[227] Ibid.

[228] Shortland, 'tenure of Maori land', NZMs998/2, fos.36–7, APL.

The increasingly accurate surveying of New Zealand's littoral and hinterlands also assisted Grey, especially as he presented a sense of an administration at Auckland acting in accordance with a revisionist outlook on pursuing settlement locations. The availability of fertile pasturage in the South Island was stressed in the search for settlement sites, as with the results of Stokes' voyage in the steamer *Acheron* during early 1849. A consequence of this expedition was to enlarge the extent of the 'great southern plain' (Canterbury Plains) in the South Island as they appeared on New Zealand charts.[229] Grey stated that 'Your Lordship will be gratified at finding that the country in the neighbourhood of Port Cooper is so well adapted to the purposes of colonization, as also that the Middle Island of New Zealand appears to be so much broader than was imagined, and that the increased extent of territory is of so fertile and *available* a character'.[230] Rutherford accurately observed that Grey proceeded much more cautiously with territorial acquisition in the North Island than in *Te Waipounamu*.[231] Indeed, this governor's administration produced a series of paper transactions that embraced that extensive island with charts signifying ambitious imperial claims to territory as opposed to any prior claims of Ngāti Toa, Ngāi Tahu, or a corporation. A still youthful Grey was clearly responding to instructions stipulated in Westminster circles. In this sense, Grey cannot be unqualifiedly seen as fulfilling the role of an independent 'great man', acting upon his own assured designs, whether one is confronting his hagiographers or demonizers in the historiography, or authors seeking an increasingly subtle *via media* between these two extremes.[232] Flourishing settlement sites were sought after. Aboriginal tenure was to be avoided if possible, or unlocked in areas where intelligence on local Māori was strongest. These were Grey's principal objectives from November 1845. The Office established his framework for activity and performance. His peculiar skill was in appearing to fulfil the expectations of this framework initially created by Stanley in 1845 and therefore eventually earning the confidence of Earl Grey. His despatches encouraged a sense of comfort on the part of imperial administrators in Westminster. Grey, as a forager of intellectual sources and persons like Hadfield, Selwyn, and William Martin, the chief justice, was fully prepared to countenance the use of particular sources on native title in certain limited areas of administration, if not in others.

229 Grey to Earl Grey, 15 May 1849, 'Papers relative to New Zealand', *GBPP1850*, xxxvii [1136], 152; 'sketch of Middle Island (New Zealand), shewing the east coast as laid down by Captn Stokes', [facing 152]; Stokes to Grey, 4 May 1849, *GBPP1850*, xxxvii [1136], 153; Hamilton to Stokes, 3 May 1849, *GBPP1850*, xxxvii [1136], 153–5.

230 Grey to Earl Grey, 15 May 1849, *GBPP1850*, xxxvii [1136], , 152 (emphasis added).

231 Rutherford, *Sir George Grey*, 176. See also Gladstone to Grey, March 1846, BL AddMss44363, fo.294: 'I deem it probable that the middle island may be regarded as in no respect subject to the native claim of property in gross'.

232 For a nuanced recent account of Grey, his political thought, and policy, see Cadogan, 'Constituting the settler colony and reconstituting the indigene'. For those scholars possibly opting for a *via media*, see Francis, *Governors and Settlers*, 221–9; Ward, *A Show of Justice*. Peires provides a highly critical account of Grey in *The Dead will Arise*, 51–5, as does Keegan, *Colonial South Africa and the origins of the racial order*, 288. An earlier criticism of Grey can be located in McLintock, *Crown Colony Government in New Zealand*, 281, 285. For a discussion of Grey's role in the constitutional historiography of New Zealand, see McHugh, 'The Historiography of New Zealand's Constitutional History', in Joseph (ed), *Essays on the Constitution*, 344–67, 350–1; McHugh, 'Australasian narratives of constitutional foundation', in Neumann and Ericksen (eds), *Quicksands*, 101.

One illustration of this development can be found in a court decision to be explored in the following section.

SYMONDS CONTEXTUALIZED

Regina v Symonds, delivered on 9 June 1847, charted the outline of a formal jurisprudence on native title within New Zealand.[233] It was a sketch drawn expressly from northern American sources concerning *ius gentium* indigenized via the opinions of the Marshall court as a common law of the United States. *Symonds* performed a key role in the early colonial legal history of New Zealand, as it formally transmitted United States jurisprudence concerning 'Indian title' to New Zealand and treated it as relevant to analysing Crown–Māori relations. This was no less contestable a transmission than it had been in 1840 or 1844. But the case represented a judicial marker in the shifting sands of political argumentation about native title in the late 1840s. As a court decision, it performed the role of janitor, distilling a tidier, self-contained narrative from what might otherwise have appeared messily contestable and unresolved. The broad outline of a juristic approach to aboriginal title was there, although, as the United States experience demonstrated, it harboured tensions and disagreements as between judges. Insofar as Chapman and Martin were concerned, on the basis of *Symonds* a thin consensus could be sketched as to the presence of native title in New Zealand, its vulnerability to extinguishment by means of cession through purchase, and the Crown's pre-eminence as a purchaser of lands from indigenous populations in colonies, and, implicitly, recognition in these processes of 'rights' to be quieted or removed. Colonial New Zealand was already set on a trajectory of purchase, having inherited such a practice hinging upon multiplying deeds of purchase since Marsden's efforts at Rangihoua in 1815. With *Symonds*, however, the colonies in New Zealand were now also tied to northern American jurisprudential comparators despite the discomfort of early policy-formulators such as Stephen in London. At the very least, as a judgment for which native title served as a context, *Symonds* attested to the suitability of others, such as colonial judges, drawing these comparisons explicitly with reference to northern American sources. In particular, it encouraged resort to Kent's *Commentaries on American Law*, which both Martin and Chapman cited.

Both judges agreed in *Symonds* as to the primacy of Crown grants issued under the public seal of the colony, a point subsequently confirmed in decisions such as *Scott v Grace* in May 1848, where Chapman stated 'it has already been decided by this Court after much consideration, in the case of the *Queen v Symonds*, that the Crown can convey nothing to the subject, except under the public seal of the colony'.[234] Insofar as tying indigenous populations within New Zealand to a broader, trans-oceanic

[233] Now, most accessibly printed as *The Queen (on the prosecution of CH McIntosh) v Symonds* (1847) [1840–1932] NZPCC 387. The decision of *Symonds* was initially printed in an official form in the *New Zealand Government Gazette*, 6 July 1847 (referred to as '*M'Intosh v Symonds*'), and was forwarded to the Colonial Office in London (CO209/53, fos.45–47a, TNA). I have dealt with this case in Hickford, '"Vague Native Rights to Land"', 190–3. Owing to a misprint, the date of the *Symonds* judgment is incorrectly recorded as 19 June 1847 in '"Vague Native Rights to Land"', whereas it ought to read 9 June 1847.

[234] See *Scott v Grace* (13 May 1848) in Hickford, '"Settling some very important principles"', 71

narrative, Chapman was the principal innovator in the New Zealand context, transmitting a jurisprudential literature minted and honed in the United States. As seen, he had contended in the fifth issue of *The New Zealand Journal* published in London in April 1840 that the 'judges of the Supreme Court of the United States . . . base their decisions on what may be called the customary law of nations'.[235] Through this contention, Chapman was able to generalize the application of this legal reasoning to novel settings, such as New Zealand. Indeed, he observed how the American judges referred constantly to 'certain principles, as well recognised among the nations of Europe, and, like our judges, they affect to be the depositories and interpreters of the law, and not its makers'.[236] Chapman's opinion in *Symonds* represented an ongoing implicit sensitivity to allegations that the jurisprudence of the United States Supreme Court was an *ex post facto* innovation or novelty—a tidily presented invention of Marshall and his fellow jurists contemplating the messily varied and particularist practices of some two centuries. These 'principles of universal application to the respective territorial rights of the Crown, the aboriginal natives, and the European subjects of the Queen' flowed 'not from what an American writer has called the "vice of judicial legislation" '.[237] But, as Lindsay Robertson has explored, such a claim rested on uncertain foundations, with Marshall himself acting as a judicial innovator with regard to northern American juridical history.[238] Robertson also observed how Marshall dislodged his preferred historical narrative in *Johnson v M'Intosh* when he revisited the question of European discovery and its impact upon Native American polities in the *Worcester v Georgia* opinion. He sought to 'dismantle the discovery doctrine by overruling that part of the doctrine assigning the fee title to the discovering sovereign' but it would be revivified in *Mitchel v United States* in 1835.[239]

Placing the Treaty of Waitangi—native title and court decisions as a resource for colonial government disciplining subjects

Upon receiving the *Symonds* decision in November 1847, the third Earl Grey stated, '[t]his judgment is a most important one and the reasoning quite conclusive'.[240] The rejection of FitzRoy's preceding measures in the Supreme Court opinions of the chief justice, Martin, and Justice Chapman represented Grey's principal objective, one that he had augured in despatches to the Colonial Office. Indeed, Grey's administration engineered the submission of a writ of *scire facias* to the Supreme Court at Auckland, opting for a contrived testing of a certificate issued pursuant to FitzRoy's proclamation of 10 October 1844. Yet Grey was sufficiently concerned about the possibilities of an

[235] Chapman, 'The English, the French and the New Zealanders', 1.

[236] Ibid.

[237] Ibid. The phrase the 'vice of judicial legislation' appeared in Hoffman, *A Course of Legal Study, Addressed to Students and the Profession Generally*, II, 566.

[238] Robertson, *Conquest by Law*, 100–3, referring to, among other things, Marshall's historical narrative *The Life of George Washington, Commander in Chief of the American Forces*.

[239] *Worcester v State of Georgia* 6 Pet 515, 31 US 350 (1832); *Mitchel v United States* 9 Pet 711, 9 L Ed 283 (1835). Robertson, *Conquest by Law*, 133, 138–9. The notion of the underlying fee residing with the Crown was an analytical approach that Salmond, solicitor-general for New Zealand from 1910 to 1920, also favoured: see Hickford, 'John Salmond and Native Title in New Zealand', 853–924.

[240] Earl Grey to Hawes, minute, 3 November 1847, CO209/53, fo.38a, TNA; Earl Grey to Grey, 3 December 1847, CO209/53, fo.44.

uncongenial judicial result to instruct the Colonial Secretary in Auckland to ensure that 'the Attorney General . . . make the requisite preparations for an appeal to the judicial committee of the Privy Council'.[241] Nevertheless, the Supreme Court ruled in favour of Grey's preferred view. In doing so, it provided his administration with an additional means of disciplining settlers disposed towards a free trade in territorial transactions with Māori. The gravamen of the claim was based on the certificate obtained by Charles McIntosh, a clerk in the Auckland surveying office, pursuant to a FitzRoy proclamation. The certificate was obtained in consequence of McInstosh's purchase of an island 'called "Taratoroa", situated in the Frith of the Thames, a little to the eastward of Waiheke [an island in the Hauraki Gulf to the east of the settlement at Auckland]', comprising some 401.5 acres, according to the survey McIntosh paid for.[242] Grey's native secretary, Symonds, was provided with an overlapping Crown grant for this land and Grey arranged for McIntosh to commence his legal action. The proceedings constituted a direct assault on FitzRoy's policies. In essence, Martin and Chapman held that such certificates constituted a breach of the 1842 legislation concerning the management of imperial 'waste lands' in the Australasian colonies. Chapman corroborated this emphasis in personal correspondence, remarking: 'in the face of the Australian Land Sales Act [the imperial waste lands statute of 1842] no grant except for *money* and at *Auction* is valid hence an Act of Parliament was necessary'.[243] FitzRoy's executive council and law officers at Westminster in 1844 and 1845 respectively had already determined that this statute either did not apply to New Zealand or was not breached by any such 'waiver' proclamations.[244] The possibility of notionally granting lands to settlers which was still in the possession of indigenous populations on the assumption that they might be subsequently confirmed (or not) was not novel. Stephen in the Colonial Office may have disapproved or presented himself as disapproving in 1840, preferring tidy and Crown-mediated purchases as precursors to Crown grants; but there were a number of judicial precedents for a less-controlled approach. In *Marshall v Clark* (1791) the Supreme Court of Appeals in Virgina held:

> the Indian title did not impede either the power of the legislature to grant the land to the officers and soldiers, or the location of the lands on treasury warrants, the grantee, in either case, must risque [*sic*] the event of the Indian claim, and yield to it, if finally established, or have the benefit of a former or future extinction thereof.[245]

In closing his opinion in *Symonds*, the chief justice noted the *Symonds* judgment did not affirm the absolute validity of the grant to the defendant, as the case decided only that the grant could not be set aside 'on the grounds which are set forth *on the Record*'.[246] The record in the case, on which the writ of *scire facias* turned, alleged that by virtue of the certificate and FitzRoy's waiver of the right of pre-emption, McIntosh 'acquired the right of pre-emption over the said island, and that

[241] Grey to Sinclair (Colonial Secretary), 29 May 1847, NZMss227, fo.280, APL: 'If the Supreme Court should be in favour of the power of the Governor to waive the right of pre-emption,—the Attorney General should make the requisite preparations for an appeal to the judicial committee of the Privy Council'.

[242] OLC1/1116–1117, ANZ(W).

[243] Chapman to Chapman senior, 19 August 1847, qMs-0420, ATL (emphasis in original).

[244] 'Minutes of executive council [extract]', 17 July 1844, CO209/28, fo.306a, TNA.

[245] *Marshall v Clark* 4 Call 268, 8 Va 268 (Va), 1791 WL 325 (Va).

[246] *'M'Intosh v Symonds'*, *New Zealand Government Gazette*, 6 July 1847, vol 7, no 1, 68.

he accordingly . . . exercised that right by purchasing the . . . island from the native owners [on 12 January 1845] . . . , thereby [acquiring] an equitable right and title' to the island.[247] McIntosh reportedly paid consideration of £32 in cash, four breeding ewes, 10 blankets, one piece of cotton duck, and one black cloth waistcoat. Despite the legal result in *Symonds*, McIntosh was not precluded from enjoying the fruits of his acquisition. Following his purchase, he erected a wooden hut, flocked the land with sheep, goats, and pigs, and employed a labourer. Ultimately, McIntosh obtained a deed of Crown grant dated 27 October 1848, confirmed by Swainson as Attorney General, for 204 acres on Taratoroa Island in accordance with the processes outlined in clauses 11 and 14 of the Land Claims Ordinance 1846.[248] Indeed, McIntosh was already embroiled in Henry Matson's investigations of pre-emption waiver certificate land claims when the *Symonds* litigation was on foot. Matson was appointed commissioner, as recently as 14 December 1846, in accordance with clause 1 of the Land Claims Ordinance 1846 with a view to inquiring into such claims.[249] Embarrassingly, when Grey replaced FitzRoy in November 1845, no Crown grants had yet been issued to any of the pre-emption waiver claimants. Some 67 per cent of pre-emption waiver certificate claims fell within the Auckland area alone. Many land transactions conducted beneath the auspices of FitzRoy's pre-emption waiver proclamations lay fallow—the merits still to be investigated and secure legal tenure obtained. On 5 August 1847, a mere 57 days after the *Symonds* determination, Matson recommended a confirmatory Crown grant be issued to McIntosh on the basis of the testimony of four Māori witnesses, aided by Charles Davis and Edward Meurant as interpreters, the evidence of McIntosh having been in 'undisputed possession of the land since the purchase', and the improvements he had made to the land (such as erecting a house).

Symonds also set out the general pre-eminence of a Crown grant issued in accordance with the precepts of the judgment's understanding of Crown pre-emption. This was important, as pre-emption waiver certificates could also result in Crown grants under the then recently enacted Land Claims Ordinance 1846. A critical distinction for McIntosh, however, is that he was already engaged in a process to secure a Crown grant in respect of the lands he claimed in Tarataroa Island. It is to be recalled that a central issue for the two judges in *Symonds* was not the substance or content of proprietary claims of Māori (as parties), but rather a contest between two European claimants relative to the interest obtained from the Crown. If a Crown grant was alleged to be void or voidable, the appropriate procedure under the common law to revoke a deed of grant was that of the writ of *scire facias*.

An important implicit context for the *Symonds* litigation consisted of the peculiar legal norms relating to the writ of *scire facias* and Crown grants developed in the anglophone courts. These were norms, which had already acquired a layering of colonial understandings through court proceedings in British North America, New South Wales and elsewhere, associated with the power of governors to alienate Crown lands

[247] 'Reports of cases in the Supreme Court of New Zealand', 1844–1852, vol 104, 33, Hocken Library, Dunedin.

[248] 'An Ordinance to authorize Compensation in Colonial Debentures to be made to certain Claimants to Land in the Colony of New Zealand', 10 Vict, number 22, 18 November 1846.

[249] The details of these processes still remain under-researched. For an overview, see Daamen, 'The Crown's Right of Pre-emption and FitzRoy's Waiver Purchases'.

in accordance with their commissions and royal instructions under the Royal Sign Manual. Royal commissions, issued under the great seal, were treated as public documents in contradistinction to royal instructions, which were viewed as private communications. If a governor exceeded the authority afforded him in a royal commission, he was at risk of acting *ultra vires*, as in *Cameron v Kyte*.[250] The Privy Council had considered the legal effect of royal instructions in *Camm v Hansford* in 1766.[251]

At base, *Symonds* represented a degree of juristic reflection on the place of the Crown within the innovated constitutional order in New Zealand, adapted to the presence of pre-existing indigenous populations but consonant, nevertheless, with the assumptions then obtaining in the Supreme Court of New South Wales. Martin analysed the voyaging Crown as state, or as a generator of new states subordinate to the Crown in its imperial guise, through the lens of Vattel's text on *ius gentium*, although Martin's own reading was, in its turn, inculcated through common law reasoning in a decision of *Attorney-General v Brown* determined in New South Wales in February 1847. Martin quoted a key passage from *Brown* concerning how the Crown was to be comprehended within New South Wales:

> In a newly-discovered country, settled by British subjects, the occupancy of the Crown with respect to the waste lands of that colony is no fiction. If, in one sense, these lands be the patrimony of the nation, the Sovereign is the representative and the executive authority of the nation; the 'moral personality' (as Vattel calls him, Law of Nations, bk 1, chap 4) by whom the nation acts, and in whom for such purposes, its power resides. Here is a property depending for its support on no feudal notions or principles.

In *Brown*, the Crown was treated as the embodied and institutional 'representative' of the 'nation' at work. In *Symonds*, Martin was clear as to the authority of Kent's *Commentaries on American Law*. He cited passages from Kent's third volume concerning the 'exclusive right [of the state] to grant a title to the soil, subject only to the Indian right of occupancy' and recognizing the 'natives... to be the rightful occupants of the soil'. Yet he cited Kent 'not as an authority in an English Court, but only as a sufficient testimony that the principles contained in the rule of law [that no British subject could acquire a title against the Crown in a 'new country' without authorization from the Crown]' derived from the period when the various United States were once British colonies.[252] Martin tied these principles, together with his conception of the task of Crown pre-emption, to colonial state-building. As he put it, 'colonization is a work of national concernment—a work to be carried on with reference to the interests of the nation collectively; and therefore to be controlled and guided by the Supreme Power of the nation'.[253] In essence, language of this complexion, combined with asserting the significance of Crown grants under the public seal, gave an additional fillip to the proclivities of imperial policy and Grey's colonial administration to discipline settlement niches. The jurisprudence of Marshall, a moderate federalist, was used to strengthen the policy arm of colonial government in New Zealand.[254]

[250] *Cameron v Kyte* (1835) 3 Knapp 332, 344.

[251] Smith, *Appeals to the Privy Council from the American Plantations*, 624.

[252] '*McIntosh v Symonds*', CO209/53, fo.47.

[253] Ibid, fo.46a.

[254] On Marshall as a 'moderate federalist', see Wilentz, *The Rise of American Democracy*, 99–100.

Whither the Treaty of Waitangi? The conditionality of United States jurisprudence applied to New Zealand

Although neither extensively acknowledged nor reported in the judgments of *Symonds*, Bartley, legal counsel for McIntosh, based his argument on the Treaty of Waitangi. Michael Belgrave, in his significant work *Historical Frictions*, contended, '[a]lthough [*Symonds* was] a victory for Maori land rights, the decision saw the end of the Treaty of Waitangi as *the primary source for discussion of Maori rights*'.[255] Yet, as subsequent chapters reveal, the Treaty did not retreat but remained a key presence in intra-anglophone political (including constitutional) arguments and also a way of presenting colonial administration to Māori. In this sense, the patterns of intra-anglophone debate in the 1840s persisted—a mingling of sources, including those drawn from mid-nineteenth-century adaptations of a law of nations and stadial analyses of proprietary rights, each able to be viewed as a contributing influence but not necessarily primary in and of itself. In *Symonds*, the parties agreed that the Treaty of Waitangi, as translated in the parliamentary papers printed by order of the House of Commons on 11 May 1841, would be taken to be the 'true version of the said Treaty'. Bartley, in opposing the Attorney General, endeavoured to invoke the language of the Treaty and to place its open-textured text at the heart of the litigation. He failed. In his Treaty-based argument, he focused on its second article. He averred that in the Māori language text of the Treaty, 'there was no such word as "exclusive"', and, with the word 'anake' signifying '"only" or "exclusive"', he noted that 'there is no such word in the original'.[256] Thus, he contended, '[i]f the words "exclusive right of pre-emption", meant... "exclusive right of purchase", why was not the indisputable and unequivocal word "purchase" used, and not "pre-emption" which admitted and bore a different meaning?'[257] The Attorney General responded that 'the treaty [was not one-sided, as Bartley had claimed, but] must be necessarily taken as a whole, and if so taken, that it was not one-sided for it would be found that expressly in consideration of what the chiefs of New Zealand has contracted to do, Her Majesty by the 3rd article conferred upon the natives all the rights of British subjects'.[258] Bartley submitted that, irrespective of the policy intent and design at the formation of the colony to control the spatial extent of settlement and to raise funds from the Crown's management of the sale of land at fixed prices, those Māori 'who formed a party to the Treaty of Waitangi', could never have intended the 'prevention of sale' by 'natives to settlers'. He judged that the control on land transfer, 'if carried into effect', as operating 'injuriously to, rather than positive of, emigration'.[259] What remains noteworthy was Chapman's elegant side-stepping of the Treaty of Waitangi, a manoeuvre of common law reasoning that gave rise to a resilient and oft-cited phrase 'in solemnly guaranteeing the native title, and in securing what is called the Queen's pre-emptive right, the Treaty of Waitangi, confirmed by the charter of the colony, does not assert either in doctrine or in practice anything new and unsettled'.[260] Bartley's argument was marginalized as

[255] Belgrave, *Historical Frictions*, 70 (emphasis added). See Hickford, '"Vague Native Rights to Land"', 191.

[256] *Supplement to The New-Zealander*, 8 May 1847.

[257] Ibid. [258] Ibid. [259] Ibid.

[260] *'M'Intosh v Symonds'*, CO209/53, fo.45a, TNA. This phrase has been cited since, proving to be one of the most resilient passages in *Symonds*: see *Ngati Apa v Attorney-General* [2003] 3 NZLR 643, para 16.

'rather philological than legal', thereby evading the possibilities of permitting Māori communities to act unimpeded, as they had before 1840 in the nascent land market.[261]

Neither Chapman nor Martin was compelled to accept United States jurisprudence as particularly persuasive. Furthermore, even if one were to accept reasoning as persuasive for certain purposes, such a stance did not necessarily signify its wholesale acceptance. Unremarkably, aspects of literature could be scavenged to the extent that they were perceived to be congenial or applicable. Mere admission of distinct characteristics of United States Supreme Court decisions did not equate to complete acceptance or approval on the part of colonial jurists. Other parts of a *corpus juris* could be omitted or ignored. In his judgment, Chapman resorted to the favoured literature of the New Zealand Company and certain of its Whig and Tory advocates (Eliot). Thus, he drew support from the Marshall court opinion in *Cherokee Nation v Georgia* (1831), although the proposition for which he relied on that decision was incorrectly reported.[262] At first, he claimed that the northern American courts would 'not allow a grant to be impeached under pretext that the native title has not been extinguished, yet they would certainly not hesitate to do so in a suit by one of the native Indians'.[263] Chapman then proceeded to say in his *Symonds* opinion that 'in the case of the *Cherokee Nation v the State of Georgia*, the Supreme court threw its protective decision over the plaintiff-nation, against a gross attempt at spoliation; calling to its aid, throughout every portion of its judgment, the principles of the common law as applied and adopted from the earliest times by the colonial laws'.[264] Yet that case could not be construed so bluntly. Chapman's rendition of *Cherokee Nation v Georgia* was misleading to say the least. In those proceedings before the United States Supreme Court, the Cherokee nation brought a motion seeking an injunction to restrain the state of Georgia from executing or enforcing certain state laws within the Cherokee territory, as that territory had been designated by treaty between the United States and the Cherokee nation. One of the objectionable state measures included legislation authorizing the governor of Georgia to 'take possession of the gold, silver and other mines, lying and being in that section of the chartered limits of Georgia commonly called the Cherokee country'. Marshall, in delivering the opinion of the court, observed that a preliminary issue had to be addressed as to whether the court had jurisdiction to entertain the application for an injunction at all.[265] The procedural bill filed on behalf of the Cherokee nation, signed by John Ross, who was presented as their principal chief, characterized the plaintiffs collectively as 'the Cherokee Nation of Indians, a foreign state, not owing allegiance to the United States, nor to any State of this Union, nor to any prince, potentate or State, other than their own'.[266] The third article of the federal constitution limited the judicial power of the United States to controversies between 'the State or the citizens thereof, and foreign states, citizens, or subjects'. A majority of the court concluded that the Cherokee nation was not a 'foreign state' within the meaning of the constitution. Indian tribes may 'more correctly, perhaps', said Marshall, 'be denominated domestic

[261] Ibid.

[262] *Cherokee Nation v State of Georgia* 5 Pet 1 (1831) (USSC), cited in *Regina v Symonds* [1840–1932] (1847) NZPCC 387, 390, per Justice Chapman.

[263] *'M'Intosh v Symonds'*, CO209/53, fo.45a, TNA.

[264] 'Reports of cases in the Supreme Court of New Zealand', 1844–1852, vol 104, 36.

[265] *Cherokee Nation v State of Georgia* 5 Pet 1 (1831), 15.

[266] Ibid, 3.

dependent nations'. Given the nature of their complaints, Marshall signalled that their proper redress was political rather than judicial and that the appropriate forum to adjudicate their claims was a political one as opposed to the 'judicial department'.[267] The dissentient, Justice Thompson, treated the Cherokee nation as a 'sovereign state' under the law of nations and in accordance with the treaty practices of the federal government. He was further 'authorized by [his] brother Story to say that he concurs with me in this opinion'.[268] Story expressed his pleasure with Thompson's dissent in correspondence to the reporter of the *Cherokee Nation* decision, Richard Peters, in June 1831: 'I rejoice that Mr Justice Thompson has done what I requested, that is, stated my concurrence with him', adding, 'I am more and more satisfied we are right; and when I feel this, I am ready to meet all consequences'.[269] Subsequently, Story confessed in 1832, when hearing the arguments in *Worcester v Georgia*, that he 'blush[ed] for [his] country, when I perceive that such legislation, destructive of all faith and honor towards the Indians, is suffered to pass with the silent approbation of the present Government of the United States'.[270]

In rendering *Cherokee Nation v Georgia*, Chapman resorted to Kent's *Commentaries on American Law*, specifically the fifty-first lecture entitled 'Of the Law concerning Real Property'.[271] Chapman's predilections to do so were implicit in his personal past. Had Chapman been so minded he could have cited *Mitchel v United States* (1835), as it was discussed relatively extensively in the 1836, 1840, and 1844 editions of the *Commentaries*.[272] Indeed, that decision was distinctly referred to with reference to, *inter alia*, the following propositions: 'the ultimate fee was in the crown or its grantees, subject to this right of possession, and could be granted by the crown upon that condition; that individuals could not purchase Indian lands without license, or under rules prescribed by law; that possession was considered with reference to Indian habits and modes of life, and the hunting grounds of the tribes were as much in their actual occupation as the cleared fields of the whites, and this was the tenure of Indian lands by the laws of all the colonies'.[273] Given that Chapman mentioned *Cherokee Nation* in the absence of any submissions, it was open to him or the chief justice to do likewise with *Mitchel v United States*.[274] Despite what FM Brookfield might have hoped, Chapman did not. Quite properly, even though one might disagree with him, Chapman might

267 Ibid, 20. 268 Ibid, 80.

269 Story to Richard Peters, 24 June 1831, in Story, *Life and Letters of Joseph Story*, II, 46.

270 Story to Mrs Joseph Story, 26 February 1832, in ibid, II, 84.

271 This lecture was formerly included as 'lecture L' in the earlier 1826–1831 edition but figured as the re-numbered 'lecture LI' in the 1836, 184,0 and 1844 editions of Kent's *Commentaries on American Law*.

272 *Mitchel v United States* 34 US 711 (1835).

273 Kent, *Commentaries on American Law*, 3rd edn, III, 386, note a; *Commentaries on American Law*, 4th edn, III, 385, note a; *Commentaries on American Law*, 5th edn, III, 385, note a.

274 Cf Brookfield, 'The Doctrine of Aboriginal Title in New Zealand: A Defence' where Brookfield argues unconvincingly and rather earnestly in defence of Chapman: 'Had the matter come before him judicially again, and had *Mitchel v United States* been drawn to his attention and properly considered, he might well have decided against the Lockean limitation. We do not know'. Subsequently, Brookfield contends, 'But, as I suggested two decades ago, the answer of the Marshall Court [to the Lockean comprehension of proprietorship] is provided in the last of its Indian cases, *Mitchel v United States*. There Baldwin J's judgment (for the Court) is clearly against the Lockean restriction: "Indian possession or occupation" must be considered "with reference to [the Indians'] habits and modes of life, their hunting grounds [being] as much in their possession as the cleared fields of the whites"' (draft on file with author).

have had his own conceptions as to what aspects of American jurisprudence were applicable to colonial New Zealand's circumstances in 1847 and what aspects were not. *Mitchel*, however, was not cited in the *Symonds* decision. Furthermore, as a distinct point, it should be recalled that Chapman had signalled how the logic of stadial theory rendered the reference to the 'hunting grounds of the [Native American] tribes' irrelevant to the situation of Māori within New Zealand.[275] Accordingly, Chapman, on his own intellectual trajectories, may have considered the *Mitchel* opinion as reported in Kent's *Commentaries* broadly inapplicable to New Zealand circumstances insofar as Māori economic practices were perceived distinctively. Chapman had long perceived Māori to be ambulatory horticulturists rather than pursuers of game, requiring less-expansive territories than those who could be classified as hunters and foragers. Although not acknowledged in the relevant passage in Kent's discussion of *Mitchel*, the final sub-limb of this sequence of propositions was extracted from Baldwin's opinion in that decision. It resonated with a developing acknowledgement of possession at common law (although it did not necessarily imply the distinctions drawn in *Regina v Marshall; Regina v Bernard* (2005)[276]). If anything, the intellectual assumptions regarding distinctions between what was exclusively used and occupied as opposed to claimed pursuant to non-territorial use or activity-based entitlements remained latent in assessing the intensity or quality of indigenous relationships with particular landscapes or areas, and have continued to do so.[277] The aftermath of *Symonds* reveals distinct intellectual approaches to native title lurking within the underlying imperial and colonial contexts— which continue to confront to this day.

Chapman was also able to shape the agenda of what would become the decision in *Symonds* through preparing a draft judgment, and sending it to Martin in Auckland on 28 May 1847 who subsequently prepared his own. In personal correspondence to his father, he reported, 'I am very familiar with the history of our [i]ntercourse with the American Indians for 200 years'.[278] There was no doctrinal predictability in the application of this jurisprudence, or even in the fashion in which those who employed it understood its substance or chose to do so. Certainly, Chapman was sufficiently cautious not to enter into the myriad disputes as to the substance or extent of aboriginal title recognized under this law on *ius gentium*. With care, Chapman corralled his

275 Hickford, '"Decidedly the Most Interesting Savages"', 123.

276 *R v Marshall; R v Bernard* 2005 SCC 43: exclusive use and occupation means the intention and capacity to retain exclusive control and, to that end, a reasonable inference must be able to be drawn that the group could have excluded others had it chosen to do so (ibid, paras 57 and 65). In other publications (particularly on the foreshore and seabed question), Brookfield commended the distinction between 'exclusive use and occupation' and non-territorial rights, although this sort of approach need not have been implicit in the statements of Justice Baldwin in *Mitchell* in 1835, nor coincide at all with the test for 'Māori customary land'—'held in accordance with tikanga Māori'—under s 129(2)(a) of Te Ture Whenua Māori Act 1993. In *Da Silva v Aotea Maori Committee and Hauraki Maori Trust Board* [1999] 25 Tai Tokerau MB 216, 217, for instance, the Māori Land Court held that the 'change in approach' signalled by s 129 of Te Ture Whenua Māori Act required the 'Court to make its determination according to tikanga Māori—from the inside'. It considered that the term 'held' in s 129(2)(a) possessed 'no connotation of ownership but rather that it [land] is retained or kept in accordance with tikanga Māori'.

277 As with the Canadian spectrum of rights and aboriginal title, where title is recognized as a right to exclusive possession of the land itself. See also s 32 of the Foreshore and Seabed Act 2004 (territorial customary rights) and s 58(1) of the Marine and Coastal Area (Takutai Moana) Act 2011 (customary marine title) in New Zealand.

278 Chapman to Chapman senior, 15 June 1847, qMs-0419, ATL.

thoughts, restricting them to the directly engaged question of the validity of certificates issued under FitzRoy's proclamation. Tantalizingly, he signalled his appreciation of a variety of lurking assumptions and views as to the nature and extent of native title. But he was sufficiently astute to avoid engaging with these views in the open, especially in circumstances where Martin did not necessarily concur with him. Thus, '[w]hatever may be the opinion of jurists as to the strength or weakness of the native title, whatsoever may have been the past vague notions of the natives of this country, whatever may be their present clearer and still growing conception of their dominion over land', Chapman did not proceed to examine these proprietary rights in any detail.[279] Hence, he opined that native title ought to be respected, but did not proceed to analyse its contents beyond sporadic inklings: 'Technically, [pre-emption] contemplates the native dominion over the soil as inferior to what we call an estate in fee'.[280] Chapman merely hinted at an opinion of 'aborigines' using only those lands that they required in accordance with their habitual ways of life, such as these were—the resilient motif of 'occupancy' emerging here: 'Practically, it secures to them all the *enjoyments* from the land which they had before our intercourse, and as much more as the opportunity of selling portions, useless to themselves, affords'.[281] Such language was generally consistent with the tenor of the Marquis of Normanby's instructions to Hobson of 1839.

Chapman's ideas were not fully disclosed in *Symonds*. It is to his extra-judicial commentary that we must resort, amongst which we find a set of notes broadly contemporaneous with the *Symonds* decision. They enjoyed a subsequent afterlife as the basis for a 'law lecture' to the University of Melbourne. The notes were not subsequently disowned as remnants or symbols of youthful waywardness or apostasy. They represented Chapman's efforts to construct a cogent account or theory of native title relative to emerging colonial settlements and legal systems. For one thing, Chapman surmised that the notes would be helpful for 'the purpose of informing the inferior magistrates and *the protectors* as of warning and instructing the native population' (emphasis added)'. The protectorate department in New Zealand was remodelled and effectively abolished in 1846. Chapman also adverted to particular events in 1842 (at Kauaeranga on the Thames) and in 1844.[282] The provenance of Chapman's notes is suggested not only by references within the manuscript text itself, but also through Chapman's personal correspondence. In June 1847 Chapman reported that he had been at work on preparing 'some parts (say Chapters)' on the subject of native title as an area of 'colonial law'.[283] His extant notes comport with just such an effort.

In these notes, the judge spoke to his underlying views as to the non-justiciability of native title and its incommensurability with English legal concepts of tenure—concepts which bound the jurisdiction of the colonial courts. Beneath the heading 'Title to Land', Chapman began with the proposition that the 'rights and dominion which native tribes exercise over land are not such as come within the cognizance of the Tribunals'. In speaking of 'the Tribunals', Chapman was referring to the colonial

279 *Regina v Symonds* [1840–1932] (1847) NZPCC 387, 390, per Justice Chapman; *Regina v Symonds*, CO209/53, fo.45a, TNA (reported in *New Zealand Government Gazette*, 6 July 1847, 63–8).

280 Ibid, 391; CO209/53, fo.46, per Justice Chapman, TNA.

281 Ibid, CO209/53, fo.46, TNA (emphasis added).

282 See also Dorsett, 'Sworn on the Dirt of Graves'.

283 Chapman to Chapman senior, 15 June 1847, qMs-0419, 438, ATL.

courts generally, unless an ordinance or act of the legislature constructed a competent jurisdiction for a body to investigate native title and to ascertain proprietors or those with an interest in it. He did not merely focus on justiciability, however. Something richer than a mere assertion of non-justiciability in the colonial courts undergirded Chapman's memorandum. Entwined with his statement about the 'cognizance of the Tribunals', he also suggested the absence of 'analogy' between English conceptions of real property tenure and native title. To put it another way, these concepts were not commensurable or well aligned. In characterizing the *sui generis* qualities of native title, Chapman noted how '[t]heir dominion bears no analogy to that full and complete dominion which we call an *estate in fee* which is also something less than the pure allodium of some countries'.[284] Each bore different incidents or attributes. A different state and stage of political economy and different historical narratives also underlay the estate in fee simple when compared with native title. Chapman's appreciation of the logics of stadialism mingling with a developing sense of what amounted to 'possession' of land by tribal communities was in evidence: 'Savage tribes do not adopt the custom of reducing land into private possession'. Here, Chapman based his view on the economic and agricultural practices of Māori and how they seemed to organize their communities. The country inhabited by 'savage tribes' remained 'for the most part... waste in a perfect state of nature unbroken by the foot of man'. When required, '[p]arts were occupied for cultivation not for private use but in common and when such parts are worn out the tribe removes to & breaks up other land sufficient for this *temporary possession*'.[285] As such, averred Chapman, '[a] mere right of occupancy... is all that the Native tribes comprehend, and if Europeans teach them that they can obtain money for such lands and they part with their rights, the sale is sure to be disputed by the co-occupants'. Nor did Chapman seem to envisage indigenous 'customs' as determining the nature and extent of native title on a permanent and stable basis. Such customs were not determinative. On the contrary, assessing the modes of subsistence or economic behaviours of indigenous communities relative to land from a distance and adjudging their behaviours to be consistent with 'temporary possession' seemed sufficient. Chapman's view of European discovery as legally foundational in the British claim to New Zealand, aligned as it was with his interpretation of a congenial United States jurisprudence, remained unhinged. Thus, the 'Waitangi treaty considered (erroneously) as the foundation of the Queen's sovereignty has led', he averred, 'to [the] difficulty' of permitting chiefs to 'take the law into their own hands'.[286]

Pre-emption in favour of the Crown was prudential. It allowed European settlers to avoid the risk of such disputes, as the Crown's officials bore the risk of any disputed transactions in the first instance. The Crown represented a single portal through which Māori transactions concerning land could pass, rather than the multiplicity of settlers with all of the various risks of misunderstanding, violence, and heightened transaction costs associated with many potential buyers.[287] If the courts were to recognize an interest passing to the European settlers through a direct sale-and-purchase transaction,

[284] Chapman, legal notes, undated [1846], Ms-Papers-8670-0417, ATL (emphasis in original).

[285] Ibid (emphasis added).

[286] Ibid, 25. Dorsett, in 'Sworn on the Dirt of Graves', considers this point in detail relative to the question of abrogating indigenous customs.

[287] There was no such restriction on dealings with chattels, such as shipping vessels, and other items of personal property.

it would be limited to the nature of the interest in the possession of the vendor. For Chapman, this was an expression of the 'rule', as he put it, that 'a man can only [sell] such estate as he has'. Accordingly, a European purchaser would simply obtain 'an estate of occupancy in common with the conveying tribe and not the right to reduce any piece of land into perfect possession'. This statement sat squarely in accordance with Marshall's view in *Johnson v M'Intosh* (1823), where the chief justice considered an individual European purchaser, acquiring land from Native Americans or being allowed to occupy, perforce had to rely on the forms of recognition internal to that Native American community. Chapman viewed rights of native title to be 'so weak—weaker even than the easement of a commoner in England that the courts would find it next to impossible to deal with it in accordance with the English law by which they are bound'.[288]

Given these circumstances, he ventured that the pre-emption rule was 'perhaps fortunate', as it effectively prevented 'dealing with native tribes for the acquisition of land' on a broad-ranging basis. Regarding customary law relating to native title and Māori communities, Chapman was no legal positivist in the Austinian mould. He did not need to be. Indeed, he simply treated the system of English real property tenure as generally incommensurable with Māori conceptions and norms. He envisaged points of communicability mediated by negotiated purchases, protectors of aborigines, and directly authorized magistrates. Unlike Martin, Chapman did not express a strong commitment to seeing native title as encompassing broad swathes of territory despite what Māori polities might have asserted to the contrary. Rather, Chapman's suggestion, certainly concealed in *Symonds* and left unanswered with care, appeared to head in the opposite direction—a doubt that Māori could claim proprietorship of areas they did not exclusively occupy and possess. In this vein, Chapman did not appear to adapt developments in English common law to indigenous populations in New Zealand. *Jones v Williams*, for instance, had been decided in 1837, determining how acts consistent with a possessory claim in one area of land might be sufficient in contextual circumstances to warrant a finding of de facto possession to the whole area claimed. Baron Parke had stated how, 'If you prove the cutting of timber in one part, I take that to be evidence to go to a jury to prove a right in the whole wood, although there be no fence, or distinct boundary, surrounding the whole'.[289] The primacy of Crown grants was defended: 'No grant can be disputed to the subject on the ground that the Crown has not extinguished the native title'.

We see alignment between political authority of indigenous communities over territorial space and rights in the land itself. Chapman was comfortable with a form of political authority over territorial space theoretically subordinate to the supervisory jurisdiction of Britain.[290] Thus, legal-conceptual strategies were available for jurists to assert de facto exceptions (the continuing power of tribes to prosecute wars) as consistent, nevertheless, with overarching albeit insufficiently nested or embedded

[288] Chapman, Ms-papers-8670-047, ATL.

[289] *Jones v Williams* (1837) 2 M & W 326, 331, per Baron Parke.

[290] I have previously approached this question from the specific angle of property rights: Hickford, '"Decidedly the Most Interesting Savages"', 165; Hickford, 'Law and Politics', 261–2, 265; Hickford, 'Framing and Reframing the *Agōn*'. This issue has been approached from the jurisdictional angle by Shaunnagh Dorsett in 'Sworn on the Dirt of Graves'.

jurisdiction. As a technique or device, this approach was neither startling nor novel.[291] These anomalies or exceptions, seen as merely transitional and in being denuded of any *de jure* significance, such as that which obtained in the United States, allowed Chapman and Martin to ensnare Māori conceptually within the supervisory jurisdiction of the Crown even though the jurisdiction was not fully embedded or nested institutionally through effective courts and magistrates. These were the circumstances of New Zealand as construed by two of its colonial jurists. Chapman and Martin interpreted New Zealand as an experiment in incorporating Māori as subjects *de jure* even though practically embedding this claim was still a work-in-progress. Thus, in his personal notes, Chapman cautioned that in 'considering the question of what laws prevail in a newly settled country where a civilized people come into contact with a rude people, the idea of sovereignty must not be confounded with that of laws either generally or in relation to the title to the land'.[292] Martin's later musings suggest satisfaction with 'discovery' as the central arbiter of when external dominion relative to other European powers could be claimed. 'A Proclamation in the London Gazette suffices', as occurred with New Zealand in October 1840.[293]

In view of the overall context, Martin's conclusion in *Symonds* is not puzzling: 'Upon the whole, then', the chief justice opined, 'Mr McIntosh is simply a purchaser from the Natives, without authority or confirmation from the Crown'. As such, 'He cannot possibly stand in a better position than did the original land claimants. He cannot possess, any more than they did, a title against the Crown or the Crown's grantee'.[294] It is conceivable that Martin was most likely envisaging the 'original land claimants' as the Māori vendors in this passage or, alternatively (and less probably), the claimants who had putatively acquired territory directly from Māori prior to 14 January 1840. Whichever alternative applied, the interests acquired from Māori—whether by McIntosh or other land claimants—were defeasible and fragile relative to the pre-eminence of the Crown expressed through its grants. The settlers could only obtain a title as strong as that which the Māori vendors had to give, and no more. Only a Crown grant could convert the title into something stronger—a fee simple title. For those who disagreed as to the validity and extent of Māori claims to territory and whether such claims were properly characterized as a form of territorial dominion or an interest in the land itself, or a combination of both, deeds of purchase were broadly accepted as the way forward. Under such deeds, the price per acre could be kept relatively low. An important feature in Martin and Chapman's shared tendency to avoid discussing the question of title substantively was the assumed eagerness of Māori to transfer territories to Europeans. Martin stated, '[t]he readiness of the natives generally, to sell their lands—and even to do so at the sacrifice of their own permanent interests—is *assumed as a known fact* in the judgment of Mr Justice Chapman'.[295] This point undeniably stressed the capacity of Europeans to obtain sufficient acreage for settlement in spite of the recognition of aboriginal proprietary rights vesting in Māori. Such reasoning

[291] Ward, 'Constructing British Authority in Australasia'.

[292] Chapman, legal notes, undated [1845–1846?], Ms-Papers–860-047, 16–17, ATL.

[293] Martin, 'Observations on the Proposal to take Native Lands under an Act of the Assembly', *GBPP1864*, (326), xli, 5.

[294] *Symonds*, 398.

[295] Martin, *England and the New Zealanders*, 52, 54 (emphasis in original).

within *Symonds* was intended to suggest the innocuous qualities of acknowledging aboriginal title.

Symonds established a thin consensus on the broad outlines of a jurisprudence of indigenous property rights, at least in colonial New Zealand—a preference for extinguishing native title by Crown purchase. The American jurisprudence was no steady state doctrine either, as Robertson, Banner, and Christian McMillen have made clear, although some authors elsewhere, like Brookfield in New Zealand, seem to have ignored this, preferring those cases according with their preferred views.[296] But *Symonds* concealed lurking tensions—fine, albeit important intellectual differences between the judges. The decision's importance as an artifact for subsequent use in the later twentieth century relied significantly on the point that these subterranean tensions or differences were not aired within its text. Outwardly, observable practice overtook the unresolved intellectual or theoretical distinctions in any event, although they resurfaced from time to time. This not only emerged in 1847, 1848, and 1858, but also with the discussions of indigenous customary law, tribal authority, and *mana*, as well as territorial and non-territorial customary rights in the foreshore and seabed disputes of 2003 and subsequently.[297] These unresolved theoretical disputes also materialized when discussing the degree to which Māori customary norms ought to shape what amounts to legally or politically meaningful authority over territory, how and to whom territory is to be allocated and on what terms, and who possesses that authority. The nature of the incompletely theorized approach was to leave these topics unresolved and continued to create political disruption when a 'sentinel' event occurred, such as the foreshore and seabed decision of the Court of Appeal in 2003.[298]

Custom and its discontents, part II—Martin, Merivale, and the third Earl Grey

Martin would not corral his thoughts concerning native title in a supposedly anonymous pamphlet in 1847 supported by that other ally of Grey, Selwyn.[299] He referred approvingly to passages of his own opinion in *Symonds*. The significance of United States jurisprudence was expressly acknowledged: 'the principle thus recognized in the case of North America, has been solemnly asserted by the Supreme Court of New Zealand, as directly applying to the rights of the native people of this land'.[300] Excerpts from Sir Howard Douglas' speech in the Commons debate concerning New Zealand, referred to previously, were scavenged by Martin in his pamphlet, but Douglas' rejection of Marshall court jurisprudence was studiously ignored. Thus, Martin meshed intellectual sources associated with the Marshall court and

[296] Robertson, *Conquest by Law*, 131–44; Banner, *How the Indians Lost their Land*, 150–227; McMillen, *Making Indian Law*.

[297] For one insight, see Jackson, 'Tipuna Title as a Tikanga Construct re the Foreshore and Seabed'.

[298] *Attorney-General v Ngati Apa* [2003] 3 NZLR 643 (NZCA).

[299] Martin, *England and the New Zealanders*. On the issue of this pamphlet's dissemination, see Selwyn to Grey, 5 October 1848, GL NZ S16(6), APL, where Selwyn accepted responsibility for publicly issuing it. In addition, Grey's manuscript note on his copy of this pamphlet reads 'written jointly by Bishop Selwyn & Sir William Martin [APL]'. See *New Zealand National Bibliography to the year 1960*, I, 937.

[300] Martin, *England and the New Zealanders*, 25.

intelligence collected in parts of New Zealand. In venturing this composite impression, Martin produced an intermingling reminiscent of a crudely entwined or composite collection of information purporting to represent substantive 'knowing' as to what Māori territorial rights and interests were. Martin viewed native title as a species of right determined by 'native usages'. Seeing customary property rights as informed by the norms of indigenous populations wherever they might be found and interrogated, he disputed the third Earl Grey's assumptions as to the proper generic interpretation of indigenous rights in lands subjected to British settlement. He characterized Earl Grey's principle as a 'general' one: 'That we may enter into any other Country similar to New Zealand, and, *without any reference to the usages or customary rights of the people of the country*, may lay down our own definition of right, and confiscate the soil of the country in conformity with that definition'.[301] Throughout the North Island, Martin regarded it to be 'absolutely certain', excluding those lands already acquired from Māori, that 'there is not an acre of land available for purposes of Colonization, but has an owner amongst the natives according to their own customs'.[302] The chief justice appreciated the intra-Māori complexities: 'There might be several conflicting claimants of the same land'. Yet, he said, 'however the natives might be divided amongst themselves as to the validity of any one of the several claims, still no man doubted that there was in every case a right of property subsisting *in some one* of the claimants'.[303] Martin contended that what he characterized as the 'territorial rights' of the 'New Zealanders' were, in the main, areas that various descent groupings were disposed to defend by force of arms.[304] The general tenor of Martin's pamphlet was to emphasize peaceable ways of extinguishing native title. Ultimately, processes of land-acquisition proved to be the focal point, the outcome on which a consensus could be fashioned if not on the underlying theories and assumptions about native title. Therefore, the very contentiousness of legalistic intellectual sources—and their interpretations—dislocated them from the practices of extinguishing aboriginal title and emphasized the significance of 'knowing' Māori through intelligence and concentrating upon the procedures of land-acquisition. Disagreement and confusion remained beneath this surface recognition of native title despite the varying disputes, especially since 1837, bequeathing, in its turn, an impression of political and intellectual instability. If anything, the disputes in 1847 and 1848 concerning the third Earl Grey's instructions of 23 December 1846 revealed that Grey could not extensively rely upon hitherto provisional albeit influential intellectual resources in formulating policies regarding Māori territoriality. To the extent that he did so, this reliance was confined to non-official correspondence passing between Grey and his advisors or superiors. Indeed, correspondence signified as 'private' or 'confidential' might generally contain much more explicit references to these intellectual influences.[305] The consumption of these sources still occurred, but could be concealed compared to their explicit eruption into published sources in Select Committees of the House of Commons in 1840 and 1844.

[301] Ibid, 42 (emphasis in original). [302] Ibid, 47.
[303] Ibid (emphasis in original). [304] Ibid, 51.
[305] For instance, Hadfield to Grey, memorandum, 1846, 'system of government among the New Zealand tribes', GNZ Mss17, 73–96, APL; Hadfield to Grey, 15 June 1847, enclosing 'notes', GL NZ H1(2), APL.

Earl Grey's despatch dated 23 December 1846 to Grey was drafted with the assistance of Buller, his parliamentary under-secretary, Hawes, and Stephen, although Earl Grey, Buller, and Hawes were the principal authors. Briefly, this despatch stated, 'the word "occupancy" is susceptible of many meanings, and as thus employed it must mean something more than can be duly alleged of the hunter, the fisherman or the nomadic tribes who first explore the waste regions of the world, and first consume a part of the herb[i]age'. Continuing, it suggested that the 'prior occupation, which ripens into title, must be a real use and enjoyment of the land, or of its products derived from the expenditure of human labour on the production of them'. In preceding chapters, we have already located these sources and sentiments as those associated with imperially oriented Whigs (Earl Grey and Russell for instance), radicals, and Company functionaries. Company representatives appeared more comfortable with citing United States jurisprudence on legal aspects of relations with Amerindians. With Earl Grey's relationship to these sources (evident in 1844) and to Buller, the Company benefited from a convergence of sympathies not witnessed since the *concordat* of 18 November 1840 supervised by Russell. In December 1846, an ornate machinery for ascertaining native title was suggested. The instructions to Grey under the Royal Sign Manual and Signet proposed the protector of aborigines or any like officer to transmit to a district land registrar a statement of the extent of any lands 'to which... natives, either as tribes or as individuals, claim either a proprietary or a possessory title'. Those claims would be provisionally registered and land courts would ascertain the accuracy and validity of the registration. Clause 9 of chapter xiii of the instructions gave a sense of the particularity envisaged. The land courts had to be satisfied the '[Māori] claimants or their progenitors, or those from whom they derived title, have actually had the occupation of the lands so claimed, and have been accustomed to use and enjoy the same, either as places of abode, or for tillage, or for the growth of crops,... or otherwise for the convenience and sustentation of life by means of labour expended thereon'. Here was an attempt to provide 'occupancy' with analytical content.

In his despatch of 23 December, Earl Grey recited the 'liberal Anglican' historian Arnold's views upon the historical emergence of proprietorship. Arnold's intellectual influence cannot be underestimated. He was treated as a prominent historian and theologian by a bevy of senior Whigs, including Earl Grey and Russell's confidante, Morpeth, son of the sixth Earl of Carlisle. Moreover, Grey's mentor, Whately, had not only instructed each of Senior and Hinds but had also profoundly influenced Arnold.[306] Earl Grey's despatch remains instructive as it repeated those viewpoints expressed in his 1844 Select Committee report. Evidently, it was self-aware in its use of intellectual sources and summarized intellectual assumptions underlying this Whig's conceptions of aboriginal proprietorship interacting with colonial settlement. It also reflected assumptions that had been represented and strenuously argued by Company advocates such as Buller since 1842. Quoting Arnold, Earl Grey's despatch stated, '[m]en were to *subdue* the earth—that is to make it by their labour what it would not have been by itself; and with the labour so bestowed upon it came the right of property in it'. This pertained to Māori since Arnold had said, 'so much does the right of property go along with labour that civilized nations have never scrupled to take possession of countries inhabited only by tribes of savages—countries which have been *hunted over*

[306] Brent, *Liberal Anglican Politics*, 138–40, 146.

but never *subdued* or cultivated'.[307] Arnold acknowledged it to be 'true [that 'civilized nations'] have often gone further, and have settled themselves in countries which were cultivated, and then it becomes a robbery; but when our fathers went to America and took possession of the mere hunting grounds of the Indians—of lands on which man had hitherto bestowed no labour, they only exercised a right which God has inseparably united with industry and knowledge'.[308] Here was the voice of Vattel and *ius naturale* entwined with *ius gentium* and stadialism. Unsurprisingly, given his intimacy with the internal counsels of the Company, Earl Grey publicized this despatch directly to the Company directorate, 'in terms which fully justified them in sending it to a newspaper'.[309]

Contrary to some accounts of his despatch, Earl Grey was not insisting that Grey rigorously follow this theory; merely that he was mindful of the preoccupation of securing settlement land for emigrants, a feature lurking within his use of Arnold.[310] Hence, he accepted that Māori engaged in rudimentary forms of agriculture: 'But the extent of land so occupied by them was absolutely insignificant when compared with that of the country they inhabited; the most trustworthy accounts agree in representing the cultivated grounds as forming far less than [one-hundredth] part of the available land'.[311] Thus, these cited passages accorded with the expectations of imperial administration. They supplied a framework of approach—a reminder that settlement space was to be vigorously pursued. Earl Grey would be at pains to illustrate this very point when responding to Grey's sending of protests from Selwyn.[312] Earl Grey responded with dismissive comments. He claimed that his despatch of 23 December 1846 merely said, 'if this question were now open for consideration, that is, if we were commencing the colonization of New Zealand at the present time, the doctrine to which the Bishop objects would, in my judgment, be the best foundation of our proceedings, as I conceive it to contain the true principle in regard to property in land'.[313] Earl Grey thought that the *Symonds* opinions sustained his reading of the theoretical basis of aboriginal proprietorship. As an additional protestor, Martin rejected a 'colonization' conducted by 'seizure' of the sort that he assumed Earl Grey's sentiments and the resort to Arnold supported.[314] Further evidence, however, suggests that Earl Grey's intentions were

[307] Earl Grey to Grey, 23 December 1846, CO209/47, fos.271–2, TNA (emphasis in original). These passages were cited from Arnold, 'The labourers of England', in Arnold, *The Miscellaneous Works of Thomas Arnold, D.D.*

[308] Ibid, 157.

[309] Earl Grey to Grey, private, 31 December 1846, GNZ Mss35, fo.6, APL.

[310] Cf Rutherford, *Sir George Grey*, 167–71; Ward, *An Unsettled History*, 108–11, where Ward accepts that, theoretically, there existed a 'widespread view that Maori were entitled to be regarded as proprietors only of the lands they actually cultivated' (108), but then does not fully account for the substantive impact of such a perspective upon imperial practices. Indeed, he appears to endorse the position that Grey readily retreated from the theoretical and substantive implications (also, ibid, 2: 'Although this narrow view was partly rejected by 1847, and Maori rights to uncultivated lands were acknowledged administratively by the Crown, many officials and settler politicians still held that such rights were confused, inchoate, and precarious, not able to be asserted and defended in the courts until replaced by a British type of tenure such as a Crown grant, after adjudication by some State-empowered tribunal').

[311] Earl Grey to Grey, 23 December 1846, CO209/47, fos.273–3a, TNA.

[312] Selwyn to Grey, 1 July 1847, protest (enclosed in Grey to Earl Grey, 7 July 1847), *GBPP*1847–1848, xliii [892], 82.

[313] Earl Grey to Grey, 30 November 1847, *GBPP1847–1848*, xliii [892], 83.

[314] Martin, *England and the New Zealanders*, 43.

not dramatically inimical to practices adopted eventually relative to Māori reserves in accordance with his 23 December 1846 instructions. Earl Grey did not propose a simplistic 'Waste Lands doctrine'. He adapted a Vattelian waste lands approach to New Zealand circumstances, reflecting a measure of practical inflection in a new setting with consequences for policy and practice. In a critical albeit neglected excerpt, Earl Grey averred:

> To that portion of the soil, whatever it might be, which they really occupied, the aboriginal inhabitants, barbarous as they were, had a clear and undoubted claim; to have attempted to deprive them of their patches of potato ground, *even so to have occupied the territory as not to leave them ample space for shifting, as was their habit, their cultivation from one spot to another, would have been in the highest degree unjust*; but so long as this injustice was avoided, I must regard it a vain and unfounded scruple which would have acknowledged their right of property in land which remained unsubdued to the uses of man.[315]

Here we have a modified approach to 'waste lands' or Lockean understandings as portrayed by Vattel.[316] Elsewhere in early 1848 he noted how securing 'an ample extent of land to meet all their real wants' required paying attention to the economic realities of Māori life as 'native inhabitants'. Again we see a modified form of Vattelian (*ius naturale* and *ius gentium*) as well as stadial analyses entwined:

> Their habits would have to be considered and though it certainly w[oul]d not have been held that the cultivation & appropriation of tracts of land capable of supporting a large population must be foreborne because of an inconsiderable number of natives had been accustomed to derive some part of their subsistence from hunting & fishing on them, on the other hand settlement of such lands w[oul]d not have been allowed to deprive the natives even of these resources without provision for them in some other way.'[317]

Importantly, Grey's private correspondence to Earl Grey indicates that he had no difficulty with the Colonial Secretary's stance on 'waste lands' and he received printed draft copies of this despatch before its publication.[318] It remains probable—although not yet recognized in the historiography—that Grey was completely aware of Earl Grey's Arnoldian references and had not only adjusted to this tendency within his superior's despatch but also harboured viewpoints consonant with it. Thus, an extract of Arnold's quotation appearing in Earl Grey's correspondence of 23 December 1846 also materialized as an isolated passage within Grey's personal papers, as well as Earl Grey's own collection.[319] Within New Zealand, Grey's official stance was presented as ambivalent vis-à-vis Arnoldian 'occupancy', but he was sympathetically aligned with theoretical

[315] Earl Grey to Grey, draft, 23 December 1846, Gre/B147/37, fo.11, DUL.

[316] On the Vattelian renditions of Locke's labour and spoliation principles, see Tuck, *The Rights of War and Peace*, 195–6. See also Hickford, '"Decidedly the Most Interesting Savages"'.

[317] Earl Grey, notes, undated [March 1848], CO209/64, fos.374a–5, TNA.

[318] Grey to Earl Grey, 'private', 9 April 1847, Gre/B99/6A/1, DUL; Earl Grey to Grey, 'private', 27 November 1846; Gre/B99/6C/1, DUL: 'I think it advisable to transmit to you thus privately & confidentially the accompanying drafts which have been printed for the consideration of the Government of the despatch, the new Charter, & Royal Instructions'.

[319] 'Dr Arnold Lord Grey to Govr. Grey. Draft instructions. November 1846', GNZ Mss36(1), APL, where the passage commencing with 'men were to subdue the earth; that is to make it by their labour what it would not have been by itself' may be located. For instances of historiographical and interpretative neglect that emphasize Grey distancing himself personally and politically from Earl Grey's notorious despatch, see Ward, *An Unsettled History*, 110–11.

assumptions underlying the Whig Earl Grey's commentaries.[320] In a despatch to Earl Grey dated 15 May 1848, referring to Earl Grey's exposition of Arnoldian precepts, Grey succinctly summarized his task in engaging with convoluted conceptions of indigenous property rights within New Zealand. Posing his objective as an exercise in pragmatic administration he noted that 'the question which would always arise would really be, Would it [be] better to endeavour at all hazards to enforce a strict principle of law, or to endeavour to find out *some nearly allied principle which should be cheerfully assented to by both parties*'.[321] This was the stuff of 'incompletely theorized agreements' (as Cass Sunstein puts it) and *modus vivendi*.[322]

Commenting also upon the North Island specifically, Grey evidently rejected the perspective: 'there is no waste land in this colony which can be appropriated to the Crown without purchase'. He continued, 'it is my belief that even in the most densely inhabited portions of the northern part of this island there are very large tracts of land claimed by contending tribes to which neither of them have a strictly valid right'.[323] Grey conveyed a remarkable confidence in his exploitative capacity, lacing his account with assertions and supposed anecdotal evidence: 'When these tracts of territory come to be occupied by Europeans, the natives will cheerfully relinquish their conflicting and invalid claims in favour of the Government, *merely stipulating that small portions of land, for the purposes of cultivation*, shall be reserved for each tribe'.[324] Hence, contested Māori historical narratives, initially produced through officers of a now disbanded protectorate department, were to be manipulated and exploited for imperial advantage. Crucially, Grey was echoing the assumptions of Earl Grey in spite of what certain scholarly observers and apologists might subsequently have asserted.

Significantly, whilst there was a political closure of sorts to tensions between the Company and Office concerning aboriginal title, there had not been a corresponding intellectual closure. Disputes continued to erupt over the choice and interpretative use of intellectual sources in discussing native title. These sources remained latent, available for politicians to use at other moments of contention. In 1847, for instance, a barrage of protests from Martin and Selwyn concerning Earl Grey's published stipulations on an accurate approach to aboriginal proprietary rights-status reinforced the political instability and contentiousness of such sources. Martin's pamphlet *England and the New Zealanders* occasioned discomfort and irritation, although Merivale, as permanent under-secretary, regarded it calmly on account of its limited circulation. He considered Grey's official irritation with Martin justifiable: 'On this the Governor has animadverted and I think justly: (though it may be suspected the Gov[erno]r is just now a little sore with the Ch[ief] Justice on account of the recent decision in Mr Clarke's case)'.[325] Yet, thought Merivale, 'the Governor has not added what certainly strikes me, viz. [t]he inconvenience of a Ch[ief] J[ustice] laying down principles of law

[320] This is denied in Frame, 'Property and the Treaty of Waitangi: a Tragedy of the Commodities?', in McLean (ed), *Property and the Constitution*, 228–9. But compare with Ward's comments in *An Unsettled History*, 110–11 (and 167) where, in part, he appears to concur with the findings suggested here.

[321] Grey to Earl Grey, 15 May 1848, *GBPP1849* [1120], 22–6, 23 (emphasis added).

[322] Sunstein, 'Incompletely Theorized Agreements'.

[323] Grey to Earl Grey, 15 May 1848, *GBPP1849* [1120], 24.

[324] Ibid (emphasis added).

[325] Merivale to Hawes, memorandum [chiefly concerning protest of Bishop of New Zealand, George Augustus Selwyn], 29 November [1847], CO209/159, fo.456a, TNA.

in a pamphlet: on which he may have officially to decide' as a judge.[326] Merivale concluded that had Martin 'done this in the way of publication, he would have been very wrong: mere private printing, of course, is a less serious matter'. London tolerated the chief justice's infelicities.

The Wesleyan Missionary Society, the incidents of native title, and living with abstract disagreement

The dispute was a slow-burning fuse. In 1848 Wesleyan missionary interests levelled belated and politically salient protests against Earl Grey's 1846 despatch, purchasing little impact on intellectual assumptions within Earl Grey's office.[327] Yet they did oblige Earl Grey, Hawes, and the permanent under-secretary, Merivale, to consider the relationship between the Treaty of Waitangi and the reasoning in *Symonds*. 'The doctrine of the Judges', said Merivale in March 1848, 'though perhaps not absolutely necessary for the determination of the case before them—appears to me to be this: that (independently of treaty) there is, or may be, a native title to *all* lands, waste as well as cultivated; but that the Crown alone can extinguish that title by purchase.' In contradistinction to this, Merivale took the 'doctrine of the land instructions and dispatch [of 23 December 1846] to be... (independently of treaty) there is no native title in any waste land: that it all belongs to the Crown'. Merivale observed how the judgment was delivered before the instructions might have reached New Zealand. Grey, in New Zealand, had seen an early draft but Chapman was certainly aware of them in mid-June 1847. On 15 June, he reported to his father that the 'principles that [Earl Grey] lays down in relation to the native title to the land are precisely what I have asserted'.[328] Earl Grey authored extensive notes on the topic himself. Again, he expressed narrow agreement with *Symonds* on the pre-eminence of the Crown in acquiring land from indigenous populations. From this principle he was able to argue that the Wesleyan Missionary Society was incorrect if it interpreted the property rights of 'uncivilized tribes' as 'absolute'. As 'an absolute right of property involves the right of alienation [as with fee simple estates]', indigenous populations had something less—circumscribed rights of property.[329]

In bolstering his own theoretical supposition, Earl Grey was content to say that the 'question therefore... is whether the natives of NZ[d] be regarded as the absolute proprietors of the lands they claim with the unrestricted power of alienating them at their pleasure, or whether on the contrary the Crown sh[oul]d be held to be the general owner of the soil as trustee for the public good, or more particularly as guardian of the native races?'.[330] The restriction of alienability could be presented as something profoundly historical and legalistic. '[T]he last', observed the notes, 'is the rule to which the general consent of all civilized nations for at least three centuries has given the authority

[326] Ibid.

[327] *Correspondence between the Wesleyan Missionary Committee and the Right Honourable Earl Grey*, 5. See also 'New Zealand and its charter', *The Colonial Intelligencer; or Aborigines' Friend*, 183–5, discussing Earl Grey's despatch; Chamerovzow, *The New Zealand Question and the Rights of Aborigines*.

[328] Chapman to Chapman senior, 15 June 1847, qMs-0419, 437–8, ATL.

[329] Earl Grey, notes, undated [March 1848], CO209/64, fo.378a, TNA.

[330] Ibid, fos.379–9a.

of a recognized principle of national law' and it was this principle 'conclusively shown in the very important judgment of the Supreme Court of NZ^d.'[331] He regarded the restriction on alienation as applying to native title as a 'tribal' title. '[A]s individuals', he said, 'they should be as free as any of the other inhabitants of New Zealand to acquire and to dispose of property in land.'[332]

Hawes thought that the *Symonds* court had overreached itself. Although he might also disagree with its reasoning, it had strayed into the proper domain of the executive and political dimensions of the Crown: 'Whatever may be considered the abstract rights of the Crown to wild & waste land—[the] Treaty recognized a large & practical exception to, or interference with it'. Yet, the 'act of the Executive alone gives effect to the Treaty—could alone define native possessions &c—c[oul]d alone exempt either the lands held by tribes or individuals from the jurisdiction of Local Courts'.[333] The Treaty was an act of state and, within the purview of the political constitution, something subject to the legal scrutiny of the courts. '[U]ndoubtedly', he accepted, 'the natives as the judges appear to have decided might have a claim under the Treaty to all waste lands.' Nevertheless, he argued, '[t]his was for the Executive to decide'. Hawes characterized *Symonds* as ruling that 'all waste lands not thus reserved *by the Treaty* became vested in the Crown', an angle dramatically different to Martin in *England and the New Zealanders*.[334] As Hawes saw it, the Treaty of Waitangi afforded a distinct interpretative route to that of the law of nations.

In his account of 'native title to waste lands', published in 1851, William Fox, principal agent for the New Zealand Company in the colony following the death of William Wakefield, stood fast to the approach of Emerich de Vattel in Joseph Chitty's 1834 edition as definitive on such title. That is, he claimed, 'in an unreclaimed country, "in which there are none but erratic natives, incapable of occupying the whole, they cannot be allowed exclusively to appropriate to themselves more land than they have occasion for, or more than they are able to settle and cultivate"'.[335] Fox characterized the alternative theory as holding that the 'savage inhabitants of an unreclaimed country have an absolute right of proprietorship in its soil, based upon the mere fact of their residing on some portion of it'.[336] To this theory, Fox alleged, the Anglican Bishop of New Zealand, George Selwyn, and the missionaries adhered, an influence that had already been noted in debate in the House of Commons in 1847.[337] Allowing the politics of

[331] Ibid, 379a–80.

[332] Earl Grey to Grey, 23 December 1846, *GBPP1847*, [763], 70.

[333] Hawes to Earl Grey, 21 March 1848, CO209/64, fos.394a–5, TNA.

[334] Ibid, fos.395–5a (emphasis added).

[335] Fox, *The Six Colonies of New Zealand*, 89–90, citing 'Law of Nations, Ed. 1834, by Chitty, p.100'. Henry Sewell allegedly wrote the section on 'waste lands' (ibid, 98). For the reception of Emerich de Vattel, *The Law of Nations* in arguments concerning colonial New Zealand at this time, see Hickford, '"Decidedly the most interesting savages"', 130–1; Hickford, 'Making "Territorial Rights"', 38–9, 172–4. The reference to Chitty on the part of Fox is to Joseph Chitty the elder (1776–1841). Joseph Chitty's son, Joseph Chitty the younger, a special pleader of the Middle Temple, authored *A Treatise on the Law of the Prerogatives of the Crown*, which was published in 1820.

[336] Fox, *The Six Colonies of New Zealand*, 89.

[337] See the report of R Vernon Smith's remarks in support of a motion to suspend certain provisions relating to the proposed government of the colony of New Zealand: 'He [Vernon Smith] expressed regret that Governor Grey had such a Bishop as coadjutor in the government of New Zealand, for his evident intention was to interfere with the civil and political rights of the Colonists' ('New Zealand and its Charter', in *The Colonial Intelligencer; or Aborigines' Friend*, 179).

negotiation to address information concerning customary usages and norms permitted the sides in these disputes to hold to their preferred intellectual views irrespective of practices within the field. Colonial and imperial politics would see the continuation of these sorts of dispute into the 1850s.

Grey undoubtedly played upon ambiguities in his political manoeuvrings, placating both Selwyn and Martin, yet remaining responsive to the general parameters of the requirements established by his superiors in London. Selwyn's perspective was evident from personal correspondence. He explained that the 'only difference between Governor Grey on the one hand, and Mr Martin and myself on the other, has been this, that the Governor thought that the instructions [despatch] were only a satisfaction to Lord Grey's theoretical opinions, to which he was pledged, and that he neither would nor could carry them into practice in New Zealand'.[338] Selwyn continued, 'we, on the contrary, affirmed that the abstract injustice of the principle was in itself an evil to be protested against'. Considering accessible evidence, however, Grey was clearly deceptive. Intriguingly, Selwyn favoured a composite image of 'English and native rights in equal proportions' rather than a thoroughgoing confidence in deploying unqualified 'English' legal or political economic conceptions.[339] Grey was also operating within this notion of an abstract *via media* with concrete significance, combining Māori conceptions of territorial relationships with anglophone intellectual resources; but the emphasis on seeking settlement areas was that of Stanley, Gladstone, and Earl Grey. In any event, the intellectual sources underlying perceptions of aboriginal title were increasingly concealed within the trails of confidential correspondence. Importantly, however, Merivale supported Earl Grey's view as correct as late as 1861, 'on very strong grounds of abstract reason, and in conformity with the general understanding of nations', knowing full well that the principal sources were Arnold and Marshall court jurisprudence.[340] Moreover, the Company had received what it required—financial relief with a loan of £100,000, for instance—irrespective of continuing debates concerning the intellectual languages of native title.

A number of interpretative possibilities were available. 'Occupancy' survived in Grey's policies on Māori reserves despite what Selwyn and Martin thought. What was *cultivated* was construed as definitely occupied and not merely 'claimed'. Thus, Māori were thought to exclusively possess or 'own' what they 'occupied'—a practical survival of New Zealand Company and senior Whig thinking. These areas were treated as meriting intensified forms of protection or recognition. FitzRoy himself identified this distinction. The minutes of his executive council on 17 July 1844 noted that 'every portion of the surface of these islands (containing in the whole not less than [sixty million] acres) is owned or claimed [read disjunctively] by one or more tribes or individuals of the Aboriginal race, whose "territorial rights as owners of the soil" have been

[338] *Memoir of the Life and Episcopate of George Augustus Selwyn, D.D.*, I, 272–3: Selwyn to Reverend E. Coleridge, 4 September 1848.

[339] Ibid, Selwyn to Coleridge, 7 October 1848, 275: 'But I would rather that [Earl Grey] cut me in pieces than induced me by any personal compliments to resign the New Zealanders to the tender mercies of men who avow the right to take the land of the New Zealanders, and who would not scruple to use force for that purpose. There is a Cerberus in New Zealand which cannot be sapped by any other cake than one composed of English and native rights in equal proportions'.

[340] Merivale, *Lectures on Colonies and Colonisation*, 2nd edn, 497 (note). Merivale rated Grey favourably in 1861, commenting that he seemed 'to possess the rare faculty of entering into the savage mind and becoming [himself] intelligible to it' (ibid, 511 (note)).

guaranteed'.[341] Crown grants in 1845 also evidenced this broad approach. There was a realization that areas of territorial claiming beyond fortified sites or cultivations were also subject to proprietary claims albeit much more difficult to identify without frustrating overlapping cross-claimants. In future, reserves would reflect this constrained idea of ownership. Grey's skill as a politician was to generally satisfy both sides of the argument. Hence, we find that the jurisprudence initially advocated by Company sympathizers in Westminster was restricted to court settings and not admitted into politics unless it could assist Grey's management of government (as in *Symonds*). These intellectual sources remained influential paradigms within which administrators operated—*ius gentium*; assessing the historical placement of Māori. As such, references to histories of proprietary rights shared by Māori and Anglo-Saxon or medieval European populations intruded into Martin and Hadfield's assessments of proprietorship and customary practices. Hadfield considered Māori wars of reprisal as analogous to those 'practised in Europe in the fourteenth century'.[342] These sources supplied an explanatory framework—a means of analysing what was observed in alien situations—and enjoyed a resonance in the *making* of native title. That is, these observers and formulators of imperial policies expected to locate 'tribal' peoples animated by historical tendencies towards migratory diffusion, to warring in competition for resources, subsistence, and territorial spaces. They located such evidence. They construed Māori as crude agriculturists such that cultivated sites or areas for future cultivation were often privileged in Crown 'purchase' transactions as falling within 'reserves' established for the pursuit of subsistence practices.

Intrusions of intellectual expectations about 'aborigines', 'uncivilized', or 'tribal peoples' glimmered in political practices and negotiations involving Māori. Complicated disputes between Stanley's Colonial Office and the Company, together with intelligence collected on Māori tenure in New Zealand, produced a nuanced, intermingled understanding. By the later 1840s, Hadfield, Shortland, Grey, and Earl Grey exhibited ambivalent approaches to aboriginal proprietorship. Claims to territory represented the blurred outward extent of terrestrial space defended through histories of warring and a predilection to resort to the contest of arms. A descent-grouping would 'occupy' discrete sections of this space, as Shortland advised Hawes, Earl Grey's parliamentary under-secretary. Hence, Shortland could say, 'I now advert to some of the principal causes, which have operated to extend native claims over a greater space than is requisite for their present use, and *than would at first seem probable to European ideas*'.[343] He listed these 'causes', including the 'value set on eel-fisheries, which causes every stream to have its weirs, and every large swamp its embankments, and channels to direct the eels into the weirs during a flood'.[344] Occupation was identified through the presence of vegetable plantations or fortified and residential sites. This assessment of 'use' and 'occupation' was clearly associated with notions of aboriginal 'proprietorship'—what was expected of 'uncivilized' populations. Evident meta-assumptions indicated what these observers and formulators of policy expected to find (so-called 'customs') and

[341] 'Minutes of the executive council [extract]', 17 July 1844, CO209/28, fo.306a, TNA (emphasis added).

[342] Hadfield to Grey, memorandum, 1846, 'system of government among the New Zealand tribes', GNZ Mss17, 77 (the 'weregild' of the Anglo-Saxons was also mentioned at 78), APL.

[343] Shortland to Hawes, 25 February 1847, Ms86B, Hocken Library, Dunedin (emphasis added).

[344] Ibid.

also guided their 'investigation'—locating negotiators who would extinguish or minimize Māori claims to larger tracts of land, as in the Wairau transaction. To paraphrase Richards, 'an archive' composed of intelligence (often scattered fragments of information) together with a series of travelling intellectual expectations—travelling with persons and embodied texts themselves—was subjected to attempts at unification and ordering.[345] The fictitious claims of this archive to profoundly 'knowing' Māori tenure were revealed in the subsequent misplaced confidence of Grey's officers (McLean and Kemp) in ambitiously extinguishing Māori claims to vast territorial swathes and led to warring in Taranaki and elsewhere in the early 1860s.[346] Just as crucially, those events showed the inherent dynamism and adaptability of the indigenous communities' politics, as they endeavoured to manage multi-dimensional problems of intra-*hapū* politics as well as relations with bridgehead colonial settlements and expanding options for participating in colonial economies.

'Occupancy' was not jettisoned. It persisted. 'Occupancy' was the hard, less-disputed core of a tribal group's area of territorial interest and authority. A broader area or penumbra consisted of a claimed territory over which a tribe was disposed to assert its authority or jurisdiction with force if need be. As seen, Martin subscribed to the view that areas subject to territorial rights amounted to those swathes of land which indigenous communities were disposed to defend by arms, although he also considered such territories to have coextensive 'owners' (even if contestable ones). Another possibility, albeit far more abstractly jurisprudential than Martin's, was to treat these broader areas as types of public property residing with indigenous peoples or princes, as per Hugo Grotius' view in *The Rights of War and Peace*: rivers, lakes, ponds, forests, and uncultivated mountains.[347] Shirley Woolmer of Sergeant's Inn expressed this perspective in 1848 for the Aborigines' Protection Society.[348] For a number of imperial and colonial politicians and officials, 'occupancy' was enveloped as a kernel within a broader understanding and calculus of Māori historical and political narratives and the relevance of these narratives to the effective placement of British settlers.

In any event, these intellectual resources based on observing indigenous practices could be presented as procedurally and politically meaningful in transacting with aboriginal inhabitants such as Māori. They posed as 'knowing' and were presented in the midst of languages of observation and analysis mediated by stadial histories and *ius gentium*. They were shared, interpreted, and contested by literate European advisors and formulators. Hadfield's memoranda to Grey figured in this account as much as the internal deliberations of the Colonial Office. In his notes concerning 'native policy' in June 1847, he precisely recounted his principal sources, including tomes by Saxe Bannister, George Cornewall Lewis, Arnold, James Mackintosh, Blackstone, and Brougham.[349] He also embraced Kent's commentaries on United States jurisprudence transmitting passages from Marshall's *Johnson v M'Intosh* opinion. But he read this source as Martin did without troubling himself with the ambiguous contents of 'occupancy': 'The natives admitted to be the rightful occupants of the soil, with a *legal* as

345 Richards, *The Imperial Archive*, 4.
346 See Chapters Five and Seven.
347 Grotius, *The Rights of War and Peace, in Three Books*, II.4, 148.
348 Woolmer, opinion, 4 February 1848, 23 in Chamerovzow, *The New Zealand Question*.
349 Hadfield to Grey, 15 June 1847, enclosing 'notes', GL NZ H1(2), APL.

well as just claim to *retain possession* of it, and to use it according to their own discretion, though not to dispose of the soil at their own will'.[350] Here, Hadfield contributed his own gloss, stating that 'the Crown acquires a *paramount* title to all *waste lands* not to wild lands (as has been ignorantly asserted), but lands without owners'.[351] This memorandum is intriguing for its indication of Hadfield's access to a range of texts that travelled and were used in New Zealand locations. It also illustrated the survival of questions about 'occupancy' and its meanings in intra-European conversations in spite of serious disputes throughout the 1840s.

Grey did not escape this intermingling. For instance, he considered the Māori 'use' of territory when discussing the propriety of Te Atiawa returning to Taranaki from Waikanae and insisting upon the restriction of pākehā to the approximate 3,500 acres authorized under FitzRoy's rejection of Spain's award. He stated that 'upon my pointing out that they were *actual occupants* of large tracts of land along Cook's straits,—that they did not *use* any land in the neighbourhood of Taranaki, and that they could not remain here upon account of their enemies [Waikato], if it were not for the presence of the Europeans:—they stated, that some of them intended to come and live there themselves'.[352] Grey supported Spain's decision stating that 'I do not understand, nor can I think that he [FitzRoy] intended that the original purchase should be set aside, in as far as those natives are concerned, who had originally sold their land in a *bonâ fide* manner and received payment for it'. Yet Taranaki remained discomfiting for Grey in 1847, who expressed anxieties over his ability to enlist sympathy from Te Ātiawa and other Māori. This was not Wairau, Heretaunga, or Porirua, where Grey successfully enlisted the support of certain Ngāti Toa against Te Rangihaeata. In Whanganui, Grey informed local *rangatira* that 'I have seen that the chiefs do not require this [purchased land] for their own use [other land] *sufficient* for *all their wants* having been reserved for them'.[353] There was a realization that, politically, native territorial rights embraced a concept of 'claiming' even though there were clear indications that conceptually and in policy terms Maori title was considered most efficacious in cultivated or physically occupied areas—*pā*, villages, and vegetable plots. Grey traded in paper presentations of territorial alienation to his superiors. But these presentations largely responded to discursive anglophone conceptions of native title—to the idioms and expectations of pākehā negotiators and not to Māori interpretations.

Theorizing and formulating practices on aboriginal proprietorship was still profoundly a question of intra-European vocabularies and anxieties. Procedural calculations remained paramount in assessments of aboriginal proprietorship. Elite discourse in the salons of policy and the jurisprudence of empire about the substance of indigenous property rights compared to fee simple estates was less influenced by concrete *modus vivendi* worked out in local areas of empire. Yet practices on the ground, focusing

[350] Ibid.

[351] Ibid (emphasis in original).

[352] Grey to Earl Grey, 2 March 1847, CO209/51, fos.286–6a, TNA (emphasis added). Compare Grey to Earl Grey, 4 March 1847, CO209/51, fo.303: 'once the cupidity of the natives is excited, it is impossible to satisfy them;—indeed I have never seen the native character under so bad a point of view as at Taranaki'.

[353] Grey to 'Te Honi Kingi, Te Hoani Wiremu and to all the other chiefs of Wanganui', NZMss227, fo.125, APL (emphasis added). Cf Dalziel, 'Southern islands: New Zealand and Polynesia', in Porter (ed), *The Oxford History of the British Empire*, 581 (this argument contributes to an understanding why '[r]eserves set aside for Maori, as in the South Island, were usually totally inadequate to their needs' (ibid, 581)).

on process, local custom, and *modus vivendi* with indigenous vendors, inflected the intellectual assumptions of certain anglophone interlocutors like Martin. Earl Grey advised Grey that it 'will further be necessary that before any such Crown grant be issued, the [Attorney General] should certify to you that the natives from whom the purchases have been made were, *according to native law and customs*, the real and the sole owners of the land'.[354] This sentiment reasserted Stanley's initial instructions to Grey concerning the possible acquisition of sites in the Wairarapa and in finalizing the 'several purchases of the Company'. Hence, 'you will not fail to bear in the mind the importance of endeavouring to ascertain as far as circumstances will permit, that the natives by whom or on whose behalf the sales are made, are actually the parties who have the right and title to the lands'.[355]

Conceptions of indigenous territorial rights in Britain's new empire in Australasia became increasingly layered, passing from moments of tentative emergence in 1837 to an era of noticeably convoluted albeit unresolved discussions. Upon reflection, therefore, 'humane' sentiments understood generically as a sympathetic disposition, although not unimportant, were not as significant or crucial as scholars such as Alan Ward continue to insist.[356] Nor was South Australia as informative or defining an instructor for the development of policies concerning aboriginal proprietorship, as Reynolds has argued. Rather, a decided tentativeness, even during Glenelg's supposedly sympathetic tenure, was in evidence on the part of Glenelg and his principal advisors in considering questions of native title throughout New Holland (as in Port Phillip). Imperial anxieties concerning the configuration and behaviour of British settlement predominated in these musings materializing within correspondence, with occasional sensitivities expressed towards the possible 'improvement' of aboriginal populations and the probabilities of their assumed fate (extinction of communities) when confronted with ambulatory empires. The concrete policy prescriptions and practices of various jostling strands of 'humane' or 'philanthropic' politics and theology already implied this sort of pragmatic approach. We saw these strains at work in Chapters Two and Three. Disciplining settlement was one key aspect and consequence of recognizing native title: a particularly tangible and paternalistic expression in the 1830s and 1840s of what is now called 'humanitarianism'.[357] Analytically, imperial conceptions of

[354] Earl Grey to Grey, 10 February 1847, fo.343, TNA (emphasis added); ibid, fo.335: Stephen to Hawes, minute, 13 January 1847, CO209/44, fo.335; Earl Grey, minute, 13 January 1847, CO209/44, fo.335a.

[355] Stanley to Grey, 15 August 1845, CO209/39, fos.433–3a, TNA.

[356] *An Unsettled History*, 9–10, 17. Ward's comments at 167 indicate the sheer analytical and historical difficulty of resorting to phrases such as 'British humanitarians and officials' at ibid, 17. See also his comments in Ward and Hayward, 'Tino rangatiratanga: Maori in the political and administrative system', in Havemann, *Indigenous Peoples' Rights in Australia, Canada, & New Zealand*, 379.

[357] Saxe Bannister employed the term 'humane' in his *Humane Policy or Justice to the Aborigines of new settlements*; Bannister, Saxe, 1790–1877, educated at Queen's College, Oxford (Master of Arts, 1815); barrister (Lincoln's Inn), appointed Attorney General for New South Wales, 23 October 1823; advocated permitting settlers in New South Wales to slay aborigines (Kociumbas, *The Oxford History of Australia*, 142). See also Stephen to Vernon Smith, 28 December 1840 (reference to 'philanthropy'), CO209/8, fo.446a, TNA; sympathy of the philanthropist 'New Zealand', *The Colonial Intelligencer; or Aborigines' Friend*, vii (1847), 99. Merivale uses the following phrases to characterize 'humanitarian' strains of thought in Merivale, *Lectures on colonization and colonies*, 1st edn, II, 150: 'philanthropic orators and writers'; ibid, 175: 'sentiments of humanity and justice have so far gained ground among us'. For 'humanitarianism', see Hickford, 'Making "Territorial Rights"', 3–14; Porter, *Religion versus Empire?*, 136–48.

aboriginal title, rather than having been perceived as a creature of common law, could be integrated with developing approaches to hitherto undisciplined transactional behaviour, specifically relating to the early nineteenth-century occupation of diverse territories. The significance of whiggish ministerial political preoccupations and their momentary coalescence with additional sources of political opinion (such as theories propounding 'scientific' or 'systematic' settlement) have been duly weighted in such an analysis.

The Aborigines' Protection Society—'magisterial jurisdiction' and 'territorial jurisdiction'

Louis Alexis Chamerovzow's 1848 treatise in London, addressing the 'rights of aborigines', directly engaged with northern American jurisprudence and the law of nations. Written with knowledge of the *Symonds* judgment, Chamerovzow, assistant secretary to the Aborigines' Protection Society, deferred to Vattel on questions of '*jus gentium*', to Grotius as a complementary source, and to Kent's *Commentaries* on United States law. He unexceptionably advocated the procedure of 'purchase' as sufficient to extinguish 'native title' rather than assuming that 'waste lands' belonged to the Crown: 'It remains for us to prove that the custom has been generally observed, of acquiring, by purchase, lands appertaining to Aborigines, and consequently of recognising their title thereto, independently of the expenditure thereupon of any labour'.[358] For this demonstration, he uncritically relied upon Marshall court jurisprudence as transmitted via Kent's tomes and the treatment of northern American imperial histories postulated in that jurisprudence. Hence, the imperial proclamation of October 1763 relating to Amerindian territories westward of British settlement was interpreted in conjunction with the interpretation of Marshall in *Johnson v M'Intosh* and Kent. The proclamation 'distinctly recognises the territorial dominion of the Indians, as existent antecedent to their cession of the soil, and asserts the practice of acquiring the same by cession and purchase, even prohibiting the latter, unless effected in the name of the Crown, at a public assembly of the Indians'.[359] Chamerovzow argued that the Supreme Court of the United States 'distinctly disavowed' principles constraining the substance of aboriginal proprietorship to territories physically cultivated. This disavowal was treated as significant since that court was, 'an authority the most competent as being the most deeply implicated in the question'.[360] Chamerovzow's novelty was to advocate 'purchase' as a principle of unqualified application to imperial relations with aboriginal populations. He suggested that it might even be applied to Australia despite recognizing that 'the Aborigines are scanty in number, scattered in their occupancy of the soil, miserable in their resources, limited in capacity'.[361]

A key source for Chamerovzow in framing relations between Māori property rights and abstract principles of jurisprudence was the official English language version of the Treaty of Waitangi, subsequently translated into Māori and forwarded to London.[362] Critically, for Chamerovzow's purposes, Article I of the Treaty was rendered as giving to 'Her Majesty, the Queen of England, absolutely, and without reservation, *all the*

358 Chamerovzow, *The New Zealand Question and the Rights of Aborigines*, 202.
359 Ibid, 203–4. 360 Ibid, 204. 361 Ibid, 212.
362 On this version of the Treaty, see Parkinson, '"Preserved in the Archives of the Colony"', 86–7 (and note 45).

rights and powers of sovereignty which the said confederation or individual chiefs respectively exercise or possess, or may be said to exercise or possess, *over their respective territories* as the sole sovereign thereof'.[363] This was the provision which in the Māori text marked at Waitangi used the neologism '*kawanatanga*' or 'governorship' (government) for 'sovereignty'.[364] Chamerovzow interpreted Article I the Treaty as giving the Crown 'magisterial jurisdiction', but not 'territorial jurisdiction', which was retained by Article II. Article II guaranteed 'to the chiefs and tribes of New Zealand, and to their respective families and individuals thereof, the full, exclusive, and undisturbed possession of their lands, estates, forests, fisheries, and other properties which they may collectively or individually possess, so long as it is their wish and desire to retain the same in their possession'. Under Article I, the Crown merely acquired the 'sovereignty' of individual chieftains or, more precisely, that which they could alienate: 'perfect independence, and of magisterial control, (though rude) over their subordinate chiefs and the tribes themselves; with the power of making laws; of declaring either war or peace; in a word, . . . the individual jurisdiction over the country which Sovereignty is generally supposed to confer'.[365] As such, in conjunction with one of the founders of the Aborigines' Protection Society in 1838, the physician Thomas Hodgkin, Chamerovzow did not countenance any constitutional prospectus for Māori that contemplated the maintenance of legal diversity and pluralism. As they noted in an extensive critique, the tenor of section 71 of the New Zealand Constitution Act 1852, which echoed section 10 of the proposed 1846 constitution, contemplated a pluralistic order within the pale of the constitutional setting. The provision allowed the proclamation of native districts in which native customary laws would prevail (a situation prevailing in practice anyhow).[366] The secretary and assistant secretary of the Aborigines' Protection Society criticized permitting the formal emergence of a non-British jurisdictional reserve.[367]

What was not alienated to Britain, however, was the so-called 'collective sovereignty in respect of the soil generally' residing in tribes. Article II, therefore, 'completely annul[led] the claim set up [by some under Article I that the Treaty conferred] Sovereignty absolute [on Britain]'.[368] This 'right of property in the soil itself', whether or not cultivated, was held conjointly with the entire tribe and did not belong to the chiefs as 'sole sovereigns': 'Although the head Chiefs could not control the chieftains in the disposal of such lands as to them belonged, the whole of the latter, together with the tribe, enjoyed a right to control the head chiefs in the alienation of the lands held in common'.[369] In 1849, the Aborigines' Protection Society reiterated the value of the distinction between 'magisterial jurisdiction' and 'territorial jurisdiction', claiming that the *The Times* was echoing these concepts and 'only now, for the first time, defining the exact nature of the sovereignty the Crown has acquired'. The

363 The English text dated 6 February 1840: Hobson to Gipps, 6 February 1840, *GBPP1840*, xxxiii (560), 10–11 (emphasis added).

364 Parkinson analyses the historical translations of the Māori language text in '"Preserved in the Archives of the Colony"', 47–8.

365 Chamerovzow, *The New Zealand Question*, 175.

366 See pages 239–240, and Chapters Five, Six, and Seven.

367 *The Colonial Intelligencer; or, Aborigines' Friend*, nos 3 & 4, June and July 1852. Submission to Pakington signed by Thomas Hodgkin and Chamerovzow. This point is also recognized by Cadogan, 'Constituting the Settler Colony', 251.

368 Chamerovzow, *The New Zealand Question*, 178.

369 Ibid, 175–6.

Crown acquired 'a simply magisterial, and not a territorial jurisdiction; that is, not a right of property in the soil in virtue of the royal prerogative'.[370] Magisterial jurisdiction seems closer to later twentieth-century and early twenty-first-century notions of the Crown's underlying 'radical title' to land in settler societies.[371] The Aborigines' Protection Society's sense of 'magisterial jurisdiction', informed by its reading of the Treaty of Waitangi and not common law, was not akin to what the leading writers on American jurisprudence were saying about the dominion obtained by the discovering sovereign at law relative to indigenous populations. Story, in his *Commentaries on the Constitution of the United States* (1833), described the Native American 'right of occupancy' in a Marshallesque fashion, drawing on *Johnson v M'Intosh*: 'They were admitted to be the rightful occupants of the soil, with a legal as well as just claim to retain possession of it, and to use it according to their own discretion'.[372] Read simply, these were fine-sounding words. Yet Story glossed this proposition with further analysis: until the land was transferred to the discovering sovereign, 'they were generally permitted to occupy it as sovereigns *de facto*'. Irrespective of the right of occupancy, however, 'European discoverers claimed and exercised the right to grant the soil, while yet in possession of the natives, subject however to their right of occupancy; and the title so granted was universally admitted to convey a sufficient title in the soil to the grantees in perfect dominion, or, as it is sometimes expressed in treatises of public law, it was a transfer of *plenum et utile dominium*'.[373] Elsewhere, Story clarified 'Indian title' as not a 'right of propriety and dominion; but . . . a mere right of occupancy'.[374] Such was the fragility of what Native Americans were deemed to possess.

MODUS VIVENDI AND PROPRIETARY RIGHTS—THE POLITICS OF NEGOTIABILITY AND LIVING WITH INDETERMINACY

Modus vivendi prevailed in the absence of underlying consensus and untrammelled power to enforce one's preferred meanings or in circumstances where fluid clusters of individuals secured moments of concurrence through incompletely theorized agreements. In this sense, it compares with (but is not identical to) Richard White's concept of a 'middle ground', albeit the particular forms of these *modus vivendi* often stressed the interpretative risks posed to indigenous communities through deeds of purchase.[375] One risk was to presume consensus or the thoroughgoing completeness of consensus as parties entered into mutually convenient arrangements for the

[370] 'The New-Zealand Question', *The Colonial Intelligencer; or Aborigines' Friend*, March 1849, 163.

[371] In that 'magisterial jurisdiction', as presented by Chamerovzow, entailed a notional form of entitlement to administrative influence or interference (through enacting legislation, for instance, or exercising the rights of *dominium eminens*, in acting on a dispositive power regarding property) rather than the view that the Crown held the underlying fee subject to the burden of indigenous rights of occupancy. For an illustration of officials acting on a view of the Crown's underlying title as approximating with a fee simple estate, see Hickford, 'John Salmond and Native Title', 872–3, 922.

[372] Story, *Commentaries on the Constitution of the United States*, I, 7–8.

[373] Ibid, 8.

[374] Ibid, 135.

[375] White, *The Middle Ground*, x, 50–3.

time being, where no such state of affairs could be presumed to exist casually or unqualifiedly.[376] Certainly, the possibilities of violence or applying force were not precluded in such a setting but the prevailing tone or temper was one suffused by the politics of negotiability. Pownall represented a certain late eighteenth-century archetype of political thought on *modus vivendi* in relations between European colonial settlements and pre-existing communities, at least in the second edition of his tome *The Administration of the Colonies* (1765). Pownall's account hinged on 'Indian politicks', as in his view '[t]he different manner in which this globe of earth is possessed, and occupied by the different species of the human race which inhabit it, must form the specific difference in their interests and politicks'.[377] Techniques familiar to eighteenth-century stadialism intruded. Thus, Pownall stated how the 'Tartars are in one part wandering herdsmen, and in other parts hunters and fishermen'.[378] Native Americans were adjudged as 'the same race or family as the Tartars, precisely of the same colour, if the same form of skull, of the same species of hair,—not to mention the language and their names'.[379] Whereas Europeans were settlers and 'landworkers from the beginning, who, wherever they have spread over the face of this globe, have carried with them the art of cultivating vines, and fruit trees', the inhabitants of northern America were 'naturally . . . not land-workers, but hunters; not *settlers, but wanderers*'.[380] The fauna, as well as the geographical and climactic circumstances of northern America, encouraged these attributes in Native Americans. As 'America, in its natural state, is one great forest of woods and lakes, stocked not with sheep, oxen, or horses; not with animals of labour, and such as may be domiciliated, but with wild beasts, game, and fish', all that furnished raiment or sustenance 'must be hunted for'.[381] But Pownall's sense of the pre-eminence of bespoke practices was one largely mediated by these differences, and the fashioning of inter-cultural communicability through commerce or trade. Compromise (and the hard business of politics) occurred in these circumstances. Hence, he explained, '[f]rom the European desire of having the furs and peltry of the Indian hunters, and from the Indian desire of having the more useful and necessary tools and instruments of improved life, an artificial reciprocation of wants has arisen between the European settlers, and the original inhabitants of America'. Out of this 'has arisen a necessary relation of politicks [*sic*] between them'.[382] Pownall resurfaced in Merivale's published Oxford University *Lectures on Colonization and Colonies*, both in the original edition and the subsequent 1861 reprint with additional commentary. In 1861, Merivale saw the circumstances of New Zealand and southern Africa in the 1850s and early 1860s as 'analogous to that of the first settlers of America: in contact with numerous and powerful tribes of uncivilized men,—imperfectly subjugated, or not at all,—sufficiently intelligent to be at once dangerous in warfare, and capable more or less of friendship and of improvement'.[383] Such circumstances compelled the operation of delicate, relationship management politics and negotiability if warring was to be avoided.

[376] Cf the useful analysis in Promislow, '"Thou Wilt Not Die of Hunger"', in Webber and McLeod (eds), *Between Consenting Peoples*, 80–4, 103–6.
[377] Pownall, *The Administration of the Colonies*, 155.
[378] Ibid, 156–7. [379] Ibid, 157. [380] Ibid (emphasis in original).
[381] Ibid. [382] Ibid, 159.
[383] Merivale, *Lectures on Colonization and Colonies*, 2nd edn, 514.

Hazel Petrie has observed that these negotiated practices operated between Māori and settlers in commercial or mercantile affairs.[384] Hutton and Head have also explored permutations of these relations in considering questions of territorial space and dealings with agents of colonial administration.[385] The politics of negotiability, as witnessed by these various *modus vivendi* crafted in localities between Māori polities and colonial administrators, were as much conditioned by the relative weakness of colonial officials and the imbuing of native title with a transactional (sale and purchase) and intellectual significance (as a political economic category). Donald McLean had been an assistant protector of aborigines for the western district of the North Island.[386] In that role he was called upon in 1844 to assist negotiations to resolve the New Zealand Company's purchase claims in the area around the settlement at New Plymouth in Taranaki. In November 1844, McLean walked, in the company of 'natives', the proposed boundaries of the parcel of land containing the fledgling New Plymouth settlement.[387] McLean undertook the perambulation of the intended boundaries at the governor's direction, who, in his turn, was following a suggestion of the Wesleyan missionary, John Whiteley. Whiteley advised that '[a]s there [had] been so much stupidity and misunderstanding on the part of the natives relative to the boundary line . . . nothing further be attempted with them until the line has been completely traced not only on the map, *but on the land* from one end of it to the other'.[388] A minute in FitzRoy's hand stated: 'Mr McLean—I wish you to act in conformity with these suggestions—and ask Mr Forsaith and Mr Carrington to accompany you'.[389] McLean's personal papers and those of FitzRoy's personal secretary, JW Hamilton, illustrate how the negotiated lines of the block were walked along and marked on at least three separate occasions from 13 November 1844 to 15 November 1844.[390] Cultivations were reserved within a parcel of land comprising some 3,300 acres.[391] Reflecting upon his approach in the Taranaki some 12 years later in 1856, McLean commented that he 'did not think . . . it . . . practicable to issue Crown grants to natives by defining the boundaries of individual rights to land'.[392] He alleged that 'there is really no such thing as individual title that is not entangled with the general interest of the tribe, and often with the claims of other tribes who may have migrated from the locality'.[393] He recounted how he endeavoured to pursue 'this system' of identifying individual interests at the suggestion of the Anglican bishop, George Selwyn, in the negotiations regarding the New Plymouth block at Taranaki. McLean reported that it occasioned considerable delay. Furthermore, participating Māori appeared to regard the arrangement premised on individual entitlements 'as altogether imaginary, and it did not appear to effect [*sic*]

[384] Petrie, *Chiefs of Industry*, 196–214.

[385] Hutton, '"Troublesome Specimens"'; Head, 'Land, Authority and the Forgetting of Being', 168–73.

[386] George Clarke senior to McLean, 2 August 1844, Ms-1306, ATL.

[387] McLean, journal, 13 November 1844, vol I, Ms-1284, ATL.

[388] This communication from Whiteley to FitzRoy, 14 November 1844, appears in the papers of McLean, Ms-0032-0634, ATL (emphasis in original).

[389] Ibid.

[390] McLean, journal, 13 November 1844, vol I, Ms-1284, 80–1, ATL; McLean, journal, 14 November 1844, vol I, Ms-1284, 82, ATL; Hamilton, journal, 15 November 1844, Ms-2303, ATL.

[391] McLean to Clarke senior, 17 December 1844, CO209/33, fo.201a, TNA.

[392] 'No. 33. Mr McLean, Chief Commissioner, 17 April 1856', *GBPP1860*, [2719], 303–5, 304.

[393] Ibid.

in the estimation of the natives the general or tribal right'.[394] He concluded: 'When I considered the title settled of some individuals on this basis, I found the natives quarrelled among themselves about the boundaries, and prevented any definite arrangement being carried out until I afterwards purchased the *whole of the tribal claim*, in order to secure a clear title'.[395]

An aggregative approach to indigenous descent-groupings and purchase was deployed rather than a minute process of disaggregating distinct territorial claims. By 1848, McLean, now inspector of police under Grey's appointment, adapted the face-to-face technique of walking the boundaries of a block to be acquired with elite figures of the relevant Māori claimant groups for the unresolved Wanganui purchase, some of whom were referred to as 'chiefs'. Reporting to the lieutenant-governor, Edward Eyre, in May 1848 on the proposal to settle the purchase of the Wanganui block, McLean signalled an approach predicated upon addressing the range of possibly relevant claims to the space in question. 'The names of the principal chiefs and claimants in each tribe', said McLean, 'were written in the letters [forwarded as circulars] and after their names the following words were added "and to all others who have any claim to the lands for the Europeans at Wanganui" this distinctly giving them to understand in the most public manner that all who could prefer just claims should be recognized.'[396] McLean noted that he would organize a 'public meeting of the natives' with a view to 'obtaining a sufficiently definite idea of the extent or position of the separate claims of the several tribes who own this district, so as to enable [him] to have a satisfactory and equitable division of the payment'.[397] Ultimately, McLean requested the preparation of a map to accompany his negotiations for settling the purchase of the Wanganui block, which included the New Zealand Company settlement at Wanganui near the mouth of the eponymous river.[398] The map, prepared by Alfred Wills, the surveyor for the New Zealand Company at Wanganui, was used to assist McLean's negotiations with Māori chieftains as the deed of purchase for the Wanganui block was read orally at the signing site in the Wanganui settlement.[399] Signed by McLean it was inscribed with the words '[m]ap made for the natives in explanation of the boundaries of the block and of the native reserves (coloured yellow) as described in the final deed of sale'.[400] The deed for completing the acquisition of the Wanganui block itself and setting out the reserves within its boundary lines bore some 207 names. This last feature may be seen as something of an innovation in official practice but was essentially directed towards ensuring the broadest coverage of markings and, on McLean's approach, 'claimants'

394 Ibid. 395 Ibid (emphasis added).

396 McLean to Eyre, 12 May 1848, qMs-1208, McLean papers, ATL. See also IA1 1878/1499, ANZ(W). Notices in Māori were prepared and circulated: see McLean, journal, 3 May 1848, vol II, Ms-1285, ATL.

397 Ibid. McLean explained that Ngāti Apa had already supplied adequate information regarding their claims towards Whangaehu.

398 Alfred Wills, the surveyor for the New Zealand Company at Wanganui, reported: 'On preparing the final Deed of Sale Mr McLean requested me to write the descriptions of the external boundaries of the Block and also those of the reserves mentioning the names of whatever natives had at different times accompanied me when engaged in the survey, and he desired me to make a skeleton map only for the Deed so that both the Deed and the map should be easily and thoroughly understood by the natives': Wills to William Wakefield, Principal Agent, New Zealand Company, 23 June 1848, NZC3/8, fo.411, ANZ(W).

399 Wills to William Wakefield, 23 June 1848, NZC3/8, fo.412, ANZ(W).

400 The map can be located at ABWN8102, W5279, fo.47, Wgn 286, ANZ(W).

at the 'public meeting'. McLean was aware that the location of graded authority within Māori communities and amongst their negotiators was less clear, and therefore the capacity to make unchallenged, authoritative pronouncements was much less pronounced.

NEW ZEALAND'S LOST WHIG FOUNDATIONS—DIVERSITY AND BALANCE IN A 'BAROQUE' CONSTITUTION

Although assailed with politically hectoring mirth on the part of the philosophic radical Molesworth as a 'Brobdignagian measure for a Lilliputian colony', the New Zealand Constitution Act 1852 was an exemplar of whiggish legislative design—of a type combining the conservative gradualist temper of Burke and Macaulay.[401] While Molesworth saw 'the immense quantity of government which was to be imposed upon the scanty population of New Zealand', the 'Act to grant a representative constitution to the colony of New Zealand' permitted and constituted a transposing of ancient (eighteenth-century) whiggish discourses concerning the representation of the legitimate interests of the state, as adapted in the broth of early nineteenth-century politics, both at Westminster and in the counties.[402] The New Zealand constitution's apparent messiness, through having multiplied formal sites for political discussion and disagreement, was an exercise in producing whiggish-conservative diversity. Decentralization and ensuing thickets of localism (municipal and provincial government) were viewed as protectors of political liberty against a potentially overweening or despotic central government. Institutional pluralism in the form of distributing formal sites of authority across a range of institutional forms or configurations was in evidence. Sir John Pakington, in defending his measure during its second reading in the House of Commons, stated:

> 'Why', said the hon. Baronet [Molesworth], 'are you going to have all this cumbrous machinery; why divide a small population of 26,000 persons into communities?' But the House was bound to consider of whom these communities consisted; they were bound to consider that they were composed of men of education, men of property, men who desired naturally in going out there to enjoy still the institutions of this country; and they would also bear in mind the advanced state of civilisation among the native tribes.[403]

In the House of Lords, the fourteenth Earl of Derby (Stanley) expressed the 'hope that in New Zealand, which was a most important and promising colony, there would arise in time a class of men possessing large property, out of whom might be taken those who would represent the aristocratic element in the colony'. A Whig turned liberal Tory, Derby (formerly Viscount Stanley)

> thought, looking forward to that period, it was important that the Crown should have the power of nominating, not a body of men who would be the mere representatives of the Government of the day, but men who, being chosen personally, retained their full rights of legislation, wholly independent of the Government, for their lives, and who should not be capable of being dismissed, and who would in consequence exercise a great deal of influence both on the popular will on the one hand, and on the will of the Governor on the

[401] Molesworth, *HPD*, 3rd series, 21 May 1852, vol 121, col 922.

[402] On the 'representation of interests', see the excellent discussion in Pole, *Political Representation in England and the Origins of the American Republic*, 442–57.

[403] Pakington, *HPD*, 3rd series, 21 May 1852, vol 121, col 977.

other; and that influence would go on extending and increasing as the aristocratic element developed itself, until it might ultimately approximate to the principles of the British Constitution.[404]

Yet these essentially whiggish philosophical foundations have been forgotten. They have been replaced by a sense of the inexorability of responsible colonial self-government and shifts towards universal suffrage away from institutional pluralism, representing propertied interests as opposed to mere numbers or individuals, as well as political pluralism within the colony itself, with Māori engaging in a politics of negotiability with the governor and his officials. The fixation within much of the historiographical literature on the 1852 constitution has been on representative institutions, democratization, and responsible self-government, rather than the importance of tropes of pluralism and overlaid rivalrous constitutional forces to mid-nineteenth-century political and legal debates.[405]

Institutional pluralism, constitutional adjustment, and native title—constitutions as process and negotiability

For a scattering of not-especially populous colonial settlements, the New Zealand Constitution Act was certainly baroque in execution and design. But overlaid messiness had its uses. It recalled the compliments that Guizot paid to rivalrous and contending forces within historical political constitutions—'all principles of social organisation co-exist therein; powers spiritual and temporal; elements theocratic, monarchical, aristocratic, democratic; all orders, all social arrangements mingle and press upon one another'.[406] Guizot, along with Tocqueville, was widely read amongst mid-Victorian liberals, whether inclined to the Peelite interpretations of liberal-tory (conservative) politics, philosophic Whiggism, or philosophic radical strains, and Whigs.[407] Burrow, Boyd Hilton, and Ghosh have commented on the inherent ambiguities of Victorian liberalism in the mid-nineteenth century.[408] It was to Tocqueville that many within politically active English elites turned for insights to debate on questions of political representation of a community, including the place of minorities. Tocqueville was familiar with John Stuart Mill in London, along with Henry Hallam, the whiggish historian and author of *The Constitutional History of England from the Accession of Henry VII to the Death of George II*, George Cornewall Lewis, a classics scholar and author of *An Essay on the Government of Dependencies* (1841), the radical JA Roebuck, as well as the historian of classical Greece, George Grote (1794–1871), and his spouse, the biographer, Harriet Grote (1792–1878). The Whig appreciation of the lessons to be drawn from democratic representative institutions in the United States, including insights on

[404] Derby, *HPD*, 3rd series, 25 June 1852, vol 122, col 1287. On 30 June 1851 Stanley's father died and he succeeded to the title as the fourteenth Earl of Derby.

[405] McHugh, 'The Historiography of New Zealand's Constitutional History', in Joseph (ed), *Essays on the Constitution*, 350–4.

[406] Guizot, *General History of Civilisation in Europe*, I, 22, 24.

[407] Burrow, *Whigs and Liberals*, 19, 45–6, 123. See also Crook, *American Democracy in English Politics 1815–1850*, 166–98.

[408] Hilton, *A Mad, Bad, and Dangerous People?*, 518–24; Burrow, *Whigs and Liberals*, 1–20, 126–8; Ghosh, 'Gladstone and Peel', in Ghosh and Goldman (eds), *Politics and Culture in Victorian Britain*, 55 (note), 71–2.

democratic governance in Tocqueville's ranging analysis, grappled with the risks of corruption and the emergence of tyrannical majorities, as well as the tendencies of democracies towards monied acquisitiveness and factionalism.[409] The Whig writer, James Spedding, envisaged the United States as a place for the mingling of races, leading to unforeseen changes in political formations: 'The four races of men, too, which compose that vast population,—the Saxon, the Celt, the Negro, and the Indian,—whatever their separate fortunes, must mingle their blood, more or less; and, as Nature makes nothing in vain, we know not what political results may come of that'.[410] Through the New Zealand Constitution Act the Crown sought to be represented within the so-called representative colonial institutions itself, enacted as part of the legislative process in the form of giving or withholding assent to legislative measures. Responsible government had not yet materialized. But when it did, from 1856, the Crown assumed a permanent share in the electoral system, with an interest in obtaining advisors (ministers) responsible to the legislature from time to time.[411] In the heated forums of Westminster politics, liberal Conservatives, such as Stanley, Whig-liberals, like Russell, Morpeth, and the third Earl Grey, as well as those of radical dispositions within the House of Commons, including Molesworth, actively participated in the parliamentary debates concerning what became the New Zealand Constitution Act.

Yet debates had already preceded this enactment, not merely in the wake of the foiled constitutional arrangements of 1846 but also in the drafting of what eventually emerged in June 1852 as 'An Act to grant a representative constitution to the colony of New Zealand'.[412] Its multi-layered complexities of provincial legislatures—elected provincial superintendents, a legislative council of appointed members, an electorally determined house of representatives, and a governor—admitted institutional pluralism. Each aspect and layer represented a potentially rivalrous interest. In this way, vigorous local government was thought to act as a constraint on any centralizing tendencies. Municipalism rather than federalism was the trope underscoring the design of what became the New Zealand Constitution Act 1852.[413] Later, Earl Grey exhorted municipalism as the best training ground for those needing to learn how to exercise a 'larger measure of political power' appropriately.[414] The New Zealand Constitution Act did not reflect the simple sense of a balanced constitution adumbrated by Polybius of Megalopolis in his account of the republican Roman constitution.[415] Institutional pluralism in the form of distributing formal sites of authority across a range of institutional forms or configurations was in evidence. Native title evidenced the presence of still other forces and centres of competitive or, at the very least, potentially rivalrous authority dispersed throughout the archipelago. Areas subject to native title were thought of as places yet to be incorporated within the day-to-day, ambulatory operation

409 For example Spedding, 'A Second Visit to the United States of America', 339–71.

410 Ibid, 366.

411 See Chapter Six. Cf Pole, *Political Representation in England*, 396.

412 'An Act to grant a representative constitution to the colony of New Zealand', 30 June 1852, 15 & 16 Vict, c72 (Imp).

413 For example, Merivale to Peel, 1 January 1852, CO209/159, fos.221–2a, TNA. Important arguments emerged within settler politics as to whether the constitution was properly viewed as 'federal' despite the intentions of the policy-formulators in London.

414 Earl Grey, *The Colonial Policy of Lord John Russell's Administration*, I, 32.

415 Polybius, *The Rise of the Roman Empire*, 303–18.

of the constitutional body politic, as purchase transactions purported to extinguish pre-existing territorial rights or claims.

Interest-based representation, rather than merely representing numbers, was another whiggish feature of the Act. In this fashion, it reflected preoccupations of English constitutional thought tied to Burke in the eighteenth century and Whig discussions in favour of electoral reform in 1832.[416] These questions of balancing and calibrating the representation of interests—different property-based franchises—with the representation of numbers (electors as individuals) are re-cast in the late twentieth and early twenty-first centuries as contests between recognizing groups or collectivities constitutionally as opposed to mere majoritarian interests (howsoever that majority is produced from time to time). As his private correspondence with the governor suggests, Earl Grey wanted minorities to have their say, and meaningfully too.[417] Concepts of liberty in these varied senses were worked out in a number of localities within and alongside empire—New Zealand afforded yet another set of sites for these processes of working out. As Jonathan Parry, Catherine Hall, and Thomas Holt identified, 'liberty' or 'freedom' was a problem under construction, a work-in-progress in Victorian times as much as the early twenty-first century.[418]

Regrettably, New Zealand's constitutional architecture has been prone to passing caricature in recent legalistic and political studies.[419] Often the accounts are purely descriptive. Yet aspects of the historiographical literature in the period following the Second World War were sensitive to fragmentary albeit interlocking complexities of the constitutional situation obtaining in the colony after the implementation of the New Zealand Constitution Act 1852.[420] These features have also received recent historiographical attention.[421] In being so sensitized to complexity of the institutional configuration, these scholars recall the perspectives of various commentators in the mid-nineteenth century. A former colonial Attorney General, William Swainson, noting the tendency towards 'provincial isolation' in 1856, adjudged that the formal constitutional setting left it to the 'colonists themselves', especially in the General Assembly, as to whether New Zealand would simply be 'a collection of insignificant, divided, and powerless petty states'.[422] As is well appreciated, the 1852 constitution introduced representative institutions—its focal point was representation rather than responsible self-government, an issue on which it was silent.[423]

Victory has a thousand fathers and defeat is an orphan. With the Constitution Act being seen as combining elements of strategic victory and defeat, we find diverse groups claiming credit for those details most convivial to their aspirations. As a statute, its conceptual ancestry was manifold, with a number of individuals claiming primary authorship. Charles Adderley was credited with having drafted the 'independent constitution of New Zealand' at Hams Hall in 1850, it being said that the constitution of

[416] Pole, *Political Representation in England*, 443–4, 494–9.

[417] Earl Grey to Grey, private, 19 February 1851, GNZ Mss35, fos.45–51, APL.

[418] Parry, 'Liberalism and Liberty', in Mandler (ed), *Liberty and Authority in Victorian Britain*, 71–100; Hall, *Civilising Subjects*; Hall, McClelland, Jane Rendall, *Defining the Victorian Nation*; Holt, *The Problem of Freedom*.

[419] For example, see Johansson, *The Politics of Possibility*, 55–6.

[420] Sinclair, *The Origins of the Maori Wars*, 94.

[421] Ward, 'Civil Jurisdiction'.

[422] Swainson, *New Zealand. The Substance of Lectures on the Colonization of New Zealand*, 32.

[423] Sorrenson, *Report of the Royal Commission on the Electoral System*, B-13.

the other colonies followed this precedent.[424] By his own account, Adderley drafted an alternative constitution to that already enacted in 1846 during Earl Grey's tenure as Secretary of State for Colonies: 'As to the detail of the New Zealand Constitution Act, I cannot do better than continue quoting Mr Gladstone's criticism, agreeing as I do with his general approval of the measure, which indeed was based on a draft I drew up under the guidance of Gibbon Wakefield'.[425] Adderley's autobiographical notes conveyed a more subtle impression as to authorship. In mid-1851, he recorded, 'I got on with the New Zealand Bill and Constitution, which had been drafted on the terrace at Hams with Gibbon Wakefield... Fox, Sewell, and Lord Lyttelton assisting'.[426] Adderley's underlying view, matured most visibly by 1860, was to transfer responsibility to settlement colonies so that they would bear the risks and burden of error together with the associated costs. What better way to incentivize peace with indigenous populations than to foist the costs of failure and war on colonial settlements instead of the imperial government? That, at least, was a view Adderley and Gladstone began to assume more strongly from this period onwards. There can be no doubt that Earl Grey was the main conceptual driver of the 1846 constitution, and also the primary driver of the subsequent 1852 Constitution Act.

Although readily forgotten, well before the twenty-first century New Zealand's constitution was not simply focused on majorities of individuals determining who might have the confidence of representative institutions following elections. It was directed towards the relation of the state to the representation of interests and associations of interest (not merely voters as individuals)—an issue topical both then and now. An heir to the verities of ancient whiggism through upbringing, parentage, and cousinage, Earl Grey was an advocate for representation of interests with a propertied stake in the community through diverse forms of franchise and not for the mere representation of numbers.[427] A £10 householder franchise was introduced. Edward Gibbon Wakefield and others appreciated the significance of the proprietary franchise relative to native title. When Wakefield proposed a provincial councils bill for New Zealand in a memorandum circulated to Gladstone in 1850 or 1851, he commented how requiring a 'franchise amounting to a £5 annual occupancy of a separate tenement, will it is believed confer the privilege of voting for members of the constituent council on all bona fide colonists adult and male, while it will exclude the mere transient visitor and the bulk of the natives who are undoubtedly unfitted for such a privilege, and who by the limitation of the provincial boundaries will practically be little affected by the proposed constitution, few of them residing within the limits of the provinces'.[428]

424 de Montmorency, rev Matthew, 'Adderley, Charles Bowyer, first Baron Norton (1814–1905)', in *Oxford Dictionary of National Biography*.

425 Rt Hon CB Adderley MP, *Review of 'The Colonial Policy of Lord J. Russell's Administration'*, 137.

426 Childe-Pemberton, *Life of Lord Norton*, 99.

427 Earl Grey, *Parliamentary Government Considered with Reference to a Reform of Parliament*, 64–5.

428 Memorandum, EG Wakefield, *circa* 1850–1851, BL AddMss44566, fos.312–16a.

Native title illuminating British political debates about colonial constitutional design

The presence of native title illuminated whiggish, tory, and radical tendencies in constitutional design. Merivale, Frederick Peel (Hawes' successor as the parliamentary undersecretary at the Colonial Office from 1 November 1851 until 27 February 1852), and Earl Grey entered into extensive discussions on the topic of framing a constitution. Merivale distilled the question of constitutional design to 'a choice between two plans': first, a project 'Of municipalities: Provincial Councils transacting most ordinary business: and a general legislature seldom meeting; [second, one] [o]f Provincial Councils with limited powers of a municipal character, & a general Council transacting the ordinary legislative business'. He characterized the former of the two as the governor's proposal. Peel, he thought, inclined 'to the second—so should I under different circumstances from those of N[ew] Zeal[an]d'. Yet, he cautioned, 'the experiment of a single & strongly democratic legislature, to govern a country so large, & so broken by natural obstacles into small & distant neighbourhoods, seems to me a hazardous one'.[429] True to radical and whiggish predispositions, a vigorous form of local government was sought after to counteract any tendencies towards centralization. In expressing these views, Merivale revealed his advice to be closer to the position of Fox than might have been thought. Merivale stated, '[s]ince it is impossible under existing circumstances to constitute such a legislature with any aristocratic or other check on the immediate pressure of popular power, the check which independent local legislatures might afford seems (as in America) something of a practical substitute'. Again, a trans-Atlantic comparator was drawn upon as an illustration: 'New England, which has always been a collection of provinces with separate legislatures, is hardly larger than New Zealand'.[430]

Regarding Māori, the reach of the constitution was largely ambulatory—something that was incipiently mobile by way of design, able to incorporate Māori politically through adjustment, as they were 'civilized' and gained property cognizable in English law. Until that happened, section 71 of the Constitution Act could be invoked although, as will be seen in Chapters Five and Six, in practice that was not necessary. Section 71 provided for Her Majesty to have the power of setting apart districts by letters patent for the maintenance of the 'Laws, Customs, and Usages of the aboriginal or native Inhabitants of New Zealand, so far as they are not repugnant to the general Principles of Humanity, . . . for the Government of themselves, in all their Relations to and Dealings with each other'. Section 10 of Earl Grey's proposed constitution of 1846 anticipated this provision.[431] Earl Grey saw the provision as animated by the principle 'that the laws and customs of the native New Zealanders, even though repugnant to our own laws, ought, if not at variance with general principles of humanity, to be for the present maintained for their government in all their relations to and dealings with each other'.[432] Both in a draft and a formal despatch, the third Earl Grey mused as to whether there would be any practicable necessity for using such a power.[433] The practical persistence of Māori authority proved sufficient, as will be made clear in subsequent chapters. In

[429] Merivale to Peel, 1 January 1852, CO209/159, fos.221a–2, TNA.

[430] Ibid, fos.222–2a.

[431] 'An Act to make further Provision for the Government of the New Zealand Islands', 28 August 1846, 9 & 10 Vict, c103.

[432] Earl Grey to Grey, 23 December 1846, *GBPP1847*, 38 [763], 70.

[433] Earl Grey to Grey, February 1852, CO209/159, fo.238a, TNA.

recognizing customary political and legal authority over areas subject to native title, there was no logical or necessary inconsistency between such recognition and the first and second articles of the Treaty of Waitangi.[434] The second article was not breached by the maintenance of customary authority to determine to whom the use or occupation of territory might be allocated. This sort of authority could be seen as political or jurisdictional authority residing in a chief (*rangatiratanga* or chieftainship). Others could see it as merely proprietary—the entitlement to determine what was to be done with one's own property—or as a claim to a right. In any event, insofar as deeds of purchase were concerned, it was seen as a claim or a right to be assuaged, satisfied, and extinguished (or transformed into a different interest under a Crown grant). It need not have been textually explicit for this to occur. On occasion, however, it was expressly noted at least. Indeed, in a deed of purchase of January 1840, Nōpera Panakareao purported to transfer to Taylor '*te rangatiratanga me te mana i taua whenua*'.[435] Earl Grey considered the chiefs of indigenous communities to be critical parts of the political constitutional architecture. In writing to Governor Grey in 1853 on the publication of his *The Colonial Policy of Lord John Russell's Administration*, he thought the 'absence of any provision for maintaining the position in society of the Chiefs' to be unsatisfactory: 'Experience in Kafraria, in Ceylon & wherever barbarous tribes have been brought under British dominion seems to me to show that this may be a source of danger hereafter'. Binding indigenous sources of authority to the British government required placating those customary elites. Enabling the 'Chiefs to maintain their accustomed station amongst their countrymen' was needed if they were to 'remain really affected to the Government & contented'.[436]

In looking at the New Zealand Constitution Act, we find the propensity to see the main lesson of whiggish-liberal constitutionalism to be that of judicious adjustment to changes in general social circumstances—aligning the constitutional frame to perceived changes by degrees over time. In this way, a constitution was seen as a process rather than as a static textual fact. Pragmatic Burkean Whigs sought less to contrive abstract designs predicated on *a priori* principles than to harmonize and adjust the complex and historical givens of a community or communities. As Earl Grey appreciated, freshly settled colonial niches challenged these approaches. They required constitutional and legislative design to frame the interior lives of a sprinkling of start-up colonial settlements—workings of what Belich characterized as 'instant townships', such as Auckland, Wellington, Nelson, Christchurch, and New Plymouth.[437] But New Zealand (as well as the neighbouring Australian settlements) presented a way in which the rhythms of adjustability and gradualism could be transposed colonially by outlining a baroque constitutional setting. To radicals, these overlaid and competing features, with a governor at the apex holding reserve powers regarding native title areas and indigenous populations, might seem inefficient and corrupt. Paradoxically, however, a distrust of centralization (often equated with despotism) on the part of liberal radicals aligned these radicals (including colonial reformers such as William Fox) with Tories stressing another element to be found within Burke's *oeuvre*—defending

[434] As appears to be surmised by Head in 'Maori Land Tenure and Chiefly Authority in Whanganui, 1840–1865', 105–6; and Brookfield, *Waitangi and Indigenous Rights*, 116–19 (but see 171–2, where Brookfield seems to argue differently).

[435] See deed of purchase, 20 January 1840, Ms papers-0075-106C, John White papers, ATL.

[436] Earl Grey to Grey, 24 August 1853, GNZ Mss35(13), fos.63–4, APL.

[437] Belich, *Making Peoples*, 188.

ancient privileges. Indeed, Burke enjoyed an afterlife in the hands of Tories suspicious of centralization within the state—whether imperial or colonial—as well as radicals. Joshua Toulmin Smith, an advocate of the principles of local self-government within the English constitution, proved sceptical of centralization within the state.[438] This chimed with the younger Benjamin Disraeli (a Tory radical) who in his *Vindication of the English Constitution* (1835) chastised the Whigs for favouring oligarchic centralization above localized customs and ancient heritage.[439] For Adderley, too, the empire of colonial settlements deserved local self-government rather than the survival of centralized authority answerable to London, from which emanated numerous governors armed with personal instructions and commissions from a Secretary of State. The philosophic radical James Mill, in *The History of British India* (1817), warned of the unhelpful results of not adapting a scheme of government 'to the state of the people for whose use it is intended', adding '[i]n those diversities in the state of civilization, which approach the extremes, this truth is universally acknowledged'.[440] For a number of political actors figuring prominently in New Zealand's early colonial history, such as the Peelite liberal, the fifth Duke of Newcastle (styled the Earl of Lincoln until 1851), or the third Earl Grey, a Whig, an approach of this sort was seen as reflexive. Newcastle, writing to Gladstone, surmised that the 'mistake of France and the cause of her present fate was too great and obstinate a resistance to a fair and necessary expansion of the democratic element in her government and that the resistance of Louis Philipe & Guizot to any Electoral Reform was one of the main causes of the Revolution of 1848'.[441] Māori, as will be argued in Chapters Five, Six, and Seven, were also seen as relevant subjects for deliberative constitutional tuning and adjustment. Here was the language of 'civilization' mingling with the genres of liberal and Whig constitutionalism. Merivale adjudged the position of the indigenous peoples of New Zealand to be distinct. 'It is evident', he said in November 1848, 'that this is a perfectly new state of things: a state for which there is no precedent at all in the whole history of British colonization.'[442] He explained how '[n]o such circumstance has ever occurred, as that a mass of British settlers, [and] a mass of semi-civilized natives, should live together in the same districts & under the same government', even if only nominally, it might be added.

As witnessed, native title was certainly tied to a certain stage in historical and contemporary political status and political economy. But this was not a static conception. It was not seen as a steady state but as a fragile category able to be transformed. Earl Grey anticipated the incorporation of Māori within the embrace of the electoral franchise 'by degrees' as they 'advance[d] in civilization and [acquired] property'.[443] In accordance with a theme of constitutional adjustment, two broad approaches were canvassed as ways of dealing with large areas still subject to native title in the North Island. Merivale noted that under 'Lord Grey's plan... fixing the

438 Smith, *Local Self-Government and Centralization*.

439 Disraeli, 'The Spirit of Whiggism', (1836), published as an addendum to the 'Letters of Runnymede', reprinted in Hutcheon (ed), *Whigs and Whiggism*, 331. On Disraeli as a 'Tory-Radical', see Hilton, *A Mad, Bad, and Dangerous People?*, 519.

440 Mill, *The History of British India*, I, 429.

441 Newcastle to Gladstone, 26 August 1852, BL AddMss44262, fos.126–6a.

442 Merivale to Hawes, 29 November 1848, CO209/64, fo.388, TNA.

443 Draft, Earl Grey to Grey, 29 January 1852, CO209/159, fo.335a, TNA.

boundaries of the provinces was left to the Governor: [b]ut it was intended that he should be instructed so to limit them as to include in them as nearly as possible the *settled* [that is, European] lands'. Indeed, the 'rest was left under the control of the General Legislature, but with power to the Governor to set apart aboriginal districts where native usages should prevail'.[444] Merivale observed how one alternative draft for the constitutional arrangement of representative institutions in New Zealand—known as the 'MS project'—endeavoured to obtain the same objective differently. It suggested that the '"provinces"... consist only of such lands as have been actually purchased from the natives'.[445] The remaining territories would be the preserve of the governor's legislative authority (executive proclamations, for instance). Merivale adjudged this approach to be a 'more complete method, but... difficult in practice'. He noted how 'lands are purchased from the natives, not in compact districts, but in bits here & there, there will be as it seems to me much intersection & confusion between districts within the provinces & districts subject to the Governor'.[446] Merivale characterized the MS project as quite different from Earl Grey's proposal: 'Lord Grey's frames a constitution, [whereas] the M.S. Project makes a constituent council to frame a constitution, subject to very slight restrictions'. In the time-honoured fashion of managing expectations in politics, the MS project set up a process rather than an answer. 'Consequently', said Merivale, 'almost the whole of Lord Grey's bill consists of details which are quite omitted in the M.S.'[447] The MS project bore the colonial reformers' stamp of liberal conservatism in the Peelite mode, combined with allies in radicalism (two *elective* chambers in each province; a constituent council to determine matters of constitutional design locally rather than having them framed in London). Although one would not know it from some of the secondary literature, Earl Grey's 'baroque' colonial constitution survived—eased no doubt through the assured and persuasive advice of Merivale to Earl Grey's Tory successors, Pakington and his parliamentary under-secretary, Lord Desart—and was enacted.[448]

CONCLUSIONS

This chapter has addressed the reaching of a thin, 'incompletely theorized' consensus on the metes and bounds of native title in empire. What this situation represented was an agreement to disagree as to the true test for ascertaining what native title was—whether it required tangible or physical occupation of territorial space in the form of dwellings, fortified sites, and cultivations, or whether broader-ranging uses and claims to territorial space in accordance with the customary norms of the claimant group were sufficient. As Ballara has implied, the presence of European settlements and a land market, reflected by deeds, stabilized broad tribal areas of authority and influence.[449] European newcomers analysed this stability in terms of the language of property rights and occupation. We have traversed the persistence of seeing 'occupancy' as something

[444] Merivale to Pakington, 24 March 1852, CO209/159, fos.291–1a, TNA.

[445] Ibid, fos.291a–2, TNA. [446] Ibid, fo.292. [447] Ibid, fos.289–9a.

[448] See also Merivale's marginal notes comparing the MS project to 'Heads of [a] Bill [for the Government of New Zealand] submitted to Sir J. Pakington on 25 March 1852': CO209/159, fos.157–64a, TNA.

[449] Ballara, *Taua*, 454–7.

distinct from unoccupied land over which political authority was claimed. It was theorized as something distinct from unoccupied land over which political authority was claimed. New Zealand Company advocates contended for these views in the press in Britain and New Zealand, in the Parliament at Westminster, and through direct lobbying. Others insisted that customary law and practice needed to be consulted. Yet those who argued against narrow interpretations of occupancy moved the argument towards focusing on purchase without minute investigations of the particular forms of indigenous interaction with a landscape—whether territory was cultivated or used for hunting or fishing. Such thoughts concerning occupancy were never truly resolved. This ought not to be surprising, as debates concerning *occupatio* or occupation were of longstanding. These disputes continued as indigenous property rights were conceived as part of a non-indigenous debate concerning who had pre-eminence in sorting out the patterns of colonial settlement. In 1847, Marshall court jurisprudence on 'Indian title' formally landed in New Zealand through a case in the colonial Supreme Court (*Symonds*). A former New Zealand Company agent, Chapman, was the prime actor in deploying this imported jurisprudence within a juridical-colonial context. The decision formed part of a broader narrative of colonial administration reasserting primacy in sorting out the authority of settlers to occupy space on the ground.

5

Extricating 'Native Title from its Present Entanglement'—Recognizing Diversity and the Problem of a Liberal Constitution

Hinging on the preceding discussion, this chapter considers the problem of a liberal political constitution for colonial New Zealand and its relations with native title during the period from 1852 until 1860. Native title and numerous well-armed Māori polities posed distinct and troublesome questions for the whig-liberal aspects of a mid-nineteenth-century constitutional setting. The following questions may be discerned—how to recognize diversity and whether such recognition was to be merely transitional; how to balance disparate interests, including those of indigenous descent-group-based communities, in a constitutional framework purporting to be liberal; how the *demos*—the politically relevant population—should be constituted and taken into account and whether it could accommodate Māori collectivities and collective interests in natural resources such as land distinctively from settlers' concerns; and whether pre-existing albeit changing indigenous interests in territory also continued to invoke questions of customary authority and, if so, how such interests should be accommodated in a new constitutional frame.

As will be explored in this context, anglophone conceptions of native title were considered through the entwined but subtly distinct notions of jurisdictional incommensurability, conceptual incommensurability, and non-justiciability. Each of these approaches posed significant consequences both for legal-political thought and for practically interacting with areas perceived to be subject to native title claims. Thus, a stress upon experimental legislative proposals endeavouring to craft portals of legal recognition for native title, as well as institutional design in the form of circuit courts, emerged, as colonial and imperial politics pursued ways of formalizing engagements with Māori beyond the negotiability of purchase and merchant commerce. In this fashion, Chapters Six and Seven also demonstrate how, within imperial and colonial political practices, fundamentally whiggish tropes about encouraging and managing uneasy transitional stages or states ensnared in processes of change, as well as adjusting forms of government and legalism to these transitive conditions of change, were adapted to the perceived circumstances of indigenous communities within New Zealand and their place within histories of progress and regression. As Burrow has said, the early to mid-nineteenth-century forms of whiggism were 'not assimilable to contractarianism and doctrines of natural rights'. Rather, they tended to stress 'a conception of civilization as the spontaneous, unintended transformation and (for the most part) improvement of society and manners, which tended to make the relation of government to society one primarily of adjustment and mediation'.[1]

The implications of filling out the content of humanitarian impulses with concrete policy objectives and outcomes in the 1850s and early 1860s illustrate a significant point about strands of thought and individuals ordinarily associated with liberal-tory and whiggish politics and with humanitarianism itself. That is, under the press of contingent events and policy disputes, humane policies already contained the seedlings of the transition in approaches to indigenous populations ordinarily ascribed to mid-nineteenth-century trends in favour of 'positivism' or 'social Darwinism' or to wars and the Indian rebellion of 1857.[2] Those individuals conventionally described as belonging to a humanitarian strain of thought on colonial policies, including William Martin, the first chief justice of New Zealand, the former Attorney General William Swainson, and George Augustus Selwyn, the Bishop of New Zealand, often nurtured and gave expression to these very seeds. In doing so, they may not necessarily have appreciated all of the implications of certain policy proposals that they supported. Yet the wars themselves were not decisive factors in any policy shift. The implications of policies concerning native title, adapted to the expansion of colonial niches, whether at a gradual or, less preferably, more explosive pace, were already clear and present. Violence was already an aspect of colonization but organized warfare in earnest from 1860 simply attracted an intensification and increase in imperial resourcing in certain locations, echoing the growing availability and injection of imperial funds in the later 1840s addressed in Chapter Five. The trinity of Austinian 'positivism', 'social Darwinism', and brewing warfare were not the authors of these troubled consequences for native title and the legal status of indigenous communities. They already inhered in the range of interpretations of native title and customary law operating in colonies of settlement.[3]

A JURISPRUDENCE IN THE SHADOWS—BALANCED CONSTITUTIONS AND NATIVE TITLE

As before, during the hinge years of 1859 and 1860, the tangible lives of native title were to be found not in the courts but in the memoranda and places of political contest, especially amongst key advisors and colonial ministerialists, as well as negotiations with Māori. We see native title in the making, as an activity or process of working out and working through. It is in these workings—these activities—that we may see the illuminations of native title and how it related to the jurisprudence of empire. Rather than reflecting an elaborately presented and argued hoard of high-level juristic texts comprising a *corpus juris*, ideas about native title were made, contested, and unpacked in politically driven debates. Legalistic genres proved to be highly relevant. Yet these ways of speaking were deployed in an array of nuanced political activities and practices. They mingled with other political idioms, including early nineteenth-century treatments of the techniques of stadial history lurking within theories of political economy.

[1] Burrow, *Whigs and Liberals*, 126.

[2] Cf Bank, 'Losing Faith in the Civilizing Mission', in Daunton and Halpern (eds), *Empire and Others*, 364–83; Mantena, *Alibis of Empire*, 1–4, 190 (note 14).

[3] This would also appear to be an implication of Ford's *Settler Sovereignty*.

It was a jurisprudence in the shadows so to speak, certainly perceptible to contemporaries. But, for posterity, it was a less legible and visible strain of juristic thought, mingling with politics and at the real risk of being treated as the ephemera and detritus of legal-policy musing and design, only to be forgotten by subsequent generations. The footprint of this working through was registered in the minutiae of manuscripts—handwritten and printed papers—not in the authoritative reports of judicial decisions of colonial courts. Its archives were scattered. London, too, remained a potential source for remedial policy attention. Colonial lobbyists, voyaging between colony and metropole, and British-based sympathizers sought remedies either through the Colonial Office in the form of policy directions to governors or the imperial legislature in Acts of Parliament. This thinking and acting on native title were multi-dimensional, to be found across the seas and in many places, imperial and colonial. It is possible, therefore, to speak of a jurisprudence in the shadows worked out, disaggregated, and critiqued from differing points of view in both elite political discourses and 'from below'.[4]

With issues seldom litigated authoritatively in a judicial sense in the Supreme Court, except in *Symonds* (1847), officials and politicians resorted to legal opinions to supply broad guidance or resources for action in policy. The recorded volume of colonial litigation in the resident magistrates' courts involving Māori was slight relative to the estimated indigenous population and its concentrated distribution in parts of the North Island. Settlements at Auckland and Wellington recorded higher numbers criminal cases,[5] with Wanganui in the Wellington province returning lower numbers than Wellington in most years, except for 1854, where fourteen cases were recorded, as opposed to nine in Wellington. In New Plymouth, a mere two cases of assault were brought against Māori in 1856 (with two convictions counted). A summary of offences in the resident magistrates' and magistrates' courts for the years from 1853 to 1858 suggested that no Māori were proceeded against for breach of the Cattle Trespass Ordinance, except three in 1854 and five in 1857. Civil cases in which only Māori were concerned were comparatively rare. The province of Auckland accounted for no cases in 1853, one in 1854, two in 1855, and 12 in 1856.[6] The numbers accounted for raise intriguing questions as to why and how the native land court proved to be so efficacious in luring in Māori participation, especially after 1865. Even with *Symonds*, and the presence of northern American jurisprudence, a lot of interpretative detail remained to be worked through as to what native title was as a class of interest in territory, how it related to concepts of indigenous political authority, and the guarantee of 'full chieftainship' (*rangatiratanga*) in the Treaty of Waitangi, or how it operated in specific factual circumstances, such as customary transfers or dispositions to pākehā settlers—pastoralists pursuing grazing territories or individuals cohabiting with Māori families or *whānau*. The apparent meanings of *Symonds* were neither idly nor quiescently accepted as setting out the content of native title or preferred legal policy in any authoritatively convincing or even persuasive way. In 1864 the then representative

[4] Salesa, *Racial Crossings*, 5–6, makes a comparable point about discourses on race in the mid-nineteenth century.

[5] Broken down into categories of assault, drunkenness, felony, and 'all other cases': *Statistics of New Zealand for 1853, 1854, 1855, and 1856*, table 64.

[6] Ibid, table 86, 'Summary of Convictions for the undermentioned offences in the resident magistrates' and magistrates' courts in New Zealand, during the years 1853, 1854, 1855, 1856, 1857, and 1858, distinguishing the European and Maori Cases', in *Statistics of New Zealand for 1858*.

for the Auckland electoral seat of Newton, Hugh Francis Carleton, hearkened to the legal opinions of Joseph Phillimore and Shirley Woolmer obtained by the Aborigines' Protection Society and reprinted in Louis Alexis Chamerovzow's *The New Zealand Question and the Rights of Aborigines* (1848), supporting the 'native interpretation of the pre-emption clause' in the Treaty of Waitangi.[7] By this he meant to refer to Phillimore's statement that the Crown had merely:

> acquired a right to purchase the fee simple of all lands in New Zealand, which fall within the scope of the Treaty—in preference to, and exclusive of any other individual—but if the Crown should decline to purchase, I am at a loss to ascertain by what rule the native proprietor, to whom the treaty has imparted all the rights and privileges of a British subject, can be barred from disposing of his property by sale to any one of his fellow-subjects.[8]

Moreover, it was not apparent, for instance, whether all aspects of United States jurisprudence, as understood through the texts of James Kent and Joseph Story predominantly, would be applied to Crown–Māori relations in New Zealand. Claims to overarching territorial jurisdiction throughout New Zealand relative to external European powers such as France and the United States in 1840 or subsequently did not preclude arguments in favour of treating Māori communities as jurisdictionally distinct in de facto practice and, more contestably, *de jure*. Practices may obtain a juridical significance. This was a feature of the law of nations and customary law. Some commentators considered the de facto situation as sufficiently enduring or embedded to warrant a *de jure* interpretation of its significance. How the introduced legal orders of the colonial settlements were framed also posed challenges, as we shall see in relation to qualification for the electoral franchise under the Constitution Act.

Yet, in view of the small volume of litigation in the ordinary courts addressing native title, the New Zealand setting tended to furnish juristic accounts in the activities of politics, where protagonists offered and contested opinions regarding the relationship of native title to the colonial constitution and to questions of how colonial settlements might access areas of territory subject to native title. Northern American jurisprudence and the form of the Treaty of Waitangi (the express reference to pre-emption in the second article) supplied some pieces to the puzzle of native title. But arguments as to the detailed content of such title and particular applications to concrete situations remained. These processes of working out were not static but iterative, as befitted common law and policy frames of reference principally adapted to problems or questions of the moment rather than grandiose abstract schemes in advance:

> Politics is the sphere of the unsettled, the locus of those issues not fully governed now by the unconscious play of tradition or the conscious control of administrative rationality; it is also the sphere in which collectively binding decisions sometimes must be made even though the available resources of reason and tradition are insufficient to determine the outcome'.[9]

[7] Carleton, 'New Zealand', 430 (note).

[8] 'Appendix to the New Zealand Question being the Opinions thereupon of Joseph Phillimore Esq., D.C.L. and Shirley F. Woolmer, Esq. of the Middle Temple, Barrister-at-Law', 10–11, in Chamerovzow, *The New Zealand Question*. It should be noted, however, despite Carleton's suggestions to the contrary, that Woolmer did not address the issue in the same way as Phillimore.

[9] Connolly, *The Terms of Political Discourse*, 227.

As Maurice Cowling noted:

> Political practice.... involves making decisions, taking chances, arriving at choices between one course of action and another, often in conditions of extreme uncertainty, often where no one course is self-evidently preferabl[e] to any other.[10]

We see a halting, episodic approach to questions of native title. It is in the occasional decisions of the courts, as well as the juristic musings of legalists, coupled with the real life of the constitutional legal and political practice, that we see the production of the jurisprudence of native title; a process never completed supplying increased detail over time. In part, various protagonists were endeavouring to find or establish the scope of an *Ur*-principle as to native title in the real life of a particular colonial polity and its legal system.[11] These processes of argument, borne on the airs of contingent events, were vital in challenging opinion, prompting and crystallizing new ways of characterizing legal-political understandings, and posing novel questions of material transposed from other parts of the empire or jurisdictions presented as potentially analogous, such as the United States. In the intimate, familial spaces of colonial settlements, the professional distance assumed to exist between legal advisors, politicians, and officials was slight. Legal doctrinal positions were worked out in specific circumstances as policy questions or debates emerged, often without the guidance of the courts, but with the assistance of views expressed by William Martin, the former chief justice, together with the former Attorney General, Swainson, who sat in the legislative council. Court decisions yielded little at this stage in the way of practical guidance to formulators of policy. Indeed, the imprint of court decisions was absent from the discussions of the former chief justice, Martin, as much as the chief justice from 1 March 1858, George Arney. Court decisions of the Supreme Court on native title in the first two-and-a-half decades of colonial settlement, whether directly or indirectly, were relatively rare but remained as shards and artefacts. *Symonds* proved to be the most extensive of judicial considerations in the period addressed in this study.

A General Assembly was not constituted until 1854. Sorting out the political constitutional relations between the governor and his responsible ministers on the question of overseeing and administering Crown–Māori relations assumed primary importance. As noted, the New Zealand Constitution Act was silent on the issue of whether or not a responsible ministry was necessary. However, once Thomas Gore Browne assumed office as governor on 6 September 1855, the move towards responsible ministries soon followed. A compact was achieved in April 1856 expressed in the form of a minute laid on the table of the House of Representatives in May. Generally, the governor would act on the advice of responsible advisors, irrespective of whether or not it was 'in accordance with his own opinion on the subject in question'. In matters 'affecting the Queen's prerogative and Imperial interests generally', however, the governor would be disposed to receive ministerial advice, 'but when he differs from them in opinion, he will (if they desire it) submit their views to the consideration of Her Majesty's Secretary of State, adhering to his own until an answer is received [which might be contrary to his

[10] Cowling, *Mill and Liberalism*, 107. See also Sharp, *Justice and the Māori*, 163–4.

[11] I am grateful to G McLay of the faculty of law at Victoria University of Wellington for helpful discussions on this point (September 2010).

preference]'.[12] 'Among Imperial subjects', the minute continued, 'the Governor includes all dealings with the Native tribes, more especially in the negotiation of purchases of land.'[13] A memorandum dated 18 April 1856 annexed to the minute explained that the governor saw no problem with the House of Representatives defining specific lands to be purchased but that it would not be compulsory for the governor to make purchases 'if, in his opinion, political reasons render[ed] it inexpedient to do so'.[14] The subtleties of these relations were sorted out further in subsequent correspondence. Responsible ministers prepared a minute of 22 August 1856 together with a second minute of 2 September 1856. To test his position, the governor went so far as to consult with a relatively broad base of politically influential opinion in the colony, particularly a range of members of the Anglican and Wesleyan missions but also the former chief protector of aborigines, George Clarke senior, Major Nugent of the 58th regiment, late Native Secretary during Grey's recent governorship. With the granting of representative institutions, the politically relevant colonial *demos* were not completely electorally driven. Consensus on the relations between governor and responsible ministers, if only understood to be ultimately temporary, was reached without responsible ministers having to resign. McLean was to be designated Native Secretary.[15]

Jurisdictional incommensurability, conceptual incommensurability, and non-justiciability—the electoral franchise and native title

Diversifying the political marketplace through the establishment of new configurations of political resource under the New Zealand Constitution Act—provincial legislatures, a bicameral general legislature comprising a House of Representatives and a legislative council, and provincial superintendents—promoted new challenges for native title, which increasingly converged with questions of whether tribal proprietors were entitled to exercise the electoral franchise under the Constitution Act. Section 7 of the Constitution Act provided for three qualifying classes of property interests under real property law, provided a man was 21 years old or more. First, such a person could be entitled to vote if registered in circumstances where he held 'a freehold estate in possession, situate within the district for which the vote is to be given, of the clear value of £50 above all charges and incumbrances [*sic*], and of or to which he has been seized or entitled either at law or in equity for at least 6 calendar months next before the last registration of electors'. Secondly, a man of the relevant age could vote if he had 'a leasehold estate in possession, situate within such district of the clear annual value of £10 held upon a lease which at the time of registration shall not have less than 3 years to run or having a leasehold estate so situate and of such value as aforesaid of which he been in possession for 3 years as aforesaid next before such registration'. Finally, section 7 stipulated that 'a Householder within such District occupying a *Tenement* within the Limits of a Town (to be proclaimed as such by the Governor for the purposes of this Act) of the clear annual Value of Ten Pounds, or without the Limits of a Town of the

[12] 'Ministerial Government. Minute of his Excellency as to the relations between himself and his responsible advisers', *Votes and Proceedings of the House of Representatives; session iv—1856*, volume 1, A-13.

[13] Ibid. [14] Ibid, 'Memorandum', 18 April 1856.

[15] Sinclair, *The Origins of the Maori Wars*; Ward, *A Show of Justice*, 93; Morrell, *British Colonial Policy in the Mid-Victorian Age*, 214–15.

clear annual Value of Five Pounds, and having resided therein Six Calendar Months next before such Registration as aforesaid, shall, if duly registered, be entitled to vote at the Election of a Member of Members for the District' (emphasis added).

Certain Māori were registered on the general and provincial electoral rolls, but in small numbers and with noticeable variations from province to province.[16] Complicating the issue was an unresolved debate as to whether unextinguished native title was sufficient to qualify Māori dwelling within political formations such as *hapū* to exercise the franchise. The electorates established in 1853 did not cover New Zealand in its entirety. They would not do so until the Electoral Districts Act 1858 when Wanganui and Rangitikei were extended to embrace hitherto excluded territory in the North Island. William Fox, based in the province of Wellington, saw the issue combatively. Jousting with William Martin in the 1860s on the question of open war with Māori communities, Fox did not consider Māori as precluded from the general franchise under the Constitution Act 1852 within that province. Hugh Francis Carleton, a member of the General Assembly for the Bay of Islands electorate until 1857 and the City of Auckland electorate in 1859, noted as late as 1858, with no discernible sense of unease, that 'the European settlers themselves succeeded in keeping the natives with a few exceptions, off the Electoral Roll'.[17] Carleton sympathized with Māori concerns, albeit from a Church Missionary Society perspective developed in northern New Zealand (the land claims of missionaries) and in alignment with the FitzRoy policy on the so-called waiver of pre-emption in 1844. Educated at Eton and Trinity College, Cambridge University, Carleton had studied law at the Middle Temple but refrained from practising.[18]

Thus, provinces and their people had their own tales to tell on the question of native title and the franchise. Divergences in interpretation and approach were noted between provinces, and between provinces and the general government of the colony. Although overseen by the Colonial Secretary's office based in Auckland, the registration of voters was primarily a local matter of implementation and interpretation, driven by registration officers in various electorates. In Taranaki, the provincial superintendent, Brown, reported in 1856 how 'many [Māori] asked the reason why they were not allowed to vote for the Superintendent'.[19] 'Maori enfranchisement', as the *Otago Witness* classed the issue in May 1853, arose where moves were undertaken to register electors, the concern being that large numbers of inappropriate individuals might be recruited as electors. In the South Island, a pressing issue was whether Māori communities dwelling within native reserves set aside under deeds of purchase had a sufficient proprietary interest

[16] The classic accounts on the franchise within the first decade following the New Zealand Constitution Act 1852 are to be found in Herron, 'The Structure and Course of New Zealand Politics, 1853–1858'; Herron, 'The Franchise and New Zealand Politics, 1853–8', 28–44; Herron, 'Provincialism and Centralism, 1853–1858' in Chapman and Sinclair (eds), *Studies of a Small Democracy*, 10–32. See also Atkinson, *Adventures in Democracy*.

[17] Carleton, 'Memorandum', CO209/150, fos.547–7a, NA.

[18] Hugh Francis Carleton, 1810–1890, in *The Dictionary of New Zealand Biography—Volume I, 1769–1869*, 70–1.

[19] Brown, 22 April 1856, evidence before the board of inquiry, 'New Zealand. Return to an address of the Honourable the House of Commons, dated 24 July 1860;—for, "copies or extracts of despatches from the Governor of New Zealand, relating to the management of native affairs and the purchase of native land, and the proposed establishment of a native council; and of the answers returned to such despatches by the Secretary of State", *GBPP1860* [2719], 284.

to qualify for the franchise. These reserves were not necessarily treated as identical to areas still subject to native title. Some reserves may have been construed as places still clothed with native title; that is, areas subject to pre-existing rights, excluded or preserved from the effect of deeds of purchase.[20] Others, such as the *residuum* of the New Zealand Company's so-called 'tenths reserves', were not necessarily viewed in such a way. Rather, they were seen by some (not uncontroversially) as areas to which native title had been extinguished but which were then effectively granted to Māori residents in the area purchased as reserves.[21] In this vein, Henry Sewell's journal entry for 4 April 1853 set out his view that the reserves could not possibly qualify, as they 'belonged to the Crown; and were vested in the Crown for the benefit of the Natives, just as if they were infants or lunatics, not having legal capacities'.[22] Sewell, colonial premier from 18 April 1856 until 20 May 1856, confided in his journal that the 'native interest in reserves' was not legal, 'for the legal interest [was] vested in the Crown which alone has the *jus possessionis* ['right of possession'], as well as the *jus dispositionis* ['right of disposition']'.[23] Nor did he consider that it was an equitable interest, as he doubted that a petition of right in a court exercising the equity jurisdiction of Chancery 'calling on the Crown to execute the legal estate in favo[u]r of the natives' would succeed.[24] The governor's stance by 1858 was subtle. He was familiar, as were others, with the conceptual neutrality of the language in section 7 of the imperial New Zealand Constitution Act. It did not expressly deny any entitlement to the electoral franchise on the basis of race. In speaking on the subject of the controversial Native Territorial Rights Bill and the Qualification of Electors Bill, the governor wrote to the native minister, Christopher Richmond, stating that 'I repeat that I shall regret to see natives possessing votes other than in exceptional cases but I cannot sanction a disqualification which has been so carefully avoided by the Imperial Parliament [in the drafting of the New Zealand Constitution Act]'.[25]

The Qualification of Electors Bill was introduced to the House of Representatives at the behest of responsible ministers in 1858. Clause 1 of the Bill stipulated 'that no estate, house, tenement, or hereditament, shall be deemed to confer a qualification as aforesaid unless the same be held or occupied by title derived from or through the

[20] This cannot be casually assumed, however, as the Court of Appeal (comprising Arney, the chief justice) in *Regina v Fitzherbert* (1872) 2 NZCA 143, 172–3, was of the view that '[f]rom and after the purchase of these lands by the [New Zealand Land] Company from the Natives, they became, by virtue of the alienation itself, part of the demesne lands of the Crown, insomuch that even if the purchase by the Company had been investigated by Commissioners under the Land Claims Ordinance No. 1, and the same had been approved, and the Commissioners had recommended grants or a grant to the Company accordingly, it would have remained at the discretion of the Crown to make or refuse such grant'. Sewell's comments in his journal appear to be aligned with this conclusion, at least insofar as the South Island is concerned.

[21] Depending on the words used in the deeds of purchase or conveyance, however, this view was not always correct or sustainable. A number of deeds, and the legally effective Crown grants deployed to give effect to them, appear to except from purchase various sites or a quantity of acres, which were excluded from the effect of the purchase (therefore remaining as areas of unextinguished native title). This was a matter of some complexity in the construction of deeds of purchase as to reservations and exceptions, as noted in the decision of Chief Justice Denman in *Doe v Lock* (1835) 2 Ad & El 705, 745; 111 ER 271, 287.

[22] Sewell, 4 April 1853, in McIntyre (ed), *The Journal of Henry Sewell 1853–7*, I, 229.

[23] Ibid. [24] Ibid.

[25] Browne to Richmond, 7 June [1858], in Scholefield (ed), *The Richmond-Atkinson Papers*, I, 407.

Crown'.[26] Although the Bill passed through the House of Representatives unscathed, the offending clause was removed in the upper chamber, the legislative council. The former Attorney General, Swainson, was cautiously but influentially critical: 'There was no man in the colony', he said, 'more averse than himself from the immediate and indiscriminate admission of the Natives, as a body, to the exercise of the elective franchise.' Yet he added, 'when the proceedings of the Assembly should become a matter of history he thought it would redound but little to their credit if, after obtaining a large measure of representative self-government, the very first act of the colonists in the exercise of their newly-acquired constituent powers was to deprive their Native fellow-subjects of the political privileges which had been conferred upon them by the British Parliament'.[27] Gilfillan objected to the clause 'not only on account of the disfranchisement of the Natives which it would effect, but also because it would similarly affect those Europeans whose land claims had not been settled'.[28] Whitaker, speaking from an Auckland perspective, observed that he wished to see the 'Native and the European... placed precisely in the same relation; but, if it were proposed to extend the franchise to Natives occupying lands over which their title had not previously been extinguished, he, for one, could not agree to it'. He explained how the population of Māori within the Auckland province outnumbered colonial settlers. To qualify Māori *in toto* as electors would be to 'create Native electors in the proportion of three or four to each European elector'.[29] The ministerialists within Stafford's government did not act in unison. Whitaker, the Attorney General, voted with Swainson and a majority in the legislative council in favour of expunging the closing words of clause 1. Whitaker averred again that he could 'see no valid reason why the Native should be favoured more than the European', and 'strongly objected to any measure which drew a distinction between the two races'.[30] The chief justice, Arney, was in the minority opposing the deletion of the paragraph.

This turn of events occasioned the lower chamber to adopt a resolution, proclaiming that:

> the New Zealand Government ought to endeavour to obtain an opinion from the Law Officers of the Imperial Government, on the subject of claims to vote, preferred by Aboriginal Natives under the seventh and forty second sections of the Constitution Act, whether natives can have such possession of any land that is used or occupied by them in common as tribes or communities, and not held under title derived from the Crown, as would qualify them to become voters under the provisions of the forecited sections.[31]

The responsible ministers, in reporting to the Colonial Secretary's office in Auckland on the fate of various statutory proposals in the legislative session, stated that, 'A great difference of opinion existed in the Legislature as to the amendment of the qualification of electors, and especially in reference to the extent to which the franchise should

[26] These words are extracted from the Clerk of the House's copy of the Qualification of Electors Bill appearing in LE1/16 1858/1, ANZ(W). See also the discussion in Browne to G Bulwer Lytton, 18 July 1859, CO209/150, fo.517a, TNA.

[27] Swainson, 29 July 1858, *New Zealand Parliamentary Debates—1858–1860*, 62.

[28] Ibid.

[29] Whitaker, 29 July 1858, ibid, 62.

[30] Ibid, 63.

[31] Carleton, 'Memorandum', CO209/150, fos.545–5a, TNA.

be enjoyed by the Aboriginal Native Population'.[32] The difference of viewpoints was characterized as 'irreconcilable', meaning that the resultant measure was compromised in that it embodied 'a few of the provisions of the Bill on which there was no difference of opinion, but which were calculated to meet some potential difficulties that had arisen'. A separate communication on the 'question relating to the natives' was anticipated.[33] Underlying the dispute was interpretative ambiguity. Provinces had dwelt with a sense of different interpretations for some years. Clarity can be politically costly, especially in circumstances where it is pragmatic for political leaders to avoid resolving ambiguities where collective action has effectively occurred on agreed outcomes in spite of discordant views as to the correct interpretation.[34] Ambiguity allowed provinces to hew their own pathways. Nevertheless, clause 1 represented a desire on the part of certain politicians, such as Hugh Carleton from the province of Auckland, to clarify the matter through statutory action and to generalize the clarification to all provinces. In an extensive memorandum supporting the reference to the law officers of the Crown in England, therefore, the following sentiments were conveyed:

> It is unnecessary for the purpose of this memorandum, to enter into the legal question, whether land held in common by tribal tenure and not in severalty can confer a qualification under the Constitution Act. It suffices that there is a doubt, and that the restriction imposed by the before cited clause was introduced by the Government for the purpose of placing the question beyond a doubt.[35]

Two prominent strains of concern and argument converged. First, advocates for clarifying the relevance of native title to the franchise qualification through statutory means claimed that Māori so qualified would be prone to the political machinations of the governor or other representatives inclined to purchase support. This was presented as an argument against despotism, a point to which Carleton proved to be particularly alive. A memorandum prepared in support of a reference to the law officers averred that '[t]he practical result of a mixture of native men in the assembly would be to invest the Governor with almost despotic authority notwithstanding responsible government'.[36] The rationale for this proposition was presented in terms of the particular constitutional place of the governor relative to managing and negotiating Crown–Māori relations: '[The governor's] influence with the native members in the House would be paramount', it was assumed, 'because of the large powers retained by him in the management of native affairs'. Through use of the civil list monies for native purposes guaranteed to him under the New Zealand Constitution Act, the governor could, '[b]y means of the votes of the native members, . . . oust any ministry that differs from him in opinion, and replace them by such as, for the name of office, might be willing to obey'.[37]

[32] Responsible advisors of the Crown to the Colonial Secretary's Office, Auckland, 9 October 1858, CO209/147, fos.94–4a, TNA.

[33] Ibid, fo.94a.

[34] On the utilities of ambiguity and vagueness, see Sunstein, 'Leaving Things Undecided', 4–101; March and Olsen, *Ambiguity and Choice in Organizations*; Goodin, *Political Theory and Public Policy*, ch 4.

[35] Carleton, 'Memorandum', CO209/150, fo.546, TNA.

[36] Ibid, fos.552a–3.

[37] Ibid, fo.553.

In this fashion, the civil list for 'native purposes' established under section 66 of the Constitution Act and amounting to £7,000 was seen as a source of discretionary and arbitrary patronage for the governor.[38] Applying funds from the guaranteed civil list sum would ensure the independence of the governor but at the cost of introducing placemen to representative institutions: 'In New Zealand we are aware that we have to deal with a race whose point of honor consists in receiving payments, as ours in refusing them'.[39] Carleton insisted that his motives were not driven by any dissatisfaction with the governor retaining pre-eminence in Crown–Māori relations as per the compact of 1856: 'The object of these remarks is merely to shew [*sic*] the absolute incompatibility of his retainment of that power with the election of natives to the House of Representatives'.[40] Secondly, a decided preference for Crown-derived proprietary interests to form the basis for electoral qualifications was also aired. Accepting Crown grants was seen, without any analysis, as importing an additional demonstration of loyalty to the Crown: 'a native who accepts a Crown title does actually feel himself bound to render true allegiance to the British Crown'.[41]

The observation that there was no abstract right or entitlement to vote as a given inhering in British subjects was also noted. Carleton stated, 'It would seem scarcely necessary to refute in argument, which has never the less been seriously adduced, that the natives, being British subjects have a natural or inherent right to vote even though unable to exercise that privilege with advantage to the state'.[42] With reference to the electoral situation in the United Kingdom, he treated this position as readily rebuttable, noting, 'No such abstract right is acknowledged in the mother country; for if it were, manhood suffrage would be the logical consequence'.[43] Admitting native title as qualifying Māori electors would be to upset the balance of the constitutional setting, tilting it considerably in favour of the governor's (and McLean's) system of political diplomacy with Māori chieftains and communities.

Carleton's arguments spoke to the balance of powers within the colonial constitution—a classical Whig position: not, as Carleton observed, a broad suffrage for the sake of it but rather a suffrage to which there was no abstract entitlement. This moderate interpretation from the liberal-whiggish spectrum of British political thought was transposed and adapted to peculiarly antipodean circumstances. There were no aristocratic social eminences within colonial New Zealand; certainly none to approximate with the Whig and Tory grandees in the United Kingdom. Indeed, the third Earl Grey thought that legislative councils as upper chambers could be unhelpful, implicitly denuding the lower, elected chambers of much-needed elite talent.[44] The hemmed-in territorial nature of early colonial bridgehead settlements, coupled with the absence of large-scale, heritage-family proprietors within colonial politics, meant that a Tory and

[38] The amount of £7,000 was set out in the schedule to the Constitution Act.

[39] Carleton, 'Memorandum', CO209/150, fo.548a, TNA.

[40] Ibid, fo.553. [41] Ibid, fo.550a. [42] Ibid, fos.548a–9. [43] Ibid, fo.549.

[44] Earl Grey, *The Colonial Policy of Lord John Russell's Administration*, II, 98: 'Legislative Councils composed of Members appointed by the Crown have, in general, had little real influence over public opinion, while they have been attended with the great disadvantage of rendering the Assembly less efficient, by withdrawing from the scene where their services might be most valuable, some of the persons best qualified, by the enjoyment of a certain degree of leisure, by their character and ability, to be useful members of the popular branch of the Legislature. The number of such men in the small circle of Colonial society is necessarily limited; hence it seems inexpedient that any of them should be taken away from the Assembly, which must always exercise the largest share of power and influence'.

Whig grandee approach to the constitutional significance of territorial patrimonial estates and the politics that went with them did not emerge.[45] Yet, what became the nominated legislative council under the New Zealand Constitution Act was favoured in debate in the House of Lords, for instance, owing to its relative imperviousness to the vicissitudes of public opinion. Thus, the Earl of Desart had defended it on that basis:

> What the Government wished to see in the colony of New Zealand, was not a system similar to the House of Lords—for that was impossible, and he might add Utopian—but they aimed at creating something analogous to the House of Lords; for he considered the great benefit they derived from that institution was, that they had a legislative body with certain powers, which were not liable to be affected by the influence of popular feeling.[46]

Desart 'thought they could constitute a body in the colonies, which, not being elective, would not be subject to be influenced by popular feeling, which might be transitory'. A balanced representation of interests or forces within the disparate colonial political communities was sought—a property-based franchise yielding general and provincial level representatives, nominated members of a legislative council in a General Assembly, elected provincial superintendents, and a governor. Such balance between these constitutional actors could only be preserved through a measured, gradualist incorporation of Māori. The implications of anything other than that would be liable to allow the power of mere numbers to engross the colonial settlements, particularly when combined with the ability of the governor to distribute monies and places from the civil list for 'native purposes'. Swainson's arguments were in favour of ongoing concealment and allowing ambiguity or vagueness as to who was entitled to exercise the franchise to persist.

Failure in the legislative council prompted resort to the Colonial Office, revealing once more not only the varied and potentially lengthy life cycles of policy issues but also the diverse range of politically relevant sources of opinion in an imperial framework. Through the guiding hand of Christopher Richmond, ministers within Stafford's government pointed out, by way of contrast, 'that in the Imperial Act 9 & 10 Vic: c.103 (called Lord Grey's Constitution of 1846) there is clear indication of an intention to exclude this kind of franchise which does not exist in the Act of 1852 [adding that]—Under the Act of 1846, the electoral or municipal districts are confined to "such parts of the islands as are or shall be owned, or lawfully occupied by persons of European birth or origin"'.[47] Furthermore, '[p]ersons are also disqualified who "are not able to read and write in the English language", which is the condition of almost the whole native population at the present time'.[48] The debate on Māori qualification for the electoral franchise under the imperial constitutional framework demonstrated a thickening discussion of native title and its content. Contributing to this debate was a resort not

[45] This early pattern converges with Boast's remarks in *Buying the Land*.

[46] Earl of Desart, *HPD*, 3rd series, 25 June 1852, vol 122, col 1286. See also the Earl of Derby, ibid, col 1287: 'He quite agreed with the noble Earl (the Earl of Harrowby) that it was important to have property represented as well as population; and that was precisely what would be done in New Zealand under this Bill—for the Governor of New Zealand would depart from his duty to the State if he did not take care that the members who were nominated to the Upper Chamber were *men of large property and of respectability and standing*, and who had a large stake in the colony of New Zealand' (emphasis added).

[47] 'Case for opinion of Law Officers of the Crown', CO209/150, fos.533a–4, TNA.

[48] Ibid, fo.534.

simply to legalistic genres but to musings on information regarding the nature of Māori dwellings and whether these comported with concepts of, say, 'a *Tenement* within the Limits of a Town (to be proclaimed as such by the Governor for the purposes of this Act) of the clear annual Value of Ten Pounds, or without the Limits of a Town of the clear annual Value of Five Pounds'. The ministers themselves observed how economic tangibles shaped behaviour on the ground despite the risks of illegality according to the colonial legal system. They noted therefore how '[i]n point of fact notwithstanding the Native Land Purchase Ordinance [1846] many European settlers have located themselves on native lands in various parts of the colony under arrangements in the nature of lettings—Those persons occupy as tenants and (in some cases, but rarely) pay rent—subject of course to the risk of the Native Land Purchase Ordinance being enforced against them—but practically undisturbed'.[49] Their memorandum admitted that the 'rent and value of holdings is in many instances no doubt sufficient in amount to be the basis of qualification if the land were held under ordinary English tenure'. But, the paper continued, 'whether in the eye of the law land so held can be regarded as of value, ie marketable value, to satisfy the requirements of the Constitution Act seems to depend in some degree on the effect of the local ordinances referred to—in particular, of the Native Land Purchase Ordinance, which renders all dealings with natives for land illegal, and subjects the parties so dealing to penalties'.[50]

A memorandum on the domiciliary habits of Māori accompanied the report of the governor's responsible ministers in support of the Qualification of Electors Bill. What was emphasized in this account was the lack of fixity in the residences of Māori: 'Rude temporary huts constructed in a few hours with rough poles cut from the forest, and thatched with *toetoe* a species of grass, and the sides covered with *raupo* or bulrush, are the domiciles of the common people, whose migratory disposition and indifference to the comforts of life lead them to regard the labor of erecting a substantial and roomy house as superfluity'.[51] Even the more substantial dwellings located within *pā* or fortified sites were presented as communal. The extent to which the jurisdiction of the colonial courts was adapted to addressing questions of native titles in land *inter se* arose. The responsible ministers in Stafford's ministry noted, under the authorship of the colonial treasurer, Christopher William Richmond, that 'No case has occurred in which the Supreme Court of the colony has assumed jurisdiction where the native title or right of occupancy was in question *between* natives'.[52]

Governor Browne called on the former chief justice, Martin, to offer an opinion on the interpretation of section 7 of the Constitution Act. In doing so, however, Browne found his own preferred interpretation to be unseated. Prior to receiving Martin's memorandum, Browne considered 'that a native residing within the limits of a British settlement; or in a district proclaimed to be under the Native Districts Regulation Act and possessing any one of the following qualifications should be entitled to the franchise and would probably use it quite as well as many Europeans who exercise it without question and not infrequently abuse it'.[53] The qualifications to which Browne alluded

[49] 'Case for opinion of Law Officers of the Crown', CO209/150, fo.533, TNA.
[50] Ibid, fos.533–3a.
[51] 'Note on dwellings of New Zealanders', 23 June 1859, CO209/150, fo.542, TNA.
[52] 'Case for opinion of Law Officers of the Crown', CO209/150, fo.534, TNA (emphasis added).
[53] Browne to G Bulwer Lytton, 18 July 1859, CO209/150, fos.522–2a, TNA.

were unrelated to anything in section 7 of the Constitution Act, representing at best an administrator's sense of how statutory clauses might be interpreted practically on the ground. Thus, Browne set out three qualifications: first, the 'use and occupation of land not less than (say five) and fenced'; secondly, the 'habitual occupation of a house with a chimney and a portion of land not less than a quarter of an acre fenced'; and, thirdly, the 'possession of an acre of land under a Crown title'.[54]

Martin's legal conclusions confounded Browne's expectations. Martin noted the three classes of qualifying property status for the electoral franchise: first, 'a freehold estate in possession of a certain value'; secondly, 'a leasehold estate in possession of a certain annual value'; or, thirdly, 'being a householder occupying a tenement of a certain annual value'.[55] In focusing on native title as communal or tribal rather than individually held, Martin's opinion despatched the idea of Māori qualifying under the fee simple estate criterion swiftly. He considered that 'If the ***native tribal ownership*** were held to be equivalent for these purposes to the freehold tenure of our law, & if our politicians were to act largely upon such a view, the consequences would be very mischievous'.[56] He foresaw that a 'great number of wholly unfit persons would be added to the list of Electors & the natives would be exposed to the wholesale action of the most corrupting influences'. Turning to the question of the household qualification, however, Martin saw no such negative consequences attaching to it. He apprehended the 'number admitted under such a qualification [to be] small'. Moreover, to Martin, qualification under the household franchise suggested civilizational progress: 'the fact that a man has abandoned the gregarious habits of the *pa*, & set up for himself & his family a separate house, is in itself one of the best evidences of his advancement in civilization'.[57] For that reason, he presumed, 'the Resolution of the House of Representatives (19 August 1858) makes no reference to any form of qualification, except such as may be supposed to arise from "possession of any land that is occupied by them in common as tribes or communities, & not held under title derived from the Crown"'.[58] This debate regarding native title and the electoral franchise under the imperial New Zealand Constitution Act reached Britain in 1859. Merivale incorrectly thought it to be a 'subject... of such interest, but diminishing importance, as the Europeans are so rapidly outnumbering the natives'.[59] The demographics of British settlement would render the political vulnerability of the European electorates to swamping by Māori increasingly irrelevant.

The formal legal response from London, however, would be to assert conceptual incommensurability between native title and English real property law concepts of freehold, leasehold, and tenement, rendering the closing paragraph of clause 1 of the Qualification of Electors Bill unnecessary at law. In addition, it proclaimed the non-justiciability of native title in the ordinary colonial courts (the Supreme Court particularly), a conclusion to be taken up subsequently in 1860 and 1863 by William Martin. In practice, then, we see three strategies for analysing the place of native title within the colonial legal system, within the jurisprudence of empire: non-justiciability, conceptual incommensurability, and jurisdictional incommensurability. All three yielded a similar practical result in legal-policy terms, namely a recommendation (eventually) in

[54] Ibid, fo.522a.
[55] 'Memorandum by the late Chief Justice Martin', 12 July 1859, CO209/150, fo.555, TNA.
[56] Ibid, fos.555–6 (emphasis added). [57] Ibid, fo.556. [58] Ibid, fo.556a.
[59] Merivale, 21 October 1859, CO209/150, fo.524, TNA.

favour of using legislative resources to craft statutory portals of recognition and statutory tribunals or courts able to cope institutionally and conceptually with native title. Nonetheless, conceptual incommensurability suggested that the common law was not as accommodating a recognition tool for native title or customary norms regarding Māori territorial claims as some scholars may have thought.[60]

For Richard Bethell and Henry Keating, the law officers of the imperial Crown in England, the starting premise was whether the proprietary interests of Māori were 'such a holding, habitation and occupancy that English law would take cognizance of and protect'.[61] Bethell became solicitor-general in 1852 and received a knighthood, and in 1856 he was made Attorney General.[62] Keating, a Queen's counsel since 1849, was appointed solicitor-general in May 1857, and knighted; he lost the position on Palmerston's resignation in the following February, but regained it in June 1859 when Palmerston again became Prime Minister.[63] The question to be addressed for their opinion was '[w]hether natives can have such possession of any land, that is used or occupied by them in common as tribes or communities, and not held under title derived from the Crown, as would qualify them to become voters under the provisions of the 7th and 42nd sections of the Constitution Act of New Zealand, that is the 15th and 16th Victoria c72'.[64] Section 42 of the Constitution Act provided that members of the House of Representatives were to be electors within an electoral district meeting the requisite qualifications for exercising the electoral franchise. Regretting the relative absence of information from New Zealand as to the underlying practical context for the question, the law officers assumed it to be as follows:

> The electoral districts, which have been constituted in New Zealand under the 41st section of the Constitution Act do in many instances comprise within their limits or boundaries... and districts which still belong to and are occupied by the aborigines and have never been ceded to the Crown of Great Britain and a question has arisen whether the ownership or occupation of such lands by natives under native authority can confer the electoral franchise.[65]

The law officers concluded that conceptual incommensurability existed. The legal concepts of English real property law used in section 7 of the Constitution Act and the concept of native title simply did not speak to each other. 'Now', the law officers said, 'whatever may be the nature of the ownership of these lands by the natives, it is clear that in the first place... it cannot be described by the terms "Freehold Estate" or the term "Leasehold Estate".' Bethell and Keating averred '[t]hese words [to be] terms of art in English Law, and plainly presuppose the existence and establishment of the English law of tenure in any place to which they can be considered applicable'. To them, it was 'plain that such native ownership or possession cannot be denominated either freehold

60 I address this issue broadly and in relation to the 1840s in Hickford, 'Law and Politics'.

61 Bethell and Keating to Newcastle, 7 December 1859, CO209/152, fo.290a, TNA. Bethell (1800–1873) would ultimately become Lord Westbury (and would also become Lord Chancellor). For a brief account of Bethell as solicitor-general (he was appointed in 1852), see Edwards, *The Law Officers of the Crown*, 48. Henry Keating (1804–1888) was solicitor-general from May 1857 to February 1858, and again in June 1859, during the two administrations of Viscount Palmerston.

62 Cocks, 'Bethell, Richard, first Baron Westbury (1800–1873)', in *Oxford Dictionary of National Biography*.

63 Hedley, 'Keating, Sir Henry Singer (1804–1888)', in *Oxford Dictionary of National Biography*.

64 Bethell and Keating to Newcastle, 7 December 1859, CO209/152, fos.288a–9, TNA.

65 Ibid, fos.289–9a (emphasis added).

or leasehold'.[66] Their opinion resonated with recognizing difference but without any attempt to use recourse to conceptual analogies in order to bridge the perceived cultural and conceptual incommensurability between concepts of English tenurial estates, on the one hand, and native title. That is, native title was not analogized with proprietary estates or interests already comprehensible within English real property jurisprudence, such as usufructuary rights or qualified terms of freehold (qualified in the sense of these being, say, restrictions on the ability to alienate to any parties other than the Crown). Having addressed these two elements underpinning qualification for the electoral franchise, the law officers supposed 'the chief difficulty [to arise] under the third head of electoral qualification, which is, the being a "household within an electoral district, occupying a tenement within the limits of a town (duly proclaimed) of the clear annual value of ten pounds, or without the limits of a town of the clear annual value of five pounds, and having resided therein six calendar months before registration".' Noting the limitation imposed by the words 'within the limits of a town' in respect of the first limb of the householder qualification, Bethell and Keating opined: 'First we presume the question can never arise as to tenements within the proclaimed limits of a town—No native land can be supposed to be within such limits'. As to households beyond the limits of a township having the clear annual value of £5, Bethell and Keating observed once more how 'all the terms of description are taken out of the vocabulary of English law, which is assumed by the Act to be applicable to the subject of which it speaks'; that is, the 'Elector must be a householder, and the occupier of a tenement'. In other words, 'these must be such a holding, habitation and occupancy that English law would take cognizance of and protect'.

Strictly speaking, such a conclusion was uncontroversial, as native title was not necessarily to be regarded as falling within a system of English tenure but as a proprietary interest acknowledged to exist by English law albeit sourced elsewhere. To speak of 'tenure' was not necessarily proper when analysing customary interests, as the use of tenure is ordinarily taken to imply the doctrine of tenures and the hierarchically tiered tenurial regime of land-holding either mediately or immediately of the Crown.[67] Yet there was nothing in section 7 of the Constitution Act, the law officers insisted, that contemplated 'many persons promiscuously using one common habitation', for instance. Fundamentally, the only form of occupancy recognizable was that in severalty only and 'such as is known to English law'. To demonstrate their underlying point, the law officers posed a query:

> But suppose in a district of native land, lying within the limits of an electoral district, that one native by consent of the rest is permitted to have exclusive possession of a piece of land, on which he builds a native hut for his habitation, but is afterwards turned out, or trespassed on by another native; could he bring an action of ejectment or trespass in the Queen's Court in New Zealand? Does the Queen's Court exercise any jurisdiction over real property in a native district?[68]

By way of answer, they presumed that 'these questions must be answered in the negative, and that it must of necessity therefore follow that the subject of householding occupancy and tenement, and their value in native districts, are not matters capable of being recognized, ascertained, or regulated by English law'.[69]

[66] Ibid, fos.289a–90.

[67] This remains an important conceptual issue, for instance, as the category of 'Māori customary land' under Te Ture Whenua Māori Act 1993 (NZ) is not necessarily consistent with this sort of technical approach to the doctrine of tenure: see Hickford, '"This Intricate Question"', 2, note 4.

[68] Bethell and Keating to Newcastle, 7 December 1859, CO209/152, fos.290a–1, TNA.

[69] Ibid, fo.291.

Subsequently, some 21 years later in 1880, legal strategies were gathered to address this question, as in the use of the Statutes of Forcible Entry of the English Parliament (1381–1429), a point that Brookfield has noted, although with a view to demonstrating how Māori autonomy could not have been regarded as anything other than *de facto*.[70] At that stage, the Court of Appeal in *R v Niramoana* (determined on 31 May 1880) treated the *de jure* jurisdiction of the Crown as sufficiently nested or embedded in practice. Justice Johnston, for one, in a reported exchange with counsel in *Niramoana*, stated how the 'Queen's writ runs *de jure* over every part of the colony'.[71] By that time, colonial institutions were projected much more effectively into Māori territories. The material presence of courts and the coercive arm of the state had dramatically changed from the tentativeness and experimental forays of the 1850s. The judge bolstered his sense of the efficacy of the 'Queen's writ' in 1880 through reference to the criminal jurisdiction of the ordinary courts—a key indicator of the visibility of an embedded rather than the merely aspiring efficacy of colonial or settler jurisdiction (as Lisa Ford has argued).[72] Justice Johnston dealt with the issue as primarily one of jurisdiction: 'The house was on land which could not ordinarily be held by private individuals under English title; but the land was *within the Queen's dominions*, and persons living there are *within the Queen's peace*, and any breach of the Queen's peace is to be punished there as elsewhere'.[73] In *Niramoana*, an indictment had been brought for forcible entry at common law. The five defendants were Māori. They had been convicted of forcible entry before Justice Richmond in the circuit court held in Auckland, with the judge imposing a fine of £10 upon each of the defendants subject to conviction being affirmed by the Court of Appeal. The identified defendants, in conjunction with others not brought before the court, had entered a wooden inn or public house at Ohinemutu in the possession of Isaac Wilson and, according to the indictment, 'with sticks stocks staves and other offensive weapons unlawfully violently forcibly injuriously and with a strong hand' expelled Wilson from the building. The chief justice, James Prendergast, concluded that the 'mere fact of the native title not [having been] extinguished does not afford ground for quashing the conviction'.[74] The difficulty historiographically is whether this subsequent development ought to be treated as enfolding the situation obtaining more than two decades earlier in the 1850s when the question of embedded, as opposed to overall supervisory, jurisdiction was still a matter of serious dispute or tentativeness at least within anglophone juristic and political circles. That is, it is one thing to identify a court decision as reflecting an underlying *Ur*-principle as to the breadth and content of how a legal doctrine may have been approached or understood at the time of its argument and decision. Yet, historical dynamism is such that it cannot be assumed that an approach in, say, 1880 necessarily or readily reflects what a similarly constituted court may have determined in differing circumstances two decades previously. If anything, it may reveal the degree to which change may be witnessed in the doctrinal proclivities of a particular jurist or the alteration of applicable circumstances in the

[70] Brookfield, *Waitangi and Indigenous Rights*, 148.

[71] *R v Niramoana* (1880) Olivier, Bell and Fitzgerald's New Zealand Law Reports 78 (New Zealand Court of Appeal).

[72] Ibid. Ford, *Settler Sovereignty*, 181–2; Ford, 'Before Settler Sovereignty and After Aboriginal Sovereignty', in Attwood and Griffiths (eds), *Frontier, Race, Nation*, 185–205.

[73] *R v Niramoana*, 80 (emphasis added).

[74] Ibid, 79.

colony. It remains critical, therefore, to examine the concrete reception of sources and understandings at particular times with sensitivity to the particularities of those times and circumstances.

In the Bethell and Keating law officers' opinion of December 1859, the question was fundamentally treated as one of jurisdiction, but their collective sense of jurisdictional incommensurability interacted with conceptual incommensurability as a key driver: 'it seems to us to be clear that no electoral title can be conferred by the statute, except in respect of property *known by that law* [English law] and *within the pale of its jurisdiction*'.[75] The conclusion was accordingly pronounced:

> we therefore think that the electoral franchise as conferred by the Constitution Act (sections 7 and 42) is constituted by the ownership tenancy or occupation of such lands and tenements only as are holden under a Crown title;—and in direct answer to the questions put to us, we are of opinion that natives cannot have such possession of any land, used or occupied by them in common as tribes or communities, and not held under title derived from the Crown, as would qualify them to become voters under the provisions of the 7th and 42nd sections of the 15th and 16th Victoria c.72.[76]

This opinion, unexpectedly stark in its conclusions in colonial political circumstances adapted to supposed interpretative ambiguity, prompted differing responses.

The political significance of native title was further heightened by the stance of the Supreme Court bench as to the procedural and evidential amenability of questions of native title to consideration within the jurisdiction of that court. In May 1861 the then chief justice, George Arney, and the other two justices of the Supreme Court bench, Alexander Johnston and Henry Gresson, appeared to consider simply that 'the constitution and mode of procedure of the Supreme Court as it exists at present are not well adapted for the investigation and determination of questions relating to Native Title *generally*'.[77] They were responding to two queries posed by Governor Browne, specifically whether the 'constitution and mode of the Supreme Court can be adapted for the investigation and determination of questions relating to Native Title', and, secondly, whether 'an efficient Court could be established for such purpose, and what should be the nature of its constitution and procedure'.[78] Familiar with *Symonds* in 1847, the judges acknowledged that the procedure and constitution of the Supreme Court could, nevertheless, 'be sufficient for the purpose when such questions arise incidentally in the course of other proceedings'.[79]

Arney and his fellow judges did not go so far as to suggest that native title was not cognizable in the Supreme Court in every circumstance. Rather, they suggested a jurisdictional incommensurability, and then only *sotto voce*. Indeed, to say in May 1861 that the constitution and procedural *modus operandi* of the Supreme Court were not 'well adapted' to investigating and determining questions 'relating to Native Title *generally*', implied a softer, less determinative view of the question than that expressed by the law officers of the Crown in England on the electoral franchise issue. They were stronger,

[75] Bethell and Keating to Newcastle, 7 December 1859, CO209/152, fos.291–1a, TNA (emphasis added).

[76] Ibid, fo.291a.

[77] Arney, Johnston, and Gresson to Browne, 9 May 1861, *AJHR—1861*, E-3, 13 (emphasis in original).

[78] Browne to Arney, Johnston and Gresson, 6 May 1861, *AJHR—1861*, E-3, 13.

[79] Arney, Johnston, and Gresson to Browne, 9 May 1861, *AJHR—1861*, E-3, 13.

however, in their view as to what could conceivably be done in the near future. 'We do not think', they wrote, 'the constitution and mode of procedure of the Supreme Court can be practically adapted so as to deal with the investigation of such questions *generally*, in a satisfactory manner, and without materially interfering with the efficiency of the Court in other respects'.[80] To explain further, the judges said:

> Even with the element of a Maori jury introduced, and the treatment of Maori Customs as matters of fact and not of law, we think that the system of pleading and procedure, and the law of evidence, which bind the Supreme Court could not be practically applied in such cases to the satisfaction and with the concurrence of particular litigants or the mass of the Native community; so that the Court would have to set aside the general law of New Zealand in those respects, in order to enable it to deal efficiently with the great mass of investigations of this kind.[81]

The bench of the Supreme Court did not recommend placing the court in such a position because 'the status and the organization of the Court would thereby be seriously affected'.[82]

On the second question, the judges did not doubt that 'an efficient Court' could be established for the purpose of investigating and determining questions of native title. Yet they refrained from offering any views on the 'precise nature, constitution, functions and procedure of such a tribunal', sensing that they did not 'possess sufficient materials, either respecting the requirements of the Native Race, the policy of your Excellency's Government, or the means at its command'. The judges were also of the view that the question seemed so 'necessarily involved with political considerations, that it might be improper for us to give our opinion, as Judges, respecting matters more strictly within the duties of statesmen or politicians'.[83] Subject to those points, Arney, Johnston, and Gresson offered a number of suggestions, albeit spare and tentative:

> A competent tribunal might probably be established by the formation of a Land Jury, selected by lot or otherwise, from members of the various tribes in previously defined districts, nominated by such tribes as competent to act in that capacity, to be presided over by a European Officer or Commissioner (not being an Agent of the Crown for the purchase of land)[84] conversant with the Maori language, and assisted if necessary by a Native Assessor.[85]

In a pre-eminently political constitution, legalistic genres could be deployed in sites other than courts. A powerful judicial and legal presence was also noticeable in the General Assembly's upper chamber, the legislative council. Arney had been appointed from 20 February 1858. Swainson, the former Attorney General, was also a member. Legal skills were certainly accessible and drawn upon, but so was experience in the field in the form of legal-policy advisors, such as Christopher Richmond, Francis Dart Fenton, and the non-lawyer but practised negotiator, Donald McLean, who positioned himself as a pre-eminent authority in matters to do with extinguishing native title through purchase transactions.

Despite the legal scaffolding of the Constitution Act, there was no emergence of constitutional cultures whereby the ordinary colonial courts (the Supreme Court)

80 Ibid (emphasis in original). 81 Ibid. 82 Ibid. 83 Ibid.

84 Here the judges were mindful no doubt of the recent disputes around the Waitara purchase in 1860, a situation canvassed fully in Chapter Seven.

85 Arney, Johnston, and Gresson to Browne, 9 May 1861, *AJHR—1861*, E-3, 13–14.

scrutinized the quality of political behaviour against the provisions of the colonial constitution. There was no outbreak of what might be called 'negative constitutionalism' whereby constitutional arrangements were envisaged as principally directed towards restraining state activities, often through legally enforceable means.[86] Native title, in being considered as not necessarily well suited to direct consideration in the courts, was not exceptional in this regard. The conceptual approach was one of relative institutional competence or function in the constitution, as well as constitutional comity between the various layers and branches of authority in the colonial constitution. In assessing the appropriate role for the courts, a number of judges considered the relative institutional competence of the courts when compared with legislatures, determining that political relations and accountabilities regarding revenue were best remedied politically. Fiscal impecuniosity was a feature of both provinces and the general government. Struggles for control of revenue in the provinces and attempts to discipline provincial superintendents consumed much attention within the scattered provinces themselves. One case illustrated the significance of legal opinion-making within the executive part of the colonial administration, as opposed to court decisions and judicial remedies, to discipline political activities. In that instance, 'a motion was made on the 2nd day of September 1858 on behalf of Mr E[dward] J[erningham] Wakefield, for an Injunction to restrain I[saac] E[arl] Featherston, as Superintendent of this Province [Wellington], from issuing any money to the public service'. Justice Gresson, presiding in the Supreme Court in the case of *Wakefield v Isaac Earl Featherston, Superintendent of Wellington Province*,[87] however, refused the application for an injunction, treating the matter as not appropriate for a legal remedy. In *Wakefield* the 'plaintiff moved for an Injunction to restrain the defendant from paying any money on account of public works or otherwise, on the grounds stated in the plaintiff's affidavit, viz., that no Appropriation Act had been passed by the Provincial Council of Wellington for the year 1858, although the Council had been sitting from March until September, 1858; and that the defendant nevertheless had lately paid a sum of £28 11*s* for Stationery furnished for the use of the Government since last July'. Gresson considered such an application 'wholly untenable'.

Justice Gresson observed that provincial legislation could have been used to discipline the superintendent and his officials but that the province had failed to do so. Thus, the 'Executive Government Act of the Province vests in the Superintendent, with the advice of his Executive Council, the entire administration of the Province'. He added, 'It might have imposed restrictions if it had thought fit to do so, but it has not'.[88] Section 1 of the Executive Government Act 1853 vested the 'entire Administration of the Provincial Executive Government…in the Superintendent alone acting by and with the advice of an Executive Council'.[89] The appropriate remedies were to be found in the legislature and not in the courts. 'In England', the judge stated, 'the remedy would be, in a case as nearly as possible analogous, not in the Courts at Westminster

86 Ivison, 'Pluralism and the Hobbesian Logic of Negative Constitutionalism', 83–99.

87 *Wakefield v Isaac Earl Featherston, Superintendent*, 23 September 1858, Supreme Court of New Zealand, Wellington (unreported).

88 *Wakefield v Isaac Earl Featherston, Superintendent of Wellington Province*, CO209/151, fo.407, TNA.

89 Executive Government Act 1853 ('An Act to establish an Executive Government for the Province of Wellington', 3 November 1853), Wellington, session I, number 1.

but by impeachment.' He concluded that '[h]ere too, I apprehend, the remedy is to be looked for from the Provincial Legislature'. The judge reasoned: 'The sole ground upon which I am asked to stop the whole machinery of the Government is that an Appropriation Act has not yet passed'. Yet, he said, '[i]f I were to grant this application the principle of the decision would oblige the Court, if an Appropriation Act had not been passed by the General Assembly, to stop the whole machinery of the Colonial Government'. Gresson observed that there was no allegation of fraud against the superintendent or of misappropriation of public monies for his own use. As such, it appeared to Gresson that the plaintiff had 'mistaken his course'. Nonetheless, the Supreme Court judge was sufficiently circumspect to say 'I carefully abstain from saying that in no case would this Court interfere by Injunction against a Superintendent who was misapplying public money: I merely say that in this case I see no grounds for granting an Injunction which would cause such monstrous inconvenience to the public'.[90]

The colonial Attorney General, Frederick Whitaker, advised the governor that 'neither the Constitution Act, nor the Acts of the General Assembly provide any remedy for the illegal expenditure of the Public Money by the Provincial Authorities, nor am I aware of any mode by which a Provincial Council can make the Superintendent of a Province and his Executive responsible for spending public money without authority'.[91] Nevertheless, where a provincial superintendent expended monies authorized by the General Assembly and paid to the provincial treasury, he stated that 'I am of opinion that the Superintendent of a Province is not invested with the power of spending at his discretion public money paid over under acts of the General Assembly to the Provincial Treasury and not appropriated by the Provincial Council'. In his legal view, 'Such a doctrine in my opinion is clearly both unconstitutional and contrary to law'.[92] As such, he regarded 'the recipients of this money [in the latter situation to be] accountants to the Crown;—[and] liable as such to render an account,—and are chargeable with any sums of money not expended under legal authority. They are answerable in the Supreme Court on the prosecution of the Attorney General'.[93] The broader background to the dispute inside the Wellington province concerned the provincial council passing a Public Money Control Bill, endeavouring to discipline the public finances in the hands of the executive government of the province, which the superintendent disallowed. Henry Tancred, the member for Canterbury in the legislative council, advised the speaker of the Wellington provincial council from the Colonial Secretary's office in Auckland: 'It is proper to observe that the existing remedies against illegal acts of the nature in question, as entailing consequences of undue severity, *appear ill suited to the present political constitution of the colony* and his Excellency's advisers therefore contemplate the proposal of measures in the General Assembly for adapting the law to the circumstances of the colony'.[94] The provincial council was discharged with the political responsibility to judge the conduct of the executive. Where unauthorized expenditure was involved, 'the Provincial Council is

[90] *Wakefield v Isaac Earl Featherston, Superintendent of Wellington Province*, CO209/151, fo.407, TNA.

[91] Whitaker to Browne, 7 October 1859, CO209/151, fos.427–7a, TNA.

[92] Ibid, fo.427a. [93] Ibid, fos.427a–8.

[94] Tancred to Speaker of the Provincial Council, Wellington, 8 October 1859, CO209/151, fos.431–1a, TNA (emphasis added).

the Constitutional Judge of the conduct of the Superintendent'. Thus, 'If the Council should approve of or acquiesce in the course taken by the Superintendent it will give effect to its decisions in his favo[u]r by making a retrospective appropriation covering the unauthorised expenditure'. Alternatively, the provincial council could 'refuse the indemnity which it alone can grant, leaving the Executive exposed to the liabilities incurred by an illegal expenditure of the public money'.[95] The issue made it into the Auckland press. The *Daily Southern Cross* rounded on the financial state of the provincial government of Auckland, urging a 'Public money control bill' to be passed similar to the one introduced in Wellington: 'If the Constitution Act (a point on which we are by no means clear) be insufficient to restrain Superintendents from disposing of the public revenue at pleasure, without the authority of the Council, a specific enactment ought to be passed, that we may at least have something tangible to refer to'.[96] It recommended legislation of the General Assembly to restrain executive expenditure: 'A bill to settle the doubtful point, for it appears to have been left in doubt by Mr Justice Gresson,—to supplement the incomplete clause [of the Constitution Act], ought to have been sent down long since by the Government to the General Assembly'.[97]

With representative institutions in place in the wake of the Constitution Act, statutes were available as legally expressed political resources to whosoever managed to obtain the confidence of the legislature and secure the assent of the governor or the royal assent in London. These resources were expanded and their possible sources multiplied. Colonial New Zealand was no longer merely a world of ordinances, imperial statutes enacted in Westminster, prerogative powers, the charter for the colony in 1840, royal instructions, and commissions.[98] Now that there were provincial councils and a representative General Assembly with competence to legislate, legislation was in the offing as an appropriately politically driven legal adaptation to a perceived remedial lacuna. Law-making powers were distributed throughout the colonial settlements. A sequence of steps was involved and lobbyists, to be effective, had to be familiar with these steps. Section 18 of the Constitution Act empowered 'the Superintendent of each Province with the Advice and Consent of the Provincial Council thereof, to make and ordain all such Laws and Ordinances (except and subject as herein-after mentioned) as may be required for the Peace, Order, and good Government of such Province, provided that the same be not repugnant to the Law of England'. It was not lawful for the provincial superintendents and councils to make laws in relation to a range of topics set out in section 19, including any affecting 'Lands of the Crown, or Lands to which the Title of the aboriginal native Owners has never been extinguished' (section 19(10) of the Constitution Act). Legislative supremacy within the geographical limits of the colony resided with the General Assembly by virtue of section 53 of the Constitution Act.[99] The General Assembly comprised the governor, the legislative council, and the

[95] Ibid, fos.429a–30.

[96] 'Raising the Wind', *Daily Southern Cross*, vol 16, issue 1257, 4 October 1859, 2.

[97] Ibid.

[98] See, eg Hickford, '"Settling some very important principle of Colonial Law"', 30.

[99] Section 53 of the Constitution Act provided: 'It shall be competent to the said General Assembly (except and subject as herein-after mentioned) to make Laws for the Peace, Order, and good Government of New Zealand, provided that no such Laws be repugnant to the Law of England; and the Laws so be made by the said General Assembly shall control and supersede any Laws or

House of Representatives (section 32 of the Constitution Act). Under section 56 of the Constitution Act, the governor was entitled to assent or refuse assent to bills. The discretion of the governor to assent was 'subject nevertheless to the Provisions contained in [the Constitution] Act and to such Instructions as may from Time to Time be given in that Behalf by Her Majesty, Her Heirs or Successors'. Alternatively, he could reserve a bill for 'the signification of Her Majesty's pleasure'. Even where a bill had been assented to, the bill was subject to disallowance at any time within two years of the Secretary of State receiving a copy of the bill.

Indeed, with the emergence of the post-Constitution Act institutions, the political marketplaces for argument and position throughout colonial New Zealand diversified and expanded. Pressures in some provinces were multiplying. Some provincial inhabitants used the alleged want of accessible territorial space for settlement and the obscurities of the occult negotiations of McLean and his network of officials as a basis for waging campaigns in order to pursue increased political influence relative to the governor and other provinces. Rival constitutional interpretations were also in play. In an orphaned letter in the Colonial Office archive, written on the very day the ministry of William Fox gave way to that of Edward Stafford, Browne characterized Fox and his coterie of sympathizers as 'American' in their constitutional predispositions:

> Mr Fox and his party (the upholders of American opinions) though few are united and able men: they consider the election of the Superintendents [of the provinces] to be "the apple of the eye of the Constitution" and it may be a question as to whether the present ministerial party though more numerous could hold their own against the activity of an united & determined ministry.[100]

Of the first three ministries in the colony's experience of responsible government in the 1850s, Stafford's was the most enduring and stable. His two predecessors experienced brief tenure. Sewell, conventionally regarded as the first colonial premier in this constitutional period, held the role from 18 April 1856 until 20 May 1856. William Fox, as Attorney General and holder of the first seat in the ministry, was premier from 20 May 1856 until 2 June 1856. Yet Stafford would lead his ministry for five years, with Fox reassuming the position of premier on 12 July 1861. At its beginning, Stafford's ministry comprised Christopher Richmond (the member in the House of Representatives for the town of New Plymouth electorate) as Colonial Secretary, Frederick Whitaker, as Attorney General (in the legislative council), Henry Sewell, as colonial treasurer until 4 November 1856 when Richmond assumed the Treasury role, a position Richmond largely held continuously until the fall of the ministry,[101] and John Logan Campbell, as a responsible minister without portfolio (representative for the city of Auckland electorate although he resigned on 24 November 1856).

Ordinances in anywise repugnant thereto which may have been made or ordained prior thereto by any Provincial Council; and any Law or Ordinance made or ordained by any Provincial Council in pursuance of the Authority hereby conferred upon it, and on any Subject whereon under such Authority as aforesaid it is entitled to legislate, shall, so far as the same is repugnant to or inconsistent with any Act passed by the General Assembly, be null and void.

[100] Browne to Merivale, 2 June 1856, CO209/159, fo.601, TNA.

[101] Sewell was designated colonial treasurer for a brief period from 25 February 1859 until 26 April 1859. In spite of his absence from New Zealand, Sewell was treated as a member of the executive council in the Stafford ministry from 4 November 1856 until 26 April 1859, at which point he assumed his independence from the ministry.

Jurisdictional incommensurability continued—a board of inquiry in 1856

Native title was undeniably tied to questions of jurisdiction. As we will see, this point was demonstrated not only in relation to the electoral franchise but also in the disallowance of the Native Territorial Rights Bill in London in 1859. It also emerged in the context of a board of inquiry into native title in 1856. Fittingly, Donald Loveridge has noted the degree to which Browne as governor 'displayed a marked predilection for tackling problems by collecting information and opinion *en masse*' throughout his tenure.[102] He evinced this quality early on with the commissioning of a board of inquiry into native title to be headed by the surveyor-general, Ligar.[103] In his letter to Merivale in London, Browne advised the Colonial Office of his intention to forward the material obtained by a commission (or board of inquiry) appointed to explore the native title question and land-acquisition policies as soon as it was assembled. After reflecting on matters of intra-European constitutional politics, Browne wrote that the 'native question causes me more uneasiness than anything connected with the Europeans'.[104] 'The pith of the matter', he advised, 'is that the natives are sufficiently advanced in civilization to watch our prosperity with great jealousy and alarm and to observe that they wax weak as we wax strong'.[105] Browne appreciated the undeniable significance of negotiation and diplomacy to Crown–Māori relations. Using illness as a metaphor, he explained how '[i]n every case of outrage or disturbance I have hitherto succeeded in obtaining redress and I hope to continue to do so but it has been by diplomacy and not as a recognized right: a chronic state of disease has been treated with anodyne but it may assume an aggravated form any day'.[106]

Governor Browne conceived the work of Ligar to be that of collecting 'a mass of evidence... containing the opinions of all the persons best acquainted with the subject'. Ligar was assisted by Nugent, recently the Native Secretary to Sir George Grey during the latter's first governorship in New Zealand, Thomas Smith, and William Crush Daldy, a member of the House of Representatives (City of Auckland electorate). Smith had been a resident magistrate based at Rotorua but was also acting Native Secretary at the time of the board of inquiry's investigations. Soon he was to become Assistant Native Secretary under Donald McLean. Daldy had been appointed as much for the value of the contrariness of his views as his experience. Browne considered it useful to have access to a diversity of opinion, noting that Daldy 'takes a different view in many cases from myself and my advisers'.[107] Browne posed a series of discrete questions concerning the 'present system of purchasing land from the natives', including whether 'Crown titles [could] be given to Maoris for land (not previously transferred to the Crown), with or without restriction that it cannot be sold or let to an European until after the grant has been in possession of the native proprietor for a given term of

[102] Loveridge, 'Origins of the Native Land Acts and Native Land Court in New Zealand', 48.

[103] CO209/138, TNA.

[104] Browne to Merivale, 2 June 1856, CO209/159, fo.601a, TNA.

[105] Ibid. [106] Ibid, fo.602.

[107] Browne to Labouchere, 23 July 1856, 'New Zealand. Return to an address of the Honourable the House of Commons, dated 24 July 1860;—for, "copies or extracts of despatches from the Governor of New Zealand, relating to the management of native affairs and the purchase of native land, and the proposed establishment of a native council; and of the answers returned to such despatches by the Secretary of State"', *GBPP1860* [2719], 235.

years'.[108] Tribal structures were seen as sources and focal points of Māori loyalty. They provided security for individuals sharing in the protective communal cloak of tribal title. Individuals would be loath to extricate themselves from tribal loyalties unless the benefits were clear: 'While they continue as communities to hold their land, they will always look to those communities for protection, rather than to the British laws and institutions, which, although brought so near, *does not embrace them in regard to their lands*'.[109] Native title, tied to the normative systems and control of tribal communities, proved to be an effective jurisdictional lever, setting apart such lands from 'British laws and institutions'.

Here, then, was a basis for an interpretation of native title as importing a concept of jurisdictional incommensurability rather than non-justiciability. Seeing jurisdictional incommensurability as the key to analysing the place of native title in the jurisprudence of empire was potentially a softer approach than one of non-justiciability in the colonial courts, although the two views could be blended in accounts in spite of their underlying conceptual distinctiveness. In this sense, it is important to appreciate that this jurisdictional incommensurability was not necessarily a radical form of incommensurability as envisaged by John Gray.[110] That is, the jurisdiction could be explicitly amended, with the assistance of legislation if required, in order to ensure or to clarify that the jurisdiction could be extended to the subject of native title. Certainly, it was possible to present the incommensurability as stark or as a radical form, admitting that it was inconceivable for the colonial courts to deal with native title questions. On a softer account, however, the Supreme Court could be seen as not ideally adapted to dealing with unresolved questions of native title procedurally. Legal and institutional techniques, particularly statutes giving rise to bespoke or specialized institutions able to bridge interpretative worlds, were seen as a possibility. As noted, incommensurability may be seen as conceptual or jurisdictional. Neither was mutually exclusive, as the Bethell and Keating opinion on the electoral franchise and native title made clear. Both could be seen to subsist and apply simultaneously. Each spoke to a particular dimension of incommensurability. But seeing incommensurability of whatever sort encouraged the politics of negotiability seen through the medium of sale and purchase. It also encouraged crafting law codes and building institutions with a view to bridging and translating seemingly incommensurable worlds, discovering meeting places and pathways. Hence, we see resident magistrates of varying competence and energy appointed under Governor Grey's Resident Magistrates Courts Ordinance 1846 and for eight areas, namely Waikato, Napier, New Plymouth, East Cape, Russell, Mangonui, Rotorua, and Whaingaroa (treated together), and Wanganui. As will be explored in the following section, their abilities to insinuate themselves in Māori politics were highly variable and not always welcome. Yet they formed a key part of the strategy to connect or intersect with Māori communities and ways of governing people and territorial spaces. Returns of expenditure on resident magistrates paid out of the civil list funds of £7,000 for the financial period from 1 July 1856 until 30 September 1857 gave a figure of

[108] Browne, memorandum, enclosed with Browne to Labouchere, 23 July 1856, *GBPP1860* [2719], 235.

[109] Report, board of inquiry, *GBPP1860* [2719], 237.

[110] Gray, *Enlightenment's Wake*, 104–6, 126.

£1,280.2.3.[111] This amount was spread across a number of individuals, including WB White, officially operative in the Mangonui area from 1 July 1856 until 30 June 1857 and who received £75; JR Clendon, who operated in the Russell (Bay of Islands) district from 1 July 1856 until 30 June 1857 and who received £200; Thomas Smith, who was paid £200 and was responsible for the Rotorua and Whaingaroa from 1 July 1856 until 20 February 1857, when he was succeeded by Francis Dart Fenton, who received £175 for the period from 20 February 1856 until 30 June 1857.

'They are all entangled or matted together'

Complexity governed. Everywhere one turned this complexity proved inescapable and unremitting: 'They are all entangled or matted together'—so said Riwai Te Ahu in explaining whether there were indeed individual claims to native title. He held that there were no such claims, all being subsumed within the interlocking and overlapping rights of the community.[112] Riwai Te Ahu, a Māori deacon of the Anglican Church, undoubtedly saw the gaming and politics underlying native title, behaviours that the colonial emphasis on a market in land had only exacerbated:[113] 'The natives mark off their boundaries, without reference to other tribes, who may dispute the boundary'.[114] In his evidence, Selwyn, the Bishop of New Zealand, ruminated on the practicable ease of identifying the sum total of claimants in respect of an area: 'They ['the New Zealanders as a body'] know the parties who claim the land; by care in taking down the names there will not be much difficulty'—a rather sanguine assessment. Yet, he admitted, there were, 'many properties which cannot be disentangled, as in some of our own titles to landed property, and these must be left as encumbered estates, which nobody would wish to buy'.[115] Local official experiences corroborated these narratives of mingling complexities. John Rogan, the district commissioner at New Plymouth in Taranaki in 1856, recorded how he had never met with any Māori whose individual title was sufficiently distinct for the purposes of purchase. He recounted the complexities of the negotiations at Mokau where he 'endeavoured to survey... into two parts, a piece of land of about 2,000 acres' on account of the land being 'claimed by two distinct sections of a tribe,—one favourable to the sale of land, and the other not'.[116] He met with failure: 'The whole of their claims were in such a state of confusion, that I found it impossible to effect a settlement of their respective boundaries'.[117] In conclusion, Rogan would only express comfort with giving Crown grants in circumstances where the 'whole tribe and the *neighbouring tribes* consented to the subdivision'.[118]

Beneath the heading 'Claims of Individual Natives to Land', the board explained that '[e]ach native has a right in common with the whole tribe over the disposal of the land of the tribe, and has an individual right to such portions as he or his parents

[111] Expenditure on resident magistrates referred to in a return accounting '[f]or the expenditure from the 1st July 1856 to the 30th September 1857 on account of civil list fund for the financial year ended 30th June 1857', CO209/152, fos.346–6a, TNA.

[112] Riwai Te Ahu, 10 April 1856, evidence to board of inquiry, *GBPP1860* [2719], 278.

[113] On Riwai Te Ahu generally, see Williams, *A Gift or a Grant? The Wi Parata Case in New Zealand Law and History*.

[114] Riwai Te Ahu, 10 April 1856, evidence to board of inquiry, *GBPP1860* [2719], 278.

[115] Selwyn, evidence to board of inquiry, *GBPP1860* [2719], 272.

[116] Rogan, April 1856, evidence to board of inquiry, *GBPP1860* [2719], 276.

[117] Ibid. [118] Ibid (emphasis added).

may have regularly used for cultivations, for dwellings, for gathering edible berries, for snaring birds and rats, or as pig runs'.[119] In general, the board concluded that 'there is no such thing as an individual claim clear and independent of the tribal right'.[120] The overall tenor of such remarks from a policy perspective was to further entrench and encourage the stance of treating all possible claimants the same, without ascertaining whether there was any distinction as to the status of those claimants in accordance with Māori norms. Yet this approach was arguably an innovation on account of the emphases on asset transfer in land. Lyndsay Head contends that it was the 'power to make decisions over land' that represented the 'Maori meaning of what is expressed in English as "land ownership"'.[121] The pre-eminence of chiefs in this sense was intimated in the recollections of a number of the witnesses before the board of inquiry, but these recollections were mixed with a sense of the transitional state ushered in through the land market. Hence, as Head explains, we see Wīremu Maihi (Te Rangikaheke) of the Te Arawa confederacy, supplying evidence to the board of inquiry to an increasingly challenged past and the transitions occurring subsequently:

> I had an individual claim... in my youth, to a block of land which may have contained from [ten] to 20,000 acres, but since then my individual right has been disputed. Formerly I could have sold it after talking to the natives, even against their consent, but I must have divided the proceeds of the sale, or they would have seized the land from the person to whom it had been sold.[122]

The report of the board argued that Crown grants supplied a sufficient security of tenure. The so-called 'unimproved', 'waste', or 'surplus' lands subject to native title—those not used for dwellings or cultivated sites, or not used regularly—would benefit passively from the increase in value of adjacent land fenced in by Europeans or used as roads. As the European settlement of these lands intensified, native title areas increased in value inexorably. 'It was well known', argued the board, 'that even among European settlers themselves an absentee proprietor, or one who leaves his land in a state of nature, reaps an advantage by the value given to it through the cultivation and improvement of the adjacent land.' Given this overall context, the board's preference was to obtain Māori consent to the alienation of unimproved lands to the Crown in return for 'individual natives' or 'heads of families' obtaining a Crown grant 'for such portions of land as may be *actually required for occupation*'.[123] No mechanism or policy device, whether legislative or otherwise, was prescribed or even suggested for inducing Māori to consent to such a course of action. All that may be garnered from the report is an implicit expectation that the willingness to engage with colonial administration in this particular way would be generated internally. Consent was sought. The vectors for this change would be endogenous—internal to the political and social fluidities of Māori communities—rather than exogenous. In these various foregoing senses, then, the presence of native title as a classification of status and as a proprietary interest represented a vital hinge and form of leverage in the politics (and economics) of negotiability. It continued to act as a mode of discipline upon the territorial aspirations of largely coastally bound colonial settlements.

[119] Report, board of inquiry, *GBPP1860* [2719], 237. [120] Ibid.

[121] Head, 'Land, Authority and the Forgetting of Being', 190.

[122] Maihi Te Rangikaheke, Board of Inquiry, *GBPP1860* [2719], 279. Head discusses this evidence and more in 'Land, Authority and the Forgetting of Being', 190 *et seq.*

[123] Report, Board of Inquiry, *GBPP1860* [2719], 238 (emphasis added).

To ease the transfer to Crown-derived titles, the board of inquiry report advised that 'it would be necessary that the native title to the piece of land should, as a preliminary step, be transferred to the Crown' before a Crown grant could be issued to an individual Māori.[124] Moreover, 'in order to prevent any claims being raised to the land, after it was granted, the same forms should be gone through as if the native title were about to be extinguished by a sale to the Crown for the purposes of resale to Europeans'. Yet, '[t]o give clear and undisputed titles to individual natives, would require mutual concessions on the part of the natives themselves, and the whole of the claimants to the land should be ascertained and be made parties to the transaction, and sign the transfer to the Crown'. Rather optimistically, the board of inquiry thought that there would then be 'no danger of any after claims'.[125] McLean, too, mindful of the interlocking complexities of North Island Māori politics, casually referred to a real distinction between Māori populations in the South Island and the North Island in September 1856. He recommended that a system to individualize Māori property in the South Island be trialled 'owing to the paucity of the native population, and the nature of their tenure'—that is, places where native title had been largely extinguished and Māori communities resided within reserves (some of which were sites of unextinguished native title while other communities were already on particular reserves treated as Crown land on the basis of prior purchases or Crown grants having extinguished any pre-existing native title).[126]

Finally, the board of inquiry report reflected a broader debate as to the political significance of native title and how to prise open native title. Should officials and institutions proceed first or should the policy of acquiring and transforming lands by purchase be pursued? Should a combination of techniques be deployed, including those of purchase and building institutions within districts where native title prevailed? An astute missionary observer based in the Whanganui region, Richard Taylor, reflected on this point in a London publication in 1855. In a chapter on 'native chiefs', he noted how *rangatira* might have been appointed 'assessor, and as such a right to sit with the [resident] magistrate; but even this hono[u]r is not intended to raise them'.[127] He added that it was 'only in purely native cases they are entitled to sit, those they are enticed to bring before the magistrate, in order to accustom them gradually to submit to British law', which, he said, merely applied 'nominally'.[128] How Taylor characterized the situation was meant as a criticism: government seldom resorted to chiefly elites as 'native assessors' by 1855 because of their perceived 'unfitness' and the parsimonious level of salaries. The focus of the board of inquiry report was directed towards obtaining Māori land by purchase. As Lyndsay Head expressed it, '[the board's] was not a disinterested investigation, but read the needs of the colony into custom by viewing custom through the urgent, narrow lens of land purchase'.[129] Issuing Crown grants was seen as one technique for making inroads into areas subject to native title. With the transformation of native title into a Crown-derived title, institutions and norms associated with real property law and general English law would follow. Or so it was assumed.

124 Ibid. 125 Ibid.

126 McLean, Chief Commissioner, memorandum, 4 September 1856, *GBPP1860* [2719], 395.

127 Taylor, *Te Ika a Maui, or New Zealand and its Inhabitants*, 274.

128 Ibid, 274 and 271 ('British law is nominally established in the land, but it is only nominally, and likely to be so for years, unless some measures are taken to obtain the co-operation of the native chiefs').

129 Head, 'Land, Authority and the Forgetting of Being', 118.

Yet the underlying difficulties of these forms of abstraction and a policy of purchase were alluded to in several of the witness statements before the board of inquiry. Bishop Selwyn advised the board of inquiry on the tactics that Māori resorted to in managing large groups of strangers. Although he did not say so explicitly these tactics would not be sustainable politically in the longer term as British settlements acquired access to greater financial and military resources. Thus, '[t]here is a great difference . . . between those who come "taketahi", one by one, and the "tokomaha" wholesale coming'.[130] This remark, reported Selwyn, was 'occasioned by my asking how it was that a certain European was left in undisturbed possession of his claim, while all those around him were subjected to constant annoyances'. Strangers who came 'one by one' could be incorporated within the hosting group or community. The levers of indigenous Māori political management were strained by larger forms of pākehā settlement. These recounted remarks resonated with the changes wrought by extensive and systematic European settlement—the movement of peoples across oceans. In its report, the board of inquiry stated: 'When the natives first came into contact with the Europeans in the relative position of sellers and buyers of land, the evidence of which before the Board extends as far back as the year 1822 [at least in the far north of New Zealand], it has been shown that the natives in disposing of their land intended only to convey a title similar to that that which they, as individuals, hold themselves;—the right of occupancy'.[131] Such Europeans were 'considered as one of the tribe, among whom he had cast his lot'.[132] The onset of organized settlement in numbers, however, prompted changes in approach. Whereas '[f]ormerly, to obtain a town in their neighbourhood, large tracts of land would have been ceded for such purposes, and for farms around it', a noticeable change in behaviour was occurring, as Māori communities adapted to the presence of larger numbers of strangers. 'Now natives', the board of inquiry reported, '[having found] that with their improved means of communication one or other of the various settlements affords a market not too remote for the sale of their produce, and that they can at these places purchase everything they require, think it is to their advantage to keep their large tracts of land, which the European settlements have enhanced in value'.[133] Such a sentiment, the board counselled, would continue to operate amongst Māori *hapū* for a time, although the board of inquiry's analysis was principally tied to behavioural economic incentives.

In principally trimming its analytical approach to such a way of seeing, the board failed to present the underlying constitutional and political significance of a gradual slowing of the pace and spatial extent of territorial acquisition by Crown purchase. Yet its report did acknowledge that it was 'known that almost every spot chronicles some well remembered tradition, and when they are asked to part with these places to strangers, who cannot be supposed to enter into their feelings on the subject, and whom they see destined at no very remote period to place them in a secondary position in their own country, it is no wonder they hesitate to take the step'.[134] Furthermore, rivalrous

[130] Selwyn, evidence to board of inquiry, *GBPP1860* [2719], 270.

[131] Report, Board of Inquiry, *GBPP1860*, [2719], 237. In fact, the initial deed dated from 1815.

[132] Ibid. [133] Ibid, 238.

[134] Ibid, 240. European analogies were also cited. Hence, the report stated, 'In old European countries attachments to hereditary property exist to such an extent, that very tempting offers would not induce some proprietors to part with what [has] long been associated with the history of previous generations' (ibid).

overlapping claims required delicate political management, both amongst colonial officials and within Māori political elites. Although the report was mistaken in assuming a simplistic bilateral possibility of contested claims, as multilateral *hapū* descent-group claims were most probable in many areas, it stated, '[A]s long as neither [Māori] party exercise any very decided act of ownership, are allowed to lie dormant, but which would be called forth and give rise to serious quarrels immediately it was understood that either party meditated a sale of the land so circumstanced'.[135] The presence of strangers operating a colonially driven market in territorial space, therefore, was seen as crystallizing otherwise congenially dormant sources of political dispute.

CONSTITUTIONAL CONDOMINIUM OR CONSOCIATION—RECONCEIVING CROWN–MĀORI RELATIONS IN COLONIAL NEW ZEALAND

A number of Māori communities were volunteers for and vectors of change but preferably on terms that could be negotiated and renegotiated episodically with incoming pākehā settlers together with the norms of behaviour, the intellectual sources, and the ways of seeing they brought with them. A local *rūnanga* at Te Hautōtara in the Wairarapa to the east of the Wellington settlement independently resolved a territorial dispute between the descendants of two ancestors while invoking the authority of the deity and the law of the Queen to sustain their judgment.[136] *Rūnanga* were indeed active, adapting a variety of indigenous and introduced strains of thought, either accepting the 'English system' or 'jurisdiction' or rejecting it 'merely as a matter of interest or convenience'.[137] Dynamism and the possibilities of novel commercial, familial, and political relations were not admitted on any terms. Influential leaders and sources within fluid Māori politics were conscious of needing to manage both anticipated and unanticipated change and its risks. In an important analytical study, Brookfield has suggestively spoken of an intensifyingly effective normative and practical 'revolution' wrought through introducing British legal norms to Māori-governed or dominated New Zealand during the course of the nineteenth century.[138] But it was an intermittent Kelsenesque 'revolution' occurring in a variety of localized places at different times, requiring a sensitivity to variations across time and place. Certain affiliates of the Kīngitanga interpreted their movement as an experimental exercise in parallel government, of that there can be little doubt:

> I have taken away half of the property of those Pakeha's [*sic*] who are living without payment on the King's land, half is to be for the Pakehas, and half for the King. If the Pakeha's [*sic*] do not divide their property, they shall be sent back on to the Queen's land. Enough of that word.[139]

In effect, a constitutional condominium or consociation (with divided decision-making autonomies and are at mutual or shared influence) was envisaged—embracing a set of polyvalent sites of authority and parallel governments in the North Island

135 Ibid.
136 *Te Karere o Poneke*, 30 August 1858, 3–4.
137 Hanson, 20 November 1861, *AJHR-1862*, E-5a, 7.
138 Brookfield, *Waitangi and Indigenous Rights*, 2nd edn, 108–35.
139 Te Tapihana [teacher at Kawhia] to Browne, 16 October 1858, CO209/150, fos.25–5a, TNA.

with each Māori community having its relationship with the representatives of the imperial monarch from across the seas interpreted in ways particular to that relationship. Chiefly elites dealt with the officers of colonial administration as an increasingly familiar but still relatively alien or novel power or source of influence. This introduced administration could be seen as a potential or actual competitor for authority in respect of peoples, territorial space, and natural resources. But it could also be seen as a deliverer of other benefits albeit with undoubted political risks to the incumbent indigenous elites, as these officials carried different interpretative expectations and understandings with them. The term 'condominium' itself resonated with Rusden's characterization of the relations between governors and colonial ministries, as Cadogan has observed.[140] Chiefly figures in the eastern reaches of the North Island, such as Te Hāpuku of Ngāti Te Whatuiāpiti based near Te Mahia (albeit aligned also with Ngāti Kahungunu), represented one interpretation of this relationship. Te Hāpuku controversially presented himself as able to command the transfer of spaces to the settlements—to act as a pre-eminent purveyor of land and natural resources to European newcomers. His preferred technique was selling land, as well as his ability to insist on not selling it. Both were presented as demonstrations of authority. He tactically positioned himself as a particular sort of congenial ally and mediator, able to introduce colonial resources to his areas of activity and able to elevate his own political placement relative to other aspiring leaders such as Te Ropiha through direct correspondence with colonial officials.[141] Similarly, the female *ariki* Hineipaketia and Hōri Niania Te Aroatua also exhibited this tendency. Civil strife and warring erupted in Hawke's Bay as a result of these practices in 1856 and 1857, as opponents of such tactics plied different interpretations of how to interact with bridgehead pākehā settlements.[142]

The emergent Kīngitanga represented another such interpretation. A central theme of withholding lands from sale amongst Kīngitanga affiliates represented an adaptation to the emphases that colonial administration placed upon proprietary claims to territorial space and the market in land. In pursuing such a course of policy, the Kīngitanga broadly coalesced with a temper or inclination exhibited by a number of descent groups not necessarily affiliated with the Kīngitanga in any formal sense. Indeed, the so-called 'land league', which was more a loose disposition towards a policy of withholding territories from sale (a '*tikanga pakeke*' or obstinate policy or proclivity to withhold), need not have been associated with any confederacy or alignment with Pōtatau Te Wherowhero.[143] As early as April 1856, Tamati Ngāpora, then residing at Māngere to the south of Auckland, advised the board of inquiry that 'Waikato tribes have determined not to sell any more land to the Government; [adding] the alleged reason is, to prevent disputes amongst themselves, through parties offering lands for sale to which they have not a just claim'.[144] Sorrenson observed how the Kīngitanga was 'an effective land league—in that all chiefs who owed allegiance to the King accepted his veto over

[140] Cadogan, 'Constituting the settler colony', 301. The term 'consociation' is not used in the defined technical sense in which it is used by Nico Krisch in his important *Beyond Constitutionalism*, 61–5, as common or shared decision-making. Rather, it is used to suggest fluid forms of association (and possibly shifting or even stable alliances) predicated on areas of shared influence as well as the persistence of autonomous decision-making powers amongst indigenous politics, even as some experienced a diminution of such autonomy over time.

[141] Head, 'Land, Authority and the Forgetting of Being', 239.

[142] For example, Ballara, *Iwi*, 261.

[143] Sinclair, 'Te Tikanga Pakeke', in Munz (ed), *The Feel of Truth*, 79–92.

[144] Ngāpora, 24 April 1856, board of inquiry, *GBPP1860* [2719], 286.

their sale of land'.[145] In addition, the Kīngitanga illustrated the competitive political autonomies operating in New Zealand.[146] It established its own magistracy. In 1861, for instance, a European 'married to a half-caste woman' endeavoured to bring a claim for the loss of sheep in consequence of marauding dogs on his pastoral run licensed by local Māori. He approached the relevant 'King Magistrate' at the *rūnanga* to seek a remedy but the 'Chief Magistrate' declined to adjudicate. When his wife approached the magistrates, the case was heard and adjudicated in her favour, with costs awarded.[147]

Senior elements within the Colonial Office were less than sanguine at this dynamic turn of events in the Waikato and neighbouring Taranaki. Merivale, as permanent under-secretary, thought the situation precarious and in advice of October 1857 to the parliamentary Under-Secretary of State for Colonies, Edward George Bulwer Lytton, considered constitutional adjustments necessary albeit possibly too impracticable (with a view to eliciting a sense from Bulwer Lytton of the political practicalities or otherwise). The spare response of the Secretary of State for Colonies, Labouchere, suggests the possibility of an oral discussion on the topic, one which remains inaccessible: 'Mr Merivale... Pray let me speak to you on this'.[148] Yet, whatever the content of such discussions, no distinct policy adjustment or statutory activity was forthcoming within the circles of imperial administration, with the Colonial Office awaiting further reports from Browne in New Zealand. The source of disturbance was an article in the Auckland publication *The Southern Cross* of 5 June 1857 reporting on 'The Native Question'.[149] It discussed in plentiful detail the gradual emergence of the Kīngitanga and gave brief intimations as to the political thought of a number of its leading advocates, including Wīremu Tāmihana Tarapīpipi Te Waharoa, through reciting summary accounts of their speeches. Waata Kukutai was described as heading a procession of Waikato 'bearing the [Union] Jack', and occupying the 'side of the square opposite to that taken by the King party, immediately after which another body advanced bearing the Union Jack No. 2, and took possession of the ground to the left of the other party, when both Jacks were planted in the ground opposite to the white flag with the red cross'.[150] In appraising the article, Merivale ruminated: 'The Maoris are an exceedingly changeable race—even beyond the ordinary capriciousness of half reclaimed savages. And we have seen clouds of this kind form & disperse often enough before'. 'Nonetheless', he added, 'there is plenty of occasion for watchfulness and anxiety.'[151] Merivale reiterated his view in favour of treating the Auckland and New Plymouth settlements as constitutionally distinct: 'I still believe the best solution for N[ew] Z[ealand] would be a change throwing [thrusting?] back Auckland & New Plymouth more under the power of the Crown. But this is not now practicable'.[152] He wondered why 'the Governor has not used the power left to him by the constitution of proclaiming native districts'. He doubted, without elaborating further, the reasoning underlying its suggested inapplicability: 'The reason suggested against this in [correspondence item] 8021 [dated 9 May 1857 from Governor

[145] Sorrenson, *Report of the Royal Commission on the Electoral System*, B-15.

[146] Hill, *State Authority, Indigenous Autonomy*, 33–5.

[147] *Taranaki Herald*, vol 10, issue 479, 5 October 1861, 2.

[148] Labouchere, 3 October 1857, CO209/141, fo.691a, TNA.

[149] Enclosure, extract from *The Southern Cross*, Friday, 5 June 1857, 'The Native Question', CO209/141, fos.692–3, TNA.

[150] 'The Native Question', *The Southern Cross*, vol 14, issue 1037, 5 June 1857, 3.

[151] Merivale to Labouchere, 1 October 1857, CO209/141, fo.690, TNA.

[152] Ibid, fo.691. This view would be echoed in the second edition of his *Lectures on Colonisation and Colonies*, 521 (note). See also the discussion at page 417 *et seq*, Chapter Seven.

Browne to Henry Labouchere]—that the Crown could by the constitution maintain native usages but could not make laws modifying those usages—seemed to me rather to savour of legal subtlety than reality'. In view of his minute, and as with the then colonial premier, Edward Stafford, Merivale implicity saw the potential to use special legislation to shape or to prise open windows of communicability between indigenous law and introduced colonial legal systems, whereby indigenous law could be modified or adjusted and not merely maintained in stasis.

This 'tendency to self-organization'—colonial administration looking for inroads, intersections, and uptake

Stafford's ministry observed the moves towards localized expressions of Māori self-rule. In an important paper of May 1857, the colonial premier, Stafford, remarked how the 'peculiar feature of the time is the tendency to self-organization now being exhibited by a large section of the Maori people'.[153] The emergence of the Kīngitanga was one example.[154] In the works of one of its primary theorists, Wīremu Tāmihana, there was little expectation of a hierarchy of subjection but instead one of association and alliance with a trans-oceanic imperial Crown. It was an imperial Crown both distant and present; both a metaphor able to be invoked by Māori political actors when suggesting desired behaviour—how colonial political authority *ought* to be distributed, understood, and applied—and a tangible person to whom chieftains might have recourse over and above the distant monarch's colonial officials in New Zealand. Stafford saw the 'numerous meetings... being held throughout the country;—the recent attempts at legislation which have taken place at the villages of the Waikato Tribes, and the agitation for the appointment of a Native King', as 'the signs of this movement'. Diverse, underlying viewpoints were not elided. Stafford's ministry appreciated the myriad complexities at work. Intelligence sources identified nuanced shades of opinion. Thus, Stafford reported, '[w]ith some amongst the natives there is reason to think that social organization is sought chiefly, if not wholly, as a means to the ulterior end of counteracting the growing predominance of the European, preventing the further alienation of territory, and maintaining the national independence'.[155] Other possibilities were aired within the memorandum: 'Another class appears purely to desire the establishment of law and order, and to be at the same time sensible that this benefit is only to be attained by the cooperation of the British Government'. Stafford observed how between the two poles of the spectrum there were 'probably many shades of opinion'.[156] The symbology of the Crown and its ties to the Church of England were appreciated. Indeed, colonial resident magistrates in other areas remarked how Māori leaders were aware of the symbolism and meaning of the prayers of the Anglican Church. In 1858, Herbert Wardell recorded the chief Kemera stating, 'I for one will never join the church service and hear the Queen prayed for lest the potae [*pōtae* or cap used here in the sense of overarching authority or supremacy] should slip over us and smother us & our children'.[157]

153 Stafford, memorandum, 6 May 1857, LE1/19, 1858/232, ANZ(W).

154 Pei Te Hurinui, *King Pōtatau: An Account of the Life of Pōtatau Te Wherowhero the First Māori King.*

155 Stafford, memorandum, 6 May 1857, LE1/19, 1858/232, ANZ(W).

156 Ibid.

157 Wardell, 21 May 1858, qMs-2121, ATL. See also Wardell, 23 August 1861, *AJHR-1862*, E-7, 31.

Stafford's memorandum noted that the ultimate object of 'native policy' represented a continuous theme: 'Successive governors have promised, in the name of the British Crown, that the colonists and the Maories should form but one people, under one equal law; and no effort must be spared to redeem this pledge'. His memorandum predicated the extension of amalgamating or incorporating policy devices—civil institutions (magistrates and itinerant courts)—on Māori consent. For legislation to be effective, it had to accord with Māori conceptions. The Treaty of Waitangi had set out the broad frame in outline, with further details engrained through particular provisions within the Constitution Act. But amalgamation—the union or fusion of peoples—was still to occur. Institutional devices to encourage or procure incorporation were to be calibrated to concrete circumstances on the ground. In a distinctly early-to-mid-nineteenth-century whiggish constitutional mode, reminiscent of Macaulay, the need was presented as one of extending to 'Native Districts a *social organization suited to their actual condition*'.[158] Macaulay had famously said that the 'great cause of revolutions is this . . . while nations move onwards, constitutions stand still'.[159] Implicitly, institutional and legal adaptation to concrete social circumstances was required. Osmosis through mere proximity to European settlements was not seen as a sufficient device for encouraging Māori communities to embrace British laws and institutions. The memorandum criticized what it characterized the 'dominant political ideas' on how to engage with Māori. Those ideas amounted to leaving them 'politically to themselves'. Both osmosis and rational voluntarism were the central themes underpinning such a stance. On this theory, wrote the premier, 'their own advancing civilization, consequent upon the efforts made for their individual improvement, and upon their extending intercourse with the Europeans, would gradually, but surely lead to their voluntary adoption of British Law, grounded upon practical experience of its superiority to their own usages'. Stafford anticipated criticisms of his suggested approach from some quarters. For one thing, any 'special legislation . . . has by some been reprobated as inconsistent with the promise to the Natives of a national unity with the British Settlers'. Stafford's ministerial proposal was not a liberal-radical measure of the sort Charles Adderley or Robert Lowe would necessarily countenance in the United Kingdom: it savoured of leveraging-off particularist and plural legalities rather than exerting forms of legal and constitutional uniformity. Adderley may have favoured a continued laissez-faire approach. Yet, Stafford observed, 'it is not reasonable to expect that a barbarous race should be able to adopt, *per saltum*, the complex institutions of a free British colony'.[160] A transitional period had to be contemplated, advised Stafford. Such a period required 'special treatment; and it may reasonably be objected to the Theory of Native Treatment above stated, that the civilization which is expected to lead to the adoption of British Law can itself only be attained through the medium of

158 Ibid (emphasis added).

159 Macaulay, *The Miscellaneous Writings and Speeches of Lord Macaulay*, 583.

160 Stafford, memorandum, 6 May 1857, LE1/19, 1858/232, ANZ(W). By contrast, Browne acknowledged the Kingitanga (say) might promulgate its own law codes (provided they could be characterized as 'the law and customs of the Aborigines') but thought section 71 of the Constitution Act did not permit 'the establishment of any other law'. In the same advice he considered there was no 'power conferred by the Constitution Act on her Majesty enabling Her to enact laws differing from but not repugnant to, English laws, yet such alone are suited to the present condition and civilization of the Māori case'. (Browne to Labouchere, 9 May 1857, CO209/141, fos. 510–510a, TNA).

fitting institutions; institutions which, taking the actual condition of the Aboriginal population as the point of departure, provide for its present necessities and for this transition state'.[161] Special, customized legislation would perform the role of signalling and enabling the delivery of these extensions into areas where unextinguished native title predominated.

Having said that, Stafford's memorandum proceeded to explore what might be done in the meantime without the assistance of legislation. To that end, three main ventures were proposed. First, '[t]he simple measure', suggested by the governor himself, 'of directing the Resident Magistrates to hold circuit courts, will, we think, not merely greatly increase the efficiency of those Officers; but...will afford a safe basis for important changes'. Secondly, the institution of Māori assessors was to be bolstered by increasing their number and allowing them to be elected by popular vote in each village—'a broad popular basis' was desired. Yet the need to avoid alienating the chiefly ranks was recognized. Chieftains had to be 'consulted on any appointment'. Furthermore, the ministerialists concurred with the governor's suggestion that classifying separate levels of assessor would provide a 'means for avoiding the offence to men of rank, which might otherwise possibly arise from associating them in the office of Assessor with their inferiors'.[162] Assessors of the first class would exclusively comprise 'the higher chiefs', who would be remunerated by sums of £20 to £50 per annum. Such assessors would have a 'distinct jurisdiction' extending 'over all the settlements of their tribe'. In this manner, too, they would be distinguished from assessors of the second rank or class who would receive from £5 to £20 per annum and merely have jurisdictional competence in respect of their own villages. Stafford's memorandum anticipated the legislative programme of the session of the General Assembly in 1858. The colonial premier looked forward to the time when the 'Circuit Court will ultimately assume jurisdiction over cases when territorial rights are in dispute between members of a tribe,—decision being given according to native usage'. In this context, '[i]ntertribal differences may also prove susceptible of similar adjustment, until such time as the extinction of native tenure shall have done away with questions of that kind'. Extinguishing native title, therefore, was seen as a means of pacifying Māori social orders by reducing or eliminating causes of intra-*hapū* and inter-*hapū* strife.

It was not enough, however, Stafford wrote, to supply a 'judicature commanding the confidence of the native people'. Thirdly, the memorandum argued, there had to be an administrative function, also consented to by the Māori communities to which this function would apply. As the circuit courts themselves could be treated as 'natural occasions of popular assemblages', when and where 'subjects of political interest' could be mulled over, 'public feeling' or sentiment could be ascertained at such moments. This was one of the mechanisms, presumably, by which Māori consent would be obtained—the *agōn* of a popular assembly attending a circuit court. A British magistrate's presence might guide opinion and 'objectionable customs might be got rid of', especially those of 'making tauas [raiding or warring parties] upon the innocent relatives of an offender; of punishing the imaginary crime of witchcraft; and of the tapu'.[163] Legal sanction had to be given to the deliberations of such meetings ('village assemblies') called together through the presence of a circuit court. Thus, Stafford advised how his ministry proposed to introduce in the

[161] Ibid.
[162] Ibid.
[163] On this point, compare with Shaunnagh Dorsett's excellent discussion of Justice Chapman's views on objectionable customs in the late 1840s in 'Sworn on the Dirt of Graves'.

next session of the General Assembly a 'measure enabling the Governor in Council to put in force local bye-laws of this character in native districts, to be defined for the purpose'—in essence, the provision of local legislative power. Fenton was proposed as the appropriate person to shepherd the first trial of a circuit court as a magistrate in the 'Waikato country', particularly at locations like Tuakau and Rangiriri. As it was, in the wake of the Stafford memorandum, Fenton departed the Auckland district for the Waikato by sea in mid-July 1857 en route to various Māori settlements, including Taupari, Tuakau, Rangiriri, and Paetai, as envisaged by the premier's memorandum. In those places Fenton presented to his superiors in Auckland—corresponding through the colonial treasurer, Christopher Richmond—as one presiding over a circuit court or resident magistrates' court, although his journal of proceedings revealed a much more nuanced situation as we shall see.

Fenton's prolonged foray into the Waikato from July 1857 to March 1858 was treated with particular interest. Resident magistrates largely busied themselves in areas of colonial settlement or in immediately contiguous areas with occasional expeditions into the hinterland on discrete matters. Their power beyond settled areas was limited, depending very much on interpersonal relations with elite Māori, such as Fenton's relationship with Waata Pihikete Kukutai in the Waikato in 1857.[164] Waata Pihikete Kukutai was a leading chieftain of Ngāti Tīpā of Waikato, a *hapū* dwelling along the western coast of Waikato between Kāwhia and Waikato Heads, as well as along the banks of the Waikato River to Onewhero. Fenton reported on what he referred to as circuit court proceedings at Taupari in the Waikato in July 1857, listing the cases of '*Hapurona v Tamati and John*' (concerning the destruction of fencing and the consumption of the plaintiff's potato crop by pigs belonging to the defendant) and '*Tamihana v Pairama*' (taking of a horse with a claim for damages of £60).[165] In '*Hapurona v Tamati and John*' it was the accompanying person, described as the 'native magistrate', who issued the decision, none other than Waata Pihikete Kukutai himself. When holding a court in Pungapunga in February 1858, Fenton mused on how the cases of cattle trespass were 'already beginning to disappear under the influence of the regulations made by the village "runangas"'.[166] As the lone resident magistrate in the Waikato, Fenton's problem was to become associated with offering alternative options and opportunities for new aspirational Māori leaders to the irritation or at least concern of those tied to recollections of the status quo ante or of long-standing lineage preferring the political status quo ante in the Waikato. For many long-standing or conservative Māori leaders, innovators amongst Māori politics were seen as a management challenge and a problem for Māori control and normative systems. A *tapu*-removal movement known as the Kaingarara founded by Tamati Te Ito, a former Wesleyan teacher from the Taranaki area, supported land retention and independent local government for Māori.[167] Denuding *tapu* of its significance had the potential to denude chiefly authority of much of its power in the spiritual and temporal realms. Although acting in a way that could not be characterized as collaborating with colonial government, Tamati Te Ito's innovations received criticism from other leaders, such as Rewi Maniapoto, a chief within the Kīngitanga, in December 1859, who commanded him to halt his 'sorcery' at once.[168]

164 On Waata Pihikete Kukutai (?–1867): *The People of Many Peaks*, 17.

165 Fenton, Resident Magistrate, and Kukutai, Native Magistrate, 'Specimen of Proceedings in Circuit Courts', CO209/156, fos.343–67, TNA.

166 Fenton, 25 February 1858, 'Journal of F.D. Fenton, Resident Magistrate of Waikato, commencing 12 July 1857', 30.

167 Goode, 'The Kaingarara Letters', 120–5.

168 Toma Whakapo and Rewi Maniapoto to Tamati Te Ito, 29 December 1859, Ms-Papers-32–74, McLean Māori letters, ATL.

The meeting of Te Wherowhero and Tamati Ngāpora with Browne some time after these events in 1858 at Māngere suggested the frustration of two politically influential Māori chiefs with Fenton's co-option *inside* the complexities of multifarious Waikato politics and what he represented by way of an alternative chiefly politics.[169] Browne's rendition of the meeting suggested the precariousness of Fenton's position in aligning himself too closely with those such as Kukutai who had other political agendas. Thus, with Browne reeling from criticisms of his unwillingness to continue Fenton's project in the Waikato in the late 1850s, the governor reported to the Duke of Newcastle in November 1860: 'It was not however until some time after this that Potatau and his half brother [cousin] Tamati Ngapora, called on me—And here I must observe that I never invited any expression of opinion by Potatau as stated by Mr Richmond in his answer (n[umber] 971 p[age] 54)'.[170] He recorded how someone of the long-standing status of Te Wherowhero exhibited quietude in displeasure: 'The former was silent as usual when not pleased, but Ngapora impressed me that Mr Fenton had neglected Potatau and allied himself with the younger men of the country who desired to emancipate themselves from his control: that we should find the young men a rope of sand which would separate instantly if Potatau [Te Wherowhero] did but move his fingers'.[171] Here, Browne touched upon what became a vital policy challenge for his administration generally. Yet, as late as April 1861, Fenton's report of his labours in the Waikato in 1857 and early 1858 received endorsement from the Colonial Office. The parliamentary under-secretary, Chichester Fortescue, remarked, 'In fact the object w[oul]d be to introduce into Native Districts very much the system wh[ich] Mr Fenton tried to introduce into the Waikato country, & in wh[ich] he seems to have failed, not from faults of his own, but for want of support, want of money & departmental jealousies (I sh[ould] be disposed to advise the Governor, at any rate, to avail himself again of Mr Fenton's services)'.[172] To Frederic Rogers, Merivale's successor as the permanent under-secretary in the Colonial Office, Fenton's report on his sojourn as resident magistrate in the Waikato, 'certainly leaves on my mind the impression that the responsible government and Mr Fenton have made a very vigorous and correct effort for the amelioration of the Waikato tribes—an effort which promised extraordinary success when it was crushed by the Governor and Mr McLean'.[173]

Variations in enforcing legal provisions against squatters or Māori were in evidence. One key exception to the general tendency not to prosecute or to report any prosecutions, however, was the resident magistrate in New Plymouth, Josiah Flight. Flight proceeded against squatters allowed onto Māori land at the behest of Māori claiming authority over the land concerned and collecting rents. In an official return, he recorded eight prosecutions under the Native Land Purchase Ordinance 1846 from August 1847 through to May 1856.[174] Flight remains an anomalous puzzle. Others did not prosecute. Taranaki was peculiar, but so was everywhere else, each region sporting its own local ways of getting things done and looking the other way. The different local or micro-level

[169] Browne's chronology is not at all clear and appears somewhat elusive.

[170] Browne to Newcastle, 26 November 1860 [received at Colonial Office, 18 February 1861; answered 16 April 1861], CO209/156, fos.257a–8, TNA.

[171] Ibid, fo.258.

[172] Fortescue, 'Notes on Sir F. Rogers' mem[orandum]', 1 April 1861, CO209/156, fo.171, TNA.

[173] Rogers, memorandum, 21 February 1861, CO209/156, fo.141, TNA. On Rogers, see Parris, *Constitutional Bureaucracy*, 143, 145, 159.

[174] 'Return of Europeans in the Occupation of Native Land in the Northern Island of New Zealand', *AJHR—1863*, E16, 13.

motivations at play in these variations are difficult to explain in the absence of closer studies. Taranaki was characterized by what was in effect a civil war simmering amongst local Māori descent-groups and occasionally erupting. Indeed, the entire Te Waitere Katatore affair in the Taranaki was treated as a crisis of colonial governance, as it played out, even though it perplexed Māori systems of governance predominantly. Elsewhere, Fenton, as magistrate, behaved differently to Flight. According to one account, a 'native arrived to ask assistance against a European neighbor, who would not pay rent for a cattle-run'.[175] The settler, aware that there were several indigenous claimants to the land, 'judiciously denied all their titles'. Fenton advised the complainant that 'as the dispute concerned a Maori title, the magistrate could not interfere; and that the law could afford him no protection until he held by legal [English] tenure'.[176]

A number of these pākehā pastoral run-holders throughout the colony, whether or not prosecuted, liked the idea that Māori had an inside edge, as they saw it, on the question of property rights—the power of command over territorial space. Either way, such power could be imbued with *de jure* rights-status, de facto significance, or both. George Law, the civil commissioner and resident magistrate for Taupō, had, since 1862, by what was described as an 'agreement signed by the principal men of the tribe', paid no consideration for his property, which was reportedly worth £35.[177] Chapman and Synott, described as sheep farmers, paid £330 per annum for a 12,000 acre run in the Hawke's Bay region on the eastern coast of the North Island under a lease with effective occupation from May 1861. In practice, localized understandings were favoured in spite of the breaching of provisions within ordinances. Indeed, unfenced lands—whether claimed by European settlers or Māori—proved to be a persistent problem. In one instance, Flight recorded how Northcroft found 16 horses on his parcel of land 'which he drove to the Pound; his land is not fenced, he therefore claimed no damages'.[178] The Northcroft matter swiftly became an issue for the local provincial administration in Taranaki because the 'poundkeeper[,] misinterpreting a proclamation of the Superintendent whereby he empowered the poundkeeper to receive two and sixpence per head for the damages to which any one was liable for allowing his cattle to wander in the roads or public places[,] claimed that amount from the [unspecified] Maories'.[179] The relevant Māori 'offered one shilling and sixpence being sixpence per head above the sum the poundkeeper was authorized to receive; as this was refused they proceeded to remove some of the bars and let their horses out'.[180] Flight noted that no formal complaint was made to him as resident magistrate. Nonetheless, the entire matter was sorted out peaceably, though not in strict compliance with the ordinances.

However, the resident magistrates and their instructing ministers were all too familiar with the overall precariousness of the situation, as well as the requirements for negotiability. It was well appreciated that the colonial administration did not have a monopoly on organized coercion—that sign of a tangible state: the physicality of constraint and fear as the ultimate arbiter of subjects. Swainson cautioned how Māori were 'jealous of their liberties' and disinclined to be administered or controlled by others.[181] Adopting a rhetorical style reminiscent of David Hume and Macaulay, he assumed that:

[175] Gorst, *The Maori King*, 66. [176] Ibid. [177] Ibid, 9.

[178] Flight to McLean, 19 April 1857, Ms-Papers-0032-0276, McLean papers, ATL.

[179] Ibid. [180] Ibid.

[181] Swainson, *New Zealand. The Substance of Lectures on the Colonization of New Zealand, delivered at Lancaster, Plymouth, Bristol, Hereford, Kirkby Lonsdale, Richmond, and the Charter House, London*, 61.

in some far distant age, when the 'Present' of New Zealand shall have become time-honoured, and shall be dimmed in the antiquity of the 'Past', it will be regarded as an historical fact of curious interest, that a little band of Englishmen, strong only in their weakness, were sent forth by the parent state to found a colony in these islands, and to govern and control, no only their own countrymen, but a barbarous, well-armed, warlike native people.[182]

Māori leaders remained central to enforcing preferred norms or customs in areas close to European settlements without any reference to colonial officials. Thus, in December 1854, John Rogan, the district commissioner for Taranaki, reported how Īhāia Te Kirikumara of the Waitara 'shot a young man from Onairo the other day, who was accused of adultery with his wife'. He explained rather cursorily and inaccurately that Wīremu Kīngi Te Rangitāke organized a *taua* or war party and 'so therefore the matter passed away very quietly'.[183] Further south in the Whanganui district, the resident magistrate, Durie, advised the governor of a 'barbarous murder' at one of the *pā* of Topene approximately 150 miles from the European coastal and riverine settlement at Wanganui.[184] Durie noted:

From the information I have received it appears that Waiato Potango one of Topene's men, and a chief of some consequence, with his son Pohipo, two women and a child (the nephew of Kuru Kanga), were proceeding homewards towards Topene's place at Maraekowhi, when they were pursued by Henu [?] and the Ngatitus, who shot and tomahawked the above party when asleep in their w[h]are at daylight in the morning.[185]

To suggest a certain measure of European engagement, Durie noted that the 'Rev[eren]d [Richard] Taylor intends, as soon as possible, to proceed up the river, in order to pacify, if possible, the belligerents'.[186] Keeping the peace remained very much a function of local Māori notables. Furthermore, Māori chieftains obtained information from European informants as to the martial experiences and failings of Britain's empire: 'The loss of our army in Cabul [Kabul in Afghanistan] in 1841', reported the Bishop of New Zealand, 'with full particulars, was communicated to me by Taraia, the chief, on the Thames, in June 1842'.[187] In a private and confidential despatch of February 1858, Richmond, in referring to the growing disturbances amongst Te Ātiawa in the Taranaki, told the resident magistrate that the 'means placed at the Governor's disposal are . . . as everyone knows, very limited, and it is his first duty not to undertake more than he can perform'.[188] He added, 'Empty threats, therefore, he will not deal in [as it would] be a bad day for New Zealand when the Natives can declare that our bark is worse than our bite'.[189] These settlers also had a keen sense of the frailties of their situation from a military perspective, as did colonial policy-formulators.[190] In mid-1862, an important source of intelligence for the secretaries of the Church

[182] Ibid.

[183] Rogan to McLean, 2 December 1854, Ms-Papers-0032-0540, McLean papers, ATL. See entries on 'Oraukawa, Tamati Hone', in *The People of Many Peaks*, 81 (Ian Church).

[184] Durie to Attorney General, Auckland, 6 January 1859, CO209/150, fo.27, TNA.

[185] Ibid, fos.27–7a.

[186] Ibid, fo.28.

[187] 'His Lordship the Bishop of New Zealand', 'New Zealand. Further Papers relative to the Affairs of New Zealand', *GBPP1860* [2719], 271.

[188] CW Richmond to J Flight, 8 February 1858, in Scholefield (ed), *The Richmond-Atkinson Papers*, I, 348.

[189] Ibid.

[190] Noted also in a sophisticated study of Hauraki by John Hutton: '"Troublesome Specimens": A Study of the Relationship between the Crown and the Tangata Whenua of Hauraki 1863–1869', 5–6.

Missionary Society in London, the Reverend John Morgan, was writing of Waikato that it was difficult to assess whether peace or war would prevail.[191]

The philosophy and political economy of individualizing native title through Crown grants—1856–1860

In these increasingly restless environs, native title was still seen as a transitional and problematic prelude to incorporating Māori communities within the ambulatory carpet of colonial settlement. The transition to be wrought was that of transforming Māori into individual subjects within the scope of the colonial body politic and political economies of settlement, rendering Māori as wage-labourers or landlords, merchants or farmers. In short, native title was both a conceptual and practical hinge and precursor to what may be called an incorporating and 'capacitarian' vision of colonial settlement polities.[192] It had come to be regarded as a useful category of political economy—an implicit statement as to what was to be but was not yet in existence. It was, however, seen as a category of land title requiring a terminal point, a time when it would need to be transmuted into something cognizable in the language of English real property. Property rights recognized within the colonial legal system were vectors of civil liberty. Holders of native title were to be liberated and enfranchised—to have their autonomy as individuals accorded recognition. Transforming native title into Crown-derived titles was to give the holders a right to liberty understood within the colonial political economy—an entitlement to alienate or to hold and an entitlement to vote under the electoral franchise of the Constitution Act if registered.

Crown grants were seen as vehicles for performing a sort of temporal shift by updating localities hitherto clothed with native title—a customary collective interest seen as indicative of historical pasts. They were also perceived as ushers of change to a locality by introducing the area subject to such a grant to a set of normative understandings operative within the colonial political economy. Noteworthy and influential colonists, such as Sewell, the first premier (albeit briefly) countenanced the transformation as one from the barbarism of tribal kin groups to the powers of individuality as settlers or colonists themselves in a broader, less geographically, and economically constrained colonial community. While in London in 1857 he wrote in a miscellaneous letter to John Ball, parliamentary under-secretary at the Colonial Office from 5 April 1855 until 22 May 1857: 'The policy of the colonial government is in fact to make colonists of the natives on their own land'.[193] Thus, the 'legislature with this view, in the last session, passed an Act (the Native Reserves Act) for the first time enabling the native reserves to be granted to the natives by individual titles, the first step towards raising them from their present wretched condition of tribal barbarism, in which so long as they remain no permanent measures of amelioration can be

[191] Morgan to secretaries of the Church Missionary Society, London, 1 July 1862, qMs-1390–1392, ATL.

[192] Hickford, 'Making "Territorial Rights"', ch 4. For the term 'capacitarian', see Kahan, *Liberalism in Nineteenth Century Europe*, 6; Cadogan, 'Constituting the Settler Colony', 44, 64, 83, 166, who has expressly used the term 'capacitarian' in the context of George Grey's policies within New Zealand.

[193] Sewell to Ball, 8 May 1857, CO209/144, fo.402, TNA.

applied'.[194] The first step in securing this transformation peaceably, alleged Sewell, was 'to obtain by purchase the voluntary cession by the natives of their seignory of the soil'.[195] Funds were needed. Indeed, for Sewell, adequate imperial funds remained the outstanding issue, a question that would lead in part to his mission to the United Kingdom to agitate for an imperial loan in 1857.

However, the pace of transition varied depending on a range of influences, including the proximity of coastal colonial settlements, nodes of commerce providing coastal and trans-oceanic access to other markets, and sources of credit. Here, then, we see a point of intersection with a rich vein of discourse in emergent liberal-whig and liberal-radical vocabularies, ways of speaking associated with an early nineteenth-century adaptation of an older Harringtonian and civic republican theme, which the late John Burrow noted as supplying an earlier but persistent analogy for the developing trope of 'individuality' and 'character' in nineteenth-century liberal tracts.[196] Shorn of any nostalgic qualities for an English past dominated by independent aristocratic proprietors bearing arms, supplying tenurial protection recognized *within* a colonial legal system performed a functional, liberty-enhancing role, at least in the context of providing points to access the emergent colonial political economies. That is, the lands subject to interests cognizable in English real property law could be used as security for raising funds. As it was, jurisdictional forays of English law pursued the chattels of British settlers rather than the space they occupied at the behest of Māori hosts, who may or may not have charged rent depending on their respective arrangements. A Wool and Oil Securities Act enacted in 1858 illustrated this very point:[197] 'An Act to enable the proprietors of sheep and whaling stations to give valid security on future produce of wool oil and bone' allowed negotiable security to be given to any proprietor of sheep or of a whaling station 'on condition of receiving wool of the next ensuing clip, or oil or bone to be caught in the next ensuing whaling season' (section 1).[198]

The mid-to-late 1850s were critical years, as new questions regarding native title emerged, especially regarding the status of Māori communities within the new colonial body politic. Within anglophone constructions of native title, one sees a myriad of experiments proposed in memoranda or through bills in the General Assembly. An abiding theme underlying these proposals was the effort to attract Māori to adopt anglophone legal norms relative to property. Two main techniques were developed. First, efforts were made to explain English law and to understand it, as well as how to manage it in the novel circumstances presented by Māori communities yet to be persuaded of its worth. Secondly, many statutes were introduced. A veritable deluge was put through in the 1858 session of the General Assembly in New Zealand. Thus, in a session commencing on 10 April 1858 and ending on 21 August 1858, the Native Districts Regulation Bill,[199] the Native Territorial Rights Bill,[200] the Native Circuit

[194] Ibid, fos.402–2a. [195] Ibid, fo.402.

[196] Burrow, *Whigs and Liberals*, 88–90.

[197] See also Belich, 'How Much Did Institutions Matter?, in Greene (ed), *Exclusionary Empire*, 248–68, 261.

[198] 'An Act to enable the Proprietors of Sheep and Whaling Stations to give Valid Security on future produce of Wool Oil and Bone', 3 June 1858, 21 & 22 Vict, number 12 .

[199] 'An Act to regulate the Local affairs of Native Districts', 4 August 1858, 21 & 22 Vict, number 41.

[200] 'An Act to enable the native tribes of New Zealand to have their Territorial Rights ascertained, and to authorize the Issue in certain cases of Crown Grants to Natives', 21 August 1858, 21 & 22

Courts Bill,[201] and the Bay of Islands Settlement Bill passed both chambers of the General Assembly. A number of these forays failed as political speculations, in their implementation if not in their passing. By March 1861, the parliamentary under-secretary at the Colonial Office in London, Chichester Fortescue, frustratingly characterized the '"Native Districts" & "Native Circuit Courts" Acts of 1858 [as] hav[ing] been dead letters'.[202] Yet, as statutory ventures they experimented with the possibilities of setting out windows of communicability between the colonial settlements and Māori communities located in areas where native title remained unextinguished. None of these proposals was thought of as operating singly without succour from other legal-policy techniques. The strategy was oriented towards providing an entwined package of options. Statutory experiments and fashioning codes of law were seen to operate in tandem. Each remains of interest, as they reflected views on the nature and content of native title and how it interacted with concerns regarding colonial government and the distribution of constitutional authority.

However, these sorts of proposal also proved attractive to policy aspirants wishing to come to the attention of the governor or other influential leaders in the colonial settlements. In a still relatively infantile colonial political marketplace, in which individuals vied for patronage, and official (bureaucratic) and elected places, the challenges posed by relations between colonial administration and Māori polities afforded opportunities for self-dramatization. A key individual emerging at this time was Francis Dart Fenton. Henry Sewell and Christopher Richmond used policy proposals to further build or to cement reputations for astute diagnoses and policy innovation. Despite initial encouragement on the part of his superiors in the administration at Auckland, Fenton's reputation suffered at the hands of McLean and the governor, Thomas Gore Browne. Fenton's fate in this regard became especially noticeable when Browne and McLean came under concerted pressure from the House of Representatives in 1860 with war in the Taranaki and various members scenting the possibility of wounding the McLean system of negotiated engagements with Māori based on the sale and purchase of land subject to native title. Browne's opinion turned against Fenton in 1859 when he suspected Fenton of disgruntlement at having been removed from the Native Department and of being the source for various newspaper criticisms of the governor's management of Crown–Māori relations.[203] Yet Fenton's fall in favour was one from which his posthumous reputation has not fully escaped. Alan Ward, in his superb groundbreaking study of 'racial "amalgamation" in nineteenth century New Zealand', has characterized Fenton as an 'ambitious, conceited, and fractious man' and elsewhere as 'narrow and legalistic'.[204] To a significant degree, the blame for inciting the emergence of the Kīngitanga, leading it to draw up ranks and to end all active association with European resident magistrates in the Waikato, has been heaped upon his

Vict, number 80; reserved for the signification of Her Majesty's pleasure. Disallowed, *Gazette*, 27 July 1859.

201 An Act to make better provision for the Administration of Justice in Native Districts, 4 August 1858, 21 & 22 Vict, number 42.

202 Fortescue, 12 March 1861, CO209/156, fo.168a, TNA.

203 'Remarks by the Governor' on William Daldy MGA, Edward King MPC, M Cooper MPC, Thomas Forsaith MGA, Hugh Carleton MGA, Thomas Henderson MGA *et al*, to Newcastle, 20 October 1859, CO209/152, fo.136, TNA.

204 Ward, *A Show of Justice*, 94 and 102.

shoulders. So the allegations went. That very issue, however, was a question in dispute in the highly charged year of 1860 rather than 1858 or 1859. They were allegations associated with a governor and his officials in the Native Secretary's office deploying all means available to stave off criticism for the increasingly potent Kīngitanga or Māori king movement. It is by no means clear that the governor's account or that of McLean, as self-serving as they were, should be given any more credence than that of their critics in the House of Representatives.

The short point, as we shall see, is that Fenton's power and ability to influence as a single individual in the midst of the Waikato was more limited than pretended—to invest his presence with the power to cause instability within Waikato in and of itself without more is to overstate the case. More critically and influentially, indigenous politics internal to Waikato also played their part. In this sense, Fenton afforded options to ambitious newcomers from within Waikato descent-groups, searching for novel interpretative options with which to elevate and embed their own leadership ambitions. To put his role into perspective, the recorded volume of intra-Māori matters engaging resident magistrates was slight relative to the overall indigenous population scattered throughout the islands. Arthur Thomson calculated that in 1854 a mere 'thirty-one purely native cases were tried by the resident magistrates' courts in the colony', whereas by '1856 the numbers had risen to sixty-six'.[205] Official statistics closely mirrored Thomson's calculations, with twenty-one solely Māori civil cases recorded in 1854 and some sixty-three in 1856.[206] The role of Waata Pihikete Kukutai, a leading chieftain of Ngāti Tīpā of Waikato, and what he represented to older or alternative interpretations of how Waikato-based descent-groups ought to proceed in relation to the colonial administration, was a vital ingredient internal to fluid intra- and inter-*hapū* politics. Against this background, Fenton was much more of a tool in the hands of nuanced Māori political activities and thought than his foes and critics subsequently allowed him to be.

How to transform native title—indigenous communities as vectors of, and volunteers for, change

In his thirties, Fenton, legally trained, and undoubtedly ambitious, driven and industrious, deployed intellectual sources as a currency for networking with like-minded personnel throughout colonial officialdom and politics. One of his aims was to collect, if possible, sympathetic audiences and potential patrons. He not only endeavoured to attract such attentions but sought to nourish them also, as had Grey during his first governorship in New Zealand. His means of access to these networks was as a person bearing an official title and role. His contemporary, Henry Sewell, understood this point well. In his journal Sewell matter-of-factly recorded how 'Ceasing to be of importance, I cease to have influence, or the means of accomplishing objects which I may think most necessary'.[207] Born in Huddersfield in Yorkshire, Fenton belonged to a family living off well-established legal practices. Fenton's father was a solicitor

[205] Thomson, *The Story of New Zealand, Past and Present*, II, 272.

[206] See *Statistics of New Zealand for 1853, 1854, 1855, and 1856, compiled from official records presented to both Houses of the General Assembly by Command of His Excellency*, 30 April 1858, table 67.

[207] Sewell, 25 March 1859, journal of Henry Sewell, I, 5, qMs-1786, ATL.

practising in London, while his uncle maintained a practice in Huddersfield where the younger Fenton first laboured as a solicitor.[208] We still know too little of Fenton's background, intellectual influences, and early professional training before he departed for New Zealand in 1850.

As a resident magistrate at Whaingaroa and Rotorua from 20 February 1856, Fenton developed on-the-spot views as to managing native title in a broader context of questions regarding the government of indigenous populations as distinct communities. In doing so, Fenton presented himself to others as an appropriate source for correspondence and advice on the subject of Crown–Māori relations. His set-piece accounts of the conditions of native title and Māori communities were leavened with a seasoning of the sort of sources familiar to readers of a liberal-radical political persuasion in Britain, or at least those acquainted with such sources. Well-worn elements of stadial historical analysis, mingling with sources on political economy, suffused his views on the place of native title and Māori within a history of progress and civilization. In setting out his prospectus for civilizing Māori, Fenton posed the question: 'What then are the conditions required by natural laws affecting civilization?'[209] His initial answers and proposals, captured in a minute of 13 October 1856, vaunted a familiarity with Robert Chambers' *Vestiges of the Natural History of Creation* (1844).[210] The work *Vestiges of the Natural History of Creation* was used to set out these conventional elements of stadial theory, specifically the emphasis on sedentarizing human communities—fixing their habitations in particular places—and an increase in population to further grow and diversify the wants of people within the communities for products. These two core elements, said Fenton following *Vestiges of the Natural History of Creation*, were the prerequisites for civilization: '*Fixity of residence* and *thickening of population* are perhaps the prime requisites for civilisation'.[211]

Again, we find what Mandler might characterize as a 'civilizational perspective' in play.[212] We see its stress upon features of political economy as a key ingredient in appraising the quality of Māori ways of life and indigenous power over how to understand property rights in land. On the point of 'fixity' or sedentarization, Fenton cited as additional evidence the work of George Catlin on the North American Indians: *Letters and Notes on the Manners, Customs and Condition of the North American Indians* (1841).[213] At this juncture, Fenton touched upon the example of the Mandans—'a

208 Renwick, 'Fenton, 1820 (1825)?–1898', in *The Dictionary of New Zealand Biography: Volume One*, 121.

209 'Minute by Mr Fenton in reference to Native Affairs', 13 October 1856, *AJHR—1860*, F3, 133–40, 136. This minute was printed in the *Appendices to the Journals of the House of Representatives* in 1860 as part of the Waikato Committee report in the House of Representatives.

210 'Minute by Mr Fenton in reference to Native Affairs', 13 October 1856, *AJHR—1860*, F3, 133–40, 136. The controversial work, *Vestiges of the Natural History of Creation*, was published anonymously: Chambers, *Vestiges of the Natural History of Creation*, 1st edn, 1844); Chambers, *Vestiges of the Natural History of Creation*, 3rd edn, 1845. On the controversy, see Desmond and Moore, *Darwin*, 320–3; Bowler, *Evolution*, 141–7.

211 'Minute by Mr Fenton in reference to Native Affairs', 13 October 1856, *AJHR—1860*, F3, 133–40, 136 (emphasis in original). Chambers, *Vestiges of the Natural History of Creation*, 5th edn, 316.

212 Mandler, '"Race" and "Nation" in Mid-Victorian Thought', 231.

213 Catlin, *Letters and Notes on the Manners, Customs and Condition of the North American Indians*. It is conceivable that, other than Chambers' references to the Mandans, Fenton was using the review of Catlin's work in Joyce, 'Catlin on the North American Indians', 415–30. After reviewing Catlin's account of the Mandans' advancement, which relied on the speculative existence of a civilized but

tribe, far placed amongst those which inhabit the vast region of the North West, and quite beyond the reach of any influence from the whites' but amongst whom 'a remarkable civilisation existed'.[214] Fenton's minute used a Chapmanesque type of stadial reasoning, of the sort discussed in Chapters Two and Three tied to Henry Chapman's early musings on the condition of Māori within New Zealand: 'The Maori, possessed of tastes eminently agricultural, and prevented, by the entire absence of animals of the chase from a tendency to predatory or roving habits, presents few or no points of resemblance to the rude hunter of the North American plains'.[215] Yet the propensities towards cultivation were not free from frailty: 'Though eminently a people of agricultural tastes, the Maories, in their own system of cultivation, are careless and improvident to a degree that is astonishing to any person who is acquainted with their covetous disposition'. He explained that at the 'moment a succession of crops has lessened the productive powers of land, it is abandoned, and immediately becomes covered with a prolific crop of docks and other noxious weeds, which spread their seeds into the adjoining plantations'.[216] Again, we are reminded of Donald Winch's statement that '[a] philosophy of history is required to establish the stage of civilisation'.[217] Fenton set his remarks within a historical frame but it was a relatively thin disquisition, focusing in particular on how recently published sources on the circumstances of Amerindians supplied insights as to the political-economic past.

By temperament an innovator and floater of ideas inclined to trial his concepts experimentally, Fenton was an advocate for pilot schemes. There was an undeniably practical element to this temperament. In order to manage the risks of failure, and as a believer in the educative properties of a discretely successful and flowering example to others, Fenton advocated pilot experiments at first, rather than wholesale application: 'The endeavours made on this behalf should be devoted to one tribe at most, and would be more under the guiding hand of Government, and more likely to have complete success, if the initiation were attempted with only the subdivision of a tribe (*hapu*)'.[218] Moreover, these efforts ought to be '*concentrated*, and when marked success has attended the experiment in one instance, the adjoining tribes will quickly see the advantage of the new system, and will *spontaneously* hasten to adopt it'.[219] Fenton proposed techniques to arrest and change the customary agricultural economy of Māori seen to be directed towards the short term. Initially, 'a *fixity of residence*' would be attained through establishing a pilot farmlet, a prospect regarded as achievable given

now extinct precursor 'race' containing perhaps the blood of European travellers (lost followers of the legendary Madoc in 1174), Joyce says (pp 423–4): 'To us, their advancement seems sufficiently explained by their settled mode of life. They have always lived in the presence of the numerous and warlike Sioux; and necessity has compelled them to establish themselves in dwellings more permanent and capable of defence;—thus giving them, what in England we should call "a stake in the country", and enabling them to cultivate arts which could not flourish in a roving community'. For the significance of Madoc to Catlin's work, see *Letters and Notes on the Manners, Customs and Condition of the North American Indians*, 319, 416, 748, 781,782.

214 'Minute by Mr Fenton in reference to Native Affairs', 13 October 1856, *AJHR—1860*, F3, 136.

215 Ibid, 137. See also the discussion on Chapman's approach in Hickford, '"Decidedly the Most Interesting Savages on the Globe"', 144–5.

216 'Minute by Mr Fenton in reference to Native Affairs', 13 October 1856, *AJHR—1860*, F3, 137.

217 Winch, 'The cause of good government', in Collini, Winch, and Burrows, *That Noble Science of Politics*, 118.

218 'Minute by Mr Fenton in reference to Native Affairs', 13 October 1856, *AJHR—1860*, F3, 137.

219 Ibid (emphasis in original).

Fenton's view of Māori predilections towards agricultural pursuits. Once a sedentary residence was obtained, then '[t]he success of a small body of new farmers will quickly raise up imitators, many of whom will settle in the immediate vicinity of the exemplar farm, and thus will gradually be secured the *thickening of the population*'.[220] The minute proceeded to argue in favour of securing material economic and social advances of the pilot or exemplary community before attempting any adjustment of laws and institutions.

The lessons and insights to be drawn from 'history' were allegedly clear and reveal Fenton's tendencies to find historical analogies for circumstances observable in his own time. 'Let it... be remembered', he said, 'that history and past experience teach the lesson, that some social advancement must be made by a people before the desire or necessity for any fixed code of laws, or machinery for the administration of them, can be entertained or recognized.'[221] He demonstrated this observation with a swift aside: 'No man feels the want of rules for the conservation of property, who has no property to lose; and laws for the protection of civil rights, are little esteemed by those [for] whom civil rights are wholly a myth'.[222] In meeting the challenges of history, he advocated an internally driven and voluntarist Māori approach to generating institutions to deal with new commercial and social options as the pilot communities developed to a sufficient level. An initial seed could be sown, however, through a 'majority of the tribe' selecting a 'native magistrate' or 'warden'.[223] Such a warden or magistrate would 'hear and decide all matters civil and criminal originating in his tribe, and may, with the assistance of the other residents, to be named by himself, make such bye-laws as may be found necessary for the order and good management of the community'.[224] Fenton pointed out how 'no difficulty [would] attend the establishment and development of this scheme', as 'something of a similar nature has been spontaneously originated by the tribe whom I have proposed'; and Waata Kukutai was the person chosen.[225] Indigenous communities, and indigenous elites in particular, were to be vectors of change and volunteers in the period of transition. Fenton's proposals were about ensnaring or rather converging congenially with the transition already occurring in some select indigenous communities, particularly through the medium of well-selected, congenial chieftains and well-disposed Māori populations. The then recent case of 'Manuka v. King' (as Fenton expressed it) in the Taranaki was highlighted as an instance 'if any such proof were needed, of our utter incapability of obtaining obedience to laws that are distasteful to a people, if we have no allies amongst those people, beyond the few chiefs who are in receipt of eleemosynary pensions'.[226]

Fenton suggested both institutions and the co-option of Māori opinion leaders to carry English law to Māori communities and to work with it adaptively. He was also a party to preparing a compilation of English law translated into the Māori language. A so-called 'code' of *The Laws of England compiled and translated into the Maori language*, prepared by Fenton, and presented to the House of Representatives on 16 June 1858, reflected the view that anglophone norms on real property at common law were ill-adapted for simply accommodating indigenous attitudes towards power and authority over land. The Attorney General, Frederick Whitaker, explained the background to the legislative council in July 1858, stating how in the summer of 1857–1858, it was

220 Ibid (emphasis in original). 221 Ibid, 139. 222 Ibid. 223 Ibid.
224 Ibid. 225 Ibid. 226 Ibid, 140.

the governor's idea 'that it would be necessary to exempt [Māori in the Bay of Islands and Waikato districts] from the operation of British law, and to create an entire Native code'. Nevertheless, '[f]urther consideration...made it appear that the British law would prove the better adapted to the exigencies of the case; and, accordingly, a careful selection had been made, and a translation prepared in the Native language'.[227] In *The Laws of England compiled and translated into the Maori language*, 'law' ('the Law of England,—the Law of the Queen') was presented as an autonomous discipline to be cherished. It was treated as distinct from the law of the divine but as distilled, universally applicable 'human law' about which the British had refined their knowledge through the centuries and the presence of Christianity.[228] Cleaving to the language of the adherents of the Kīngitanga at Ngāruawāhia, the 'code' leveraged off a sense of the legalistic and constitutional apparatus or framework already present in the rhetoric of chieftains such as Wīremu Tāmihana. Thus, in the introductory passages to *The Laws of England compiled and translated into the Maori language*, we find a presentation of law as hinging upon dimensions spiritual and temporal: 'Divine Law is that which is written in the Holy Scripture'; '[t]hose to whom the Divine Law is committed, and whose duty it is to expound it, are the Bishops, Ministers, and Teachers'.[229] Temporal or human law laid down 'rules for the guidance of the bodily and outward relations of men'. Irrespective of whether the law was human or divine, the deity was the fount of both: 'good Human Law is built up by man upon Divine Law'. Historical references were resorted to in order to explain the value of this human law as a source for peaceable dispute-resolution: 'Formerly, when the ancestors of the Pakeha lived in ignorance, England possessed no good Law' and there was 'no Restrainer of the wrong'.[230] Law was represented as transcending cultural differences. Similarities between that state of affairs in the perceived situation of New Zealand Māori were starkly drawn:

> Then a man's own strength was his Law; a law of oppression towards the weak. Men lived then in anarchy and fear. It was a state of things like that which prevailed throughout New Zealand but a short time ago. Men lived in disorder, strife, and mutual aggression;—killing each other, and doing every evil thing natural to a state of ignorance.[231]

On native title the code was clear. Turning to the question of 'land' in the second part of the code devoted to 'civil injuries' (or '*hara hiwhiri*' in Māori), it was said that the 'rules with respect to actions at Law in reference to Land will not be stated here, because the Maori tenure of land is quite different from that of the Pakeha'.[232] The code commented that the 'Law of the Pakeha in reference to land, does not apply to land held under the Maori title'.[233] 'If, however', it continued, 'the Maori tenure were made similar to that of the Pakeha, the provisions of the Law of the Pakeha, in reference to land, might be brought into operation for the adjustment of those disputes

[227] Whitaker, 5 July 1858, *New Zealand Parliamentary Debates—1856–1858*, 578–9.

[228] Fenton, *The Laws of England compiled and translated into the Maori language by direction of His Excellency Colonel Thomas Gore Browne CB*, i: version presented to the House of Representatives, LE1/1858/229, Archives New Zealand, Wellington ('ANZ(W)').

[229] Ibid. [230] Ibid.

[231] Ibid. See also ibid, ii: 'The people of England were not so fortunate in days of old as are the people of New Zealand now. When they began to frame for themselves laws, in generations long past, they had no example to direct them'.

[232] Ibid, 45. [233] Ibid.

which now arise among the Maori people, and cause strife between their tribes.'[234] The core feature of English real property law was said to be that of individual titles: 'If their lands were divided, and each individual had his own portion, and held it under the same kind of title as the Pakeha holds his land, that is, under a title which could be recognized by the Law, the Pakeha Law might then with propriety and advantage be brought to bear upon all cases of disputed ownership'.[235] This view coincided with a number of such views swirling throughout the official literature. Individualizing property had been seen as a necessity by Dr Arthur Thomson of the 58th regiment in his memoir of December 1856 on 'the state and progress of civilization among the Maoris, with remarks on the means requisite to promote this object'. Tying systems of landholding to moral and broad behavioural qualities, Thomson asserted that the 'common property system now in force paralyses the mind, checks the industry of the active, and encourages the idleness of the lazy'.[236] The 'most civilized New Zealanders', he alleged, were 'those holding land with Crown titles'.[237] Amalgamation or a fusion of British settlers with Māori was seen as undoubtedly critical to any long-term strategic policy on civilizing New Zealand.

Institutional jurisdiction, title, and law were entwined. Browne made a passing reference to the underlying purpose of the law code when noting how 'English law prevails in the English settlements, but in native districts the Maoris are not yet willing to accept it'. In order to 'encourage them to do so [to accept English law], an abstract of English law has been complied & translated into Maori, & special Acts of the Assembly having the same object have received H.M.'s assent'.[238] Sewell in Britain endeavoured to bring Fenton's digest to the favourable attention of the fourth Earl of Carnarvon in March 1859: 'I send you a manual of British Law which has been compiled for the purpose of instructing them in the exercise of our law in substitution for their own barbaric customs—I may state that although as yet it has been sparingly circulated it is received with the greatest interest & amiability'.[239] *The Laws of England* was predominantly descriptive, distilling key features of introduced English law. After preparing his own spartan but prescriptive version of a law code in early 1860, Martin, the former chief justice, subsequently criticized this relatively baroque code as 'far too multifarious and complicated'.[240] He considered '[m]uch of it [as] occupied with matters, which must always be confined to the English Courts', adding, '[t]here was little or nothing adapted to the very peculiar needs and difficulties of the Maories at the time'.[241] Its circulation as a whole was minimal, with extracts reprinted in *The Maori Messenger* and *Te Karere o Poneke* although it was advertised for sale at 10 shillings and sixpence in *The New Zealander* on 2 July 1858.

Meanwhile, in Britain, Merivale continued to muse on the nature of native title as a proprietary right, offering an extensive appraisal of his views in the Colonial Office, at least in the late 1850s, before a Select Committee of the House of Commons in 1857.

234 Ibid. 235 Ibid.

236 Thomson, 'On the Progress of Civilization among the New Zealanders, with remarks on the means requisite to promoted this object', December 1856, enclosed with Thomson to Steward, 9 December 1856, *GBPP1860* [2719], 419.

237 Ibid.

238 Browne, 'Remarks by the Governor on Mr Daldy's letter', CO209/151, fo.259a, TNA.

239 Sewell to Carnarvon, 18 March 1859, Auckland, BL AddMss60782, fos.72–3.

240 Martin, *The Taranaki Question*, 103. 241 Ibid.

In doing so, he diagnosed the peculiarities of native title in New Zealand when seen through the eyes of a senior British official and compared with other colonies. The venue for Merivale's analysis was a Select Committee appointed 'to inquire into the expediency of guaranteeing by Act of Parliament the liquidation of a Loan, to be contracted in pursuance of an Act passed by the Legislature of New Zealand, for defraying the debt of the colony to the New Zealand Company, towards extinguishing the native title to lands in certain portions of the colony, and for other purposes'. Only two witnesses were examined—Merivale and Henry Sewell, the last having recently arrived back from New Zealand. The Select Committee comprised eight members, all with a professed interest in policies regarding colonial settlement, including the Secretary of State for Colonies, Henry Labouchere, Lord John Russell, Stanley, Sir John Pakington, Adderley, Robert Lowe, and John Abel Smith. It convened for three days from 6 July 1857 to 8 July 1857. '[I]n most colonies of the Crown', Merivale explained, 'the natives have been recognised only as possessing certain possessory rights over the soil, and they have paid comparatively trifling sums for those rights.'[242] New Zealand was seen as distinctive as, 'by the interpretation put upon the Treaty of Waitangi by the Home Government, it was considered that the New Zealand tribes had a right of proprietorship over their lands'. Merivale analysed this 'not simply [as] a general right of dominion, but a right of proprietorship, like landlords of estates, for which the Crown was bound to pay them'.[243] Here, in suggesting an intriguing distinction between a 'general right of dominion' and proprietorship in his evidence, Merivale signalled a right of dominion as an entitlement to be regarded as importing jurisdiction or authority over a territory. In 1863, the former chief justice of New Zealand, Martin, would dispute Merivale's construction on this point, suggesting that this 'dominion' (which he called 'internal dominion') had already been lost to the Crown with indigenous rights of property remaining.

Merivale sensed that the market in land, coupled with the interpretative approach adopted under the Treaty of Waitangi, had encouraged a particular set of circumstances: 'It is alleged that the natives, from having this territorial right admitted, acquire a notion that it is connected with the right of dominion, and are apt to consider themselves *politically lords of the land as well as landlords*'.[244] Through the combination of these interpretative features underlying Crown practice, alleged Merivale, the colonial administration had been 'impressed . . . with the necessity of buying off this title, and have made it so very onerous to them to buy off'. Harking back to the first governorship of Grey and the acquisitions under his auspices at Wairau and elsewhere, Merivale characterized the costs incurred in quieting native title in the South Island as less than those experienced in the North Island. Thus, he reported to the Select Committee, the 'whole Middle [South] Island (more than fifty millions of acres), having little or no native proprietary, has been purchased at a trivial cost, and the waste lands comprised in it have been included in the three provinces of Nelson, Canterbury, and Otago, in whose hands they constitute an immense source of wealth, for which they have given little or no consideration'.[245] Turning to the North Island, however, Merivale saw a multitude of indigenous communities 'being in comparison [to the South Island]

[242] Merivale, 7 July 1857, 'Report from the Select Committee on New Zealand; together with the Proceedings of the Committee, Minutes of Evidence, and Appendix', *GBPP1857*, sess. 2, ix (HC171), 10.
[243] Ibid. [244] Ibid (emphasis added). [245] Ibid, 7.

densely peopled by the aborigines, [and] as yet only partially purchased'.[246] This qualitative distinction implied by Merivale in respect of native title in the North Island as opposed to the South Island was not anomalous. Gladstone had fallen prey to this view in 1846. McLean, too, casually expressed it as a real distinction in September 1856. He recommended trialling a system to individualize Māori property in the South Island, 'owing to the paucity of the native population, and the nature of their tenure'.[247]

Although conventionally deployed to denote an interest in real property, the term 'territorial right' could be used in conjunction with the concept of government or dominion, a usage with which Merivale was familiar having sought advice from the law officers of the Crown in June 1857 on the 'validity of the several claims of territorial right of government, exclusive trade, and taxation insisted on by the [Hudson's Bay] Company'.[248] The law officers advised that 'with respect to any rights of government, taxation, exclusive administration of justice or exclusive trade, otherwise than as a consequence of the right of ownership of the land, such rights could not be legally insisted on by the Hudson's Bay Company as having been legally granted to them by the Crown'.[249] In the Select Committee on New Zealand, in responding to questioning from Labouchere, the Committee chair and Secretary of State for Colonies, Merivale, expressed the view 'that the native title in the Middle Island was nominal or nearly so; whereas the native title in Auckland, and part of New Plymouth, and Wellington, was a very substantial title indeed'.[250] Before this Select Committee, Sewell asserted that the 'extinction of their tribal right and the substitution of an individual title to land is the first step, and the most important step, towards, if possible, saving them'.[251] He considered that Māori sold those lands in deeds of purchase to which 'they have an unprofitable abstract right'. Those lands they cultivated, which Pakington classified as 'actually possessed.... in the sense of property', were 'in all cases reserved'. When Pakington asked whether Māori 'in any case derive[d] a value from those tribal rights in the same sense that a North American derives a value from the territory over which he roams for the purposes of hunting ground[s]', Sewell replied, 'No'.[252] Sewell also took the opportunity to quote from a letter written to him by William Martin on the

[246] Ibid.

[247] McLean, 4 September 1856, in Browne to Labouchere, 24 September 1856, *GBPP1860* [2719], 395.

[248] Merivale to Bethell and Keating, 9 June 1857, 'Report from the Select Committee on the Hudson's Bay Company; together with the proceedings of the committee, minutes of evidence, appendix and index', *GBPP1857*, sess. 2 (224), (260), 402.

[249] Bethell and Keating to Merivale, July 1857, ibid, 404. See also ibid: 'on every legal principle the Company's territorial ownership of the lands and the rights necessarily incidental thereto (as, for example, the right of excluding from their territory persons acting in violation of their regulations), ought to be deemed to be valid'. In addition, its use by Merivale before the Select Committee on New Zealand may be compared with the reference to correspondence of the superintendent-general of the Indian Department in Canada where he said: 'the Six Nation Indians have strong and peculiar claims to the protection of the Government, and that their property is not held in virtue of *undefined territorial right as Indians*, but on a different and far more solid tenure [specifically the granting of a reserve in return for their adherence to the Crown during the revolutionary war in the 13 colonies from 1775]': R Bruce to McNab, 10 July 1851, 'Copies or extracts of representations to the Secretary of State, on behalf of the settlers on the Grand River, in Upper Canada; together with copies or extracts of the replies thereto, and correspondence on the subject with the Governor-General of Canada', *GBPP1852–1853* (1003), 6 (emphasis added).

[250] Merivale, 7 July 1857, *GBPP1857*, sess. 2, ix (HC171), 9.

[251] Sewell, 7 July 1857, ibid, 23.

[252] Ibid, 26.

question of native title: 'purchases should be made as soon as practicable, not only because the extension of the Crown title carries with it a practical extension of English law and usages, the Maoris readily acquiescing in the principle that Maori customs are not to be followed on the Queen's land'.[253] Sewell pointed out the 'converse of that is true; that until they have surrendered their territorial rights they do not consider themselves practically subject to British law'.[254] In his correspondence with Sewell, Martin had no doubt 'as to the soundness of the policy of buying up the native lands largely and without delay... provided such policy be pursued quietly and patiently'.[255]

For Fenton in the late 1850s, Anglo-Saxon antecedents unearthed in Henry Hallam's historical studies on medieval Europe (*View of the State of Europe during the Middle Ages*) supplied adequate if not complete guidance. In conducting the first official census of the Māori population in August 1858, he took the opportunity of composing an especially powerfully expressed set of closing paragraphs and an appendix on indigenous property rights in New Zealand and their reformation. The note to the published version of his tables and report on population stated that the 'object of the publication by the Government of this Paper is to draw attention to the fate of the Native Population,—especially to its demise in numbers,—with a view to invite inquiry as to the cause, and suggestions of a remedy'. Published in 1859, his *Observations on the State of the Aboriginal Inhabitants of New Zealand* announced that the device of a 'Crown grant' was one remedy directed to arrest the ambulatory nature of Māori communities. The underlying philosophy of liberating the denizens of a tribal community or clan from the despotism or whims of the chief or tribe was critical. A Crown grant, given to an individual, was to be an engine of political and commercial liberty, whether for Māori or for European settlers.

There was more, however. Undergirding Fenton's prospectus was a philosophy of history as progress and regression. The assumption was that:

> Securing to an individual [as opposed to a group] by means of a crown grant his holding, even if it be but a small area, will, in inducing continued residence on the spot, its improvement year by year, and the natural collection around it of the appliances which lead to comfort;—such security of tenure, will, I believe, conduce more to the improvement of the Maori, than any plan that has yet been proposed, and will cause him and his successors to respect the laws of the power, which in their first exercise secured to him a status and an independence, an immunity from the encroachments of the chief or tribe.[256]

The times of the chieftain and the tribe were to be eased away. The maximum period of usefulness of chieftains and tribes in supplying security and a sufficient circle of liberty to group members was seen as now having passed. Fenton did not treat this sense of historical distance as an excuse for any cultural chauvinism. 'It must be remembered', he advised, 'that the process of separating common titles and apportioning

[253] Ibid, 25. Sewell introduced the correspondence from Martin as follows (ibid, 24): 'I wrote to him [chief justice Martin] to ask if he could, without risk to his health, attend the Committee to-day for the purpose of speaking upon this subject, as to the purchase of native lands; he says,—"My dear sir, The short time I spent in town threw me back so much that, after a week's absolute rest, I am not rid of the unpleasant sense of weakness in my back, you will not be surprised therefore at my shrinking from another visit to London at present..."'.

[254] Ibid. [255] Ibid.

[256] Fenton, *Observations on the State of the Aboriginal Inhabitants of New Zealand*, 42.

lands is not yet completed even in England'.[257] Crucially, then, these Crown grantees would not be subject to chieftains or not *as* subject to the discretion of chieftains. Individualizing title would assist in prying individuals from the assumed despotism or arbitrariness of chieftains and the potential stagnation of proprietary rights held in collective ownership where individual preferences and choices were subsumed. In writing thus, Fenton's argument resonated with themes in the histories of progress explored by the liberal Anglican theorist, Thomas Arnold, as long ago as 1830 in 'On the Social Progress of States' (as discussed in Chapter Two). Tribalism and clannishness were seen as signs of a lack of improvement.[258] Palgrave, in the *The Rise and Progress of the English Commonwealth*, remarked that the 'first and most obvious right accrues to the people, or nation, as is the case with the Aborigines of North America'.[259] He surmised that the residue of such historical approaches was to be found in the English present: 'The same doctrine is established under another guise, in the fictions of the law, which teach that all land is held of the Crown'. 'History', Palgrave claimed, 'affords sufficient proof of the slow development of individual possession, and the difficulty of arriving at the principles upon which such an exclusive claim is founded'.[260]

But Fenton appreciated that one could not undermine customary forms of authority and sympathy abruptly. He, as with others in the colonies, foresaw a relatively lengthy process of troublesome transition. As an abstract concept, Fenton's suggestions to extricate or liberate individual members of tribes or clans from the binding oversight of tribal superiors or elders would anticipate the musings of Henry Maine on the significance to histories of progression of initially developing collective proprietorship (usually in village communities) and thence passing to individualized proprietary tenure.[261] John Burrow has identified a developing mid-nineteenth-century strain of progress in and through time reflected in the 'emergence of individualism, of the free individual, from the kin-group, and then from serfdom; its accompanying movement in property-holding was from the initial collective ownership of the village community, through feudal tenures, to the modern form of outright untrammelled ownership of disposable property'.[262] This broad sense does not, however, capture the subtleties of transitional periods anticipated by Fenton, as implied by his reference to the incomplete state of change in England itself. As he appreciated, communal proprietorship could hardly be characterized as something of simply antiquarian interest. In his paper, therefore, the decision-making ability of these grantees vis-à-vis the uses of land would *not* be subsumed within the tribe as a whole, although they would remain individual members of the tribal grouping. As such, a preservationist ethos towards communal ties (preserving the tribal back for as long as possible) mingled with a transitional state towards a broader sense of community affiliation, specifically that of increasing connection to newly established colonial communities within New Zealand as a whole. There was nothing in Fenton's prospectus to suggest that the bonds of genealogy would

[257] Ibid.

[258] Arnold, 'On the Social Progress of States', 111.

[259] Palgrave, *The Rise and Progress of the English Commonwealth*, I, 71.

[260] Ibid.

[261] On which, see Burrow, 'The Village Community and the Uses of History' in McKendrick (ed), *Historial Perspectives*, 272–3. For a discussion of Maine and a development of his approach to 'village communities', see also Stocking, *Victorian Anthropology*, 117–128.

[262] Burrow, *Whigs and Liberals*, 110.

be sundered; merely that the decision-making of individual grantees would not, as matter of law, be circumscribed by tribal or chiefly concerns.[263]

Supplying Crown grants in substitution for native title was a vehicle for 'giving security and permanence to the occupation and possession of land'. Recalling his minute of October 1856, Fenton elevated 'fixity of residence' as the 'grand requisite of civilization'.[264] A number of practical material advantages would flow from the presence of a sound Crown grant. In exercising the power of alienation accompanying a title secured by a Crown grant under English common law:

> a class of European settlers will be brought amongst them, who will by example and instruction wean the Maoris from their present desultory plan of agriculture to a system vis-à-vis based upon the feeling of a perpetual right in the cultivator and his successors, and, who will moreover cause them to apprehend, that the secret, which they have for many years been trying to find out, viz:—the art of living without labour, is one which will never be discovered.[265]

In this context, the necessity of permanent fences would be recognized: 'The cultivated grasses, which will *immediately follow or which may precede the division and legal tenure of land*, will maintain sheep to furnish an annual income from their wool, and cows, whose milk will supply a nutritious food to the young and may reduce the mortality among that class of the population'.[266] Building these sorts of economic practices was intended to distract Māori from feeding practices suited to roving communities. In this vein, Fenton expressed concern about the 'diversion of the habits of the people' into unsustainable economic practices. He noticed, in particular, the tendencies of Māori to head into 'new and unprofitable channels such as results from the possession of a breed of light horses fit only for tribes of hunters, or the ownership of seagoing vessels which they are incompetent to manage, and which not uncommonly end a short career in loss and disappointment'.[267] These tendencies were 'not so beneficial a direction of their energies as the encouragement and instruction of their natural tastes and ancient habits as cultivators of the soil'.[268]

Native title was not, therefore, merely a legalistic category of analysis. It was also a category for historical analysis, situating Māori ways of life and economic practices in historical time (the history of progress) and Victorian political economy in the mid-nineteenth century. The phenomena of particular indigenous populations and how they related to territorial land in the colonies were treated as broadly *sui generis*. High-level texts on the law of nations, constitutional histories, and political economy supplied broad categories and techniques of analysis but were inextricably entwined with intelligence sourced from the ground in a host of colonies, each with its own set of customized relations to the metropole. Colonies in this sense were provincial outcrops, customizing their own relations with indigenous populations and inflecting British metropolitan discourses and politics in particular ways. As policy-formulators ventured to develop and adapt an imperial jurisprudence and a theory of political economy on native title suited to the mid-nineteenth century, one sees an empire of variations.

263 The political influence of chieftains, for example, might be a different matter altogether, as their influence might still be sufficient to affect the decisions of Crown grantees.

264 Fenton, *Observations on the State of the Aboriginal Inhabitants of New Zealand*, 41.

265 Ibid. 266 Ibid, 41–2 (emphasis added). 267 Ibid, 42. 268 Ibid.

Other places of anglophone settlement throughout the globe might supply analogies but were not necessarily determinative, and nor was it accepted that these analogies, as useful and informative as they were, provided complete answers. Thus, responsible ministers, in defending the suite of legislation considered in the 1858 session of the House of Representatives—the Native Circuit Courts Bill, the Native Territorial Rights Bill, the Bay of Islands Settlement Bill, and the Native Districts Regulations Bill—were minded to draw links with other colonial settings, but not in a fashion suggesting that they were mastered by such precedents or examples. The Attorney General, Frederick Whitaker, in specifically referring the Native Districts Regulations Bill in July 1858, touched upon how Māori were dispersed throughout New Zealand, but contrasted 'their agricultural and other operative habits, with the wandering and hunting propensities of North American Indians, and the cattle rangings of the natives of Caffraria and South Africa, to show that the primary difficulties to civilization of other savage tribes had not to be contended with in [Māori]'.[269] Indeed, Whitaker, in moving the second reading of the Native Districts Regulations Bill in the legislative council, explored these comparisons at some length, tying them into the logic of stadial theory: 'Barbarous tribes might be separated into three grand divisions—the hunters, the nomad tribes, and the agricultural class—of which divisions the last had the advantage in civilization over the nomads'.[270] The New Zealanders, said Whitaker, 'were eminently agricultural, living for the most part on the produce of the soil; their villages were fixed places of abode, or, if they moved, only for the exigencies of cultivation'.[271] With New Zealand, the Attorney General averred, 'we are at the point at which they that have tried to civilize the American Indians and others have striven to attain, namely, to bring them to a fixed place of residence'.[272] Subsequently, as the debate proceeded, the Attorney General said that ministers 'had... been charged with mystifying the subject by referring to Arkansas, Caffraria, and Natal'. Yet, he responded, '[w]here else were they to look for instruction as to the probable working of their Bills, if not to analogous cases in the histories of other nations?'[273] The 'New Zealanders' were already 'so fixed' in places of residence. The ultimate objective was to 'incorporate' Māori completely into the body of the colonial political and legal system—'to civilise and make settlers of them'.[274]

Here, the example of Arkansas was portrayed as salutary. Whitaker 'entered into a comparative statement of the facilities or difficulties of Aboriginal civilization, referring to a speech of the American President, which he allegedly quoted from a late number of the "Times"'.[275] 'The speech', said the Attorney General, 'was in reference to the settlement of Arkansas, where, so successful had been the progress of Indian

[269] Legislative Council, [5] July 1858, 'New Zealand. Return to an address of the Honourable the House of Commons, dated 24 July 1860;—for, "copies or extracts of despatches from the Governor of New Zealand, relating to the management of native affairs and the purchase of native land, and the proposed establishment of a native council; and of the answers returned to such despatches by the Secretary of State"', *GBPP1860* (492), 8.

[270] Whitaker, 5 July 1858, *New Zealand Parliamentary Debates—1856–1858*, 578.

[271] Ibid.

[272] Legislative Council, [5] July 1858, *GBPP1860* (492), 8.

[273] Legislative Council, 6 July 1858, *GBPP1860* (492), 12.

[274] Legislative Council, [5] July 1858, *GBPP1860* (492), 8.

[275] Ibid. Note that there is no reference to *The Times* as a source in the record of his second reading speech in the relevant *New Zealand Parliamentary Debates* volume.

civilization, that the President hoped it would be ere long incorporated into one of the sovereign states'.[276] The official record of Whitaker's speech in the legislative council related how '[i]n 1830 the United States Government formed an aboriginal settlement on the Arkansas'.[277] In expressing the view that there was no reason why Māori could not demonstrate comparable progress and 'ascend to a place beside the colonists in the scale of civilization', Whitaker recounted how the president of the United States (James Buchanan) had advised the Congress that '[t]he tribes of Cherokees, Choctaws, Chickasaws, and Creeks, settled in the territory set apart for them west of Arkansas, are rapidly advancing in education and in all the arts of civilization and self-government; and we may indulge the agreeable anticipation that at no very distant date they will be incorporated into the Union as one of the Sovereign States'.[278]

The necessity for courts to investigate native title—'Negotiations and diplomatism will have no force, and no public support'

Flexing his notion of Māori voluntarism further, Fenton argued in his *Observations on the State of the Aboriginal Inhabitants of New Zealand* that a 'simple scheme for settling the Native title to land somewhat analogous to the system pursued by our Anglo-Saxon forefathers is appended to this paper, the operation of which would be simple and without risk to the European government or people;—the whole management and responsibility of the transaction resting with the Maori alone, *guided* only by the judicial officer of the district'.[279] The appendix to his paper set out the Crown grant proposals in further detail. Starting from the premise of Māori agreement to any change, he noted that 'Crown grants cannot except in rare instances be issued, even in cases where sole and unencumbered ownership is clear and undisputed, for the Native owner will not accede to a proceedings which infers that his own title is imperfect'.[280] Fenton suggested that a 'certificate testifying that the parties named therein are the owners of the lands therein described' was required. The process of ascertaining such owners was key, as a certificate was not to be issued unless 'due enquiry has made it clear that the right parties have been discovered, and that no adverse claims are outstanding'. The risks of investigating title were to be internalized within Māori communities. The Crown and its grants were to be freed from any taint: 'The whole conduct of the investigations and the responsibilities of them, as well as the duty of maintaining the award, should be thrown upon the Maories, so that the dignity of the Crown should in no case be compromised, or its interference be needed'.[281] The machinery most 'admirably adapted' for investigating proprietorship and partitioning the common lands of Māori communities was the 'species of Court Leet and Great Court Baron recently created by the Native Circuit Courts Act 1858'.[282]

[276] Legislative Council, [5] July 1858, *GBPP1860* (492), 8.

[277] Whitaker, 5 July 1858, *New Zealand Parliamentary Debates—1856–1858*, 578.

[278] Ibid. The speech was President James Buchanan's first annual message to the Congress dated 8 December 1857.

[279] Fenton, *Observations on the State of the Aboriginal Inhabitants of New Zealand*, 42.

[280] Ibid, 43. [281] Ibid.

[282] Ibid. On questions of courts baron and courts leet, as well as copyhold, see Scriven, *A Treatise on Copyhold, Customary Freehold, and Ancient Demesne Tenure, with the Jurisdiction of Courts Baron and Courts Leet.*

For Fenton, the proceedings of courts had to be authoritative. In a barely concealed criticism of the governor-centric regime of land purchase managed by McLean as native minister, Fenton proclaimed that the artifice of '[n]egotiation and diplomatism will have no force, and no public support'. Native title would be extricated from the politics of anglophone negotiability but not necessarily that of intra-Māori politics, as indigenous communities sorted out who was entitled to be characterized as having an interest in the relevant land. Fenton set out a process for '*legalizing* tenure', for rendering native title a legally cognizable species of proprietary right, able to be considered in the courts.[283] The judicial process would be conducted in the investigative manner of 'an enquiry before the Commissioners under an Act for inclosing lands of common would be conducted in England'.[284] Only at the conclusion of this enquiry could the jury (assisted, if necessary, by the resident magistrate) give a verdict as to whether the claimant was entitled to the land or whether the land ought to be divided amongst a group of contending claimants. Where a number of claimants were successful, the resident magistrate and 'native magistrates', assisted by the jury, could then partition the land, causing 'all sufficient posts and boundary marks to be set up'. Any subsequent alienations or changes in ownership, whether by virtue of descent or otherwise, would be presented by a jury at a court leet, and entered on the rolls. The original copy of the roll would be surrendered and a fresh one issued. 'Thus', said Fenton, 'will be established a very tractable tenure resembling the copyhold or base tenure of England, each District of a Court representing a Manor.'[285] Where land was proposed to be alienated to a 'pakeha, a certificate of title from the Crown can be issued with ease to the Native proprietor whose name appears at the time on the Rolls of the Court as the owner, all doubt as to title and boundaries having been removed by the foregoing operations'.[286] Addressing the question of how revenue was to be obtained from the European purchaser, Fenton proposed that '[o]n the transfer of the certificate to the purchasing pakeha, and the issue of a Crown Grant to such purchaser' the due sum had to be paid to the Crown for the release of its right of pre-emption. He saw how such a right could not 'at present be foregone, as by the recent Imperial Act [the New Zealand Loan Act] the whole territorial revenue is mortgaged to the Crown'.[287]

Unlike Chapman, Martin, or Henry Sewell, Fenton, as a lawyer (and subsequently as a judge), did not display a desire to deploy examples on 'Indian title' drawn from US jurisprudence concerning Native Americans. The sheer historical contingency of the attraction of these sources and forms of analysis must always be borne in mind, recalling that Chapman was a major conduit of the transmission of United States jurisprudence from the United Kingdom to New Zealand and to Martin, while Gipps in Sydney was another transmitter courtesy, most possibly, of Bourke's experiences with the Port Philip Association and Justice Willis of the New South Wales Supreme Court.[288] What may prove useful at a generic level might not satisfy those hungering to lead in policy efforts to transmute native title into a species of property under English real property law.

283 Fenton, *Observations on the State of the Aboriginal Inhabitants of New* Zealand, 43.
284 Ibid, 43–4. 285 Ibid, 44. 286 Ibid. 287 Ibid.
288 John Walpole Willis, 'Notes on the acquisition of New Zealand as a Dependency of New South Wales with reference to lands obtained by British Subjects from the Aborigines'.

State-building and experimentation—the Native Territorial Rights Bill and the 'exclusive use and occupancy of any lands'

Christopher William Richmond also gained pre-eminence at this time. As colonial treasurer in the ministry of Edward Stafford from 2 June 1856, he combined legal training with an appreciation of the significance of maintaining and building public revenue with a view to further building an infantile colonial state. Born in London in 1821, he enjoyed enduring friendships from his University College, London days with the poet Arthur Clough, William Shaen (the friend of the Italian Giuseppe Mazzini), and the editor of the *Spectator* in England, Richard Hutton. Entering Middle Temple in 1844, Richmond was called to the Bar in 1847 while practising with Charles Hall, a future vice-chancellor of England.[289] Arthur Samuel Atkinson and Richmond's political correspondence of protégé to mentor flourished with the easy familiarity of relaxed references to John Stuart Mill and to the poetry of Alfred Tennyson—'For nature brings back not the mastodon'[290]—in reminiscing on their developing relations (what is could no longer be what was).[291] Richmond supplied much of the intellectual orientation underlying the Native Territorial Rights Bill of 1858 and made considerable efforts to persuade others on it. As Native Secretary, his memorandum on behalf of responsible ministers supplied the principled ingredient—the *raison d'être* of statutory innovation—'the extrication of Native Title from its present entanglement'.[292] To liberate native title required reducing the native title of occupancy to 'fixed rules' and 'subjecting it to the jurisdiction of regular tribunals' independent from the governor and the governor-centric politics of negotiability.[293] The logics of stadial theory in political economy underscored these views. Far from dissipating, this theory proved a potent means for analysing native title and the place of Māori property rights in historical time. During the first reading of the Native Territorial Rights Bill in the House of Representatives on 1 June 1858, Richmond proclaimed that '[g]reat evils would arise should there grow up in this country a wandering and lawless class of natives, occupying a position like that of the gipsies in Europe, without fixed habitations, and uninfluenced by those principles and institutions which would gradually civilize them, and prepare them for the enjoyment of their rights and privileges as British subjects'.[294] The *Symonds* decision in the Supreme Court (1847) was drawn on to establish the support of Martin for 'colonization' as a field of 'national concernment' best left in the hands of government. Richmond explained how he was 'strongly opposed to the Government meddling with matters beyond its proper sphere; but in a matter of such importance as colonization he believed that the chief control should be exercised by the Government'. He gave in support of his views 'the opinion of that philosophical writer, Mr J.S. Mill'.[295] Richmond also saw statutes as providing avenues for containing and pacifying disputes as to tenure by committing their resolution to particular specialist

289 *A Dictionary of New Zealand Biography*, Scholefield (ed), II, 236.
290 Alfred Tennyson, 'The Epic/Morte d'Arthur' (1842), l.36.
291 AS Atkinson to Richmond, Taranaki, 7 August 1859, in Scholefield (ed), *The Richmond-Atkinson Papers*, I, 478.
292 Richmond, memorandum, 29 September 1858, CO209/154, fo.472, TNA.
293 Ibid.
294 Richmond, 1 June 1858, *New Zealand Parliamentary Debates—1856–1858*, 45.
295 Ibid, 45–6.

forums—the native circuit courts. Browne, as governor, was behind the scenes, at least in part, hoping to use proposed legislation in the General Assembly to test, crystallize, and elicit the views of the Colonial Office in London as to how to approach the question of managing areas of native title and Crown–Māori relations. In March 1858 he asked Richmond whether the Attorney General was 'still of opinion that it is necessary to reserve for Her Majesty any bill enabling me to secure to the natives['] property to which they can prove their individual or joint title'.[296] If such was the case, Browne 'beg[ged] that the subject may be brought before the House at the earliest possible opportunity in order that I may send the bill home for approval without delay'.

Supplying a conceptualization of the policy problem of native title, Richmond's approach was to begin with underlying policy concepts—legal architecture was to be suited to the manner in which relations with indigenous populations were conceived. At its crudest, the general principles of 'native policy' could have conformed to one of two shapes (although, in practice, a far from pure intermingling could be in evidence). Imperial policy might have 'addressed itself to the maintenance of the Natives as a separate race under distinct institutions and a Government wholly or in great measure independent of the ordinary Colonial Government'.[297] As has been noted elsewhere, such a stance accorded with the temper of the Buxton Select Committee on Aborigines reporting as long ago as 1837.[298] Alternatively, thought Richmond and his colleagues, the policy of the British government 'might have been directed to promote the eventual absorption of the Maories into the European population'.[299] Such a course would have amounted to the policy aspiration of 'amalgamation' or, to use Richmond's expression, 'fusion'.[300] If one were to abide by the former approach, said Richmond, one ought to have seen a policy marked by the maintenance rather than the obliteration of 'such Native customs as were not repugnant to humanity'. Furthermore, 'it would have been essential to set up, and rigidly to guard, a territorial division between the Races'.[301] In essence, however, territorial division had occurred. Areas subject to native title were seen as less permeable than anticipated in that they had not been as readily transferable through purchase as some pākehā had initially contemplated. The process of amalgamation by osmosis on account of mere proximity of Māori settlements to colonial niches—the 'nuclei of civilization'—leading Māori to adopt 'the laws and usages of the Settlers, and resorting to the European Tribunals for the settlement of their differences', was viewed doubtfully.[302] The empirical evidence was all to the contrary.

As William Renwick recognized in his thesis almost half a century ago, Richmond was 'confronted with a formidable problem of government and, very short of men and money, he devised [along with his colleagues] a system that would make a virtue of necessity'.[303] The conceptual and practical difficulties were profound. Colonial administrators were contemplating a period of change and how to calibrate policy and legal devices to that dynamism in the absence of a reliably considerable revenue. Harling

[296] Browne to Richmond, 29 March 1858, in Scholefield (ed), *The Richmond-Atkinson Papers*, I, 374.
[297] Richmond, memorandum, 29 September 1858, CO209/154, fo.470a, TNA.
[298] Hickford, 'Making "Territorial Rights of the Natives"', ch 2.
[299] Richmond, memorandum, 29 September 1858, CO209/154, fo.470a, TNA.
[300] Ibid. [301] Ibid. [302] Ibid, fo.471.
[303] Renwick, 'Self-Government and Protection', 368.

argues that the 'legitimacy of the mid-Victorian State stemmed in large part from its "weakness", if we understand by "weakness" its inability to do very much either to help or to hinder "respectable" interest groups'.[304] The irony is that the very features of fiscal prudence contributing to the increasing legitimacy of the Victorian state in the United Kingdom were at the same time contributing to a marked lessening of the colonial state-building exercise in New Zealand. Those associated with indigenous orders of jurisdiction and authority were less than impressed with a colonial governmental presence at best transient and ephemeral, unable to exert any significant influence beyond European settlements. It was appreciated that Māori contributed to the customs revenue of the colony. But these revenue collections occurred in settlements and not in the Māori-dominated hinterlands.

The ultimate objective was to achieve amalgamation of Māori with European settlers. Richard saw the period of the mid-nineteenth century as one of gradual rather than dramatic transition. He accepted that 'the administration of native affairs [could not] consistently with good faith, be entrusted to any but Her Majesty's Representative, while the Maories continue a distinct and separate people'.[305] There was to be no rapid descent into unconstrained individualization of communal titles.[306] Richmond, hailing from the precarious borderlands of Taranaki, and others amongst the Stafford ministerialists, would have appreciated the need for gradualism. Yet, '[a]s [Māori] bec[a]me incorporated and amalgamated with the colonists, they should take their proper position under Colonial institutions'. Calibrated legislative design was in evidence. The Bay of Islands Settlement Bill was designed to apply to what Richmond characterized a 'mixed district'. The precept was to form a 'special settlement on the western side of the Bay of Islands, for colonization by Her Majesty's subjects, without distinction of race'.[307] In the explanatory memorandum of the responsible ministers, Richmond wrote how the Native Districts Regulation Act and the Native Circuit Courts Act were intended to apply 'in parts of the country which may be described as progressive Maori Districts'.[308] This remark was explained as: 'Districts over the whole of which the Maori Territorial right subsists, and in which there has latterly existed (as has been fully reported to Her Majesty's Government) a marked political activity, accompanied by a disposition to resist the further exclusion of European settlement'.[309] By way of contrast, there were 'other Native Districts still too little advanced for any measure of this kind', as well as other 'localities in which the population is already *so much intermixed* as to require a distinct treatment'.[310]

[304] Harling, 'The Powers of the Victorian State' in Mandler (ed), *Liberty and Authority in Victorian Britain*, 33.

[305] Richmond, 'Memorandum by Native Secretary', 13 October 1858, *GBPP1860* (492), 51.

[306] It is for this reason (as well as the clauses of the Native Territorial Rights Bill) that a more cautious reading than that advanced by Sorrenson in *Report of the Royal Commission on the Electoral System: 'Towards a Better Democracy'*, B-14 is required. There, Sorrenson said, 'In 1859 [*sic*] the General Assembly passed a Native Territorial Rights Bill which abolished Crown pre-emption and allowed settlers to purchase land directly from individual Maori'.

[307] Preamble, 'An Act to enable the Governor to establish a Settlement for Colonization in the Bay of Islands', 19 August 1858, 21 & 22 Vict 79 (New Zealand).

[308] Richmond, memorandum, 29 September 1858, CO209/154, fo.471a, TNA.

[309] Ibid. [310] Ibid (emphasis added).

'No well-defined law' to guide and 'exclusive use and occupancy'

The Native Territorial Rights Bill was conceived as an aid to what Richmond presented as the 'individualization of native title'.[311] As with the functionality of recognizing native title as a means of disciplining colonial settlements, proposing a statutory portal of recognition for native territorial rights revealed connections between processes of state-formation and discourses on rights.[312] Yet, in keeping with a pragmatic appreciation of these processes, the language of its provisions envisaged a gradual deliberative and permissive process rather than a wholesale transformation or mandatory process. The Bill's rationale was clearly expressed, however. Recalling the Stafford memorandum of May 1857, Richmond's policy paper ascribed disputed titles to land as a driving cause of many of the 'most frequent and bloody Maori feuds'. Hence, the overlapping and contestable qualities of native title were presented as in need of pacification through managed tenurial change—transforming native title into determined parcels of land with ascertainable proprietors and supplying a means for their transmutation into Crown-derived titles. These concerns in Richmond's paper addressed internal and external politics of *hapū*, their own *innenpolitik* and *aussenpolitik*. Socio-economically, Richmond's memorandum promulgated the view that the 'communistic habits of the Aborigines are the chief bar to their advancement... [s]eparate landed holdings are indispensable to the further progress of the people'.[313] In a passage reminiscent of Martin's concerns in July 1859 regarding the 'gregarious habits of the *pa*', Richmond's ministerial memorandum stated that '[c]hastity, decency, and thrift cannot exist amidst the waste, filth, and moral contamination of the Pas'.[314] It was to 'strike at the root of these evils', wrote Richmond, that the Bill provided 'first, for the ascertainment and registry of Tribal Title—Secondly, for the issue of Crown Grants to individual Natives of Lands ceded for the purpose by their respective Tribes'. The ministerial memorandum considered that the policy of 'at least' attempting to 'provide means for the extrication of Native Title from its present entanglement, for reducing it to fixed rules, and for subjecting it to the jurisdiction of regular Tribunals, can hardly admit of a doubt'.[315]

Deploying statutorily created native circuit courts was a way of detaching the processes of ascertaining native title from the executive branch of colonial administration but not completely: 'The interference of the Executive Government to adjust land disputes *remains under the Bill purely optional*'.[316] Richmond's paper took care to reassure its political audiences—including the governor and the Colonial Office—that the provisions of the Native Territorial Rights Bill were 'permissive, and the plan must by no means be confounded with the Compulsory Registration of Native Title provided for by the Royal instructions of 1846'.[317]

The Native Territorial Rights Bill threw up the incomplete theorization of native title in empire once more. Fundamentally, Richmond and his ministerial colleagues expressed concern with what they saw as an erroneous doctrinal understanding of Māori territorial rights to and in land. This state of affairs demonstrated once again

311 Ibid, fo.472.

312 As recognized in Ivison, 'The Nature of Rights and the History of Empire', in Armitage (ed), *British Political Thought in History, Literature and Theory, 1500–1800*, 191–211.

313 Richmond, memorandum, 29 September 1858, CO209/154, fo.472, TNA.

314 Ibid. 315 Ibid. 316 Ibid (emphasis added). 317 Ibid.

the unresolved nature of disputes regarding the content of native title in the 1840s. For some, a debate was needed to clarify whether native title was a property right deserving recognition in English law through an 'absolute grant in fee simple'. This concern arose because of two main interconnected reasons. First, anglophone commentators—colonial and imperial politicians and officials, judges, and news media—entertained continuing doubts about the legal incidents or characteristics of native title as an interest held in common subject to communal or tribally based strictures as to how the land should be used. In short, was an 'absolute grant in fee simple' with all the powers that estate entailed, including a complete liberty to alienate, consistent with the nature of a communal title? Secondly, there were continuing doubts as to whether the nature or quality of the relationship of an indigenous community to every acre of land was such as to justify a full fee simple estate. That is, did the community merely use the land sporadically and non-exclusively from time to time so that members of other groups could also use the area without needing to seek the permission of any other group, or was it occupied to the exclusion of all others?

This question of legal translation between a native title in occupancy and a fee simple estate emerged because clause 9 of the Native Territorial Rights Bill empowered the governor in council to 'authorise the granting of Lands, over which the Native Title shall have been duly ceded to Her Majesty for the purpose, unto, or in trust for the benefit of, any person or persons of the Native Race, either in Fee Simple, or for any less Estate or Interest'.[318] Not all of the legal incidents of a fee simple estate would necessarily flow from a Crown grant. The power to alienate land by way of sale, mortgage, or through granting a leasehold estate to strangers to earn rent, for instance, could be restricted. Under clause 12, then, it would be lawful for the governor alone 'by the provisions of any [deed of grant] to prohibit the alienation, or restrict the alienability of any Estate or Interest created by such Grant, any rule of Law or Equity to the contrary notwithstanding'. The jurisdiction of the colonial courts regarding questions of native title or right of occupancy of Māori, *inter se*, was ousted by virtue of clause 8:

> It is hereby declared that no Court of Law or Equity within the Colony hath, or ought to have, cognisance of any question of or affecting the Title or right of occupancy of the Aboriginal Natives, *as amongst themselves*, to or over any Lands or Hereditaments over which the Native Title is not extinguished, except so far as the Native Circuit Court may have such jurisdiction under and by virtue of any regulation made in pursuance of 'The Native Districts Regulation Act, 1858'. (emphasis added)

In his first-reading speech on the Native Territorial Rights Bill, Richmond explained that this provision had been inserted because of his 'understanding of the law'.[319] 'No Court of law', Richmond claimed, 'could decide questions arising between Natives themselves, though it might be able to protect Native rights—whether founded on treaty or on the law of nations—against Europeans'.[320] The operations of the native circuit courts were seen as undeniably linked to questions of clarifying native title within Māori communities. Resident magistrates and circuit courts were to be the cuckoo hatchlings of a thinly resourced colonial state. Yet indigenous magistrates supplied

[318] Under cl 15 of the Native Territorial Rights Bill, 'Half Castes shall, for the purposes of this Act, be deemed to be persons of the Native Race'.

[319] Richmond, 1 June 1858, *New Zealand Parliamentary Debates—1856–1858*, 474.

[320] Ibid, 474–5.

other advantages to their own communities—usually access to political or commercial communities within the colonial settlements. Thus, John Gorst recorded how Te Huirama Tiakiawa, a Ngāti Mahuta *rangatira*, advised 'that he was going to Auckland to ask for £100 to buy iron-work and stones for a mill, but intended his friend [Hone Kingi Te Paki, a probationary magistrate] to ask for it, because, being a loyal man and a Queen's magistrate, he was more likely to get attention from the Government'.[321]

As far as native title as a property right was concerned, the starting point was not the power to issue a Crown grant under the Native Territorial Rights Bill. For the responsible ministers, what was characterized in their explanatory memorandum as a 'native title of occupancy' could be provided a 'certificate of registration'.[322] As seen, 'occupancy' was not especially reducible to precisely agreed definitions between contending anglophone parties in politics. Additional complications emerged on account of the implicit definition of native title used in clause 1 of the Native Territorial Rights Bill. That provision stipulated that:

> Upon the application of any Tribe, Community, or Individuals of the Aboriginal Inhabitants of New Zealand, and upon the Governor in Council being satisfied that such Tribe, Community, or Individuals are entitled, according to Native Custom, to the exclusive use and occupancy of any lands within the Colony over which the Native Title has not been extinguished, it shall be lawful for the Governor at his discretion, to issue under his hand to the Tribe, Community, or Individuals, so appearing entitled, a Certificate of their Title to such Lands.

The non-analysed phrase 'entitled, according to Native Custom, to the *exclusive use and occupancy* of any lands', corresponded to the right of exclusive occupation of land seen as an incident or attribute of ownership.[323] The words controlling the meaning of 'exclusive use and occupancy' were contained in the phrase 'entitled, according to Native Custom'. As presented in clause 1 of the Native Territorial Rights Bill, 'exclusive use and occupancy' was something the 'Tribe, Community, or Individuals' were entitled to. This measure addressed native title with much more precision than section 4 of the Native Circuit Courts Act, which deemed certain lands to count as subject to native title.[324] Such broad language made sense where the aim was to ensure maximum jurisdictional coverage for a circuit court.

[321] Gorst, *The Maori King*, 98–99.

[322] Richmond, memorandum, 29 September 1858, CO209/154, fo.472a, TNA.

[323] As a phrase, 'exclusive use and occupancy' emerged sporadically in various contemporaneous sources. Thus, Alden Bradford in *History of the Federal Government*, 253 stated: 'These purchases had been affected on friendly terms, and the value at which they were estimated by the Indians was paid by the government; and when desired, tracts were reserved for the exclusive use and occupancy of the natives'. A variant phrase was 'exclusive use and occupation': see Bell, *Principles of the Law of Scotland*, §940: 'The right to the *exclusive occupation and use* of land leads, in its exercise, to many difficult cases of interference between coterminous proprietors; and between land-owners and the public. The proprietor of land has the exclusive right to the use and occupation, not merely of the surface, but of what is below, and what is above the surface, "a cœlo usque ad centrum"' (emphasis added).

[324] Section 4 of the Native Circuit Courts Act stipulated: 'Provided that lands granted by the Crown to any person of the Native race, or to any person or body politic in trust for religious educational or charitable purposes, or in respect of any purchase made prior to the proclamation of the Queen's sovereignty, or specially granted as homesteads to persons of European race domiciled in Native districts, shall, where the same respectively abut upon lands over which the Native title has not been extinguished, be deemed for the purposes of this Act to be lands over which the Native title has not been extinguished, and may accordingly be included within any such district as aforesaid'.

Presumably, an *entitlement* to 'exclusivity' within the meaning of the Native Territorial Rights Bill was as much defined by a *present* material capacity or propensity to go to war over territory. If so, this view recalled Martin's analysis of Māori property rights in 1847, an analysis rooted in power over space and natural resources—the ability to exclude strangers (or to invite them) had the claimant group decided to do so.[325] Similarly, the board of inquiry in 1856 viewed the 'native title to land as tribes' as existing only insofar as and so long as it 'could be defended from other tribes'.[326] It is conceivable, therefore, that ministerial users of the phrase 'exclusive use and occupancy' envisaged, at least in theory, even transient uses of territory as activities potentially consistent with the legal concept underlying the phraseology, provided the claimant group could effectively demonstrate an ability to repel transgressors from time to time.

At this juncture in 1858, however, we have no sense of drawing distinctions between some types of Māori relationship with land as justifying a finding of 'exclusive use and occupancy' and other types of relationship being so transient or intangible to justify a finding of rights less than exclusive or less than an interest in the land (non-exclusive rights of use, for instance). Indeed, the language of the Native Territorial Rights Bill was not a simple replay of the arguments between the third Earl Grey and Martin, the Wesleyan Missionary Society, and others in 1847 and 1848. Nevertheless, while the text of the Native Territorial Rights Act did not seem to harbour such tensions, commentators on the Bill and on the subject of territorial rights did not necessarily agree. The lurking conceptual tensions regarding the assumed nature and extent of native title identified in Chapter Four still remained. There was, for instance, little agreement amongst commentators as to the nature of 'occupancy'. The Assistant Native Secretary, Thomas Smith, wrote in September 1859 that the '*unimproved* lands [of the Māori] are regarded as the property of the colony, merely encumbered with a certain native right of occupancy, of which it is the duty of the Government to clear them, as from time to time they may be required by the settlers'.[327] 'Unimproved lands' referred to those allegedly surplus lands not cultivated or occupied in the form of villages or fortifications. In Smith's view, '[f]ew would admit that the extension of European settlement must be contingent on the consent of the aboriginal owners to cede their territory'.[328]

At base, Richmond's memorandum treated Crown grants in substitution for native title as '*gratuitous* transmutations of the Native Title of occupancy into an English fee-simple'.[329] The key word was 'gratuitous'. It implied that a benefit passed, for which the replacement of the substance of the native title of occupancy was insufficient as the recipient of a Crown grant, obtained a better value than required. To that extent, the grantee received a gift. No true exchange of equivalent value occurred. What the recipient of the Crown grant received was a legal benefit of considerably higher value. Richmond accepted that it was a 'difficult question whether land so granted should, or should not, be alienable to Europeans'.[330] 'Perhaps', he surmised, 'no general rule can be laid down', believing it judicious to recognize the possible range in conduct on the part of holders of Crown grants. 'In some cases', he explained, 'it might be desir-

325 Martin, *England and the New Zealanders*, 51.
326 Report, Board of Inquiry, *GBPP1860* [2719], 237.
327 Smith to Browne, 20 September 1859, CO209/151, fo.182a, TNA (emphasis added).
328 Ibid.
329 Richmond, memorandum, 29 September 1858, CO209/154, fo.472, TNA (emphasis added).
330 Ibid.

able to secure the heirs of a spendthrift chief against the effects of his extravagance'.[331] Nevertheless, in other circumstances, 'no sufficient reason might exist for withholding the *full powers of ownership*'. On this basis, therefore, discretion was imparted to the governor under clause 12 of the Native Territorial Rights Bill. Richmond's memorandum noted a 'doctrine so mischievous and unfounded' to the effect that the 'native is *really entitled* to an absolute grant in fee-simple of whatever territory his tribe may think fit to make over to him in severalty, however extensive'.[332] The words 'really entitled' were used deliberately to illustrate the opposite—native title was not an interest in land to justify the granting of a fee simple estate under English real property law as a matter of right. According to the responsible ministers, proponents of a doctrine of native title claimed that 'to refuse such a grant, at least to impose any condition which does not operate for the sole and exclusive benefit of the natives, is unfair'. These proponents went further in professing that '[t]o make the Crown's right of pre-emption productive of a land fund, either in the way in which it is now made productive, viz., by means of sales of land ceded to the Crown at a low rate, and disposed of at an increased price, or by the proposed tax on alienation, is regarded as essentially unjust to the natives, who, it is thought, ought fairly to receive the whole purchase money'.[333] Expressing the alleged injustice in this way, the ministerial memorandum considered that the 'doctrine' reduced 'the Crown from the possession of a substantial power over the whole territory of New Zealand; which power it is bound for the benefit of all its subjects, to the condition of a bare trustee for the Maories'.[334]

Richmond's memorandum disagreed with this analysis of the relationship between the right of pre-emption under the Treaty of Waitangi and native title. In the view of the responsible ministers, the 'Crown's right of pre-emption (which no officer of the Crown, at least, will venture to question) was reserved avowedly for colonizing objects; viz., to enable the Government to promote and systematize the settlement of the country'.[335] For the purposes of his despatch to the Secretary of State for Colonies, Browne read Richmond's points rather narrowly, seeing in them a repetition of the disputes regarding the nature and extent of native title in the late 1840s and early 1850s. Turning in particular to the doubts expressed by Richmond as to whether 'the native title is really entitled to an absolute grant in fee simple of whatever territories his tribe may think fit to make over to him in severalty, however extensive', Browne said: 'If by these expressions it is intended to invalidate the rights of the aboriginal natives to *their unoccupied lands*, the subject is one which involves the peace of the colony'.[336] Rather dramatically, because the points in Richmond's memorandum had been directed towards the sensitive question of whether a native title of occupancy was necessarily equivalent to an estate in fee simple recognized under a Crown grant, Browne acknowledged 'the rights of the natives secured to them by the Treaty of Waitangi, and the fulfilment of engagements made by successive Governors, and confirmed by successive Secretaries of State'.[337]

Where Browne's concerns would have been on surer ground would be in doubting whether 'exclusive use and occupancy' (possession) would necessarily equate with all

[331] Ibid. [332] Ibid, fo.473 (emphasis added). [333] Ibid. [334] Ibid.
[335] Ibid.
[336] Browne to Lytton, 14 October 1858, CO209/154, fo.469, TNA (emphasis added).
[337] Ibid.

the areas of land that Māori groups claimed but did not occupy or use exclusively. There was no effort to distinguish, as has occurred in Canada or in New Zealand under the Foreshore and Seabed Act 2004 or Marine and Coastal Area (Takutai Moana) Act 2011 respectively, between exclusive use and occupancy approximating with an interest in the land itself and non-territorial rights (what Brian Slattery refers to as 'floating rights').[338] In 1862, the Native Lands Act neatly skirted this issue, using the broader formula of native title determined by 'native custom': 'All Lands in New Zealand over which the Native Title shall not have been extinguished may[,] save as hereinafter excepted and after the respective owners by Native Custom of the same shall have been ascertained as hereinafter provided[,] be dealt with and disposed of under the provisions of this Act'.[339]

Yet these profound questions of colonial policy on the nature and extent of native title were also addressed indirectly through the issue of colonial revenue. The proposed legislation concerned both state-formation and state projection, tied ineluctably to questions of land revenue. Māori were already estimated to figure predominantly in the collection of customs receipts but policy-formulators continued to pursue ways of bringing their land into the revenue system much more effectively. Clause 11 of the Native Territorial Rights Bill envisaged the payment of a tax of 10 shillings per acre by a purchaser of land subject to native title. The aim of the tax was to supply a fund for the colony to be used for public works and improvements on the purchased parcel of land, or within its neighbourhood. Setting the tax rate at '[t]en shillings per acre [was to align it with] the ordinary price of waste lands in all the provinces of the Northern Island; and the amount of the tax will consequently operate differentially in favour of the ordinary mode of purchase'.[340] The governor responded with the view that the 'effect of this tax would be to induce Europeans to select coveted plots of land, and to leave in the hands of the Maories large tracts, the alienation or retention of which is supposed to convey or retain a *right of sovereignty*'.[341] The governor was equating indigenous political authority and autonomy with land retention.

These issues about native title and the direction of colonial policy also arose in the context of ongoing debates about the distribution of constitutional authority within the colonial settlements. It did not escape notice that the governor was not authorized to act alone under the Native Territorial Rights Bill in issuing Crown grants. Rather, he was empowered to authorize the making of such grants 'in [executive] Council'; that is, in conjunction with a group comprising responsible ministers.[342] An interpretative

338 See s 32 of the now repealed Foreshore and Seabed Act 2004 (territorial customary rights), which refers to 'exclusive use and occupation of an area of the public foreshore and seabed' and s 58(1)(b)(i) of the replacement foreshore and seabed legislation—the Marine and Coastal Area (Takutai Moana) Act 2011 (customary marine title)—which refers to 'exclusively used and occupied [a specified area] from 1840 to the present day without substantial interruption'. Slattery, 'Making Sense of Aboriginal and Treaty Rights', 212. See also Slattery, 'A Taxonomy of Aboriginal Rights', in Foster, Raven, and Webber (eds), *Let Right Be Done*, 111–28.

339 'An Act to provide for the ascertainment of the ownership of Native Lands and for granting Certificates of Title thereto and for regulating the disposal of Native Lands and for other purposes', 26 Vict, number 42 (NZ).

340 Richmond, memorandum, 29 September 1858, CO209/154, fo.471, TNA.

341 Ibid, fo.472a (emphasis added).

342 See cl 11. Under cl 12, however, it would be lawful for the *governor alone* 'by the provisions of any [deed of grant] to prohibit the alienation, or restrict the alienability of any Estate or Interest created by such Grant, any rule of Law or Equity to the contrary notwithstanding'.

point was raised because of the relationship between the New Zealand Constitution Act as an imperial enactment and the native territorial rights measure of the colonial legislature. Section 73 of the Constitution Act provided that:

> no Conveyance or Transfer, or Agreement for the Conveyance or Transfer of any such Land [land of or belonging to or used or occupied by them in common as tribes or communities], either in perpetuity or for any Term or Period, either absolutely or conditionally, and either in Property or by way of Lease or Occupancy, and no such Release or Extinguishment as aforesaid, shall be of any Validity or Effect unless the same be made to, or entered into with, and accepted by Her Majesty, Her Heirs or Successors.

A statute purporting to effect such transfers, rather than the Crown itself, was seen as problematic. In appraising the Native Territorial Rights Bill and Richmond's memorandum, the governor clearly stated: 'The government of aboriginals is not conceded to the representatives of the civilized races either in British America or in other English Colonies'.[343] He added, '[i]f it were so, the English residents in Ceylon, or even in India, might reasonably claim to govern the coloured population of these countries'.[344] In approaching the question from the perspective of identifying who ought to control the public revenue of the colony, and aligning that answer to that question with the identity of those who were responsible to the public (the ministers acting in concert with the governor), there is a suspicion of despotism in Richmond's memorandum. And here the governor was seen as both the practitioner and prey of despotism—the sorcerer and the sorcerer's victim: 'Looking at the question as one of abstract constitutional principle, no Ministry could propose to entrust a power vitally affecting the relations of the settlers and natives, and the pecuniary resources of the Colony, to the discretion of a single individual, however elevated his position, who must commonly possess only a limited experience and a transitory interest in the affairs of the country'.[345] Richmond's paper recorded how '[e]ven in a Crown Colony, acts of so high a nature are often required to be done with the advice of the Executive Council'.[346] It is important to appreciate, however, that the troubles of the Native Territorial Rights Bill notwithstanding, the governor and his responsible ministers within Stafford's ministry had collaborated since 1857 on the broad principles underlying the legislative programme launched in the session of 1858. Indeed, in June 1858, Browne authorized Richmond to say publicly to legislators that Browne, as governor, 'entirely approved the Native Districts Regulation Bill, the Native Courts Bill and the Bay of Islands Bill'.[347]

As with Māori elites, however, colonial politicians perforce had to be multidirectional in their tactics. The Native Territorial Rights Bill was disputed in London, having been perceived as threatening to subvert the supervisory imperial element in the administration of relations with Māori groupings. Stafford, the premier at the time of the passage of the Bill, was not especially fond of it, expressing his reservations in private correspondence with Richmond when it was refused support in the United Kingdom. 'I cannot say I regret this much', wrote Stafford from Lucerne in Switzerland, adding that 'I was always... half afraid of that Bill in every shape in wh[ich] it was considered.'[348]

343 Browne to Lytton, 14 October 1858, CO209/154, fo.469a, TNA.
344 Ibid.
345 Richmond, memorandum, 29 September 1858, CO209/154, fo.472a, TNA.
346 Ibid.
347 Browne to Richmond, 22 June [1858], in Scholefield (ed), *The Richmond-Atkinson Papers*, I, 411.
348 Stafford to Richmond, 19 June 1859, in Scholefield (ibid), I, 465.

He acknowledged it to be 'on the whole a useful experiment'—'[w]ith it', he concluded, 'we might have staved off the direct purchase agitation until other means of placing would-be Colonists on land still held by Natives had palpably superseded the direct purchase cry'.[349] The Native Territorial Rights Bill was critiqued across the oceans. Disallowance of the Bill was signalled by an early Carnarvon's despatch of 18 May 1859. Carnarvon, the youthful parliamentary under-secretary in the Colonial Office under Bulwer Lytton, alleged the measure to be 'opposed to the spirit' of section 73 of the New Zealand Constitution Act by permitting individuals to purchase native title lands directly from Māori. Carnarvon held it to be 'far more advisable that Government should purchase territories, than that individuals should purchase properties, so that the line which separates the purchased lands on which European law is to prevail, from the unpurchased on which the Native usages will continue to subsist, though always advancing, will be broad and unequivocal'.[350] This sense of distinction between areas mantled with native title and those acquired through purchase was tangibly represented in mapping. We find illustrations in 1861, for instance, by Charles Heaphy, and in 1863 in a sketched map prepared in conjunction with local Whanganui *rangatira* distinguishing 'Native land' from 'European land' in the Whanganui region.[351] It is difficult to be categorical as to what Carnarvon's use of 'territories' to describe what government actors purchased meant when compared his description of individuals as purchasing 'properties'. Nevertheless, native title was once more tied to jurisdictional limits and boundaries; its presence suggested places where English real property law could not run—real property law inextricably linked to the elective franchise under the Constitution Act and to the absence of native title.

Reflecting on the course of the measure from the perspective of the House of Commons in 1861, Carnarvon's successor as parliamentary under-secretary at the Colonial Office, Chichester Fortescue, observed: 'The best friends of the natives [implying the Bishop of New Zealand and Martin, for instance] believed that nothing could be more desirable than an improvement in the native tenure of land, and some approach to the system of individual property'.[352] He acknowledged that:

> Several attempts had already been made to effect the desired change. In 1858 a Bill, called the Native Territorial Rights Bill, was sent home; but, upon full consideration by the Government of the day, the Colonial Office being then presided over by the right hon. Baronet the Member for Hertfordshire (Sir Bulwer Lytton) was not assented to, on the ground that in endeavouring to improve the native tenure of land the Bill gave the authorities in the Colony too large a discretionary power as to the purchase of land, and enabled them to issue to native owners certificates of title which the Crown could not assume the responsibility of maintaining.[353]

In New Zealand, advisors to the governor within the Native Secretary's office (Donald McLean and Thomas Smith) were unremittingly negative. Smith, reflecting on the disallowance of the Native Territorial Rights Bill, noted that '[h]owever desirable it may be that the natives should hold their lands in severalty, it is not true that any general desire exists to exchange the native title to one derived from the Crown nor are the

[349] Ibid.

[350] Carnarvon to Browne, 18 May 1859, *AJHR–1860*, E-1, 37.

[351] For key features redrawn from Charles Heaphy's map of March 1861, see plate 1 below. For the Whanganui map, see plate 2: White to Mantell, 20 May 1863, JC-WG1/4, 86, ANZ(W).

[352] Fortescue, *HPD*, 19 April 1861, vol 162, col 826.

[353] Ibid, cols 826–7.

aborigines of this country yet prepared for the introduction of any general individualization of title'.[354]

Provincial politicians in Auckland in particular responded negatively to the disallowance of the Native Territorial Rights Bill. A lengthy memorandum prepared for the new Secretary of State for Colonies in Viscount Palmerston's ministry, the Duke of Newcastle, spoke directly to the obstacles to 'civilization' occasioned by the failure of the imperial administration to countenance a Native Territorial Rights Bill regime that contemplated the individualization of native title. Saying that the 'great hindrance to the rapid individualisation of native title, without which, we are convinced that no continuous progress can be made' was the well-spring of difficulty, the Auckland provincialists referred to the liberal Anglican, Richard Whateley, and John Bird Sumner (Archbishop of Canterbury from 1848 until 1862) as accessible authorities. Thus, ' "I have spoken of *security of property*" says Archbishop Whately, in his introduction to the study of political economy, "as the most essential point; because, though no progress can be made without a division of labour this could neither exist without security property, nor fail to arise with it" '.[355] Sumner's *A Treatise on the Records of Creation* was cited for setting out how property '[was] this mainspring...which keeps the arts and civilised industry in motion'. He was also quoted for outlining the significance of property rights to peaceable affairs: 'The first who, having enclosed a spot of ground has taken upon himself to assert—*This is mine*, given a new aspect to society and lays the foundation, not of crimes and wars, and murders, as if these were unknown to the savage; but of improvement and civilisation'.[356] They expressed concern at the reducing return on the territorial revenue of the colony: 'It thus appears that the Auckland revenue derived from land, which in 1855, had risen to £60,137, had decreased in 1858 to £2433; and this, not from the want of demand to purchase, but from want of land to supply'.[357] Their exercise was one of *paradiastole* or 'rhetorical redescription' certainly—in their case, to cast something in a less unfavourable light.[358]

This cynical form of redescription—to speak expressly of 'enfranchisement'—operated in two ways: politically and as rationale. At the outset and most literally it mantled their proposals with liberal objects—to liberate individuals within Māori communities from the economic monopoly of the Crown in the land market by ensuring their access to the complete 'rights and privileges of British subjects' under the third article of the Treaty of Waitangi. The second dimension, however, was to invite government to respond to the challenge of liberating the market for potential purchasers. Carleton, for one, had expressed considerable faith in the Native Territorial Rights Bill before its disallowance was pronounced officially. In July 1859, Browne reported to Bulwer Lytton, 'Mr Carleton states that "a native is free to exchange his Maori

[354] Smith to Browne, 21 November 1859, LE1/1861/300, ANZ(W).

[355] William Daldy MGA ('Member of the General Assembly'), Edward King MPC ('Member of the Provincial Council'), M Cooper MPC, Thomas Forsaith MGA, Hugh Carleton MGA, Thomas Henderson MGA *et al*, to Newcastle, 20 October 1859, CO209/152, fos.71a–2, TNA (emphasis in original).

[356] Ibid, fo.72 (emphasis in original).

[357] Enclosure, William C Daldy, MGA; Edward King, MPC; IR Cooper, MPC; Thomas Forsaith, MGA; Hugh Carleton, MGA; 14 February 1859, printed, CO209/152, fo.104, TNA.

[358] Hickford, 'Framing and Reframing the *Agōn*'. For an account of *paradiastole*, see Skinner, 'Moral Ambiguity and the Renaissance Art of Eloquence', in *Visions of Politics*, 276; Runciman, *Political Hypocrisy*, 30.

title for a Crown title: the machinery is provided: every encouragement is given"'. The governor supposed that 'Mr Carleton alludes to the Native Territorial Rights Bill which I was unable to recommend for Her Majesty's assent; but that Bill would not have attained this object even if it had become law, because "Crown Grants were only to be issued under a restriction which might practically become a prohibition,—and in no case after the year 1861", (vide memo. by the late Chief Justice—attached;)'.[359] In addition, Browne noted that 'the complication of native title to land is such as to prevent the possibility of any one individualizing his property without the consent of very many others, and unless he is a chief of some influence; this is so difficult as to be virtually impossible without the assistance of the Government'.[360]

The Auckland politicians' memorial, trading in the language of 'enfranchisment', sought to withdraw the curtain from the Browne-McLean policy on the basis that it was insulated from material contestability in the colonial legislature, and by highlighting the perceived imbalance between the liberties of Māori as individual British subjects (counting as autonomous numbers) and the political and economic constraints operating upon Māori as members of customary political communities privileged by the Browne-McLean policy of negotiating with large groupings *qua* collectivities. The concept that the processes, norms, characteristics, or values of some particular configuration of a 'community' or clan ought to be preserved or laminated from change brought about through the decisions of individuals or sub-groups (certain families, for instance) doing something different from the wishes of the 'community' as a whole posed an ongoing problem for policy-formulators, as it did for Māori elites. The memorialists were arguing, self-interestedly, in favour of providing a less-rigid 'choosing context' for individual Māori, a situation where there would be fewer constraints on what counted as acceptable than what might have been the case with, say, a very stable, less-mutable cultural polity or grouping. So they assumed. For Carleton, William Daldy, and Thomas Forsaith, for example, their proposals represented an appropriately calibrated response to the troubled period of cultural transition for negotiating colonial and Māori communities, where these communities were affected by the presence of other sources of cultural meaning. Here, then, lay a fundamental and persistent tension in imperial and colonial constitutional philosophy, not readily answered or resolvable as a question of political thought or practical policy. This tension reflected an historical juxtaposition of the desire of certain individuals within indigenous descent-groups to obtain particular benefits (as they saw them) by entering into commercial transactions with colonial settlers and the norms of community-based control over territorial space and the political authority of chiefly elites. In so doing, some pursued these transactions with a view to evading intra-hapū hegemonies or forms of influence. The presence of strangers in the guise of colonial settlers—new pākehā—supplied these sorts of options together with risks that tactics of evasion, insubordination or simple participation in novel relationships would be interpreted in ways not aligned with broader

359 Gore Browne to G Bulwer Lytton, 18 July 1859, CO209/150, fos.520–20a, TNA. Martin had written, 'The proposal to make the franchise depend solely on a Crown title was not even accompanied by any provision under which a Crown Title might be readily obtained, when desired. Crown grants were only to be issued under a restriction which might practically become a prohibition, & in no case after the year 1861 (Native Territorial Rights Bill s 12)' ('Memorandum by the late Chief Justice Martin', 12 July 1859, CO209/150, fos.558–8a, TNA).

360 Gore Browne to G Bulwer Lytton, 18 July 1859, CO209/150, fos.520–20a, TNA, fos.520a–1.

whānau interests. That culture changes is a truism. Yet this tension between preserving the culture of community control regarding territorial space and the liberties of individuals *qua* British subjects[361] to participate in the colonial political economy on individual terms resonated in later periods, such as the late twentieth and early twenty-first centuries.[362] What it suggested in 1859 was to permit indigenous communities to respond to exogenous forces as well as ones endogenous to the group—individuals, according to the memorialists, ought to be permitted to engage at liberty with colonial actors regarding territorial space.[363] It was the sort of tension that emerged dramatically in 1860 in the crisis regarding the putative Waitara purchase, as will be explored in Chapter Seven.

In the main, there is no doubt that colonial policy-formulators and others, like Selwyn, Martin, and Swainson, were not prepared to tolerate the unvarnished survival of community title collectively owned (as native title was perceived). That is, neither the colonial ministry nor the governor would accept that community title was to be insulated from any form of individual engagement with the colonial legal and economic systems in the form of Crown grants held individually. Unremarkably, colonization, as conceived in the sense of transposing a political community to settle new lands, contained the very seedlings of normative innovation and disturbance as it encountered strangers. Ossification of existing Māori communal structures, even assuming that the metes and bounds of what existed in terms of Māori political formations could be accurately identified,[364] was not sought after. Rather, disagreements persisted as to the processes that ought to be pursued in order to introduce the possibilities of Crown-derived tenure into areas subject to native title. A ploy of the Auckland politicians adhering to

[361] Accepting that not all participants need have thought of themselves as 'British subjects' even though others might have characterized them thus.

[362] Appiah, *The Ethics of Identity*, 124, 130–8; Kymlicka, *Multicultural Citizenship*, 104–5, for example; Ivison, *Postcolonial Liberalism*, 66–7. It also materializes as an issue in Waitangi Tribunal proceedings, including *Turanga Tangata, Turanga Whenua—The Report on the Turanganui a Kiwa Claims* (Wai 814; 2004), which largely addressed the Native Lands Act (especially the Native Land Act 1873), II, 398, 446. In an important passage in *Turanga Tangata, Turanga Whenua—The Report on the Turanganui a Kiwa Claims* (Wai 814; 2004), the Waitangi Tribunal recognizes that certain land sales were 'fully consensual' (ibid, II, 446). It then noted, 'There will be others in which *some* or all *of the owners* did not wish to sell, or did not agree the price, yet were forced by circumstance or tricked by purchasers into joining the transfer' (emphasis added). 'Some' is an extraordinarily slippery category. It could mean a significant minority on the basis of a vote or show of hands in a majoritarian system or perhaps a lesser minority. In short, this sort of expression—'some... of the owners'—crystallizes one of the difficulties with the Tribunal's notion of consensus. It calls into question what 'consensual' might signify, as well as what it would look like from the perspective of process. Furthermore, the use of the term 'some' in the quote above appears to suggest that there could be no dissentients for a consensual transfer (or, more fundamentally, a community decision) to occur. These extracts also raise the question of what have been referred to as 'juridical histories' or histories that are teleological in being directed towards the ends of judicial (or judicial-like) appraisals in historical accounts: Andrew Sharp, 'History and Sovereignty: A Case of Judicial History in New Zealand/Aotearoa', 159–181; Sharp, 'Recent Juridical and Constitutional Histories of Maori', 31–60.

[363] Cf Kymlicka, who in *Multicultural Citizenship*, 104, stated: 'It is natural, and desirable, for cultures to change as a result of the choices of their members'. Yet, he counselled, 'We must, therefore, distinguish the existence of a culture from its "character" at any given moment'. Appiah contends that 'it is far from clear that we can always honor... preservationist claims while respecting the autonomy of future individuals' (*Ethics of Identity*, 135), a tension that comes into sharp focus as Kymlicka and Appiah appreciated in colonial settings.

[364] Ballara suggests the difficulties of assuming this: *Iwi*, 55–87.

the memorandum was to lay open this very tension with a clear preference for a permissive laissez-faire regime whereby individual members of Māori communities would be unconstrained by governor-centric controls (or, implicitly, any constraints operating within a relevant indigenous polity, such as a given *hapū*). As it was, the memorialists took umbrage with distinct aspects of the Earl of Carnarvon's despatch communicating the disallowance of the Native Territorial Rights Bill. They considered it undesirable for ' "the line which separates the purchased lands on which European law is to prevail, from the unpurchased lands on which the native usages will continue to subsist", [to be one that was] "broad" '.[365] If such a line were to be 'maintained at all, we certainly desire that it should be "unequivocally" drawn by law in accordance with the provisions contained in the seventy first section of the Constitution Act, and *not by the tacit or equivocal understanding* from which only a temporising system can result, and a continual risk of bringing the Queen's authority into contempt'.[366] Their preference was to lay bare through transparent legal means the divide between native districts where customary norms continued to predominate and those areas where British law and its jurisidictional apparatus operated unhindered.

Three main objections to the governor-centric system of interaction with native title and areas of Māori pre-eminence were sounded. First, the memorialists considered the pre-eminent legal role of the governor in acquiring territories from Māori on behalf of the Crown as problematic in situations where disputes arose as to the quality of the purchase or whether the vendors were properly identified. In endeavouring to resolve such disputes, Māori only had recourse to representatives of the colonial government: 'But as the Government whose mediation they seek, is not only an interested party, but, through its agents, the originator of the difficulty, the interference of the Crown, which under other circumstances would be all powerful, is from this cause shorn of its influence and authority'.[367] The memorialists could not have anticipated that they were envisaging the very nature of the Waitara dispute as it would be characterized by the former chief justice, Martin, in the following year. Yet Browne was dismissive. He despatched their concerns with the comment, 'Since I have been in N[ew] Zealand scarcely a single difference of opinion has occurred between the natives and the Government after a purchase has once been made, and in no case has there been a difficulty in arranging any misunderstanding which may have arisen'.[368]

Secondly, tying their arguments to a particular interpretation of the Treaty of Waitangi—one seen portrayed in argument before *Symonds* in the Supreme Court and circulated by advocates of direct purchase during FitzRoy's administration—the Auckland-based remonstrators said, 'The theory of the Government, as propounded in the Treaty of Waitangi, in virtue of which the cession of sovereignty was originally obtained, and as invariably explained and illustrated to the natives in subsequent oral

[365] William Daldy MGA, Edward King MPC, M Cooper MPC, Thomas Forsaith MGA, Hugh Carleton MGA, Thomas Henderson MGA *et al*, to Newcastle, 20 October 1859, CO209/152, fos.8-8–8a, TNA.

[366] Ibid (emphasis added).

[367] William Daldy MGA, Edward King MPC, M Cooper MPC, Thomas Forsaith MGA, Hugh Carleton MGA, Thomas Henderson MGA *et al*, to Newcastle, 20 October 1859, CO209/152, fos.68a–9, TNA.

[368] 'Remarks by the Governor' on William Daldy MGA, Edward King MPC, M Cooper MPC, Thomas Forsaith MGA, Hugh Carleton MGA, Thomas Henderson MGA *et al*, to Newcastle, 20 October 1859, CO209/152, fos.59–100a (reported at CO209/152, fo.122, TNA).

and documentary communication, is—that they, the natives are British subjects, entitled to all the rights and privileges which a subject of the British crown can claim'.[369] In a pugilistic passage, the Auckland memorialists then alleged that the:

> practice of Government, as exhibited in the present system of acquiring land, and as expressed by the natives themselves, is this—'You allow us to sell our pigs, our potatoes, our flax, and our spars to whomsoever we please, and at the best prices we can obtain; but you forbid us selling our land to any one but yourselves, and you will not give us nearly so much as we could obtain from the settlers. We cannot sell the trees that are growing on our land, because you have made a law forbidding the Europeans to buy. And yet you say that we are British subjects. If we desire to sell land, and make you the offer, we are not always certain that you will buy; and if it does suit your convenience to purchase, you only give a trifling sum per acre for land which we see you after a short time resell at 10s or 20s'.

In addition, the Auckland memorialists discounted one of the usual arguments made in favour of Crown-monitored and overseen purchase, namely the contingent benefits of the proximity of colonial settlement. Hence, they alleged it to be:

> useless to argue with the natives, and say that the contingent advantages which they derive from the sale of their lands to the Government are so numerous and valuable that they must be taken into consideration as part of the price they obtain, because they are quite witted enough to reply—'True, but these contingent advantages would still be ours if we sold to the Europeans at higher rates. When we sell to the Government it often happens that a long time elapses before any Europeans come to reside upon the piece of land we have sold, and thus no advantage is derived from the sale, beyond the mere nominal amount for the purchase money'.[370]

Browne disputed whether this statement accorded with the general opinion of Māori, although he confessed that individual Māori may have expressed such views. In this extract alone, the memorialists assailed a number of the complicated statutory features in play, circumscribing the options for *modus vivendi* between Māori and settlers directly. Fenton's opinions were cited. In this context, we find the governor reporting to the Colonial Office: 'Mr Fenton's opinion is probably quoted because he was recently employed in the Native Department where his conduct did not meet my approval: he is still in the employment of the Government, but there is a remarkable similarity between his opinions and those published in a local newspaper where columns are constantly occupied with attacks upon the Native Department'.[371] Asked to respond to the detail of the Auckland provincial politicians' 'enfranchisement' proposals, Thomas Smith, the Assistant Native Secretary, commented: 'However desirable it may be that the natives should hold their lands in severalty, it is not true that any general desire exists to exchange the Native title for one derived from the Crown; nor are the aborigines of this country yet prepared for the introduction of any general system of individualization of title'.[372]

A third limb of objection to the governor and Native Department's predominance and oversight of Crown–Māori relations hinged on the alleged formation of a 'land

[369] Ibid, fo.69, TNA. [370] Ibid, fos.69–70a.

[371] 'Remarks by the Governor' on William Daldy MGA, Edward King MPC, M Cooper MPC, Thomas Forsaith MGA, Hugh Carleton MGA, Thomas Henderson MGA *et al*, to Newcastle, 20 October 1859, CO209/152, fos.59–100a (reported at CO209/152, fo.136, TNA).

[372] Smith, Assistant Secretary, Native Secretary's Department, Auckland, to Gore Browne, 21 November 1859, CO209/152, fo.150, TNA.

league' of Māori with a policy against transferring lands to the colonial government. The Auckland politicians averred: 'One of the evil effects of the present system has been the gradual formation of a league or conspiracy amongst the natives, the object of which is to hinder altogether the sale of land; and thus a serious impediment to the progressive settlement of the country has been raised'.[373] To this, Browne riposted: 'This is an assertion which can only be paralleled by that relative to the Tenterden Steeple and the Godwin Sands [meaning a nonsensical assertion]'. Explicitly linking native title or territorial rights to political autonomy, he claimed, 'The league existed before I arrived only because the natives feel that when they have divested themselves of their territorial rights they will no longer be able to maintain a separate nationality. The league is quite as strong against the purchase of their lands by individuals as against that by the Government; and the reason above given is the only one used by delegates sent about the country to obtain adherents to it'.[374]

Opposition was mounted against various colonial measures in London demonstrating the ongoing significance of sustaining political networks within the metropolitan heart of Britain's trans-oceanic empire. Often the opposition had a provincial colour. James Fitzgerald, for one, contended against various pieces of colonial legislation in the imperial metropole. Fitzgerald had resigned his seat in the General Assembly in New Zealand in 1857 and acted as emigration agent for the province of Canterbury for three years based in England, refusing offers of the governorship for British Columbia and Queensland. Stafford reported on Fitzgerald's efforts in the United Kingdom opposing various legislative efforts of the Stafford ministry, keeping his co-ministerialists alive to the multi-directional aspects of colonial politics. He also advised Richmond on the latest political developments and rumours in Britain. On one such occasion, Stafford in visiting the United Kingdom reported on the developments in favour of party organization, writing to Richmond that New Zealand colonial politicians ought to grasp that future too: 'The one subject all men in office in Engl[an]d think of is to *keep in*... conduct their departmental business as did those whom they have displaced!'[375] He concluded, 'we in New Z[ealan]d are in our own persons far behind the age in the matters of Parliamentary Gov[ernmen]t, & should change our course & consider alone how we are to create & *keep* a *strong party*'.[376]

Richmond and his colleagues amongst Stafford's small coterie of ministerialists were well aware of the complexities of policy and legal design—the craft or 'science' (as Adam Smith would have put it) of the legislator. The vexing question of what was to be done, if anything, waylaid them. Aware that they could use the legislative resources available to them in the House of Representatives to assume the initiative, they sought self-dramatization in producing statutes, thereby aspiring to open up novel avenues for patronage beyond the gift of the governor and his Land Purchase system (centred on McLean) and for addressing the policy stasis on native title since the end of Grey's tenure as governor. These ministerialist newcomers, having legislative timetables and

373 William Daldy MGA, Edward King MPC, M Cooper MPC, Thomas Forsaith MGA, Hugh Carleton MGA, Thomas Henderson MGA *et al*, to Newcastle, 20 October 1859, CO209/152, fo.70a, TNA.

374 Remarks by the Governor, CO209/152, fo.123.

375 Stafford to Richmond, 19 June 1859, in Scholefield (ed), *The Richmond-Atkinson Papers*, I, 469 (emphasis in original).

376 Ibid (emphasis in original).

resources at their disposal, encouraged an enthusiasm for legislative adventures. In these ventures they endeavoured to shape political agendas for the colony trans-regionally, to wrestle with provincial politics and their relations to general colonial government.

In 1858 and 1859, a temper of experimentation prevailed amongst responsible ministers vis-à-vis native title. This temper set up a dynamic whereby the governor engaged in counter-experiments and counter-memoranda, seeing statutory ventures as a way of building gubernatorial resources through constructing new institutions. For responsible ministers in a time when political parties of a disciplined nature had not yet crystallized, legislation was conceived as a means of keeping otherwise ill-disciplined and restive members of the House of Representatives occupied and fashioning points of political convergence, as well as for supplying ways of setting out legally contained forms of interaction between Māori communities and niches of colonial settlement. Other than these ventures in statutory design, we see reactive reflections on the nature of native title, as new problems emerged throughout the second decade of the colony, requiring advice and answers as to what to do in particular circumstances. Hence, in 1850 Merivale, in the Colonial Office, had trialled an extensive opinion on the question of native title and gifting territory in accordance with localized, customary norms to those from outside of the relevant gifting group. Merivale was unsuccessful in obtaining complete endorsement from the third Earl Grey, as his opinion proceeded more as an idea than a proper solution to the problem in hand. In the view of the Secretary of State, two despatches were warranted: 'Mr Merivale—I concur generally in the views you have embodied in this draft & I consider them of much importance. I am of opin[io]n however that it will be better to divide the despatch into two, the one a public one confined to Mr Meurant's case (on which this draft seems to me quite right) the other a confidential one referring to the former & stating my views on the more general questions'.[377] Merivale's position on customary gifting by individuals within a tribal or communal framework was as follows: 'I think that, with respect to the allotment of lands held in common by the tribes by individual members of those tribes, native usage must be respected: such a power in the chiefs must be maintained where it exists, conformably not only with the general principle to be followed in dealing with them, but also, perhaps, with the words of the Treaty of Waitangi'.[378] On the specific question of a power to alienate, however, it appeared to Merivale that 'land so allotted [to individuals] does not acquire the incidents of real property in the English sense of the word'. He wrote, 'I think the native obtaining any such allotment has no right to alienate the land: or, if this be too broadly stated, certainly no right to alienate except to the Crown, whose right of pre-emption is not affected by the allotment'.[379]

On the question of a pākehā settler (in this case Edward Meurant) incorporated within Māori *whānau* and occupying customary land with a Māori spouse, he considered that a 'European marrying a native woman acquires no further rights in such land, whether allotted before or after his marriage, than she possessed herself: consequently that he is under the same restraints as to alienation, and certainly has no claim to a Crown grant of such land'. In all the circumstances, which he regarded as 'confused' on account of Meurant 'not accurately distinguishing between his claims for land

[377] Earl Grey, minute, 4 November 1850, CO209/159, fos.133–3a, TNA.
[378] Merivale, minute, to Hawes, 28 September 1850, CO209/159, fos.134–4a, TNA.
[379] Ibid, fos.134a–5.

alleged to have been granted to his native wife by native chiefs, and other land which it now appears he purchased from native chiefs', Merivale concluded that Meurant's allocation of acreage was fair and appropriate. Indeed, in applying 'these principles to Mr Meurant's case, it appears to me, that he acquired no right of property in the 30 acres: that he could only enjoy them in right of his wife: and that he could have no greater right of disposing of them than could have been claimed by herself'.[380] As to the thirteen acres which 'he has purchased [from the Māori chieftains], I conclude that he could not claim a Crown grant of them as of right'. He found, then, in responding to Meurant's memorial, 'I have no reason to doubt that the issuing of a Crown grant for [twenty four] acres to him as his absolute property in lieu of those imperfect and ill-defined claims to a somewhat larger amount, was a fair and even a favourable adjustment'.[381] Such was the answer to the distinct immediate inquiry on the facts as suggested by the Colonial Office.

In considering Meurant's memorial, however, a more profound issue had emerged as a matter of legal policy, namely that of allowing the recognition within English law of certain forms of Māori alienation or perhaps adapting these customary forms of disposition. Thus, Merivale stated:

> I think it is a fair question whether this right of disposal of land, which from having belonged in common to a tribe has become private property, may not be conceded, under proper precautions to prevent its being made use of as a pretext for evading the Crown's right of pre-emption: For instance, if the system of registration planned in the Land Instructions be gradually adopted, a native might perhaps be allowed to alienate such land, if it had been registered as his or hers for a certain time: perhaps if it did not exceed a certain amount.[382]

At this point, the third Earl Grey interpolated an extensive comment, including thoughts as to whether it would be apposite, '[i]n making an arrangement also for the purchase by the Crown of lands claimed by the natives... to allow so much of the land as can be usefully held by the natives to be divided among them & held by the same terms & the same absolute right of disposing of it which is given to British settlers by obtaining a Crown grant'.[383] The so-called 'case of Mrs. Meurant' occasioned a petition from Hugh Carleton to the Secretary of State for Colonies in January 1852 in which it was noted that 'the [Meurant] family was content with a Maori title, and would at the present moment much prefer the whole under a Maori title, to a portion under a Crown grant', concluding that '[n]o practical inconvenience resulted from that peculiar tenure'.[384] Indeed, Carleton averred, the 'ground was occupied, before the interference

[380] Ibid, fos.135–5a.
[381] Ibid, fos.135a–6.
[382] Ibid, fos.138–9.
[383] Ibid.
[384] Carleton to Earl Grey in 'The Case of Mrs. Meurant', *Daily Southern Cross*, 30 November 1852, 2. See also ibid, 'The question is strictly confined to the wrongs of Kenehuru his wife, from whom thirty acres were taken, ten of which were afterwards granted to the husband and family. I maintain that the New Zealand Government had no more right to grant those ten acres to the husband, than it had to take the thirty acres from the wife. The case is entirely misconceived. The land was originally given to the wife by her friends as an endowment; and was in justice and in reason her sole and separate property. The whole is taken from her, the Government and the husband dividing that to which neither was entitled. Mr. Meurant's fault consisted in becoming a party to the transaction; but being a Government officer, he dared not refuse'.

of the Government, by two, rent-paying tenants, and the mesne profits of the land, from the time of that interference, are due by the Government to the family'.[385]

Merivale and the third Earl Grey revealed an abstract willingness to calibrate the legal system's accommodation of Māori proprietary interests, as Māori communities transitioned, in their view, from ruder forms of society. Over time, claims to more complicated forms of 'social rights' were anticipated, 'social rights' being a term conventionally used in the contemporary political literature to describe individual liberties to engage in civil transactions with others and individual liberty in acts of conscience.[386] 'Considering the great advance which the natives of N[ew] Zealand appear to be making in the arts of European life and their partial adoption of the manner and sentiments of Europeans', wrote Merivale, 'I cannot but imagine that complicated difficulties may soon arise out of the insufficiency of native usages framed under the influence of former barbarism, to satisfy the various cases of claims to *social rights* which must occur among them as they advance in civilization'.[387] Furthermore, they signalled the possibility of adapting colonial modes of legal recognition to allow some forms of alienation of property so that Māori could participate in the colonial economy with increased ease.

By comparison, the *Meurant v Keir* case in the Supreme Court at Auckland was spectacularly uninformative, although published (and criticized) in the newsprint media. Becoming embroiled in disputes as to civil procedure and the ritualistic observances and pedantries of colonial barristerial culture, the court failed to pronounce on the key points at issue. The media identified the main points arising in the *Meurant* proceeding, including the power of the Crown to 'confiscate' the lands belonging to the 'Maori, British subject,— Mrs Meurant'.[388] It also raised the issue of the authority of lieutenant-governor Pitt to issue grants of Crown lands, and the legality of the Quieting Titles Ordinance.[389] The *Daily Southern Cross* reported how the case was of 'great interest, not merely as settling the important law questions raised,—their effects upon the natives, and the amalgamation of the races; but likewise on account of this being the first occasion here on which the Courts of law have been appealed in order to test whether a Governor and Council can do as they ch[oo]se;—that their unathorised acts are the Law of New Zealand, and cannot be questioned'.[390] No remedy was forthcoming. The hoped-for assistance of judges was absent. Underlying the case were the notoriously 'many and fruitless efforts which were made, before the late Mr Meurant's death, to recover the land conveyed to his native wife and her children, by the chiefs Te Hira, Te Tawa, and Te Keene, which had been confiscated and sold by Governor Grey, in direct contravention of the Treaty of Waitangi, and of the rights of the natives

[385] Ibid. A key issue was the marital status of Kenehuru. Thus, 'if Kenehuru had lived in concubinage with Meurant, she would have retained her native right of holding land without a Crown grant. This right she is alleged to have lost by being lawfully married [within the meaning of English law]' (ibid).

[386] For example, Villier, *An Essay on the Spirit and Influence of the Reformation of Luther*, 62;, *On Liberty*, ch 4 ('Of the limits to the authority of society over the individual').

[387] Draft, Earl Grey to Sir George Grey, draft September 1850 [Merivale—28 September 1850; Hawes—29 September 1850; Grey—[5 October/November? 1850]], CO209/159, fos.140–40a, (emphasis added), TNA.

[388] *Daily Southern Cross*, 1 December 1854, 3.

[389] An Ordinance for Quieting Titles to Land in the Province of New Ulster, 25 August 1849, session X, no 4.

[390] Ibid.

guaranteed thereby'.[391] The *Daily Southern Cross* in Auckland reported how '[d]uring the lifetime of Mr Meurant the recovery had been sought by means of correspondence only; for [he] was a Government officer, and dared not risk the loss of his situation'.[392] His death left his widow ('his native wife'), Eliza Meurant (Kenehuru), as potential plaintiff. The 'proverbial uncertainty of the law was risked', according to the newspaper, when the plaintiff's counsel, Rochfort, arrived in the colony from Melbourne, who, in taking 'so clear and comprehensive view of the case, and, we must admit, so novel a view', advised his client to approach the Supreme Court.[393]

Exchanging parcels of land subject to native title for a Crown grant remained a persistent theme of ministerial proposals, as much as those of Selwyn, the Bishop of New Zealand, and Martin.[394] Responsible ministers put forward a 'Native Crown Grants Bill' in 1859 with a self-explanatory long title as follows: 'A Bill to authorise the Grant of Crown lands to natives in consideration of the surrender of their territorial rights; and also the grant of Crown lands in certain cases to Europeans resident amongst the natives'.[395] The difficulty, as the governor appreciated, was one of political economy—how to incentivize Māori to forego the negotiated status quo in favour of a situation that carried with it new and foreign legal norms enacted by a distant colonial legislature? Indeed, the political-economic relations of colonial-settlement niches and adjacent hinterlands incentivized a status quo favouring localized *modus vivendi* without necessarily accepting by way of negotiation colonial legal norms. Commenting on lands adjoining the settlement of Napier in 1859, Browne stated: 'A large tract of valuable land very much required by the Europeans, remains uncultivated in the hands of the Maoris who get so much for trespass and illegal licence to pasture that there is no probability of their alienating any portion of it'.[396]

FASHIONING STATUTORY WINDOWS OF COMMUNICABILITY BETWEEN INDIGENOUS CUSTOM AND ENGLISH LAW

Once proposed in June 1858, the colonial native territorial rights legislation crystallized a statutory form purporting to address how, in addition to deeds of purchase, native title might be gradually replaced by Crown-sourced titles. Upon the communication of the disallowance of the Native Territorial Rights Bill, a legislative-policy aspiration to

391 '*Meurant v Keir*', *Daily Southern Cross*, 23 May 1854, 2.

392 Ibid. On the procedural missteps that held up the case, the newspaper commented: 'We had thought that at this time of the nineteenth century we had got quit of all these cobwebs which obstruct and obscure the path of justice, but we were mistaken' (ibid).

393 The sorry irresolution of this case was referred to in Carleton, 'New Zealand', 440–1. See also *Daily Southern Cross*, 14 December 1867.

394 In May 1860, Selwyn continued to advocate Crown grants as remedies for the problems associated with native title (Selwyn, 8 May 1860, *AJHR—1860*, E-1, 25): 'The remedy appears to be simple, viz:—An unqualified recognition of the Native Land Title to the fullest extent, and with every legal security that would be given to any landed proprietor of our own race.... In what respect is the Native owner inferior to the English purchaser? Why is the land which a tribe has sold to be secured by a Crown Grant, and not the land which it retains?...Crown Grants are the remedy for this evil'.

395 'Draft of Bill by Ministers with remarks thereon by the Governor', CO209/151, fos.220–4, TNA.

396 Ibid, 'remarks by the governor', fo.221a.

supply a means for ensuring the translation of native title into English tenurial estates still remained to be addressed. Indeed, despite its disallowance, the Native Territorial Rights Bill suggested a way forward to certain colonial politicians, especially in the North Island provinces of Auckland and Taranaki. Certainly, once it was off the table, a vacuum abhorred by political nature stood in its place. Yet its way of addressing the conundrum of native title shaped subsequent ventures and experiments. Now the distinct question was ignited of what, if any, statutory regime ought to be crafted to comprehensively address the ascertainment of native title and its possible substitution by Crown-derived titles. There was a rush to consider other statutory stand-ins.

The pace of land acquisition was slowing. As discomforting as it might have seemed to the governor, figures suggested less interest amongst Māori *hapū* in large-scale acquisitions of territory via deeds of purchase. An approximate return reporting acreage purchased pursuant to deeds of purchase from 1850 until 30 September 1859 suggested declining success in producing territorial land for colonial settlements.[397] Overall, seen from this perspective, the situation in the Taranaki appeared especially parlous. From 5 July 1850 to 31 March 1854, some 31,015 acres were acquired, whereas in the period from 31 March 1858 to 30 September 1859, a mere 14,000 acres were reported as acquired, yielding a total of 45,015 acres. For the Wellington and Hawke's Bay provincial areas, some 3,391,065 acres were reportedly acquired from 5 July 1850 to 31 March 1854. Yet only 402,000 acres were acquired in the period from 31 March 1856 to 31 March 1858.

In Auckland, still then the seat of gubernatorial administration, the *Daily Southern Cross* kept up, in the words of the governor, a 'continual agitation on the subject of enfranchising native lands: reminding its readers that "one well written address placarded in every kainga [village] in the country would raise a fever of excitement (among the natives) which all the anodynes and opiates of the native department would be incompetent to allay" '.[398] Indeed, these words, taken from the 16 August 1859 issue of the *Daily Southern Cross*, constituted part of an extensive argument against the imperial administration's reasons for disallowing the native territorial rights legislation.[399] Subsequently, the newspaper continued its condemnation of the disallowance of the Native Territorial Rights Bill, a measure which it saw as a 'first step in advance towards the enfranchisement of the native lands'.[400] Both the governor and the responsible ministers participated in this discursive exploratory exercise. Far from denying the increasing difficulties of acquiring territorial space for settlement purposes, Browne now admitted his government's predicament, although he stressed the relative absence of funds subject to the governor's control. Yet Browne's despatch also anticipated elements of the arguments to be posed by the Auckland provincial memorialists in the following month. These were arguments, as we have seen, that Browne would seek to marginalize unless expressed and construed through the medium of his approved despatches: 'With the increase of the European population land has necessarily acquired an additional value: the natives have seen the lands they alienated for farthings resold for pounds; they feel that dominion and power, or as they term it "substance",

[397] 'Approximate return of all lands purchased by the Crown in the northern Island of New Zealand; From the 5th of July 1850 to the 30th of September 1859', CO209/152, fo.153a, TNA.

[398] Browne to Newcastle, 20 September 1859, CO209/151, fos.139–9a, TNA.

[399] 'The Territorial Rights Bill', *Daily Southern Cross*, 16 August 1859, vol 16, issue 1244, 2.

[400] 'The Territorial Rights Act', *Daily Southern Cross*, 23 August 1859, vol 16, issue 1246, 2.

went from them with the territories they alienated, and they look with apprehension to the annihilation of their nationality'.[401] Browne carefully set out the timing of the consequences of these sentiments as predating his assumption of office: 'The consequence of this feeling has been the formation of a league to prevent the alienation of land, commenced by the tribes in the Waikato before my arrival in the colony, and which has since combined with the so-called King movement'.[402]

To address the policy impasse, the governor forwarded a copy of 'Heads of a Bill promoting the colonization of lands in New Zealand whereof the native title is at present unextinguished by Mr Sewell', along with various responses to it, including those of Martin and Richmond. Once again, Browne revealed a strong proclivity to have views tested and to disclose the testing of these views to the Colonial Office. Sewell's proposal envisaged an intermediate body between the politics of a settler ministry and the politics of Māori communities. The intermediate body would engage with Māori, mainly insulating Māori from the full diversity of colonial politics, and vice versa. The executive council would continue to have a role but largely in relation to revenue or money matters. Clause 2 of Sewell's sketched outline Bill empowered 'Her Majesty [to] appoint not more than—nor less than—[left blank] persons to be a Native Council for the purpose of this Act with the usual powers of removal and new appointment with power to delegate such authorities to the Governor personally'.[403] Clause 11 set out that 'The Governor may by proclamation define and declare any lands in New Zealand whereof the native title is at present unextinguished to be a district subject to the provisions of the Act'. Each proclaimed district was to be referred to as a 'native land district'. Clause 17 envisaged an institutional apparatus for any such proclaimed district: 'In every district a Native Circuit Court to be established under the Native Circuit Courts Act 1858 and a Resident Magistrate and at least two Assessors to be appointed for the district'. Setting out a revenue stream to finance the activities of the governor and permanent council was a critical tool of power and provided ways for Sewell's proposals to exert concrete effects throughout designated parts of New Zealand. Under clause 5 the governor was empowered, albeit acting in accordance with the advice of his executive council, to 'raise from time to time not exceeding £250,000 on the security of the General Revenue of the Colony to be applied to purposes to be defined in the Act'.[404] The objects to which such monies could be put were outlined in clause 6. These purposes included 'obtaining the assent of the aboriginal inhabitants to the cession of their title either by way of direct payment or in public works beneficial to them or by way of loan to individuals or annual payments to chiefs or others or in the establishment or maintenance of habitations for their benefit'. Although officially forwarded to London in September 1859, there is evidence to suggest that Sewell had worked on this measure in the winter of 1859. Sewell noted in his journal for 3 July 1859, 'I have prepared a Bill for the management of Native Lands'.[405]

The responsible ministers supplied their own commentary, again signed by Richmond, as with so many memoranda previously: 'The distinctive feature of

[401] Browne to Newcastle, 20 September 1859, CO209/151, fos.135a–6, TNA.

[402] Ibid, fos.136–6a.

[403] 'Heads of a Bill promoting the colonization of lands in New Zealand whereof the native title is at present unextinguished by Mr Sewell', fos.206–6a, TNA.

[404] Ibid, fos.206a–7.

[405] Sewell, 3 July 1859, journal of Henry Sewell, I, 41, qMs-1786, ATL.

Mr Sewell's proposal is the constitution of a Board of Commissioners appointed by the Crown, having the Governor at its head, to which are to be transferred the important questions[:]—First—of conducting land purchasing operations[;] Secondly—of regulating the sale and disposal of lands acquired from the natives[;] Thirdly—of supervising the survey & preparation for settlement of such lands'.[406] Richmond and his colleagues not unexpectedly moved to characterize the status quo as they understood it and the ways in which Sewell's proposals might unseat the preferred features of the status quo. Commenting on each function separately, the ministers referred to those areas where the governor's political judgment might prevail over that of his responsible advisors: 'Under existing arrangements, the first of these functions is exercised by the Governor, who acts upon the advice of his Responsible Ministers as to what Blocks shall be purchased and what prices shall be paid; subject however to His Excellency's right of veto if political reasons render it, in his opinion, inexpedient to make a particular purchase'.[407] In practice, the ministers observed that McLean, 'the Chief Land Purchase Commissioner (over whose appointment and removal the Governor retains a personal control, and who is the sole medium of communication on the subject of land purchases between the Government and the natives), exercises a very large influence over the conduct of land purchasing operations'.[408] Yet the 'second function' they noted as belonging to the 'General Assembly; and the third & last to the Provincial Governments'.[409] Any combination of such responsibilities in a permanent council or board of commissioners was seen as inconsistent with the representative institutions of the colony granted under the Constitution Act. 'His Excellency's Responsible Ministers', they said, 'are decidedly of opinion that the union of these powers in a permanent Board could not fail to excite strong public dissatisfaction; and that the proposal cannot be made to the legislature with a chance of success.'[410] The governor contributed his own assessment of his responsible ministers' commentary when the ministers remarked that it appeared 'improbable that such a system could work in harmony with the representative institutions of the Colony' and concluded that the proposals hardly seemed congruent with the 'existing institutions' of the colony in appraising the 'scheme abstractly' without reference to public opinion. He merely posed the point: 'Is there any greater incongruity than in the present system which vests the power in the Governor alone?'

Responsible ministers developed a suite of proposed counter-bills, including 'A Bill to authorise the Grant of Crown lands to natives in consideration of the surrender of their territorial rights; and also the grant of Crown lands in certain cases to Europeans resident amongst the natives'. They also suggested 'A Bill to provide for the colonization of native districts' and 'An Act for the partition of lands over which the Native Title is not extinguished between the Native Owners thereof' (the short title of which was the 'Native Land Partition Act 1858'). The aims of the Native Land Partition Bill were considerable. It sought to ensure that Māori communities would be volunteers for the individualization of title. According to its preamble:

> Whereas the partition of land held in common by Native tribes and the individualization of the title to such lands would greatly conduce to the gradual advancement and promote

[406] 'Remarks by Ministers on Mr Sewell's draft Bill', 19 August 1859, CO209/151, fo.212a, TNA.
[407] Ibid, fo.213. [408] Ibid, fos.213–3a. [409] Ibid, fo.213a.
[410] Ibid, fos.213a–4.

the civilization of the native race, and it is expedient that such partition and individualization should be effected by the natives themselves with the assistance of the Resident Magistrate of the district, in such a manner as to avoid the necessity of the interference of the Government for the purpose of conducting such proceedings or of upholding any awards decisions or arrangements made in furtherance of the objects aforesaid.[411]

In commenting on the last of these measures, Browne noticed how the responsible ministers had assumed that the legislative measures passed in the previous session in 1858—the Native Districts Regulation Act, the Native Circuit Courts Act, and the Native Territorial Rights Act—had all come into full operation, which, he said, could not be assumed. He observed that the heights of the ministers' ambition were not warranted by the actual state of affairs on the ground—all was aspiration: 'The £7,000 granted for native purposes provides only for four magistrates who are already fully employed in four comparatively small districts', adding 'also that the funds are insufficient to pay the assessors at present employed; while such a scheme as this would require magistrates and assessors in every district'.[412]

'How to reconcile this work of civilization with the fair claims and rights of the natives is the problem which the Government has to solve'

In New Zealand we see rich veins of constitutional reflection and argument in connection with indigenous property rights. Reflecting on the constitutional situation in April 1859, Sewell noted the constitutional import of native title and Crown–Māori relations. In keeping with mid-nineteenth-century strains of whiggish-liberal as opposed to radical-liberal thought, Sewell was not in favour of unimpeded democracies—the despotism of sheer numbers or swamping. In this sense, his thoughts reflected well-worn and traversed whiggish strains of politics: 'Democracies without very powerful correctives are the worst kind of governments'.[413] He expressed the not uncommon concern with the quality of education, political mindedness, and thought in colonial New Zealand—the absence of 'public opinion of a high tone'—noting that the relative weaknesses of these qualities tended to 'exaggerate popular power without preserving the true *balance*'.[414] While the independence of the governor was largely preserved in the arena of Crown–Māori relations, he apprehended that this '*imperium in imperio* will become intolerable and is only now carried on by great judgment on the part of Richmond assisted no doubt by the Governor's personal respect and liking for him and the general agreement of opinion between them'.[415] He was critical of the manner in which responsible government had been understood in the Australasian colonies. It seemed to him that it had been 'carried to a preposterous extreme and that not in New Zealand alone but in all the Australian Colonies'. A consequence was that the 'Governor has been practically pushed off the Throne'.[416] This was not to say that Sewell was an advocate for double government—far from it. He displayed his unease

[411] 'Draft of Bill by Ministers', 'An Act for the partition of lands over which the Native Title is not extinguished between the Native Owners thereof', CO209/151, fos.288–9, TNA.

[412] 'Remarks by the Governor on the Draft of a Bill by Ministers—marked F', CO209/151, fos.236a–7, TNA.

[413] Sewell, 5 April 1859, journal of Henry Sewell, I, 29, qMs-1786, ATL.

[414] Ibid, 28 (emphasis added); 'Public opinion of a high tone', ibid, 29.

[415] Ibid, 26. [416] Ibid, 25.

in private musings. Both responsible ministers, in seeking to obtain complete control of Crown–Māori relations, and the governor, in reserving these relations from the complete authority of his ministers, were 'wrong' he said and 'I see evil in the distance'.

Writing in his journal in April 1859 at least, which he intended to use to inform others,[417] he recommended a system of complete party government, with the governor simply acting as one member of the executive council, but subject to an important constraint. He proposed a discursive setting where each party could state their views in writing in executive council proceedings and submit these views to the 'Imperial Government whose decisions should be acquiesced in'.[418] His notion was predicated on broadening the expected behaviour on native affairs recorded in Browne's memorandum of April 1856 and applying it to government generally. In Sewell's proposal, the imperial administration would assume an adjudicative role between different colonial views. A delicate balance in a constitutional setting was a precondition of liberty certainly; but maintaining such a balance also preserved the political community from a sudden lurch towards despotism and degeneration. This sort of whiggish analysis was not an argument in favour of the predominance of mere numbers. Nor was it a simplistic transposition of William Blackstone's version of the Polybian balance in his swift, mechanically driven recitation of the mixed classical constitution. In the first volume of his *Commentaries on the Laws of England* (1765), he characterized the executive, the people, and nobility within the legislature as akin to 'three distinct powers in mechanics': 'they jointly impel the machine of government in a direction from what either, acting by themselves, would have done; but at the same time in a direction partaking of each, and formed out of all; a direction which constitutes the true line of the liberty and happiness of the community'.[419] Both Sewell and Carleton, although coming from different points of emphasis, were adapting aspects of English liberal constitutional thought in relatively sophisticated ways to a situation comprising relatively isolated provincial colonies.

An innovative proponent of policy solutions himself, by 1859 Sewell was something of a soloist as far as Stafford was concerned, and possibly a political prima donna—somewhat aloof from Stafford's political coterie, of whom Sewell occasionally disapproved as tainted by commercial interests in pastoral runs in Otago. Stafford's ministry was no stranger to petty interpersonal jealousies: 'From the little I saw of him [Sewell] in Sydney I was reluctantly forced to the conclusion that he was in a state of mind...wh[ich] would militate against his acting cordially with us & heartily casting in his lot with ours'.[420] Sewell's salaried involvement with a British-based company searching for investment opportunities within the colony, particularly by obtaining contracts for the carriage of mail by steam vessels, also complicated matters considerably. Stafford was damning on this point:[421]

[417] With Sewell's journal, there is a willingness to forward it or parts of it to those individuals, such as Lord Lyttelton, he identified as political patrons: see, for instance, 2 November 1860, journal of Henry Sewell, I, 183, qMs-1786, ATL. In the entry for 25 March 1859 he recorded how he would endeavour 'to keep (though perhaps irregularly) a diary of my proceedings, as the most compendious mode of informing all our friends in England of what may be of interest' (ibid, 1).

[418] Sewell, 5 April 1859, journal of Henry Sewell, I, 24, qMs-1786, ATL.

[419] Blackstone, *Commentaries on the Laws of England*, I, 151.

[420] Stafford to Richmond, 19 June 1859, in Scholefield (ed), *The Richmond-Atkinson Papers*, I, 465.

[421] Stafford was offered a salary of £250 per annum: Sewell, 25 March 1859, journal of Henry Sewell, I, 7, qMs-1786, ATL.

> How, too, he could for a moment have supposed that we could place ourselves in so false a position with the public as to have a member of the Ministry in the most unconstitutional position of being at the same time the paid agent of a Company receiving a large pecuniary subsidy under conditions always susceptible of dispute—& that the Treasurer too—almost raise suspicions one would not willingly entertain of the character of the proposer.[422]

As with other colonial politicians on the make, the political marketplaces in New Zealand afforded Sewell opportunities for self-dramatization; but he was content in 1859 to retain independence as an advisor to the governor and to ministers. He was well connected in the United Kingdom. His brother, the Reverend EJ Sewell, of New College, Oxford University, hosted him at times during his sojourn in Britain from 1856 until 1859, while another brother, the Reverend William Sewell, White's professor of moral philosophy at Oxford University from 1836 until 1841, became a well-known Tractarian associated with Frederick Denison Maurice (who lost the competition for the Drummond chair in political economy to Herman Merivale).[423] He was also interested in a number of investments, including the failed Manukau and Waitemata Company project, and busied himself as a litigating lawyer in various proceedings. In July 1859, he proved unsuccessful as a plaintiff arguing for a mandamus to compel to the commissioner of Crown lands to select land (*Sewell v Pollen*[424]). He had argued in favour of mandamus in this litigation *ex parte* in June 1859. Having written a letter to the Auckland provincial government and received no answer, Sewell had felt obliged to seek a judicial remedy. His intention had been to compel the 'Waste lands Commissioner to permit us to select the land we claim', namely an additional quantity of 18,000 acres in dispute.[425]

Sewell was a reader of tracts on colonies, and was noticeably familiar with the third Earl Grey's study on the *Colonial Policy of Lord John Russell's Administration* (1853), a copy of which he borrowed from the Auckland provincial council library to elucidate his points to Governor Browne. In that book he could 'see from pencil marks that Whitaker or Richmond have been drawing on it for ideas'.[426] By late May 1860, after an evening meeting with the governor, Sewell expressed concern that Browne was 'veering away from what I consider the right opinions, which he held last year [in 1859]'.[427] He thought the governor to be in a 'sort of despair' about what was to be done and where to turn for policy solutions, let alone what those solutions would look like.[428] Not for the first or the last time, a New Zealand administration was uncertain as to what to do privately—the pressure to do something decidedly weighed heavily. Sufficiently anxious because of this perceived turn, Sewell 'called his attention to the cases of attempts made to organise native government in Western Africa, the Gold Coast and Natal; referred to in Lord Grey's Colonial Policy (see appendix)'. He was at pains to point out how New Zealand was a very different case:

422 Stafford to Richmond, 19 June 1859, in Scholefield (ed), *The Richmond-Atkinson Papers*, I, 465.

423 See Sewell to Richmond, 20 October 1858, in Scholefield (ed), *The Richmond-Atkinson Papers*, I, 433. For a discussion of William Sewell, see Hilton, *The Age of Atonement*, 27, 47–8, 144, 172, 268–9.

424 'Supreme Court (Sittings In Banco)', *Sewell v Pollen*, *Daily Southern Cross*, vol 16, issue 1237, 19 July 1859, 3.

425 Sewell, 12 June 1859, journal of Henry Sewell, I, 39, qMs-1786, ATL.

426 Sewell, 21 May 1860, journal of Henry Sewell, I, 87, qMs-1786, ATL.

427 Ibid, 86–7.

428 Ibid, 88.

In Western Africa we were dealing with mere frontier tribes, with whom we did not propose to have any other relations than those of trade and protection—that as to Natal, we were dealing with a conquered territory, which offered no embarrassment as regards the territorial question—but that here in New Zealand, we had to solve the complicated problem, both of governing and civilizing the natives and at the same time colonizing their territory.[429]

Sewell surmised that 'to adopt a policy of mere protection, recognizing them that is, as an independent people and only assisting their efforts at self-government, would be fatal to them in the long run'.[430] To Sewell's mind, the record of history anticipated the likely results of recognizing Māori polities as truly independent, with Britain discharging a protectorate role: 'To train them into an independent people side by side with the settlers might for the present have a shew [*sic*] of good in it, but would end in a struggle for the mastery between the two races which must be fatal to the weaker'.[431] Rather pessimistically, the apprehended disaster of acknowledging Māori independence beyond the colonial settlements appeared to be a recurring theme. Advising the secretaries to the Church Missionary Society in London, Morgan, reporting from Otawhao in July 1862, stated: 'Allow them all they ask, a Maori king and independence of British authority, and what would soon be the state of such Maori districts—civil war would soon break out, and law and order would be an impossibility'.[432] Yet, in 1860, with Browne appearing to be in a slump, and supposing that 'nothing [could] be done towards colonization', Sewell heard the governor suggesting the prudence of preparing to 'submit to the native demand and practical independence'.[433] Practical independence was already in existence, however. This point has not escaped the notice of New Zealand historians and legal scholars.[434] Yet, as will be seen in Chapters Six and Seven, a number of commentators in New Zealand mused upon the *de jure* or juristic significance of such independence as well as its de facto properties.

CONCLUSIONS

The 1850s witnessed concerted efforts to construct windows of communicability through the language of property rights between Māori customary authority and law concerning territorial space and English tenure. Uncertainties concerning the mutual intelligibility of the pre-existing 'customary' norms relating to authority over territorial space and English real property law—whether arising through, say, jurisdictional or conceptual incommensurability, or otherwise—prompted experiments in the forms of a 'code', *The Laws of England compiled and translated into the Maori language* (1858), a Native Territorial Rights Bill, and resident magistrates on circuit (Fenton's circuit in the Waikato). The machinery of luring Māori polities to partake in these experiments did not always succeed (let alone proceed, as with the Native Territorial

429 Ibid, 87. 430 Ibid. 431 Ibid, 88.

432 Morgan to secretaries of the Church Missionary Society, London, 1 July 1862, qMs-1390–1392, ATL.

433 Sewell, 21 May 1860, journal of Henry Sewell, I, 88–9, qMs-1786, ATL.

434 Belich, 'Governors and Maori (1840–72)', in Sinclair (ed), *The Oxford Illustrated History of New Zealand*, 75–6; Belich, *Making Peoples*, 224–8, 229; Brookfield, *Waitangi and Indigenous Rights*, 2nd edn, 114–9.

Rights Bill of 1858), with many indigenous communities preferring to negotiate and clarify relations on a case-by-case basis. Some Māori leaders drew in Crown resources, whether through purchase transactions for land or admitting resident magistrates. Others refrained from doing so and adapted novel strategies, including the Kīngitanga, to address intra-Māori politics and the challenges posed by strangers. In these circumstances, native title became embroiled in explicit discussions about authority over territorial space, or became a proxy for such discussions. Tensions still lurked as to whether indigenous voices were to be treated as pre-eminent in determining the content of such authority, whether expressed as proprietary rights or as rights of government, or whether tropes of *ius gentium* or political economy ought to discipline such voices. Given the events witnessed in Chapters Two to Four, this was not strikingly novel. But it was complicated through the formal expansion of Her Majesty's advisors in New Zealand to include responsible ministers. Indeed, to adapt a phrase of JGA Pocock, policy processes within the imperial and colonial Crown were pressed to include new categories of counsellors and representatives, drawn from outside Parliament, which provided new sites for contesting the content and meaning of indigenous property rights.[435]

[435] Pocock's memorable phrase referred to the 'medieval technique of expanding the king-in-parliament to include new categories of counsellors and representatives' in *The Machiavellian Moment*, 547.

6

Exploring the Dynamics and Consequences of 'Occasional Association'

THE METAPHOR AND PROBLEM OF 'OCCASIONAL ASSOCIATION'

> '[T]he Government', he said, 'conducts its relations with the native tribes by occasional *negociation* [sic], (as to Land buying, surrender of criminals &c) as though it were with foreigners, and performs scarcely any of the functions of a Gov[ernmen]t towards its *subjects*'.[1]

Amongst the most contested proposals to access territories not yet segued into transposed English notions of real property tenure were the initiatives concerning a native council. Emerging most clearly as a distinctive exercise in constitutional experimentation in 1859 under Sewell's hand, the native council option envisaged a nominated cluster of so-called specialists on relations with Māori. From these exploratory beginnings, two clear options crystallized. One proposal, soaring into contention in 1860 and resurging briefly in 1861, was an imperial, Colonial Office-driven option pursuing political sustenance amongst ministers and within the legislature at Westminster. Under such a native council, nominated council members were to be appointed by the governor, with the council and its powers enshrined permissively in imperial statute. As a device or model it recalled, in vague outline if not in precise content, the Council of India, which was provided for under the Act for the Better Government of India in 1858.[2] In London, with a view to luring aristocratic Tory support in the House of Lords in 1860 and 1861, such as the fourteenth Earl of Derby (previously Viscount Stanley), suggestive proposals, albeit inconclusive, were also aired for a native council to contain Māori chieftains as members. As it turned out, the Native Council Bill, as proposed in London, passed the House of Lords in July 1860 but was withdrawn from the House of Commons on 21 August 1860.

A second option was that of a measure prescribed by the colonial legislature and answerable to it. To this end, a Native Council Bill was enacted by the General Assembly in New Zealand in November 1860.

These proposals have been treated sparsely in parts of the historiographical literature.[3] Yet the travails of the native council as an experiment reflect three key points—first,

[1] Fortescue, minute, 12 March 1861, CO209/156, fo.168a, TNA (emphasis in original).

[2] 'An Act for the better Government of India', 2 August 1858, 21 & 22 Vict, c106 (Imp).

[3] Donald Loveridge supplies the best chronological account to date in two reports prepared for district inquiries of the Waitangi Tribunal: 'Origins of the Native Land Acts and Native Land Court in New Zealand', 128–55; 'The Development and Introduction of Institutions for the Governance of

a continuation on the theme of crafting and framing legalistic windows of communicability between chiefly sources of indigenous political authority in Māori communities and *anglophone* notions of proprietary rights in land; secondly, an underlying contest as to adjusting the new colonial constitution with a view to enfranchising Māori territories clothed with native title; thirdly, if enacted, it was proposed to act as a scheme for broadening the scope and meaningful influence of the colonial polities on Māori communities and for incorporating Māori within colonial politics. What it also demonstrated were ongoing doubts in certain, especially Whig, quarters as to the merits of colonial self-administration. But these doubts were tied to persistent whiggish tropes as to the propriety of certain institutional forms of governance relative to the placement of indigenous populations in political history where those same populations were interspersed with European settlements or dwelt in proximity to them.[4] Had the imperial native council prospered, colonial New Zealand may well have embarked on a somewhat different constitutional trajectory.

'Occasional *negociation*' and the metaphor of 'occasional association'—an extended essay in two parts

While presuming to afford a means for admitting and domesticating Māori polities—of ensuring, at least in aspiration, that they could be authoritatively rendered subject to introduced colonial legal orders—for some, the proposals for a native council also reflected the persistent influence and power of *ius gentium* as an analogical tool, casting into doubt the extent to which Māori were indeed subjects or completely administered as if subjects. Fortescue, Whig parliamentary under-secretary at the Colonial Office, characterized the issue crisply in an internal memorandum of March 1861 in deploying a metaphor of limited association both temporally and geographically bound. '[T]he Government', he said, 'conducts its relations with the native tribes by occasional *negociation* [sic], (as to Land buying, surrender of criminals &c) as though it were with foreigners, and performs scarcely any of the functions of a Gov[ernmen]t towards its *subjects*.'[5] Thus, Fortescue concluded, 'The *writ* of Government is scarcely felt by the natives and has had a very great share in producing the "Maori King movement", as a substitute for European rule'.[6]

An implied metaphor of 'occasional association', mediated by the activities of episodic, case-by-case negotiation, was not only a concept deployed astutely by Fortescue. Notions of intermittent association rather than British subjecthood underlying it were also used by significant elements amongst Māori political elites in the Ngāti Haua *hapū* of the Waikato, for instance. Inextricably entwined by virtue of shared chronologies

Maori, 1852–1865', 113–15. Morrell offers an effective narrative of the fate of the Native Council Bill in the United Kingdom: Morrell, *British Colonial Policy in the Mid-Victorian Age*, 251–5. Other secondary accounts treat the proposals for a council incompletely and in passing: Sinclair, *The Origins of the Maori Wars*, 231–2; Dalton, *War and Politics in New Zealand 1855–1870*, 91, 119–21; Orange, *The Treaty of Waitangi*, 150–1; Ward, *A Show of Justice*, 108; Ward, *National Overview*, II, 211.

[4] On the significance to constitutional design of locating populations relative to a place in political history, see Burrow, *Whigs and Liberals*, 44; Collini, Winch, and Burrow, *That Noble Science of Politics*, 91–126, 111, 116–24.

[5] Fortescue, minute, 12 March 1861, CO209/156, fo.168a, TNA (emphasis in original).

[6] Ibid, fo.168a (emphasis in original).

and networks of political interest, Chapters Six and Seven address the dynamics of 'occasional association' in two substantial, interconnected parts. First, the present chapter considers the legislative experiments in 1860 and 1861 to further institutionalize the conduits—the windows of communicability as this book has referred to them—between the colonial niches of European settlement and areas of native title through developing a native council. In traversing this question, it will also demonstrate the connectedness of political configurations and networks—colonial and imperial. It will seek to display, through the narrative arc of the imperial native council option, how practices of politics, domestically located within the metropole, intersected with forays of colonially derived political anxieties and agendas directed into the cauldron of metropolitan political concerns. Conversely, it will explore how these political activities and drawing on constitutional genres constrained the possibilities of whiggishly orientated intervention in New Zealand. Secondly, the discussion in Chapter Seven will examine the stresses placed upon these proposals by the intensifying disputes in the aftermath of the much-criticized Waitara transaction of 1859–1860, leading to warring in the Taranaki. It will use the Waitara imbroglio as a means of accessing various interpretations of native title in relation to property rights and *de jure* rights (or de facto powers) of government—colonial and indigenous. It will also see the discussions surrounding Waitara as a substantial hinge for a number of reflections on what the context suggests about the operations of the real life of the political constitution and how it lived with indeterminacy and the sheer fact of persisting disagreement.

Implicitly, a concept of 'occasional association', hinging on 'occasional *negociation*', suggested a *relational* emphasis on the phenomena of transactional engagement in negotiations, whether for deeds of purchase, for the release of alleged Māori offenders against pākehā settlers, for the presence of resident magistrates, or otherwise. Underlying this metaphor was a sense of swathes of territory subject to persistent (unextinguished) indigenous claims to title and extant areas of political autonomy. Because of these factors, there was an undoubted stress on the element of *conditionality* as well as the contestability of these engagements and the need for Māori consent (with all of the practical decision-making difficulties that that necessarily entailed remaining unaddressed).[7] Unsurprisingly, therefore, Fortescue could fittingly resort to 'occasional *negociation*' as a feature lying at the heart of the entwined histories of association between indigenous communities and an incoming Crown whose tangible presence was principally confined to coastal settlement niches. Conceptually, then, 'consent' was itself deployed as an ill-defined background value, not so much to suggest a distinct process to be observed but to be issued as a broad caveat—a reminder that the dynamics of 'occasional association' were suffused with contestability and conditionality. This chapter specifically examines the challenge of legislative design for the Colonial Office, and demonstrates how such design and the question of native title became a problem for imperial politics entwined with colonial agendas at Westminster. It brings the politics of negotiability into clearer view. As will be explored in Chapter Seven, in the context of the Waitara dispute in 1860 and 1861, anglophone jurists certainly had a conceptual repertoire to overcome or to gloss over the tentativeness and instability of 'occasional association', at least for anglophone audiences. Chapter Seven will also

[7] On the problem of 'consent' and the utility of 'contestability', see Ivison, 'Consent or Contestation?'.

observe how any meanings or interpretations assigned to these particular associative engagements amongst and between Māori and European interlocutors were not necessarily secure but rather ephemeral, vulnerable to reinterpretation and reconsideration. Fittingly, a permissive approach was taken to defining native title. Although evidently recognized in policy and legalistic genres deployed with reference to New Zealand, the content of native title was supplied via customary norms (referred to as 'native laws, customs, or usages') rather than exogenous legal sources, thereby driving a distinctive New Zealand approach within empire (as with a distinctive British northern American approach). But the point is that officials such as Rogers, and Whig politicians like Fortescue, knew the phenomena gathered within the phrase 'occasional association' to act as concrete political factors—ones which inflected the manner in which relationships were approached and managed and which exerted an influence on the episodically agreed outcomes of these relations.

Fortescue's analysis in early 1861 was not the stuff of secrecy and concealment. In the House of Commons on 19 April 1861, Fortescue reported:

> The natives in the northern island were, to a great extent, merely nominal subjects of the Crown, living apart from the Europeans in a state of semi-independence, and all dealings with them, as in the case of those respecting land, had hitherto been carried on by means of negotiation rather than of the regular and ordinary law of the Colony.

Thus, he continued, 'In the purely native districts, in short, the natives were not wholly in the position of British subjects, and... the small portion of them who were now engaged in hostilities with the Crown could not justly be regarded as being wholly in the position of rebels'.[8] Indeed, almost three months subsequently, with open warring between British regulars and Māori having recently ceased by way of a brittle truce in the Taranaki, Newcastle observed in June 1861 that the relevant indigenous participants could 'scarcely be looked upon as subjects in rebellion'.[9] He referred to 'the fictitious uniformity of law' prevailing in colonial New Zealand.[10] Looking back from the vantage point of 1870, Sewell, by then a minister of justice and a member of the legislative council in New Zealand, said that the 'great bulk of the lands of the Northern Island which belonged to the Native... were *extra commercium*—except through the means of the old land purchase system, which had entirely broken down'.[11] Sewell's passing reference to '*extra commercium*', meaning 'beyond commerce', barely obscured the implication that transposed anglophone intellectual languages of legalism, and forms of colonial authority had failed to make substantive inroads beyond the coastal fringes of colonial New Zealand. His use of a term conventionally used to denote things beyond the realm of buying and selling, such as flowing navigable rivers, public roads, and titles of honour, was revealing. Its use as a term spoke to a perceived incommensurability between what were thought to be the 'customary' norms of Māori claims to proprietorship and authority over natural resources, on the one hand, and the introduced notions of English real property law, on the other.

In this sense, the underlying conundrum recalls a paradoxical pattern identified by Lauren Benton in analysing the later nineteenth century, albeit in the circumstances

[8] Fortescue, *HPD*, 3rd series, 19 April 1861, vol 162, col 826.
[9] Newcastle to Grey, 5 June 1861, CO209/156, fo.244, TNA.
[10] Ibid, fo.248a.
[11] Sewell, 29 August 1870, *New Zealand Parliamentary Debates*, 361.

of British pretensions in southern Asia.[12] Legalistic genres had already adapted useful technologies to cope with such problematic relations. Vitally for Māori descent-groups, however, sources drawn from literature addressing *ius gentium* were treated as remaining analogically apposite and permitted both commentators and policy formulators to contend with the degree to which such groups were incorporated within the new body politic. As Sewell contended reflectively in a pamphlet published separately, with minor differences, in London and Auckland in 1864, the 'acknowledgement of sovereignty by the New Zealanders was the same in effect as in the case of the American Indians'.[13] 'Did the New Zealanders', Sewell asked rhetorically, 'any more than the American Indians imagine that by placing themselves under the guardianship of the British Empire they forfeited their inherent rights to govern themselves according to their own usages, and to retain the ownership of their land?' He argued that '[a]s to the latter, the treaty of Waitangi expressly reserves to them their territorial rights'. On 'inherent rights' of self-government, Sewell acknowledged it to be 'true they surrendered to the Queen the "Kawanatanga"—the governorship—or sovereignty; but they did not understand that they thereby surrendered the exercise of the right of government over their internal affairs, a right which we never have claimed or exercised, and could not in fact exercise'.[14] As such, Sewell cautioned, '[w]e have left them the internal management of their own affairs; we have refused to extend the jurisdiction of our courts to the settlement of their disputes; we deny them the electoral franchise'. He stressed the diplomatic quality of relations with Māori: 'When we go to war with them we make treaties of peace; and we have always heretofore extended to them the rights of belligerents'.[15]

Sewell acknowledged that spatial jurisdiction was not completely nested or embedded. But he was able to reconcile the absence or relative lack of materially embedded empire in some areas by analogizing the analytics of northern American jurisprudence to Māori polities. Section 71 of the Constitution Act was seen to afford analogical support for the application of this principle to New Zealand. In providing for the setting-apart of districts in which the 'laws, customs, and usages of the aboriginal or native inhabitants of New Zealand, so far as they are not repugnant to the general principles of humanity, should for the present be maintained for the government of themselves', the statutory constitution was said to accord in principle with United States legal thought (which could apply in any event without resort to positive legal action). On this question, however, others, including Martin, disagreed. By asserting that such jurisprudential insights drawn from the United States did not apply—a reprise of earlier contests regarding the relevance of United States case law on 'Indian title',—they proposed to stress the status of Māori merely as incompletely incorporated subjects.[16]

The concept of a 'native council' proved to be resilient. As an episode of failure in political-legal design in the United Kingdom and New Zealand, it yields insights as

[12] See Benton, *A Search for Sovereignty*, 238–9, who is discussing a later period: 'The [Indian princely] states seemed to international lawyers to represent an intermediate case in the continuum from subordinate society to semiautonomous and potentially independent state. They retained significant control over internal affairs while being stripped of rights to engage in foreign relations. Their regulation seemed to belong to the realm of imperial administration rather than international law. Yet, even for John Westlake... international law continued to have the power of analogy'.

[13] Sewell, *The New Zealand Rebellion*, 11. [14] Ibid. [15] Ibid.

[16] See the discussion in Chapter Seven.

to analytic rather than banal, complacently unreflective forms of imperial constitutionalism. This is because the episode ignited both temperate and fiercely contested appraisals of the constitutional significance of these native council proposals. From 1859 to 1861, the possibilities of a native council—a collection of nominated specialists—was explored through two distinct policy life cycles leading to distinct statutory proposals in both Britain and New Zealand. But a native council, and variations on the themes of a permanent council, remained a living concept for years after, with William Martin advocating a native council option in 1870. A representative Māori commission would be advocated by James Fitzgerald and others in 1865, resulting in the Native Commission Act 1865.[17] As a proposal the concept of a native council boasted influential supporters and opponents, whether in New Zealand or the United Kingdom, although, amongst its erstwhile supporters, disagreement ranged on the details of any such proposal. In July 1860, as the House of Lords considered Newcastle's native council option, Alexander Johnston, a justice of the colonial Supreme Court, considered a 'council for Maori affairs' prudent. He envisaged it as including a 'European minister, a few Europeans with special knowledge of Maori matters, and a certain number of leading Maori Chiefs from different parts of the country'.[18] The absence of convergence on such a key proposal amongst its proponents contributed to its eventual demise.

PART I—THE NATIVE COUNCIL BILL OF 1860—AN EXCEPTIONAL EXPERIMENT IN LEGISLATIVE DESIGN AND IMPERIAL CONSTITUTIONALISM

Nothing less than a constitutional experiment, as conceived in London, the proposed native council would not be answerable to representative institutions in colonial New Zealand. It would be disparaged by opponents in the House of Lords as an exercise in modernity—closer to British India and southern Africa—and not in keeping with the preferred older system of localized, colonial self-administration for tran-oceanic British settlements. Tendering advice to the governor directly, this predominantly advisory council was to consist of 'no more than seven persons' (although, circumspectly, the number of appointees was not revealed in the version of the Bill in the House of Lords, leaving the number to political negotiation as the Bill proceeded through its parliamentary stages).[19] As envisioned within the Colonial Office, then, the Native Council Bill kept to the theme of aligning a council of nominees with a governor. As such, the acts of the governor concerning native affairs under the Constitution Act 1852 could be classed as the governor acting in native council rather than in the executive council (which generally comprised advisors responsible to the General Assembly in the colony).[20] As initially presented to Newcastle, Fortescue, and

[17] Sorrenson, *Report of the Royal Commission on the Electoral System*, B-15.

[18] Johnston, *Notes on Maori Matters ('Notes for the Formation of an Opinion on Maori Matters')*, 41.

[19] See a printed version of the Bill as introduced into the House of Lords in *AJHR-1861*, E-6b, 3–5.

[20] It need not have simply comprised responsible ministers. The governor had signalled in a memorandum of 18 April 1856 that he would 'not object (having the Queen's sanction to that effect) to limit the members of the Executive Council to his responsible Ministers': Memorandum, 18 April 1856, *Votes and Proceedings of the House of Representatives; session iv—1856*, A-13.

Merivale, by way of analysis of the colonial land and emigration commissioners in January 1860, it amounted to 'a proposal for establishing in New Zealand by authority of the Crown a permanent Council, independent of the Responsible Government, to assist the Governor in the purchase of the Native Lands and (as we understand) in the administration of Native affairs'.[21] The council could be appointed by 'any Letters Patent to be issued under the Great Seal of the United Kingdom'.[22] The governor would act as president of the council (clause 3). It would be funded from imperial sources. In doing so, it spoke to a sense of an imperial legislature acting as a 'bargaining table capable of resolving conflicts at a central level but also of devolving solutions back to local and "national" level[s]'.[23] The keystone for legalistic intervention in such fluid constitutional settings, therefore, was to manage and adjust constitutional relationships at the level of principle. But legislative design was intended to establish an institutional form and powers rather than prescribing or predetermining how the constituent parts might decide a particular question in substance.

In proposing to interpose a nominated conciliar body, the Colonial Office in early 1860 spoke to a peculiarly whiggish sub-strand of interventionist thought, previously associated with the colonial policies of the third Earl Grey. It would operate distinctly and independently with indigenous communities and their laws, expressly recognizing jurisdictional pluralism within New Zealand. With the native council, technocratic management was to augment the role of the governor in relating to indigenous communities, thereby further centralizing the capacity of colonial administration. It would not, as a proposal, diversify the pool of relevant political voices by tying the nominate council to responsible ministers answerable to the colonial legislature. Rogers considered it to be, rather loosely albeit appropriately, an essentially whiggish proposal—assuredly a proposal of political Whigs in the person of Fortescue (and Rogers himself)—but it could be interpreted by some as harbouring family tensions, not least of all with another strain of whiggish political thought, as exemplified by Macaulay. If a constitutional setting or artificial polity stood still, disabled or unable to adapt flexibly to shifts in political influence and economic change within communities, then imbalances emerged inexorably.[24] At the heart of this type of stance was a concern for any circumstances suggesting a disjunction between the artifice of a political constitution and the practical state of civil society. Underlying this trope was, as Burrow reminded us, a Burkean and nineteenth-century Whig conception of 'working with, not against the grain of society and manners', an approach 'certainly not reducible to the individualism of market economics, though it could include it, nor did it reduce government to a nullity'.[25] Others might suggest that the proposal was perfectly consonant with just such a way of thought—in setting out machinery thought to be peculiarly fit for purpose in engaging with communities beyond the formal writ of colonial settlements, operating with their own laws, customs, and usages. Such, however, was its vulnerability as a proposal—the possibilities of doubt, anxiety, and disagreement on so many profound as well as technical points in a legislative process extending across

21 Rogers and Murdoch to Merivale, 1 January 1860, CO209/158, fos.179–9a, TNA.

22 Clause 1 of the Native Council Bill.

23 Mandler, *The English National Character*, 34.

24 On Macaulay's characterization of this point, see Burrow, 'Introduction', in Macaulay, *History of England*, 8.

25 Burrow, *Whigs and Liberals*, 35.

two Houses of the imperial Parliament. As a measure, it certainly did not accord with non-interventionist liberal strains of thought, associated with the likes of Gladstone and Adderley, both of whom proved either sceptical or, in Adderley's case, profoundly opposed.

As with earlier efforts, such as the disallowed Native Territorial Rights Act of 1858, the Native Council Bill, as formulated in London in early 1860, reflected a desire to design windows of communicability on the question of native title between Māori communities and those legal orders associated with the bridgehead settlements such as New Plymouth, Auckland, and Wellington. To do so, it endeavoured to establish an imperially sanctioned, statutorily contained portal of legal recognition, whereby the governor in native council (as opposed to the governor in council) would constitute the main intermediary of political suasion between settlements and Māori communities that inhabited territories subject to native title. The preamble noted that it was expedient to 'make more effectual Provision for ascertaining, recording, and amending... native laws, customs, or usages... and for declaring the districts within which the same shall be maintained'. Its other main objective was to allow for 'ascertaining and recording the rights of the said aboriginal natives in lands to which the native title shall not have been extinguished, whether such lands shall be held in common or in severalty'. Tied to this objective was that of 'regulating the management of such lands, and for facilitating the extinguishment of such title'.

The porous distinction drawn between settled colonial areas, on the one hand, and those districts predominantly remaining subject to native title and the practical normative authority of Māori polities, on the other, was seen as impermanent, albeit real nonetheless. In London, on reviewing the native council proposal received from Auckland, the colonial land and emigration commissioners noted that '[p]olicy and charity alike require that the existing order of things should be treated with the utmost tenderness—but those who are entrusted with the authority of the Crown should never for a moment forget that however long it may be destined to last, it is by its very nature merely provisional'.[26] These commissioners cautioned that 'the institution of a Council might be [a] production of much evil, if its members acted on the notion of maintaining permanently by *artificial means* in the centre of a British colony a society governed by other than British laws and independent of the colonial authorities'.[27] Consistent with the tenor of these sentiments, the native council option was presented as transitional and not one to impair the processes of transition, which were assumed to operate inexorably. Thus, '[t]he gradual extinction of the native titles and consequent amalgamation of the races must at no distant period leave the Council without any subject on which to exert its powers'.[28] As a concept, native title itself suggested the ability to claim the incipient incorporation of Māori political communities within the pale of colonial administration as Crown-driven purchases proceeded to consume space, even though such a claim was premature and merely aspirational in practical terms. In essence, therefore, a proposed native council was 'for the present an exceptional

[26] Rogers and Murdoch to Merivale, 1 January 1860, CO209/158, fos.200–200a, TNA.
[27] Ibid, fo.200 (emphasis added).
[28] Rogers, '1858/59—New Zealand—Proposal for a Native Council' [*circa* 20 April 1860], CO209/159, fo.744, TNA.

instrument intended to facilitate a transition from an exceptional and anomalous state of things to one which is natural and permanent'.[29]

As an option overall, the native council proposal reflected a gradualist, deliberative approach to amalgamating Māori into areas of colonial settlement—to incorporating Māori deliberatively through piecemeal, case-by-case arrangements entered into with defined districts. Within the New Zealand archipelago, the relativities, meanings, and geography of diverse and plural allegiances—let alone the question of 'to whom?'—remained complicated and nuanced. The situation obtaining with the nascent Kīngitanga was seen as a problem of an absence of colonial government, as well as the resilience and adaptability of indigenous tropes and practices of government. Native title was ineluctably tied to this question of political authority and autonomy in the stance of policy-formulators, whether in Auckland or London. The constitutional framing of this core question was open and far from settled, being very much a place of ongoing discursive play and argument. It was indubitably ensnared in issues concerning the distribution of nodes of political authority within colonial settlements and the negotiated qualities of politics at Westminster in circumstances where parties still comprised diverse and shifting coalitions of interest. Initially, a 'Sketch of an Act creating a "Native Council" for the management of Native affairs in N[ew] Zealand' was developed. The sketch clearly outlined that the legislative proposal would be empowering and permissive rather than prescriptive. Hence, the draft Bill would state (as it ultimately did): 'Subject to such instructions as the Governor may receive from Her Majesty the Native Council to have the powers... (1) of declaring districts within which Native Law shall prevail—provided Native Law shall not prevail when native Title to land has been extinguished'.[30] The proposed council would also have the power 'of enquiring into questions of Native Title to land of granting of title certificates tribal or individual and of making rules respecting the use of such native lands and the effect of such certificates provided that such certificates shall not confer a power of alienation'.[31] That a proposal for imperial legislation was subjected to significant deliberation and shepherding throughout 1860 and early 1861 was in part, and quite coincidentally, testament to the relative stability of the positions of the principal Secretary of State for Colonies and the parliamentary under-secretary at this time, the fifth Duke of Newcastle and Chichester Fortescue respectively. Newcastle would be Secretary of State from 18 June 1859 until April 1864, whereas Fortescue occupied the role of parliamentary under-secretary from 18 June 1859 until November 1865.[32]

Newcastle had at first appeared to be a reluctant supporter of imperial legislation. He considered that 'Imperial legislation for its settlement is full of objections but I have come to the conclusion that it must be attempted'.[33] Subsequently, as reported in the House of Lords on 6 July 1860, Newcastle admitted a sense of caution but also recognized the essentially experimental and mediatory nature of the Native Council Bill: 'Without being too sanguine as to the result of this attempt at mediation, he felt that it

[29] Ibid, fos.744–4a.

[30] 'Sketch of an Act creating a "Native Council" for the management of Native affairs in N[ew] Zealand', CO209/159, fo.757, TNA.

[31] Ibid, fo.757a.

[32] For Newcastle, see *London Gazette*, number 21396; for Fortescue, see CO324/154, fos.267–8; CO701/12, TNA.

[33] Newcastle, minute [April 1860], CO209/159, fos.740–40a, TNA.

was only right that the experiment should be made, and hoped their Lordships would not retard the progress of the Bill'.[34] Newcastle envisaged the council as an entity capable of being presented to Māori as a disinterested body aligned with the imperial Crown: 'Whatever might be his opinion of individual Members of the Legislature of the colony, he had nothing to say against it collectively, but at the same time there was no disguising the fact that the Natives did not repos[e] in it the same confidence as they would do in a body appointed by the Crown'.[35] Fortescue later assessed the rationale for resorting to the imperial legislature as twofold: first, 'because such legislation was, in their view, within the spirit of the Constitution Act, being intended to operate only within those limits of Imperial authority wh[ich] that Act had laid down'.[36] Secondly, he ascribed the reference to the Parliament in Westminster to both:

> immediate and imperial action [having] the advantages of preventing further delay, where too much had already taken place, of avoiding the discord & party strife wh[ich] the previous reference of such questions to the colonial legislature might possibly occasion, of giving stability and authority to the improved system wh[ich] it was proposed to establish, and of enabling the Crown to exert its powers efficiently for the benefit of its subjects of both races, instead of resting satisfied with putting a veto upon enlightened measures of local legislation wh[ich] might impose conditions on the Governor, to which the Crown could not properly be advised to assent.[37]

In Newcastle's absence from the United Kingdom, as a member of the prince consort's official suite bound for a tour of northern America from 10 July 1860 (departing on the *Hero*) until October of that year, the elegant Fortescue assumed a driving role behind the scenes.[38] Upon reaching the House of Commons in August 1860, the Bill became his formal responsibility. Fortescue, a student at Christ Church College, Oxford, had been content with his studentship and the prospects of scholarship before being enticed into political life, obtaining the predominantly Roman Catholic constituency of County Louth as a Liberal in 1847.[39] He and Rogers, who succeeded Merivale as permanent under-secretary from 3 May 1860, were principal movers behind the particular drafting, although Rogers would attribute the measure privately as 'his [Fortescue's] Bill'.[40]

A version of the Bill introduced to the House of Lords was forwarded to New Zealand on 26 July 1860.[41] In advising the governor of its introduction, Cornewall Lewis noted, 'You will not fail to observe that in framing this Bill great care has been

[34] Newcastle, *HPD*, 3rd series, 6 July 1860, vol 159, col 1519.

[35] Ibid.

[36] Fortescue to Gore Browne, 27 August 1860, CO209/159, fo.776, TNA.

[37] Ibid, fos.776–7a.

[38] The official party escorting the prince consort arrived in St John's, Newfoundland on 23 July 1860. On Newcastle's participation in the tour, see Martineau, *The Life of Henry Pelham, Fifth Duke of Newcastle, 1811–1864*, 291.

[39] On Fortescue's background, see '. . . *And Mr Fortescue*' 1–6; Matthew, 'Fortescue, Chichester Samuel Parkinson, Baron Carlingford and second Baron Clermont (1823–1898)', in *Oxford Dictionary of National Biography*.

[40] Rogers to Lady Rogers, undated, apparently 20 August 1860, in Marindin (ed), *Letters of Frederic Lord Blachford, Under-secretary of State for the Colonies 1860–1871*, 229.

[41] Cornewall Lewis to Gore Browne, 26 July 1860, CO209/159, fos.768–71, TNA. Lewis also noted by way of a marginal note in the Colonial Office records, 'I have no objection to this despatch, but I have no knowledge on the subject/GCL' (ibid, fo.768).

taken to adhere to the spirit of the 71 72 & 73rd sections of the Constitutional Act'.[42] In an ameliorative tone, Lewis' despatch advised, '[t]he quasi-legislative functions of the Council are confined to those districts within which Her Majesty is empowered to provide for the maintenance of Native Law; and provision is made that neither directly nor indirectly shall the Council have the power without the consent of the local legislature to effect the extinguishment of a Native Title or to anticipate the revenue arising from the resale of native lands'.[43] A brief Bill, it contained no more than six clauses. The fifth clause was the provision tasked with setting out the powers of the native council, subject to any royal instructions to the contrary. These broad, permissively expressed powers were contained in 10 sub-clauses.

Under clause 5(1) of the version of the Bill in the House of Lords, districts were to be set apart in which 'Native Law shall be maintained for the Government of the said Aboriginal Inhabitants in all their Relations to and Dealings with each other: Provided always, that Native Law shall not be maintained in any District or Part thereof after the Native Title to the same shall have been extinguished'. As a term appearing in the draft Bill, 'native law' was 'deemed to mean the Laws, Customs, and Usages of the Aboriginal Inhabitants of any Part of New Zealand, so far as the same are not repugnant to the general Principles of Humanity'. Pursuant to clause 4(2) of the proposed measure, the native council (or the governor acting alone) would be authorized to 'declare, record, and amend the Native Law', provided that any such declaration or amendment obtained the consent of relevant Māori subject to that law. Such consent would be 'ascertained and signified in such manner as the said Council shall appoint'. The native council would also have the power to alter and revoke a particular piece of legislation of the General Assembly in colonial New Zealand, namely the Native Districts Act 1858. Clause 5(3) empowered the council to 'make rules respecting the use, occupation, and devolution of native lands'. An adjudicative function for the native council was envisaged. Clause 5(4) enabled the council to 'investigate and to make Rules respecting the investigation of Native Titles, and to issue Certificates of such Titles when duly established'. A proviso to this power was that no certificates would confer the power of alienating the lands to which the certificates referred without the consent of the General Assembly.

'Native lands' were defined non-exhaustively as including 'all lands, not being comprised in any Crown Grant, which shall at any time belong to, or be held in trust for, the said Aboriginal Inhabitants, or any of them, or which shall have been *used or customarily occupied in common* by such Inhabitants as Tribes or Communities' (emphasis added)'. The term 'native title' was defined in clause 1 to mean 'the rights of the said inhabitants to *any "native lands"*' (emphasis added): title represented a bundle of rights to land. The 'native owners' were the 'possessors of such title'. The breadth of the definition of 'native lands' is illuminative, as it was directed to ensuring the proposed council's pre-eminence in engaging with indigenous property rights of whatever variety or type. It was also aiming at 'facilitating the purchase of native lands' howsoever conceived, as per the long title of the Bill. In keeping with earlier disputes on the metes and bounds of Māori proprietary interests, it appeared to imply a disjunction between those lands '*used*', on the one hand, or 'customarily *occupied*' in common, on the other. As it was merely permissive, this provision did not signal a commitment to determine

42 Ibid, fo.768. 43 Ibid, fos.768a–9.

authoritatively which lands were simply 'used' in common as opposed to those 'customarily *occupied*'.

Yet, given its broad, inclusive definition of 'native lands' and in tying 'native title' and 'native owners' to such lands, broadly conceived, the tenor of the Bill was to avoid any minute inquiry into the nature of indigenous customary interests—its framers were content to treat all such lands as having been brought within the compendious, rights-orientated term 'native title'. In keeping with colonial New Zealand-driven precedent, therefore, a precise investigation as to whether certain tracts of territory were possessed or exclusively used and occupied was not to be pursued.[44] As it turned out, therefore, the manner in which 'native title' was to be defined was less porous than the deemed definition operating under the Native Districts Regulation Act enacted by the colonial legislature in New Zealand.[45] Section 10 of that Act deemed the following lands to be spaces over which native title had not been extinguished for the purposes of the Native Districts Regulation Act:

> Lands granted by the Crown to any person of the Native race, or to any person or body politic in trust for religious educational or charitable purposes, or in respect of any purchase made prior to the proclamation of the Queen's sovereignty, or specially granted as homesteads to persons of European race domiciled in Native districts, shall, where the same respectively abut upon lands over which the Native title has not been extinguished.

As Fortescue summarized it in March 1861, the Bill:

> not only dealt with the *Land* question, but also with the '*Government* of the native inhabitants'—by extending the powers reserved to the Crown by the 71st section of the Constitution Act,—& enabling the Gov[erno]r & Native Council not only to set apart Native Districts, but to '*amend* the Native Law' (a very wide word) within them—with, however, the very important, perhaps distinctive, proviso—'that Native Law sh[ould] not be maintained in any District or part thereof after the Native Title to the same shall have been extinguished'.[46]

In addition, the measure 'conferred on the Gov[erno]r & Native Council no power of giving Crown grants or rendering native land alienable to purchasers other than the Crown, or of borrowing money, except with the consent of the General Assembly'.[47] None of these powers were provided, leaving uncertain the question of supply of revenue for the native council.

A Bill 'for the better government of the native inhabitants of New Zealand, and for facilitating the purchase of native lands' eventually received its first reading in the House of Lords on 28 June 1860, although no first reading debate took place.[48] Opposition sounded with the second reading on 3 July 1860. Newcastle's second reading speech attributed the very provisionality of colonial government in New Zealand as a source for the measure. Māori 'dreaded a complete absorption among the colonists, and, fearing to lose the possessions which they regarded as their birthright, they

[44] Cf Hickford, '"Decidedly the Most Interesting Savages"'; Hickford, '"Vague Native Rights to Land"', 194–7.

[45] 'An Act to regulate the Local Affairs of Native Districts', 4 August 1858, 21 & 22 Vict 41 (New Zealand).

[46] Fortescue, 12 March 1861, 'New Zealand—Memorandum on Native Council Act &c', CO209/156, fo.168, TNA (emphasis in original).

[47] Ibid.

[48] *HPD*, 3rd series, 28 June 1860, vol 159, col 1069.

showed an increasing indisposition to part with their land, even upon fair and equitable terms'.[49] Newcastle saw New Zealand's circumstances as 'exceptional', warranting a bespoke, customized response. He added:

> It almost involved a question of good faith as regarded the Natives were they to place this power in the hands of the local Government; because it was not to the English inhabitants of New Zealand, it was to the Crown that these territories had been ceded by the Natives; the Natives had submitted themselves to the good Government of the Crown, and hitherto, though occasions had arisen when they had shown distrust towards the local Government, they had reposed confidence in the Imperial Government.[50]

In the Lords on 6 July, the Earl of Derby queried whether it was a 'point worthy of consideration how far advantage might be taken of the services of Natives in the proposed Council'.[51] Responding to this query, Newcastle replied there was 'nothing to prevent natives being on the Council, but he was not sure he would encourage their appointment'.[52] People began to take sides, making points, arguing with vigour—pursuing the possibilities of delay, the intimate foe of many a legislative or policy measure. Defenders of the Bill, such as the Whig, the second Earl Granville (George Granville Leveson-Gower), in the House of Lords, countered that a council of nominated specialists would assist disinterested deliberation on questions relating to native title. Hence, if 'the Crown could appoint persons to this Council who would command the confidence both of the settlers and the Natives, the result would not only be that the Government would work more smoothly, but greater concessions would be obtained from the Natives with regard to lands than could be obtained by any measures passed by the Legislature'.[53]

Elements of Westminster and New Zealand colonial politics converged. Sceptics alleged that the Bill was unnecessarily innovative and provocative, perceiving it as an attempt to engineer a constitutional force external to representative institutions and responsible advisors drawn from the colonial legislature. Further, throughout the life of the native council option in 1860, critics made much of the stealth and suddenness of its appearance as a mature proposal.[54] In the House of Commons on 14 August 1860, Sir John Pakington, in counselling delay, noted that the 'Bill was opposed to the views of the existing ministry and legislature of New Zealand, and was brought forward behind the backs of the people whom it concerned in the most interesting points'.[55] In this vein, the well-connected James Fitzgerald denounced the Bill, circulating printed memoranda and private correspondence to key figures, and endeavouring to build diverse pressure points both within and without Palmerston's cabinet. To Fortescue's dismay, Fitzgerald proved influential, especially with members of the House of Commons. Reflecting on Palmerston's withdrawal of the Native Council Bill on 21 August 1860, Fortescue remarked, 'Fitzgerald & Adderley were indefatigable in priming members of the House [of Commons] against it—& they had got Graham, Stanley [the son of the fourteenth Earl of Derby] &c to take that view'.[56]

[49] Ibid, 3 July 1860, vol 159, col 1326. [50] Ibid, col 1327.
[51] Ibid, 6 July 1860, vol 159, col 1519. [52] Ibid, col 1519.
[53] Earl Granville, 31 July 1860, *HPD*, 3rd series, vol 160, col 422.
[54] See, eg Fitzgerald, 'Memorandum, No 2 relating to the conduct of the Native Affairs in New Zealand, as affected by a Bill now before Parliament', 30 July 1860, 1.
[55] Sir John Pakington, *HPD*, 3rd series, 14 August 1860, vol 160, col 1317.
[56] Fortescue to Newcastle, 27 August 1860, NeC10, 931/1, Nottingham University.

Fitzgerald's first memorandum, dated 5 July 1860, was prepared in advance of the Bill being reported to the House of Lords in committee on 6 July 1860. Blandly entitled a 'Memorandum relating to the conduct of the Native Affairs in New Zealand, as affected by a Bill now before Parliament', it affected an air of policy neutrality in its tone, expressing doubts as to the Colonial Office's command of the local circumstances in New Zealand and its vulnerability to a narrow faction of colonial opinion. In a further pamphlet of 30 July, Fitzgerald classified the views in favour of an imperially enacted native council as finding their source in three main parties of colonial opinion, each presented in his rhetoric representing a brand of conservatism troubled by representative institutions—a 'missionary party', a 'Native Land Purchase department', and an 'old Government party'.[57] Fitzgerald saw the proposed council as 'entirely *irresponsible* [constitutionally], probably a secret Board which is to be independent of the ordinary Government of the Colony'.[58]

Gladstone, mindful of the fiscal impact of imperial expenditures and known to be unsympathetic to continued imperial oversight of settlement colonies, received a copy of the pamphlet from Fitzgerald at this time. In so doing, Fitzgerald, long a correspondent with Gladstone on colonial questions and as one who treated Gladstone as a patron, apprised the Chancellor of the Exchequer of his anxieties regarding the native council proposals. In early July 1860, in informing Newcastle of his having received Fitzgerald's pamphlet, Gladstone noted, 'I should be very loath to trouble you [with it;] perhaps you will ask Rogers and Fortescue to let me know their answers to the statements, which Mr Fitzgerald has made in objection to the Bill'.[59] Rogers had also been within Gladstone's orbit of personal correspondence and patronage for a number of years. Both individuals had corresponded extensively with each other on church and theological matters during the 1840s, with Gladstone an occasional source of patronage.[60] Gladstone, committed to fiscal rectitude, was by no means in a politically commanding position personally, despite his role as Chancellor of the Exchequer. In 1859, as Ghosh points out, Gladstone was coming out of a personally 'bleak and even disastrous' thirteen-year period—the period of 'party disorganization'.[61] Tories, such as the youthful Carnarvon, expressed dismay at having lost him, especially given that Gladstone had joined an administration whose 'first Minister [Palmerston]... is a man of whom I have heard Gladstone express the most unmitigated distrust'.[62] Carnarvon, just shy of turning twenty-eight when Palmerston formed his cabinet, remarked of Newcastle: 'I do not esteem his defection a loss as I have long looked upon him as incurably incompetent and self-conceited, a combination of qualities more dangerous to his friends than injurious to his enemies'.[63] Palmerston's success in luring Gladstone into the fold, at least for a time (or so it was hoped), was resented. Gladstone's Peelite and colonial networks, however, proved critical to Fitzgerald. In communicating privately

[57] Fitzgerald, 'Memorandum no. 2 relating to the conduct of the Native Affairs in New Zealand, as affected by a Bill now before Parliament', 30 July 1860, 8.

[58] Fitzgerald, 'Memorandum relating to the conduct of the Native Affairs in New Zealand, as affected by a Bill now before Parliament', 6 July 1860, 9 (emphasis in original).

[59] Gladstone to Newcastle, 6 July 1860, BL AddMss 44531, fo.24.

[60] See Gladstone to Rogers, 3 December 1841, BL AddMss44107, Gladstone papers, fos.205–12.

[61] Ghosh, 'Gladstone and Peel', in Ghosh and Goldman (eds), *Politics and Culture in Victorian Britain*, 62.

[62] Hardinge, *The Life of Henry Howard Molyneux, Fourth Earl of Carnarvon 1831–1890*, I, 145.

[63] Ibid.

with Fitzgerald, Gladstone saw the Native Council Bill as a 'firmly departmental measure', advising that he knew 'nothing of the New Zealand Bill as a member of the Gov[ernmen]t'. In composing such a message, Gladstone signalled the Bill's lack of exposure in advance to cabinet opinion—the sort of exposure that flushed out early signs of opposition, socialized potentially controversial proposals, and permitted adjustments or preparations to be made for disagreements ahead. He owned that 'Lord Lyttelton is aware to it', whereas, 'I am unaware of its particular grounds or objects'.[64] Lyttelton and Charles Adderley, two of Gladstone's parliamentary fellow travellers within the broader Canterbury Association circle, were adamantly opposed to the native council concept as expressed in Newcastle's suggested imperial measure. As Chancellor of the Exchequer, Gladstone proved content to signal opposition behind the scenes in private correspondence and oral communication.

In purporting to make native laws and regulating the sale of land to settlers, Fitzgerald assailed the native council proposal in his subsequent memorandum of late July as 'really and virtually...a new irresponsible nominee Parliament'.[65] This statement was a reprise of his earlier characterization of the proposal as creating 'two Governments' in New Zealand.[66] Such a criticism was adeptly calculated to agitate those, such as Adderley, who were critics of the 'inevitable confusion of double government' as a broad theme in imperial constitutionalism and governance.[67] In the debate during the third reading of the Bill in the House of Lords, Lyttelton noted Fitzgerald's concerns in this context: 'on the authority of Mr Fitzgerald, who had been prime minister of the colonial administration, that the disputes with the natives had commenced, almost without exception, with the government or their agents, and in no instance through any act of the colonists'.[68] Lyttelton construed the proposal not only as innovative but also as an option in keeping with alleged modernity in imperial policy. Hence, he saw the proposed measure as 'constitut[ing] a divided authority, by creating a new council, based not on the old, well-known colonial system, but according to the bad *modern* plan of *nomination*'.[69] Lyttelton also expressed concern at the narrowness of the interests in favour of the native council option: 'The Governor was supported by the Bishop of New Zealand, the late Chief Justice, the late Attorney General, and a considerable number, though not all, of the missionary clergy of the colony: while in the opinion of the members of the Council the measure could not fail to excite strong public dissatisfaction, and such a proposal could not have been made to the Colonial Legislature with any chance of success'.[70] He proclaimed it curious that 'in the eighth year after giving a representative constitution to New Zealand they should propose

[64] Gladstone to Fitzgerald, 6 July 1860, BL AddMss 44531, fo.25.

[65] Fitzgerald, 'Memorandum, No 2 relating to the conduct of the Native Affairs in New Zealand, as affected by a Bill now before Parliament', 30 July 1860, 16.

[66] Fitzgerald, 'Memorandum relating to the conduct of the Native Affairs in New Zealand, as affected by a Bill now before Parliament', 6 July 1860, 12. A version was published officially in New Zealand in the *Appendices to the Journals of the House of Representatives*, as the second enclosure to Cornewall Lewis to Browne, 26 July 1860: 'Memorandum relating to the conduct of the Native Affairs in New Zealand, as affected by a Bill now before Parliament' although the memorandum was dated 'London, 5th July 1860' (*AJHR*, 1861, E-6b).

[67] See Rt Hon CB Adderley MP, *Review of 'The Colonial Policy of Lord J Russell's Administration'—by Earl Grey, 1853*, 142.

[68] Lyttelton, *HPD*, 3rd series, 31 July 1860, vol 160, col 420.

[69] Ibid (emphasis added). [70] Ibid, col 418.

to pass a measure without the sanction of the constituted ministers of the colony, or the concurrence of the Administrative Assembly, ousting the regular authorities of the colony from the control of a large portion of their domestic affairs'.[71] There was a sense that those opposing the imperially enacted native council option portrayed it—along with the concept of Crown nomination—as profoundly out of step with a self-determining colonial-settlement society.

Opposition on this count was not necessarily expressive of identical concerns or agendas. Merivale, in his reprinted *Lectures on Colonization and Colonies* in the first half of the succeeding year, also expressed criticism of a system that effectively established two sources of European government in an outpost of empire without establishing, however, two distinct sources of revenue. In a note to the 1861 reissue of his *Lectures* he remarked, 'I must add that I cannot but regard the suggestion of establishing in the same colony "responsible" government for the settlers, and a separate administration of native affairs under the Home authorities, as unpractical'.[72] The concept of 'two governments in the same community' was thought injudicious 'unless some mode can be devised of having two public purposes'.[73] Merivale at least appeared to contemplate the possibility of crafting two distinctive sets of 'public purposes'. Neither Adderley nor Fitzgerald was so accommodating. At pains to establish the credentials of electorally responsible colonial administration, Fitzgerald highlighted what he construed as its disinterested conduct in formulating policies on relations with Māori. To this end, he referred to the Native Circuit Courts Act, the Native Schools Act, and the Bay of Islands Settlement Act.[74] Moreover, he referred to his own proposals for a board consisting of Māori chieftains, constituted by the colonial legislature and subject to its oversight. Overall, his memoranda reflected a commitment to the principle of localized colonial management—what Adderley later characterized as 'self-administration'.[75] Fitzgerald perceived the 'policy of the Ministers and the Assembly [as that of saving] the native race, by amalgamating them with the English; by extending to them English laws and English civilization'.[76] In defending the policy of 'self-administration', Fitzgerald claimed 'for the present [colonial] Ministers and for the present Assembly [in New Zealand] the credit of inaugurating far more liberal, generous and far-seeing policy, in respect of native affairs than was ever contemplated by any Government which has preceded it in New Zealand'.[77] Coincidentally, although not expressly mentioned, Waitara spoke to the failure of gubernatorial diplomacy—of negotiation and purchase centred on a governor and his officials, a factor increasingly exploited as the year proceeded and reports of military difficulties in New Zealand multiplied. Fitzgerald could ably demonstrate his prescience, as the brewing cauldron that was Waitara raised questions as to the prudence of governor-centric purchases from Māori, even before it erupted into

[71] Ibid.

[72] Merivale, *Lectures on Colonisation and Colonies*, 2nd edn, 521 (note).

[73] Ibid.

[74] Fitzgerald, 'Memorandum relating to the conduct of the Native Affairs in New Zealand, as affected by a Bill now before Parliament', 6 July 1860, 5–6.

[75] Rt Hon CB Adderley MP, *Review of 'The Colonial Policy of Lord J Russell's Administration'—by Earl Grey, 1853*, 418–23. On Adderley generally, see Beasley, *Empire as the Triumph of Theory*.

[76] Fitzgerald, 'Memorandum, No 2 relating to the conduct of the Native Affairs in New Zealand, as affected by a Bill now before Parliament', 30 July 1860, 17.

[77] Fitzgerald, 'Memorandum relating to the conduct of the Native Affairs in New Zealand, as affected by a Bill now before Parliament', 6 July 1860, 6.

war, with reports of military reverses not reaching London in *The Times* until Thursday, 13 September 1860.[78] Fitzgerald also criticized legal superfluity within the draft Bill, specifically the provision to empower the 'Crown to set aside certain districts in New Zealand within which the native law is to be maintained instead of English law'.[79] It merely repeated, he said (and not unfairly), section 71 of the Constitution Act.

A sense of colonial provincial rivalries underlay the politicking in London, intersecting with the play of imperial-level politics at Westminster—the metropole as a province of parochial politics in a distant colony. An Auckland colonist with substantial commercial interests in New Zealand, William Smellie Grahame wrote from England in late July 1860 that an Auckland deputation present in London was in favour of the Bill passing through its stages. 'I think under such a Bill', he said 'that much could be done in individualizing the titles of the tribal lands and furnishing them with alienable Crown grants.'[80] Grahame supposed that this would 'make their lands available and open the Waikato districts for colonization where thousands and tens of thousands of European population could be located'.[81] 'Of course', he added, 'Fitzgerald and the southern island people don't care how long Auckland is kept in the background, what is our loss & ruin is their gain'.[82] Throughout the second half of 1860, Grahame continued to provide McLean with a steady diet of intelligence on political activities on colonial matters, apprising him with rumours of social and political failure or embarrassment. Grahame's reportage and activities, along with those of Fitzgerald and his allies, demonstrated the fashion in which colonial agendas might converge with the erstwhile domesticity of Westminster politics. We see, then, as Laidlaw so ably analyses it, that settlers did not disappear permanently over the oceanic horizons.[83] A number of aspiring elite colonial figures sought to contribute, and did contribute, to vibrant, discursive, unsettled politics in Westminster circles as comfortably as in Auckland or Christchurch.

Newcastle had not yet tilled the political field of his senior colleagues in cabinet.[84] At least he had not done so effectively. His lengthy absence from the United Kingdom during a tour of northern America in the official party of Albert, the prince consort, only exacerbated this seeming neglect. Ultimately, the Bill suffered on account of this failing of foresight and energy, together with the scarce resource of legislative time with the sheer press of business in the Commons and the Lords—for a controversial measure with a negative fiscal impact, these factors proved fatal. Cabinet was strewn with political disagreements and factions; but navigating these shoals was increasingly vital to securing political objects, and it had begun to emerge at this time as a body 'with not only executive but also legislative predominance'.[85] Indeed, although Walter Bagehot would not invoke his well-known characterization of cabinet as a 'connecting link'

[78] 'The Native War in New Zealand', 13 September 1860, *The Times*, issue 23724, col C.

[79] Fitzgerald, 'Memorandum relating to the conduct of the Native Affairs in New Zealand, as affected by a Bill now before Parliament', 6 July 1860, 8.

[80] Grahame to McLean, 26 July 1860, Ms-Papers-0032-0298, fo.5, McLean papers, ATL.

[81] Ibid. [82] Ibid. [83] Laidlaw, *Colonial Connections*.

[84] In itself, this is unremarkable although it turned out to be injudicious. In 1860 Gladstone aroused irritation amongst some of his colleagues in the ministry (and indifference amongst others) by negotiating a commercial treaty with France 'largely independently of Cabinet', as Colin Matthew expressed it: Matthew, *Gladstone 1809–1898*, 113. On Gladstone and Palmerston, see, generally, Hoppen, *The Mid-Victorian Generation 1846–1886*, 209–19.

[85] Cox, *The Efficient Secret*, 45 and 51.

in the 'efficient secret of the English Constitution' until an article in the *Fortnightly Review* in May 1865, its increasing influence as a collective able to exert a pre-eminence in the legislature was coming to particular notice by the early 1860s.[86] In his commentary for the year 1860 in the multi-volume account of Gladstone's life, John Morley captured something of the colour and heightening significance of cabinet in saying, 'Severer than any battle in parliament is a long struggle inside a cabinet. Opponents contend at closer quarters, the weapons are shorter, it is easier to make mischief'.[87] As we will see, Newcastle belatedly consulted with cabinet colleagues collectively in January 1861 in seeking to revisit and revive an imperial native council option. By then, however, having tilled too late, his timing proved astray. Much later, Rogers' praise of another Secretary of State for Colonies, the second Earl Granville (George Granville Leveson-Gower), suggested the significance to the Colonial Office permanent undersecretary of a certain type of minister adroitly able to muster political capital with the senior colleagues in cabinet where the minister's civil servants did not possess belligerent status: '[Granville's] merits as a chief were . . . that he saw his way clearly and would act vigorously in what may be called ministerial as distinguished from departmental policy, and he was ready to act with promptitude and authority in matters which none but a chief could handle, matters requiring action in the House of Lords or the Cabinet or the Treasury'.[88] In commenting on the fourth Earl of Carnarvon, Rogers stated further that it was a 'great recommendation to a chief in the eyes of his subordinates' if '[h]e was not in the least afraid of the House of Commons'.[89]

In 1860 Palmerston's cabinet was, in essence, a coalition cabinet. Palmerston had fashioned an administration on 12 June 1859 comprising a fragile collection of Peelites, including Gladstone as Chancellor of the Exchequer, and the fifth Duke of Newcastle as Secretary of State for Colonies. Amongst senior ministers, Palmerston had also gathered representatives of aristocratic Whigs, with Russell at the Foreign Office, Cornewall Lewis at the Home Office, Granville as president of the council, and Charles Wood as Secretary of State for India.[90] Factional fault lines and intersections inside and outside of cabinet nevertheless complicated this overarching coalitionary canvass even further. Indeed, Fitzgerald's efforts, coupled with the place of one of Gladstone's closest political allies in cabinet, Newcastle, in leading the proposal in the House of Lords, pointed to the overlapping plurality of political sympathies and loyalties. The relationship between Newcastle and Gladstone was familiar and long-standing, ranging across personal familial issues and constitutional matters. Newcastle shared with Gladstone his ruminations on WR Greg's constitutional analyses in 1852.[91] As with settler politicians and fluid Māori elites, imperial actors were not readily pigeonholed. In ranging against the proposal, opponents and, if not outright opponents, critics or sceptics, reflected a variety of possible motives and agendas, whether internal to Palmerston's ministry, in the House of Lords, or in the House of Commons. Some merely advocated delay on

[86] Bagehot, 'The English Constitution (Part I): The Cabinet', 9.

[87] Morley, *The Life of William Ewart Gladstone*, II, 42 (the chapter concerns the 'Battle for Economy' from 1860 until 1862).

[88] Marindin (ed), *Letters of Frederic Lord Blachford*, 264. See also Parris, *Constitutional Bureaucracy*, 130.

[89] Marindin (ed), *Letters of Frederic Lord Blachford*, 263.

[90] Brown, *Palmerston*, 431–4; Ziegler, *Palmerston*, 110.

[91] Newcastle to Gladstone, 26 August 1852, BL AddMss44262, fos.125–30.

the measure until a subsequent parliamentary session. In such circumstances, it proved sufficient for opponents to lean on these various pressure points as sources of anxiety and to alert the anxious or doubtful. In Fitzgerald's pamphlet, the very architecture of the Constitution Act 1852 was cast as wanting in key respects. Core parts of it were presented as inherently mistrustful of the public assembly within colonial New Zealand. The Constitution Act explicitly reserved to the governor a sum of £7,000 per annum to be expended on native affairs.

Disagreements mounted as to whether the proposed Bill was indeed constitutionally innovative or merely reflected and expressed the aims of the Constitution Act of 1852 supplying further detail as to what section 71 of that Act contemplated operationally. Marginalia in Fortescue's hand on a Colonial Office copy of a draft version of the Bill dated 7 August 1860 emerging from the House of Lords revealed the scorched marks of its passage through that chamber. The Bill was headed with the telling words: 'This is the shape into which the Bill of 1860 was reduced by Sir F[rederic] Rogers & myself—and into wh[ich] it was intended to alter it in Committee of the H[ouse] of C[ommons]. (As amended by Mr Fortescue)'.[92] The draft differed subtly albeit significantly from that introduced to the House of Lords. A newly drafted clause 2 admitted a role for the executive council in appointing a single member to the native council. In thus conceding a minority place for the responsible colonial ministry within New Zealand, this proposed clause represented a minor relaxation on Fortescue's part in preparation for the House of Commons.[93] Against clause 4(1), which provided for the maintenance of native law in stipulated districts pending the extinguishment of native title (what had been clause 5(1) when before the House of Lords), Fortescue queried: 'a bad provision?' In this, Fortescue was undoubtedly mindful of the criticisms of legal superfluity in view of section 71 of the Constitution Act. In the wake of its passage through the House of Lords on 31 July 1860, a further amended version of the Bill was published—this time dated 8 August 1860. The sequencing of its clauses was slightly reorganized, but nothing of substance was altered.

Once the Native Council Bill was sent to the House of Commons, William Smellie Grahame, a commercial partner to the then colonial Native Secretary in New Zealand, Donald McLean, recorded how 'Fitzgerald redoubled his exertions and got about 20 of the Southern people with Newman & Brodie (the only 2 from Auckland) to petition against the Bill!'[94] Writing from Berkshire, he claimed how Fitzgerald approached every Member of Parliament known to him 'then in town', alleging that he used the most exaggerated language to induce opposition to the Bill. 'Amongst other things', reported Grahame, '[Fitzgerald] said the Constitution Act was invaded *&c&c* [whereby] under these circumstances, it was necessary for the Auckland Colonists to petition in favo[u]r of the Bill which we did'—too late as it so happened.[95] The campaign of those against an imperially enacted native council proved remorseless. Fitzgerald penned a letter to the editor of *The Times* contending that the Bill could only be 'worked at considerable

[92] Fortescue, marginal note, 7 August 1860, CO209/156, fo.188, TNA.

[93] For membership of the executive council at this time, see Wilson, *New Zealand Parliamentary Record, 1840–1984*, 61.

[94] WS Grahame to McLean, 23 August 1860, Ms-Papers-0032-0298, fo.3, McLean papers, ATL. Grahame was named as the executor in McLean's will drawn up in 1860. Cf Fargher, *The Best Man Who Ever Served the Crown?*, 237.

[95] WS Grahame to McLean, 23 August 1860, Ms-Papers-0032-0298, fo.4.

expense; and as the supplies will certainly not be voted by the colonial parliament, they must be provided by the English taxpayer'.[96] He asserted that the Bill was 'opposed by Sir John Pakington, with all of the Tory party who have paid any attention to it' and 'by many of the Whigs'.[97] The Aborigines' Protection Society also signalled its opposition to the Bill at the House of Commons stage.[98] The sense of somewhat dejected frustration amongst officials at the Colonial Office was palpable. Yet the committee of the Church Missionary Society, although suggesting an amendment to clause 5, 'look[ed] upon the Bill as likely to have a decidedly beneficial tendency; and regard[ed] it as important that the Bill should pass during the present session of Parliament'.[99]

In the midst of this contestable mixture of material, information from the governor of New Zealand arrived on 10 August 1860, attaching, amongst other things, memoranda on 'native affairs' from the former chief justice, Martin, the former Attorney General, William Swainson, and the Bishop of New Zealand, Selwyn. Forwarded to Rogers in the Colonial Office on 14 August 'as bearing upon the Native Bill now before Parliament', the papers of this trio of advisors to Governor Browne supplied broadly consonant diagnoses of the New Zealand question in 1860. These documents, dating from New Zealand in May 1860, remain worthy of careful consideration, as they signalled the significance of establishing, subordinate to the native council, a secondary tier body—a specialist tribunal or court—for the purpose of ascertaining, by 'careful investigation', the ownership of native lands.[100] Moreover, they counselled the attainment of permanency and stability institutionally by enlisting imperial legislation to embed the structure and to secure a clear demarcation of authority between responsible ministries and the function of a governor acting in native council. An important context for these papers, congenial to the then aspirations of Fortescue regarding the Native Council Bill, was the anticipated conference of various Māori chieftains at Kohimarama near Auckland settlement. With a view to combining their distinct views, the three authors provided a united 'recommendation', drawing together a set of policy recommendations distinctly unsympathetic to the expansion of the jurisdiction of the colonial legislature. Included as the second recommendation was a suggestion in favour of a native council answerable to the governor and, ultimately,

[96] Fitzgerald, 'The New Zealand Bill', letter to the editor, *The Times*, Monday, 20 August 1860, issue 23703, col A, 7.

[97] Ibid.

[98] FW Chesson, secretary of the committee of the Aborigines' Protection Society, to Fortescue, 13 August 1860 [received 14 August 1860], CO209/158, fo.295, TNA. Gairdner, minute, 14 August 1860, CO209/158, fo.296: 'The Society appear to be very imperfectly informed on the subject on which they write. They might advantageously receive a copy of Mr Richmond's pamphlet, but their great gift [?] always has been to keep themselves alive by discussion, and a simpler acknowledgement may be best'.

[99] J Chapman, secretary of the Church Missionary Society, to Fortescue, 16 August 1860, CO209/158, fo.300a, TNA. The proposed amendment was as follows: 'Provided that no rules respecting the use occupation or devolution of native lands or respecting the investigation of native titles or the leasing of native lands by the native owners or the terms on which or the mode in which the extinguishment of native titles shall be effected shall be of force without the consent of the native owners of the land to be affected thereby such consent to be ascertained & signified in such manner as the Council shall appoint But all such rules so made as aforesaid and testified by the signature of the Resident published in the Gazette shall be conclusive evidence of such consent having been given'.

[100] See, eg, Selwyn, Martin, and Swainson, [undated], 'Recommendation', CO209/154, fo.64, TNA.

imperial authorities: 'for the present and until the natives shall have become entitled to the elective franchise under the provisions of the Constitution, the Governor in the management of native affairs be advised, not by the Responsible Ministry, but by a Council appointed by the Crown, responsible to the Crown, and holding their offices at the pleasure of the Crown'.[101] Critically, the financial independence for such a policy of managed engagement was considered vital and would be achieved by ensuring the availability of a statutorily mandated sum distinct from the annual appropriations vote of the General Assembly. The thrust of this recommendation proposed:

> for the management of native affairs, the Governor [having] at his disposal independently of an annual vote of the Assembly, such a sum, chargeable upon the General Revenue, as may be sufficient for the maintenance of an efficient native department, for the payment of native magistrates and assessors,—and of such other expences [*sic*] as may be necessary for promoting the gradual introduction of law and order amongst them, in their relations with each other.[102]

Again, the tenor of the advice was to treat the circumstances within New Zealand as transitional; a complicated process of gradualist, managed regime and legal change was already underway in indigenous communities. The jointly authored paper of recommendations noted 'the growing desire of the natives for a better and more efficient system to control them in their relations with each other'.[103] It advised that such a course 'should be encouraged, and that the government should prepare for their acceptance, but as open to amendments to be suggested by themselves, a simple system of local self government, suited to their present condition and circumstances; and be prepared to make some contributions towards the payment of the native magistrates and others who may be required to carry the system into effect'.[104] The ultimate aim was to provide for and recognize such forms of 'local self-government as may prepare them to acquiesce in the ordinary administration of English law'.[105] Managed points of intersection between the native council and indigenous communities were required, together with guidance in the form of a law code prepared by Martin entitled 'Rules for the Proper Administration of Justice, being a translation of the rules put forth in Maori by the Governor in February, 1860'.[106] As such, these rules contained provisions for localized Māori *rūnanga* or councils, already in evidence, and the distribution of penalty payments by way of income.[107] They also set out requirements for a quorum in

[101] Ibid, fo.60a, TNA. The ultimate responsibility to imperial authorities would be secured by adherence to the first recommendation, specifically that 'a definite line of policy, based upon the principles on which, with reference to the rights of the natives, New Zealand was erected into a British colony, and to the obligations contracted by the Crown of England in subjecting them to British rule should be prescribed by the British Cabinet, and that every Governor, on his arrival in the colony, should personally assure the natives on behalf of Her Majesty that the policy so prescribed will be faithfully adhered to' (ibid, fos.60–60a)'.

[102] Ibid, fos.60a–1. [103] Ibid, fos.64a–5. [104] Ibid, fo.65.

[105] Ibid, fo.65a.

[106] These rules are to be distinguished from those developed by Francis Fenton, presented to the House of Representatives in New Zealand on 16 June 1858: *The Laws of England compiled and translated into the Maori language by direction of His Excellency Colonel Thomas Gore Browne CB, Governor of New Zealand &c.*

[107] Clause 14 stated, in part (paragraph divisions omitted): 'The penalties which are paid to the Queen are to be deposited with such persons as the runanga shall appoint, for safe keeping until the end of the year. At the end of each year the runanga will assemble to appropriate the money. Part shall be for the magistrate, part for the assistants, part for the church, mill, school, house &c, or whatever

any *rūnanga*. Applying these rules to a given community, however, was predicated on obtaining prior consent, although how the assent of the 'whole tribe' was to be assessed or through whom (or indeed what was to count as a 'tribe') was unclear: '*If the whole tribe agree to the rules*, here written, they will thenceforward be followed in all proceedings between one native and another'.[108] Martin's 'rules' presumed a selection of the *rūnanga* or council within a 'tribe'. Its members were to be 'chosen by the Tribes and the names certified by the kai-whakarite [magistrate] to the Governor'.[109] These rules traversed matters of people *as* forming or becoming institutions—*rūnanga* and kai-whakarite—to oversee processes and procedure, as well as questions of wrongs, including classes such as 'adultery', 'eating rotten food', 'drinking spirits', 'theft', and 'any malicious act'. The notion of 'any malicious act' entailed an act 'by which the house, or clothing, or property, or food of another person is injured'. Under the proposed rules, the penalty was to consist of two parts: 'One part of the penalty is the value of the property injured. If growing crops be injured, the value of such crops at harvest time is to be considered. The other part is the fine for the offence, not less than twenty shillings, nor more than ten pounds'.[110]

Martin's own memorandum, which supported the concept of a native council, analysed the 'practical problem' of Crown–Māori relations as comprising two dimensions: first, '[t]o obtain from the natives by fair and peaceful means a transfer of their superfluous lands'; secondly, '[t]o establish the natives upon the residue in orderly communities, obedient to law'.[111] Martin's proposals were, as with the native council option as a whole, seen as transitional, permitting a body to operate until, for instance, indigenous communities dwelt on lands secured to them under English tenure. 'The functions of such Board would continue', he said, 'until the superfluous lands of the natives were purchased, and the conditions of the purchase performed, and until the native communities were sufficiently organized for their internal government and good order, and that upon soil secured to them by Crown grants.' Once these results were accomplished, 'the functions of the Board would cease'.[112] Māori communities would have become fully incorporated within the scope of English legal norms: 'The Maoris would then be under the protection of the courts of law, and on the same footing as their English fellow subjects'. Furthermore, as an opinion of the law officers of the Crown in 1859 had held 'that occupation under the native title does not in any case entitle the occupant to

object they shall think best. But let not the money be actually paid away, until the Governor shall have assented to the proposal of the runanga. For the Governor's assent is the assent of the Queen'.

[108] 'Rules for the Proper Administration of Justice, being a translation of the rules put forth in Maori by the Governor in February, 1860', CO209/154, fo.67, TNA.

[109] The term 'magistrate' is used rather than 'kai-whakarite' in the above February 1860 version, whereas a further manuscript version was prepared for printing, which used 'kaiwhakawa', a term replaced in the printed version by the word 'kai-whakarite': see 'Rules for the Proper Administration of Justice', CO209/153, fo.361 (for 'kaiwhakawa' appearing in cl I.2, for example) and to the printed 'He Tikanga enei mo te Whakarite Whakawa kia pai ai' [received at the Colonial Office on 10 August 1860], CO209/153, fos.370–3a, TNA. The version of the rules presented by way of message from the governor to Māori assembled at the Kohimarama conference on Monday, 16 July 1860 used the term 'kai-whakawa': see Monday, 16 July 1860, as reported in *The Maori Messenger—Te Karere Maori*, vol 7, number 14, 31 July 1860, 3.

[110] 'Rules for the Proper Administration of Justice, being a translation of the rules put forth in Maori by the Governor in February, 1860', CO209/154, fos.68–8a, TNA.

[111] Martin, 'Memorandum on Native Affairs', 12 May 1860, 'Tararua', CO209/154, fo.38, TNA.

[112] Ibid, fos.44–4a.

a vote', the colonial legislature could not 'claim dominion over a race which it does not represent, and the necessity becomes more urgent of constituting some special body to carry out the policy of the Crown in respect of that race, until it be placed completely on the same legal footing as our own race'.[113] Martin thought it prudent for policy to lever off the development within Māori communities of various councils or *rūnanga*, as these nascent forms of organization could be used to insinuate Crown-appointed magistrates. He concluded it to be 'in our power by adopting what is sound in their own scheme so to improve and control it as to make it an efficient instrument for keeping peace and good order amongst them, and carrying the authority of the Queen effectively into every nook of this Island'.[114]

Swainson, the former Attorney General and another trusted advisor to the governor, was mindful of a need to ensure that the person of the governor remained central in mediating relations with indigenous communities. Responsible ministries were inexorably ephemeral in the eyes of Māori political elites, whereas permanence and longevity were respected: 'They [the natives] know little and they care less about a responsible ministry—here today and gone tomorrow—the members of which they hardly know by name, and for whom they can have no respect'.[115] In line with earlier advice advanced in 1859, Swainson advocated a renewed institutional emphasis on this central role for the governor in order to maintain the prestige of that office.[116] Swainson's suggestion for the treatment of native title was to multiply the tenurial options available to Māori descent-groups, albeit with a clear assumption that an estate in fee simple would afford increased economic opportunities. Nothing less than a tenurial transformation was recommended, however, in respect of particularly identified 'surplus lands', rather than territories subject to indigenous claims as a whole: 'With a view to facilitate[ing] the acquisition of the surplus lands of the natives for [the] purposes of colonization I have already suggested in a previous memorandum (6 Sept[embe]r 1859) that the partition of land held by them in common should be encouraged'. Once the:

> ownership shall have been ascertained after careful enquiry by a competent tribunal; and when it shall have been divided amongst them by mutual agreement amongst themselves, that it should be competent for the Governor and Council nominated by the Crown (and either with or without an intermediate transfer from the natives to the Crown) to issue Crown grants to each member of the tribe of his own allotted portion, either in fee simple absolutely, with full power to dispose of it, or under such limitations and restrictions, and with such powers of leasing &c, as to the Governor in Council may, in each case, deem meet.[117]

The award of a 'fee simple estate to the individual members of the tribe of a specific portion of the common land', said Swainson, 'would confer a title much more valuable in every respect than that which they possess while holding the land in common under the Treaty of Waitangi'. An invidious difficulty with the communal nature of native title was its inherent indeterminacy and complexity, as these factors impeded turning land to economic account. Thus, he argued, 'so long as it is held in common by the tribe, it cannot be sold even to the Crown without the consent of all the claimants; and even when all are willing to sell, it can be disposed of to the Crown alone; and

[113] Ibid, fos.44a–5. [114] Ibid, fo.45.

[115] Swainson, memorandum, 7 May 1860, CO209/154, fo.48a, TNA.

[116] This course of action was recommended in conjunction with Selwyn and Martin: see Selwyn, Martin, and Swainson, [undated], 'Recommendation', CO209/154, fos.60–6, TNA.

[117] Swainson, memorandum, 7 May 1860, CO209/154, fos.56–6a.

there being but a single buyer and no competitors, the price given is below the market value'.[118] But once grants from the Crown were received securing recognition of 'land divided in severalty..., [then] each claimant receives both a better *holding* title and a better *selling* title'.[119] As such, while a claimant continued to hold such land, 'he has the security of a grant from the Crown, and he may not only sell when he pleases, and without reference to other members of the tribe, but he may sell not only to the Crown but to any of Her Majesty's subjects, and obtain the full market value of his land'. Swainson undoubtedly envisaged the expansion of European settlement, although by degrees in a disciplined and deliberative fashion.

Yet Palmerston's attitude as Prime Minister remained deliberately obscure at this time, leaving Fortescue and Rogers to surmise on his disposition after a meeting with him in late August 1860. An interview between Palmerston, Fortescue, and Rogers, occurring before Monday, 20 August 1860, not only revealed the Prime Minister's absence of commitment, but also his political abilities in sounding softly placatory, albeit elusive and disengaged. The conference had been sought because 'Chichester Fortescue, [was] in a great fright that his Bill (New Zealand) would be abandoned'.[120] Rogers observed how, on seeing them, Palmerston 'sat us down, put his hands between his knees and assumed a kind of fixed resigned look, drooping his shoulders and sinking his eyes like a man who was to undergo a shower-bath'.[121] At that point, 'Fortescue [then] began ['it being understood that Palmerston was in doubt about proceeding'], and, as I should say, rehearsed his speech for the House, stating the case and invoking me occasionally'. Rogers characterized Palmerston as saying 'in a kind of obedient way, "Well, then, I have got my lesson; and I shall say that alterations will be made in the Bill that will remove any of the objections, and that the Government will state the reasons for introducing it on Monday (now put off till Tuesday [21 August 1860])" '.[122] Rogers had 'expected a kind of arguing and cross-examination, and the whole thing was despatched by [Palmerston] in such a free and easy way and with so little trouble to himself (except hearing [Fortescue's] speech) that as soon as we got into the cab I burst into a fit of laughter, in which [Fortescue] joined'.[123] Rogers reportedly inquired of Fortescue, 'Well, what do you think he thinks of you and your case?' Fortescue allegedly replied, ' "Oh, I don't know", with an amused look', adding that, "I would give some thing to know" '. As Rogers recounted the discussion, Fortescue suspected that Palmerston's 'impression was that it would go down with the House of Commons', and then [Fortescue] laughed and said: "This is being behind the scenes" '.[124] The intricacies of political negotiation were telling in that Rogers' account captured the sense of the

118 Ibid, fos.56a–7. 119 Ibid, fo.57 (emphasis added).

120 Rogers to Lady Rogers, undated [August 1860], in *Letters of Frederic Lord Blachford*, 229. As Dalton also notes in *War and Politics in New Zealand 1855–1870*, 120 (note 39), the letter could not have been written on 20 August 1860.

121 Rogers to Lady Rogers, undated [August 1860], in *Letters of Frederic Lord Blachford*, 229.

122 Ibid, 229–30. 123 Ibid, 230.

124 Ibid. Rogers went on to note: 'He [Fortescue] had quoted to Palmerston with great force a passage in favour of his present proceedings from a despatch of Lord Carnarvon's. "Of course I shall read that in the House", as if it were the testimony of an enemy. So when we got into the cab I told him that that despatch was my writing, so that when the Whig Under-Secretary quotes the Tory Under-Secretary in favour of the Whig measure it will be in fact quoting Sir F.R.'s despatch as a hostile testimony to the merits of Sir F.R.'s Bill. I told him this and he laughed and said, "Behind the scenes again"'.

temporally and politically contingent together with the vulnerability of a departmental measure to being overturned. Rogers expressed respect for Fortescue's temperament: 'He is very pleasant and uncommonly plucky, for we have the whole world against us'. The permanent under-secretary confessed that he could 'hardly believe even now that it will pass'. At this juncture, Rogers noted the assistance of the Attorney General on the Native Council Bill, Bethell having been 'quite keen and a valuable help', especially in view of the disagreement on how to relate section 71 of the Constitution Act to the Bill.[125] Palmerston, however, was increasingly mindful of the deteriorating military situation in the Taranaki region of the North Island in New Zealand, having been apprised of the requirement for additional regiments in July 1860.[126] Fortescue was also reflecting on the situation there, with Grahame recording how he had 'several interviews' with the parliamentary under-secretary of the Colonial Office '[w]hen the excitement was going on about the Bill'.[127]

In announcing the decision to withdraw the Bill from the House of Commons on 21 August, Palmerston claimed that '[w]e are of opinion... that the powers which the New Zealand Constitution gives to the Crown of making regulations bearing upon the interests of the aborigines will, if properly used, be sufficient for the purpose we have in view; and if it should appear that those powers are inadequate it will be then for the Government at some future time to have recourse to legislation on the subject'.[128]It appears from Fortescue's subsequent despatch to Browne that Bethell's advice concluded that the 'power [authorizing the governor and "Native Council to declare districts in which Native law was to prevail and (within these districts of course) to declare, record and amend the Native law" [was a power] (I am advised) Her Majesty already possesses, and the Bill merely recognizes a particular mode of exercising it'.[129]

Governing subjects as strangers and legislative design—double government, British South Asia, the Cape Colony, and New Zealand

Fortescue's continuing defence of the Bill as constitutionally conservative and astutely adapted to the peculiar circumstances of the settlements within New Zealand was evident: 'The Bill would not have transferred power from the Colonial to the Home Government, but would only have furnished a machinery for the exercise of a power already given'.[130] As such, he acknowledged that opposition to the Bill had characterized it as a 'retrograde step'. He noted that '[f]rom a misapprehension (as I think) of its provisions [the Bill] was threatened with an obstinate opposition on behalf of certain influential colonists, who considered that it invaded the existing privileges of the Legislature'. Fiscal concerns had also proved critical in converging with opposition

[125] Ibid. Bethell, first Baron Westbury (1800–1873), Lord Chancellor, born at Bradford-on-Avon, Wiltshire, 30 June 1800; son of Richard Bethell MD (*d.* 1831) of Bristol, and Jane Baverstock (*d.* 1825): see Cocks, 'Bethell, Richard, first Baron Westbury (1800–1873)', in *Oxford Dictionary of National Biography*.

[126] WS Grahame to McLean, 23 August 1860, Ms-Papers-0032-0298, fos.1–2, McLean papers, ATL; Grahame to McLean, 26 July 1860, Ms-Papers-0032-0298, McLean papers, ATL; Barrington to Grahame, 25 July 1860, Ms-Papers-0032-0298, McLean papers, ATL.

[127] Grahame to McLean, 23 August 1860, Ms-Papers-0032-0298, fo.5, McLean papers, ATL.

[128] Viscount Palmerston, 21 August 1860, *HPD*, 3rd series, 21 August 1860, vol 160, col 1640.

[129] Fortescue to Gore Browne, 27 August 1860, CO209/159, fo.782, TNA.

[130] Ibid, fo.783.

mounted on the basis of constitutional opposition: 'And it was viewed unfavourably in other quarters from an apprehension that any fresh parliamentary interference in this direction would be used as an argument for throwing on Great Britain more than her share of the cost of any future native war'.[131] But he regarded these views as unfortunate on account of the broadly elaborative aspects of the Bill, which were intended merely to detail the means by which existing constitutional powers could be exercised. It was not seen as modifying the constitutional membrane. Rather, it was said to elaborate and finely grain what was already implicit. He conceded, however, 'one or two points of detail in respect of which the Bill confers upon the Governor and Council a power not conferred on the Crown by the Constitutional Act'.[132] 'Of these the most important', advised Fortescue, 'is that which authorizes the Council to make rules under which the natives may lease land for not more than [five] years.'[133] Pakington, on hearing of Palmerston's decision to withdraw the Bill, gave as a parting shot the view that the interposition of a council would have retarded the processes of amalgamating Māori:

> It would have created an irresponsible Council to act concurrently with the constitutional legislature of the colony; and he thought that every one who considered the subject must be persuaded that the action of two such bodies must have produced constant ill-will and collision, and would have created bad feeling between the colonists and their Governor, between the colonists and the Imperial Government, between the European settlers and the Natives, and must have tended to retard that amalgamation of the races which every wise and benevolent statesman must be anxious to promote.[134]

Yet Fortescue persisted in seeing the issue as something not readily reducible to uttering the maxim of 'responsible government' blithely. Instead, the particular conditions of colonial settlement in the North Island of New Zealand posed two profound questions for legislators. He advised the Commons at the moment of the measure's withdrawal that 'Two questions had long been disputed between the Home Government and British colonists. One was, should they govern themselves? [A]nother, and a totally distinct one, was, should they govern *others*?'[135] While he suggested that the first question had been answered appropriately through the granting of 'responsible government' to the colonists, 'wherever it had been possible', the second question remained moot, albeit merely postponed until the next parliamentary session. On that outstanding issue, 'the Crown held its ground, and maintained its right and duty of protection and control over Native races and Native questions, wherever and so far as it could usefully and practically exercise such control'.[136] Here, Fortescue drew comparisons not with the neighbouring colonies of New South Wales and Victoria, but with 'British Caffraria, Natal, Ceylon, most of the West India colonies, or, to take a gigantic example, British India itself'.[137] Within the House of Commons, the reference to British South Asia would have called to mind the very spectre of 'double government' in the case of India, going back to its presence as a principle underlying and animating an independent board of control (the 'commissioners for the affairs of India') in the late eighteenth century and, more recently, in the revised constitution of the East India Company in the 1850s. But at least in structural design the principle was broadly employed to

131 Ibid, fos.778a–9. 132 Ibid, fo.784. 133 Ibid, fos.784–4a.
134 Pakington, *HPD*, 3rd series, 21 August 1860, vol 160, cols 1641–1642.
135 Ibid, col 1644 (emphasis added). 136 Ibid. 137 Ibid.

the same extent as regards the Council of India established under the Government of India Act 1858. In proposing to establish a permanent native council to support the governor in New Zealand, Fortescue was summoning comparisons with similar constitutional frames and prospectuses considered as applicable to British government in India. As imperial legislation, the design of the Government of India Act was considered to have imbibed at least some of the influence of John Stuart Mill's protestations in favour of 'double government' for British India before the House of Lords in June 1852. When presenting before the Select Committee of the House of Lords in mid-1852, Mill was one of the assistants to the examiner of Indian correspondence and remained at the East India Company until its disestablishment in 1858. Presenting to the House of Lords Select Committee in June 1852, he had said: 'I am inclined to think that such a double Government would be useful, wherever it was necessary to have a body of a permanent character specially conversant with a subject not generally studied by politicians in this country, while, at the same time, the general Government of the country must also have a voice'.[138] Reporting on what he thought to be the satisfactory operations of the then current regime, Mill was asked whether he would recommend introducing 'the system of double Government with reference to the [fifty-two] colonies of the Crown'. Admitting his relative lack of knowledge regarding the Colonial Office, he conceived 'that there might be great advantage from having some body analogous to the Court of Directors as a Council to assist the Colonial Minister'.[139] He adjudged Canada and Australia to have 'local representative bodies perfectly competent to exercise that antagonistic discussion, which seems to me an essential element of good government everywhere; but for India you cannot have any local body which shall produce that result'.[140] Mill composed a major paper in defence of the East India Company administration in 1858, but it failed to turn the preponderance of political opinion against terminating the Company's pre-eminence in administering British interests in southern Asia, leading to the Government of India Act.[141] The petition of the East India Company, presented to the House of Commons by Thomas Baring on 9 February 1858, also failed to persuade. Mill's recollection of this time was less than positive: 'To the letters and petitions I wrote for them [the East India Company], and the concluding chapter of my treatise on *Representative Government*, I must refer for my opinions on the folly and mischief of this ill-considered change'.[142]

[138] Mill, 21 June 1852, 'Report from the select committee of the House of Lords, appointed to inquire into the operation of the Act 3 & 4 Will IV, c.85 for the better government of Her Majesty's Indian territories; and to report their observations thereon to the House; and to whom were referred the petitions of G.J. Gordon, respecting education in India, and of C.H. Cameron, respecting the establishment of universities in India; and to whom were also referred several papers and documents relative to the subject-matter of the inquiry: together with the minutes of evidence, and an appendix and index thereto', *GBPP1852–1853* (411), 309. On Mill, generally, see Harris, 'Mill, John Stuart (1806–1873)', in *Oxford Dictionary of National Biography*. On Mill and empire, see Bell, 'Empire and Imperialism', 882–886.

[139] Ibid. [140] Ibid.

[141] Mill, *Memorandum of the Improvements in the Administration of India during the last Thirty Years, and the Petition of the East-India Company to Parliament*. A copy also appeared in *GBPP1857–1858* (75), xliii, 1–38, enclosed with Melvill, 11 February 1858, 'Copy "of a memorandum (prepared at the India House) of the Improvements in the Administration of India during the last thirty years"'.

[142] JS Mill, *Autobiography* in Robson (ed), *Collected Works of John Stuart Mill*, I, 249.

Although the legislation of 1858 had replaced the classical form of 'double government' of which Mill was speaking in 1852 and which he again favoured in 1858 in pleading for the retention of the East India Company and its court of directors, as RJ Moore observed, 'The Act preserved the essential [structural] principle of the double government—the dual authorities of the minister and an independent council'.[143] The Government of India Act was noticeably more detailed, baroque, and ambitious than the Native Council Bill in outlining the functions of the Council of India.[144] India was to be governed directly by the Crown acting through a Secretary of State to be assisted by a council of fifteen members, eight of whom were to be appointed by the Crown and the remaining seven elected by the East India Company directorate.[145] What became known as the Indian Councils' Act of 1861 was not yet before the House. However, John Stuart Mill had spoken favourably of the preceding experiment of 'double government' operating in Britain's southern Asian territories. He lamented its passing in his *Considerations on Representative Government*, published in 1861, regarding a permanent delegated administration as a fitting institution for the 'government of a semi-barbarous dependency by a civilised country'.[146] His fond wish, tinged with regret, was that the lessons imparted by the East India Company would be recognized as the 'true theory of government' for such dependencies: 'When the home government and Parliament are swayed by those partial influences in the exercise of the power reserved to them in the last resort, the intermediate body is the certain advocate and champion of the dependency before the imperial tribunal'.[147] The proposed native council for New Zealand would be but a shadow of the principle of 'double government' institutionally deployed through the East India Company and the board of control. In appraising constitutional proposals for the administration of Britain's territorial interests in India, Mill, Charles Trevelyan (Macaulay's brother-in-law), and Sir James Melvill, the secretary of the East India Company, perceived the 'perfect simplicity which is called for [in constitutional government as] not consistent with our National habits'. 'The British Constitution', it was admitted, 'is a most complicated machine but we should not do so well with one of simple construction.'[148] A diversity of powers and institutions in rivalrous contention assisted the finding of balance and equilibrium.

However, alive to his precedents, whether in southern Africa, British India, or Ceylon, Fortescue noted: 'In all of [these territories in] which the Crown retained more or less control', a guiding nostrum underscoring policy towards such colonies was 'not [to] commit unrepresented Native races to the government of the settlers under the extreme doctrines of responsible government'.[149] In this vein, Fortescue urged:

> It was felt that the Natives could not possibly—at all events, for a long time to come—be included in such a representation; it was felt that it would be difficult and dangerous to govern them and tax them without giving them any voice in the matter; it was felt also that it was to the Crown, and not to the settlers, that they had ceded the sovereignty over their country; and that the Crown had, in return, by solemn treaty taken them under its protection.[150]

[143] Moore, *Sir Charles Wood's Indian Policy 1853–66*, 34.

[144] Section 19 of the Government of India Act 1858, 21 & 22 Vict, c106.

[145] For a brief overview, see Ilbert, *The Government of India*, 95–6.

[146] Mill, *Considerations on Representative Government*, in Mill, *Utilitarianism, On Liberty and Considerations on Representative Government*, 427–8.

[147] Ibid, 423.

[148] Moore, *Sir Charles Wood's Indian Policy*, 30.

[149] Fortescue, *HPD*, 3rd series, 21 August 1860, vol 160, col 1644.

[150] Ibid.

Fortescue's account, therefore, expressly rendered section 71 and section 73 of the Constitution Act as 'the *charter* of the Native race' in an enacted form.[151] The rich intellectual capital upon which Fortescue drew was informed by a sense of the fragility and combustibility of politics within Ireland, as well as an entwined liberal Anglican-whiggish tendency to adapt legislative interventions to the observable state of society in the history of progress—southern Asia and the Cape colony.[152] Needless to say, disputes as to ways and means of particular forms of intervention would arise, as with the native council proposals. Intellectual milieu did not predetermine particular policy or statutory design options.

Adderley complained in his notebook: 'I was recalled by a letter from R[obert] Lowe from grouse shooting with Wynne of Voelas, for the New Zealand Government Bill, and found on my return it had been withdrawn'.[153] Fortescue reported to an absent and ailing Secretary of State for colonies, 'I left nothing undone to explain the Bill', but there was 'much opposition to it, of which there was plenty, both within & without the Cabinet, & the official circle'.[154] Fortescue explained that 'Lowe was violent against it—& I have no doubt', he surmised, 'wrote the article in the Times of Wednesday or Thursday last'. At least to Newcastle, Fortescue suspected, 'Palmerston [still] thought the Bill right, & was inclined to go on—but on Monday, after taking counsel with Bethel[l] [the Attorney General] & C[ornewall] Lewis, & seeing the violent opposition it was since to encounter, and the plausible arguments against it afforded by the lateness of the moment at which it was to be debated, he decided to withdraw it'.[155] Lowe was a figure outside of cabinet but with a post in the Privy Council. In that role he was given considerable responsibilities in the areas of the committee of council on education and the medical department.[156] Since April 1851 he had been a regular leader writer for *The Times*, a fact with which Fortescue was familiar.

As Fortescue surmised, Lowe possibly prepared the leader in *The Times* of Thursday, 23 August 1860, which contended against the withdrawn Bill. Resonating with the tenor of Lowe's well-known aversion towards narrowly circumscribed and self-interested sources of politic advice and his constitutional arguments against vested interests, the piece in *The Times* proclaimed: 'Let no one trust too much to general maxims, or believe that there is in any class or in any clique a monopoly of reason and good sense, any more than of prejudice and folly'.[157] Thus, '[w]e have seen the men of peace deep in the preparation for a Chinese war; and we have seen the colleagues of the late Sir William Molesworth all but involved in the reversal of our colonial policy, and returning to the

[151] Ibid, col 1645 (emphasis added).

[152] On Fortescue's intimate awareness of Ireland and the political resonances there, see, eg Fortescue to Newcastle, 5 September 1861, NeC10,935, Nottingham University.

[153] Childe-Pemberton (ed), *Life of Lord Norton 1814–1905*, 177.

[154] Fortescue to Newcastle, 27 August 1860, NeC10, 931/1, Nottingham University.

[155] Ibid. In the House of Commons on 21 August 1860, Cornewall Lewis observed, 'It was only last night [Sunday, 20 August 1860], after full consideration of the means which the Crown already possessed of accomplishing the object aimed at by the Bill, without having recourse to Parliament, that they decided it would be consistent with their duty not to proceed with the Bill at present' (*HPD*, 3rd series, vol 160, col 1647).

[156] Parry, 'Lowe, Robert, Viscount Sherbrooke (1811–1892)', in *Oxford Dictionary of National Biography*.

[157] Anon [Robert Lowe?], 'It is fashionable to say that in Government…', *The Times*, 23 August 1860, issue 23706, col E, 8. This article was reprinted in New Zealand in the *Taranaki Herald*, 3 November 1860, vol 9, issue 432, 4, the *Colonist*, 20 November 1860, vol 4, issue 322, 3, and in the *Wellington Independent*, 13 November 1860, vol 15, issue 1471, 5.

doctrines and acts worthy of the darkest days of Colonial-office folly and meddling'. In saying this, *The Times*' leader then proceeded to state, '[w]e allude, of course, to the New Zealand Bill, which came to a well-deserved end on Tuesday night'.[158] The author reiterated his concern as to the narrowly drawn, circumscribed range of colonial opinion supporting the proposal: 'It is now desired by some local authorities—among whom are the Governor, the Bishop, and the late Chief Justice—to establish a native Council to assist the Governor in his dealings with the natives, and to give to that Council more extended powers than the Governor originally possessed'. Speaking of the Native Council Bill, the article commented on the alleged absence of consultation with colonial administration and the settlements: 'Of this attempt to legislate on affairs of which Parliament knows absolutely nothing the colonists have never heard up to the present moment'. 'We may ask', it was said, 'whether New Zealand is an exception to the rest of the world, in which it is found that two co-ordinate Governments having jurisdiction over the same subject cannot long go on in harmony.'[159] Better, remarked the author, for the United Kingdom to accept the risk of failure on granting self-government to colonial settlements: 'We must be content to take the evil with the good', as 'we gain in exchange for this licence the privilege of being free from the necessity of determining questions of intricate colonial policy such as this very difficulty about the natives of New Zealand'.[160]

As Fortescue appreciated, however, in the timing of these debates, the inaccessibility to other sources of colonial opinion proved telling. In the House of Commons on 21 August 1860, the parliamentary under-secretary reported that he 'had a petition to present from fourteen gentlemen of Auckland, New Zealand, who stated that the petition against the Bill came from the Southern Island, in which the Native question did not exist, and where no necessity had arisen for the services of the army and navy'.[161]Fortescue ruefully recorded how he 'got into communication with several leading Auckland men who are in England & found them not at all pleased at the agitation got up by Fitzgerald & his Southern I[slan]d friends, and very anxious that the Bill sh[ould] pass'.[162] One such Auckland colonist, WS Grahame, in writing to his business partner, Donald McLean, from Sunninghill, Berkshire, on 23 August 1860, lamented the fate of the measure in the House of Commons. In doing so, however, he characterized Fitzgerald's success as incomplete. He thought that the main aim of obtaining an authoritative transfer to the General Assembly within the colony of administrative control in policy-making on questions pertaining to Māori in New Zealand had not transpired.[163] '[A]t the same time', he opined, having read the speeches of ministers and their supporters in the House of Commons in *The Times*, 'I am satisfied they will retain thro' the Governor the control of these native affairs.'[164] In this regard, the relativities of the colonial settlements in the North Island and South Island respectively were well appreciated. Strategically, individuals such as Selwyn, the Bishop of New Zealand, anticipated that the substantial extinction of native title in the southern island,

[158] Anon [Robert Lowe?], 'It is fashionable to say that in Government…', *The Times*, 23 August 1860, issue 23706, col E, 8.

[159] Ibid. [160] Ibid.

[161] Fortescue, *HPD*, 3rd series, 21 August 1860, vol 160, col 1643.

[162] Fortescue to Newcastle, 27 August 1860, NeC10, 931/1, Nottingham University.

[163] Grahame to McLean, 23 August 1860, Ms-Papers-0032-0298, fo.4, McLean papers, ATL.

[164] Ibid, fo.5.

thereby attracting a 'more free and rapid immigration into that part of the Colony', would lead to a 'proportionate increase of legislative influence in the hands of persons practically unacquainted with the Native questions'.[165] Nevertheless, in contemplating Palmerston's decision to withdraw the proposal, Fortescue concluded in his own missive to Newcastle, 'there was no help for it, and I could only submit to the decree of the higher powers'. Ultimately, there was insufficient support from their own governmental colleagues for Newcastle and Fortescue to draw on the Palmerston ministry's legislative resources in the House of Commons—mustering both the requisite numbers (votes) and the necessary legislative time in the parliamentary session.

PART II—THE CONDITIONALITY OF THE INTRODUCED COLONIAL CONSTITUTION—THE REVIVAL AND DENOUEMENT OF AN IMPERIAL NATIVE COUNCIL OPTION

Warring in the Taranaki contributed additional stresses, troubling the political system with increased costs to the imperial Treasury. Media reports of various military reverses in the campaign at Waitara led Fortescue to write to Newcastle, stating that '[t]oday's news from N. Zealand are bad', and advising that '[t]his day's Times will tell you, I think, all that we know'.[166] Even so, Gladstone did not consider the balance of opinion as necessarily favouring his own views of imperial policy. As late as 23 January 1861, he wrote to Selwyn, the Bishop of New Zealand and his long-standing correspondent on ecclesiological matters: 'I ever revert to my old & rooted conviction which I have now a days little or no success in propagating, that it is the height of folly approaching to madness, for us to undertake to regulate and be responsible for the management . . . of such business in New Zealand'.[167] Gladstone's primary concern with warfare in the Taranaki (and, it would be fair to assume, on account of his favouritism towards colonial self-administration, the native council option) was that it diverted political resources and capital into what he thought to be distractions from the main preoccupations of policy.[168] Similarly, along with Newcastle, he doubted the prudence of committing scarce political capital to distant New Zealand affairs in a fractious cabinet so preoccupied with a range of pressing policy questions: 'With so little powder and shot in store I feel reluctant to waste time for so small an object'.[169] 'Perhaps, at Cabinet tomorrow or otherwise', he suggested, 'you will kindly tell me what you mean to do.'[170] Certainly, his own predilections towards fiscal economy as Chancellor of the Exchequer encouraged Gladstone to caution Newcastle about the

[165] Selwyn, memorandum, 8 May 1860, CO209/154, fo.481, TNA (received at the Colonial Office on 10 August 1860).

[166] Fortescue to Newcastle, 14 September 1860, NeC10932/1, Nottingham University, referring to 'The War in New Zealand', Friday, 14 September 1860, *The Times*, issue 23725, col A.

[167] Gladstone to Selwyn, 23 January 1861, BL AddMss44531, fo.110, Gladstone papers.

[168] Ibid. Newcastle's chief concern was with Selwyn writing directly to Gladstone in criticism of policies in New Zealand, as his private correspondence dated 21 January 1861 suggested: Martineau, *The Life of Henry Pelham, Fifth Duke of Newcastle, 1811–1864*, 319.

[169] Gladstone to Newcastle, 30 January 1861, BL AddMss44531, fo.113, Gladstone papers.

[170] Ibid.

'hopeless & incurable faults of our plan of attempting to manage such controversies whether on paper or in the field from the other end of the world'.[171] No doubt considering the varied factional dispositions of Palmerston's ministry, he concluded that the 'doom of that system is written even if its hour be not yet come'.[172] Such sentiments did not coincide with those of Fortescue or Rogers in January 1861.

To confound the withdrawal of the Colonial Office's option further, the General Assembly in New Zealand, on 5 November 1860, enacted its own legislation to 'establish a council to assist in the administration of native affairs', whereupon it was 'reserved for the signification of Her Majesty's pleasure'.[173] Royal assent was withheld on Colonial Office advice. The preamble to the Native Council Act set out the intention to establish a council 'on a constitutional basis, to whom the Governor and his Responsible Advisers may have recourse for advice'. There could be no doubt that the role of the native council was to be strictly advisory and a body with whom the colonial administration would consult. Under this proposal, the 'duties of the council' were enumerated in section 12 and were cast as threefold. First, a duty of the native council would be that of advising 'upon all matters relating to Native affairs upon which they shall be consulted by the Government' (section 12(1)). Secondly, it was obliged to 'submit for the consideration of the Government such measures as may appear to the Council desirable for promoting the civilization of the Natives; for establishing law and order amongst them; for preparing them for the exercise of political power; and generally for promoting the good government welfare and advancement of the native people' (section 12(2)). Finally, under section 12(3), the council was to 'assist, when called upon, in the preparation of the drafts of any laws regulations or other legislative measures which it may be deemed desirable to submit for the consideration of the General Assembly for the purpose of effecting any of the before-mentioned objects [under subsections (1) and (2)]'. McLean's source of political intelligence in Britain, his business partner, William Grahame, characterized the 'great inquiry for the Home Government [as to the colonial proposal for a native council] is, will the Maories have *confidence* in such men as will accept office! If not then the Council will be of no use whatever'.[174] Although not mentioned in the Colonial Office deliberations on the colonial native council option, it appears that the colonial ministers did not support the measure themselves, at least not wholeheartedly, possibly relying upon the Colonial Office to bear the burden of withholding approval to it. Sewell, who was a proponent of the Native Council Bill in the House of Representatives in New Zealand, expressed concern that what he viewed and hoped to be a 'good work', was being trusted to 'the present [colonial] Government who accept it coldly if not reluctantly and who vowed at the commencement of the session that they would resign rather than submit to such a measure'.[175] Barely appreciating the complicated politics of the issue, Sewell observed

[171] Ibid. [172] Ibid.

[173] The short title was 'The Native Council Act, 1860'. Section 15 provided that 'This Act shall not come into operation until the same shall have been confirmed by Her Majesty, with the advice of her Privy Council, and Proclamation of such confirmation shall have been made by the Governor in the *New Zealand Gazette*'.

[174] Grahame to McLean, 23 January 1861, Ms-Papers-0032-0298, fo.9, McLean papers, ATL (emphasis in original).

[175] Sewell, 6 November 1860, journal of Henry Sewell, I, 190, qMs-1786, ATL.

how it was a 'strange government which alternately kicks and submits and accepts a policy forced upon it by [its] opponents without a thought of surrendering power'.[176]

In a cutting assessment of the colonial Bill, Fortescue said: 'It looks & sounds as if it were a concession *to* the Imperial Gov[ernmen]t—while in reality I believe it c[oul]d be a concession *by* the Imperial Gover[ernmen]t in the matter of native administration'.[177] While the colonial legislature's version of a native council option presented the outward trappings of an independent body of advisors (including authorization of funding up to £2,350 per annum for salaries), the measure 'carefully avoids connecting [?] the Council with the *Governor*—it gives the Council no initiative—it subordinates it to the "Government" i.e. the Ministers of the day in all its action—& it only concedes to it *administrative functions* in "special cases", & "of [at] the [text unclear] of the *Governor in Council*" i.e. with the consent of his Ministers'.[178] The preamble was also noted as tending towards an interpretation of the colonial Bill as '[placing] the control and *ordinary departmental administration* of Native affairs [being] under Responsible Ministers'. In the circumstances, Fortescue counselled the Secretary of State for Colonies to advise withholding royal assent from the Bill: 'My own idea w[oul]d be to send the Gov[erno]r a desp[atch] by the mail of the 26th [February] withholding the confirmation of the Act on the grounds both of its encroachment upon the Governor's authority in native affairs, & its imperfect & fragmentary character'.[179] He suggested using the subsequent delay to develop an alternative plan for the 'management of native affairs', allowing a period of creative indeterminacy to resolve itself in recommendations for action.

On the same date, Rogers ventured a closely argued, broad-ranging paper on the issue of the colonial Bill, distilling a number of points that an imperial counter-proposal could suggest. First, he proposed the 'Governor & Native Council (including a responsible minister [as a member]) to have the power of legislating for natives in native districts'.[180] Secondly, he advised a reorganization of constitutional government within New Zealand, by eliminating any jurisdiction the provincial councils might claim in so-called native districts, where native title and indigenous laws, customs, and usages prevailed: '[the] General Assembly, not Provincial Council, to have powers of legislating for European or mixed questions in these districts'. Instead of a native council drawing upon imperial funds, a sum of '£25.000 [was] to be placed at the command of the Native Council subject to such general conditions as [the] assembly may impose'. The 'Native Council [was] to be empowered to give natives alienable grants of land but [, fourthly,] I would also require that the administration of native affairs should remain on its present footing'. Rogers counselled how to approach this vexed policy question tactically:

> But I should be disposed not merely to bring this as a *proposal* before the Assembly, which I fear would only elicit more counterproposals of the same illusory kind as the present (being in fact all that any N[ew] Zealand ministry will dare to make) but to take an actual

[176] Ibid. He added: 'It is a new phase of Responsible Government but I am too glad to get the measure passed upon any terms to quarrel with these things': ibid, 190–1.

[177] Fortescue to Newcastle, 21 February 1861, CO209/156, fo.130, TNA (emphasis added). The word 'c[oul]d' is read by Morrell as 'w[oul]d' in his *British Colonial Policy in the Mid-Victorian Age*, 255.

[178] Fortescue to Newcastle, 21 February 1861, CO209/156, fos.130–30a, TNA.

[179] Ibid, 131a.

[180] Rogers, 21 February 1861, CO209/156, fo.143a, TNA.

> step issuing Letters Patent to invest the Governor and Native Council (after consultation with the Law Officers) with all the powers which the Constitutional Act places at the command of the Crown.[181]

If that course were pursued, then the native council would 'thus be at once in a position to act with a certain amount of authority and effect, and to negotiate with the colonial government on the spot, instead of remaining themselves the subject of negotiation between two parties separated by the semi circumference of the globe'.[182] Newcastle, in agreeing that he could not advise the monarch to assent to the colonial Native Council Bill, could not help but notice the absence of practical power residing with the native council under the colonial statute: 'The measure, whilst it constituted a Native Council and provides funds for its payment, gives it no real power,—but on the contrary takes away from the Governor (though not by express enactment) the very little independent action which was conferred upon him by the Constitution Act and places him and the proposed Council in active subordination to the government of the day'.[183]

Newcastle was more than prepared to consider such a constitutional arrangement as either good or bad. Moreover, he admitted, '[i]t may be that when responsible government was given to the colony it was impolitic to exempt from its operation the management of native affairs', adding that it 'may be that the natives would be more liberally treated under the operation of this Ordinance [the colonial version of the Native Council Bill]'.[184] Such, however, were not his immediate concerns. In turning to what he considered objectionable about the colonial option, he surmised that the relevant provisions in the Constitution Act were 'framed in recognition of the engagements of the Treaty of Waitangi, though it may be doubted whether it [the provisions] really carried them out'.[185] Most strikingly, Newcastle's analysis suggested the inherent conditionality of the colonial constitution relative to the Treaty of Waitangi and the honour of the Crown, conceiving the colonial measure as a barely veiled constitutional innovation requiring the consent of Māori before it could be proceeded with: 'In the face of the Treaty of Waitangi this Ordinance cannot be sanctioned without injustice and bad faith to the natives'. This was the sort of argument which resonated with an imperial Crown reserving some shards of the true cross that is the Treaty of Waitangi from the colonial government of the day. The indigenization of the settler state, however—the state apparatus falling completely into the hands of settler politicians and officials—had not yet occurred. In Newcastle's opinion, Māori 'have *never been consulted as to its provisions*, and those provisions deprive them of that which they believe is their best security as given by the Treaty—the direct protection of the Sovereign of England'.[186] In this context, Newcastle considered that consultation and consent was advisable: 'Without their consent such a change would be looked upon by them as indicative of evil intention by the settlers even in times when the two races were living together in peace'.[187] In the absence of seeking such deliberative consent, Newcastle apprehended additional strife and negative fiscal results.

The overall tenor of the fluid political calculations occurring to Newcastle at this time was the necessity of placing the government of New Zealand on a different

[181] Ibid, fo.144. [182] Ibid.
[183] Newcastle, 23 February 1861, CO209/156, fos.134–4a, TNA.
[184] Ibid, fos.134a–5. [185] Ibid, fo.135.
[186] Ibid, fos.135–5a, TNA (emphasis added). [187] Ibid, fo.135a.

footing. As a result, searching analyses were made of the various options before the imperial administration, with internal debates over how political influence within New Zealand ought to be distributed. Fortescue authored two extensive memoranda dated 12 March 1861 and 1 April 1861 respectively on the subject of a native council and how to govern interaction between the colonial regime and Māori communities (including issues of native title). Fortescue remained committed until at least early April 1861 to imperial policy formulators driving overarching policies but conceding to the colonial legislature a role in tendering advice to the statutorily created native council. He suggested an option predicated on a native council receiving 'large powers of legislation in native matters (including that of land) and to be exercised within native districts but subject to the *tacit* assent of the Assembly'.[188] The import of the term 'tacit' in Fortescue's paper is ambiguous—as policy and analysis it provided neither clarity nor guidance. Yet, in his memorandum of 1 April 1861, Fortescue seemed prepared to countenance increased responsibility on the part of colonial authorities in view of the expenses associated with military action borne by the imperial Treasury: 'I think we may trust the Ministers with a larger share in native administration than at present, if the Governor is supported by a Council chosen by the Crown, and therefore less likely to be overborne by the Ministers,—for which purposes also I would require the *assent* of the Native Council in all matters of importance'.[189]

In an increasingly uncongenial ministerial climate at Westminster, an imperial enactment was no longer considered to be viable. Fortescue still preferred maintaining a degree of imperial pre-eminence. This pre-eminence would be maintained through the governor and a permanent council as opposed to a set of ministers liable to change as significant and politic. It 'ought to be laid down', he opined, 'that the direct correspondence with the natives [is] to be carried on, not by a changeable "Minister" or by a provincial officer who w[oul]d be the Minister's subordinate, but by a permanent officer of rank & consideration—say by the Secretary of the Native Council,—and by the Governor, who sh[ould] be instructed to take an active personal part in native administration.'[190] Provided these conditions were satisfied, Fortescue considered that 'native correspondence might pass through the hands of a *responsible minister*,—and the governor might consult his Ministers on native affairs, and with appointment promotion, dismissal *&c* of affairs, native or European, in the native districts & Native Department,—*though without being bound by their advice*'.[191] In order to placate colonial sensibilities, however, as well as the temperament of Newcastle's various colleagues, especially Gladstone within cabinet, but also others such as Lowe, aligned with Palmerston's ministry, Fortescue thought it apposite to propose it as necessary 'to make native ordinances of the Gov[erno]r and Native Council subject to disallowance by joint resolution of the two Houses of Assembly [in the colony]'. A way towards a compromise position was sought. In the meantime, however, he concluded that the 'first & immediate steps to be taken sh[ould] be to obtain a definition of the Crown's powers under the Constitution Act from the Law Officers,—which Sir F Rogers would [take] in hand'.[192]

188 Rogers, 21 February 1861, CO209/156, fo.138a, TNA (emphasis added).

189 Fortescue, 'Notes on Sir F Rogers' mem[orandum]', 1 April 1861, CO209/156, fo.165, TNA (emphasis in original).

190 Ibid. 191 Ibid (emphasis added). 192 Ibid.

Yet the lengthy delays after 21 August 1860 proved critical in undermining a principally imperial approach to the native council option. By late April 1861, Newcastle, now echoing Gladstone, doubted the prudence of crafting imperial solutions. 'I am sure I should be running a great risk', he confided to Browne, 'of complicating the already serious difficulties of the colony if I attempted to regulate affairs by didactic dispatches which require more than two months for their transmission.'[193] One notes an increasing sense of the inadequacy of the resources available to the imperial administration with which to bargain in order to influence colonial decision-making. Both Rogers and Fortescue doubted the threat of refusing the provision or reinforcement of imperial troops as a 'substantial check', even though the imperial resources committed to colonial defence were substantial relative to the local commitment in the Taranaki.[194]The Native Council Bill of the colonial legislature occasioned considerable comment in London albeit much of it remaining undetectable. A noticeable shift in Colonial Office temperament and approach had occurred during the first four months of 1861. Newcastle consulted with his associates in cabinet. In considering the draft despatches that Rogers and Fortescue had prepared on the question of the Colonial Office's response, Newcastle was mindful, as he had not been in mid-1860, of a need to consult with senior ministerial colleagues: 'I think however that if he will be good enough to elaborate these heads into a draft despatch I would deal with it more satisfactorily, and this is more desirable because in a case of such importance I should wish the Cabinet to see it before it is sent out'.[195]

Tipping points in imperial policy occurred in April and May 1861. By May 1861 Fortescue proved to be a major advocate for sending George Grey out to New Zealand with permissive rather than directive instructions for a reprise of his gubernatorial role.[196] Some sense of the possibilities of replacing Browne as governor had been signalled in August of the preceding year when Fortescue met with the erstwhile Auckland colonist William Grahame in the context of the Native Council Bill then before the House of Commons. Grahame had recounted how Fortescue 'asked me what I thought of Governor Brown[e]—if he was quite the man for the present emergency'. Grahame replied, 'I thought he was a good governor'. But he 'inferred it was just possible that the Government here [in the United Kingdom] might contemplate a change of governor—as Browne's 5 years are nearly up!'[197] He added, '[o]f course you must consider this as quite confidential'. A further private note in September 1860 appeared to forebode the end of Browne's tenure: 'There appears to be a want of confidence in the Governor—that he wants firmness—And I would not be at all surprised to find another sent out soon—it is reported the Government are looking out for a suitable person for

193 Newcastle to Browne, 26 April 1861, NeC10885, Nottingham University.

194 Fortescue, 'Notes on Sir F Rogers' mem[orandum]', 1 April 1861, CO209/156, fos.164–4a, TNA: 'If indeed I could believe in a "substantial check" to be imposed upon the colonial gov[ernmen]t by the refusal of troops I might lean the other way, but, I believe Sir F[rederic] R[ogers] (p.8) I have little faith in such a check,—and believe that, when the lives & properties of our colonists are in danger, the greater or less control of the Home Gov[ernmen]t over native affairs will make little or no difference in the number of troops supplied—So far therefore as military considerations are concerned, the Home Gov[ernmen]t may as well retain or exercise the amount of that control'.

195 Newcastle, 24 April 1861, CO209/156, fos.176a–7, TNA.

196 Fortescue, diary, 4 May 1861, in '. . . *And Mr Fortescue*', 179.

197 Grahame to McLean, 23 August 1860, Ms-Papers-0032-0298, fo.6, McLean papers, ATL. Newcastle, in writing to Browne, referred to six years.

the office but this may only be rumour'.[198] For Fortescue, appointing Grey in 1861 was seen as a way of addressing the ebbing native council proposal, and potentially reviving it if political stasis on policy towards Māori communities remained unresolved or opinion within New Zealand turned to it. Allowing Grey discretion to determine whether to pursue a version of the proposal on the ground permitted a testing of the waters without committing to any particular solution. In the House of Commons in April 1861, the tenor of criticism of Palmerston's ministry on the New Zealand question was beginning to venture into the territory of an 'independent tribunal' and the absence of such an institution within the colony to deal with conflicting native claims to title. George Hope asked Fortescue '[w]hether it is intended to endeavour to institute a Tribunal in New Zealand to decide upon conflicting claims of Natives in cases of proposed sales of land by them to the Government'.[199]

In the absence of an imperially designed native council, Fortescue assumed that the energetic patronage of Māori elites would be advisable—an approach associated with Grey's policies in southern Africa. In April 1861, Fortescue commented: 'There can be little doubt, I think, that the true course w[oul]d be to employ & pay selected chiefs, invited [?] and checked by Resident Magistrates'. He characterized this as 'Sir G Grey's plan in British Kaffraria, with far worse materials—Kaffir chiefs being, I suppose, inferior to Maori chiefs'.[200] In the vital despatch prepared for Grey in early June 1861, the new governor was instructed to reflect on his experiments within southern Africa: 'I may add that your experience in British Kaffraria would seem to recommend a system under which a certain number of the native chiefs should be attached to the Gov[ernmen]t by the payment of salaries & the recognition of their dignity, and should at the same time be assisted by Resident Magistrates in administering justice within their respective districts or tribes'.[201] Newcastle's own personal (unofficial) correspondence with Grey revealed the development of this theme, where he refers to the 'introduction of your Kaffrarian policy' directly.[202]

Ultimately, selecting Grey, with directions for the new governor to consider local circumstances as to whether a native council ought to be introduced, proved agreeable to a number of ministers within Palmerston's cabinet. Entries in Fortescue's diary highlighted his commitment to the Grey option, but also his inclination to record his own significance in steering Newcastle towards that appointment—'*May 4.* Wrote to the Duke pressing him to send Sir George Grey to New Zealand'.[203] These spare words do little justice to the significance of his letter in galvanizing action and setting a course

[198] Grahame to McLean, 25 September 1860, Ms-Papers-0032-0298, fo.3, McLean papers, ATL. Incidentally, it was in this letter that Grahame reported the incident of the wife of Sir George Grey on board a naval ship bound for the Cape Colony: 'Your old friend Lady Grey has made a sad mess of it—Sir George and she were going out to the Cape on board one of H[er] M[ajesty]'s ships—Admiral Keppel and report affirms that Sir George caught Keppel and Lady Grey in bed together!!! The consequence was that Sir George landed her Ladyship at Rio and sent her back to England whilst he went on to the Cape with the Admiral!' (ibid, fos.3–4). For a less salacious view (with reference simply to a possibly flirtatious letter), see Hewett, '*. . . And Mr Fortescue*', 168–70, and Rutherford, *Sir George Grey K.C.B. 1812–1898*, 427–8.

[199] Hope, *HPD*, 3rd series, 19 April 1861, vol 162, col 824.

[200] Fortescue, 1 April 1861, CO209/157, fos.397a–8, TNA.

[201] Newcastle to Grey, 5 June 1861, CO209/156, fo. 246a, TNA.

[202] Newcastle to Grey, 5 June 1861, NeC10885, Nottingham University.

[203] Fortescue, diary, 4 May 1861, in '*. . . And Mr Fortescue*', 179.

that would lead to the substantial re-conception of how imperial authority interacted with New Zealand on questions of native title. Fortescue, in forwarding Rogers' draft despatch dated 29 April 1860 to Newcastle on 4 May 1861, prepared a covering note, reinforcing the requirement for a new governor in Browne's stead, who would be given a modicum of discretion as to how to proceed on the question of colonial government in the native districts. It presaged a retreat on the part of imperial policy-formulators in driving a native council option from London by statutory means. 'The proposed despatch [of Rogers]', wrote Fortescue, 'makes me feel more and more how very much more depends upon the *man* who is to negotiate on behalf of the Home Gov[ernmen]t with colonists and Maories than upon any terms or scheme wh[ich] we may frame here'.[204] The native council was receding as an option although its recession was not yet formally acknowledged at Westminster.

The ease of expression in Fortescue's note revealed something of the intimate appreciation of the politics at play. A politics of negotiability subsisted between metropole, colonial administration, and Māori polities as much as within these various configurations and clusters of influence and opinion. The parliamentary under-secretary focused on 'two great works to be done at this crisis in New Zealand'. First, 'the restoration of peace on a footing wh[ich] will secure its continuance'; secondly, 'the imagination of an improved system of Native administration, or rather, the introduction of something like government into the native districts—not forgetting an improvement of the system of land purchase [?]'.[205] To achieve these works, an astute and commanding temperament, as well as adroit relationship-management skills, was called for. 'For these purposes', he suggested, '[another] & stronger man is wanted than Colonel Browne, and it will be hard to find any one suitable except Grey—who also possesses the great advantage of influence acquired over the Natives, wh[ich], I think, more than counterbalance hostility already incurred on the part of some of the colonists'.[206] It was vital, Fortescue signalled, to ensure a new gubernatorial appointment for New Zealand as soon as practicable and this factor also favoured selecting Grey, as it could assist in accomplishing the imperial Treasury's much-desired diminution in military expenditure in the Cape colony: 'His removal from the Cape w[oul]d also have the advantage of making it easier to cut down the military expenditure there, which it is evident must be done'.[207] Such an option also buttressed Fortescue's preferred tactical approach to instructions for any governor in the then insecure circumstances of policy on the administration of the interlocked triad of imperial, colonial, and Māori issues within New Zealand: 'If he, or indeed any near Governor, be sent out within the next few months, it w[oul]d do, I think, to make the proposals to the Colony contained within drafts before his arrival, instead of making him the bearer of them, and leaving him a certain discretion on the matter'.[208]

Fortescue explored the delicacies of how to seed this sea-change by way of announcements in the imperial Parliament in order to obtain maximum political effect and to staunch the wounds of the Colonial Office's policy on New Zealand both within and beyond Palmerston's regime. Mindful of managing presentation to politically literate opinion, he alerted Newcastle to the point that the third Earl Grey had 'told [him] yesterday that he meant to take the opportunity of the New Zealand Provinces Bill

[204] Fortescue to Newcastle, 4 May 1861, NeC934/1, Nottingham University.
[205] Ibid. [206] Ibid. [207] Ibid. [208] Ibid.

to make a speech on the general question—on some stage of the Bill'. Fortescue suggested '*[t]hat* would perhaps be an opportunity for announcing your intentions as to a new governor'.[209] In consequence, the announcement of Grey's appointment was timed to coincide with a second reading debate on the New Provinces (New Zealand) Bill in the House of Lords on 28 May 1861 following the discussions at cabinet. With the loss of the Native Council Bill in the preceding parliamentary session, Newcastle found himself in the curious position of withstanding criticisms from the third Earl Grey in the Lords as to the absence of an 'independent tribunal' to assess Māori territorial claims. In rebutting the criticisms he noted that the 'Treaty of Waitangi did not refer to such a tribunal, but it said that transactions for the purchase of land should be carried on between the native proprietors of the land and the Governor, and that was the course taken in this case [the negotiations for the Waitara purchase in 1859 and 1860]'.[210] Leaving the announcement to the last, Newcastle expressed pleasure at the appointment of Grey to reprise his role as governor in New Zealand.[211] Fortescue diarized how he 'Talked to the Duke about New Zealand affairs, & gave him hints for speaking', adding that he '[h]eard him in the Lords in answer to Lord Grey'. At this point, Newcastle 'announced Sir George Grey's appointment which is really my doing, & made use of my ideas and words'.[212]

Newcastle's urgent request on 6 May 1861 for twenty printed copies of the still-incomplete draft despatch prepared by Rogers concerning a native council suggested the political significance of the New Zealand question to Newcastle quickening with an impending meeting of cabinet: 'I wish 20 copies of this draft despatch [*with the words '& reference to Law Officers' placed in margin*] to be printed as quickly as possible—marked "private & confidential"—and as soon as they are printed the type may be broken up'. Newcastle also minuted, 'If they can be printed by Thursday let me find 16 copies in a large box with a... label on my arrival at 43 Grosvenor Place'.[213] These copies were printed privately at the Foreign Office on 10 May 1861 and a reference to the law officers was organized on 7 May. The principal utility of Rogers' draft is that it traversed the broad themes of the imperial arguments against the colonial native council option, as well as the imperial Treasury's fiscal concerns. Under Rogers' draft despatch, Newcastle refused to recommend assent to the Native Council Bill passed by the General Assembly in New Zealand. Defending the existing legal resources available to the Crown rather than denuding them proved to be an actuating spirit in Rogers' draft. To this end, the draft stated: 'As Her Majesty, acting in virtue of the Constitutional Act (15 & 16 Vict c.72) and in the exercise of undoubted prerogative has already the power of establishing a Council with greater powers than those wh[ich] it is proposed to confer upon Her, the confirmation of this Bill would involve a surrender rather an accession of authority to the Crown'.[214] To guide rather than to receive or to follow

209 Ibid (emphasis in original).

210 Newcastle, *HPD*, 3rd series, 28 May 1861, vol 163, col 170.

211 Ibid, col 177.

212 Fortescue, diary, 28 May 1861, '*...And Mr Fortescue*', 180.

213 Newcastle, 6 May 1861, CO209/156, fos.193–3a, TNA.

214 Draft, Newcastle to Browne, [Sir Frederic Rogers, signed off the draft on 29 April 1861; Fortescue, 4 May 1861; Newcastle, 6 May 1861], [CO209/156, fo.194: '[Printed privately at the F[oreign] O[ffice] 10 May [18]61]']; [CO209/156, fo.194: 'Cancelled...to Sir George Grey/5 June'], undated, CO209/156, fos.196a–7, TNA.

the vicissitudes of public opinion was preferred. As initially conceived, the imperial native council option aspired to coax Māori communities into engaging in a contained but much more regular basis with introduced colonial government. To achieve that, either statutorily enacted permanence at the imperial level was required or, failing that, the survival of a legally and politically insulated dimension of the Crown exercising prerogative powers assisted by members able to acquire the confidence of Māori elites. Permanence in these terms was construed as less vulnerable to the vicissitudes of colonial politics—so the argument proceeded. Public opinion was considered to be unavoidably unreliable and riven with potentially costly political risks in a setting such as New Zealand:

> The interests of the European inhabitants of New Zealand in some respects no doubt coincide, but in others they conflict with those of the native race. And it may be universally laid down that when society is sharply divided into two classes, the interest of one class cannot be safely left to the guardianship of the other. The more remote motive of common interest is forgotten under the pressure of some immediate and partial difference. And as the whole community is ranged either on one side or the other there is no overpowering public opinion emanating from persons not concerned in the actual dispute, and to which in a great country particular classes solicitous about their own interests are compelled to submit.[215]

On these grounds, the despatch assumed that 'effectual control' should reside with the imperial administration. Such 'effectual control' should be preserved 'over the management of the natives until either the amalgamation of the races has proceeded so far as to break down the sharp division of colour, or until such a system of government as will in itself furnish a guarantee not only in fact but also in the feelings of the natives, against oppressive or one sided treatment of the less educated race has taken firm root in the colony'.[216] By 'effectual control', however, the Colonial Office did not wish to signify that 'the imperial government should interfere in the principles on which native affairs are managed, or at all in the details of management, still less that those affairs should be conducted in a spirit of opposition or indifference to colonial feelings or interests'. What was intended was 'only that the practical treatment of this subject should for the present be in the hands of persons under definite responsibility to the Home Government, and not liable to be displaced or overborne by any of those popular feelings of which it is impossible to predict the direction or the strength'.[217] Thus, any subordination to the impermanency and political preoccupations of changeable ministries in the colony was considered inappropriate:

> If the Native Minister has the power of appointing, removing, approving, censuring, advancing and instructing the officers of the native department, subject only to the Governor's power of occasional obstruction, it is plain that the Native Minister will have in his hands the power of causing peace or war, of affronting or conciliating chiefs, of preventing or advancing the progress of a particular tribe, or of the whole native race, and the spirit in which this power will be exercised will necessarily be such as is dictated by that public opinion, the course of which, as I have said, it is not possible to calculate.[218]

Yet the despatch harboured two lines of inconsistent reasoning. On the one hand, it expressed concern as to the fiscal responsibility for warring in New Zealand, stating as a general principle of imperial finance that 'The first & most obvious answer is that the

215 Ibid, fos.216a–17a.
216 Ibid, fos.218a–19.
217 Ibid, fos.219–19a.
218 Ibid, fos.220–20a.

cost of... every other war should be exclusively defrayed by those for whose exclusive benefit it is carried on—that is to say in the present instance by the inhabitants of New Zealand'. Accordingly, '[t]he British taxpayer has no greater interest in subduing the natives of that colony than the colonists have in suppressing an insurrection in the United Kingdom'.[219] The colonial treasurer, however, contended that such a general principle was defeasible owing to the peculiar constitutional circumstances of New Zealand. Hence, 'so long as native policy is divided by the Home Government the military expenses of native wars should be treated as if New Zealand were a Crown colony'. Colonial Office counter-arguments stressed the visible constitutional practices on the ground rather than the general framing of the Constitution Act 1852. In summing up its points, the draft paper concluded:

> The truer statement of the case is this—that in acquiring New Zealand for the colonists the Home Government incurred certain obligations to the natives—that in handing over New Zealand to the government of the colonists it retained certain powers intended to secure that those obligations should be performed—that those powers have proved inadequate—that the Home Government have hitherto refused to relinquish or the Colonial Government to enlarge them—and that under those circumstances the Governor has been obliged to do not what he could have wished, but the best that his means allowed in order on the one hand to advance the settlement of the country—on the other to ensure that the natives enjoyed those advantages which were expressed or implied in their Treaty with Great Britain, and which the colonists who enjoyed the benefit of that Treaty were bound to allow them.[220]

Even if New Zealand were able to be analogized with a Crown colony, the despatch observed in a passage deleted by Fortescue that 'Ceylon contributes largely to its military expenditure; India defrays the whole of it; And rightly so too'.[221] Fortescue preferred a different comparator, namely the Cape colony. In his marginal note accompanying the deleted passage, Fortescue wrote, 'Better to omit?—The Cape can be quoted with great effect on the other side—& India differs too widely from a little colony 20 years old to form a satisfactory precedent'. Here, in Fortescue's commentary on Rogers' draft, we see the presentational influence of Godley's memorandum to the Colonial Office on imperial military expenditure.[222] And, as importantly for its dissemination to members of cabinet in May 1861 in a printed version, such a comparison would serve as a reminder to Newcastle's audience of such a link, calling to mind the peculiarities of New Zealand in Britain's empire. In this fashion, New Zealand's present predicament and the Cape colony could be aligned. After all, Godley's memorandum had re-categorized the constituent parts of Britain's empire not with reference to constitutional form (Crown colonies, self-governing colonies, and protectorates), but according to the security of the military situation and demands upon military expenditure. For the purposes of such expenditure, Godley divided the colonies into four classes. The first category consisted of '[g]reat and unmixed European communities, such as those in British North America and Australia'.[223] New Zealand fell into a second category—'European communities which are large and thriving, but in contact with powerful and

[219] Ibid, 203a–4. [220] Ibid, fos.209–10. [221] Ibid, fo.211.

[222] Godley to Colonial Office, 28 January 1860, reprinted in Fitzgerald (ed), *A Selection from the Writings and Speeches of John Robert Godley*, 278–94.

[223] Ibid, 283.

warlike natives, such as the Colonies of New Zealand and the Cape of Good Hope'.[224] Again, Godley's memorandum merely illuminated the fragility of framing a general rule or principle for such a range of imperial situations. Fortescue himself had emphasized these links in his speech to the House of Commons on 21 August 1860.

The key point in Rogers' draft paper was that expenditure on wars was a duty of government that crystallized whenever warring arose, irrespective of the particular constitutional arrangements of a given community—'whether free or absolute—native or foreign'. The expenses relating to New Zealand had been considerable. In the financial years 1853 to 1857 (inclusive) alone, '£434,360 of British money appears to have been spent in furnishing troops to New Zealand (to say nothing of naval expenditure) which may not very incorrectly be treated as a gift from the inhabitants of the United Kingdom to those of the colony'.[225] Yet the triumvirate of senior Colonial Office authors—Newcastle, Fortescue, and Rogers—appreciated that the question of military assistance extended to areas within Britain's formal imperial orbit was not to be sorted out conclusively 'as one of dry justice'. Nevertheless, it could not be alleged that the 'British Government have at any time governed New Zealand in the interest of the British Taxpayer'. Indeed, the 'inhabitants of the United Kingdom have never derived or endeavoured to derive from New Zealand any advantages other than those which the colony and metropolis enjoy in common from commerce and emigration'. Nor were the colonists 'compelled to receive English manufactures or to carry their goods to an English market'. Unlike British India, the colonists did not contribute any 'quota to the imperial army, [nor any] money to the imperial Treasury'.[226] The point was intimated—specifically the possibility of tying the constitutional situation to the provision of military assistance and imperial funds. Intimation on paper was enough for cabinet discussions.

'The incorporation of the two races in one body politic'—letters patent and an imperial native council: native title, administering native districts, and the levers of imperial military assistance and funding

What, then, was proposed? As a guide to sophisticated and contested thinking in April and May 1861 in the Colonial Office on the question of administering areas subject to native title, Rogers' memorandum remains unrivalled. In setting out the policy proposals, Rogers sounded a cautionary note: 'This must be modified or enlarged according to the opinion wh[ich] the Law Officers of the Crown may entertain on the subject'.[227] The draft paper advocated proposing 'to Parliament a grant of £10,000 per annum for a

224 Ibid.

225 Draft, Newcastle to Browne, [Sir Frederic Rogers, signed off the draft on 29 April 1861; Mr Fortescue, 4 May 1861; Duke of Newcastle, 6 May 1861], [CO209/156, fo.194: '[Printed privately at the F[oreign] O[ffice] 10 May [18]61]']; [CO209/156, fo.194: 'Cancelled... to Sir George Grey/5 June'], undated, CO209/156, fos.214–14a.

226 Ibid, fos.212–12a. In *Representative Government*, John Stuart Mill stated that 'It is essential... in all wars, save those which, like Caffre or New Zealand wars, are incurred for the sake of the particular colony, the colonists should not (without their own voluntary request) be called on to contribute anything to the expense, except what may be required for the specific local defence of their own ports, shores, and frontiers against invasion': Mill, *Utilitarianism, On Liberty and Considerations on Representative Government*, 414.

227 Ibid, fo.224.

few years to be spent on the management of the natives or the administration of native affairs in such manner as the Governor shall think fit'.[228] Rather than resorting to imperial legislation, with all the risks of diverse political scrutiny within the House of Commons and House of Lords that that entailed, the prerogative device of using letters patent was now preferred. Insulated from the glare of parliamentary process, a key strategic resource for implementing policy was to be the prerogative. These letters patent were to confer on the governor 'all the powers which can be conferred upon him by the Constitutional Act'. The main powers identified were twofold, each of which touched on native title. First, the governor would have the 'power of declaring districts within which (as between natives) native law shall prevail:—the power, within the districts, so set apart, if not of declaring and amending that law, yet of procuring and recording such declaration and amendment by the natives, whether respecting the administration of justice, the general occupation of land:—the individualization of titles:—the settlement of disputes or any other matter of a purely native character'.[229] Secondly, the 'power of promulgating rules under which alone such lands shall be allowed to be alienated to Europeans' would be expressly referred to.[230] The letters patent would 'appoint, or authorize the governor to appoint' a native council. The native council would be advisory. Under the letters patent, the native council would be instructed to consider the most effectual mode of encouraging Māori communities 'with a view to their own interests, [and] also in conjunction with the colonial legislature to concert measures for accelerating the alienation of native lands'. The exact mode of achieving this objective was to be left to the native council. Rogers' draft merely mentioned the possibilities of 'direct purchase from the natives (if sanctioned by the Local Legislature)', a 'system of long leases', 'Government purchases of large tracts of land', or any other alternatives suggested by 'local knowledge'.[231] The existing constitutional proprieties observed between the governor and the responsible ministers were to be maintained. That is, the governor 'should communicate his proceedings to [his responsible ministers] and should receive their advice, but should not be bound to follow it'.[232]

In order to maintain sound relations between the native council, on the one hand, and the responsible ministers and colonial legislature, on the other, Rogers' paper recommended that the native minister (being a member of the General Assembly in the colony) should always to be a member of the native council. It was also thought conducive to the 'good management of native districts that on the proclamation of any such district the territory compri[s]ed therein should become subject, in respect of the Europeans resident in it, to general and not provincial legislation'. The motive underlying this recommendation was the view that a 'unity of plans and procedures is all important, and ... the prevalence of purely local feelings and interests is practically dangerous'.[233] As such, the paper recommended colonial legislation to withdraw native districts from the jurisdiction of provincial legislatures. Next, the colony was to be advised to raise the sum voted for native purposes from £13,000 per annum to £25,000 per annum. This sum was to be expended under the supervision of the governor and native council 'through the native department, of whose proceedings the Native Minister will have full cognizance—and over which he will exercise considerable influence, partly (it is hoped) as Member of Council, partly because the native

[228] Ibid, fo.225. [229] Ibid, fos.225a–6. [230] Ibid, fo.226.
[231] Ibid, fos.227–7a. [232] Ibid, fo.225a. [233] Ibid, fos.228a–9.

correspondence will probably pass through his hands, as it is understood to do at present, on its way to the Governor'.[234] In considering who should receive the purchase monies on lands subject to native title, Rogers' memorandum was prepared to leave the detail to the General Assembly—'It will rest with the Assembly to make such provision as may seem fit for enabling the Natives to alienate their lands to individuals or to receive the purchase money in the shape of an annual or other charge on the Land Fund, and generally for all matters involving any lien on the Public Revenue'.[235] On these questions, the imperial government was prepared to 'place itself with little reserve in the hands of the Governor and [Native] Council' and to abandon 'all endeavour to prescribe the principles on which the acquisition of land shall be regulated so long as they are generally conducted in a spirit of fairness and consideration'.[236]

By these means, it was hoped, forbearance and cooperation in dealings between the native council and colonial ministers was enjoined. In return for such forbearance and cooperation, the imperial authorities would agree to bear the costs of imperial troops stationed in New Zealand 'for the ensuing five years', subject to the colony contributing the 'merely nominal amount of £5 a head per annum for every soldier and officer serving in N[ew] Zealand'.[237] The prefatory words were conditional—'If on these [foregoing] points [set out in the preceding paragraphs] the Local Government can promise its cordial co-operation to the proposed Council . . . '. The lessons of living with indeterminacy—the unavoidable fact of often profound disagreement on relative rights and duties, whether of the colony or indigenous populations—animated the tone and spirit of Rogers' memorandum. At the last, it acknowledged that:

> though it may be impossible to come to any arrangement as to abstract rights and duties of Great Britain and New Zealand, yet one thing is certain—that it is on the Colonists and not on the British Nation that the want of a cordial understanding must inflict the most serious and enduring injury, both because the pacification and safe occupation of the country must be arrested during any struggle for power, and because it cannot be expected that Great Britain can continue to contribute towards the defence of the settlers, while these settlers refuse to allow her the powers necessary for the protection of her own interests, and the fulfillment of her now very sacred obligations.[238]

The weathervane that is cabinet suggested that the overall balance struck in consultation with Newcastle be much more agreeable. Indeed, Gladstone's diary entry for 15 May 1861 records: 'Cabinet 4½–7¼: we did a good stroke of business on N.Z.'.[239] But what balance exactly? Cabinet discussions did not yield a result aligned with Rogers' draft despatch, initially addressed to Browne. The despatch itself was cancelled, having performed its vital role as a prompt for discussion amongst senior members of Palmerston's ministry rather than pre-determining any particular outcomes. It appears reasonable to suppose that Newcastle raised the question of Grey's appointment at the cabinet discussion and Newcastle's cabinet colleagues supported the Secretary of State's recommendation.[240] Twelve days later, Newcastle issued a private note to the governor, Browne, signalling the desirability of appointing another governor: 'With these views I naturally turn to Sir George Grey, and I propose to write to him by the next Cape mail

[234] Ibid, fos.229a–30. [235] Ibid, fos.230–30a. [236] Ibid, fo.231.
[237] Ibid, fo.231a. [238] Ibid, fos.233a–4a.
[239] Matthew (ed), *The Gladstone Diaries, Volume VI—1861–1868*, 32.
[240] For context, see Newcastle to Grey, 5 June 1861, NeC10885, Nottingham University.

(the 5th of June) sending him instructions to proceed to New Zealand as soon as he can make his arrangements'.[241] Thus, what ignited with Fortescue's note of 4 May 1861 attained fruition. Although it was not yet fully appreciated, the appointment of Grey sounded the death knell of the imperially driven native council option and a shift in favour of pursuing localized, New Zealand-driven options.

Ultimately, the sentiments expressed in Rogers' draft paper discussed at cabinet were revisited and recast in the wake of the cabinet meeting. Rogers and Fortescue hurriedly prepared a paper for despatch in mail bound for the Cape colony. Fortescue's diary entry for 5 June 1861 recorded: 'Hard at work finishing a dispatch to Sir George Grey, containing general instructions as to his New Zealand mission, which I had put off to the last, just in time for mail'. In his view, the 'Duke liked it very much'.[242] At this point in time, pending receipt of the law officers' opinion, a less-prescriptive tone was taken to the question of a native council: 'It will be for you & your Ministers', the despatch said, 'aided probably by the proposed Council, to consider whether a Colonial law might not with advantage be passed withdrawing such districts, for all purposes, from the provinces within which they are nominally included,—and whether a distinct legislation & administration, in wh[ich] the natives themselves should take part, w[oul]d not better promote the present harmony & future union of the two races, than the fictitious uniformity of law wh[ich] now prevails, or than any attempt to introduce the natives in their present condition, into the electoral body of the colony, either provincial or general.'[243] The paper directed Grey to review the governor-centric approach to the politics of negotiability relative to the purchase of territories subject to native title—what the Colonial Office referred to as the 'system of negociation [*sic*]'. While perceived to be consonant with the Treaty of Waitangi, the despatch perceived the system as requiring an early review in order to ascertain whether some tribunal might be warranted which could intervene peaceably with adjudicative power in disputed claims to land amongst or within indigenous communities.[244] For the Colonial Office, it was an open question whether such a tribunal would completely supersede the existing system of governor-centric negotiation or would play a complementary and modifying role. The central query for Grey to explore and to answer, as expeditiously as possible, was 'whether, if it [the system of negotiation] should in whole or in part be maintained, some tribunal cannot be established, entitled to the confidence of both parties, for the purpose of adjudicating upon disputed claims, when argued in a legal & peaceable manner'.[245] The imperial authorities proposed a bargain predicated on certain concessions as an inducement to the colonial politicians to settle, on the condition that Grey could report that he and the 'representatives of the colonists' had reached a 'satisfactory arrangement of native administration'.[246]

[241] Newcastle to Browne, private, 27 May 1861, NeC10885, Nottingham University.

[242] Fortescue, diary, 5 June 1861, '... *And Mr Fortescue*', 181.

[243] Newcastle to Sir George Grey, 5 June 1861, CO209/156, fos.248–8a, TNA.

[244] Ibid, fo.249: Grey was directed to examine 'whether the system of negociation [*sic*] between the agents of the Gov[erno]r, and the native owners, though in conformity with the Treaty of Waitangi & for many years successfully, may not, in the present condition of the natives & settlers, require to be modified or superseded'.

[245] Ibid. [246] Ibid, fo.249a.

Three possible and vital concessions on the part of imperial policy-formulators were enumerated. First, the imperial administration would be 'prepared to the extent wh[ich] you may think wise to waive the serious objections to such changes as those proposed by the "Native Territorial Rights Act" of 1858, which led to the non-confirmation of that measure, & were pointed out in the desp[atch] of my predecessor (signed by Lord Carnarvon) of the 18th May 1859'. The effect of such a concession amounted to the Colonial Office being 'willing to assent to any prudent plan for the individualization of native title, and for direct purchase, under proper safeguards, of native lands by individual settlers, wh[ich] the New Zealand Parl[ia]m[en]t may wish to adopt'.[247] Secondly, it would be prepared to accede to 'any ministerial arrangements for the conduct of native affairs, which may appear safe to yourself & be acceptable to the colonists'. Thirdly, on the question of military expenditures, the imperial authorities were minded to 'treat the colony with as much indulgence as their duty will permit on the subject of charges of military protection, and the number of troops to be maintained in New Zealand'.[248]

Newcastle himself penned a private communiqué to Grey confirming his appointment as governor and setting out the expectations of the Secretary of State for Colonies. It is in this private missive that we find intimations of the orientation of the imperial cabinet on the question of a native council. Newcastle had forwarded 'all the dispatches and papers connected with New Zealand affairs . . . to you to the Cape in order that you may take up the thread of events from the time you left the Colony until now and read them on your voyage'.[249] The Secretary of State provided his assessment of the Waitara purchase 'as an event of history and a state of circumstances has arisen which will require a treatment having only an indirect reference to this original cause of—or as I believe—pretext for the war'. Consistently with previously expressed sentiments in favour of a transitional state of affairs whereby territories subject to native title and 'native laws, customs, or usages' would be maintained temporarily, the ultimate objective was to incorporate Māori territories within the colonial polity. As for the future, then, Newcastle explained how 'knowledge and experience both of the natives and the settlers will be required to place the future management of "native affairs" upon such a footing as may prevent the recurrence of these unhappy disputes about land, and lead to the incorporation of the two races in one body politic, even though a more distinct separation by way of "districts" may possibly be for a time the most practical mode of obtaining this ultimate result'. With this in mind, Grey's attention 'will naturally be directed to the "Native Council" Bill which, you will find in the Blue Book and which I informed Colonel Browne by the last mail would be dealt with in a despatch addressed to you—that d[e]spatch goes to you by the present mail'.[250] Discretion as to the applicability of a native council option was to be placed into Grey's hands. Hence Newcastle advised, 'I have purposely left you the utmost latitude of action and trusted to your discretion and the view you may take upon arriving in the Colony of the state of affairs as then existing, what course you may take in reference to a measure which is fraught with such important consequences'. Newcastle, with the matter having been aired at

[247] Ibid, fos.249a–50. [248] Ibid, fo.250.

[249] Newcastle to Grey, 5 June 1861, private, NeC10885, Nottingham University.

[250] Ibid (here referring to Newcastle to Sir George Grey, 5 June 1861, CO209/156, fos.243–52, TNA).

cabinet, was able to say that the 'view of the Queen's Government is that upon the whole it would be best to adopt that measure [the Native Council Bill of the colonial legislature] or some one similar, and if Colonel Gore Browne had remained the Queen's assent would probably have been given'. Yet, Newcastle was prepared to concede to Grey a discretion on the point of whether or not to proceed with the statutory proposal. '[B]y leaving it to your discretion', Newcastle noted, 'enables you to make any bargain with your Parliament you may think desirable—by which I mean, enables you to ask as a condition a vote of money for native purposes of sufficient amount and to be provided for a certain number of years—so as to facilitate the introduction of your Kaffrarian policy into the colony as soon as the rebellion is at an end.'[251] Grey arrived in Auckland on 26 September 1861 and assumed the colonial government on 3 October 1861.[252] Nevertheless, he would have been mindful that Newcastle's private correspondence was not without warning. Indeed, Newcastle pressed upon him the:

> importance of winning over to your support and confidence the New Zealand politicians. I do not expect you to be pleased to find the system of responsible government in full work—I know your habits of mind and views of government of a colony are not strictly attuned to these ultra popular institutions,—but for good or evil they exist, and I cannot agree with Lord Grey that it would be desirable, even if it were possible, to change these.[253]

An imperial native council option confounded—the second cut

The letters patent strategy was, however, foiled. Advice from the law officers of the Crown in the United Kingdom frustrated the Colonial Office's aspirations for the letters patent. Imperial legislation could not be avoided insofar as there was a risk of the Office's proposals for a native council and the treatment of 'native law' on native title trenching upon the requirements of the New Zealand Constitution Act. As seen, on 7 May 1860, in the absence of an imperial statute entitling the appointment of a nominated native council but with a live Native Council Bill passed by the colonial legislature still in existence, a formal opinion was sought from the law officers of the Crown.[254]

The law officers noted: 'it was desirable to ascertain whether it would be competent for Her Majesty and consistent with the spirit of the constitutional act' to act in relation to seven related matters. These legal issues included, first, the power 'to appoint a council by Letters Patent or other sufficient instrument for the purpose of advising the Governor in the conduct of native affairs'; secondly, empowering:

> the Governor with or without the advice of that Council Ist to set apart districts within which Native law and usage should prevail as between natives (ss 71, 79).
>
> IInd to declare and amend the native law in those districts or at any rate to procure that declaration or amendment by the natives themselves and to prescribe the mode in which that declaration or amendment should be made and recorded.[255]

[251] Ibid.

[252] Grey to Newcastle, 4 October 1861, *GBPP1862* [3049], 1.

[253] Newcastle to Grey, 5 June 1861, private, Ne C10885, Nottingham University.

[254] Fortescue to Attorney-General and Solicitor-General, 7 May 1861, CO209/156, fos.235–42, TNA.

[255] Law Officers to Newcastle, 25 June 1861, CO209/166, fos.199a–200, TNA.

A permanent council advising the governor was not, the law officers claimed, envisaged by the Constitution Act. Statutory innovation at the imperial level could not be avoided. They concluded, 'It would not in our opinion be consistent with the spirit of the constitutional act 15th and 16th Victoria c 72, to appoint a Council for the purpose of advising the Governor of New Zealand, in the conduct of native affairs'. Furthermore, 'No mention is made of a Council of advice, or assistance, to the Governor: and we think that no such Council was in contemplation'.[256] On the question of amending indigenous law, Bethell and William Atherton opined that '[w]e are of opinion that the Governor may be empowered to declare, but cannot be empowered to amend, the native law, in the districts set apart'. On their reading of the Constitution Act 1852, in a manner comporable to the advice Thomas Gore Browne tendered Labouchere in May 1857, the 'authority conferred by the statute (s 71) is for "mainaining" the native law for the present, subject to certain restrictions; and *not for its amendment*'.[257] On reviewing this legal advice, Rogers evinced displeasure. 'This opinion', he observed, 'is directly contradictory to opinions wh[ich] I had understood to have been expressed by Sir R. Bethell when the subject was under consideration of the Cabinet last autumn.'[258] In composing these words, Rogers was expressly reflecting on the sense he had obtained of discussions between senior ministers, including Palmerston, on the tactical course to adopt towards the Native Council Bill in the House of Commons in August 1860. In essence, the Bill was presented as having been deferred partly on account of the powers outlined in section 71 of the Constitution Act being sufficient to permit extant 'native law' to persist but also to be modified. Recent cabinet conversations in January 1861 may also have contributed to this impression. He concluded pragmatically that 'The result is however that there is nothing to be done but to invest Sir G Grey with the general powers wh[ich] H[er] M[ajesty] is authorized to delegate in the same terms wh[ich] were used to confer those powers upon him when he was last Gov[erno]r wh[ich] is done, I believe, in the draft commission now in circulation'.[259] The Constitution Act, however, had reduced the flexibility available to him in that any governor would need to draw on the resources of the colonial legislature in order to secure innovation beyond the remit of his existing powers.

The legal scaffolding of the New Zealand Constitution Act, as interpreted within the imperial government by its law officers, conditioned a sense of what was politically possible. Here, then, we see facets of political and legal constitutionalism intertwined. Political constitutionalism was a mansion with many rooms, housing, allowing, and contemplating disagreement, political competition between individuals and clusters of individuals, and rich vocabularies of, for example, political economy and philosophic history and legalistic idioms—congeries of ideas both inhabited and deployed in diverse situations and issues where people disagreed not only about what was to be

[256] Ibid, fos.202a–3.

[257] Ibid, fos.203–3a (emphasis added). For Browne's advice, see the discussion in Chapter Five (pages 275–6 *et seq.*) and Browne to Labouchere, 9 May 1857, CO209/141, fos. 510–510. Browne characterized the predicament posed by the distribution of authority between central and provincial governments, as well as indigenous polities, as one occurring completely *within* the aspirational jurisdiction of the colonial polity: 'the management of what must be called an *imperium in imperio*' (ibid, fo.508a).

[258] Rogers to Fortescue, 10 July 1861, CO209/166, fo.204a, TNA.

[259] Ibid, fos.204a–5.

done but also about how to do it and why. To speak of political constitutionalism as the primary animating element in the real life of constitutionalism is not to marginalize or preclude the salience or importance of legal norms and ways of speaking. To put it another way, as Graham Gee has done (modifying JAG Griffith's aphorism), in such constitutional settings, '*whilst everything that happens is constitutional, not just anything can happen*'.[260] Significantly, reduced confidence as to whether legal interpretations of section 71 of the Constitution Act permitted non-statutory amendments or modifications of indigenous law or customs, tended to encourage institutional and process-oriented solutions that could be presented as not materially amending those underlying laws or customs but as merely recognizing and accommodating them while facilitating the transformation of native title into Crown-derived titles. Newcastle, Fortescue, and Rogers failed to persuade key political actors that a native council concept required legal casing in the form of an imperial statute—they failed to persuade others that New Zealand was a fitting place for such an intervention and the commitment of legislative resource required. In this sense, their ministerial colleagues would prove more successful in respect of India with the Indian Councils Act of 1861.

CONCLUSIONS—A STUDY IN FAILURE

How the concept of a native council proposal fared as an imperial option from 1860 until 1861 revealed a neglected but significant moment in experimenting with legal form and design, including statutory design. In purporting to establish a legally permissive structure, allowing a native council to operate, the purpose of the option was to devise the machinery for setting out and prizing open windows of communicability between native title areas—sites where 'native laws, customs, or usages' prevailed—and English law. As an experiment, it did not foresee abrupt change or prescribe details. It anticipated transitional staging posts—places where native title was to be transformed, case by case, into Crown land. Presented by its proponents as responding to exceptional albeit transitional circumstances, therefore, it also spoke to questions of how to shift or adjust constitutional assumptions about settlement colonies with responsible government (self-administration), if only for a time. In this sense, the experimental proposal brings into focus the nuances of imperial and colonial authority—the point that the politics of negotiability within a pre-eminently political constitution, albeit one suffused with legal constraints and legalistic ways of seeing and speaking, did not offer simple choices between incorporating putative subjects of the Crown or treating them separately.

Paul McHugh has noted the whiggish teleological propensity in parts of the New Zealand and broader imperial legal historiography to assume the inexorable drift to representative institutions and responsible government in an anglophone settlement colony such as New Zealand, marginalizing the powers of the governor.[261] Legal scho-

[260] Gee, 'The Political Constitutionalism of J.A.G. Griffith', 42 (emphasis in original). The aphorism of Griffith was '[e]verything that happens in constitutional [and] if nothing happened that would be constitutional also': see Griffith, 'The Political Constitution', 19.

[261] McHugh, 'The Historiography of New Zealand's Constitutional History', in Joseph (ed), *Essays on the Constitution*, 344–67.

lars like Philip Joseph have seen the narrative of a flow towards independent constitutional development as irrepressible and irresistible.[262] It was a tale familiar to Thomas Erskine May, who commented in 1863: 'To conclude this rapid summary of colonial liberties,—it must be added that the colonies have further enjoyed municipal institutions, a free press, and religious freedom and equality'. He said further: 'No liberty or franchise prized by Englishment at home, has been withheld from their fellow countrymen in distant lands'.[263] In 1860 Adderley, ever watchful and attentive, and others, were alive to its underlying fragility as a teleological narrative, regarding with the utmost jealousy and contempt any move seen to be inconsistent with its narrative arc. Indeed, New Zealand's example of native title and Crown–Māori relations as a problem for a liberal representative constitution was richer and much more nuanced than this narrative implied. As has been seen, Fortescue for one assumed the propriety of a 'double government'-based approach, whereby a permanent council of nominated members would stand alongside and distinct from the responsible ministry. John Stuart Mill also acknowledged the virtues of double government in specific circumstances. This question of design remains an issue with constitutional resonances to this day. Hanna Wilberg has recently suggested that this narrative ought not to have occurred in the absence of particular provision for Māori polities in colonial government: 'At the very least, transfer of power to a settler government should have been made formally subject to the Crown's Treaty obligations, and should have included some mechanism for ensuring that this limit was observed'.[264] 'Much preferable', she has written, 'would have been transfer a government representing both peoples, with provision of mechanisms for equitable resolution of differences between them.'[265]

Many institutional and conceptual subtleties were at play in 1859 and 1860. And these subtleties demonstrated the problems of grappling with the dynamics of 'occasional association' as seen from London, responding to proposals for a statutorily embedded native council emanating from a governor and a coterie of his advisors. What sort of institutional choices ought to be made and how and by what means might they be delivered? With whom would its architects have to negotiate? Seen in this way, then, the problem posed by the metaphor 'occasional association' and its implications for the political significance of native title was more complicated than the usual way of portraying the choices of empire as falling along a spectrum of incorporation and differentiation, as important as those analytical and policy themes might be.[266] The native council option presented a whiggish aspect or frame, at least insofar as its intel-

[262] Joseph, 'Introduction', in Joseph (ed), *Essays on the Constitution*, 25: 'Like Dr Oliver, I subscribe to the inevitability of a colonial society's evolution towards separate existence and nationhood, as a "Darwinian end-point of constitutional development", [in contradistinction to Paul McHugh's characterization of Parliament as a Hobbesian 'Leviathan' and constitutional rule of law being 'Darwinian end-point[s]' in a whiggish historical narrative] although the path need not be as regular, harmonious, and uneventful as Canada's or New Zealand's'.

[263] May, *The Constitutional History of England since the Accession of George the Third 1760–1860*, II, 577.

[264] See the discussion generally in Wilberg, 'Judicial Remedies for the Original Breach?', 714–15.

[265] Ibid, 715.

[266] For example, Cooper, *Colonialism in Question*, 154: 'Where to find a balance between the poles of incorporation (the empire's claims that its subjects belonged within the empire) and differentiation (the empire's claims that different subjects should be governed differently) was a matter of dispute and shifting strategies. Balances were continually upset by the actions of people in the colonies'.

lectual underpinnings were concerned, in that it proposed to embed an institution of nominated members, if only temporarily, thought to be appropriate to the peculiar historical circumstances of indigenous communities in New Zealand and to the problems of colonial settlement. The Cape colony and British southern Asia were treated as appropriate comparators for statutory intervention if not precise precedents. For Fortescue, precedents were servants, not masters, able to be adapted and re-engineered or rejected. Sceptics and outright opponents begged to differ, portraying the native council option as a constitutional innovation strictly inapplicable to colonies identified for predominantly British settlement where the principle of self-administration ought to prevail.

Secondly, as demonstrated, in the mooting of the option in Westminster we see the entwining of political agendas, colonial and imperial, together with their entanglements in the internecine play of British domestic politics. This intermingling of political strands at Westminster included the politics of islands and provinces drawn from across the seas, as well as the contentions of Whigs, non-interventionist liberals, and Tories. Thirdly, the two distinct life cycles of the imperial native council option in 1860 and 1861 showed a Colonial Office adapting its strategy. The need for statutorily enacted innovation to the constitutional regime in New Zealand, the Colonial Office, and its politicians were exposed to politically risky scrutiny and critique at the hands of the erstwhile colleagues of the Office's principal Secretary of State as much as Tory opinion. It proved politically risky in that Fortescue and Rogers could not be assured of getting the native council as a legislative option through the imperial legislature. In broad terms, the failure of this approach prompted a resort to royal instructions under the prerogative and letters patent in order to secure a native council, only to see this avenue closed by an opinion of the law officers of the Crown—the legal outline of the New Zealand colonial constitution—in the form of the New Zealand Constitution Act, which was sufficiently clear to constrain the aspirations of the Colonial Office. For the native council experiment to proceed, as conceived by the Colonial Office, imperial legislation would be required with all of the risks of political delay, assault, and invective such a course of action ordinarily brought to bear.

7

'Tribunals Independent of a Prince', 1859–1862—Exploring the Dynamics and Consequences of 'Occasional Association', Part II

'WHATEVER MAY BE THE TRUE THEORY OF NATIVE TENURE'—OF NATIVE TITLE, *MANA*, AND SEIGNORIAL RIGHTS

Waitara proved to be a twitch upon the threads of an intrusive and innovative colonial system. It pulled arguments on native title together in a veritable explosion of debates regarding the legitimacy of the colonial government's putative purchase of the Waitara (Pekapeka) block in Taranaki. It is well appreciated that conceptions of property rights to territorial space cannot necessarily be divorced from claims to govern the use of the space by others and to which uses that space may be allocated. This very question emerged dramatically in New Zealand with Waitara presenting as the crucible of war. The intense, ranging disputes concerning the colonial government's attempted purchase of 600 acres abutting the Waitara River in the Taranaki in 1859–1860, which led to a lengthy civil war amongst *hapū* of Te Ātiawa (Ngātiawa) and warring with colonial forces from March 1860, only serves to emphasize this point. That putative purchase was predicated on the consent of Te Teira in circumstances where Te Teira asserted the entitlement to sell the block in question but where Wīremu Kīngi Te Rangitāke (Kīngi or 'William King') was subsequently interpreted as claiming an ability to preclude such assent to sell on the basis of overarching political authority.[1] The seeming indeterminacy of this issue would vex influential observers within both colonial New Zealand and in the distant United Kingdom. Soon after it occurred, the Waitara transaction was raised as an epitome of injustice—an imprimatur it has not shaken with the passing of the years.

This section will examine the Waitara transaction together with the anglophone debates ranging around it. As this chapter will also explore, these disputes further demonstrated the place of native title in a political constitution and the politics of negotiability, encouraging participants in the anglophone debates around Waitara—imperial and colonial—to consider the possibilities of creating specialist tribunals through statute, not as associated with the whims of the prince (the governor and his officials). It will demonstrate how purchase transactions—those crystallized artefacts of the politics of negotiability around native title—generated fraught and profound ruminations on

[1] For extensive accounts of the Waitara transaction, see Sinclair, *The Origins of the Maori Wars*, 136–80.

the *loci* of political and legal power within indigenous communities, and the nature of despotism and liberty applicable to such communities and to colonial polity. This was a legacy of the challenges for developing techniques of negotiating with claimants to native title in the 1840s and 1850s—a problem of entangled complexities. But it was also the stuff of conservatism and innovation amongst various Māori of political influence, as certain figures, such as Wīremu Kīngi Te Rangitāke in Taranaki, Paora Tuhaere of Ngāti Whātua, and Wīremu Tāmihana Tarapīpipi Waharoa in Waikato developed strategies to enhance and adapt chiefly centres of authority and to manage the political risks of change introduced by the presence of increasingly larger numbers of settlers.

NEGOTIATIONS FOR THE ACQUISITION OF THE PEKAPEKA BLOCK IN WAITARA, 1859 AND 1860

In surveying the Waitara transaction, we are left with vignettes to piece together. Many of these pieces have been pawed over in historical works addressing the beginnings of prolonged periods of war in colonial New Zealand. The transaction formed part of a lengthy trail of tales about the occupation of territory for settlement in Taranaki. Resolving questions of territorial space in favour of settlement would not only ease the expansion of urban and agricultural settlement, but also afford opportunities for commercial entrepreneurship in the competition for people and funds. Richmond's brother, JC Richmond, spoke excitedly of the possibilities of allowing the mining of iron sands on the Taranaki coast: 'If the Iron Sand Co. should ever float.... and in the event of Gov[ernmen]t's relations with W. Kingi and other foreign powers allowing of the extension of the place it would well repay the corporation of N[ew] P[lymouth] to buy the Kawau pa & occupy the two acres of sand between it, the sea & the Huatoki and to raise a fresh lot of questions'.[2] Browne's minute of September 1859 to McLean stated: 'If Parris is satisfied that Teira and the others who offer to sell have an indisputable title to the land, an advance should be made to them in part payment'.[3] An instalment of £100 was not paid into the hands of Te Teira and others associated with him until 29 November 1859, with Parris reporting that he had advised Kīngi of his intention to purchase the land on 25 November.[4] The deed of purchase was signed on 24 February 1860 by twenty signatories of Te Ātiawa. The block of land was sold for £600.[5] Hinting at the complicated ways in which the conduct of Te Teira might intersect with the internal complexities of Te Ātiawa politics, the district commissioner advised McLean in early December 1859 that 'Teira stops in town [New Plymouth] since he received the instalment, considering it not safe to stop at Waitara'.[6]

[2] JC Richmond to CW Richmond, 22 December 1859, in Scholefield (ed), *The Richmond-Atkinson Papers*, I, 505.

[3] Browne to McLean, [undated], Ms-Papers-0032-0015, McLean papers, ATL. Browne to Richmond, 19 July 1861, in Scholefield (ed), *The Richmond-Atkinson Papers*, I, 716, supplies a context for this minute as follows: 'Mr Parris' reply, (printed) dated September 21 and addressed to you was referred to me and I find a minute, written upon it in my own hand writing, as follows, dated Septem[be]r 27. The word "satisfied" being underlined'.

[4] Parris to Chief Land Purchase Commissioner, 4 December 1859, CO209/153, fo.473, TNA.

[5] Waitara land purchase in English and Māori, *AJHR* 1860, E-2a.

[6] Parris, New Plymouth, to Chief Land Purchase Commissioner, 4 December 1859, CO209/153, fo.473, TNA.

On the day the instalment was paid over to Te Teira, Kīngi rode into New Plymouth with a party of 'about thirty'. At his meeting with Parris, 'W[illiam] King [allegedly] avowed his determination to oppose the sale, without advancing any reason for so doing, upon which I put a series of questions to him, which I called upon the Rev[erend] Mr Whiteley to witness'.[7] When specifically asked whether the 'land' in question 'belong[ed]' to Te 'Teira and party', Kīngi was reported to have said, 'Yes; the land is theirs but I will not let them sell it'.[8] Following up this answer with a question, Parris sought a rationale for such an assertion on the part of Kīngi: 'Why will you oppose their selling what is their own?' The answer of Kīngi was presented as a signal of what would happen, as well as a statement of power and authority: 'Because I do not wish that the land should be disturbed, and though they have floated it, I will not let it go to sea'. Prodded further by Parris to explain 'the justice or correctness of your opposition', Kīngi responded simply: 'It is enough, Parris, their bellies are full with the sight of the money you have promised them, but don't give it to them. If you do, I won't let you have the land, but will take it and cultivate it myself'.

The warnings of Kīngi were presented clearly enough. But to some English ears this oratory was not readily assimilable to the expected language of one who claimed an extant proprietary interest in the land at Waitara itself. At the very least, his recorded words were ambiguous, allowing his statements to be construed as the admonitory statements of one who claimed overriding political pre-eminence in the area. Fortescue, at the Colonial Office, eager for contestable advice on the entire Waitara affair, had asked the Auckland settler, Grahame, to express his views candidly in August 1860 when Grahame was in London. 'Mr Fortecue said', Grahame reported to the colonial Native Secretary, McLean, 'that there appeared to be some doubts as to whether the Governor was quite right about Kingi having no claim to T[e]ira's land—and enquired if Kingi might not have some claim as chief of the tribe.'[9] Grahame replied simply that this 'had not been established'. Fortescue then reportedly 'seemed to think that there must have been a good deal of pressure brought to bear upon the Governor by the Taranaki people in urging on this collision'.[10] Subsequent investigations suggested that Te Teira was merely a member of one *hapū* with an interest in the Waitara block. Mapping of the Pekapeka block south of the Waitara River revealed a bewildering complex of Māori interests showing nearly 200 proprietors—visually reminiscent of a medieval commons suffused with irregularly cut strips of cultivated interest.[11] Only about one-tenth of the block was shown as being in the name of Te Teira and the other vendors. Octavius Hadfield, an early critic of the policies of Governor Browne regarding Waitara, stated as early as 29 May 1860: 'It is true Mr Parris, the district commissioner says, that in answer to his question—"Does the land belong to Teira and his party?" [h]e replied—"Yes; the land is theirs but I will not let them sell it"'.[12] Yet, Hadfield continued, 'I am credibly informed that the chief did not intend to convey the meaning here attributed to him; that what he said was, that Teira and his party were part owners of the land, but

7 Ibid. 8 Ibid.

9 Grahame to Fortescue, 23 August 1860, Ms-Papers-0032-0298, fo.6, McLean papers, ATL.

10 Ibid.

11 Enclosed with Grey to Newcastle, 6 December 1861, CO209/165, TNA: 'Map sent by Featherston to Grey. Drawn by two Maoris, one with survey experience and approved by Te Patukakariki, 29 August 1861'.

12 Hadfield, *One of England's Little Wars*, 13.

that did not justify them in selling the whole'.[13] Hadfield noted that he could 'easily conceive how such a mistake would arise, as it is quite in accordance with the idiom of the *Maori* language to begin an objection by "Yes", *i.e.* you are right to a certain extent, but, &c'.[14]

As an authority, Kīngi proved irritated at having to account for his motivations and reasons—it was enough for him to have spoken. In the absence of long conversations and meetings, a single encounter such as this highlighted the sense of the incongruity between Parris' habit towards investigation and inquiry for reasons, and the tendency of Kīngi to consider his effortless statements of authority sufficient. This impression of difference in approach was appreciated on the part of Rēnata Tama-ki-Hikurangi Kawepō of Ngāti Kahungunu months later when his correspondence with the superintendent of Hawke's Bay, Thomas Fitzgerald, was printed in Wellingon in 1861. Kawepō chastised Fitzgerald for saying that Te Teira was a chief entitled to sell Waitara 'because his genealogy was published last winter'. Kawepō replied: 'Sir, what about his [Te Teira's] genealogy? This is the second proof that he has given you (against himself) . . . . W[īremu] King[i] would never give his genealogy because it is known throughout this island; it is not recounted'. He added that to recite one's genealogy 'is a thing for the common man to do, who never was heard of before, or for an obscure thief'.[15] The words of Kawepō resonated with the point that senior chieftains did not need to recite their genealogies or to recount lists of causes underlying their ties or claims to territory—such factors were known. Parris' repeated prodding was pressing Kīngi to utter that which he had no need to utter and to objectify relations to landscape through the tropes of indigenous law, custom, and usage.

This issue remained an ongoing dispute. In August 1860, the governor, Browne, in recounting debates in the House of Representatives in New Zealand, signalled his disagreement with the assumptions of those who insisted that the obscure words and silences of Kīngi were simply those of a chief of *mana*—he was not required to demonstrate the force of his claims with reasons: 'Rights were insisted on for W. King which he has not himself urged: his own declaration that the vendors were the proprietors of the land they sold was, in spite of the known habits of the natives, ignored on a plea that he was too great a chief to say that the land was his'.[16] Variations on these views travelled to the House of Commons, with Robert Lowe, a member of Palmerston's government, viewing the conduct of Kīngi in the following terms: 'The chief did not give any reasons, did not appeal to any court, or tribunal, or authority. He merely put forward his own will and determination. He spoke like a Sovereign to a Sovereign, an equal to an equal. He is a subject of Her Majesty, but be spoke to Her Majesty's representative in a tone of absolute and unmitigated defiance'.[17] In a speech to the House of Commons on 19 April 1861, Fortescue reported how 'The conviction of the Governor was that Wir[e]mu Kingi rested his opposition to the sale of this land on entirely a different footing, setting up, in fact, his own authority as a native potentate in opposition to that

[13] Ibid, 13–14. [14] Ibid, 14.

[15] Renata Tamakihikurangi, *Ko Te Korero me te Pukapuka a Renata Tamakihikurangi, no te Pa Whakairo; ki a te Kai-whakahaere tikanga o nga Pakeha ki Ahuriri—Renata's speech and letter to the Superintendent of Hawke's Bay on the Taranaki War Question*, 21.

[16] Browne to Newcastle, 29 August 1860, CO209/155, fo.172, TNA.

[17] Lowe, *HPD*, 3rd series, 12 April 1861, vol 162, col 533.

of the Sovereign'.[18] Even if doubts could be raised about entitlements to act—whether relating to an interest in the land at Waitara as a user and occupier or as a recognizable political authority—there is a sense in seeing Kīngi as a long-standing chieftain grappling with new worlds that required him to supply a rationale for his claims. In focusing on custom as an autonomous discipline, it is increasingly detached from the interpersonal relations *inter se* and their ties to the landscape: custom becomes a construct to be studied distinctly. That is, as has been observed in relation to English common law and its treatments of 'custom', the concept of 'custom' became further disembodied from the rich empiricities of local practices and ways of life in certain areas.[19] Custom and 'rights' were constructed as distinct subjects with diverse interpreters emerging within indigenous communities, and strangers such as officials and squatters also bringing to bear new circumstances often requiring, in their turn, novel interpretations.

The people of Kīngi obstructed surveyors sent to Waitara. Troops were then essayed to protect the surveying parties and, on 17 March 1860, British regulars attacked the fortifications of Te Kohia *pā*. The myriad complexities and circuitries of Te Ātiawa *hapū* politics ensnared the new pākehā of the coastal settlements. In so doing, the very instabilities wrought by that ensnaring exacerbated intra-*hapū* disputes regarding, amongst other things, how to manage the presence of increasing numbers of strangers. It should be borne in mind that for the settlers in the coastal settlement enclave skirting the Taranaki coast, these were times of often intense anxiety—a palpable demonstration of the vulnerability of British settlement rather than its supposed strengths. In the midst of warring in the Taranaki, New Plymouth's precariousness was keenly felt. By December 1860, the native minister's brother, James Richmond, reported it to be 'crammed full, as the country is quite unsafe except in fortified buildings and the rent of every hut inside the lines is high'.[20]

As Ward and Ballara have suggested, in focusing on the political status of Wīremu Kīngi Te Rangitāke to deflect and overturn Te Teira's preference to transfer the Waitara block, a number of these reports may have contested ghostly shades rather than tangible evidence relevant to the concrete circumstances of Waitara, where Kīngi Te Rangitāke was considered to have had an interest through familial relations in the land itself. Indeed, contrary evidence, exhibited by cultivated sites attributable to his *hapū*, existed to suggest that Kīngi had such an interest or could legitimately claim such interests.[21] Ballara argues that Te Teira was merely one claimant with an interest in the Waitara block amongst the members of four *hapū*.[22] Accordingly, in Ballara's view, 'Wī Kīngi could legitimately refuse his consent to the sale [at Waitara], not because he was "the paramount chief of Te Āti Awa", but because he was one of the owners'.[23] Moreover, Ballara notes the error in arguing that Kīngi was the senior chief of Te Ātiawa. Quite simply, she says, there was no such position. To use the title of 'senior' or 'paramount chief' is merely to persist in a romantic designation with no anthropological basis except in limited cases, such as with Pōtatau Te Wherowhero, Mananui Tūkino Te Heuheu, Te Kani-ā-Takirau of Ūawa (Tolaga Bay) on the eastern coast of the North

[18] Fortescue, 19 April 1861, ibid, col 828.
[19] For a similar approach, see Dorsett, 'Thinking Jurisdictionally', ch 7.
[20] J Richmond to Taylor, 9 December 1860, in Scholefield (ed), *The Richmond-Atkinson Papers*, I, 666.
[21] Ward, *A Show of Justice*, 115–16.
[22] Ballara, *Iwi*, 263. [23] Ibid.

Island. According to Ballara, the only areas where Kīngi could forbid sales were those areas in which his own *hapū* had an interest 'through ancestors who had first cleared or occupied them'.[24] In practice, this was just the sort of situation for which McLean and others had adapted broad, inclusive negotiations for sale and purchase transactions seeking to multiply and diversify the range of voices requiring a share of compensation—an aggregative approach.

The view that Kīngi had any interest in the land within Waitara, proprietary or otherwise, was challenged. In a letter in Māori of 24 April 1860 to the governor, four Te Ātiawa chiefs, including Mahau Turakino, disputed the claims of Kīngi to any ownership in Waitara.[25] In essence, the contested evidence within Te Ātiawa pointed to inter-*hapū* and intra-*hapū* disagreements within the Ātiawa descent-group as a whole. Kīngi had long-standing political opponents, including Ihaia Te Kirikumara, a chief of the Otaraua *hapū* of Te Ātiawa, as well as a native assessor.[26] It was Ihaia Te Kirikumara who had initially offered to sell Waitara to the colonial government in 1844, but the opposition of Kīngi proved vital then in dissuading the government from proceeding. Ihaia Te Kirikumara would support the actions of Te Teira to sell and assisted the British regulars once war began in March 1860.[27] The colonial negotiators—Parris, the district commissioner at New Plymouth, and McLean, the Native Secretary behind the scenes—and the authority behind them in the person of the governor, allowed themselves to be lured into ongoing civil strife and dissension amongst *hapū* of Te Ātiawa. In seeking out the strangers—the colonial administration and its settlers—leaders such as Mahau Turakino and Te Teira sought to supply additional recognition to their pre-eminence in decision-making and to boost access to political and economic resources obtainable through relationships with embryonic pākehā enclaves.

WARRING MEMORANDA—SETTING THE SCENE

Waitara became a weeping sore. Other than civil war amongst Te Ātiawa *hapū*, warring with British regulars from March 1860, and warring with Māori forces allied to the Crown, the disputed Waitara purchase gave rise to 'wordy warfare' as Carleton observed—a profusion of pamphlets musing on the meanings of native title. As such, indigenous property rights continued to be contested in non-curial sites.[28] The early 1860s witnessed intensifying disputes regarding native title and the mustering of otherwise dormant intellectual assumptions about the nature and content of 'territorial rights of the natives'. Martin's published contributions alone amounted to London- and Auckland-based printings of *The Taranaki Question* in 1860 and 1861 intended for circulation

[24] Ibid, 264.

[25] MA 1860/256, ANZ. This letter, with an English translation, was also printed in *The Maori Messenger*, 30 April 1860, 3–4.

[26] See also 'Maori Lands', *Daily Southern Cross*, vol 12, issue 785, 5 January 1855, 2; Dalton, *War and Politics in New Zealand 1855–1870*, 26, 72–3, 74–5.

[27] Oliver, 'Te Kirikumara, Ihaia (?–1873)', in *The Dictionary of New Zealand Biography: Volume One-1769–1869*, 461–2.

[28] For a recent analysis of the pamphleteering campaigns regarding the Waitara incident, see MacDonald, 'The Political Philosophy of Property Rights', ch 6.

amongst members of the imperial Parliament and colonial legislature,[29] together with his subsequent rejoinder printed in London, entitled *Remarks on 'Notes published for the New Zealand Government', January 1861, and of Mr Richmond's Memorandum on the The Taranaki Question, December, 1860.*[30] The publications included the colonial administration's *Notes on Sir William Martin's Pamphlet entitled 'The Taranaki Question'* (1861) and James Busby's riposte to Martin entitled *Remarks upon a Pamphlet entitled 'The Taranaki Question, by Sir William Martin, D.C.L., Late Chief Justice of New Zealand'* (published in Auckland in 1860).[31] We also have Hadfield's criticisms of the Waitara affair beginning in May 1860 and those of William Fox.[32] Other unpublished material also circulated. Still further material remained concealed or in draft, distributed to a few but exerting an influence on key governmental personnel. McLean's undated but contemporaneous comments as Native Secretary on the arguments set out in Martin's *The Taranaki Question* may be counted amongst these less-visible sources.

The debates over Waitara were enough to shatter a number of Browne's previously trusted relationships with Martin, Selwyn, Swainson, and others, and forced him to move much more closely in the direction of his responsible ministers. Martin's initial pamphlet was published in December 1860, some nine months after hostilities began in the Taranaki.[33] Privately, Newcastle disapproved of Martin's pamphlet, although he reserved his greatest displeasure for Selwyn's indiscretions in openly criticizing military action in the Taranaki once battle was joined. Judging the publication '*in the Colony* of such publications as Sir William Martin's pamphlet and others [as] most lamentable', Newcastle confessed that he was at a loss to 'reconcile such acts with a sense of duty and spirit of patriotism'.[34] Later, in expressing pleasure at Grey's arrival in New Zealand as governor, Newcastle noted that he was 'not wholly unprepared for Archdeacon Hadfield's conduct, but the Bishop of New Zealand has surprised me'. In denouncing the behavior of the bishop, Newcastle avowed that he knew him to be 'august and over bearing and assumed to be Wolsey in the little state he has devoted himself to'.[35] Newcastle's criticism of Selwyn's performance in his role as Bishop of New Zealand was telling. It implied, although Newcastle had not necessarily grasped its import, that the clergy had operated in such a way as to be treated by Māori as a form of political

[29] *The Taranaki Question* was twice reprinted in London by WH Dalton (as the second and third editions respectively). For a discussion of Martin's preparation of *The Taranaki Question* and a summary of Martin's argument, see Lennard, *Sir William Martin*, 94–6

[30] Martin's preface to *Remarks on 'Notes published for the New Zealand Government', January 1861, and of Mr Richmond's Memorandum on the The Taranaki Question, December, 1860*, recorded his location as author as 'Taurarua, Feb[ruary] 1861'. The relevant part of Taurarua is now known as Judge's Bay in Parnell near Auckland central.

[31] See also Richmond, 'Richmond's Marginal Notes' in Auckland Museum Library holding of Martin, *The Taranaki Question*; Clarke, *Remarks upon a pamphlet by James Busby, Esq., commenting upon a pamphlet entitled The Taranaki question, by Sir William Martin, D.C.L., late Chief Justice of New Zealand.*

[32] Hadfield, *One of England's Little Wars*; Hadfield, *The Second Year of One of England's Little Wars*; Hadfield, *A Sequel to One of England's Little Wars*; Fox, *The War in New Zealand.*

[33] According to Martin's own account: Martin, *Remarks on 'Notes published for the New Zealand Government'*, 17.

[34] Newcastle to Browne, private, 26 April 1861, NeC10885, Nottingham University(emphasis in original). See also Newcastle to Browne, private, 27 May 1861, Ne C10885, Nottingham University.

[35] Newcastle to Grey, private, 26 December 1861, NeC10886, Nottingham University. Newcastle also observed that he could not 'help being aroused at the tone of haughty insolence with which he writes of me and my official position in private letters which I have seen'.

governance in the colony as an alternative to that of the governor and his ministers, and as conveying political critique to European officials. It is conceivable that irritation with clergy such as Hadfield and Selwyn was already noticeable as early as late 1860, at least with Fortescue in the Colonial Office. Following his meetings with Fortescue on the Native Council Bill, Grahame's personal correspondence with McLean seems to suggest Fortescue as a likely source for the view that '[t]he general impression in England is that Bishop Selwyn interferes too much in matters which do not belong to his office and Arch[deaco]n Hadfield gets the character of being a most violent man!'[36] Yet, like Busby, the former chief justice was never adept at silence. Printed words tumbled from both of them.

Following the Waitara incident, a pamphleteering campaign began in earnest. This campaign has engaged the attentions of scholarly literature in the context of Waitara as turning point, ushering in intra-Māori warfare as well as war with Britain.[37] Foremost amongst issues of contention were native title and the contested place of the Treaty of Waitangi. Typically, as with any such pamphlets, Kidd points out the challenge of ascertaining whether their contents were presented as earnest inquiry or as principally polemic and provocation.[38] Be that as it may, the disputes in anglophone circles still revealed much about the appreciation of the technical metes and bounds of native title, the relevance of indigenous proprietary interests to the Treaty of Waitangi, and the place of the Treaty of Waitangi in anglophone constitutional discussions. Waitara, its antecedents, and its aftermath were rich in complexities, defying officials and jurists to untangle them. Yet the histories of native title produced and contested at this time also demonstrate Frederick Cooper's point that 'empire could also become a moral space, the unit in regard to which righteous political behavior[u]r was debated'.[39] The important point, however, as Lindsey MacDonald has recognised from a philosophical standpoint, is that claims to proprietary rights are as much claims to political power—a power to exert an influence on practical outcomes in the relevant area; a power requiring engagement and negotiation.[40] A cycle of claim and counterclaim emerged in the colonial legislature, preceding the publication of these pamphlets. Within the legislative forum, a report of the so-called 'Waikato [Select] committee' of the House of Representatives dated 31 October 1860 and investigating the proposals to 'introduce institutions of civil government amongst the natives of the Waikato district [in 1857]; the practical effect of the same, and the causes which led to its discontinuance' was released and circulated. This paper, received at the Colonial Office on 18 February 1861, was greeted with considerable praise by Fortescue as one of the two 'most valuable & instructive documents which have yet reached us on native affairs' (the other being Fenton's account of his sojourn as resident magistrate).

Intelligence of this sort further conspired to present an impression of the conjoining of issues of native title and government in areas subject to native title. Owing to the

[36] Grahame to McLean, 23 August 1860, Ms-Papers-0032-0298, fo.7, McLean papers, ATL.

[37] For an overview of Martin's approach as an exercise in political thought, see MacDonald, 'The Political Philosophy of Property Rights', 158–61.

[38] Kidd, *Union and Unionisms*, 86. Following Kidd, this chapter will also use the strategy of exploring questions of native title and political authority 'in its various modes, from the academic to the partisan'.

[39] Cooper, *Colonialism in Question*, 163.

[40] MacDonald, 'The Political Philosophy of Property Rights', ch 6.

overall impression of apartness and a perceived lack of incorporation of Māori polities within the new colonial body politic, native title was perceived as giving Māori a solid asset-base and a lever for effectively contesting the policies of colonial government. In particular, it provided a lever for indigenous communities to contest the pretensions of the colonial government to use the legal resources at its disposal (through the legislature for example) to construct points of intersection and communicability with the interior of Māori politics regarding land and the control of territorial space. We may discern this sense of apartness—as undeniably porous, tentative, and occasionally indeterminate as it was along its boundaries—in the reductionist mapping of 'native land' as against the class of territorial claims characterized as 'European land'. Charles Heaphy supplied one such map of the North Island in March 1861, portraying enclaves and corridors of 'European land' surrounded by large swathes of 'Native land' to which native title remained unextinguished.[41] At this stage, there was no concealing by maps the fact that colonial establishments were marginal in spatial terms, nor did officials see any need to.[42] Beyond the intimate, dispersed worlds of settlement enclaves, a penumbra skirting the settlements shaded into areas where *hapū* politics were largely preeminent.

There was, therefore, neither suppression nor concealment of this class of apartness—of the contingent quality of British territorial suzerainty beyond the colonial niches or bridgehead settlements of Wellington, Auckland, New Plymouth, and Napier situated in coastal enclaves. Rather, the essential characteristics of negotiability introduced into political circles were broadly acknowledged. Both native title and its relations with the Treaty of Waitangi were treated as matters of genuine perplexity—neither politically articulate colonial actors nor Māori assumed the significance or meanings of either subject as self-evident. Native title, then, permitted Māori chieftains to calibrate economic and political intersections with the colonial settlements as distinct political municipalities and economies, as well as with clusters of colonial settlers. Fortescue, in using the term 'occasional *negociation* [sic]', understood these points to be relatively managed and discrete as well as delicate, operating through deeds of purchase and pre-deed negotiations together with other individual arrangements between local Māori and squatters.

Waitara (and subsequent warring) also underscored the under-resourced tentativeness of colonial administration in the areas outside of colonial settlements sitting on land no longer subject to native title. The very fiscal prudence that elevated the legitimacy of imperial government in the eyes of British taxpayers was seen and interpreted otherwise by many Māori as revealing profound tactical and strategic weaknesses in colonial administration, leading to an absence of the institutional apparatus of colonial government rather than a presence. From indigenous perspectives, it could be a useful weakness. It implied that case-by-case negotiations for advantage—in the form

[41] See map drawn by Charles Heaphy dated March 1861 (plate 1 on p 448).Charts were also forwarded to London, including a 'Map of [the] North Island, New Zealand, showing the relative amount of Native and Ceded Lands', enclosed with 'Statistical notes relating to the Maoris and their territory, by Charles Heaphy, Chief Surveyor, Auckland, N[ew] Z[ealand]', annexed to Browne to Newcastle, 12 April 1861, 'Further papers relative to the recent disturbances in New Zealand', *GBPP1862* [3040], situated between 40–1.

[42] Cf Belich, *Replenishing the Earth*, 551–4.

of British currency, settlers, squatters, and goods—could still occur, with some Māori elites jockeying for a share in these spoils.

As will be seen, the Waitara episode raised complex and unresolved questions of the nature and extent of 'tribal title' and any individual or sub-tribal level forms of proprietary interest or right, as well as the nature and relevance of political authority in indigenous communities and the relationship of such authority to land. Divergent interpretations were in evidence. Secondary compacts or deeds of purchase, in addressing the persistence of native title, occurred in a negotiating space that was pre-eminently a place for politics—these compacts or deeds were the outcome of negotiations with the local, often particular, practicalities of the political and territorial autonomy of *hapū* (whether in part or in whole) or clusters of *hapū* in specific districts. Yet Waitara produced raging debates as to the role of law and independent legal institutions as autonomous sources of discipline on political behaviour. Legalistic genres proved salient in the pamphlets as they navigated the questions of how to conceive the Waitara transaction and analyse Māori relations with territorial space—questions of property, rights, and political authority. We will see this relevance in turning to the memoranda and pamphlets of Richmond, Martin, and Busby below for example.

Nevertheless, neither Fox nor Hadfield resorted exhaustively or simply to recognizably juridical idioms at least in respect of native title itself as a right, which Hadfield, at least, saw beyond dispute.[43] Hadfield considered the 'merits of the question' at issue between the colonial government and Kīngi to 'lie within very narrow limits': that is, whether a 'native chief [was] to be forcibly ejected from his land, because an individual member of his tribe tells a subordinate land agent that it is his, and the not the chief's, and that agent believes him'.[44] Hadfield's critique was directed towards the alleged injustice and 'impolicy' of the governor's conduct in the Waitara transaction and its consequences in strengthening the case for the Kīngitanga. For Hadfield, the looming menace of the Kīngitanga (which he characterized as a 'conspiracy') spoke to the potential for a ruinous war of races and extermination: 'What is demanded by the natives is, an impartial court in which their respective claims can be stated; and before which they may bring evidence to be received on oath'[45]—what was warranted was a 'competent court of law'.[46] The omission of explicit legal sources was clearly deliberate, as Hadfield was familiar with the sources of *ius gentium*, having deployed them in private memoranda in the past to George Grey in 1845.[47]

However, Fox expressly used Waitara to illuminate the underlying political and legal frailties of the colonial constitution in New Zealand. In particular, in a paper written in September 1860 he rebuked the distribution of political authority between a governor and his responsible ministers. A key ingredient was criticism of a governor-centric approach to Māori affairs, including the approach taken to such issues as to the

[43] Hadfield, *One of England's Little Wars*, 5. [44] Ibid. [45] Ibid, 18–19.

[46] Ibid, 6: 'Were Teira's title as good as I am quite certain it is bad, and had William King no valid title whatever, still the real question raised by this act of the Governor is what I have now stated it to be. Are chiefs to be debarred from all right to defend their titles in a competent court of law? Is the *ipse dixit* of an interested subordinate land agent to deprive a chief of his land, and justify the Governor in having recourse to arms? If so, of what conceivable use or meaning is the guarantee in reference to their land contained in the Treaty of Waitangi?'

[47] Hadfield dated his paper to 1845 when presenting evidence on the question of Waitara and native title to the bar at the House of Representatives in August 1860: Hadfield, Appendix A, ix, 'Extracts from opinions of various authorities [on native tenure]', *GBPP1860* [2747], 203.

nature and extent of Māori 'territorial rights' and appropriate methods of land purchase. Referring to the principle of ministerial responsibility as having been 'added practically to the British Constitution after the Revolution of 1688', Fox bemoaned the incompleteness of its reception as a custom in New Zealand.[48] Fox pictured 'ministerial responsibility' as a customary principle which had to be 'supplemented [to the New Zealand Constitution Act 1852] by consent of the Crown'. But, he alleged, 'Governor Browne', in requiring the settler politicians to 'surrender to him the entire administration of all affairs relating to the natives [in return for assenting to the application of ministerial responsibility to the colony] .... robb[ed] us of exactly half our Constitution'.[49] This arrangement, he argued, allowed Browne to enjoy, as governor, 'absolute power' in the field of managing colonial relations with Māori. To the exercise of this power, Fox concluded, 'we attribute the present unhappy crisis' emerging from Waitara. Beyond these moves in constitutional discourse, however, Fox treated the Waitara episode as symptomatic of policy failures, most particularly the failure to deploy section 71 of the Constitution Act to formally declare areas adhering to the Kīngitanga as native districts in which 'native laws and customs might prevail' in dealings of Māori *inter se*.[50] If that had occurred, 'the dangerous "King movement" [would have turned] into a source of strength, and a bond of union': 'The name, changed as it easily might have been, and its functions subordinated to the Queen's prerogatives, taken in short under the shelter of the Constitution, the "King movement" would have proved a most fortunate event, and under the semblance of separation, have afforded the means of bringing about a permanent political union between the races'.[51] Fox presented Waitara as a tragic reflection of lost constitutional opportunities.

INDIGENOUS ORDERS, THE CONDITIONALITY OF THE INTRODUCED COLONIAL CONSTITUTION, AND THE THREE STICKS OF LAW, THE DIVINE BEING, AND THE *MANA* OF NEW ZEALAND IN DISUNION

Promiscuously gathering and deploying sources or extracts from sources for immediate use or ends was as much a feature of Māori politics as of *anglophone* political conduct. It is salutary to recall that a number of Māori politicians and chiefly elites loudly criticized perceived misinterpretations of European territorial claims and the distribution of political authority within colonial politics. Indeed, the register or grammar of peace or neutrality at, for example, the conference of chiefs assembled at Kohimarama in July 1860 did not preclude criticism of anglophone interpretations of claims to territory or political constitutionalism. These criticisms suggest a venerable and importantly indigenous grammar of musing on the proprieties of the politics of settlers, pākehā territorial claims, and the patterns of constitutional authority. Māori assertiveness on these questions, within and beyond settled colonial New Zealand, was in evidence, irrespective of whether the Māori actors concerned affiliated with the Kīngitanga in the Waikato, were neutral, or were allied with the governor (whether conditionally, for a discrete period of time, or not). The proceedings of the Kohimarama conference (*rūnanga*) were reported and circulated in *The Maori Messenger*, the government's main

[48] Fox, *The War in New Zealand*, 5. [49] Ibid. [50] Ibid, 11–12. [51] Ibid, 12.

Māori language newspaper, in both English and Māori.[52] They were also reported in London, where they were awaited with much anticipation: 'We hope to hear before long of the result of a great meeting of friendly chiefs called together by the Gov[erno] r, & also of that of the Assembly—until after wh[ich] no new instructions [should] probably go out'.[53] Kohimarama demonstrated yet again that there was no monopoly of constitutional or political interpretation on the conduct of colonial New Zealand. In his own distillation of the official reports on the Kohimarama meetings, Rogers reported to Fortescue of a diverse range of views, populating his memorandum with surveys of the assorted viewpoints: 'Some desire the offer of Crown grants—better provision for the poor Maoris upon occasion of land sales—and a mixed court (English & Maori) to decide on land questions'.[54]

Even the selection of Kohimarama as a site for the conference could be read by attending chiefs as speaking to the variety of sources of authority and power in New Zealand. In reporting to London, Browne noted, 'Kohimarama, a property belonging to the Church of England Mission, was chosen as the place of meeting because the land does not belong either to the Government or the settlers; this had the advantage of relieving the speakers from a restraint upon the freedom of discussion which, according to Maori custom, they might have felt if they had been entertained as guests in houses belonging to the Government'.[55] It could be presented as a neutral space but also as a place tied to spirituality and its mediating presence on human affairs, allied to but not subsumed by the new legal system or indigenous authority. At the opening of the conference on 10 July 1860 some 112 chieftains were in attendance, including representatives from Ngāti Tama in Wellington and Ngāi Tahu from Otago and Canterbury in the South Island. Influenza in that winter season, however, had prevented many from attending.

The Treaty of Waitangi, the application of English law, and the Taranaki (Waitara) question were all subjected to discussion over three weeks. On the question of English law, a Māori language version of Martin's paper was produced for consideration. This document was a less ornate and much more functionally expressed summary or abstract of *The Laws of England* or *Ko Nga Ture o Ingarani* than Fenton's somewhat more baroque albeit revelatory 'code' of *The Laws of England compiled and translated into the Maori language* (1858).[56] Martin, subsequently critical of Fenton's effort in his pamphlet *The Taranaki Question*, had prepared the summary at the governor's request, and it had been available for circulation from February 1860. Two copies were received

[52] For example, *The Maori Messenger—Te Karere Maori*, vol 7, number 13, 14 July 1860; vol 7, number 14, 31 July 1860; vol 7, number 15, 3 August 1860; vol 7, number 16, 15 August 1860; vol 7, number 17, 1 September 1860,. The governor, Browne, recorded in his report to the Secretary of State for Colonies, Newcastle, that: 'A careful record of the speeches (which after the first two days were corrected by the chiefs themselves, and a list of names attached to the resolutions have been preserved and will be circulated through the country by means of the "Maori Messenger", and (though some English gentlemen have, I regret to say, endeavoured to throw discredit on the proceedings) they will have a great and I trust beneficial effect upon the Maori people throughout New Zealand': Browne to Newcastle, 28 August 1860, CO209/155, fos.38–8a, TNA. On *The Maori Messenger* generally, see Paterson, *Colonial Discourses*, 19–21.

[53] Fortescue to Newcastle, 27 August 1860, Ne C10931/1–2, Nottingham University.

[54] Rogers to Fortescue, 24 November 1860, minute, CO209/155, fo.42, TNA.

[55] Browne to Newcastle, 28 August 1860, [received at the Colonial Office on 19 November 1860; printed for Parliament in March 1861], CO209/155, fo.35, TNA.

[56] See Chapter Six. Analytically, as discussed previously, Fenton's effort is revelatory of an attempt to address the relations between English real property law and indigenous proprietary interests.

at the Colonial Office, although the subsequent copy was referred to as a 'draft'.[57] Henry Kemp, the district commissioner for the Bay of Islands, correctly ascribed the authorship of this 'code of laws' to Martin.[58] From the Bay of Islands district to the north of Auckland, Kemp reported in October 1860 how at various *rūnanga* the 'new "tikanga" [composed by Martin, was discussed] in its different bearings, with much interest'.[59] During the second week of the Kohimarama conference in July 1860, the gathered 'chiefs were requested to consider these rules and state their opinion as to their practicability'.[60] The introductory message conveyed from the governor stated, with reference to the conditionality of their acceptability as 'rules', that the '"Rules for the proper administration of justice" [were sent] to the chiefs assembled at Kohimarama for their consideration'.[61] The themes of change and conservatism were seen in various provisions of the code. Indeed, aspects of these proposed rules were self-consciously novel, seeking to impose change on what Martin had understood to be the prevailing customary approaches of Māori communities. Accordingly, in relation to penalties for 'adultery', the proposed 'code of laws' stated:

> The penalty not less than twenty pounds. In cases where the woman has been regularly married, the penalty not less than thirty pounds. As to these offences the penalty goes altogether to the Queen [here the rule was also referring to the 'offences' of 'drinking spirits' and 'eating rotten food']. Formerly the rule was otherwise in case of adultery. The husband recovered compensation in money. But this was seen to be evil. For it is an evil thing, that the wife's infidelity should be a means of making money for the husband. Accordingly that rule has been altered.[62]

When the proposed code was presented, the Native Secretary, McLean, reportedly said: 'Do not be hasty in forming an opinion for or against them [the 'rules'], but consider carefully whether they are adapted to your wants'.[63] The Assistant Native Secretary, Thomas Smith, recorded how a 'discussion took place'. His report interpreted the sway of those discussions as revealing that 'the rules, with one exception, [were] generally approved as applicable to purely native districts'. Crucially, however, the *rūnanga* 'decided that no definite opinion should be expressed by the conference until the rules had been considered by the various tribes each in its own district'.[64]

[57] Martin, 'Rules for the proper administration of justice', draft, CO209/153, fos.361 *et seq* (received at the Colonial Office on 10 August 1860); 'Rules for the Proper Administration of Justice, being a translation of the rules put forth in Maori by the Governor in February, 1860', CO209/154, fos.67–73, TNA (also received at the Colonial Office on 10 August 1860).

[58] Kemp, District Commissioner, District Commissioner's Office, Bay of Islands, to McLean, 10 October 1860, CO209/157, fo.401a, TNA. Doubts as to Martin's authorship have been raised in the past, as noted by Guy Lennard in *Sir William Martin*, 121–2, referring to MW Hancock's suggestion in 'Sir William Martin and the Maori People' that Fenton was the author.

[59] Henry T Kemp, District Commissioner, District Commissioner's Office, Bay of Islands, to McLean, 10 October 1860, CO209/157, fos.402–2a, TNA.

[60] Smith, Assistant Native Secretary, Auckland, 'Report on the native conference at Kohimarama', 27 August 1860, CO209/155, fo.50, TNA.

[61] Monday, 16 July 1860, as reported in *The Maori Messenger—Te Karere Maori*, vol 7, number 14, 31 July 1860, 3.

[62] 'Rules for the Proper Administration of Justice, being a translation of the rules put forth in Maori by the Governor in February, 1860', CO209/154, fos.69–9a, TNA.

[63] Tuesday, 17 July 1860, as reported in *The Maori Messenger—Te Karere Maori*, vol 7, number 14, 31 July 1860, 21.

[64] Smith, Assistant Native Secretary, Auckland, 'Report on the native conference at Kohimarama', 27 August 1860, CO209/155, fo.50, TNA.

Thus, various Māori attendees strategically reserved their positions on the abstracted form of *The Laws of England* or *Ko Nga Ture o Ingarani* without committing themselves to any distinct position.

In a comparable vein, Smith recounted that a 'second message containing suggestions for the settlement of disputes about land and for defining tribal and other boundaries was also discussed, and a similar course resolved on, the chiefs not feeling themselves at liberty to act without first consulting their people'.[65] On this subject, McLean read a second message from the governor addressed to the convocation at Kohimarama. This message expressed the view that it was 'very desirable that some general principles regulating the boundaries of land belonging to different tribes should be generally received and adopted; for, until the rights of property are clearly defined, progress in civilization must be both slow and uncertain'.[66] One principle possibility mooted was that of an agreed period of limitation: 'Very many disagreements would in future be avoided if the possession of land from any fixed date—say, 20 years,—were recognised as giving the possessor a good title'.[67] The twenty-year period of limitation accorded with that operating under English common law, at least in respect of non-Crown land.[68] 'When disputes arise between different tribes in reference to land', the governor's message suggested, 'they might be referred to a committee of disinterested and influential chiefs, selected at a conference similar to the one now held at Kohimarama'—a *rūnanga*-based system. Browne's message adverted to other possibilities:

> There is also a simpler plan universally adopted in Hindostan, which appears well suited to the circumstances of New Zealand, viz., when men cannot agree as to their respective rights, each party chooses two persons—and these four choose a chief of another tribe having no interest in the matter disputed. Then the five sit in judgment, and decide who is right and who is wrong; but before they pronounce judgment, both the contending parties solemnly engage to abide by it.[69]

The recommendations of the report echoed suggestions coursing through *anglophone* policy circles in 1859 and early 1860: 'Some land might be held in common for tribal purposes; but he would like to see every chief and every member of his tribe in possession of a Crown Grant, for as much land as they could possibly desire or use'.[70] A peaceable autonomous dispute-resolution process could be resorted to through an appropriate court.[71]

In response to this message and McLean's elaboration, notables from Ngāti Raukawa, Ngāti Whakaue, Tūhourangi, Ngātitoa, Ngāi Whatua, and Ngāti Pāoa (Hauraki) spoke, suggesting a variety of views and agendas, some seeming to compete in their protestations of sympathy with the distant but present Queen, others seeing the notion of Crown grants as a means of branding their lands, as they had already done so with livestock. There was no simple focus on a regulatory regime for land as such.

65 Ibid.

66 Wednesday, 18 July 1860, as reported in *The Maori Messenger—Te Karere Maori*, vol 7, number 14, 31 July 1860, 30.

67 Ibid, 29–30.

68 In the early twentieth century, the period of limitation thought to apply to Māori customary land was a 60 years, identical to the period of limitation for Crown land. See Hickford, 'Strands from the Afterlife of Confiscation', 181–2.

69 Wednesday, 18 July 1860, as reported in *The Maori Messenger—Te Karere Maori*, vol 7, number 14, 31 July 1860, 30.

70 Ibid, 30–1.

71 Ibid, 31.

Thus, Hukiki of Ngāti Raukawa ki Ōtaki to the north of Wellington stated: 'My name is Hukiki, the brand on my cattle is HU, but the land has not been branded (referring to Crown Grants). According to my opinion the land should be marked[, b]ecause the Chiefs are grasping at great quantities of land, leaving none for the poorer people'.[72] Inducements to pākehā to settle and the diversity of options potentially obtainable, as well as the possible risks, were also referred to:

> When the pakehas arrived, and were still at sea I took hold of the cable and drew him to land. *All things are not known*. I am not concerned to know the opinions of this person or that person: each man has his own thoughts. All that I know is, that formerly we had but one kind of garment. I had not then received this which now covers me. Remember your oaths lest they be violated.[73]

On the point of Waitara, Rogers observed in London that 'One address only (and that *Ngatiawa*) complains that the Land Purchase Commission buy from a few persons blocks wh[ich] belong to many [with reference, Rogers surmised, to Waitara, while a] Waikato proposes a mixed commission (English & Maori) to enquire into the truth of W. King's case'.[74]

Accepting the presence of another's *mana* did not, however, signal subordination or obeisance. One Kohimarama conference resolution reported in *The Maori Messenger*, therefore, is apt to mislead if '*mana*' is simply equated with 'sovereignty':

> E whakaae ana tenei Runanga, i te tikanga o nga rangatira i noho ki roto; kua tino whakaae nei tetahi ki tetahi kia kaua rawa he pakanga ketanga i runga I te kupu kua whakapuakina nuitia mo te mana o te Kuini, mo te whakakotahitanga hoki o nga iwi e rua; a kua whakaae nei tetahi ki tetahi kia whakahengia nga mahi katoa mana e taka ai ta ratou kawenata tapu kua whakatakotoria ki konei.

Translated in the official account as 'sovereignty' ('te mana o te Kuini') the resolution in English read:

> That this Conference takes cognizance of the fact that the several Chiefs, members thereof, are pledged to each other to do nothing inconsistent with their declared recognition of the Queen's sovereignty, and of the union of the two races; also to discountenance all proceedings tending to a breach of the covenant here solemnly entered into by them.[75]

In what is presented, in effect, as the colonial administration's favoured rendition of the term '*mana*' at this time in a particular site (*The Maori Messenger*) in its customized vocabulary in Māori orthography, 'sovereignty' and '*mana*' are conflated for certain purposes. This was not unconventional. The Reverend Thomas Buddle, the Wesleyan missionary, treated '*mana*' as standing for 'sovereignty' in his account of the Kīngitanga.[76] Similarly, '*mana*' was translated as 'sovereignty' in a rendering of the letter read at a meeting of Waikato and Manukau Māori at Waiuku (south of Auckland) in March 1860: 'The Pakehas say, that this vesting of authority in a King will not stand because the "Mana" of this island has passed to the Queen in virtue of: discovery by Capt[ain] Cook; the Treaty of Waitangi; the Treaty of Waikato; the right of the Crown

72 Ibid, 38. 73 Ibid, 37–8 (emphasis added).

74 Rogers to Fortescue, 24 November 1860, minute, CO209/155, fo.42, TNA.

75 'Resolutions adopted by the Conference on 10th August, 1860', *The Maori Messenger*, vol 7, 15 August 1860.

76 Buddle, *The Maori King Movement in New Zealand with a Full Report of the Native Meetings held at Waikato, April and May 1860*, 54, note.

to the gold of New Zealand'.[77] Kohimarama revealed ongoing and developing strategies of Māori accommodation and incorporation of British settlements and their norms from an indigenous perspective undeniably mingling with the creation of new norms or sense of laws ('*ture*') as to how British settlers and Māori ought to interact. Some *rangatira*, like Paora Tuhaere of Ngāti Whātua based near Auckland, stressed the benefits of peaceable dispute-resolution introduced through the example of English legal norms: 'The best riches for us are the Laws of England. In my opinion, the greatest of all evils is war'. Paora Tuhaere noted how these legal norms were not as influential as they were required to be: 'When a Maori kills a Pakeha, the Pakeha says, Let us fight; and when a Pakeha kills a Maori, then the Maori says, Let us fight. For example—if I should be killed by a Pakeha, my tribe would say, Let us fight with the Pakeha; and on the other hand were I to kill a Pakeha, even though he be a slave, the Pakeha would demand me as payment'.[78] On land questions, Tuhaere said: 'The Pakeha has his mode of selling land, and the Maori has his mode..... As to the talk about Waitangi (treaty), that is Ngapuhi's matter'.[79] The *rūnanga* or council at Kohimarama was a place for communicability and entanglements between Māori politics and the governor's preferred interpretations of Crown–Māori relations. But it also reflected how certain Māori attendees described and accounted for those inter-cultural crossings already playing out on the ground in many localized or micro-settings. Their relations with the colonial government were seen as part of an ongoing relationship, negotiated in various engagements (including trading goods and selling land). But the relations were suffused with a sense of conditionality—a sense that indigenous communities were scrutinizing and weighing up what was being delivered through the relationship. This was not the narrow sense of conditionality based on observance of the Treaty of Waitangi, which tends to be the way in which the conditionality of Crown–Māori relations (if they are seen as conditional at all) are interpreted in some sources.[80]

Insofar as the *rūnanga* at Kohimarama was concerned, the conclusions drawn and presented in *The Maori Messenger—Te Karere Maori*, published by the Native Department, were congenial to the colonial government's preferred interpretations. But even in English language presentation of the proceedings at Kohimarama, publicized in *The Maori Messenger*, ambiguities emerged of a sort that suggested that alternative interpretations were possible. In the oratory of the assembled Māori leaders, the salience of the spiritual and its entwining with political authority was a not-uncommon theme, suggesting the significance of assessing the behaviour of the introduced regime against normative values associated with scriptural tenets and teachings. But the degrees to which the colonial regime was thought to have broadly complied with this intermingling varied from descent-group to descent-group and from *rangatira* to *rangatira*. In the report of 15 August 1860, the article on Kohimarama reported: 'There is truth in the words of Tamati Waka Nene on the first day of the Conference—"When the Governor came he brought with him the Word of God by which we live; and it is

[77] TH Smith, 15 March 1860, confidential, 'translation of the document read by Patara at the Waiuku meeting referred to by Mr Halse.... Mar[ch] 13th 1860', in Scholefield (ed), *The Richmond-Atkinson Papers*, I, 541.

[78] Paora Tuhaere, 10 July 1860, *The Maori Messenger—Te Karere Maori*, vol 7, number 13, 14 July 1860, 14.

[79] Ibid, 15.

[80] See, eg Wilberg, 'Judicial Remedies for the Original Breach?', 714–15.

through the teaching of that Word that we are able to meet together, this day, under one roof"'. Rogers' reaction in London suggested a willingness to read the report against the grain, entertaining a smidgeon of doubt as to whether the chiefs were as congenial to the objects of the colonial administration as the governor claimed. Aware of empire as inextricably complicated and tentative in many places, senior officials at the Colonial Office were not mere interpretative literalists. Thus:

> On reading the addresses from the separate chiefs I observe the following points. They are universally ag[ain]st the King movement—but very generally keen for letting it alone. Some do & some do not perceive that it is in principle inconsistent with the sovereignty of the Queen. I should conjecture then wh[ether] some tribal jealousy of the Waikato is at work. There are many complaints of not being allowed to get guns & ammunition.[81]

A close reading of the chiefly speeches and minutes of the Assistant Native Secretary, Thomas Smith, from the actual sessions of the Kohimarama *rūnanga* revealed more in the way of subtlety and tentativeness on the part of attending chiefs. Smith was careful to record that 'The districts most fully represented were the Bay of Islands, Kaipara, the neighbourhood of Auckland, the Bay of Plenty, Wairarapa and the West Coast from Wellington to Whanganui'. He noted that those 'least represented were Mangonui in the north, the Thames, Waikato, Taupo, Upper Whanganui and Taranaki'.[82] Two months before the conference, the governor himself had advised the Secretary of State for Colonies that invitations were not extended to those chiefs 'who openly refuse to recognise Her Majesty's Sovereignty'.[83] The Treaty of Waitangi itself was a subject of discussion in the third week of the conference, with Smith recording the regional variations in chiefly reaction to it, illuminating the need for sensitivity in listening to diverse perspectives and voices. The Treaty suggested the sheer conditionality of the politics of negotiability in New Zealand—the fact that points of consensus or convergence were but moments or episodes prone to being revisited, renegotiated, refreshed and revised, repudiated, and broken. McLean's own papers, possibly dating to 1860, suggested the divergence of views on the significance of the Treaty.[84] A paper on the Treaty of Waitangi remarked how Māori simply regarded it as 'yielding, on their part, permissive occupation to Europeans to settle in the country, as they had been already in the habit of doing'. 'A few' Māori were recorded as 'alive to the necessity of forming such alliance with England as might prevent aggression from foreign powers'. The paper acknowledged that '[n]one, however, were aware—[although] they entertained various suspicions as to the ultimate object of the Government—that the treaty could, in any

[81] Rogers to Fortescue, 24 November 1860, minute, CO209/155, fos.41–1a, TNA.

[82] Smith, Assistant Native Secretary, Auckland, 'Report on the native conference at Kohimarama', 27 August 1860, CO209/155, fo.48, TNA.

[83] Browne to Newcastle, 27 April 1860, [received at the Colonial Office on 12 July 1860; printed for Parliament in March 1861], CO209/153, fo.428a, TNA. In reporting on the conference to Newcastle, Browne noted, 'The chiefs assembled came from all parts of New Zealand, even the tribe to which W. King belongs being well represented. Many had never met before and knew each other only by name and report. The experiment was not without hazard, and it was confidently predicted that men, who in times past had eaten each other's relatives, would only meet to fight or to combine temporarily for the destruction of the Europeans as a common enemy': ibid, fos.34–4a,.

[84] McLean, undated (*circa* 1860), Ms-Papers-0032-0138, McLean papers, ATL. Dr P Parkinson attributes the date of '*circa* 1860' to this document. The paper is watermarked 'T.H. Saunders 1858' and is possibly associated with the Kohimarama conference: see Parkinson, '"Preserved in the Archives of the Colony"', 101.

way, interfere with the free and independent exercise of their own rights, privileges, and customs'. It was noted that the 'various tribes and communities throughout New Zealand' considered themselves as 'possessing independent sovereign powers' and were mindful of retaining a balance of power between assorted groups.[85]

Kohimarama was lauded as a new step or milestone, for the time being—the expectation being that it would be succeeded by further such steps. Paora Tuhaere of Ngāti Whatua (Orakei) was reported to have said: 'But this [alluding to the conference] is more like it; this is the real Treaty upon which the sovereignty [*mana*] of the Queen [*te mana o te Kuini*] will hang, because here are assembled chiefs from every quarter, and even from the other Island, to discuss various questions and to seek out a path'.[86] Seen in this fashion, native title and the authority of the introduced colonial regime formed part of a plurality of discussions. The Treaty was read and explained. Yet, as Smith recorded, 'Many of the southern chiefs spoke of it as a thing confined to Ngapuhi which that tribe had itself repudiated and broken (referring to Heke's war)'.[87] Chiefs attending from Turanga on the eastern coast of the North Island were clear that 'It will be for the Maori chiefs to consider that document which was written at Waitangi'.[88]

As to the innovation of the Kīngitanga with its core base of support in the Waikato, these chieftains saw their own authority as distinct and independent: 'This is what we say:—we do not in any way consent to the Maori King, that he should be king over New Zealand' reportedly adding, '[l]et these tribes have the king to themselves'. By way of further response, they stated: 'We have also great names in our own district, such as Hineimatioro, Te Kaniatakirau, and Hirini; yet we should not approve of any of these being made king. No!'[89] Similarly, the Waitara dispute amongst *hapū* of Te Ātiawa and between elements of Te Ātiawa and the colonial administration was seen as a matter for the parties concerned and not for others: 'The settlement of the matter between you and Waikato and William King rests with yourselves'.[90] Again, with reference to an entwining of spiritual and temporal political tropes, the viewpoint was it would be preferable for those at Turanga on the distant east coast of the Island to look to their own preoccupations. On 6 August 1860, Metekingi of Whanganui was recorded as saying vis-à-vis the Taranaki question: 'I don't understand that subject', adding '[t]hat matter rests with you [Donald McLean] and the Governor'.[91] A powerful sense of independent localized engagements with the introduced colonial regime was conveyed in a number of the speeches.

Some chiefs, such as Tāmihana Te Rauparaha of Ngātitoa, presented explicitly as innovators, designers, and merchants of managed change. In these terms, Tāmihana Te Rauparaha opened with compliments for the *rūnanga* convened at Kohimarama as a step to be repeated. 'Let this runanga', he said, 'be a beckoner to those who are going astray, following the old customs of the Maoris, that they should come back unto the

[85] Ibid. The paper is largely written in an official hand, which Parkinson identifies as possibly that of Thomas Smith, but includes additional comments by McLean: see Parkinson, '"Preserved in the Archives of the Colony"', 101.

[86] *The Maori Messenger*, Thursday, 26 July 1860, 35.

[87] Smith, Assistant Native Secretary, Auckland, 'Report on the native conference at Kohimarama', 27 August 1860, CO209/155, fo.48, TNA.

[88] Tamati Hapimana Te Rangituawaru of Turanga and Tamihana Ratapu and Te Waka Perohuka of Turanga, 'Reply from Ngati Kahungunu—no. 1', 14 July 1860, CO209/155, fo.64a, TNA.

[89] Ibid, fo.65a. [90] Ibid.

[91] *The Maori Messenger—Te Karere Maori*, vol 7, number 17, 1 September 1860, 5.

good path which the Governor has pointed out as that by which the Maori race in New Zealand may attain to what is for their welfare; and the two races, the pakeha and the Maori, may preserve mutual friendship'.[92] The possessive (and illuminating) political language of authority of speaking about 'Europeans' as things guarded, possessed, or kept by chiefs (and the absence of Europeans in some cases) suffused the speech-making. With a view to consigning 'old customs' still alive in his present to the past, Tāmihana Te Rauparaha suggested a number of policy proposals for notice and discussion, including the establishment of a commission to consider purchases of land and to investigate the 'title' to the land. Hence, 'Future sales of land by the natives to the Government should be conducted by a commission.... [; l]et the Governor select a pakeha gentleman, and a Maori chief as an assistant and let them conduct the negociations [*sic*] for the lands sold by the Maories to the Government'.[93]

Various Māori *rūnanga* (councils) had been busily constructing laws, law-like processes, and political constitutions to marshall diverse opinion, to build power, and to discipline within and across *hapū*. The 'sanhedrim' of Ngāti Mahuta in the Waikato had proposed a set of laws, including the first commandment—'Thou shalt have no Gods but one'—and regulations exhorting people to 'live peaceably in their towns' and prohibiting theft.[94] Waitara and the arguments about the colonial government's conduct relative to Kīngi afforded further opportunities to build legitimacy and authority relative to their own *hapū* members and other tribal groupings. Among the most successful was the *rūnanga* at the base of the recently elected king of the Kīngitanga ('the king movement') in Ngāruawāhia in the Waikato. Before Waitara, Ngāruawāhia had already witnessed moves to establish localized Waikato genres of legal order. On 3 June 1858, following a meeting at Ngāruawāhia on 1 June at which Te Wherowhero accepted election as king, Wīremu Tāmihana Tarapīpipi Waharoa, the so-called 'king maker', was responsible for engineering a brief statement of legalistic rules, predicated on the protection of the norms of the scriptural deity.[95] These rules were constitutional in import to Māori government and property, being presented simply in the first instance as the 'power [of the elected king] to exercise over men and land', specifically the 'power of protecting them against quarrels, wars, and murders,—a power to extend to all the chief and councils of all the tribes'.[96] Secondly, it was stated: 'Every man is to live upon his own land, and the king is to defend him against all aggressions against his land or person'.[97] Overall, such activity tended to be interpreted publicly in colonial official circles as demonstrating Māori ill-feeling and disappointment at a want of colonial administration in the considerable territories remaining beyond coastal settlements. Such interpretations were used consistently with an interpretation of overarching British legal and political authority. In this sense, these interpretations were exemplars of *paradiastole* or 'rhetorical redescription'—in this case, to cast something in a much more palatable light.[98] Yet, as with Stafford's ministry in New Zealand, the Colonial Office was certainly cognizant of this nuanced state of affairs. No false

[92] Tāmihana Te Rauparaha, 'Reply from Ngatitoa no 1', 20 July 1860, CO209/155, fo.85, TNA.
[93] Ibid, fos.85a–6.
[94] 'Proposed Code of Laws', in *AJHR-1860*, F3, 113.
[95] Buddle, *The Maori King Movement*, 13–14.
[96] Ibid, 14. [97] Ibid.
[98] Skinner, 'Moral Ambiguity and the Renaissance Art of Eloquence' in *Visions of Politics*, 276; Runciman, *Political Hypocrisy*, 30.

consciousness was required. Rogers reported with some sensitivity and concern in July 1860 that 'the formidable Waikato are assuming the position of *an independent power, calmly judging* between W[iremu] King[i] and the Government, and, avowedly, ready to take part with him under their (reluctant) king if they think him in the right'.[99] Rogers' attribution, in an internal Colonial Office minute in London, of reluctance to the elected king was significant, as it resonated with the sense in which Te Wherowhero had reluctantly assumed the kingship and his reservations about contending militarily with the colonial settlements.

Taken as a whole, Rogers' comments captured the sentiments expressed amongst Waikato leaders astutely. An illustration of alternative government and autonomy—an independent power—had dramatically presented itself in New Zealand. In May 1860, Tāmihana organized a large meeting at Ngāruawāhia to discuss the merits of the governor's behaviour on the land question in Taranaki, as well as that of Kīngi, and to consider whether to respond to the *cri de couer*—the request for assistance from Kīngi. These meetings supplied the political leaders within the Kīngitanga with a diverse range of voices and opinions drawn from within and outside the king movement on which to judge the balance of the relevant public opinion on given issues of the day—not unlike the role of the colonial legislature in that particular respect. Thomas Buddle, the missionary, estimated some 3,000 people in attendance. They come not only from Waikato, but also other descent-groups from Taupō and Auckland. One aspect that remains striking, however, is not merely the commitment to one side or another of the argument about claims of Te Teira relative to Kīngi. What is noticeable is that Māori allies of Kīngi did not unquestionably agree with his view of the situation. For elements of those inclined to sympathize with the position of Kīngi, the matter was to be tested by investigation. The vocabularies deployed in discussing the Waitara situation were indigenized versions of ecclesiology. The entwined spiritual-political dimensions of the islands of New Zealand were seen as symbolized by three sticks or pillars—some presented the Queen as distinct from that of the religious orders of the missionaries and the *mana* of the chiefs (expressed by Te Wetini of Ngāti Haua as the 'mana of New Zealand'). He described a quasi-conditional union or association of distinct authorities, something certainly akin to an alliance but with much less convergence or alignment than the concept of an alliance would suggest.[100] The 'first [stick] is the mana of the Queen, this gave us the law'; '[t]he second, is the Divine being who sent the word and is the origin of the law'; 'the third is the mana of New Zealand'.[101] Rather radically, the ties that bound could be progressively unravelled or broken. A single episode or serried patterns of conduct over time could be sufficient, and therein lay the conditionality to the sense of union relayed at Ngāruawāhia. The union was *quasi*-conditional in that the union between the word of the divine being (the scriptures and God) and the '*mana* of New Zealand' was treated as binding and permanent—it was not subject to any conditionality, at least not at this time. The *mana* of each was distinct but had been brought together in union (a form of association rather than the sublimation of the *mana* of New Zealand by the *mana* of the Queen). Te Wetini proclaimed that

[99] Rogers to Fortescue, 12 July 1860, CO209/153, fo.462, TNA (emphasis added).

[100] Angela Ballara speaks of an alliance between Te Wherowhero and the British monarch: Ballara, *Te Kīngitanga*, 46.

[101] Buddle, *The Maori King Movement*, 45.

the divine being had become an enemy of the first 'stick' and a keeper of the third. A fourth stick was embedded in the soil to represent Taranaki, the place where Waitara was located: the 'Governor has been there and done wrong'. In so doing, he had 'cut the thread that bound us and severed the union'.[102] The speech of Te Wetini conflated the position of the Queen with her officials in colonial New Zealand, the institutions of colonial government, including the ordinary courts, judges, and magistrates—in essence, all of the visible vestiges of the Crown. *Mana*, as presented in these speeches, was plural and not singular or uniform.

Tāmihana, however, drew a distinction between the Queen (the Crown) and her officials in New Zealand (the executive). Resonating with the legal doctrine that the Crown could do no wrong (but its officials could), he saw the Queen as the 'minister of God, and the minister of God is not supposed to do wrong'. He added, 'If wrong be done it is the fault of the executive (te Kaihapai)'.[103] Tāmihana carefully set out the case for calmness and deliberation rather than a rush to judgment and war, a course of action presented as profoundly different from the course of the governor. Hastiness was to be deplored. 'W[illia]m King says the land is his; Taylor [Teira] says it is his', but, said Tāmihana, 'I say let us find out the owner.'[104] The letter presented at Waiuku in mid-March 1860 had already indicated the view in favour of investigation. As translated by Thomas Smith, the sentiments supporting investigation were tied to the issue of whether conflict between Te Ātiawa allied to Kīngi and Europeans had already commenced: 'If hostilities have not actually taken place, the Chiefs and the Magistrates, Maori and Pakeha, should go to Taranaki that they may together see whether Te Rangitake (W. King) or the Governor is in the wrong or whether Te Rangitake or the Governor is in the right'.[105] Wī Tako Ngātata conducted an investigation on behalf of the elected king, Pōtatau Te Wherowhero, reporting in April 1860 that the 'sin is W[illiam] King's [Kīngi Te Rangitāke on the question of the Waitara episode]'.[106] In directing his comments to Te Wetini and others inclined to support Kīngi Te Rangitāke militarily, Wī Tako Ngātata counselled, 'Friends listen to me—former days were days of error, the days that succeeded were days of truth, let this be your work to obey the word of the Great Father in heaven'.[107]

Recalling Rogers' comments on Waikato above, some Māori, such as Wetini and Tāmihana, as much as Wī Tako Ngātata in his investigation, presented themselves as leaders in conditional association with aspects of Britain's empire. This sense of association harboured various interpretations and tensions, which were never resolved. Tāmihana, speaking in favour of peaceable and calm deliberation at Ngāruawāhia, implied the maintenance of association with a concept of the Crown understood as the imperial monarch across the seas but doubt as to whether her advisors based in the colonial settlements had properly interpreted the meanings of forms of association mediated

[102] Ibid. The death of Te Wetini Taiporutu in battle with the British was recorded by *The Times* in London on Monday, 14 January 1861, issue 23829, 9.

[103] Buddle, *The Maori King Movement*, 37–8.

[104] Ibid, 37.

[105] TH Smith, 15 March 1860, confidential, 'translation of the document read by Patara at the Waiuku meeting referred to by Mr Halse.... Mar[ch] 13th 1860', in Scholefield (ed), *The Richmond-Atkinson Papers*, I, 542.

[106] Wī Tako Ngātata, 10 April 1860, CO209/153, fo.460, TNA (translation).

[107] Ibid.

by 'occasional *negociation* [sic]'. In discussions reported with Gorst, Tāmihana apparently 'stuck in the ground two sticks, "One (he said) is the Maori King, the other is the Governor" '. Gorst allegedly reported that Tāmihana then 'laid on the top of the sticks a third horizontally [adding] "This (he said) is the law of God and the Queen" '. Tāmihana proceeded to trace a circle on the ground 'enclosing the two sticks [saying] "That circle is the Queen, the fence to protect all" '.[108] The conference at Ngāruawāhia was a site for debate and searching conversation, for ritualized speech-making and flourishes of rhetoric. It was also a prime place for criticisms of the governor's conduct and government to be aired. These criticisms were not made in the language of subjects but in the language of independent associates in government. In a report of April 1860 to the Secretary of State for Colonies, Browne, the governor, referred in frustration to the tendency of 'the King's Council [*rūnanga*] openly assum[ing] the right to decide on the justice of my proceedings'.[109] In discounting the claims of Kīngi to Waitara, Browne set the scene for treating the dispute as one of constitutional significance:

> It is quite true that this Sovereignty [claimed by Britain], as relates to the Maoris, has always been more nominal than real; but it is now evident that the Maoris desire a separate nationality and union in order that they may exert a real Sovereignty, the existence of which would be incompatible even with that very mild and imperfect exercise of authority which has been hitherto maintained and could not fail to bring a collision between the races.[110]

The Colonial Office itself would be treated to papers outlining the adaptability, relativities, and plurality of '*mana*' as a concept and linguistic term. Indeed, Buddle, the superintendent of the Wesleyan Mission, had already recorded in his pamphlet *The Maori King Movement* (1860), reproduced by the governor for sending to London on the Waitara dispute, that '*mana*' could be construed as signifying 'authority, power, influence'—qualities that ebbed and flowed over time and which could be found in different people at different places and times.[111] Similarly, earlier (12 July 1860), the Colonial Office had received a copy of Thomas Smith's 'Narrative of a visit to Waikato', which recounted a reference to 'W[illia]m King's right or mana as a chief over the land' albeit without any interpretative elaboration or analysis.[112] Duncan Ivison has cautioned that '[t]aking culture seriously entails taking its internal complexity seriously'.[113] He has argued persuasively that '[c]ultures are.... made up of negotiable, replaceable stuff, more patched-together and reassembled than woven of the same cloth'.[114] As befits this image of complexity, Buddle suggested (reluctantly and sceptically it must be added) a dynamic picture of political thought within the Kīngitanga: 'This word

[108] Martin, recounting a report from Gorst in 'Memorandum on our Relations with Waikato', 3 May 1861, *GBPP1862* [3040], 51, enclosed with Smith, Native Secretary's office, to Browne, 7 May 1861, 49–50 (ibid). Thomas Smith disagreed with Martin's conclusions, however, that the kīngitanga or an influential part of it did not purport to 'aim at a system wholly separate or independent'.

[109] Browne to Newcastle, 27 April 1860, CO209/153, fo.424a, TNA.

[110] Ibid, fos.425a–6.

[111] Enclosure xii in Gore Browne to Newcastle, 4 December 1860, despatch number 126 [received at the Colonial Office on 18 February 1861], CO209/157, fos.2–92a, TNA.

[112] Thomas H Smith, 'Narrative of a visit to Waikato', CO209/153, fo.436a, enclosed with Gore Browne to Newcastle, 27 April 1860 [received at the Colonial Office on 12 July 1860; printed for Parliament in March 1861], CO209/153, fos.422–31a, TNA.

[113] Ivison, *Postcolonial Liberalism*, 36.

[114] Ibid.

[*mana*] has *of late* been used in reference to land, and *now* we hear of the *mana o te whenua*—the mana of the land. What distinct idea is attached to it, is difficult to say. The disputed land at Waitara is claimed by the Maori King party because the King's mana has reached it: *Kua tae te mana o to matou Kingi ki reira*'.[115] Originally, he said, '*mana*' was a concept associated with a person's abilities to muster human resources through forming a war party for a lengthy expedition ('*he tangata whai mana*'—'a man possessing *mana*'), or to persuade others through influence ('*kupu whai mana*'—'words having influence').[116] The core impression, however, is one of adaptation and change rather than political stasis.

In any event, at a meeting at Ngāruawāhia, Buddle, Thomas Smith (the Assistant Native Secretary), Ashwell, Morgan, and Reid were made aware that Kīngi in person and Waitara as a place were regarded as subject to the effortless authority of Te Wherowhero—'the King's mana has reached it': 'With reference to W[illia]m Kingi's position at Waitara he [Te Wherowhero] said that he, W[illia]m King, had been *invited by him to return* to the land owned by his ancestors in consequence of what Governor Hobson had said to him on the subject'.[117] This authority was demonstrated by the power of invitation and direction to other Māori: '[Te Wherowhero] stated that W[illia]m King had removed to the south for a short time before the conquest by the Waikato of the Ngatiawa at Pukerangiora, he also stated that immediately previous to W[illia]m King's return the Ngatimaniapoto were occupying the Waitara but abandoned it at his request'. Smith, who had written the report for the governor, cast doubt on the bona fides of these claims to authority, pointing to the express language of the deed of purchase entered into between Hobson and Te Wherowhero and his brother. In Smith's view, their agreement to Hobson's arrangement for the purchase of land between 'Tongaporutu and Waitotera' and their acceptance of payment was sufficient to extinguish any claims that Te Wherowhero might have: 'It was evident to me that this specious line of argument had been devised for a special object, that of saving W[illia]m King's right or mana as a chief over the land—and I stated distinctly the view taken by the Gov[ernmen]t founded on the unmistakable language of the deed referred to'.[118] Yet this point captured rather nicely the different interpretations at play and the fatal lack of consensus.

Colonial officials were portrayed as incapable of bringing peaceable resolution and order to the question of territorial claims and settlements. As late as November 1860, the *Hawke's Bay Herald* reported on a meeting at Pā Whakairo (the *pā* of Tāreha Te Moananui) convened on 7 November 1860 at which attending Māori chieftains critiqued the conduct of the governor in the presence of the local Hawke's Bay provincial superintendent, Thomas Fitzgerald.[119] Land tenure, Waitara, and the Kīngitanga were all discussed. Approximately 200 Māori assembled, with Rēnata Tama-ki-Hikurangi Kawepō of Ngāti Kahungunu delivering an address and Fitzgerald responding. At that

115 Buddle, *The Maori King Movement*, 18 (emphasis added).

116 Ibid, 17.

117 Smith, 'Narrative of a visit to Waikato', CO209/153, fos.435–5a, TNA.

118 Ibid, fos.436a–7. Smith reported how 'Reference was made by me to the purchase by the Gov[ernmen]t of the whole district between Tongaporutu and Waitotera for which payment was received by himself and his brother'.

119 'Meeting at the Pa Whakairo', *Hawke's Bay Herald,* 10 November 1860. I am grateful to Richard Boast for discussing this particular *Hawke's Bay Herald* reference with me.

gathering, Kawepō invited the superintendent and all influential Europeans of Ahuriri to join with the assembled chieftains of Ahuriri 'in a sweeping vote of censure on the Governor'.[120] His speech was animated with the language of investigation: 'We were taught by former Governors that it was wrong to fight, but that everything should be settled by investigation'.[121] As with the language of Te Wetini at Ngāruawāhia, there is evidence of the perceived conditionality of the association between distinct indigenous communities and the colonial administration. Kawepō felt entitled not only to contest but to warn his listeners about the possibilities of consent to the new interpretative order of things being withdrawn if sufficient allowances were not made for generic judgments as to the qualities of colonial administration or interpretations particular to his descent-group and his locality. In referring to the monarch and the governor, Kawepō proclaimed: 'Now, my duty to that mother of mine [the Queen] is *ended, unless* she will look upon the fault of this Governor who feeds us with guns, powder, and ball and recall him, and give me a Governor who will feed me with digestible food, with Councils, with Courts of Justice, with love, and with good deeds'.[122] The richness of the language was replete with references not only to the conditionality of support for (or alignment with) the monarch but also with the hoped-for normative or moral characteristics of the Crown as a harbinger and bringer of generosity, peaceable order rather than civil strife or warring, and institutional forms able to act upon such expectations.

Allegations were made as to whether the sentiments expressed in the speech of Kawepō were the work of 'some English Missionary', operating as a ventriloquist.[123] In consequence, a printed account of the sentiments expressed on behalf of Hawke's Bay Māori gathered at Pā Whakairo was published in 1861 along with a letter from Kawepō to the superintendent of Hawke's Bay. Translating the metaphors and allusions in the speech of Kawepō proved problematic. The words '[i]t is not easy to convey an intelligible interpretation of this passage' or '[t]his is a difficult sentence to render intelligibly into English' appeared in the translator's notes.[124] In his letter to Fitzgerald, Kawepō, for one, deliberately deployed indigenized scriptural and other sacred metaphors to criticize the conduct of the governor and his officials. A key theme was to construe the behaviour as problematically novel, as disturbing the balance of forces and giving rise to unwanted instability. Such conduct was also seen as politically inept, comparing the governor unfavourably with his erstwhile competitor for pre-eminence, Pōtatau Te Wherowhero, the self-effacing, elected leader of the Kīngitanga. The narrative was laid out skilfully with reference to the pre-missionary past and to Te Wherowhero expressing disappointment at the governor's unwillingness to discuss the Waitara purchase dispassionately at a meeting convened in Waiuku. Kawepō recounted how Te Wherowhero—'the old man'—being 'vexed at the Governor avoiding a quiet discussion and investigation .... said—"Uenuku, the man-eater, used to be my god, but when the clergymen came to this land, I was told to put away my god, for the Pakeha's God was a true one, Jehovah, the preserver of man, the Creator of heaven and earth"'.[125] This change, Kawepō observed, was meant to yield a resort to the peaceable airing of

[120] Ibid.
[121] Tamakihikurangi, *Ko Te Korero me te Pukapuka a Renata Tamakihikurangi*, 10S.
[122] Ibid, 11S (emphasis added).
[123] Tamakihikurangi, *Ko Te Korero me te Pukapuka a Renata Tamakihikurangi*, preface.
[124] Ibid, 15S.
[125] Tamakihikurangi, *Ko Te Korero me te Pukapuka a Renata Tamakihikurangi*, 13L–14L.

grievances along with deliberative investigation of grievances and their possible remedy. 'When I accepted your God', so the trail of his letter went, 'I thought all wrongs were to be made the subject of investigation on great wrongs as well as little ones.'[126] This sort of language resonated with the language of a printed proclamation issued by Pōtatau Te Wherowhero through the missionary Robert Maunsell on 13 March 1860. It expressly stated how '[i]n former times your god was Uenuku the maneater' whereas 'you have a different god now, the God of Heaven'.[127]

In effect, Kawepō as much as Te Wherowhero was orphaned as a result of the Waitara affair, as 'I alone was left to worship his God, whilst he, the Governor, went off to pick up (ki te hamea haere) my castaway god, Uenuku, the cannibal'.[128] In thereby portraying the governor as an innovator and revolutionary inverter of the preceding order of things, he said, 'the Governor, the foundation of Jehovah, [has] risen up and taken Uenuku-kaitangata to Taranaki, as his god for the extermination of the people!'[129] It was the governor who had departed the actively negotiated constitution of occasional association. In doing so, such indigenous commentators and political elites could present themselves as better interpreters of the appropriate constitutional place and conduct of the incoming Crown and colonial administration than any government officials or judges. Waitara, and the acts of colonial officials in using it as a pretext to resort to war, were portrayed as acts worthy of derision and challenge. If the incoming Crown was indeed a bringer of civil peace rather than civil war as its officials claimed, then its officials were looked upon as lacking. Some Anglican clergy—Māori and European—were certainly engaged in critiquing the conduct of colonial government in the Waitara transaction and its aftermath, and marshalling Māori opinion to forge alliances of sympathy on the question. Hadfield, in particular, was associated with criticisms of Browne's policies in Taranaki. In another alleged instance of ventriloquism, the governor blamed Hadfield for inciting Māori at Ōtaki (to the north of Wellington) to prepare and sign a petition criticizing the governor for his 'unwarrantable' behaviour in the Waitara affair and recommending his recall from office.[130] Subsequent investigations by the resident magistrate Turton suggested that Hadfield and his Māori catechist had prepared the petition and pressed local Māori to sign it and claim it as their own. Turton's account reported:

> Ihakara informed us that he had had an interview with Mr Hadfield before the signing of the petition who acknowledged to having advised the procedure, but did not wish his name to be mentioned in connexion with it—that the work was really done by him & his assistant Rewai [Riwai Te Ahu], the catechist: but that Mr Hadfield did not attend the meeting so that it might appear to the English residents as the spontaneous act of the natives—that the signatures of those present were written down off hand, without much reference to the parties—that the names of the absentees &c were entered without any ref-

[126] Ibid, 14L.

[127] Translation appearing in Parkinson, '"The Path of the Perfected Law"', in *The Māori Language and its Expression in New Zealand Law*, 17, note 54.

[128] Tamakihikurangi, *Ko Te Korero me te Pukapuka a Renata Tamakihikurangi*, 14L.

[129] Ibid. For a discussion of the views of Rēnata Tama-ki-Hikurangi Kawepō, as expressed to Thomas Fitzgerald, see Head, 'Land, Authority and the Forgetting of Being', 256–7.

[130] Browne to Newcastle, 28 April 1860 [received at the Colonial Office on 12 July 1860], CO209/153, fos.483–4, TNA.

erence at all—and that his own name & those of many others of Manawatu were actually affixed under protest.[131]

Officially, the Colonial Office proved more circumspect.

An 1860 paper on Māori attitudes to the Treaty of Waitangi recounted that 'The various tribes and communities throughout New Zealand regard themselves as possessing independent sovereign powers', adding that they 'declare war and make peace, at pleasure; exercising full sway and dominion within their several territorial limits, and are extremely jealous of any direct interference with whatever they conceive as appertaining to their own political rights'.[132] The manner of speaking at, say, Ngāruawāhia was redolent of political autonomy retained with a material territorial base in contradistinction to the *mana* of the Crown—the *mana* of each being distinct. For autonomy to exist, there must be (and there was) a de facto power to exert an influence on practical outcomes and relationships with outsiders or strangers (those not of the relevant team or group). The 'material basis of autonomy is crucial', as Andrew Sharp reminds us, because 'if there is no basis, there can be no autonomy'. This very materiality denotes a power as well as the mere assertion of a right to do certain things. Autonomy 'depends for its exercise on the material capacity to deliberate and act effectively in the world'.[133] As at 1860 and 1861, native districts in which native title and customary laws prevailed were in existence—there was no need to invoke the Constitution Act to declare them to exist.

CONSTITUTIONAL REFLECTIONS—LIVING WITH INDETERMINACY AND DISAGREEMENT

From the vocabularies of Wīremu Tāmihana, Kawepō, and Te Wetini, it appeared that Māori political elites preferred their own sophisticated senses of whom or what '*the* Crown' (or '*the* Queen') was. Despite its use of the definite article 'the', the conceptual metaphor of 'the Crown' played host to a rich plurality of interpretations. These interpretations were sensitive to the empiricities of behaviour on the part of officials and itinerant magistrates, such that elements could be critiqued for different reasons and purposes at certain times but not necessarily others. Māori elites were contending with the puzzle of 'the Crown' or 'the Queen', as much as anglophone interpretative communities dwelling in worlds that were both imperial in scope and intimately colonial in dispersed settlements. It is in the practical historical engagements with these concepts that we may discern some illuminating senses of how this complicated juristic and political person 'the Crown' was understood in various settings.

As conceived here, *the* Crown was porously multi-dimensional and composite—personal (in the person of the monarch and the governor), executive, legislative, and adjudicative. These dimensions were not necessarily strictly or purely severable in that they often shared personnel or aspects of functions (adjudicative functions in dispute-

131 'Mr Turton RM to the Governor', Henry Turton to Gore Browne, 12 May 1860, CO209/154, fos.167a–8, TNA.

132 McLean, undated (c.1860), Ms-Papers-0032-0138, McLean papers, ATL.

133 Sharp, 'Justice, Self-government and Current Theories of Maori Organisation', 4.

resolution).[134] In mid-nineteenth-century colonial New Zealand we see an appreciation of these dimensional or functional aspects. Māori leaders displayed both an ability and willingness to critique features of these aspects without necessarily critiquing the person of the monarch. In its multi-dimensional guise, this conception of the Crown recalled Blackstone's references to the 'mixed nature of the crown, which is a part of the legislative, and the sole executive magistrate',[135] although, as presented here, the dimensions were broader and multifarious, traversing imperial and colonial fields. The Crown, in consisting of these various, porous dimensions, was able to engage in discursive, internal criticisms of its parts (and they of each other). These criticisms could lead to changes in elected advisors, appointed officials and councillors, resident magistrates, and jurists. Responsible ministries could be refreshed and reconfigured by electoral mandates. As such, advisors *to* and *within* the Crown changed. The Crown, as a metaphor, was something harbouring discursive processes. Indeed, the changeable denizens inhabiting the incoming Crown—whether, say, officials or politicians—mused upon the place and role of the Crown in its varied dimensions, as much as others, as well as what was to be done or what *ought* to be done.

The governor could, as Māori political leaders like Wīremu Tāmihana of Ngāti Haua and Kawepō of Ngāti Kahungunu appreciated, be severed from the Queen's person across the seas. At other points, these identities or personalities could be conflated. Still others could present the monarch rhetorically as speaking to the realm of the temporal, and the word of the deity as speaking to concerns of a spiritual nature. Hence, Tamati Hapimana Te Rangituawaru of Turanga and Tamihana Ratapu and Te Waka Perohuka of Turanga alluded to this not uncommon trope in saying 'There is but one law, the law of God for the spirit and the law of the queen for those things which concern the body and our temporal welfare'.[136] In accounting for the place of the Crown in a pre-eminently political constitution in these ways, we see not merely a descriptive series of imperial, indigenous, and colonial accounts of a political constitution, but also a set of normative accounts. That is, in the language of Hadfield, Martin, Kawepō, Tāmihana Te Rauparaha, and Wīremu Tāmihana, we discover diverse senses of what ought to occur in a moral sense and efforts at persuading others to conform to expected patterns and niceties of behaviour.

These contributions, together with those addressing the native council options in London and colonial New Zealand, also revealed three important interconnected qualities to understandings of the real life of political constitutionalism in New Zealand and its nexus with empire. First, the historical constitutional settings in the United Kingdom and colonial and indigenous New Zealand permitted a variety of interpretations about what *should* be done on a day-to-day basis in matters of politics as well as how political authority and influence *ought* to be distributed in such discursive constitutional settings. Secondly, in dealing with myriad Crown–Māori relations, the place and relevance of the Treaty of Waitangi, and native title, the strains of mid-nineteenth-century political constitutionalism as interpreted through a colonial New Zealand-

[134] Cf Hickford, 'Strands from the Afterlife of Confiscation', 171–4.

[135] Blackstone, *Commentaries on the Laws of England*, I, 151.

[136] Tamati Hapimana Te Rangituawaru of Turanga and Tamihana Ratapu and Te Waka Perohuka of Turanga, 'Reply from Ngati Kahungunu—no. 1', 14 July 1860, CO209/155, fo.67a, TNA. See also ibid, fo.66: 'So also the Queen's authority is ever whatever pertains to the body, or which concerns our temporal welfare'.

imperial nexus demonstrated that these were not worlds of court-expounded principles. Thirdly, these constitutional settings were not hermetically sealed capsules but semi-permeable and dynamic interpretative fields, regularly washed by waters driven from other shores and preoccupations. In spite of the New Zealand Constitution Act 1852, therefore, the settings of this political constitutionalism were principally left open. To put it another way, in the words of Richard Bellamy, the constitution 'must be left open *so we may rebuild the ship at sea*—employing, as we must, the prevailing procedures to renew and reform these self-same procedures'.[137] Māori chieftains presented themselves as participants in these processes and as commentators on and within a broader British world-system (of which they were members).

COMMUNAL OR TRIBAL RIGHTS, POLITICAL AUTONOMY, AND RIGHTS OF GOVERNMENT AS A PAROCHIAL AND TRANS-OCEANIC THEME—THE POLITICAL CONSTITUTIONALISM OF NATIVE TITLE, NEW ZEALAND, ALGERIA, AND THE LAW OF NATIONS

The general tenor of the official ministerial position assumed by Christopher Richmond in 1860, if not by Sewell (now out of office for a time), was that the rights of chiefly Māori *iure gentium* at the tribal or communal level to authority over territorial space, including the entitlement to determine how such space could be used by others, were seriously denuded by the first article of the Treaty of Waitangi. Richmond's analytical starting point was *ius gentium*. Prior to the Treaty, Māori communities consisted of many discrete 'nations'. It was the 'assumption of the sovereignty of the islands, under the provisions of the Treaty of Waitangi, [that] extinguished these separate nationalities, together with the rights flowing out of them'.[138] Richmond was running an argument that looked at what pre-existing Māori 'nations' had lost by virtue of the Treaty. What he denied was the retention of the customary authority of Māori chieftains *inter se* or regarding non-Māori. 'At the same time', however, 'the Treaty saved all *proprietary*, as distinguishable from *national* rights, and (subject to Her Majesty's right of pre-emption) confirmed to the native land owners the power of alienation which they had already begun to exercise'.[139]

In running this argument, Richmond further explored a theme already begun in his work on the Waitara question some seven months beforehand. In May 1860, writing for responsible ministers, Richmond said that the 'right set up by King[i] is simply the old title of the Maori chief', an imprecise characterization.[140] Treating the claims of Wīremu Kīngi Te Rangitāke as purely arbitrary, Richmond construed the behaviour of Kīngi as a mere assertion of a claimant without reason or foundation, entwined with what he characterized as a 'manorial right' or 'a species of minor sovereignty—over

137 Bellamy, *Political Constitutionalism*, 174 (emphasis added). This emphasis is also noted in the excellent article by Graham Gee and Grégoire Webber, 'What is a Political Constitution?', 288.

138 Richmond, memorandum, 3 December 1860, CO209/157, fos.125a–6, TNA.

139 Ibid, fo.126 (emphasis added).

140 Richmond, 'Memorandum by Ministers', enclosure number III, 25 May 1860, CO209/154, fo.98a, TNA.

the whole district'.[141] He doubted the bona fides of certain elite settlers supporting the claims of Kīngi—'the European apologists of King' as he called them. He believed those opposing the Waitara transaction to have concocted a mixture of English and Māori norms. Richmond averred that the right asserted on behalf of Kīngi, '[b]eing based upon neither the English nor the Maori rule, but upon a compound of the two, uniting the advantages afforded by either law to antiquated claims, this right is supposed to be also unaffected by the Waikato conquest, the consequent slavery and dispersion of the remnant of the tribe, and the transfer of the title of the conquerors to the British government'.[142] His main target here was the protest brought by Selwyn, the Bishop of New Zealand, alleging the errors of the colonial government's conduct in the Waitara purchase. Richmond considered the gravamen of Selwyn's protest to lie in the following passage:

> 1. An investigation of all questions relating to their title to land before a regular tribunal, with the usual safeguards against partiality or error, viz evidence on oath; arguments of counsel, and a right of appeal.
> 2. That military force shall not be employed till the civil power shall have been tried, and shall have been found insufficient to carry out the judgment of the court.
> 3. That inasmuch as this colony was avowedly formed, not for the acquisition of territory for the European race, but for the protection of the New Zealanders, this primary object shall not be sacrificed to the aggrandisement of the English provinces.[143]

Richmond was, however, prepared to recognize a modicum of complexity. Hence, he acknowledged, at least in May 1860: 'It may be true as is alleged, that where a tribe has a *recognised head*, such head has, according to Maori usage, a power distinct from any right of ownership, of prohibiting the alienation of any part of the lands occupied by members of the tribe'.[144] Here, the nub of the issue for Richmond was the position at *ius gentium* prior to entry into the Treaty at Waitangi and elsewhere and the legal situation following the assertion of British sovereignty from 1840. In his subsequent memorandum of December 1860, with the Waitara dispute raging through colonial politics, Richmond concluded that the second article of the Treaty of Waitangi was inconsistent with the survival of such a 'power'. In May 1860, however, he was much more circumspect, allowing his memorandum to wonder out loud, so to speak. He argued:

> The question does not, it is repeated, arise in the present case, or it would deserve consideration how far the exercise of such a right is consistent with the stipulations of the Treaty of Waitangi whereby the chiefs, parties to the Treaty 'yield to Her Majesty, the exclusive right of pre-emption over such land as the proprietors thereof may be pleased to alienate at such prices as may be agreed upon between the respective proprietors and persons appointed by Her Majesty to treat with them on their behalf'.[145]

Richmond's analysis on behalf of the responsible ministers revealed a shift since his correspondence to T King on 18 May 1857 on the authority of chieftains relative to the alienation of lands to others. There, he ventured the view that the 'right of putting a veto upon sales seems to be recognized as belonging to chiefs who do not possess the *dominium utile*', a term drawn from Roman law and *ius gentium* but noted in

[141] Ibid, fo.99a.
[142] Ibid, fos.99a–100. [143] Ibid, fos.95a–6.
[144] Ibid, fo.101a (emphasis added by Colonial Office).
[145] Ibid, fos.101–2 (emphasis added by Colonial Office).

Blackstone's *Commentaries* as well as Edward Coke's *The First Part of the Institutes of the Laws of England, or, a Commentary upon Littleton*.[146] As a term of art, *dominium utile* had been distinguished from *dominium eminens* in contemporary treatises drawing on these concepts in the law of nations. Thus, in 1846, Twiss had analysed *dominium utile* as signifying an individual's useful domain in land erected by that individual in contradistinction to 'eminent domain', or a nation's 'exclusive right of command in all places of the country which it has taken possession of'.[147] By 1857, Coke's distinction between *dominium utile* (the usufruct) and *dominium directum* was still used as a means of illustrating the point that the subject did not have absolute property in the soil but merely the usufructuary rights.[148] What is evident in 1860, however, is that Richmond did not use Sewell's conceptual strategy aired in 1864 to cope with the relations between native title and chiefly political authority over territorial space through analogizing American jurisprudence extracted from *Worcester v Georgia* (1832).[149] He did not opt for treating the conduct of Kīngi as consistent with the maintenance of internal self-government. The degree to which Richmond was expressing an official ministerial view in 1860, as distinct from a personal view (1857), is difficult to disentangle. It is conceivable that subsequent searching analysis of the question initially addressed *en passant* in personal correspondence some three years previously led to a substantive change further reinforced by a need to analyse the Waitara situation with a view to having an official policy on what was to be done.

Calls for an independent judicial tribunal to investigate the merits of the contending territorial claims of Te Teira, Kīngi, and others to the Waitara block were disputed. Purely political dimensions of the Crown and constitutional setting were seen as better suited to such labours than courts of law. A court or tribunal's legally authoritative ruminations exerting discipline on others would only impede the fluidity of political negotiations. Richmond's reasoning was presented explicitly. Investigating 'native title to land offered for sale has been left to the officers of the executive government, partly because, from the habits of the natives, the truth can be better got at by desultory conversations and examinations extending over a long space of time than by peremptory procedure of a court of law, partly, because reasons of policy ought to be taken into consideration by government which could not be admitted as elements in the decision of a judicial officer'.[150] In this manner, Richmond was alive to the complexities inherent in the human realities of disagreement and negotiation of disputed matters. Negotiation and its potential to compromise *à priori* nostrums, if any, were defended as something of value to this way of conducting politics. Richmond also admonished the bishop for his tendencies towards fixating on single issue politics rather than wider circles of concern. He commented: 'It should, however, be remembered that the philanthropist notwithstanding the high ground that he takes, which gives him perhaps an

146 Richmond to King, 18 May 1857, in Scholefield (ed), *The Richmond-Atkinson Papers*, I, 266.

147 Twiss, *The Oregon Question Examined*, 151.

148 Blackstone, *Commentaries on the Laws of England*, II, 102: 'A subject, therefore, has only the usufruct, and not the absolute property of the soil; or, as Sir Edward Coke expresses it, he has *dominium utile*, but not *dominium directum*. And hence it is, that, in the most solemn acts of law, we express the strongest and highest estate that any subject can have by these words: "he is seised thereof *in his demesne as of fee*"'.

149 As discussed in the opening to Chapter Six.

150 Richmond, 'Memorandum by Ministers', enclosure number III, 25 May 1860, CO209/154, fos.104a–5, TNA.

undue advantage in public opinion over those who are discharging the ordinary duties of life, is often found to be liable, even beyond other men, to the disturbing influences of prejudice and passion'.[151] Accentuating his point, he referred to the abolitionists in the United States: the 'Abolitionists of North America, for example, are certainly disinterested, but few statesmen will hold that they take a sober and just view of the great question of humanity to which they have devoted their lives'.[152]

Moreover, in describing the very politics of negotiability and the possibilities for departing from abstract norms of legal reasoning, Richmond advised that the 'flexible practice of the Land Purchase Department (which is under the direct control of the imperial government) admits of concessions to the natives not justifiable upon any ground of strict principle'.[153] In Richmond's opinion, it could not be unknown to the 'Bishop that the arrangement of which he complains is beneficial to the interest of the natives—if indeed it be beneficial (as his Lordship generally appears to think it) to yield to them on almost every occasion upon which there is any shred or likelihood of resistance or dissatisfaction on their part'.[154] The minister did not let matters rest there. Revelling in the analogy, he cautioned his audience that Selwyn had publicly signalled support for acquiring the Bell block in New Plymouth in the Taranaki in a pastoral letter to the members of the Church of England at New Plymouth in 1855, despite the observation that the techniques of purchase deployed in the negotiations for Bell block were comparable to those used for Waitara. Sounding a note of irony, Richmond observed that 'One of the grounds lately assigned by the imperial government for withholding the Royal Assent from the "Native Territorial Rights Bill 1858" was the likelihood that the award of the Governor in Council, or of such tribunal as His Excellency in Council might appoint for the investigation of native title, would not be acquiesced in by the contending parties'.[155] It would not have escaped Richmond's notice that the responsible ministers had recommended an adjudicating tribunal to sift through 'native territorial rights' claims in 1858 but that the chorus of opposition in the colonial settlements was voiced loudly by persons such as the Bishop of New Zealand.

Further precision on behalf of the responsible ministers within colonial New Zealand emerged later in 1860. Thus, in an elaborate memorandum dated 3 December 1860, Richmond asserted that 'the unrestricted right of alienation has in practice accompanied the right of property, whether subsisting in the tribe or in any smaller native community and that no seignorial or tribal right of controlling sales by the native owners has ever been exercised, or in anywise asserted, since the commencement of land purchases in New Zealand'.[156] He supposed that this so-called 'seignorial or tribal right' was a de facto power exercised in practice politically but without any basis in customary law. Indeed, Richmond averred that the notion of land as a 'marketable commodity' could not have emerged before the advent of Europeans: 'whatever alienations may have taken place amongst themselves were of a totally different character from such as followed upon the settlement of the country'.[157] For Richmond, it was a nonsensical exercise to pursue precedents for alienations of territory or exercises of chiefly oversight or supervi-

[151] Ibid, fos.94a–5.
[152] Ibid, fo.95. [153] Ibid, fo.105.
[154] Ibid, fos.105–5a. [155] Ibid, fos.103a–4.
[156] Richmond, memorandum, 3 December 1860, CO209/157, fo.128, TNA.
[157] Ibid, fo.126.

sion in pre-European Māori communities. To do so would be to waste research efforts in locating the non-existent or to analogize so thinly as to do so perversely. The colonial land market was the key novelty. According to Richmond, 'The subject, therefore, can receive no real illustration from the investigation of native ideas and customs prior to the advent of European, but the inquiry to be made is simply this—whether or not has the alleged right of control been recognized, or asserted, since the settlement of New Zealand'.[158] 'If not', he concluded, 'no such *right* can be supposed to exist.'[159]

In his memorandum of December, Richmond analysed deeds of purchase as having been used to acquire two classes of interest, specifically 'those made of leading chiefs, representing whole tribes (iwi): secondly, those made of sub-tribes (hapu), or of families or other comparatively small groups of individuals'.[160] He distinguished the two classes on the grounds of the level of community interest in the question and the nature of the territory. He associated transactions of the first category with the negotiations of the 'conquerors'—builders of indigenous empires, such as Pōtatau Te Wherowhero in the Waikato, and the elites of Ngātitoa associated with Te Rauparaha, for the disposition of 'large unoccupied' territories in the Taranaki and lower North Island respectively. Of the two classes of transaction, the second was the most orthodox. His illustrations of this sort of alienation included 'all' those purchases to the north of Auckland, whether by colonial officials on behalf of government or individuals, transactions with Ngāti Kahungunu in the Hawke's Bay and Wairarapa on the eastern coast of the North Island, and those with Te Ātiawa in Port Nicholson and Taranaki (Te Teira most recently). With the first class—'sales of *vacant territory*'—Richmond averred that 'the principal chiefs.... themselves [had] been the vendors'.[161] To the contrary, in 'sales of occupied territory an absolute and unquestioned right of alienation has always gone along with the *right of occupancy*, which is generally exclusive in certain Hapus or families, and not common to the whole tribe'.[162] On this basis, Richmond saw the right of alienation as an 'unrestricted' one, whether residing with the principal chieftains at the level of the *iwi* (a confederation of *hapū*) or at the more intimate *hapū* and *whānau* levels. Importantly, then, Richmond was merely doubting the claimed chiefly right of controlling transactions entered into by others within the descent-group as a distinct class of right from the right of the community to the lands it customarily used and occupied. However, due to prudential policy-driven concerns, Richmond was cautious. He counselled that 'The distinction between right and power is still faintly drawn by the natives themselves; and—dealing with them as in some sort of foreign power—it will generally be prudent to respect any authority or influence established amongst them, *de facto*, without too nice an inquiry whether that authority and influence exist strictly *de jure*'.[163]

Underlying this willingness to countenance ambiguity, Richmond was in no doubt that the justifiable 'right' was that of Te Teira's title on behalf of his own group in Waitara. It was the legitimacy of Te Teira's claim, then, that needed to be recognized as a constraint on the power claimed by Kīngi. Richmond undoubtedly appreciated that diplomacy preceding purchase required sophisticated relationship management. But this management did not extend to accepting the claimed pre-eminence of Kīngi

[158] Ibid, fos.126a–7. [159] Ibid, fo.127 (emphasis added). [160] Ibid, fo.126.
[161] Ibid, fo.128 (emphasis added). [162] Ibid (emphasis added).
[163] Ibid, fos.128a–9 (emphasis in original).

in supervising the Waitara transaction as a 'right'. If pursued, Richmond's analysis had the effect of unravelling the authority of chiefs who might present themselves as overlords of larger descent-groups or endeavour to claim such status. If understood in this way, the practices underlying this analysis would encourage competitors to principal chiefs or other sources of political influence and authority to assert their own entitlement to negotiate with outsiders, including officials of the Crown. As a maxim of government policy applied *ex post facto* to Waitara, it appeared to highlight the possibilities for exploiting potential political fractiousness within groups—inducing some *hapū* members to negotiate with colonial officials if not others. Understood in this way, the 'tribal title' was riven with internal fault lines, revealing different interpretations of what the group or varying parts of it ought to do.

Richmond's views on a manorial or seignorial right of chieftains received support from the superintendent of the Wesleyan mission, Buddle. Clearly sceptical, Buddle characterized 'manorial rights' as 'imaginary rights when claimed for New Zealand chiefs'.[164] Buddle's cautiousness was driven by intelligence to the effect that chiefs or persons of influence were not necessarily able to command territorial space. At Ngāruawāhia, Buddle recorded that 'a Waikato chief, who was adducing reasons for the King movement, remarked, "*hoko tahae*" (dishonest sales of land) was one reason'. That is, a 'chief offered land to Government and, because he was a chief, it was taken for granted the land was his own; "but", he added "you must not suppose that every chief, because he is a great man with a great name, is a great landowner. There are many great chiefs who have no land, and therefore have no right to sell".' All this left Buddle to pose the rhetorical question: 'How does this accord with manorial rights?', begging the likely answer that some chiefs of influence but no direct territorial interest other than an interest in asserting authority and political pre-eminence over others may very well have wished to assert such a claim (turning the question back on itself as to whether such behaviour reflected a de facto power or a right *de jure*).[165] Four years later the Auckland politician Carleton implied that a chieftain's entitlement to exercise political authority regarding a sale was proper and recognized by the Māori language version of the Treaty of Waitangi. Under the second article of the Treaty, 'the "entire chieftainship" [*rangatiratanga*] of their lands, of their kaingas, and of all their property, was guaranteed'.[166] It was '[o]f this chieftainship, it must be observed, no mention is made in the English version of the treaty; and it was for the exercise of this by Wiremu Kingi in 1860, that war was declared against him at Waitara'.[167]

McLean's own assessment of tribal title was also *hapū*-based. And, like Richmond, he disagreed that Kīngi had the pre-eminent voice through some overlordship status. McLean's comments were marshalled as 'remarks on a pamphlet by Sir W[illia]m Martin on the Taranaki Question': 'To assume [as Martin seemed wont to do in *The Taranaki Question*] that the whole of the Ngatiawa tribe formed but one community under one Chief holding their territory at Taranaki in common, is to ignore the actual state of things; and to take up a position which has never been held by the Ngatiawa themselves in their transactions with the Government for the sale of land'.[168] 'In previous

[164] Buddle, *The Maori King Movement*, 19. [165] Ibid, 18.

[166] Carleton, 'New Zealand', 430. [167] Ibid.

[168] McLean, undated, 'Remarks on a pamphlet by Sir W[illia]m Martin on the Taranaki Question', Ms-Group-1551, fo.1, McLean papers, ATL.

transactions', he said, 'the sub-tribes or hapus have been dealt with, and no general consent of the whole tribe, or of any Chief not immediately interested in the land under negotiation has been sought or deemed necessary by either party.'[169] He conceived of Kīngi's voice being irrelevant where his own *hapū* did not have an interest in the land concerned. If his *hapū* did have an interest in the land, then that would be a different matter.

Others consulted by the governor in private settings revealed the contest of views at work. Sewell's own reflections in April 1860 were broadly sympathetic with the position of the colonial government contra the claims of Kīngi. Yet he acknowledged 'what beyond a doubt exists and which cannot be disputed—namely a seigniorial right in the chiefs of the different tribes a sort of Dominion or Feudal Lordship, irrespective of their actual rights of occupation but confined to their proper territorial possessions'. In Sewell's view '[e]very tribe with its chief has peculiar and independent rights': 'Sometimes there is.... a Manor within a Manor, a superior lordship with a kind of subinfeudation'.[170] His musings revealed that he was initially minded to agree with the views of the Bishop of New Zealand, Selwyn, and Archdeacon Hadfield contrary to the government's preferred position on Waitara and the rights of Kīngi. Both, he noted, had assumed a 'strong *ex parte* view against the governor'. But, in examining the question for himself, 'by reference to blue books and documents connected with the purchases at Taranaki', as well as through conversations with McLean and Forsaith, he tended to support the governor's view of the Waitara dispute.[171] While supportive of a manorial or seigniorial right residing in a chieftain in respect of land in which the chief had a distinct territorial possessory interest, he did not accept the broader view of chiefs having a right of veto over tribal lands generally. 'But, says the Bishop, William King is the chief of the Taranaki Tribes and as such, abstractedly from all questions of territorial title, has a right to forbid the sale.'[172] On this issue, Sewell said '[t]hat is one of the points which is sought to be established by a sort of Land League formed amongst the natives, but which I am satisfied has no foundation in Maori custom', characterizing it as a 'mere usurpation'.[173] Understood in those terms, he regarded the claim of Kīngi as a 'sort of tyranny': 'The principle is that of a Trades Union "You shan't do as you please with your own"'.[174] Selwyn confounded this 'usurped claim', thought Sewell, with the superior lordship rights of a chieftain in a territory possessed by his descent-group. Sewell also regarded it as one of the pretences of the Kīngitanga.

Sewell, too, was critical of the role of the local Church Missionary Society and the Bishop of New Zealand. On 5 May 1860 he reported that the governor received a letter from Selwyn critical of Browne's conduct at Waitara: 'It casts all blame on the Governor and Government, and demands on behalf of the Maoris a Tribunal of Appeal against the Governor! As if the Governor were not the proper Tribunal in himself and as if his dealings with the rights of the natives had not been just'.[175] Sewell considered Browne to have made a strategic error in not having already called the General Assembly together, as he thought that body would have supplied the governor with support against the blandishments of Selwyn and Hadfield. Sewell may not have

[169] Ibid, fos.1–2.
[170] Sewell, 23 April 1860, journal of Henry Sewell, I, 65, qMs-1786, ATL.
[171] Ibid, 64. [172] Ibid, 64–5. [173] Ibid, 65.
[174] Ibid, 65–6. [175] Ibid, 80.

appreciated Browne's earlier strategic decision to await receipt of a response from the Colonial Office as to the proposals for a native council contained in the governor's covering despatch of 20 September 1859. Delays in London occasioned by the resort to the legislature in Westminster had effectively weakened Browne's favoured strategy. As it was, a new session of the General Assembly did not begin until 30 July 1860.

Richmond's memorandum of December 1860 formed part of a lengthy report furnished by the governor at the request of Fortescue. Fortescue's request of 27 August 1860 revealed an earnest desire to test the merits of the Waitara imbroglio, the conduct of Kīngi, and, implicitly, the conduct of the colonial administration.[176] Received at the Colonial Office on 18 February 1861, the purpose of Browne's report was to furnish information 'upon the question of an alleged right, distinct from one of property, existing in the chief of a tribe to assent to or forbid the sale of any land belonging to the members of a tribe, in cases where all the owners are willing to sell, and how far such a right has been or ought to be recognised by the Crown'.[177] In addition, Browne was asked to give Newcastle his 'own views, and all the information in my power, on the further questions whether "there are reasons, apart from the Treaty of Waitangi, in favo[u]r generally of the recognition of such a right, and whether they justify the claims of Wiremu Kingi on the present occasion" '.[178] Browne consulted with Richmond, but also referred to a host of other opinions extracted from recent or less-recent sources, including the views of Selwyn, the Bishop of New Zealand, together with those of Martin, Clarke senior, William Spain, the Native Board of Enquiry of 1856, the Reverend Thomas Buddle, superintendent of the Wesleyan mission, Archdeacon Octavius Hadfield, Archdeacon Maunsell, and the former Attorney General, William Swainson. Some of these opinions were consciously historical in that they did not purport to be *au fait* with the troubled events of 1860, as with the report of the Board of Inquiry, issued in 1856.[179] To officials at the Colonial Office, this flotsam of reported elite opinion was received as congenial to the governor's preferred interpretation of the Waitara purchase, with Fortescue noting it as 'greatly confirm[ing] my own belief that the Gov[erno]r has acted with substantial justice in the matter of W. King. Print above—add to the papers for Parl[ia]m[en]t?'[180]

Yet the opinions on native title were various, leading the governor to write in his report: 'whatever may be the true theory of native tenure, there is nothing more certain than that there exist among the native tribes themselves no fixed rules by which the practice of Government in its dealing with them for land could be grounded'.[181] The result, said Browne, was that government had to negotiate case by case with a range of different communities and effectively to find out what modes of dealing were best adapted to securing a sound alienation of land—sound in the sense of being less prone to exciting agitation and objection. Resorting to McLean's presentation to the House of Representatives in August 1860 as evidence of an official 'whose experience

176 Fortescue to Gore Browne, 27 August 1860, CO209/154, fos.133–7, TNA.

177 Browne to Newcastle, 4 December 1860, CO209/157, fo.2a, TNA.

178 Ibid, fos.2a–3.

179 For the report of the board of inquiry, see Ligar, Nugent, Daldy, and Smith, 9 July 1856, enclosed with Browne to Labouchere, 23 July 1856, *GBPP1860* [2719], 236 *et seq.*

180 The papers were printed in 'Papers relating to the Recent Disturbances in New Zealand', *GBPP 1860* [2747] (printed March 1861), 169 *et seq.*

181 Browne to Newcastle, 4 December 1860, CO209/157, fos.9a–10.

extends over more than twenty years, and who has bought twenty millions of acres for the Crown', Browne highlighted the political and conceptual fluidity of the situation. McLean viewed the 'tribal right' as something which 'varies so much in different parts of the country' owing to variations in custom from location to location.[182] If asked to explain the 'tribal right', McLean said, 'I should like to know what particular part of the country is referred to, as the custom which prevails in one place does not in another'. Reminiscent of the English notion of the *lex loci*, McLean stressed the sensitivity of tribal rights in land to time and place.[183] There were 'very wide exceptions to any general rule, and the exception is wider than the rule'. A tribal right was seen as *sui generis*, not susceptible to abstract theorizing in advance. As a result, McLean saw a 'tribal right' as suggesting a process rather than a substantive concept—identifying who possessed authority to consent to a transfer of territory in circumstances where the market in land might incentivize a multiplicity of claimants requiring satisfaction. With some descent-groups or tribes, therefore, 'the different *hapus* (*families*) must be consulted, in others the Chiefs'. In the main, the 'various *hapus* which comprise a tribe most frequently have the right of disposal, but not always'.[184] What was required, McLean averred, was a process of ascertaining the range of possible interests rather than any searching and discriminating inquiry into the relative quality and content of particular claims: 'You must discover the rights of the parties by enquiry of the people in the district where land is situate and elsewhere'.[185] Because customs varied in different areas, identifying the 'who' was fraught with the risks of igniting irritation on the part of potential vendors or even worse forms of response: 'In the Ngatiawa tribe [in the Taranaki area, including the Pekepeka block adjoining the Waitara River] a family of three or four people has been regarded as empowered to dispose of its common property: they have enjoyed this right for the last eighteen years'.[186] A major difficulty was that the forging of native title as a substantive concept consisting of recognizable attributes or characteristics was inextricably tied to the question of alienating native title (transferring lands subject to native title to strangers)—a relatively novel practice associated with the introduction of the land market in New Zealand and the proliferation of deeds of purchase.

The key point distilled by the governor on the nature and extent of native title was that 'The result of all these enquiries has certainly not been to present a very clear idea of what native title is, and still less of what it is not'.[187] In the midst of the unsettled nature of the substance of native title, the governor could only 'look forward.... to the time when the Natives will be prepared for the establishment of a tribunal in which their varying customs may acquire some settled form, and to the decisions of which they will yield a peaceful submission'.[188] To colour the reading of the disparate views, the governor could only report: 'Chief Justice Arney said on the Legislative Council the other day, "I have found much inconsistency and contradiction but no novelty, and have derived this consolation, namely of reflecting that little as I know of the native title, of the (so called) maori law of real property, the generality of people, even of the learned—the '*periti*', know little more" '.[189] Orthodox techniques to collect a range of specialist viewpoints

[182] Ibid, fo.10.
[183] Cf Thompson, 'Custom, Law and Common Right', in *Customs in Common*, 97–8.
[184] Browne to Newcastle, 4 December 1860, CO209/157, fos.10–10a, TNA.
[185] Ibid, fo.10a. [186] Ibid. [187] Ibid, fos.5–5a.
[188] Browne to Newcastle, 4 December 1860, *GBPP1860* [2747], 196.
[189] Ibid, 170.

based on experience yielded little in the way of exact consensus. Yet, claimed Browne, 'there is no reason to doubt that notwithstanding the variety of rules in different localities and among different tribes, the title to land among the natives of this country was a tribal rather than an individual title'.[190] Indeed, the substantive relationship between a broadly collective interest, such as 'tribal title' or a 'tribal right' in respect of territorial space, and those interests to which, say, individuals might lay claim exercised many of the gathered opinions. In presenting the views of the contributors, the governor's dispatch claimed with reference to Selwyn's views that the 'individual's right to possess whatever portion of land was *subdued by the labo[u]r of each member of the tribe*, was undoubtedly recognised and transmitted by descent from generation to generation, but the right to alienate land so held was one, the exercise of which was undertaken by the obvious necessity of maintaining the rights of the tribe of securing its right to service of from each member, and of preserving its land from going into the hands of strangers'.[191] This was the language of a tribal *demos*, all of whose members were relevant to decision-making, and not the language of deference to a smaller chiefly class or elite exerting constraint. The consequences were significant, as the process of quieting 'tribal rights' prompted government negotiators to resort to a broader grouping of claimants as having rights collectively, and not merely chieftains.[192]

We see concepts of native title and customary rights more broadly conceived under pressure in the Waitara context. Locating Kīngi as having a right in the land itself neatly evaded the conceptual challenges posed by a notion of customary powers of decision-making or regulatory powers over the alienation of territorial space to others—at its crudest, the political ability and authority to say 'yes' or 'no' to a particular course of action. Buddle saw this as an innovation, possibly due to the Kīngitanga (and others) adapting a concept of European provenance—the uniting *mana* of the Queen across disjointed and scattered rather puny albeit increasingly populous colonial settlements. The conceptual repertoire of legalism, as practised by authorities as diverse as McLean, Busby, Buddle, and Hadfield, was not treated as being especially adept at dealing with or inculcating a sense of change and dynamism within Māori approaches to the colonial land market. Change within Māori communities vis-à-vis land was seen as inauthentic and politically capricious.

Although critical of the Waitara acquisition, Hadfield's views before the House of Representatives from August 1860 were appended to Browne's report as those of an authority on native tenure. In presenting evidence at the bar of the House of Representatives at that time, Hadfield recognized his comments to be restricted to the state of Māori political communities, as he understood them to be in the period before 1840. He wished to 'guard himself' by 'premising' what he was saying on Māori tenure to land 'as it existed prior to the establishment of the British Government in the Colony, and not since that event'.[193] Importantly caveated in such a way, Hadfield regarded any claim that chiefs might have to 'power over some portions of land' to be a 'question-

[190] Browne to Newcastle, 4 December 1860, CO209/157, fos.5a–6.

[191] Ibid, fo.6 (emphasis added).

[192] A point also made in Head, 'Land, Authority and the Forgetting of Being in Early Colonial Maori History', 198.

[193] Hadfield, Appendix A, ix, 'Extracts from opinions of various authorities [on native tenure]', *GBPP 1860* [2747], 203.

able right or power'.[194] All this was predicated in Hadfield's account on a chief holding his position by virtue of a 'double title'. First, his title to the position 'must arise from his undoubted descent through a long line of well known ancestors from the original head of the tribe'. Secondly, his title depended on what Hadfield called a 'more democratic principle'. The chieftain 'must be the *acknowledged* and the *elected* head of the tribe'.[195] The chief was a personification of the tribe (possibly temporarily) since he was the 'representative of the territorial right of the tribe, not because he is descended from numerous ancestors of noble blood, but because he has in fact been recognized as the guardian as well as the mouth-piece of the rights of the tribe'.[196]

How change affected native title also underscored Merivale's appreciation of such title as a problem of imperial and colonial government. Coincidentally, in May 1861 Merivale saw fit to refer to the 'tribal right' as an innovative species of proprietary interest confounding the labours of colonization.[197] In this context, the perceived failures of France in colonizing Algeria allowed comparisons with settlements in New Zealand. Thus, the 'most salient difficulty in Algerian colonization seems to be precisely the same with that which we experience, on an infinitely smaller scale, in part of New Zealand'.[198] While 'individual claims of natives to landed property in Algeria' were seen as 'not very considerable', so-called '[t]ribunal claims are very large; that is to say, a native tribe claims a large tract of land for its nomade [*sic*] occupation by flocks and herds and wandering villages, in common right'.[199] 'To get rid of this class of claims in New Zealand', observed Merivale, 'has been the cautious and gradual work of many years, and as yet very far from completed.' Although 'French authorities have as yet no more than looked at the problem', it seemed agreed that 'its solution is indispensable before the work of real colonization can begin'.[200] Algeria was a fitting motif, as it was seen as a place of warring and problematic colonial settlement.[201] Once more, in the unspoken context of Waitara, Merivale was able to air his reservations regarding the particular manner in which 'tribal title' had been accorded recognition. He ascribed the 'system adopted in New Zealand as to the so-called "tribal ownership" of land by the natives' as 'one of the most unfortunate instances of the misapplication of notions founded on English law to the case of savages'.[202] The misapplication had arisen, thought Merivale, in the translation of the practices of indigenous communities into an 'absolute right of an owner to the soil, according to the strict European usage'.[203] All that Māori communities recognized, asserted Merivale, were 'some.... rights over the soil' *inter se*, whereby '[o]ne tribe respected the boundary of another, unless in cases of disputed right'.[204] Yet, 'by a few words of conveyancing language' used in the second article of the Treaty of Waitangi, the ' "tribes" in their collective character were recognized as the private landowners of the whole of a great island, into which at the same time European settlers were poured by thousands'.[205] It was here in the 1861 edition of

[194] Ibid.

[195] Ibid, 203–4 (emphasis in original). [196] Ibid, 204.

[197] Here, in using the date 'May 1861', I am simply referring to the date of the preface in Merivale's second edition.

[198] Merivale, *Lectures on Colonisation and Colonies*, 2nd edn, 68 (note).

[199] Ibid. [200] Ibid.

[201] For an overview of the early decades of French colonization in Algeria, see Rogan, *The Arabs*, 112–19.

[202] Merivale, *Lectures on Colonisation and Colonies*, 2nd edn, 497 (note).

[203] Ibid. [204] Ibid. [205] Ibid.

his *Lectures on Colonisation and Colonies* that Merivale stated how 'Lord Grey.... on very strong grounds of abstract reason, and in conformity with the general understanding of nations, [contended] "that the savage inhabitants of New Zealand have no right *of property* in land which they do not occupy, and which has remain unsubdued for the purposes of man" '.[206] The 'assertion of general principle', however, was uttered too late to 'be of much practical use' in the wake of the Treaty of Waitangi. To Merivale, the departure from 'general principle' had required a completely different policy: 'If the doctrine that the natives were the absolute owners of the soil, and not compellable to part with it, was to be maintained, British settlers should have been excluded and the Northern island maintained as a native reserve'.[207]

'Tribal title', however, was important to the New Zealand authorities consulted by Browne. These contributors to Browne's missive on native title—Richmond, Martin, Selwyn, and others—spoke a shared language without religious resonance, locating the questions of native title and political authority squarely within legalistic and historical registers. Importantly, the *loci* for these nuanced discussions were not the adjudicative spaces of the colonial courts. The making of native title—the better understanding of native title through contest and negotiation—was an exemplar of the political constitution in action. Supreme Court proceedings in *Meurant v Keir* (1854) and *Busby v White* (1859) either failed to address the issue or neatly avoided it when it was raised in the submissions of legal counsel. Even with jurists participating in disputes regarding native title and Waitara, the chosen vehicle of reference was that of the published pamphlet or memorandum. In July 1860 a justice of the Supreme Court, Alexander Johnston, recognized in a series of notes that:

> a vague idea of power, influence, right, quasi sovereignty or lordship, derived from the tribal acquisition of the land, called the 'mana' of the land,—the shadow as distinguished from the substance,—but even if this 'mana' was vested in the head Chief, or in other Chiefs, which is improbable, it does not seem to have given them any beneficial rights, or any power of disposal or control over the property in the land without, or contrary to, the assent, express or implied, of the body of the tribe.[208]

Adderley's casting of the Waitara dispute in 1869 encapsulated this point of dispute: 'In 1859, a disputed sale of land—the Waitara block, over which, through the owner, Teira or Taylor, had accepted what he considered its value, yet William King, the Chief of the Tribe, claimed seignory, and imposed his veto of sale—led to a conflict with natives'.[209] In sum, Adderley construed the case as 'one of *læsa majestas* in the eyes of the Chief, and brought to test the claims of the "Land League" formed by the natives in 1848 to prevent any further sales of land, and the pretensions of the "King movement", whereby, ignoring the paternal government, benefits, and pensions of the Queen, the natives asserted their own government still, as if in the absence of any other'.[210] These debates, then, grappled not only with questions of native title but also with issues relating to rights of government and the constitutional distribution of authority within colonial New Zealand.

[206] Ibid. [207] Ibid, 498 (note).
[208] Johnston, *Notes on Maori Matters*, 13.
[209] Adderley, *Review of 'The Colonial Policy of Lord J Russell's Administration'*, 142–3.
[210] Ibid.

'IT SEEMS AGREED THAT NATIVE TITLE IS MARVELLOUSLY COMPLEX'

Finally, for all the presentation of coherent albeit contesting and contested views from New Zealand sources, the Colonial Office and its political masters simply saw unresolved political, conceptual, and legal complexity and indeterminacy. In the House of Commons Fortescue said: 'In dealing with the natives in regard to land the Government proceeded by way of direct negotiation with the native owner, obtaining the consent to the disposal of property of those who were looked upon as having a title to sell it, being guided in each individual case by the customs prevailing in the particular district in which the land happened to be situated'.[211] Irrespective of any concerns regarding the specific details of the Waitara transaction, Fortescue expressed the view that process was undeniably significant to any question of the alienation of Māori territory. This was especially so in circumstances where 'there did not exist in New Zealand any such native title or claim to land as could be treated as a uniform and definite code of law, the native customs with respect to the ownership of land varying in different parts of the country'.[212] Although the South Island was considered to be quiescent, 'The natives in the northern island were, to a great extent, merely nominal subjects of the Crown, living apart from the Europeans in a state of semi-independence, and all dealings with them, as in the case of those respecting land, had hitherto been carried on by means of negotiation rather than of the regular and ordinary law of the Colony'.[213] These views also suffused parts of the periodical literature, with an article on 'The Maori War' appearing in the *Dublin University Magazine* published in London in February 1861 stating that 'native tenure is of precarious kind, and native title very vague' and elsewhere '[i]t seems agreed that native title is marvellously complex'.[214] This article also focused on the inability of the Supreme Court to treat native title as cognisable in the English common law of real property, citing the chief justice, Arney, in support of this view: 'Owing to the great delicacy of the questions which arise between natives and settlers, and the difficulty of adjudicating on all native affairs, the ordinary courts of the colony have no power here'.[215]

CASTING WAITARA AS A CONSTITUTIONAL MOMENT—MARTIN'S *THE TARANAKI QUESTION* AND A BEGINNING TO THE WARRING OF PAMPHLETS

Waitara was cast as a constitutional moment. And Martin treated it thus, as had Māori in May 1860 and Kohimarama in July 1860. In Martin's hands, Waitara also proved to be a fertile field. It enabled him to traverse his own sense of constitutional narratives and histories—to place Waitara in English, as well as colonial, histories. He composed a pamphlet, *The Taranaki Question*, which was divided into six tell-tale chapters: 'Native tenure of land', 'The Waitara purchase', 'The points in dispute', 'The investigation',

211 Fortescue, 19 April 1861, *HPD*, 3rd series, 19 April 1861, vol 162, cols 825–6.
212 Ibid, col 826. 213 Ibid.
214 Anonymous, 'The Maori War', 176 and 178. 215 Ibid, 179.

'The resort to force', and 'The consequences'. In his introductory salvo in *The Taranaki Question*, Martin expressly announced the pamphlet as 'printed for circulation among the Members of the Imperial Parliament and Members of the General Assembly of New Zealand'. In essence, in his opening observations on the wrongs of the Waitara transaction, Martin perceived the transaction and its consequences as demonstrating a failure of governmental process. To Martin, it revealed the presence of arbitrariness without remedy at the heart of colonial government, rather than anything conspicuously novel regarding native title. Martin lamented the absence of 'some tribunal perfectly independent of the Government, wielding the full powers of a Court of Justice, and subject to the same checks and safeguards'.[216] It echoed Blackstone's discussion, in the first volume of his *Commentaries on the Laws of England*, of the 'auxiliary subordinate rights of the subject', specifically that right to apply to 'the courts of justice for redress of injuries'.[217]

In the particular context of disputes over the acquisition of the Pekapeka block abutting the Waitara River, this absence of a profoundly cherished protection for British subjects was felt keenly. It rendered subjects prone to having a precious right impaired—a right, Martin argued, that all British subjects shared. This right was that subjects were protected against the executive government ousting them from their property or otherwise depriving them of any claimed right until 'the question between the Crown and the subject has been heard and determined by some competent tribunal'.[218] 'If there was no existing tribunal, the duty of the Government was to establish one.'[219] Previous land commissions investigating pre-January 1840 purchases from Māori operated as courts, Martin suggested, providing useful models for the sort of customized independent tribunal he considered appropriate for addressing contested evidence as to indigenous proprietary claims.[220] The divergent views of Māori political actors would be reconciled or, failing that, their disputes as to claims of indigenous property would be resolved authoritatively through the agency of a competent tribunal. In this, indigenous systems of thought regarding territorial claims and communal authority would not necessarily be determinative although Martin regarded them as informative. Implicit in Martin's approach, however, was that an arbitral or judicial authority partly or even completely extraneous to the relevant indigenous community or communities would decide. Uttered with confidence, Martin thought that independent investigation alone could resolve the relativities of these customary claims—the comparative strengths and weaknesses of each. Treating such disputes as law suits or as disagreements requiring arbitration would preserve the sense of public peace.

In presenting this argument, Martin was at pains to demonstrate an awareness of the significance of an inter-Māori-European form of customary negotiations—a lengthy set of conversations—as a precursor to any transaction to acquire territorial space from Māori. 'A sort of usage had existed from the beginning of our land purchasing',

216 Martin, *The Taranaki Question*, 46.

217 For an overview, see Lieberman, 'The Mixed Constitution and the Common Law', 345.

218 Martin, *The Taranaki Question*, 46.

219 Ibid, 60.

220 Subsequently, in 1861, Martin noted that the 'Land Claims Courts were not cited by me "as instances of the satisfactory working of a jurisdiction over Native Territorial Rights". They have no such jurisdiction. They were referred to as shewing that the Colonial Legislature had again and again created Courts of Inquiry possessing powers and means for ascertaining facts, which Mr Parris did not possess' (Martin, *Remarks on 'Notes published for the New Zealand Government'*, 49).

said Martin, 'that the outside boundaries should be laid down before the money was paid.'[221] More recently, it had become 'customary to pay the first instalment before the survey'. At that point, the survey 'was not taken as an assertion that all parties had consented, but rather that all *known* claimants had consented'.[222] Martin appreciated that the process of survey itself 'would probably bring out those claimants who were as yet unknown'.[223] These distinct steps, punctuating a series of conversational engagements, were the stuff of formulating a *modus vivendi*, recorded by way of the conveyancing text included within a deed of purchase (although the deed, in its reductionist and ritualistic format, would not necessarily reflect all that passed in these prior negotiated moments let alone the relational nuances). In this fashion, although Martin did not explore or acknowledge the point, a negotiated process of acquiring territory through deeds of purchase, with a distinctly European provenance, had been increasingly de-Europeanized and indigenized in those areas where deeds had been produced: 'When the preliminary survey, or attempt at a survey, had served its proper purpose, and brought out a large number of adverse claimants, it then became the duty of the Government to take one of two courses'.[224] It could, explained Martin, 'either.... stay its hand for a time, after the manner of former Governments, until the adverse claimants agreed to the sale'. Alternatively, 'if it was thought wise and necessary to proceed, notwithstanding the adverse claimants, [the colonial administration could then move] to disprove their claims and establish its own right before some competent tribunal'.[225] Indeed, these deeds of purchase understandably buttressed the stress placed within anglophone colonial settlement on interpreting the behaviours aired in these negotiations as preliminaries to a conveyance of land rather than a demonstration of interpersonal political alliance.

As customized as these localized forms of negotiation may have been, they remained prone to interpretations beyond the ken of Māori participants as much as European negotiators. Māori negotiators and their communities became increasingly vulnerable to a literate text-based culture of sale and the myopic focus of policy, both imperial and colonial, on the alienation of native title to ease pressures in favour of expanding colonial settlements. That is, the very legalistic repertoire of conveyancing accentuated this vulnerability. The deed of purchase itself was treated as emblematic of the extinguishment of native title. In that sense, therefore, the text of the deed played host to an inrush of norms associated with English legal interpretation, leaving native title as something vanquished and eaten up, bidden farewell, and sent away. What is not disclosed in this passage, and Martin displayed no sensitivity towards it as an issue either in *The Taranaki Question* or elsewhere, was how the *process* of identifying all possible claimants, or as many as could be identified, whether those claimants were supportive of, or adverse to, entering into a transaction with colonial officials, had the effect of redefining the relevant public for a transaction in a manner less deferential to chiefly elites.[226] In other words, the nature of the relevant *demos* to a transaction was expanded to include all persons who might have individual claims as much as collective ones. Selecting a 'competent tribunal' could potentially reinforce the underlying process of detaching questions of political authority from the claims process regarding

[221] Martin, *The Taranaki Question*, 72. [222] Ibid (emphasis added).
[223] Ibid. [224] Ibid, 72–3. [225] Ibid, 73.
[226] Head, 'Land, Authority and the Forgetting of Being', 116–17.

territorial space. None of this, then, is to argue that the grammar of custom, of tribal title or tribal rights and powers, developed within New Zealand, adequately captured the sinuosities or dynamics of Māori political economies in flux or that Māori politics completely grasped the interior discursive worlds lying behind rich, multifarious discourses, although strands of their oratory and correspondence were carried across the seas to London.

Analogizing English and colonial pasts with the present was neither unsurprising nor an unconventional technique. As witnessed in Chapter Five, Fenton had done the same in his 1858 work on proposals for native title.[227] Martin resorted to Anglo-Saxon terms of '*folcland*' ('folkland' or 'people-land') and '*bocland*' ('bookland' or 'charter-land').[228] Martin's approach to constitutional history and to the histories of legal institutions and tenure in land conformed to existing forms of analysis already well-known among literate political opinion in the United Kingdom. In citing well-known whiggish authors, Francis Palgrave and Henry Hallam, Martin selected a well-trodden path in endeavouring to persuade an imperial ministry comprising members familiar with such authors, and to present the conventionality of New Zealand. Indeed, the introductory bid of his argument in *The Taranaki Question* was to illustrate the Victorian problems it posed as anything other than quixotic or unique. Using the past as a guide to the present, he considered *folcland* as corresponding to 'the Native Tenure' and *bocland* to the tenure obtained under a Crown grant.[229] Drawing on Henry Hallam's multi-volume work *View of the State of Europe during the Middle Ages*, Martin presented Anglo-Saxon ancestors to England's present as displaying a transition from clanship to nationality, a change with which Thomas Arnold, the liberal Anglican scholar, would have been familiar. *Folcland* was the sort of proprietary interest relevant to a clan-based community. It might be occupied in common, or possessed in severalty; and in the latter case it was probably parcelled out to individuals in the *folcgemot*, or court of the district, and the grant attested to by the free men who were then present.[230] With reference to the Waitara case and the concept of 'tribal title' generally, Martin recounted, again relying on Hallam, how *folcland* could not be alienated in perpetuity: 'therefore on the expiration of the term for which it had been granted, it reverted to the Community, and was again distributed by the same authority'.[231] Quoting Hallam, Martin noted *bocland* to be territory severed from the mass of *folcland*, and converted into an alienable estate.[232] At the time of the Treaty of Waitangi, Martin proceeded to argue, the 'alleged right of an individual member of a Tribe to alienate a portion of the land of the Tribe was wholly unknown'.[233] Hallam's *The constitutional history of England from the accession of Henry VII to the death of George II* was used to demonstrate the application of tribal right in Ireland, illustrating how a chieftain was entitled to make a fresh distribution of proprietary stakes in land amongst all tribal residents (not simply progeny) upon the death of the principal proprietor: 'The policy of this custom doubtless sprang from the habit of looking on the tribe as one family of occupants, not wholly divested of its original right by the necessary allotment of lands to particular individuals'.[234]

[227] Fenton, *Observations on the State of the Aboriginal Inhabitants of New Zealand*, 42.

[228] Wickham, *Framing the Early Middle Ages*, 314–26; Wormald, *The Making of English Law*.

[229] Martin, *The Taranaki Question*, 9.

[230] Ibid, 8. [231] Ibid, 9. [232] Ibid. [233] Ibid.

[234] Hallam, *The constitutional history of England from the accession of Henry VII to the death of George II*, II, 832, cited in Martin, *The Taranaki Question*, 8.

Indigenous communities were the *loci* of 'custom'. But the point that there were many *loci*—Richmond's 'nations'—and not simply a single *locus*, was lost sight of. In Martin's account Māori were incorporated within the body politic *qua* subjects albeit insufficiently so.[235] This insufficiency was due to a lack of shared governmental and adjudicative institutions able to engage in deliberative and disinterested dispute-resolution. Exacerbating this feature was the absence of a visible institutional presence for colonial administration overall. What Martin characterized as 'one accidental function'—that of the pre-emptive negotiator for territorial space—had 'been ever active', whereas the 'proper functions of the Colonial Government', those of imparting 'law and order', had been neglected. Resonating with the theme of 'occasional *negociation* [sic]' to which Fortescue resorted in March 1861, Martin stressed that '[i]n many parts of the country, there was no indication of the Queen's sovereignty; the Natives scarcely knew the Government, except as a purchaser of Land'.[236] This want of government appropriate to the requirements of indigenous communities, coupled with a desire to obtain institutions, was ascribed to a unique conjunction of political history in both indigenous polities within New Zealand and colonial society itself. Martin asserted that significant turning points had occurred in the 'political history of both races': first, the 'earliest working of the system of Parliamentary Government amongst the Colonists'; secondly, the 'wide spread movement amongst the Natives towards some regular system of law and organisation for themselves'.[237] In exploring the Waitara quagmire, Martin argued that the circumstances called for the design of novel institutions. He implied, in particular, the creation of specifically designed courts or a native council operating in an itinerant fashion from district to district. Throughout the pamphlet, Martin disparaged the 'resort to force', condemning any approach to colonial administration predicated on 'terrorism'. His line of assault was both orientated towards deficient processes in government and the absence of appropriate institutional configurations. Similarly, diagnosing the root causes of the Kīngitanga as a 'desire for good government' allowed responsible ministers in colonial government to repeat a refrain that domesticated the movement as something that would not have arisen had British institutions been effectually employed beyond colonial settlements.[238]

This institutional deficiency was also expressed jurisprudentially in the incommunicability of native title to the norms of English real property law—the *ius privatum* of property rights. The machinery of a tribunal was required to explore ways of bridging these points of incommensurability. In a revealing passage Martin considered it unnecessary to highlight the 'practical difficulties in the way of the Native claimants, supposing they desired to protect themselves by legal means against this invasion of their land, or to consider the circumstances which disable men without knowledge of our language and our customs, and with little money, from applying to a remote Court'.[239] But by merely mentioning these issues he did, of course, highlight practical observations regarding the accessibility of the ordinary courts. In a comparable

[235] Cf McHugh, *Aboriginal Societies*, 177.

[236] Martin, *The Taranaki Question*, 106.

[237] Ibid, 85.

[238] For example, William Fox, 8 October 1861, 'Memorandum of Ministers on the position of the Colony at the date of the arrival of Sir George Grey chiefly in relation to [the] native insurrection', CO209/164, fos. fo.21, TNA.

[239] Martin, *The Taranaki Question*, 73.

rhetorical fashion, he traversed how it was unnecessary to 'inquire whether they could have proceeded effectually against officers who would have justified their acts under the authority of the Governor; the Governor himself not being liable to an action in the Colony for any act done in his public capacity'.[240] Hadfield had already anticipated Martin's line of criticism on the practicalities of access to the courts, if not its exact details, in his own first major contribution to the debate on 29 May 1860, in a letter to the Duke of Newcastle, published in London. He commented that 'If, indeed, an Englishman were the sufferer, either the Courts of law or the public press would afford a sufficient guarantee that the injustice would be remedied'.[241] Nevertheless, 'when an aboriginal chief is affected by such an act of injustice, neither of these avail him: he may be two hundred miles distant from any Judge of the Supreme Court; and he fails to enlist the sympathy of the public press'. Not unexpectedly, Hadfield had not addressed the jurists' concerns about whether native title in customary law was readily amenable to consideration in the Supreme Court of New Zealand or whether the Supreme Court would be sufficiently flexible in developing the resources to accommodate customary notions of title. Martin was, however, interested in demonstrating the alleged conceptual incommunicability between English common law and conceptions of native title.

In this context, reference was made to the officially published opinion of Richard Bethell and Henry Keating, the law officers of the Crown in London, on the question of the amenability of native title to judicial consideration in the Supreme Court. As discussed in Chapter Six, the opinion addressed the possibility of Māori descent-groups who occupied land in common under native title meeting the requirements of the electoral franchise under section 7 of the New Zealand Constitution Act. Bethell and Keating interpreted the qualifying words 'freehold estate in possession', a 'leasehold estate in possession', and a 'householder.... occupying a tenement' appearing in section 7 as creatures of English law. '[I]t must of necessity therefore follow', they opined, 'that the subject of householding occupancy and tenement, and their value in native districts, are not matters capable of being recognized, ascertained, or regulated by English law.'[242] The opinion concluded briskly that 'we are of opinion that natives cannot have such possession of any land, used or occupied by them in common as tribes or communities, and not held under title derived from the Crown, as would qualify them to become voters under the provisions of the 7th and 42nd sections of the 15th and 16th Victoria c.72'.[243] The precise extract of the opinion from which Martin quoted was that addressing the possibilities of the colonial courts considering actions for trespass where Māori complained of transgressions of native title. The relevant question, as posed by the law officers, was expressed as follows:

> But suppose in a district of native land, lying within the limits of an electoral district, that one native by consent of the rest is permitted to have exclusive possession of a piece of land, on which he builds a native hut for his habitation, but is afterwards turned out, or trespassed on by another native; could he bring an action of ejectment or trespass in the Queen's Court in New Zealand? Does the Queen's Court exercise any jurisdiction over real property in a native district?[244]

240 Ibid, 73–4.
241 Hadfield, *One of England's Little Wars*, 3.
242 Law Officers' opinion, 7 December 1859, CO209/152, fo.290, TNA.
243 Ibid, fo.291a.
244 Ibid, fos.290a–1.

In answer, they responded: 'We presume these questions must be answered in the negative, and that it must of necessity therefore follow that the subject of householding occupancy and tenement, and their value in native districts, are not matters capable of being recognized, ascertained, or regulated by English law'.[245] At this point, Martin was not committed to accepting the law officers' opinion as correct. It assisted the tenor of his argument overall, however. Carefully caveating his reference to their advice with the words '[i]f this view be correct', he observed that it followed that 'William King and his people had no legal and peaceable means of redress, through any tribunal capable of entertaining their suit'.[246] Given such a position, it was telling (Martin implied) that the colonial administration had not proposed 'any mode of settling the question by arbitration'.

The English common law itself, therefore, was not seen as supplying, at least incontestably, an especially accommodating recognition of Māori interpretations of 'custom' regarding native title. Yet it was possible to yield a comparable approach without suggesting complete incommunicability or incommensurability. As the chief justice, George Arney, and the other judges of the New Zealand Supreme Court, wrote subsequently in May 1861, this position could be expressed much more subtly. That is, the transposed English common law could be seen as not being particularly adept at providing recognition for Māori custom concerning lands. Arney, and his fellow justices on the Supreme Court bench, Alexander Johnston and Henry Gresson, appeared to consider simply that 'the constitution and mode of procedure of the Supreme Court as it exists at present are not well adapted for the investigation and determination of questions relating to Native Title *generally*'.[247] In practice, the subtle differences between these strands of thought and approach gave rise to comparable answers—a focus upon the diplomacy of land purchase negotiations between Crown officials, such as Donald McLean, and Māori communities at places like Whanganui in 1848 or Waitara in 1859–1860. As such, if there was to be a bridging of the incommunicability between notions of English real property and how indigenous communities conceived meaningful relations of power and authority over landscapes, an institutional experiment was required.

In *The Taranaki Question* Martin denuded the proprietary question of any political significance. It suited Martin to present the conundrum of Waitara in this way because it put the question of British subjecthood (colonial settlers and Māori) and its completeness or not for Māori directly into contention. 'In fact', he averred, 'the right [of Kīngi] is a simple right of property which concerns the enjoyment and alienation of land, and that only, and has nothing whatever to do with Government or administration.'[248] Here, however, in considering Waitara, Martin was not only emphasising the subjecthood of Māori but also asserting the completeness of colonial dominion throughout the New Zealand archipelago. The right exercised by Kīngi was 'a simple right of property which concerns the enjoyment and alienation of land, and that only, and has nothing

[245] Ibid, fo.291.

[246] Martin, *The Taranaki Question*, 74. Martin's point was that complainants could proceed against the officers of the Governor in tort. See McLay, 'Crown Liability in the Time of Constitutional Foxes'.

[247] Arney, Johnston, and Gresson to Browne, 9 May 1861, *AJHR–1861*, E-3, 13 (emphasis in original).

[248] Martin, *The Taranaki Question*, 27.

whatever to do with Government or Administration'.[249] Accordingly, he argued, '[i]t was just as much, and just as little, incompatible with the Queen's Sovereignty as is the ownership of land in England by Corporations, Companies, or Partnerships'.[250] Adroitly deploying the logic of property rights conceived as privatized interests, Martin countered any opposing view with the comment that '[a]s to the alleged incompatibility [of native land tenure] . . . . with the Queen's Sovereignty, the Queen's governors for twenty years had not discovered it; but on the contrary had recognised that claim in all their dealings'.[251] This point of contention lay at the heart of a contradistinction between Martin's account of indigenous property rights and that associated with the governor, Browne, and his ministerial advisors. The published governmental response was clear: 'The question raised in the original dispute with Wiremu Kingi was one of authority and jurisdiction, and not a question of the title to a particular piece of land'.[252] Indeed, it averred:

> Since ... the contest is not whether that piece of land belongs to Wiremu Kingi or Teira, but whether the Governor has authority to decide between the two, and the power to enforce his decision.[253]

In May 1861 Newcastle stated: 'I have all along said that it may be questionable whether the question of Teira's land would not have been settled without recourse to arms, but I believe that if it had, the natives would have [fastened onto] some other question which would have brought on the same result, as British supremacy was really at the bottom of their proceedings'.[254] Others also critical of the Waitara purchase did not agree with Martin's view on the 'right' claimed to have been exercised by Kīngi.[255] Martin disputed this viewpoint of Māori rights or powers of government, or at least claimed to do so in several exchanges with members of the colonial government in 1860, 1861, and 1863.

In 1863, in a lengthy memorandum entitled 'Observations on the Proposal to take Native Lands under an Act of the Assembly', Martin reflected that 'whilst in North America the external dominion was at once assumed, and the internal dominion left to be acquired afterwards in such way and to such extent as might be defined by treaties to be made for that purpose, in this case of New Zealand the attempt was made to acquire at once both the internal & external dominion by one treaty made once for all'.[256] Even if this was not the case in practice, in concrete terms, because British institutions and jurisdiction were not fully nested or embedded throughout New Zealand, the true legal and normative position for Martin was clear. To Martin's eyes in 1863, New Zealand was an indubitably modern and contemporary setting for imperial policy on indigenous populations. It was not a place for the 'old system', as he dubbed it—not a place for cutting out or leaving pockets of territory not subject to overarching British authority and supervisory jurisdiction. 'We have seen', he said, 'that under the old system the Native Tribes stood as small, but almost independent nations encompassed on every

249 Ibid. 250 Ibid. 251 Ibid.
252 *Notes on Sir William Martin's Pamphlet entitled 'The Taranaki Question'* (1860), 1.
253 Ibid.
254 Newcastle to Browne, 27 May 1861, private, NeC10885, Nottingham University.
255 See the useful summary in Dalton, *War and Politics in New Zealand*, 107.
256 Martin, 'Observations on the Proposal to take Native Lands under an Act of the Assembly', CO209/178, fos.150a–1, TNA.

side by the dominion of a great nation.'[257] As Māori were treated as having the rights and privileges of British subjects but Native Americans were not regarded as citizens of the United States but treated as semi-sovereign dependent nations in the Marshall court cases, Martin considered those parts of the Marshall court jurisprudence not to apply (*contra* Sewell in 1864). In this fashion, Martin developed a distinction between colonial New Zealand and the reasoning applicable in decisions such as *Worcester v State of Georgia* and *Cherokee Nation v State of Georgia* in the United States.[258] The difference exemplified 'two modes of colonizing: one, by which the people of the territory colonized may be locally brought within the dominion of the Crown, yet may remain in nearly everything else as independent as before; and a second, by which they may be brought (as far as possible) even from the beginning within the law and political system of the colonizers'. Under the former system the pre-existing indigenous populations remained '(at least for a time) foreigners; by the other they become subjects'.[259] What difference does a treaty make? For Martin, the third article of the Treaty of Waitangi, in imparting to Māori 'all the rights and privileges of British subjects', proved sufficient to distinguish New Zealand from the United States in respect of the putative completeness of internal dominion. He need not have argued so. The *de facto* practices of independence or autonomy—the sheer materiality of Māori political autonomy—could have justified (as Sewell endeavoured to argue in 1864) the application of *Worcester* to Māori irrespective of their assumed subjecthood.

In addition, New Zealand was a small archipelago. It was not continental in scope. Martin stated:

> A system [of quasi-independent tribes]however tolerable when applied to the wide surface of the continent of North America, would have been inconvenient in the extreme, if applied to numerous tribes occupying a small country and necessarily intermixed with the colonists scattered throughout the country: and there were special considerations of justice and humanity, which led the Home Government to desire to establish in New Zealand some settled form of government, which might restrain and protect both the natives and the settlers who were then flowing into these islands.[260]

At this point, Martin was deploying the reasoning used in *The Taranaki Question* when criticizing the policies of Browne in Waitara—the practical and conceptual incompleteness of Māori subjecthood to Britain. Turning to the Treaty of Waitangi, Martin argued: 'It is plain that the framers of the Treaty desired to bring all the natives of these islands into the position of subjects of the Crown: but it is not to be conceived that they contemplated the introduction at once amongst the New Zealanders of the minute and technical forms of English law'.[261] Indeed, all that the framers could practically have conceived as applying to New Zealand were what Martin characterized as the 'substantial fruits of government': 'legal protection for life,—legal protection for property'.[262]

Martin had no difficulties with legal pluralism in the empires of Britain, or within the United Kingdom itself for that matter. But his sense of pluralism was not that of

[257] Ibid, fo.151.

[258] *Worcester v State of Georgia* 6 Pet 515, 31 US 350 (1832); *Cherokee Nation v State of Georgia* 5 Pet 1, 8 L Ed 25 (1831) (USSC).

[259] Martin, 'Observations on the Proposal to take Native Lands under an Act of the Assembly', CO209/178, fos.145–7.

[260] Ibid, fos.151–1a. [261] Ibid, fos.153–3a. [262] Ibid, fo.153a.

coeval legal systems answering to different sources of ultimate law-making authority.[263] Each distinct legal system could still be seen as subordinate to the Crown, which, he observed, had 'never been regarded by Englishmen otherwise than as a Power acting according to settled usage and Law'. As such, 'If they be subjects of the Crown [it followed, then,] they *must be subject to some Law*'.[264] The ultimate question, therefore, was he wrote, that 'Under the single sovereignty of the Queen of England there are many systems of law'. This point was not startling. Examples abounded. 'Within Great Britain itself', he said, 'the Scottish system differs from the English.' That was not all, however. 'Even within England itself', he noted, 'there are many peculiar customs or laws (such as for example the copyhold tenure and the manifold varieties of local custom within that tenure) which differ from the common law of England, yet are of full force and validity within their own bounds.'[265] Throughout the empires of Britain, whether of settlement, trade, or otherwise, the same pluralistic varieties were in evidence: 'In our Indian possessions [for instance], divers races of men, under divers systems of law dwell together under one sovereign'.[266] 'The original theory', Martin averred, 'appears to have been this, that bloodshed was to be suppressed to that extent, at any rate the Criminal Law was to be enforced but, that, in other respects the natives were to be left to their own usages.'[267] Against this background, however, the real property law of England did not apply to Māori dwelling in areas mantled with native title. Drawing on the law officers' opinion in London on the question of the franchise in 1859 and the absence of a competent tribunal to hear native title claims, Martin stated: 'The case stands thus. No native can, in any way, enforce any right of ownership or occupation of land, held by the native tenure, in the courts of the colony'.[268] For Martin in 1863 this logic about the incompleteness and porousness of British subjecthood as a classification applicable to Māori represented an important move in arguing against any attempts to confiscate the lands of those engaged in war with imperial and colonial forces.

In a broad sense, Martin's was a form of legal analysis familiar to jurists working within the assumptions of the English common law. On closer inspection, however, as witnessed in his 'Memorandum on Native Affairs' of 12 May 1860, his pamphlets of 1860 and 1861, together with his memorandum of 1863, his analyses were not predicated on abrupt and brutally revolutionary exogenous change to indigenous legal orders as scholars acquainted with the common law reasoning aired in *The Case of Tanistry* (1608) may have assumed in other British-settlement contexts.[269] In short, then, it would be overly crude or dismissive to suggest that Martin merely accepted the view that acknowledging 'native title represent[ed] a recognition and disavowal

[263] Barber, *The Constitutional State*: 'A system is characterised by legal pluralism when it contains inconsistent rules of recognition and no institution within the system is legally empowered to resolve the inconsistency. This most commonly occurs when two legal systems overlap—or collide—and make rival demands on state officials' (draft on file with author). I am grateful to Nicholas Barber of Trinity College, Oxford University, for sharing drafts of his chapter on constitutional pluralism with me. Cf Ford, *Settler Sovereignty*, 214, note 13, who points out the notion of 'legal pluralism' as signifying, for her purposes, 'a situation in which two or more legal systems coexist in the same social field' (citing Merry, 'Legal Pluralism', 870).

[264] Martin, 'Observations on the Proposal to take Native Lands under an Act of the Assembly', CO209/178, fo.162 (emphasis added).

[265] Ibid, fos.162–2a. [266] Ibid, fo.162a. [267] Ibid.

[268] Ibid, fo.163. William Fox disagreed with this line of reasoning.

[269] *The Case of Tanistry* (1608) Dav 28, 80 ER 516.

of.... [i]ndigenous jurisdictions'.[270] He was engaging with subtleties, including the sheer tentativeness and provisional qualities of British juristic and political authority and autonomy to act throughout considerable swathes of otherwise colonial New Zealand. 'Native title' was seen as a title created through and cognizable in Māori customs but as one rendered (and recognizable) conceptually in English terms as existing by virtue of the Treaty of Waitangi and sources drawn from *ius gentium*. Native title, then, was a creature *of* Māori customary norms, with its content informed and explicated by these norms. The customary matrices in living indigenous communities from which native title was drawn predated entry of certain *hapū* (certainly not all) into a treaty relationship with the United Kingdom in 1840. Purchase was transformative in that it converted both native title and the normative regime initially underpinning its recognition into an interest cognizable in English real property law by quieting or extinguishing both. The process of purchase produced Crown land (an interim step), which could then be granted to others (a third step). Martin's advice had been to provide Māori with the opportunity (and the entitlement if they were inclined to proceed with the opportunity) to obtain a Crown grant of a fee simple estate in possession. What was recognized by that subsequent fee simple estate was both less and more than that which had predated it. But, prior to completed purchase, both native title and the associated customary normative regime addressing relations with and to the land still subsisted within the supervisory albeit not concretely or institutionally *embedded* or *nested* jurisdiction of the Crown, its officers, and its judges.

The subtle reactions to Martin's work in the Colonial Office were illuminating, revealing the persistent problems posed by native title: the vulnerability of native title to different local interpretations both in New Zealand and in the imperial metropole, its relationship to indigenous political autonomy, and the extent of its amenability to consideration in the colonial courts. His views met with much criticism not only in the context of colonial politics but also inside the Colonial Office, of which he remained unaware, although Fortescue doubted the logic of his legal analysis. Fortescue was insistent that the 'legal status of the Maories is that of subjects'.[271] At this point, the possible confiscation of Māori land was being considered. Fortescue minuted that he could not 'think however that the Treaty of Waitangi is any obstacle to the confiscation of the lands of "rebel" Natives,—and, as an argumentation *ad hominem* to the Waikato, we have the fact (see Mr Gorst's book) that they boast of never having signed it'.[272] Fortescue's reaction to Martin's paper reflected the internal tensions coursing through much British legal and political thought as to the peculiar place of Māori *inside* the colonial and imperial constitution and the continuing problem of native title and customary law *beyond* the reach of problematic concrete English laws and institutions on the ground. His reaction also highlighted the tensions in recognizing that many Māori leaders did not accept themselves to be subject or subordinate to the constitutional authority of the government in New Zealand. 'It is true', admitted Fortescue, 'that the British Gov[ernmen]t has done but little to "impart to them (practically) all the rights & privileges of British subjects".' Yet, he added, 'this failure

[270] The quoted extract is drawn from Shaunnagh Dorsett's excellent examination of custom and the common law in Dorsett, 'Thinking Jurisdictionally', ch 7.

[271] Fortescue, minute, 16 April 1864, CO209/178, fo.141a, TNA.

[272] Ibid, fo.141.

has been caused partly by negligence, ignorance, vacillation—(for our sins against the Maories have been almost altogether sins of omission) it has been caused much more by want of power, and the refusal of the Natives to accept the conditions of subjects, with all its duties of obedience'.[273] The sting in Fortescue's paper was in highlighting the very tensions operating in Martin's reasoning as to the status of Māori and how this related to their lands subject to native title:

> The state of things then which has thus arisen, must not be used altogether against the Gov[ernmen]t, and in favour of the Natives, as, I think, the advocates of the latter are apt to use it. We must not be told, for instance, that the hostile natives must not be treated as ordinary *rebels* (wh[ich] is true & right) because they are not ordinary subjects,—and, in the same breath, that it is iniquitous to take their lands from them, except under the scrupulous application of English law, because they are subjects. In the same way, it seems to me absurd for Sir W. Martin first to prove elaborately that the Natives are British subjects and then to complain of the troops crossing the Mangatawhari, and to justify or excuse 'resistance to invasion' on the part of W. Thompson, as though Ngatihauas & Ngatimaniapotos were two independent neighbouring nations, one friendly, the other hostile, and the Governor, making them suffer for the sins of the latter.[274]

Rogers, who on 8 April 1864 wrote the first minute on Martin's 'Observations', thought that the former judge's reasoning misapplied law. Rogers surmised 'Sir W. Martin's objects [to be] apparently two': first, to 'establish the principle that in all their dealings with the settlers the Maoris are to have the protection of English Law and of the ideas which regulate its application'; and, secondly, to show 'the obligation under which we lie to deal generously with them'. Rogers, alive to the practical and political sensitivities (and the moral value of these sensitivities as a guide to policy on interacting with indigenous populations), wrote: 'As to the first I can imagine no greater snare and oppression to savages than to find themselves netted as it were in a law which they cannot understand or by consequence obey'.[275] For Rogers, the application of English law was a practical question, as evidenced by his comments hinging on use of the term 'impossible', as well as a question of moral aptness and justice: 'if it is *impossible* and *unfair* strictly to enforce English Law upon the Maories, neither can you as it appears to me give them the full protection which it affords'. Hearkening back to the whiggish reasoning he and Fortescue used in support of the Native Council Bill in 1860, he set out a principle for guiding policy and action: 'You must from the *nature of the case deal with people of this kind* in a more or less anomalous, tentative and transitional way'.[276]

Expressed with ease, this principle was redolent of a practical approach to the science of legislative design or architecture, tying the statutory interventions to the conditions or circumstances of the communities at issue. Again, Rogers acknowledged the provisionality and nuances of constitutional and legal orders in New Zealand. As a normative principle, flexibly adapting political practices and principle of political action to the concrete circumstances of case-by-case facts was to be preferred to employing pure legal logic or abstraction. Rogers claimed that 'English law is an instrument of improvement not a basis of logical argument' and '[i]n the present case, I think, constitutional or legal

[273] Ibid, fo.141a.
[274] Ibid, fos.141a–2 (emphasis in original).
[275] Rogers to Fortescue, minute, 8 April 1864, CO209/178, fos.136–6a, TNA.
[276] Ibid, fo.136a (emphasis added).

arguments are especially out of place'.[277] Insofar as Martin argued from legal nostrums, therefore, against the move to forfeit the lands of those Māori engaged in war against General Cameron's forces (a perceived political emergency), Rogers thought that 'arguments of pure law or constitutional form are beside the purpose'.[278] Legislation, he contended, was intended to cure insufficiencies in existing law or to operate where there was no law: 'Legislative interference with property is *ex hypothesi* above law—and only takes place when law is insufficient for its purpose'. If one were to argue against it, then one had better use the language of 'political necessity and natural justice'.[279] Once more, these sentiments revealed a general disposition in mid-nineteenth-century Victorian political thought to appreciate what was a complicated and entangled dance between extant legal principles distilled from common law sources and the discipline of politically driven and observed conventions or arguments. These politically derived norms and contested positions, albeit not enforceable at the behest of a judicial process, were themselves a possible constraint or source for conditioning behaviour within the political dimensions of the Crown, as Geoffrey McLay has analysed in other contexts, but not necessarily remediable in the courts.[280] Critically, from time to time, these types of political-policy arguments could be given legal recognition in the form of statute law, by enlisting the legislative resources of the Crown-in-Parliament.

In responding to the Waitara dispute, the conceptual and idiomatic repertoire on which Martin and Richmond principally drew included, as its reference points, property rights and rights of chiefly government or autonomy. Alternatively, this repertoire also entailed choices between agreeing to classify the conduct of Te Teira or Kīngi as reflecting interests sounding in questions of power as a matter of fact or questions of normative entitlement (whether legalistic—a legal right—or simply a claim of moral or normative force). Martin saw the claim of Kīngi as the lawful customary exercise of a 'tribal right' (as opposed to an 'individual right' or the chiefly power of authority over others).[281] As a customary or legal abstraction, the term 'right' was necessarily conceptual in nature. It objectified a group's or individual's relationship to a particular landscape by focusing on the content of the 'right' as a bundle of constructed attributes capable of analysis divorced from the status of the person or persons claiming to wield it. The focal point became the abstract entitlements or claims to territorial space itself rather than the interpersonal political relations centred on chiefs or others of influence within Māori communities. Yet, for all that, Martin argued that property rights to land captured the empirical richness of Māori understandings on political relations regarding land, including authority over territorial space and the entitlement to allocate it to strangers.

The explicit language of 'rights' had long conditioned the fabric of elite political relations regarding territorial claims in New Zealand from an anglophone perspective. As a vocabulary, it allowed European observers to frame disputes between Māori chiefs as contests of legitimate or illegitimate rights-claimants. In analytical terms, it arguably permitted greater particularity, precision, and inventiveness in describing

[277] Ibid, fos.136a–7.
[278] Ibid, fo.137 (although Rogers agreed with those 'arguments [mounted by Martin] from policy good faith and justice, and these Mr Fox leaves untouched in his answer').
[279] Ibid, fo.137.
[280] McLay, 'Crown Liability in the Time of Constitutional Foxes'.
[281] Martin, *The Taranaki Question*, 30.

what colonial and imperial jurists and policy-formulators imagined they were seeing in concrete negotiations with Māori communities. Much of the performative work of 'rights'-talk, however, was to assist in increasing legibility in intra-European disputes, although profound arguments within a broadly shared vocabulary as to meanings persisted, or what sorts of 'rights' were engaged (if any), and whether 'rights' was indeed the appropriate way to construe the interests at issue. Even if mutual legibility could not be obtained, then, at the least, the content of some of these disputes was increasingly filled in and expanded conceptually. Richmond spoke in terms of de facto powers and rights, clearly drawing distinctions between the two where he saw fit. To imbue the actions of Kīngi with rights-status would be to elevate their status relative to the actions of Te Teira, thereby giving the actions of Kīngi either parity with the actions of Te Teira or, in Martin's view, pre-eminence (Kīngi as representative of the larger tribe). Martin's unsubtle view was that the act of Kīngi was consonant with the relevant tribe as a whole—his was an expression of the tribal right—whereas the action of Te Teira was that of an individual claimant. He drew out this issue further by relying on the board of inquiry's approach to individual claims versus tribal claims in 1856.

What Waitara suggested was that if officials were to extend lands for settlement, they may have had increasingly to make choices between different groups of Māori and different local Māori interpretations of entitlement, placing colonial administration in the invidious position of bearing the political risk of angering one group or another and imperilling the local peace (as brittle as it might be). They were confronted with the inevitable albeit difficult question for governors or for those purporting to govern others: what, if anything, is to be done in the face of difficult choices and complexities? Thus, even if it made sense to think of property rights-claims as principally explained by nostrums of private law (*ius privatum*)—the law of individuals and individual things—there was invariably a public or governmental dimension. The impenetrability and complexity of 'custom' as a body of norms and rules, and the rights supported by it, were seen as a bulwark of Māori liberty and a constraint on despotism (whether of Māori chiefs or settlers). Thematically, there was little novel in seeing customary norms in such a fashion. Although stressing fixity in circumstances where officials and jurists saw it less and less, John Stuart Mill had averred in his *Principles of Political Economy* that the 'further we look back into history, the more we see all transactions and engagements under the influence of fixed customs'. To Mill, the reason was evident, for '[c]ustom was the most powerful protector of the weak against the strong; their sole protector where there are no laws or government adequate to the purpose'.[282] But these interlocking and multiplying thickets of customary usage also presented a problem *of* and *for* government—whether government was to manage these existing entanglements for the time being or whether it ought to do something to change the state of affairs and, if so, how that should be done, emerged as a persistent challenge.

In the hands of Richmond and Martin, even though they disagreed on the details of Waitara, 'custom' and native title became a functional way of organizing *modus vivendi* in practice as well as theory. That is, if Māori and Europeans on the ground were to deal with one another and to do deals, the nomenclature of 'custom' and native title (and rights of native title) became a way of organizing modes of social and political

[282] Mill, *Principles of Political Economy with Some of their Application to Social Philosophy*, lib. 2, 240 (in Robson (ed), *Collected Works of John Stuart Mill*, vol II).

interdependence between colonial governments, neighbouring European settlements, and local Māori opinion leaders (if not all). Some Māori, such as Te Teira, became political rent-seekers in using 'custom' and interests in land in this way or allowing their actions to be interpreted in line with this way of thought. As Māori groups at the margins of colonial niches of settlement became increasingly embroiled in the systems of the local colonial political economies—the senses of value applicable to such growing settlements and commodity exchange—these particular interpretations and constructions of native title became more real and salient. It became a currency of dealing and getting along with settlers, of pursuing local advantage and endeavouring to attract various forms of economic and political good. We begin to see the cultural and institutional possibilities of why the native land court became effective in some districts at certain points in time and not others.

'A COUNTRY WITHOUT LAW AND A PRINCE'—THE TREATY AS AN USHER FOR RIGHTS-TALK; INDIVIDUAL AND COLLECTIVE RIGHTS

One ought to avoid ascribing any dominant orientation to imperial, settler, or Māori political cultures in the mid-nineteenth century. We may discern patterns and shared themes but the detailed content of positions on various issues, such as the Waitara purchase, understandably reveals complexity and a diversity of views. Therein lay the richness of the real life of constitutional debate in empire regarding the place or significance of native title together with signs as to what the content of native title might consist of as a right of property. Busby averred that 'aboriginal titles have always been restricted by the colonizing power to the "use and occupation of the land" '.[283] He perceived no difference between the 'aboriginal titles' recognized in the United States or those under the Treaty of Waitangi in New Zealand. He believed that by the 'rule of international law, as well as the customs of the New Zealanders', the guarantee within the second article of the Treaty could only extend to the 'actual possession *at that time existing*'.[284] In this vein, Busby criticized FitzRoy's decision in 1844 in the Taranaki to reduce the recommended award to the New Zealand Company to 3,000 acres as an error. His particular error was admitting 'a *right* to land as existing in such of the Taranaki tribes as had been driven from their possessions at Taranaki by the more powerful tribes of Waikato, and had located themselves on the coasts of Cook's Straits'.[285] In saying this, Busby wished to point out the sheer futility and confusion wrought in interpreting the Treaty as imposing an obligation on colonial administrators to investigate the quality of Māori tenure in land in an endless series of adjudicative inquiries.

Conceptually, then, Busby's analysis saw Māori possessory interests as set and fossilized at the time of the Treaty at Waitangi. Phraseology such as 'at that time existing' did not allow for subsequent change or adaptation. As with McLean's analysis of Martin's *The Taranaki Question*, placing a temporal limit on *when* to assess indigenous

[283] Busby, *Remarks upon a Pamphlet entitled 'The Taranaki Question*, 12.
[284] Ibid, 6 (emphasis added).
[285] Ibid (emphasis added).

interests in land posed many difficulties.[286] While McLean thought that the dead hand of custom set the rights of Māori as they were upon entry into the Treaty of Waitangi, such a point in time was difficult to fix with any precision given the different signing sites and dates throughout the length of the New Zealand archipelago. Beguilingly simple when recited as a shibboleth, whether in paper or conversation, fossilizing the nature and content of rights on making a treaty gave rise to difficult questions of timing. Concepts of rights change and adapt with newcomers, new relationships, and new options. Some people marked the Treaty documents at different times; others did not mark them at all. Neither Busby nor McLean sought to resolve these quandaries—recitation of the broad principle was enough for them. The rhetorical and analytical move was to distance the behaviour of Kīngi and his adherents or allies from the situation of 1840. McLean agreed that the 'rights of the tribe, and of [Kīngi] as its chief, were secured by that treaty'. Yet, 'it will scarcely be urged that the treaty could affect any rights beyond that which actually existed at the time the treaty was made'. In McLean's view, the Treaty could not be 'fairly interpreted as guaranteeing rights or claims subsequently acquired or assumed'.[287] Lurking within both Busby's and McLean's musings lies the vexed question of individual indigenous rights and those of a communal or 'tribal' quality. This aspect of analysis was neither novel nor surprising, as both men treated it as a question inhering in the second article of the Treaty. McLean thought that it was to 'save the rights of individuals' that FitzRoy had set aside Spain's award in favour of absentee proprietors. FitzRoy's decision, argued McLean, did not recognize a 'resumption of tribal title by [Te Ātiawa], but claims of individuals'.[288] As McLean saw it, the transaction, 'as regarded the tribes, was held to be incomplete, not a mere nullity'.[289] This disjunction between individual and community entitlements would also find expression in sections 7 and 12, for example, of the Native Lands Act 1862.[290]

With Busby, we encounter arguments that the Treaty of Waitangi set the relations of the incoming Crown with pre-existing Māori polities on an altogether different footing than that which might be supposed from a literal reading of its articles. The Treaty did not lead to the supersession and sublimation of prior acts of Māori elites in permitting settlers to occupy territorial space by treating such acts as prima facie invalid. Rather, Busby contended that the Treaty was a 'treaty of union, similar to that between England and Scotland', especially in the sense that '[m]any Englishmen possessed estates in Scotland at the period of the Union, but the Crown of England never pretended that the titles to those estates were null and void, unless allowed by the Crown'.[291] Busby, as a long-standing settler in an official capacity as 'British resident' until Hobson's arrival in January 1840 and the subsequent formal assertion of Britain's authority, and as having witnessed and participated in signal episodes such as the declaration of independence in 1835 and the discussions at Waitangi on the Treaty in February 1840, brought a distinctive and informed perspective to bear. He set up the pedigree of his authority to comment on what he characterized variously as 'aboriginal

[286] McLean, undated, 'Remarks on a pamphlet by Sir W[illia]m Martin on the Taranaki Question', Ms-Group-1551, McLean papers, ATL.

[287] Ibid. [288] Ibid. [289] Ibid.

[290] Section 12 of the Native Lands Act 1862, 26 Vict 42, for example, provided that 'the President and Members of the Court shall sign and issue a Certificate of Title in favour of the Tribe Community or Individuals whose title shall have been ascertained defined and registered as aforesaid'.

[291] Busby, *The Rebellions of the Maories*, 19–20.

titles' or 'native title' through his participation in drafting the Treaty of Waitangi and his long acquaintance with Māori in Te Tai Tokerau prior to the Treaty. It was a time when he 'had better opportunities of judging.... [indigenous communities] in their aboriginal condition than Sir W Martin could have, after they had imbibed the ideas of property which are held by civilized men, through their negotiations for the sale of land'.[292]

Sian Elias and Edwin Fletcher have demonstrated that there are still elements in Busby's history deserving analysis, including his use of legalistic genres in asserting the validity of his claimed titles in court hearings and political pleadings throughout an episodic campaign.[293] His conception of native title and the Treaty of Waitangi was by no means anomalous. Busby alleged that in 1844 he had met with Joseph Story, a renowned jurist and a member of the Supreme Court of the United States who had sat on the *Johnson v M'Intosh* decision in 1823. In recalling the substance of that meeting in a pamphlet published in 1865, Busby recounted how Story reportedly said: 'Your titles to land in New Zealand do not belong to the category of Indian or Aboriginal titles'.[294] Thus, '[w]hatever may be the social or political condition of the aborigines of New Zealand, the British Government has acknowledged and treated with them as a substantive and independent state'. In Busby's recollection, Story concluded that the imperial administration was 'bound by its own acts, and must ultimately ratify [its] titles so far as they are admitted by the natives'.[295] Striving to obtain recognition of his purchases from Māori, Busby was at odds with official policy on pre-1840 land claims. Busby's self-interested predicament saw him developing a basis for the complete legal recognition of customary transfers that pre-dated the Treaty. For Busby, such transfers were conducted in accordance with particular norms minted through negotiations on the ground with Māori elites and constituted permanent alienations under the authority of Māori as political actors and hosts. Such titles were legal and legitimate as they were 'purchased from the rightful owners when New Zealand was an independent country, and admitted and maintained by those who sold it'.[296] As a Treaty, the compact initially signed at Waitangi 'guaranteed all *existing rights* of property'.[297]

In this sense, Busby kept to the thread of reasoning that he had deployed in 1860 in critiquing Martin's *The Taranaki Question*. Busby's criticisms of Martin in 1860 centred on Martin's assumptions in a section in *The Taranaki Question*—headed 'Native Tenure of Land'—that indigenous property interests existed as enforceable 'rights'. Busby treated the misconception as twofold: conceptual and historical. He claimed that Martin's view was 'founded upon a misconception of the actual condition of the natives, who, down to the date of the Treaty, had no conception of the existence of a right implying an obligation on the part of others to respect that right'.[298] He limited his definition of 'rights of property, as they are necessarily understood by jurists and statesmen, [to those interests] implying corresponding obligations to respect such rights'.[299] As such, he argued, there was no historical evidence to suggest Māori 'ever

[292] Busby, *Remarks upon a Pamphlet entitled 'The Taranaki Question'*, 11.
[293] Elias and Fletcher, '*Busby v White* (1859', 563–604).
[294] Busby, *The Rebellions of the Maories*, 19 (note).
[295] Ibid. [296] Ibid, 21.
[297] Ibid, 19 (emphasis added).
[298] Busby, *Remarks upon a Pamphlet entitled 'The Taranaki Question'*, 4.
[299] Ibid, 5.

having possessed any rights, with the exception of those which were created by the Treaty of Waitangi'.[300] Citing the Book of Luke in the scriptures, Busby thought that the only law predating the arrival of the Crown in New Zealand was that of the 'strong arm'.[301] His argument resonated with an Austinian notion of positive law as a norm requiring an enforceable duty or right in a way that neither Chapman nor Martin shared when discussing the force of 'custom'.[302] The rules of 'native tenure of land' distilled by Martin were, Busby claimed, not historically autochthonous: 'the rules which Sir W Martin lays down as established by a singular concurrence of the best evidence are not rules of native origin'.[303] Rather, Busby saw these rules as norms inducted from later patterns of dealing between incoming pākehā settlers and local Māori—so many *modi vivendi* established by so many localized, dynamic negotiations. These 'rules' were the 'natural and necessary deductions from the proceedings which our countrymen had recourse in order to obtain an equitable title to the land which they purchased from the natives'.[304] He saw them, therefore, not as 'rules established by natives, but suggested by the precautions adopted by our own countrymen in order to obtain a title which could not be justly disputed'.[305] Some twenty-five to thirty years had elapsed since land was looked upon by Māori as having an exchangeable value—a way of luring goods and people to particular places. 'In no case', Busby asserted, 'did the land become subject to the laws regarding property until the Native title was extinguished.'[306]

Busby thus stressed the phenomenal aspects of human conduct as driving the developments around rights-talk and native title. His was not a noumenal form of analysis. For him, the phenomena of human interaction—specifically, negotiation and bargaining—sparked, crafted, honed, and inflected the sense of 'rights' to property as an innovation of practices. Such behaviour was not drawn from *a priori* principles or deductions. In this, there are shades of what Jeremy Webber has construed as inter-cultural engagement between colonists and indigenous peoples in northern America—the 'occult practices of social interaction'—leading to the emergence of aboriginal rights and a *modus vivendi* in the form of an inter-communal normative community.[307] Webber is sensitive to the point that a tangible community of interest may subsist even though its members have multiple allegiances and ties to other communities. Thus, he contends, the process of formation 'created a new, cross-cultural community—one which did not, however, displace its constituent societies'.[308] As with Richard White, Webber was willing to admit that the relations of such inter-communal communities were shaped by relations of force and domination rather than unconstrained consent.[309] These *modus vivendi*, however, were multi-dimensional and multi-directional, certainly insofar as fluid Māori groupings or configurations were concerned, let alone the colonial officials. Colonial New Zealand was not

300 Ibid.

301 Ibid. The extract from Luke 11:21 was: 'When a strong man armed kept his palace his goods were in peace, but when a stronger than he came upon him, and overcame him, he took from him all his armour and divided his spoils: and there was no redress' (ibid, 5–6).

302 On Austin's views in this sense, see Cornish, Anderson, Cocks, Lobban, Polden, and Smith (eds), *The Oxford History of the Laws of England: Volume XI, 1820–1914*, 88–9.

303 Busby, *Remarks upon a Pamphlet entitled 'The Taranaki Question'*, 7.

304 Ibid. 305 Ibid, 8. 306 Ibid, 12.

307 Webber, 'Relations of Force and Relations of Justice', 625.

308 Ibid, 628. 309 Ibid, 628–9.

a place of Manichean binaries—of the simple categories or distinctions of settlers and indigene, 'the Crown', and Māori. Each participating party or cluster of actors exhibited its own conditions and politics of interiority and exteriority—internal and external hinges at play.

Busby appeared to be moving in two directions simultaneously. On the one hand, he used a philosophical or jurisprudential definition of 'right' (as enforceable obligation) to deny that Māori had rights prior to entering into treaty relations in 1840. On the other hand, he used an empirical or 'phenomenal' conception in order to treat the post-contact rights of Māori as constituted through piecemeal *modus vivendi*.[310] Busby recognized, however, that exogenous sources were relevant in shaping and reshaping how such conduct was interpreted by those negotiating with Māori in the field (although he did not appear to acknowledge the possibilities for diverse or non-communicated interpretations to emerge or for Māori to disagree). In his account, the Treaty of Waitangi established rights and obligations, but also conveyed and drew in external interpretative sources and vocabularies with it, most notably the 'technical language [of] the right of pre-emption'.[311] Rather disingenuously, in view of his familiarity with the documents, Busby pointed out his recollection that the term 'rights' did not appear in the Treaty of Waitangi. He was correct (albeit excessively literal) insofar as he was speaking about proprietary interests in land. Under the third article of the Treaty, however, Māori were imparted the '*rights* and privileges of British subjects'. Yet, for Busby's purposes, the relevant phrasing within the treaty manuscript was that which expressed the following guarantee: 'The Queen guarantees to the natives the possession of their property in land which they may *individually* or *collectively possess*'.[312] Here, however, Busby was giving a literal reading of the second article of the Treaty. Possession could be analysed as a legal right as much as a description of how it physically related to a given landscape or area. This was as much a feature of discussions on the common law in texts such as those of Blackstone as it was of discussions on the law of nations. Blackstone had famously presented 'several stages or degrees requisite to form a complete title to lands and tenements' in a 'progressive order': first, 'mere *naked possession*, or actual occupation of the estate; without any apparent right, or any shadow or pretence of right, to hold and continue such possession'; secondly, 'the *right of possession*, which may reside in one man, while the actual possession is not in himself, but in another'; thirdly, the 'mere *right of property*, the *jus proprietatis*, without either possession or even the right of possession'; fourthly, a 'complete title to lands, tenements, and hereditaments'.[313] 'Every Title', wrote Walter Burton, 'must rest ultimately upon mere possession.'[314]

[310] I wish to acknowledge my gratitude to Ian Hunter of the University of Queensland for discussions on these passages.

[311] Busby, *Remarks upon a Pamphlet entitled 'The Taranaki Question'*, 9.

[312] Ibid, 6 (emphasis added).

[313] This discussion occurred in Blackstone (with notes and additions by Edward Christian), *Commentaries on the Laws of England*, II, 195–9, appearing in ch 13 entitled 'Of the Title to Things Real, in General' (emphasis in original). In Blackstone's account, the second category—a 'right of possession'—comprised two sub-classifications, namely 'an *apparent* right of possession, which may be defeated by proving a better; and an *actual* right of possession, which will stand the test against all opponents' (emphasis in original).

[314] Walter Burton, *An Elementary Compendium of the Law of Real Property*, 137.

Martin stated that the Treaty 'neither enlarged nor restricted the then existing rights of property'. What aspects of Māori autonomy pre-dating the Treaty of Waitangi, then, were lost or impaired? Busby put the question in these words:

> But how is such an assumption [of Martin's] to be reconciled with the clause of the Treaty, which yields to the Queen in return for their adoption into the British family, and the inestimable privileges thereby conferred, the pre-emption of their lands, relinquishing the right to dispose of their lands to individuals as theretofore, and restricting that right to the sale to the Queen, through agents appointed by her?[315]

Busby claimed that innovation was wrought by strangers from across the seas and the presence of formal British influence. Te Teira was able to clothe his individual conduct with the vocabulary and attribution of a 'right'—an entitlement to act; to demonstrate tactical generosity or hospitality: 'In offering the block of about 600 acres to the Government, Teira acted as any Native would have acted before the Treaty of Waitangi, who was bold enough to take such a step'.[316] It was this innovative quality that profoundly disturbed the hitherto unhindered abilities of otherwise politically influential chiefs with access to military power to enforce their preferences against others, including minor, less-influential leaders. Before the Treaty, alleged Busby, Kīngi and his party could have compelled Te Teira to defer to the preferred stance of Kīngi. The accessibility of settlers and colonial administration to Te Teira rendered that situation much more risky from the perspective of Kīngi. Te Teira was able to call upon the arrangements he had entered into with the colonial governor as a means of obtaining leverage against Wīremu Kīngi Te Rangitāke. For Te Teira, the proximity of European settlement at New Plymouth expanded and diversified the political marketplace in which he operated relative to other figures within Māori elites, giving him additional negotiating resources in his political repertoire against Kīngi. Te Teira could use his transaction with the governor in 1859 as a lever to contest and to enhance his political position relative not only to colonial settlement but also with regard to Kīngi. Analysed in this way, Busby perceived the ability of Kīngi to thwart, manipulate, or coerce Te Teira's choices in ways that Te Teira could not meaningfully influence as inherently constrained.[317] To Kīngi, however, the situation posed indeterminate political risks—how do we receive strangers (settlers) who have not been invited albeit invited at the behest of others? Busby was using the nomenclature of '*right*' as a cogent limit on what Kīngi, as a significant Te Ātiawa political actor, could legitimately do, and as a source of normative contestation for Te Teira.

Colonial administration could be viewed as a redistributive instrument in a thriving and contested political marketplace or marketplaces. That is, it enabled certain indigenous elites and aspiring newcomers to build power relative to competitors or other groups through patronage networks as well as by establishing particular concepts of rights recognition that recognized some individuals or groups as rights-holders while withholding recognition from others.[318] These various resources may be seen as a form

315 Busby, *Remarks upon a Pamphlet entitled 'The Taranaki Question'*, 9.

316 Ibid, 11.

317 Compare with the illuminating discussion in Ivison, 'Consent or Contestation?' in Webber and McLeod (eds), *Between Consenting Peoples*.

318 Hickford, 'Strands from the Afterlife of Confiscation', 173, 188; Hickford, 'John Salmond and Native Title'.

of political rent (or a class of political goods), or even economic rent. The presence of these resources encouraged rent-seeking behaviours on the part of certain Māori as much as settler politicians although the games and agendas at issue were multifarious and often differed. Exchange, as is well appreciated, could occur as a form of transfer to chiefs, for example, in return for permission to occupy land, with the currency given then retained or reassigned by the holders of political power in Māori communities to others (in whole or in part). Alternatively, commercial exchange could occur whereby surpluses were exchanged with others in return for capital.[319] Introduced languages of law—conveyed in the form of resident magistrates, for example, or Crown grants to certain *rangatira*—could also be viewed as resources available for co-option in the play of intra-Māori, as well as intra-European, politics. Each party might have its own interpretations of what the deployment of legalistic forms and genres amounted to in terms of who or what was exerting the most practicable influence on the relationship and who required the relationship more than the other.

WHO INTERPRETS?—'TRIBUNALS INDEPENDENT OF THE PRINCE' AND THE MEANINGS OF THE TREATY OF WAITANGI

Martin's comments were not ignored by the colonial government. A series of printed and circulated *Notes on Sir William Martin's Pamphlet entitled 'The Taranaki Question'* dating from January 1861 were issued by the government. The colonial government authors of these *Notes* disputed the existence of a 'tribal right' as conceived by Martin in *The Taranaki Question*. Such a right, if construed as applicable to Te Ātiawa, was not even admitted by the constituent *hapū* of Te Ātiawa.[320] In the matter of courts of law investigating native title, the *Notes* reflected that the 'territorial rights.... of the Natives' stood upon the Treaty of Waitangi, 'of which the Crown is, rightfully, the sole interpreter'.[321] 'No one will deny', the *Notes* claimed, 'that one of the things most to be desired in the existing state of the relations between Her Majesty's Government and the Native race, is the establishment of some tribunal in which the varying rules of Native tenure shall acquire some settled form, and to the decisions of which they will yield a peaceful submission'.[322] The Native Territorial Rights Act 1858 was seen as one attempt to design a device or means capable of beginning to address such a question. The authors were demonstrating the impracticalities of treating Māori communities as amenable to the institutional and conceptual apparatus of English common law, except on their own terms if at all practicable. There was a sense of demonstrating the practical weaknesses of Martin's reasoning. Keeping the civil peace was one such weakness. Martin's quoting of Tāmihana's speech in support of the Kīngitanga concept that the 'governor never does anything, except when a pakeha is killed', followed by the statements '[w]e are allowed

[319] For a much more extensive consideration, see Polanyi, 'The Economy as Instituted Process', in Polanyi, Arensberg, and Pearson (eds), *Trade and Market in the Early Empires*, 243–70.

[320] *Notes on Sir William Martin's Pamphlet entitled The Taranaki Question*, note on 'page 30'. Through archival references, Sinclair has attributed the authorship to FD Bell, F Whitaker and Thomas Gore Browne: *The Origins of the Maori Wars*, 282.

[321] *Notes on Sir William Martin's Pamphlet entitled The Taranaki Question*, note on 'page 59'.

[322] Ibid.

to fight and kill each other as we please' and a 'King would end these evils',[323] was interpreted as revealing Martin's lack of appreciation of the true nuances and complexities of purporting to govern territorial space and people (including erstwhile subjects who considered themselves associates rather than subjects). Such situations arose, said the authors of the *Notes,* because 'interference on the part of the Governor (except by negotiation) would be useless, unless he were prepared to go to war'.[324]

War was a term of international relations not domestic politics. Unless one was speaking of civil war, it had no place *within* or *inside* a settled polity. Criminal incidents of killing were viewed as largely having been dealt with in accordance with Māori custom—'[n]ative custom requires that life shall pay for life, and is not particular as to the victim'.[325] Illustrations of alleged intra-Māori customary management of violence outside of settlements were given, such as the 'case of the Kawau powder robbery, Sutton's case, Marsden's case', (the case of *Regina v Charles Marsden,* determined on 1 December 1855 in the Supreme Court at Auckland, regarding the murder of a Māori woman named Kerara, and where Marsden was convicted of murder and eventually executed) together with the death of an 'unknown native' in the neighbourhood of Auckland. Complexity, however, is not as communicable to broader audiences as simplicity. And Martin's overall legal argument was clear. Herein lay the trick of language. The government's *Notes on Sir William Martin's 'The Taranaki Question'* (1861) used the word 'crime' to state that '[i]n most cases of *crime,* whether committed by Natives against Europeans, or by Europeans against Natives, the latter are not very tractable'.[326] Yet, the *Notes* continued, in cases of 'crime' committed by Māori against Europeans, 'the surrender of the offender, if obtained at all, is invariably a matter of negotiation'.[327] Negotiation was required because the concrete realities on the ground suggested the very tentativeness and fragility of empire in New Zealand. Its authority, let alone its power, was not secure. As terms, war and crime did not sit very well together, suggesting very different relations to colonial authority. The jurisdictional writ of the government did run throughout New Zealand even though the government might not have accepted this in practice or, as importantly, even if Māori did not accept it. Indeed, in using the adjective 'criminal', Martin assumed that the term was the appropriate way to characterize such incidents. Characterizing something as a 'crime' suggested the supervisory role of British jurisdiction and the aspiration to embed or nest that jurisdictional oversight with concrete powers and institutions of enforcement. The word 'crime', therefore, implied that Māori communities were inside empire.

In responding to Busby's criticisms and the colonial government's *Notes,* Martin persevered with a Treaty-driven approach. The Treaty of Waitangi was the diplomatic punctuation point—the text-based usher and conduit for recognizing native title, as well as a device for reducing native title as purchases proceeded to extinguish it over time. Deeds of purchase entered into by non-governmental European actors, such as individual settlers and traders, and missionary societies, pre-dated the Treaty, but it was the Treaty at Waitangi and other sites, such as Hokianga, and the various proclamations of January 1840 and May 1840, that announced the arrival of the voyaging Crown to New Zealand shores in a formal sense.[328] As a text of diplomacy, it was interpreted

[323] Martin, *The Taranaki Question,* 88.

[324] *Notes on Sir William Martin's Pamphlet entitled The Taranaki Question,* note on 'page 88'.

[325] Ibid. [326] Ibid (emphasis added). [327] Ibid.

[328] Hickford, ' "Vague Native Rights to Land" '.

by the authors of the colonial administration's *Notes on Sir William Martin's Pamphlet entitled 'The Taranaki Question'* as assuming the Crown's pre-eminence in interpreting the articles of the Treaty. The centrality of the executive dimension of the introduced Crown (personalized through the office of the governor), rather than the judicial or adjudicative dimension of the Crown in interpreting the meanings of the Treaty, was considered vital. Martin adjudged 'territorial rights of the Natives [to] stand upon Treaty, and therefore that questions between the Government and the Natives belong to the Governor and *not* to any Court'.[329] That is, it was not only a diplomatic text in and of itself; it was also a forerunner of ongoing diplomacy between a governor and indigenous individuals and communities expressed in a variety of texts—a precursor to what Boast illuminatively refers to as 'multi-textualism'.[330]

In reporting that the only difference between Busby's account and his own was 'as to the *origin* of the rules', Martin clarified that he used the term 'right' for that 'which was acknowledged and warranted by *custom*, though there was no law in our sense to uphold it'.[331] He classified the 'tribal or communal right' exercised by Kīngi as a 'fact', which was not only in existence as at 1859 or 1860 but had been in existence from 'time immemorial'.[332] As such, it could not be criticized, as Richmond had sought to do implicitly, as a non-juristic power, although it could be interpreted as a legitimate juristic power to be exercised on behalf of the 'tribal or communal' level. Curiously, Martin's rationale for such a proposition was predicated on assumptions about the political and jurisdictional significance of the community interest in supervising the occupation of territorial space by strangers to the community, including pākehā settlers. 'For to alienate land to a stranger', he claimed, 'was to alienate to one who might any day become an enemy'.[333] As such, '[t]he whole tribe.... was interested in the matter for the sake of its own independence'.[334] Drawing on this thread of reasoning, Martin analogized it as 'something like what we call an Alien Law'.[335] He recognized that the arrival of Europeans presented new interpretative challenges and meanings. Nevertheless, it remained a significant question for an entire indigenous community 'whether a single man or a few men may, without the consent of their fellows, introduce into the midst of their cultivations an ineligible neighbor whose cattle may range over their unfenced land, or who in a variety of other ways may injure or annoy the rest of the community'.[336] Here, again, the political risks and opportunities associated with admitting strangers within the claimed area of the group came into stark relief. In the political dimension, Martin saw this very situation as incentivizing perverse behaviours, tending to unravel the customary forms of influence ordinarily exercised by long-standing elites within clan-based communities: 'It would offer an opportunity to every ill-disposed man to gratify private resentment, and to embroil his tribe with the Pakeha', adding that in the case of the Waitara, 'there are indications of something of this kind'.[337] At a much more prosaic level, Martin appreciated all too well the relatively numerous disputes that had arisen regarding unfettered and straying livestock.

[329] Martin, *Remarks on 'Notes published for the New Zealand Government'*, 22 (emphasis added).
[330] Boast, 'Recognising Multi-textualism'.
[331] Martin, *Remarks on 'Notes published for the New Zealand Government'*, 5 (emphasis in original).
[332] Ibid, 5–6. [333] Ibid, 6. [334] Ibid. [335] Ibid.
[336] Ibid. [337] Ibid.

A number of the cases that had reached the Supreme Court concerned this very issue and it proved to be a common question before resident magistrates.[338]

Martin's ultimate aspiration was clearly expressed. He regarded it as being in the 'interest of both races that individual rights should be substituted for the right of the Community, as far as possible'.[339] Nevertheless, he asserted his point of difference with colonial administrators to be that this transition could only be 'effected by rational means, not by mere force'.[340] Martin's central angle of vision remained unchanged: Māori were insufficiently incorporated as British subjects, having no ability to contest the determinations of the governor on proprietary rights except by way of diplomacy or warring—in other words, acting as incomplete outsiders or as incomplete subjects.[341] The essential point was that the third article of the Treaty, in imparting the 'rights and privileges of British subjects' to Māori, 'must mean at any rate the opposite of despotism'.[342] Political costs associated with negotiating the impenetrability of customary norms and descent-group politics were one thing. But what was required, argued Martin, was the presence of an arbitral or mediatory influence distinct from a governor who was otherwise implicated in the very negotiations to be subjected to scrutiny. Turning on this question was the issue of whether Māori had indeed been treated as if they were British subjects. On the question of the application of English law to Māori, Martin insisted that he did not mean that 'the whole complex body of English Law was at once to be applied to the Natives; but it is meant, that the plain and fundamental principles of English Law became applicable at once; that the Natives became at once entitled to the essential rights of British subjects'.[343] Amongst these rights—'surely', he said—were the following: 'life shall not be taken without a fair trial; that land shall not be taken without a fair trial'.[344]

Here, then, we discover Martin sharpening the arguments he would use subsequently in 1863 against the proposals to confiscate territories from Waikato *hapū*. Richmond's approach, Martin contended, was to give the Crown the role of 'sole interpreter of the Treaty'. Martin criticized the government's *Notes* for demeaning the name and dignity of 'the Crown' by reducing it to a minor official operating in New Plymouth (Parris) backed by a governor. Using words tinged with irony, Martin wrote: 'The majesty of the Royal word and the largeness of the national undertaking issue in the decision of an Assistant Land Purchase Commissioner'.[345] 'The Crown then', he said, 'does not mean the Queen or the Government of England'.[346] Be that as it may, the colonial administration's analysis of the Treaty left Māori beyond the realm of British subjecthood and treated them, in effect, as strangers to the Crown. Martin considered the

[338] Josiah Flight, the resident magistrate at New Plymouth, had dealt with Māori interference with unfenced horses: Flight to McLean, 19 April 1857, Ms-Papers-0032–276, McLean papers, ATL. I also note that in *R v Pita Whakaka, Marino, Mangumaugu, and Pita Te Rito*, 5 May 1865, a property damage case concerning the felonious killing and carrying away of a bullock, Justice Johnston in the Supreme Court at Wellington, when passing sentence, said: 'he did not wish to punish the prisoners more than would show to other Maories that they could not break the laws with impunity. He would not punish them as severely as he would a Pakeha, as they might not be thoroughly conversant with the laws of the land'.

[339] Martin, *Remarks on 'Notes published for the New Zealand Government'*, 6.

[340] Ibid.

[341] Martin, *The Taranaki Question*.

[342] Martin, *Remarks on 'Notes published for the New Zealand Government'*, 46.

[343] Ibid, 46. [344] Ibid. [345] Ibid, 48. [346] Ibid, 47–8.

fallacy of the government's position to rest on misreading the nature of the Treaty. He compared it to an international treaty in the ordinary sense. Thus, a 'Treaty in the ordinary sense is a compact between two independent nations, independent before the Treaty was made, and independent after it was made'.[347] Such treaties were 'not within the jurisdiction of the Courts of either nation' because 'an independent nation cannot be bound by the Courts of another nation'. Arbitration and force were the means of resolving disputes. But the Treaty of Waitangi was a different kind of compact. While the parties to the Treaty were independent before entering into it, by 'an express article of the Treaty.... one party.... bec[a]me subject to the other'.[348] Martin recounted Richmond's theory as follows: 'If the Treaty of Waitangi be (as his argument assumes it to be) a *Treaty in the ordinary sense*, then the right of interpreting and enforcing the Treaty must belong not to one party, but to both equally; that the Natives are at liberty to resort to force in support of their view, as much as the Governor in support of his; and that they cannot be charged with rebellion, if they do so'.[349] Martin considered that such a doctrine contained little theoretical value. The implications of such a stance would be to treat Māori as belligerents in war rather than as subjects in rebellion (assuming that they were indeed in rebellion). Carleton, the Auckland politician, supported Martin's view in a *Westminster Review* article in Britain, a review associated with sympathizers of Jeremy Bentham's utilitarian programmes and radical English politics. He presented the mid-nineteenth-century constitutional significance of both interpretative angles of vision distinctively, stating that all that had been 'substantially required [in 1840] was a solemn declaration that certain native rights should be preserved intact: not a treaty, but a guarantee'.[350] In his view, using a treaty was misguided: 'By adopting the *form* of a treaty, meaning thereby a compact between two independent nations, we subjected ourselves to all the incidents of treaty, hampering ourselves with the dogmas of international law'. As such, he said, '[i]t involved us in a strange dilemma; for the right of interpretation either belongs to the natives, equally with ourselves, or else to the Crown alone, the first conclusion rendering all government impossible; the second, endowing the Government with the powers of a despot'.[351] To Carleton, Richmond advocated the despotic interpretation.

Martin, Richmond, and Busby generalized custom as something rule-based and not localized to particular Māori tribes. Their versions of 'custom' applied generically in all Māori clans or tribes. Seen in this light, a key question emerges as to the purchase of the concept of native title on those indigenous communities to which it was being applied. At a much later date, considerable numbers of Māori participated in court-bound litigation, adapting the introduced legalistic registers or vocabularies of 'custom' and the ways in which these forms of legalism analysed how indigenous communities interacted with landscapes, including lakes, rivers, and the foreshore.[352] This was more than the 'ventriloquism of forms'[353] whereby individuals outwardly complied with ritualized legal argument and speech-making. Māori actively used these concepts of 'custom' and 'right'—Wittgenstein's rules of the game—adapting and contesting them, although partly caught within the institutional arena of the colonial courts.

[347] Ibid, 45. [348] Ibid. [349] Ibid (emphasis added).
[350] Carleton, 'New Zealand', 429.
[351] Ibid (emphasis in original).
[352] Hickford, 'John Salmond and Native Title'; Boast, *Buying the Land*.
[353] I owe this term to Lisa Ford.

Was Te Teira acting as an innovator? Was he one who, in conjunction with those of his 'party', adapted to the conceptual and linguistic novelties of an new land market, seeing an opportunity to obtain advantages through closer alliance with the embryonic settlement at New Plymouth and to establish himself (and his community) as people worth negotiating with? Richmond thought not. Martin thought so. Even if it was innovative as far as Kīngi were concerned, it allowed Te Teira a place to stand to contest the authority of Kīngi in Te Ātiawa. It accentuated fault lines amongst and between *hapū* within Te Ātiawa in the Taranaki, portraying old and recent lines of intra-group competition or rivalry in new guises.

THE NATIVE LAND COURT, 1861–1862: A 'TITLE SIFTED THROUGH' A STATUTORY TRIBUNAL

One unintended consequence of the Waitara disputes was to undermine the reputation of governor-centric purchase transactions. It moved politically influential colonial and imperial opinion in favour of a distinct, possibly statutorily crafted, institution or body to address native title areas within the colonial constitution—what would become the concept of a native land court, first enacted in 1862. Waitara further dramatized the inherent complexities of negotiating with native title claimants and the collective permutations of native title as something held by a set of overlapping and interlocking groups. 'Tribal title' was no simple matter, either conceptually or procedurally in terms of ascertaining who was entitled to speak, let alone for what (areas of land) and for whom. All was murkiness and complexity. Roads, seen as ribbons of either Crown-owned or administered land in the midst of native title, also proved to be testing points. A number of issues arose in relation to use of roads for the postal mail, and in the resistance to the cutting of lines of roads in the '[Māori] King's land' (1858).[354] In analysing the *Cormick and Olive v Cherokee Nation* commission of inquiry (1812), Lisa Ford notes the relevance of roads to ideas of indigenous spatial order.[355] These issues also revealed certain assumptions as to how to order relations between native title and the colonial legal system. Legal processes for taking land for roadways within native title districts were unclear. In answering a request for clarification on this issue in 1862, Sewell, as Attorney General recognized doubts as to the legal nature of native title, none of which (in his view) had been authoritatively resolved: 'whether we consider (as is sometimes done) the lands of the native as properly *lands of the Crown*, subject to the occupational right of the natives, or [whether these territories were to be construed] as land over which the natives hold *private proprietary rights* by a kind of allodial tenure'.[356] The former conceptual approach—one that would be expressed as appropriate in the early twentieth century, for instance—implicitly treated native title as a mere burden on the Crown's underlying dominion in the land itself.[357] The latter accorded recognition to a distinct normative and proprietary regime beyond the scope of Crown-managed

[354] Morgan to Richmond, 21 June 1858, in Scholefield (ed), *The Richmond-Atkinson Papers*, I, 409.

[355] Ford, *Settler Sovereignty*, 55–71.

[356] Attorney General, 22 November 1862, CO209/170, fos.221–1a, TNA (emphasis in original).

[357] For an examination of the approach assumed in legislation in the early twentieth century in New Zealand, see Hickford, 'John Salmond and Native Title in New Zealand', 853–924.

lands, and allowing no known superior or overlord in tenure. Irrespective of the correct legal description of native title, however, Sewell opined that 'by virtue of what is termed its *eminent domain* [the Crown] has in my opinion the right of making roads through such lands, in order to enable it to exercise its functions of sovereignty'.[358] Under the Constitution Act, the power to take land for making roads lay not with the Crown acting in concert with the legislature: 'power of the General Assembly, under the Constitution Act to legislate in respect of the waste lands does not arise until the land has been ceded to the Crown by the natives'.[359] '[A]s regards native lands (until they become subject to the power of the General Assembly by cession to the Crown)', Sewell wrote, 'the Crown is in my opinion the sole sovereign power.'[360] Yet, '[b]y the Treaty of Waitangi the Crown guaranteed to the natives their territorial possessions, the natives on their part ceding to the Crown the sovereignty: The power of the General Assembly, under the Constitution Act to legislate in respect of the waste lands does not arise until the land has been ceded to the Crown by the natives'.[361] Sewell considered that the right of laying roads was an incident of sovereign power in the colony. In his opinion, therefore, 'the right of passage through a country, and *ex necessitate*, the right of using and constructing all the ordinary means of passage, such as roads bridges &c is an *essential condition of sovereignty*'.[362] Beyond the process of statutory interpretation vis-à-vis the Constitution Act, Sewell's sources were telling. He resorted to Vattel on the law of nations, finding no other sources apposite for his purposes.

Officials and responsible ministers in the Fox ministry suggested formally transferring the risks of ascertaining proprietorship and other claims to Māori so that these operational and tactical risks were increasingly devolved away from the constitutional centre of colonial political activity. By the time Grey assumed the governorship for a second term, the recently installed ministry of Fox contended for a policy whereby alienation of territories subject to native title and ascertaining indigenous property rights or claims to an interest were sorted out by indigenous communities. A memorandum of 31 October 1861 acknowledged the 'subject of land [to be] a difficult & delicate one in the colony both in relation to the vendors & the purchasers'. As to Māori vendors, 'Sir George Grey is aware how much jealousy exists at the present moment in the minds of the natives on the subject'. In the view of colonial ministers, there seemed to be 'only one method of removing that feeling without at the same time absolutely abstaining from all further purchase, and that is to leave the matter substantially in the hands of the runangas'. As such, a 'title sifted through the investigations of these bodies (whose knowledge on the subject will in all, except a comparatively small number of disputed cases, be found complete) and made the subject of publicity, may be considered as pretty well ascertained'.[363] Conceptually, at least, the device of the native land courts, as conceived in 1861 and 1862, rested on this very basis of risk-transference.[364]

[358] Attorney General, 22 November 1862, CO209/170, fo.221a, TNA.

[359] Ibid, fo.220a. [360] Ibid, fo.221. [361] Ibid, fo.220a.

[362] Ibid, fos.220a–1 (the second emphasis in the passage represents underlining added in pencil at the Colonial Office).

[363] 'Memorandum by Ministers on Sir George Grey's plan for proposed institutions for the native race', Auckland, 31 October 1861, (enclosure number 6 in dispatch no 15), CO209/164, fos.360–1, TNA. Fox's second ministry assumed government on 12 July 1861.

[364] For analyses of the beginnings of the Native Land Court and its early operational histories, see Loveridge, 'Origins of the Native Land Acts and Native Land Court in New Zealand'; Boast, *Buying the Land*, 41–8, 61–7; Williams, *'Te Kooti tango whenua'*.

It reflected an increasing desire to transfer the risk of decision-making on title to fluid indigenous communities and to place the new Native Land Court in an enabling or confirmatory role albeit one operating a narrow portal through which native title was transformed. Established as a pilot in two quiescent districts in the Kaipara north of Auckland in 1864, two courts were established, with the local resident magistrate, John Rogan, named as president. Māori sat on the courts with him: two for Kaipara South district, and two for Kaipara North district.[365] The concept of native land courts resonated with earlier efforts on the part of the third Earl Grey in 1846 and Richmond in 1858 to propose legislation to lure Māori polities to increasingly enfold their indigenous narratives within a certain way of seeing relations with landscapes; that is, having a bespoke or special purpose colonial court or forum to encourage or at least to facilitate Māori to have their interests in land ascertained pursuant to an introduced regime. These relations with landscapes would be reconceived through rights-talk (rights of communities to and in land or 'tribal title') and claims to pre-eminence over a territory. Over time 'some canons of native tenure may be laid down, and the varying customs of different tribes acquire some settled form; and so that the same tribunal which ascertains title by native custom, may purge it from barbarous practices by refusing to admit these as custom at all'.[366] Section 3 of the Native Lands Act of 1862 declared that nothing in the legislation was to be 'construed as rendering the rights of the Natives in respect of such lands or the usages or customs on which such rights depend cognizable or determinable by any Court of Law or Equity or other Judicature'. Such cognizance would only be possible once those customary titles had been defined and a 'certificate of title' issued. Sewell critiqued the Native Lands Bill in 1862, informing colonial ministers that 'very ill consequences will flow from bringing native rights under the cognizance of our ordinary courts of law'.[367] In his view (as with other jurists before him), the 'only basis of title which our courts can recognize is that founded on a grant from Her Majesty under the public seal of the colony or some instrument having the like operation and effect'. Grey's ministers disagreed, as did the Colonial Office, suggesting that once a policy decision was made to encapsulate custom and native title within positive law, the ordinary courts could take cognizance of it. Rogers pencilled, 'Why not? If another is established by law the court can recognise it'. Ministers considered that there was 'no sufficient reason why native rights should not be recognised by the Courts, or why the native customary tenure, if properly defined and recorded, should be excluded'.[368]

Ultimately, then, statute resolved this question of cognizance, although, as I have noted elsewhere, certainly not always happily.[369] It meant that New Zealand jurisprudence on native title was predominantly statutory in its focus and has largely remained so. As Boast states, the impact of the Native Land Court was revolutionary in some areas, but it should not disguise the continuing significance of Crown purchase, as both Loveridge and Boast explore.[370] Boast also notes that much work remains to be done on why and how certain communities took to the court, an observation which this

[365] *New Zealand Gazette*, 1864, 168 and 273.

[366] Bell, 5 November 1862, CO209/170, fo.27, TNA.

[367] Sewell, 'Native Lands Bill', 6 September 1862, CO209/170, fos.35a–6, TNA.

[368] Ibid, fo.36.

[369] Hickford, 'John Salmond and Native Title'; Hickford, 'Strands from the Afterlife'.

[370] Loveridge, 'Development of Crown Policy on the Purchase of Maori Land' (research report 2001; Wai 1200; A77); Boast, *Buying the Land*, 104.

study's analysis supports. The statutory portal of recognition for native title opened onto an agonistic vista. Belgrave observed how the Native Land Court enabled participating Māori to 'fashion their own narratives for the court without the assistance of counsel'.[371] Yet Binney cautioned that this judicial forum 'was a competitive arena, and the oral narratives were structured for agonistic debate between Māori'.[372] In this manner, narratives could be configured and reconfigured in novel ways, as the court became a proxy for debate and contest by other means. In 1864, Carleton, writing in the politically radical, utilitarian-sympathizing *Westminster Review*, characterized the court as a fulfilment of the third article of the Treaty of Waitangi—presenting to Māori the rights and privileges of British subjects: 'The promise implied in the Maori version of the treaty of Waitangi—that natives of New Zealand should be allowed to have as good a title to their lands as Europeans, and that they should in the event of their selling or leasing, be allowed to obtain the value of such lands, has been fulfilled'.[373]

As witnessed, this view of the Treaty of Waitangi as a harbinger of liberal participation in an introduced political economy—ultimately seeking to evade the communitarian bonds of customary laws and permitting a free trade in land whereby the full market value of such territory could be obtained transactionally—was certainly not shared by all. As with the largely Whig-liberal orientation of the London advocates of the transitional Native Council Bill proposals in 1860, it illuminated once more the very ambiguities inhering in a nineteenth-century liberal setting predicated on eventually bringing diverse indigenous polities within its embrace.

[371] Belgrave, *Historical Frictions*, 27.
[372] Binney, 'History and Memory'', 84.
[373] Carleton, 'New Zealand', 468.

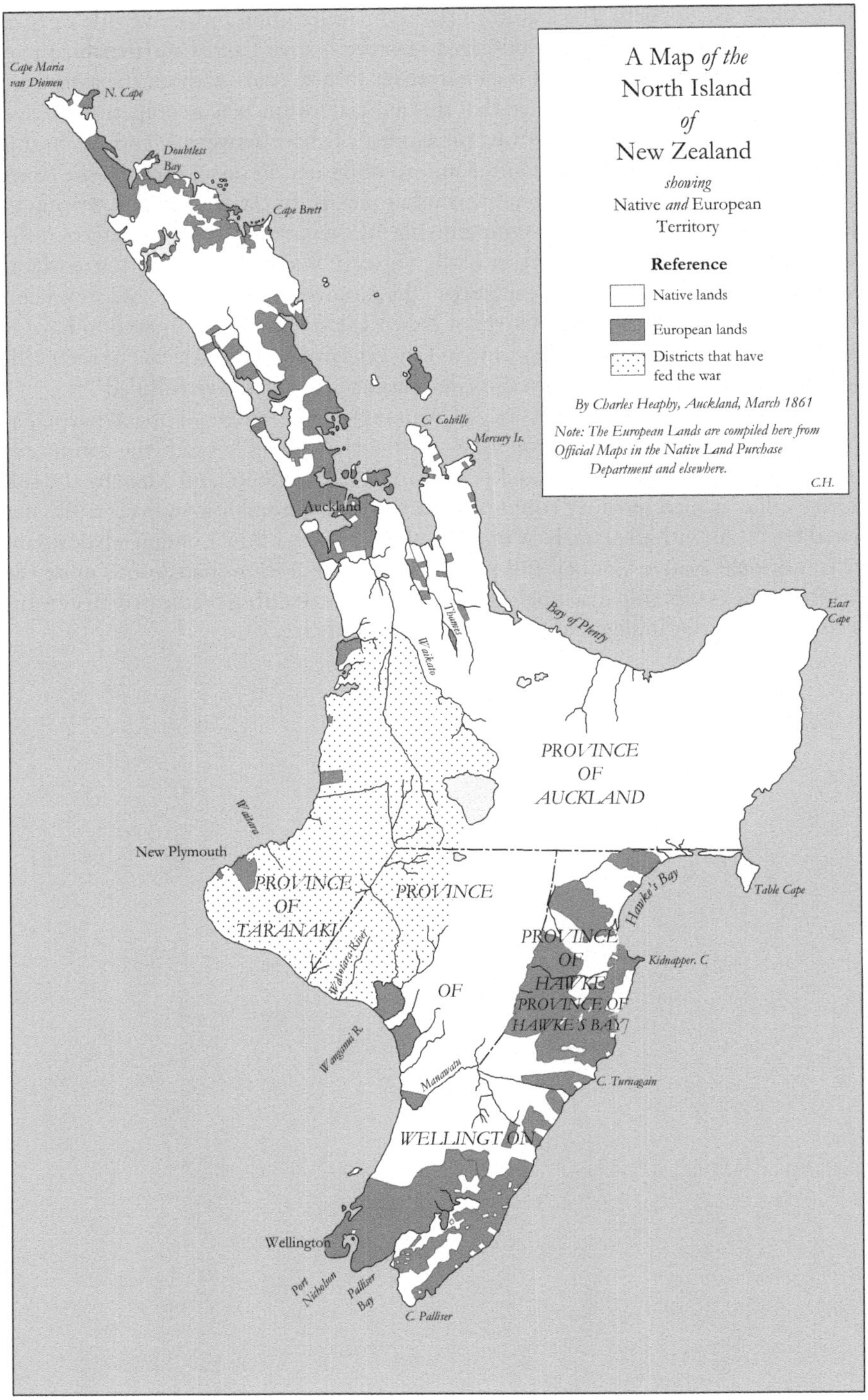

Plate 1 Based on Charles Heaphy, 'A map of the North Island of New Zealand shewing native and European territory', March 1861, NZ map 2562, Sir George Grey Special Collections, Auckland City Libraries, Auckland.

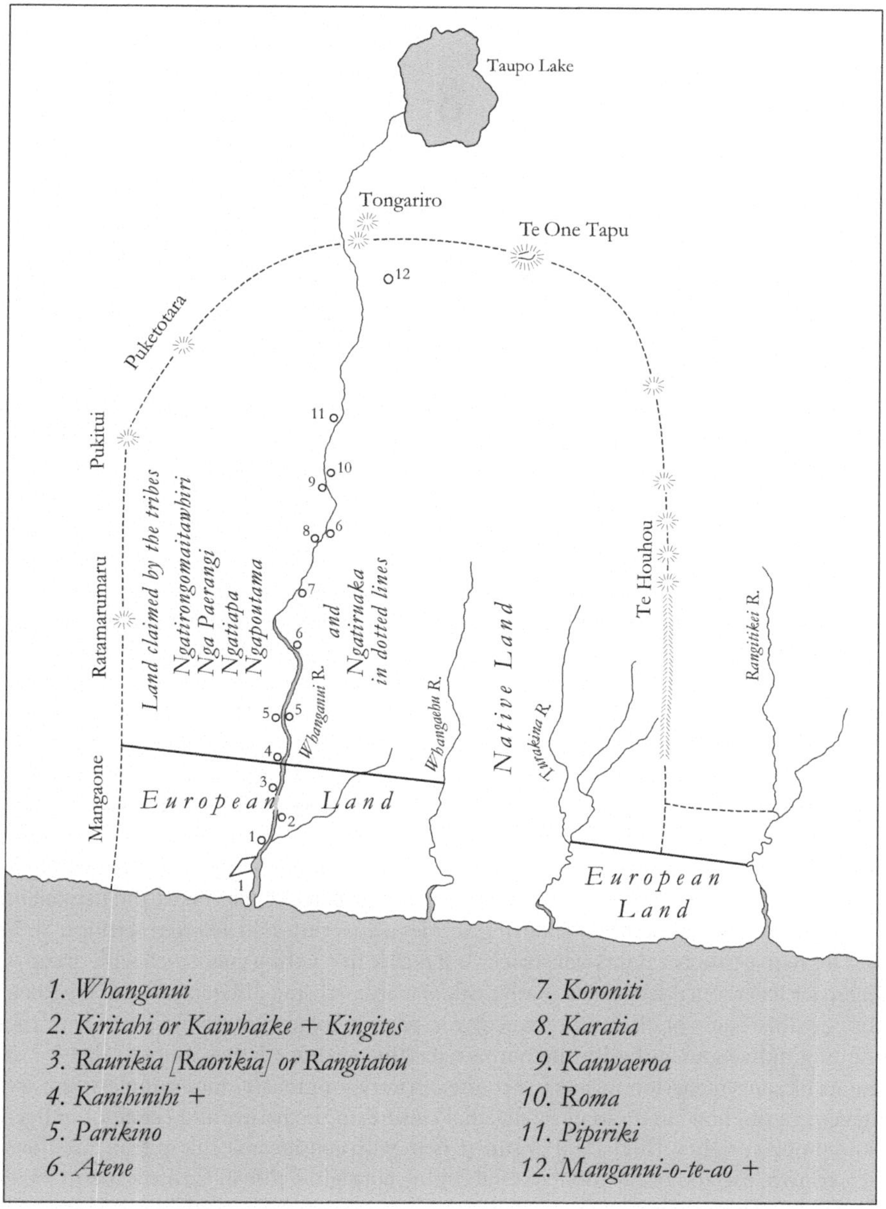

Plate 2 Drawn on the basis of the sketched map enclosed with White to Mantell, 20 May 1863, JC-WG1/4, 86, Archives New Zealand, Wellington.

8

Conclusions

CONSTITUTIONAL DESIGN AND THE TREATY OF WAITANGI: BALANCED CONSTITUTIONS, NATIVE TITLE, AND THE NORMATIVITY OF POLITICAL CONSTITUTIONALISM

Indigenous property rights in empire were made and are in the making still. Native title lay at the intersection of thought and disputes regarding indigenous political authority over territorial space, the question of English law and customary law, jurisdiction, and sovereignty. As seen in Chapters Three, Four, and Seven, it also posed the question whether indigenous views of how natives managed their territory should determine the nature and extent of the construct of native title as opposed to juristic or political economy texts transposed from abroad, or whether an exogenously imposed or negotiated mingling of these sources would come together. We see these questions emerging distinctly in Britain's relations with New Zealand. For a number of influential, early nineteenth-century academics and politicians, New Zealand was an experiment, an ignition chamber for a new colonial society, one predicated on incorporating indigenous peoples within the colonial body politic (if such peoples were not exterminated first).[1] Interwoven stories of indigenous property rights serve to illuminate rich, entwined British, colonial, and imperial histories. They tell us something about the mechanics of trans-oceanic politics and practices of empire through time. They further inform us about the transpositions, as well as translations, of intellectual sources from one arena to another through time. Rights were socially and culturally—so, thus, legally—constructed and iterated in historical contexts rather than enduring verities across time and assorted settings. So it was for native title as a rights-construct. As a puzzle in a setting concerned with occupying space for colonial settlement, native title was able to bring different threads together, to crystallize issues of discomfort, whether in relation to how to acquire territory or the status of indigenous authority and norms regarding territory. It was a subject that led to points of convergence on means to acquire territory—purchase, for example—but not agreement on 'how' to do so or intellectual closure on the nature and extent of indigenous property rights. This lack of closure persists with considerable ink spilt on questions of 'exclusive use and occupation' in establishing aboriginal title in Canada and in New Zealand to prove the presence or otherwise of 'customary marine title' in the foreshore and seabed. How these approaches compare with indigenous discourses on managing and interacting with territory and landscapes remains fraught and contested.

Jurisprudence from across the seas supplied influential satchels of sources and genres or ways of speaking and seeing. But these were not the pivots on which the making of native title turned. The application and understanding of these legal sources were

[1] Salesa also examines this idea, focusing on racial amalgamation in *Racial Crossings*.

'regionalized' and varied not merely in the localities of a colony. They were also 'regionalized' within the particular networks and politics of trans-oceanic empire, and within the imperial metropole itself. The politics of trans-oceanic empire were both global and, paradoxically, particular, intimate, and provincial, with distinct colonial settlements such as Wellington, Sydney, Auckland, Adelaide, and Port Phillip acting as provinces with metropolitan networks based in Britain.[2] Particular clusters of individuals in London, Sydney, and Auckland were connected laterally on some issues. Thus, we have seen Fox and Fitzgerald working with Gladstone in 1851 and 1852, while Chapman referred to Canada, New Zealand, and Australia when considering colonial matters. Cross-fertilization of personnel and ideas between the outlier 'provinces' also occurred: Sydney, Wellington, and Auckland intersecting—as part of a wider 'British world' system, settlers were co-owners and co-writers of British histories (and felt so entitled). As such, the English civil war that began in 1642 or the revolution of 1688 would remain as much the heritage of these distant settlers and their descendants, as it would be of those who remained in the United Kingdom. The relevance and meanings of these travelling juristic and political economy sources were often subject to fraught contestation. Thus, this study charted the uses of United States jurisprudence on 'Indian title' in British New Zealand. These United States sources were also applied to an Australian context in 1836 (the Batman treaty in Port Phillip).[3] But, unlike New Zealand, these sources did not settle. Notoriously multiplying deeds of purchase with Māori communities from 1814, as well as commerce, set a distinctive tone and temper to engagements with indigenous populations in northern New Zealand. The New Zealand Company and others pursued deeds of purchase elsewhere (1839–1840) while Sydney-based speculators used these paper forms in the South Island (1840). In *Symonds*, a former New Zealand Company agent, Justice Chapman, formally introduced to New Zealand the jurisprudence on 'Indian title' associated with the moderate federalist, Chief Justice Marshall. This jurisprudence, contesting with theories in favour of a freer market in land, aided efforts to assert the pre-eminence of colonial government in sorting out land policies.[4]

Stadial theory also entwined with jurisprudential sources, supplying key ways for framing and placing indigenous property rights. What debates on native title permit us to see is what was done to and with bodies of theory as they travelled across the seas towards novel circumstances in the early nineteenth century. Occasionally, these bodies of theory were inflected by changed circumstances even though printed, high-level theoretical or jurisprudential texts (Vattel's *Le Droit des Gens*, for example) might remain impervious. Applying stadialism developed two important insights for both proprietary rights and political authority: first, Māori were not hunters (as Native Americans were conventionally thought to be); secondly, Māori were horticulturists or planters of crops but not pre-existing users of the plough (unlike husbandmen or agriculturists in the conventional tropes of stadial theory advanced in Europe). It intermingled congenially with Christianized civilizational perspectives, as I have noted elsewhere.[5] The pervasiveness of the logics of stadialism into the 1850s and 1860s has been demonstrated in Chapters Five, Six, and Seven. Figures like Fenton, Whitaker,

[2] Hickford, 'Making "Territorial Rights"', 134.

[3] Attwood, *Possession*, 88–90.

[4] Hickford, '"Vague Native Rights"'; Hickford, '"Settling some very important principles"'; Hickford, 'Making "Territorial Rights"'. See also Rockwell, *Indian Affairs and the Administrative State in the Nineteenth Century.*

[5] Hickford, '"Decidedly the Most Interesting Savages"'.

Richmond, and Martin resorted to these logics, tying them to ways in which proprietary rights were constructed and perceived: fixed abodes allowing productive economic relations and secure property. Seeing Māori communities as predicated on horticulture allowed theorists or policy-formulators, such as Wakefield and Governor Grey in the 1830s and 1840s, to imagine approaches for incorporating Māori politically, economically, and culturally through 'amalgamation', a trope that resonated with Jeffersonian themes already advanced in the United States.[6] Such ventures of thought and practice could not be distanced from profound challenges concerning the ability to influence the legal and political meanings of how communities interacted with landscapes.

In New Zealand and British musings on New Zealand, challenging questions about whether or not to relate indigenous property rights to authority over territorial space—the ability and power to determine to whom the use and occupation of land and its resources could be allocated—gave rise to particular terms such as 'magisterial jurisdiction', 'territorial jurisdiction', 'collective sovereignty', 'territorial sovereignty', 'tribal rights', and 'seignorial rights', and generated debate about their relevance or meanings. With New Zealand we see a decidedly rich profusion of material on these subjects. These terms reflected attempts to grapple with questions of authority as much as questions of property rights. Native title combined disputes on both issues. Thus, questions emerged as to balancing the preferences or interests of individual Māori against indigenous community control concerning allocating territory to strangers. This entailed complex issues as to whether community control of land in the form of a tribal title could or would have undermined the Crown's obligations under the Treaty of Waitangi to individual Māori, particularly those who did not wish to be bound by community control, the directions of a community, or 'customary' sources of authority, such as chiefs. Such sources of authority were contested within and outside of Māori norms. They were subject to ongoing change in general, either through the presence of coastal European settlements or through chieftains endeavouring to reassert different or new forms of influence or hegemony over others, whether *hapū* members, other *hapū* or settlers.

These questions engaged conversation, debate, and still more questions. These conversations, whether temperate or intemperate, occurred against a background of often profound intra-*anglophone* disagreement. Rights often involve substantive disagreement over whether or not they actually exist and discord as to the content and incidents of such rights.[7] In New Zealand, a site for building new communities predicated on 'racial amalgamation' indigenous property rights were precursors to political incorporation within the colonial body politic. Their supersession by Crown-derived tenure was intended to lay a pathway for accessing the electoral franchise and the norms of English property law. These rights, as they were constructed and contested in such historical settings, were also constraints on action. They represented legal and political constraints in shaping policies and behaviours around purchase, and encouraged the emergence of often ornate experiments in legal design—the Native Council Bill (see Chapter Six), proposals for Native Land Courts (see Chapter Seven) and resident magistrates. Conceived and constructed as 'rights' they focused discussion on what

[6] Wood, *Empire of Liberty*, 396–9. Cadogan noted Thomas Jefferson's relevance to Grey in 'Constituting the Settler Colony', 45, 51.

[7] Waldron, *Law and Disagreement*, 11–12.

was politically plausible in particular ways: for instance, the debate about techniques of purchase as opposed to a Land Court.

As explored in Chapters Four to Seven, moments of heightened contest on these issues occurred in relation to certain pressure points, as when intra-*anglophone* as much as, or more than, intra-Māori disputes were crystallized through a particular policy decision as to the basis for occupying lands in New Zealand, as in 1846–1848, or a particular event, such as a purchase transaction in 1859–1860, for example. These disputes troubled people both in colonial New Zealand and the United Kingdom. The intensely negotiated presence of precarious bridgehead settlements in New Zealand may be profitably studied at a critical time in the middle decades of the nineteenth century when deliberate settlements were contemplated or had been implemented in South Australia, Port Phillip (Melbourne), and the Natal. Contests concerning New Zealand, Canada, and Australia shared broad thematic qualities but also revealed important distinctions and disjunctions. In Australia and New Zealand, we see a coalescence of moves to discipline the contours of European settlement through instructions on the market in Crown land. Unlicensed squatting was inevitable, it was thought. Nevertheless, the state withholding legal recognition from unauthorized transactions, or requiring European parties to go through a lengthy process of scrutiny, had a salutary effect, slowing down the release of authorized property interests. Yet, because of the materiality of indigenous power and because native title was recognized, we also witness important areas of divergence in concrete policy settings and juridical genres in spite of certain shared preoccupations and personnel, with each colonial settlement contributing its own idiosyncrasies and localized agendas.

Elite sophisticated, printed texts, including court judgments (*Symonds* and *Johnson v M'Intosh*) and books, such as Vattel's *Le Droit des Gens*, Grotius' *De Iure Belli ac Pacis*, Locke's *Two Treatises of Government*, and Immanuel Kant's *The Metaphysics of Morals* (1797–1798), survive. They now tend strongly to mediate early twenty-first-century accounts of how to analyse historical understandings of European colonization, indigenous lands, and global justice.[8] They—the extensive jurisprudential works in particular—have become subjects of textually focused analyses of their abstract principles; for instance, what Grotius, Locke, Vattel, or Kant, said or did not say. They remain accessible singular texts, more so than the disparate materials of the interior, contested worlds of political debate and negotiation, whether in the metropole or in colonial settings. High-level colonial texts can suggest ease rather than unease of course. This is particularly so when they simply purport to describe law even when the law portrays an aspirational state of affairs, a canvas of smooth completeness: presenting the worlds it purports to describe as so simply because it says so. On its own terms, *Symonds* offered this smooth sense of pre-existing legalism that would have ensnared indigenous property rights in empire anyway, erasing any sense of real contingency or messy historicity. But it is the interaction of these high-level textual sources with the interior worlds of human interaction and policy-making, together with the novel situations to which they are translated and transposed, that affords the most illuminating information on questions of indigenous property rights in the jurisprudence of empire, as well as the real life and practices of these concepts as they are inflected by different circumstances.

[8] Hunter, 'Global Justice and Regional Metaphysics', in Dorsett and Hunter (eds), *Law and Politics*, 11–29; and Ivison, 'Justice and Imperialism', in ibid, 31–48.

This jurisprudence of empire in the shadows was vulnerable to neglect as participants moved on or personnel changed, or records were neglected, mislaid, or simply forgotten. It mingled with sources of political economy and history. It often presented as a genre of legal policy oriented towards experiments in conscious legal design.

This study points to a broad consensus obtaining on some general operational characteristics of native title in New Zealand but with considerable debate as to content and application remaining. First, this consensus included seeing Crown-supervised purchase or Crown-supervised confirmation of dealings with native title as a vital element, augmented from the mid-1860s by a statutory land court. Kent McNeil rightly sees, in a passage of his important work that is overlooked, the early stress on Crown-monitored purchase or 'pre-emption' as predominantly a policy choice and not a clear jurisprudential requirement.[9] It was a contest that resonated with the experiences in British North America and subsequently in *Johnson v M'Intosh*. It had its Australasian analogue.[10] As demonstrated in Chapters Two and Three, it aligned with policies on the management of lands conceived in the 1830s (the Goderich directives). In addition, native title was not necessarily conceptually commensurable with English property law, with some jurists suggesting that a claim founded on native title could not be brought independently before the ordinary colonial courts. These points had material consequences. They were not the stuff of mere theory or abstraction.

Secondly, as seen in Chapters Four and Five in particular, theories of conceptual incommensurability between English real property law and native title conditioned policy responses and practices. In addition, some *anglophone* commentators treated the ordinary colonial courts as not jurisdictionally adapted to address native title matters or, as with Chapman in 1846–1847 and Martin in 1863, considered that native title was not legally cognizable and non-justiciable. Judges such as Gresson and Johnston thought it ill-adapted to the introduced courts and their ways of working. Indeed, the perceived non-justiciability of native title or, alternatively, its conceptual incommensurability with English tenure, encouraged a resort to customized or bespoke statutes, ordinances, and resident magistrate systems—the outcrops of experimentation. Ultimately, a statutorily contrived Native Land Court from 1862 reflected these very tendencies, as did the continuing focus on political negotiations with indigenous communities, principally for land purchase. The Native Rights Act 1865 reinforced the picture through section 5: the Native Land Court was declared to have the principal jurisdiction to adjudicate on 'issues of fact or of Maori Custom or Usage' engaged in any action involving native title, with its 'verdict or judgment as the case may be' to be returned to the Supreme Court (if the matter had initially arisen in a Supreme Court proceeding) and treated as having the 'same effect as the verdict of a jury in the Supreme Court'. This legislation was intended to declare that the 'jurisdiction of the Queen's Courts of Law extends over the persons and properties of all Her Majesty's subjects within the Colony'. By asserting that the findings of the Native Land Court could be treated as a finding of fact in the Supreme Court in circumstances where the Supreme Court found itself confronted with a disputed native title, the knot of perceived jurisdictional or conceptual incommensurability could be cut. It was expedient to remove any doubts as to the issue. Section 4 restated the significance of resorting

[9] McNeil, *Common Law Aboriginal Title*, 227, 235.
[10] Hickford, '"Vague Native Rights to Land"'.

to custom: 'Every title to or interest in land over which the Native Title shall not have been extinguished shall be determined according to the Ancient Custom and Usage of the Maori people so far as the same can be ascertained'. Statutes and institutions, such as a native council and eventually a Native Land Court, were experiments in pursuing mutual intelligibility between indigenous customary norms and exogenous conceptions of property rights.

Once formally acknowledged, native title could not easily be evaded or ignored. Although a diminishing category over time, it provided a lever for negotiation, something to be bargained. As usual, the policy-makers, advisors, and negotiators, as opposed to those simply engaging in abstraction or theory, lived the practices of native title and wrested or even theorized with these practices as new questions and difficulties emerged. This study remained alive to the intellectual dimensions, the genres of expression or language, in which these individuals, and the communities or organizations in which they participated, were involved. Hence, discourses and practices were often shaped and modified through the particular agendas and forms of community or corporate assembly in which they were conveyed or produced. The preceding chapters illustrated how these transposed sources and discrete legal instruments were deployed by, say, the New Zealand Company, the third Earl Grey, Chapman, the Aborigines' Protection Society, and Christopher Richmond, to explain and to discipline or constrain practices concerning indigenous property rights on the ground, or to try to do so. These constraints could relate to arguments about the significance of particular terms in the Treaty of Waitangi—'sovereignty', 'pre-emption', 'the full, exclusive, and undisturbed possession of their lands, estates, forests, fisheries, and other properties'—provisions in the New Zealand Constitution Act 1852 or concepts such as 'occupancy' and prior consultation with Māori before legislating change (see Chapter Six). There were also debates about the relevance of these terms and concepts. These elite texts must be seen in living dynamic relations with human use in debate and discussion. Otherwise, all too often one is left with analyses dealing in high-level abstract texts across decades or centuries, detached from the discordance and 'messiness' of human life.

The concept of 'making', which I initially used in 1999 regarding indigenous property rights, still seems apt. As with EP Thompson's contribution to English class history, the term 'making' remains relevant 'because it is a study in an active process, which owes as much to agency as to conditioning'.[11] Throughout the 1840s, this study contended that the *making* of notions regarding indigenous proprietary rights within New Zealand was a consequence of convoluted disputes and conversations principally located at Westminster, in trans-oceanic colonial bridgeheads—scattered provinces of metropolitan Britain—and *modus vivendi* with Māori polities: the complex politics of negotiability punctuated by points or episodes of congruence albeit moments of congruence vulnerable to profound interpretative risks. As Andrew Sharp characterized indigenous politics much later, 'It is clear that Māori are not one team of action but many, as Pākehā are'.[12] Native title was incorporated as a category of political economy. Bound up in 'custom', it was seen as tied to hierarchies of customary authority, which British commentators thought that they saw or needed to see in ascertaining the 'who':

[11] Thompson, *The Making of the English Working Class*, 8.
[12] Sharp, *Justice and the Māori*, 316.

with whom should they negotiate—an aggregate or a disaggregated few? Indigenous property rights were also conceived as constituting an ambulatory category. Indeed, as settlements moved, it was seen as a category of receding proportions, increasingly a relic of a prior order of things albeit one persisting into the present and associated with polities adapting to altered, colonial circumstances.

How indigenous communities actually interacted with or related to landscapes was valorized as 'custom'—at least a certain interpretation of 'custom': something cementing indigenous communities and tying them to certain political-economic practices (forms of subsistence, for example) and to the land. Any sense of local variation between indigenous groups was erased in favour of broad principles and analogizing 'custom' to British legal concepts. Discourses around 'custom' and political economy allowed native title to be seen in Whig and some liberal Tory eyes (Stanley) as a disciplining force on initially precarious bridgehead settlements, requiring deliberative engagement through the institutions of courts or the practices of purchase. These indigenous 'rights' to territory were predominantly conceived as performative—as assisting imperial management or 'discipline' of territorial transactions and anglophone settlement-dispersion within imperial fields. In this sense, they assisted state-building in nascent colonial societies throughout New Zealand, largely constraining the pace and contours of licensed settlement-dispersal. Policies concerning native title represented part of an overall intellectual and material commitment to managed or disciplined European settlement. But we find too that native title was imbued with many of the ambiguities of mid-nineteenth-century liberalism, comprising a sense of rights as constraints, as precursors to political incorporation within a colonial polity of recent migrants, and as a prelude to participating in a range of colonial market options ushered in through the land market.[13]

'Sovereignty, liberty, authority, personality—these are the words of which we want alike the history and the definition; or rather, we want the history because its substance is in fact the definition'.[14] With native title, too, it is in the histories of contest that we see the filling out of its content in jurisprudential sources, legal policies, and legal design (such as statutes). The politics of negotiability suffused questions of native title, together with the predominantly political constitutions in, or alongside which, Māori found themselves, whether as individuals, or as members of *whānau* or *hapū*. These politics were often shot through with tactical bargaining, local imbalances of power, and even violence and warring. Organized British beach-head settlements—'factories', to adapt Hobson's metaphor, taken from his experiences in India—did not suddenly suspend the historicity of Māori communities. These incoming settlements represented a new development in localized areas and new opportunities, as well as risks, in indigenous politics, economies, and cultures. Leverage varied from place to place depending on the relative size of populations, the presence of pākehā strongholds (townships and redoubts), and intra-Māori politics as groups and factions competed for economic and political relationships and trade. These places became testing grounds for understanding native title, and authority over territorial space and natural resources, such as land and pasture. But these politics allowed situations and relations to be revisited, reinterpreted, and reconditioned. What we do not see is banal constitutionalism. Vitally, however,

[13] Cf Hilton, *A Mad, Bad, and Dangerous People?*, 30.
[14] Laski, *The Foundations of Sovereignty and Other Essays*, 314.

these moments of contest also arose within the imperial metropole—the conduct of Westminster and other community politics by other means—and between colonial bridgeheads and metropolitan sites. An ability to interpret and reinterpret the multi-dimensional metes and bounds of Crown–*hapū*, Crown–*rangatira*, or Crown–Māori relations was the essence of political constitutionalism. I have spoken previously of 'conversations without end'.[15] One consequence is to see a variety of pākehā interpretative histories of, say, the Treaty of Waitangi, and its receptions, as well as indigenous histories and entangled pākehā-Māori narratives. These occasionally fraught disputes allowed the content of native title to be repolished and 'thickened' episodically, as novel circumstances or different questions required participants to explore the significance of indigenous property rights. Just as importantly, these disputes intermittently encouraged thin consensus on outcomes—what was to be done practically (as in 1846–1847)—without any agreement on the content of the underlying rights or on abstract values. At other times, one view appeared to prevail only to be challenged anew when a new dispute arose, as with the Waitara purchase dispute seen in Chapter Seven.

This iterative, work-in-progress quality readily aligned with the introduced and developing British imperial-colonial constitutions. It could even be internalized within them such that the making of native title was seen to be a part of colonial-imperial constitutions. The Treaty of Waitangi and native title, as conceived in imperial politics and law, were exemplars of a pre-eminently political and partly legalistic constitution in operation. It is not enough to say that this was 'pragmatic'. Much more was happening. There was a normative value to these practices, to the making of native title and developing Crown relations with indigenous communities through time. The politics of negotiability on native title were endemic in constitutional settings primarily animated through the workings of political contest and policy-formulation, albeit one informed by legalistic ways of speaking and seeing, and sources. The practical and normative value of this state of affairs is what Ivison has referred to as 'the possibility to challenge (and shape) those arrangements which unavoidably act on them' or, I would gloss, which others would wish to apply to them.[16] 'But then', Ivison continues, 'the obvious question is: what are the conditions required for meaningful and effective contestation? How do we distinguish between arrangements that serve to entrench relations of power into relations of domination, and those that break free of them?'[17]

These issues persisted in troubling relations between indigenous communities and incoming settlers within colonial New Zealand. There were no easy answers, no panaceas, but conversations without end. Meanings were crafted and re-crafted, negotiated and renegotiated. Localized power imbalances suffused these conversations. Some Māori politicians incorporated the Crown into their own sense of constitutionalism, critiquing its officers' behaviours—the distant monarch's less than satisfactory counsellors—while using the imperial Crown across the seas as a metaphor for satisfactory behaviour in relation to indigenous communities (see Chapter Seven).[18] The incoming Crown was also *their* Crown (a metaphor to be invoked), as pākehā could be *their* pākehā. Messiness abounded. As colonial preferences increasingly prevailed in local

[15] See Chapter One, and Hickford, 'Strands from the Afterlife', 189.
[16] Ivison, 'Consent or Contestation?', 189.
[17] Ibid.
[18] See also Hickford, 'Framing and Reframing the *Agōn*'; Hickford, 'Strands from the Afterlife', 173–4.

areas like Auckland, Wellington, and Christchurch with a sheer inrush of migrants (if not elsewhere), their preferred meanings or interpretations of rights tended to predominate. Importantly, the iterative political constitutions with which settlers and Māori grappled were characterized by political contestability and negotiability, preeminently in the 1840s, 1850s, and 1860s, but also evident in later times, including the 1920s and 1930s. It remained a feature of intra-Māori politics and of relations with (including critiques of) the Crown.[19] To expect to 'stabilize' meanings authoritatively over time, other than through the interpretations congealing in judicial decisions or political determinations from time to time, is to pursue a mistaken path.[20]

As argued in Chapter Four, the underlying Whig foundations of the New Zealand Constitution of 1852 and its relevance to questions of indigenous property rights and political authority are 'lost'. These foundations have been neglected—we see a deepening forgetting of historical and political cultural being in the late twentieth and early twenty-first centuries. Such foundations were not merely architectural but also normative. They reflected and expressed a view of what the constitution ought to be like in practice and theory. The framing of the New Zealand Constitution Act set out sketched expectations. Chapter Four revealed how the content of private and official correspondence was clearer. You do not see these underlying normative features mentioned in constitutional law texts or in constitutional histories. Even Allison, in his work on *The English Historical Constitution* (2007), avoids references to colonial and imperial constitutions. Scholars such as N Barber, Graham Gee, and Grégoire Webber have recognized the normative aspects of political constitutional arrangements in early twenty-first-century Britain.[21] Likewise, they underlay constitutional design in the 1840s and 1850s. In 1846 and in 1851–1852, Earl Grey sought a whiggishly informed balanced constitution of diverse interests, sufficient to hinder the emergence of despotic rule, whether in the form of an intemperate democratic majority or through undue centralization. Native title had its place in these worlds of constitutional design and thought. A central point, an animating normative principle, was one of rivalrous powers: setting up sites of contestation within the body politic and areas for political contestability to occur, as with questions of land subject to Māori control. The 1852 constitutional settlement formed choke-points, and divided jurisdictions, points where people had to wrest with one another and compromise if they were to get things done. This sort of design bolstered liberty in Whig and Tory eyes, although Tories tended to prefer much more local or municipal government. As a Whig aristocrat mindful of the tyranny of the majority, Earl Grey was concerned to ensure the protection of political minorities.

These concerns resonate still—the overbearing qualities of a political majority relative to the representation of minorities, for instance—although the nuanced preoccupations of, say, Whigs with these matters have been primarily forgotten.[22] Yet preferred interpretations of the imperial and colonial constitutions, whether in the imperial

[19] Hickford, 'Strands from the Afterlife'.

[20] Cf Palmer, *The Treaty of Waitangi*, 315–23, 362.

[21] Barber, 'Against a Written Constitution'; Gee and Webber, 'What is a Political Constitution?'; Gee, 'The Political Constitutionalism of J.A.G. Griffith', 20–45.

[22] As noted in Chapters Five and Six, a key source for thinking historically about mid-nineteenth-century Whig notions in these contexts, albeit in a British rather than offshore (colonial) British sense, remains Burrow, *Whigs and Liberals*.

metropole or within colonial settlements or amongst indigenous polities, were contested.[23] In the early 1850s, others, such as radical politicians at Westminster, supported majoritarian representation and expressed concerns about the unelected despotism of governors, and it is these voices that mainly attract attention in twentieth-century accounts and subsequently. These historical voices are too readily presented as heroic promulgators of colonial self-determination and harbingers of representative democracy (even if initially based on a property-based electoral franchise). Either that or they are treated in passing as forerunners of an inexorable move towards universal suffrage and fully fledged democratic institutions.[24]

This book takes seriously the historical turn in studies of legal and political thought, policy, and questions about the real life of indigenous property rights, as well as its relation to imperial and colonial constitutions rather than the abstract one of disembodied legal texts and sporadic court decisions. By no means uniquely, New Zealand's constitutions over time—and I use the plural form deliberately—were not a descriptive fact but a process, a space to be watched and lived. History, as much as the present, is a precarious source of lessons. But 'one of the uses of the past arises from the fact that we are prone to fall under the spell of our own intellectual heritage' or, more commonly perhaps, to ignore the complexities and shades of that heritage altogether—to suffer from the forgetting of being.[25] It is erroneous to simply dub these aspects of constitutionalism as 'pragmatic' (although they were that too). Richer veins of intellectual and political thought were tapped into, deployed, and contested.

Historically, New Zealand's constitutional settings illuminated both colonial and imperial British debate about the nature of British-world constitutions but also the salience of indigenous property rights and the superstructure of indigenous political authority (particularly chiefly authority) underlying or buttressing these claims to property. British designers of the Constitution Acts of 1846 and 1852—Earl Grey being a pre-eminent driver even though the 1852 legislation was enacted just after he left office—saw constitutional statutes as broad frames for incomplete pictures rather than complete codes (see Chapters Four and Five). Beneath these broad outlines each colony had its own constitutional trajectories, whether New South Wales, South Australia, Victoria, Upper and Lower Canada, or the Cape colony.[26] Similarly, as merely touched upon here, India had its own legal sophistications on constitutionalism or property rights. The so-called Great Rent Case of June 1865 (*Thakurani Dasi v Bisheshwar Mukharjya & Ors*), in dealing with the agrarian tenancy regime under Bengal's Act X of 1859, held that the ryots possessed a title to the soil anterior to that of the zamindars: a title based on custom and the practice of ryots having borne the risk and applied the labour of clearing jungle for cultivation.[27] Native title, too, with custom driving its contents, was anterior to subsequent Crown-derived titles, and required reconciliation with the new order introduced with the Crown and organized British settlement.[28] Indigenous property rights had a temporal dimension,

[23] Chapter Seven has considered (non-exhaustively) a variety of indigenous viewpoints.
[24] Johansson, *The Politics of Possibility*, 55–6.
[25] Skinner, *Visions of Politics: Volume I—Regarding Method*, 6.
[26] For Canada, see McHugh, 'The Politics of Historiography and the Taxonomies of the Colonial Past', in Musson and Stebbings (eds), *Making Legal History*.
[27] Wilson, *The Domination of Strangers*, 104–32; Sartori, 'A Liberal Discourse of Custom in Colonial Bengal', in *Past and Present*.
[28] Hickford, 'Framing the *Agōn*'.

with stadialism and jurisprudential sources imbuing them with a sense of historicity. At most, the Treaty of 1840 and the New Zealand Constitution Act 1852 were simply starting or punctuation points for a series of long conversations. Beyond their framing, one lived with considerable indeterminacy and possibility. Indigenous property rights in Britain's empire developed their own vernacular, dependent on particular colonial and constitutional contexts. Native title was as much an iterative process—something to be worked out incrementally, case by case—as were the imperial and colonial constitutions. Things could be in flux or not. Participants also dwelt with complexity and risk. And they knew it. Contestability proved to be a vital element within the historical imperial-colonial constitutions. It attested to the richness of the veins of debate on native title in mid-nineteenth-century New Zealand and Britain, as much as to its adjustability or flexibilities. None of this is to say that an account of these constitutional arrangements need be merely descriptive. Yet it is certainly common for commentators to see the British political constitution, as it has been and is now, let alone the neglected historical New Zealand colonial constitutions from the 1840s onwards, as something able to be analysed in purely 'descriptive terms, as a summation of past experiences, rather than in genuinely constitutional terms as representing the recognition of certain normative principles'.[29]

Once formally recognized, native title engaged profound questions which still perplex today. The concept of a liberally minded constitutional setting oriented towards representing politically salient interests, subjecthood, and how to accommodate cultural diversity dramatized by territories subject to practical and normative indigenous control, if at all, was one such challenge. The answers of prime Whig designers and narrators behind the 1852 constitution, although unsatisfactory to the Aborigines' Protection Society in London and to a number of liberal-radical politicians in Britain and New Zealand, encouraged a measure of practical separateness for indigenous polities. The political and legal separateness would be a diminishing category as British bridgehead settlements spread into the hinterlands and along the coasts as deeds of purchase converted native title areas into spaces of English tenure and embedded colonial jurisdiction (as opposed to indigenous authority). Native title in this guise was integrated into narratives of diversity, liberty, and despotism in an imperial-colonial constitutional framework. Custom was seen as an admittedly transitional bulwark of liberty by some, including Martin, as well as a constraint on the expansion of coastal settlements. Others, such as Richmond, contended that the conduct of some chiefs was not consistent with custom, properly understood, but amounted to despotism and that the despotic tendencies of chieftains restrained members of their *hapū*. The institutional pluralism of provincial governments, a general assembly, and a nominated legislative council would remain in play too.

As it was, the pluralism of Māori communal autonomies tied to native title persisted for a considerable time. Chiefly elites adapted to the encroachments of strangers (settlers, resident magistrates) in localized areas.[30] Some indulged in land transactions, presenting themselves as generous hosts to strangers (allowing them to settle), as well as to incoming sources of money and to novel commercial arrangements introduced by these strangers. A number of groups could present themselves as parties in a mutually sheltering alliance with the pākehā settlement enclaves, vulnerable to being considered as insufficiently

[29] Bogdanor, *The New British Constitution*, 19.

[30] It is overly blunt and geographically unspecific to say that explosive settler population growth *simpliciter* spelt the death of such autonomy, although it certainly contributed to its degradation at key points and in some areas.

subordinate to hinterland indigenous polities who may have been accustomed to exerting pre-eminent influence over these groups before the advent of major European settlements at Wellington, Auckland, or New Plymouth. Others sought coalescence or alliances around a hegemonic concept or figure, as with the Kīngitanga (see Chapters Five and Seven), in order to manage inter-*hapū* relations and relations with the bridgehead settlements. Some elements sought to evade the hegemonic pretensions of either indigenous conglomerates or European settlements. Disagreements as to which interpretations of these novel relations to prefer stoked the ashes of civil war into flame, as amongst elements of Ngāti Kahungunu and Te Ātiawa in the 1850s and 1860s. Indigenous communities were 'riders of the whirlwind' for a period.[31] Early *modus vivendi* worked out on the ground obscured what Tully refers to as broadly 'bi-civilizational' understandings.[32] Strains of thought and discourse mingled. But each participant brought with them constraints and preferred interpretations not necessarily shared by or with other participants. What Tully characterized as a 'multilogue' underlay these engagements although some texts suggested outward consensus.[33] Indeed, the interpretative risk run by indigenous actors was that the papers surviving these negotiations could be construed in ways inimical to their preferred meanings or relationships. As with any negotiated settings, even those suffused with imbalances of power or risks of violence, varied agendas were in play.

Yet, with early nineteenth-century organized colonization in New Zealand, the nomenclature of 'property rights' or 'territorial rights', as well as the languages of jurisdiction, tended to domesticate Māori politics in intra-anglophone terms, treating customary authority as contained within the introduced colonial legal system and as something less than it was in practice. At the very least, as a strategy it implicated Māori politics in the genres of colonization, internalizing Māori politics within the colonial polity through genres of jurisdiction, property rights, and subjecthood. Under this approach customary authority could be reduced to customary law to manage indigenous relations *inter se* or as an attribute or incident of a property right, such as the power to alienate land or to allocate its use to others for a brief time (leasing or licensing). Some Māori drew in the Crown and its resources (money for purchases; resident magistrates), albeit at the risk of compromising or even completely losing their 'interpretative' independence, as incoming officials interpreted indigenous behaviours as accepting the genres of jurisdiction and property rights introduced and contested on the ground in local areas. Some Māori strategists and leaders continued to assert interpretative autonomy, as much as material autonomy on the ground, as the speeches at Kohimarama in 1860 and the Waitara dispute illustrated. But these interpretative autonomies were at risk as the ability of Māori elites to exert a meaningful influence on how to define relations with incoming strangers waned in certain areas. Their own political constituencies, already dynamic and flexible, grew fragile, as individual Māori or clusters within indigenous communities could renegotiate the terms of their own political, commercial, and social engagements with settlers. Having more options of how to engage with new ideas and ways of doing things risked diversity and fragmentation, as members within communities sought to follow different pathways or were persuaded to do so.

[31] Belich, 'Riders of the Whirlwind', in Boast and Hill (eds), *Raupatu*, 33–47.

[32] Tully, 'Consent, Hegemony, and Dissent in Treaty Negotiations', 242.

[33] Tully, 'Introduction', in Gagnon and Tully (eds), *Multicultural Democracies* (Cambridge, 2001), 20.

Shifts in internal colonial and imperial politics were critical to broad changes in policy with an impact on indigenous property rights. A desire amongst Peelites and liberals in Palmerston's 1859 ministry to make colonists ultimately responsible for the ill consequences of their decision-making—and the costliness—smoothed the way to letting go of imperial designs for a native council interposing between native title areas and areas clothed with Crown-derived tenure. Arguments continued to churn. Martin reflected on the place of Māori government and property rights in the face of an incorporating imperial-colonial constitutional frame. Writing in 1870, he considered Māori as falling into two broad classes: those accepting British authority and those who did not.[34] As Victorians like Merivale, Sewell, Richmond, and Martin knew, indigenous property rights involved ongoing questions of power and authority over space. Property engages such questions as the ability to determine whether others may occupy the space and, if so, on what terms and for how long. Designers of experiments such as the Native Lands Acts of 1862 and 1865 knew this. Property rights were a contrivance used by the Victorians to grasp the realities of indigenous power and behaviours—entering deeds of purchase—and to 'domesticate' or internalize these realities: to bring indigenous communities within the pale of colonial societies. Property rights also engaged questions of government and jurisdiction: whose laws prevailed? Whose interpretations would be pre-eminent? Do rights of government reside with the occupiers and controllers of territories and, if not them, then who? Some, including jurists like Chapman and Martin, regarded these questions as resolved in one way or another. Others, such as Te Teira, Kawepō and Kīngi in 1860, did not. Yet the powers of defining and interpreting relations of power to territory were ebbing away from indigenous leaders, although at different times and places—local stories of change and reshaping relations. The early twenty-first century is engaged with such questions and is compelled to look at them anew in Canada, Australia, and New Zealand. These challenges have not departed. But, in examining histories of indigenous property rights and their relations to the jurisprudence of empire, we have not only revealed histories of the 'various peoples of [an] archipelago in their interactions with each other'[35]—their myriad meeting places as much as their places of apartness—but also a larger canvass of richly entwined histories of empire across the seas.

[34] Martin to McLean, 21 February 1870, Ms-Papers-0032-0030, ATL.

[35] Pocock, 'Removal from the Wings', 12.

Bibliography

PRIMARY SOURCES—MANUSCRIPTS

Alexander Turnbull Library, Wellington

Elsdon Best, papers
George Clarke senior, and George Clarke junior correspondence
Henry Chapman correspondence, papers and memoranda
William Colenso, papers and 'memoranda of the arrival of Lieut Govr Hobson in New Zealand 1840'
Robert FitzRoy, miscellaneous papers
Octavius Hadfield correspondence, 1833–1902
William Hobson, papers, 1833–1846, Ms papers 46
William Hobson letters, 1841–1842
George Lambton, Earl of Durham, papers
Donald McLean papers
Webster collection
William Wentworth-John Jones deeds of conveyance

Archives New Zealand, Wellington

Internal Affairs (IA), correspondence (Offices of Colonial Secretary and Chief Protector of Aborigines, Auckland)
Legislation files (LE)
Old Land Claims (OLC) commissions, archives
Thomas Gore Browne papers

Auckland Institute and Museum Library

William Hobson, letters
Henry Williams papers

Auckland Public Library

Sir George Gipps court letterbook
George Grey, 'letterbook 1846–1853', GNZ Mss227
George Grey, 'Maori letters', GNZMA (Mmss)
George Grey, correspondence, GNZ Mss (collection)
Edward Shortland, diaries and journals, 1842–1844
Edward Shortland, correspondence
Te Kanae, Wiremu Naera, 'Life and times of Te Rauparaha', Porirua, 1888, translated G Graham, Grey MNZ Ms
Tamihana Te Rauparaha, 'History of Te Rauparaha written by Tamihana te Rauparaha at his father's dictation, 1845', GNZ Mmss27 and 27a (typescript version)
Richard Taylor, letterbook and correspondence, GNZ Mss297

Birmingham, University of

Church Missionary Society archives, New Zealand mission, correspondence (general): CN/01-09; individual missionaries: CN/019, 020, 030, 039, 040, 041, 048, 054, 060, 061, 064, 065, 068, 071, 072, 076, 078, 092, 094, 096, 098, 099, 0101
Dandeson Coates, private and confidential correspondence, 1824–1847: G/AC19/1-2

Bodleian Library, Oxford University
Thomas Fowell Buxton papers, Rhodes House
Sir James Graham papers, Mss Film 118–21
Henry Taylor papers
New Zealand manuscripts, Rhodes House
Viscount Melbourne papers (microfilm)

British Library, London
BL AddMss38763, William Huskisson papers
BL AddMss44086-44835, William Ewart Gladstone, correspondence and papers
BL AddMss34611-34630, Macvey Napier papers
BL AddMss40181-40617, Sir Robert Peel, correspondence and papers, official and private
BL AddMss35261, copies of letters, 1815–1853, from Edward Gibbon Wakefield and members of his family, including William Wakefield and Edward Jerningham Wakefield, mainly relating to New Zealand affairs

Cambridge, University of
James Stephen, correspondence, papers and diaries

Durham, University of
Grey, Henry George, (the third Earl Grey), [Viscount Howick], papers: journals, correspondence concerning New Zealand, Canada, New South Wales together with personal correspondence with Viscount Melbourne, James Stephen, George Grey, Lord John Russell

Hocken Library, University of Otago
Edward Shortland, letters, HlDu Ms86A and B
Edward Shortland, 'Narrative of the origin and progress of the wars of Ngatitoa and others with Ngaitahu, by Tamihana, son of Te Rauparaha', HlDu Ms96
Hone Tuhawaiki, 'Declaration of ownership of Robucka [Ruapuke] island by John Touwaick', 28 March 1840, HlDu Ms808B

Liverpool Record Office
Edward Stanley, fourteenth Earl of Derby, papers

Nottingham, University of
Papers of the fifth Duke of Newcastle

The National Archives (formerly the Public Record Office), Kew, London
Colonial Office
CO13/1-4, South Australia, original correspondence, Secretary of State for Colonies
CO42/516, Upper Canada, report of commission on Indian affairs
CO48 (selected consultation), Cape of Good Hope colony, original correspondence, secretary of state for colonies, 1835–1837
CO201 (selected consultation), New South Wales, original correspondence, secretary of state for colonies, 1830–1841
CO209/1-178, New Zealand, original correspondence, secretary of state for colonies, 1830–1863
CO208/1-309, New Zealand Company, original correspondence
CO213 (selected consultation), New Zealand, Blue books
CO323/165-175, original correspondence, private letters, 1831–1835, to Hay, including several relating to positions in Australia, New Zealand and the Pacific islands

CO324/63-65, 176, law officers' opinions, 1797–1807 and June 1837 to December 1859, and law reports, 1794–1804
CO325/43, relations with New Zealand Company, 1840–1845
CO381/6, South Australia, instructions, letters patent, orders-in-council, 29th January 1836–25th April 1856
CO381/57, New Zealand, instructions, letters patent, orders-in-council, 30th July 1839-18th October 1854
CO384 (selected consultation), emigration, original correspondence
CO396/1, South Australia, letters from the secretary of state, domestic correspondence, entry books, 1834–1838
CO406/1-28, New Zealand, entry books, 1837–1872
CO854/1-3, circular despatches, colonies

Foreign Office
FO58/1-2, New Zealand and Pacific islands, miscellaneous correspondence

Russell papers
PRO30/22, papers of Lord John Russell, 1830–1853

Treasury
T29 (selected consultation), Treasury, original correspondence, 1830–1847

State Library of New South Wales (Mitchell Library)
Sir George Gipps, papers
Pamphlets collected by Mr Justice Wise

PRINTED PRIMARY SOURCES

I Official publications: parliamentary papers, and Hansard's Parliamentary Debates

i Select committees

Report from the select committee appointed to consider what measures ought to be adopted with respect to the Native Inhabitants of countries where British settlements are made, and to the Neighbouring Tribes, in order to secure to them the due observance of Justice and the protection of their rights; to promote the spread of Civilization among these and to lead them to the peaceful and voluntary reception of the Christian religion, *GBPP1836*, vii (538) and *GBPP1837*, vii (425)
Report of the select committee appointed to inquire into the different modes in which land has been and is at present disposed of in the Australian colonies, in the Cape of Good Hope, and the West Indies, with a view to ascertain that mode which would be most beneficial in future, both to the colonies and the mother country, *GBPP1836*, xi (512)
Report from the select committee of the House of Lords appointed to inquire into the present state of the islands of New Zealand and the expediency of regulating the settlement of British subjects there, *GBPP1837–1838*, xxi (680)
Select committee appointed to inquire into the statements contained in the petition of the merchants, bankers, and shipowners of the city of London, respecting the colonization of New Zealand, *GBPP1840*, vii (582)
Report from the select committee appointed to inquire into the state of the colony of New Zealand, and into the proceedings of the New Zealand Company, *GBPP1844*, xiii (556)
Report from the Select Committee on New Zealand; together with the Proceedings of the Committee, Minutes of Evidence, and Appendix, *GBPP1857*, sess. 2, ix (HC171)

ii *Accounts and papers—New Zealand*

Despatch from Governor Sir R Bourke to Lord Glenelg, relative to the affairs of New Zealand, with four enclosures, *GBPP1837–1838*, xl (122), 209
Correspondence with the secretary of state relative to New Zealand, *GBPP1840*, xxxiii [238], 587
Despatches from the governor of New South Wales, containing reports of Captain Hobson of his proceedings on his arrival in New Zealand; reply of secretary of state thereto, *GBPP1840*, xxxiii (560), 575
Correspondence relative to New Zealand, 1840, *GBPP1841*, xvii (311), 493
Law and ordinances passed by the governor and council of the colony of New Zealand, *GBPP1842*, xxviii (61), 223; *GBPP1844*, xxxiv (61), 783
Papers relative to the affairs of New Zealand, *GBPP1845*, xxxiii (1), (131), 1, 13
Despatches from the governor of New Zealand, received since those last presented to Parliament, *GBPP1845*, xxxiii (247), (369), 71, 239
Letters from Mr Shortland, late acting governor, and Mr Busby, late Resident of New Zealand, to Lord Stanley and Mr GW Hope, *GBPP1845*, xxxiii (108), 353
Correspondence between Her Majesty's secretary of state for the colonies and the New Zealand Company, relative to the establishment of a Proprietary Government in the islands of New Zealand, *GBPP1845*, xxxiii (357), 417
Correspondence relative to the original constitution of the legislature of New Zealand, *GBPP1845*, xxxiii (660), 373
Correspondence between Her Majesty's Government and the New Zealand Company, 19 June to 6 July; together with minutes transmitted in Mr CA Wood's letter, 8 July 1845, *GBPP1845*, xxxiii (517-I), 431
Letter from Lord Ingestre to Lord Stanley, of the 24th July, and of the Reply, relative to the affairs of the New Zealand Company, together with the decisions of the local government thereon respectively, *GBPP1845*, xxxiii (378), 475
Papers and correspondence relative to the affairs of New Zealand, *GBPP1846*, xxx (337), [712], (448), (690), 151, 333, 375, 397; *GBPP1847*, xxxviii [837], [763], 263, 271; *GBPP1847–1848*, xliii [892], [899], [1002], 251, 345, 371; *GBPP1849*, xxxv [1120], 87; *GBPP1850*, xxxvii [1136], [1280], 699, 961; *GBPP1851*, xxxv [1420], 567; *GBPP1852*, xxxv [1475], [1483], 19, 95; *GBPP1860*, xlvii [2747]
Correspondence between Her Majesty's secretary of state and the New Zealand Company relative to a loan from the public in aid of the Company's funds, *GBPP1846*, xxx (271), 435
Correspondence between the Colonial Office and Mr Halswell relating to his duties while protector of aborigines in New Zealand, *GBPP1846*, xxx (722), 421
Return to an address of the Honourable House of Commons, dated 24 July 1860;—for, 'copies or extracts of despatches from the Governor of New Zealand, relating to the management of native affairs and the purchase of native land, and the proposed establishment of a native council; and of the answers returned to such despatches by the Secretary of State', *GBPP1860*, (492)
Correspondence between Governor Sir George Grey and the Colonial Office, *GBPP1864*, xli (326)

iii *Hansard's Parliamentary Debates [2nd series, vol 19, London, 1828; 3rd series, vols 22–163, London, 1830–1861]*

iv *Appendices to the Journals of the House of Representatives, 1860–1865*

v *New Zealand Parliamentary Debates, 1856–1865*

vi *New Zealand and United Kingdom newspapers, 1837–1865 (selective consultation)*

II Articles, books, collections of letters and other documents, diaries, nineteenth-century biographies, and pamphlets

Aborigines' Protection Society, *The second annual report of the Aborigines' Protection Society* (London, 1839–1840)
—*The third annual report of the Aborigines' Protection Society* (London, 23rd June 1840)
Adderley MP, CB, *Review of 'The Colonial Policy of Lord J Russell's Administration'—by Earl Grey, 1853; and of Subsequent Colonial History, Part I* (London, 1869)
Angas, George French, *Savage life and scenes in Australia and New Zealand: being an artist's impressions of countries and people at the antipodes* (two volumes, London, 1847)
—*The New Zealanders illustrated* (London, 1847)
Anonymous, 'Earle's *Account of New Zealand*', *Edinburgh Review*, 56 (1833), 333
Anonymous, *Letters from Wanganui, New Zealand* (London, 1845)
Anonymous, 'New Zealand', *Fisher's Colonial Magazine and journal of trade, commerce and banking* (London, 1844)
Anonymous, *New Zealand, a poem* (London, 1842)
Anonymous, 'The New Zealand question', *The New Monthly Magazine and Humorist*, 84 (1848), 250–60
Anonymous, 'Principles of colonization—New Zealand', *Dublin Review*, 4 (1838), 67–96
Arnold, Thomas, *The effects of colonization on the parent state, a prize essay* (Oxford, 1815)
—*The History of Rome* (three volumes, London, 1838)
—*Fragments on church and state* (London, 1845)
—*Introductory Lectures on Modern History delivered in Lent term, 1842, with the inaugural lecture delivered in December, 1841* (Oxford, 1842)
—*Miscellaneous Works of Thomas Arnold, DD* (London, 1845)
Bagehot, Walter, 'The English Constitution (Part I): The Cabinet', *The Fortnightly Review*, 1 (1865), 1-23
Bannister, Saxe, *Humane Policy; or justice to the aborigines of new settlements essential to a due expenditure of British money, and to the best interests of the settlers With suggestions [on] how to civilise the natives by an improved administration of existing means* (London, 1830)
—'An account of the changes and present condition of the population of New Zealand', *Royal Statistical Society Journal*, 1 (1838), 362–76
—*British Colonization and Coloured Tribes* (London, 1838)
—*Memoir respecting the colonization of Natal in south-eastern Africa presented by the Cape of Good Hope Trade Society to the secretary of state for the colonies* (London, 1839)
—*British enterprise beyond sea, from the earliest original sources to the present times* (two volumes, London, 1849)
Baring, Francis, *Journals and correspondence of Francis Thornhill Baring, Lord Northbrook*, Thomas Baring (ed) (two volumes, Winchester, 1905)
Barrow, JH (ed), *Mirror of Parliament* (London, 1828–1837)
Beecham, John, *Remarks upon the latest official documents relating to New Zealand (ordered by the House of Commons to be printed, 7 February 1838)* (London, 1838)
Bell, FD, F Whitaker, and Thomas Gore Browne, *Notes on Sir William Martin's Pamphlet entitled 'The Taranaki Question'* (Auckland, 1861)
Bell, George Joseph, *Principles of the Law of Scotland* (Edinburgh, 4th edn, 1839)
Bell, KN and WP Morrell, *Select Documents on British Colonial Policy, 1830–1860* (Oxford, 1928)
Bennett, JF, *Historical and Descriptive Account of South Australia* (London, 1843)
Best, ADW, *The journal of ensign Best, 1837–1842*, Nancy Taylor (ed) (Wellington, 1966)
Bever, Thomas, *A discourse on the study of jurisprudence and the civil law* (Oxford, 1766)
Bonwick, James, *Port Phillip Settlement* (London, 1883)

Bradford, Alden, *History of the Federal Government: for Fifty Years, from March, 1789 to March, 1839* (Boston, 1840)
Bright, John, *Handbook for Emigrants, and others, being a history of New Zealand, its state and prospects* (London, 1841)
Broughton, Lord [Hobhouse, JC], *Recollections of a Long Life* (four volumes, London, 1909–1911)
Brown, William, *New Zealand and its aborigines: being an account of the aborigines, trade, and resources of the colony* (London, 1845)
Buddle, T, *The Maori King Movement in New Zealand with a Full Report of the Native Meetings held at Waikato, April and May 1860* (Auckland, 1860)
Buller, Charles, *Responsible Government for the Colonies* (London, 1840)
—*Systematic colonization: speech of Charles Buller, Esq, MP, in the House of Commons, on Thursday, 6 April 1843, on systematic colonization* (London, 1843)
Burge, William, *Commentaries on Colonial and Foreign Laws generally and their conflict with each other and the law of England* (four volumes, London, 1838)
Burton, Walter, *An Elementary Compendium of the Law of Real Property* (London, 2nd edn, 1830)
Busby, James, *Authentic information relative to New South Wales and New Zealand* (London, 1832)
—*Remarks upon a pamphlet entitled 'The Taranaki Question, by Sir William Martin, DCL, late chief justice of New Zealand'* (Auckland, 1860)
—*The Rebellions of the Maories traced to their True Origin in Two Letters to the Right Honorable Edward Cardwell, Her Majesty's Principal Secretary of State for the Colonies* (London, 1865)
Buxton, Thomas, *The Remedy; being a sequel to the African slave trade* (London, 1840)
—*Memoirs of Sir T F Buxton (with an introduction by Earl Buxton)* (London, 1925)
Carleton, Hugh, *The Life of Henry Williams, archdeacon of Waimate* (two volumes, Auckland, 1874)
—'New Zealand', *Westminster Review*, 81 OS 25 NS (1864), 420–72
Carlyle, Thomas, *Chartism* (London, 1840)
Catlin, George, *Letters and Notes on the Manners, Customs and Condition of the North American Indians* (two volumes, London, 1841)
—*Letters and Notes on the Manners, Customs and Condition of the North American Indians* (Philadephia, 1859)
Chalmers, George, *Political Annals of the present united colonies, from their settlement to the peace of 1763 Book I* (London, 1780)
—*Opinions of Eminent Lawyers on Various Points of English jurisprudence, chiefly concerning the colonies, fisheries and commerce of Great Britain* (two volumes, London, 1814)
Chalmers, Thomas, *On Political Economy: in connexion with the moral state and moral prospects of society*, introduction by David Gladstone (Glasgow, 1832; London, 1995)
—'Political economy of a famine', *North British Review*, 7 (1847), 247–90
Chambers, Robert, *Vestiges of the Natural History of Creation* (London, 3rd edn, 1845)
—*Explanations: a sequel to 'Vestiges of the Natural History of Creation', by the author of that work* (London, 1845)
—*Vestiges of the Natural History of Creation* (London, 5th edn, 1846)
Chambers, William and Robert Chambers (eds), *Chambers's Information for the People* (two volumes, Edinburgh, 1849)
—*Chambers's Papers for the People* (Edinburgh, 1851)
Chamerovzow, Louis Alexis, *The New Zealand Question and the rights of aborigines* (London, 1848)
Chapman, Henry, *The comparative prospects of our new colonies* (London, 1841)
—'The American Ballot-Box', in John Roebuck (ed), *Pamphlets for the People* (London, 1835), 11–15.

—'The English, the French, and the New Zealanders', *The New Zealand Journal*, number 5, 4 April 1840, 1–2
—'New Zealand', *Dublin Review*, 9 (1840), 189–214
—'Zealand, New', in *The Encyclopædia Britannica*, (Edinburgh, 7th edn, 1842), XXI, 979.
Clark, Charles, *A Summary of Colonial Law, the Practice of the Court of Appeals from the Plantations, and of the Laws and their Administration in all the Colonies; with Charters of Justices, Orders in Council &c* (London, 1834)
Clarke, George, *Remarks upon a pamphlet by James Busby, Esq, commenting upon a pamphlet entitled The Taranaki question, by Sir William Martin, DCL, late Chief Justice of New Zealand* (Auckland, 1861)
Coates, Dandeson, *The New Zealanders and their lands The report of the select committee of the House of Commons, on New Zealand, considered in a letter to Lord Stanley* (London, 1844)
Coates, Dandeson, William Ellis, and John Beecham, *Christianity, the means of civilization shown in the evidence given before a committee of the House of Commons on aborigines* (London, 1837)
Colenso, William, *The Authentic and Genuine History of the Signing of the Treaty of Waitangi, New Zealand, February 5 and 6, 1840* (Wellington, 1890)
—*Fifty years ago in New Zealand* (Napier, 1888)
Cooke, WB, *British Colonial Policy: Municipalities confederated under a Viceroy* (London, 1850)
Creighton, Mandell, *Memoir of Sir George Grey* (Newcastle, 1884)
Darwin, Charles, *Journal of Researches into the Natural History and Geology of the Countries visited during the voyage of HMS Beagle round the world* (London, 1845)
—*The Origin of Species*, Gillian Beer (ed) (Oxford, 1996)
Dieffenbach, Johann Karl Ernest, *New Zealand and its Native Population* (London, 1841)
—*Travels in New Zealand; with contributions to the geography, botany, and natural history of that country* (two volumes, London, 1843)
Dillon, Constantine, *The Dillon Letters: the letters of the hon Constantine Dillon, 1842–1853*, C Sharp (ed) (Wellington, 1954)
Disraeli, Benjamin, 'The Spirit of Whiggism' (1836), published as an addendum to the 'Letters of Runnymede', in William Hutcheon (ed), *Whigs and Whiggism: Political Writings by Benjamin Disraeli* (London, 1913), 327–56
Durham, first Earl of, *Lord Durham's Report on the affairs of British North America*, Charles Lucas (ed) (three volumes, Oxford, 1912)
Dyer, George, *Four Letters on the English Constitution* (London, 3rd edn, 1817)
Earle, James, *A Narrative of a Nine Months' Residence in New Zealand in 1827: together with a journal of a residence in Trista D'Accunha, an island situated between South America and the Cape of Good Hope* (London, 1832)
Ellis, William, *Polynesian Researches, during a residence of nearly six years in the South sea islands, including descriptions of the natural history and scenery of the islands—with remarks on the history, mythology, traditions, government, arts, manners, and customs of the inhabitants* (two volumes, London, 1829)
Facsimiles of the Declaration of Independence and the Treaty of Waitangi (Wellington, 1877)
Fawcett, [Mrs], *Life of the Right Hon Sir William Molesworth, Bart, MP, FRS* (London, 1901)
Fenton, FD, *Observations on the State of the Aboriginal Inhabitants of New Zealand* (Auckland, 1859)
Ferguson, Adam, *An Essay on the History of Civil Society*, Fania Oz-Salzberger (ed) (Cambridge, 1995)
Fitzgerald, James, 'Memorandum Relating to the Conduct of the Native Affairs in New Zealand, as affected by a Bill now before Parliament' (London, 6 July 1860)
—'Memorandum, No 2 Relating to the Conduct of Native Affairs in New Zealand, as affected by a Bill now before Parliament' (London, 30 July 1860
—(ed), *A Selection from the Writings and Speeches of John Robert Godley*(Christchurch, 1863)

FitzRoy, Robert, *Narrative of the Surveying Voyages of His Majesty's ships 'Adventure' and 'Beagle', between the years 1826 and 1836, describing their examination of the southern shores of South America and the Beagle's circumnavigation of the globe* (three volumes, London, 1839)
—*Remarks on New Zealand in February 1846* (London, 1846)
Forster, Johann Reinhold, *Observations made during a voyage around the world, on physical geography, natural history, and ethic philosophy*, Thomas, Nicholas, Harriet Guest, and Michael Dettelbach (eds) (London, 1778; Honolulu, 1996)
Fox, William, *Report on the Settlement of Nelson in New Zealand* (London, 1849)
—*Colonization and New Zealand* (London, 1842)
—*The Six Colonies of New Zealand* (London, 1851)
—*The War in New Zealand* (London, 1860)
Gibbon, Edward, *The History of the Decline and Fall of the Roman Empire*, J Bury (ed) (1776; seven volumes, London, 2nd edn, 1901)
—*The History of the Decline and Fall of the Roman Empire*, David Womersley (ed) (three volumes, London, 1994)
Gooch, GP (ed), *The Later Correspondence of Lord John Russell, 1840–1878* (two volumes, London, 1925)
Gorst, JE, *The Maori King* (London, 1864)
Greville, Charles, *The Greville Memoirs: a journal of the reigns of King George IV, King William IV and Queen Victoria*, Henry Reeve (ed) (eight volumes, London, 1888)
Grey, George, *Journals of Two Expeditions of Discovery in North-west and Western Australia, during the years 1837, 38, and 39, under the authority of Her Majesty's government, describing newly discovered, important, and fertile districts with observations on the moral and physical condition of the aboriginal inhabitants, &c, &c* (two volumes, London, 1841)
—*Polynesian Mythology and Ancient traditional history of the New Zealand race as furnished by their priests and chiefs* (Auckland, 2nd edn, 1885)
—*Journal of an expedition overland from Auckland to Taranaki, by way of Rotorua, Taupo, and the west coast undertaken in the summer of 1849–1850* (Auckland, 1851)
Grey, Henry George (third Earl Grey), *The Colonial Policy of Lord John Russell's Administration* (two volumes, London, 2nd edn, 1853)
Grimstone, SE, *The Southern Settlements of New Zealand* (Wellington, 1847)
Guizot, François, *General History of Civilisation in Europe, from the Fall of the Roman Empire till the French Revolution* (Edinburgh, 1848)
Hadfield, Octavius, *One of England's Little Wars* (London, 1860)
—*The Second Year of One of England's Little Wars* (London, 1861)
—*A Sequel to One of England's Little Wars* (London, 1861)
Hale, Horatio, *United States exploring expedition: ethnology and philology* (Philadelphia, 1846)
Hallam, Henry, *The Constitutional History of England from the Accession of Henry VII to the Death of George II* (two volumes, London, 1859?)
—*The Constitutional History of England from the Accession of Henry VII to the Death of George II* (three volumes, London, 8th edn, 1855)
Harris, John, *The Great Commission: or, the Christian church constituted and charged to convey the gospel to the world* (London, 1842)
Hawkesworth, John, *An Account of the Voyages undertaken by the order of his Present Majesty for Making Discoveries in the Southern Hemisphere and successively performed by Commodore Byron, Captain Wallis, Captain Carteret and Captain Cook in the Dolphin, the Swallow, and the Endeavour* (three volumes, London, 2nd edn, 1773)
Hawtrey, Montague, *An earnest address to New Zealand colonists, with reference to their intercourse with the native inhabitants* (London, 1840)
Heale, Theophilus, *New Zealand and the New Zealand Company: Being a Consideration of how far their Interests are Similar* (London, 1842)
Hewett, Osbert (ed), *'And Mr Fortescue': A Selection from the Diaries from 1851 to 1862 of Chichester Fortescue, Lord Carlingford, KP* (London, 1958)

Hinds, Samuel, *The latest official documents relating to New Zealand; with introductory observations* (London, 1838)

Hocken, Thomas Morland, *Contributions to the Early History of New Zealand [settlement of Otago]* (London, 1889)

Hoffman, David, *A Course of Legal Study, Addressed to Students and the Profession Generally* (two volumes, Baltimore, 2nd edn, 1836)

Hodgkin, Thomas, 'On inquiries into the races of man', *Report of the Eleventh Meeting of the British Association for the Advancement of Science; held at Plymouth in July 1841* (London, 1841), 52–5

Holland, Lord, *Memoirs of the Whig Party during my Time* (two volumes, London, 1852–1854)

Hunt, Thornton Leigh, *Canada and South Australia: A Commentary on that part of the Earl of Durham's Report which relates to the Disposal of Waste Lands and Emigration* (London, 1839)

Hursthouse, Charles, *New Zealand The Emigration Field of 1851* (London, 1851)

—*New Zealand, or Zealandia, the Britain of the South* (two volumes, London, 1857)

—*An account of the settlement of New Plymouth* (London, 1849)

Jameson, RG, *New Zealand, South Australia and New South Wales* (London, 1841)

Johnston, Alexander, *Notes on Maori Matters ('Notes for the Formation of an Opinion on Maori Matters')* (Auckland, 1860)

Jones, Richard, *An introductory lecture on political economy, delivered at King's College, London, 27th February 1833, to which is added a syllabus of a course of lectures on the wages of labour, to be delivered at King's College, London, in the month of April, 1833* (London, 1833)

Journal of Civilization, established for the promotion of civilization at home and abroad; and for the record of geographical discovery, colonization, and missionary enterprise (London, 1841)

Joyce, Arthur John, 'Catlin on the North American Indians', *Edinburgh Review*, 74 (1842), 415–30

Kent, James, *Commentaries on American Law* (three volumes, Boston, 1st edn, 1826–1831)

—*Commentaries on American Law*, GF Cornstock (ed) (four volumes, Boston, 1828; Boston, 11th edn, 1866)

—*Commentaries on American Law* (three volumes, New York, 3rd edn, 1836)

—*Commentaries on American Law* (three volumes, New York, 4th edn, 1840)

—*Commentaries on American Law* (three volumes, New York, 5th edn, 1844)

Keynes, Richard, *Charles Darwin's Beagle Diary* (Cambridge, 1988)

Knox, Robert, *The Races of Men: a philosophical enquiry into the influences of race over the destinies of nations* (London, 1850)

Landor, EW, *The Bushman; or, life in a new country* (London, 1847)

Lang, John Dunmore, *View of the Origin and Migrations of the Polynesian Nation; demonstrating their ancient discovery and progressive settlement of the continent of America* (London, 1834)

—*New Zealand in 1839; or four letters to the right hon Earl Durham, governor of the New Zealand Company &c on the colonization of that island and on the present condition and prospects of its native inhabitants* (London, 1839)

Latham, Robert Gordon, *The Natural History of the Varieties of Man* (London, 1850)

—*The ethnology of the British colonies and dependencies* (London, 1851)

—*Man and his Migrations* (London, 1851)

—*Descriptive Ethnology* (two volumes, London, 1859)

Lewis, George Cornewall, *An Essay on the Government of Dependencies* (London, 1841)

Library of Entertaining Knowledge [Craik, George], *The New Zealanders* (London, 1830)

—*The Hindoos* (two volumes, London, 1834)

Locke, John, *Two Treatises of Government*, P Laslett (ed) (Cambridge, 1988)

Lubbock, John, *Prehistoric Times, as illustrated by ancient remains, and the manners and customs of modern savages* (London, 1865)

Macaulay, Thomas Babington, 'Ranke's *History of the Popes*—revolutions of the papacy', *Edinburgh Review*, 77 (1840), 227–58

—*Critical and Historical Essays*, Hugh Trevor-Roper (ed) (London, 1965)

McGillivray, John, *Narrative of the Voyage of HMS Rattlesnake, commanded by the late Captain Owen Stanley during the years 1846–50: in which is added Mr EB Kennedy's expedition for the exploration of the Cape Yorke peninsula* (London, 1852)

McKay, Alexander, *A Compendium of Official Documents relative to Native Affairs in the South Island* (two volumes, Wellington, 1873)

McKinnon, W, *History of Civilisation* (two volumes, London, 1846)

McNab, R (ed), *Historical Records of New Zealand* (two volumes, Wellington, 1908)

Malthus, Thomas, *An essay on the principle of population; or, a view of its past and present effects on human happiness* (two volumes, London, 6th edn, 1826)

Maning, Frederick, *History of the war in the north of New Zealand against the Chief Heke in the year 1845, told by an old chief of the Ngapuhi tribe (faithfully translated by a 'pakeha Maori')* (Auckland, 1861)

—*Old New Zealand* (London, 1863)

Marindin, George (ed), *Letters of Frederic Lord Blachford, Under-secretary of State for the Colonies 1860–1871* (London, 1896)

Marjoribanks, Alexander, *Travels in New Zealand* (London, 1845)

Marshall, John, *The Life of George Washington, Commander in Chief of the American Forces, During the War which established the Independence of his Country, and First President of the United States, compiled under the Inspection of the Honorable Bushrod Washington, from Original Papers bequeathed to him by his deceased relative, and now in possession of the Author. To Which is Prefixed, an Introduction, Containing a Compendious View of the Colonies Planted by the English on the Continent of North America, from Their Settlement to the Commencement of that War which terminated in their Independence* (Philadelphia, 1804)

Martin, John, *A Grammar of the Tonga Language* (London, 1825)

—*An account of the Tonga islands, in the South Pacific ocean, with an original grammar and vocabulary of their language* (two volumes, London, 2nd edn, 1827)

Martin, Robert Montgomery, *The British Colonies: their history, extent, condition and resources* (London, 1850)

—*History of Austral-Asia: comprising New South Wales, Van Diemen's Land, Swan River, South Australia &c* (London, 1836)

Martin, SMD, *New Zealand in 1842* (Auckland, 1842)

—*New Zealand; in a Series of Letters: containing an account of the country, both before and since its occupation by the British government; with historical remarks on the conduct of the government, the New Zealand and Manukau Companies: also a description of the various settlements, the character of the aborigines, and the natural productions of the country* (London, 1845)

Martin, William, *England and the New Zealanders: remarks upon a despatch from the Right Hon Earl Grey to Governor Grey, dated 23 December 1846* (Auckland, 1847)

—*The Taranaki Question* (London, 2nd edn, 1861)

——*Remarks on 'Notes published for the New Zealand Government', January 1861, and of Mr Richmond's Memorandum on the The Taranaki Question, December, 1860* (London, 1861)

Mathew, Felton, *The Founding of New Zealand: the journals of Felton Mathew, first surveyor-general of New Zealand, and his wife 1840–1847*, J Rutherford (ed) (Dunedin, 1940)

Matthew, Patrick, *On naval timber and arboriculture; with critical notes on authors who have recently treated the subject of planting* (London and Edinburgh, 1831)

—*Emigration Fields: North America, the Cape, Australia, and New Zealand* (London, 1839)

—*Prospectus of the Scots New Zealand Land Company* (Edinburgh, 1839)

May, TE, *The Constitutional History of England since the Accession of George the Third 1760–1860* (two volumes, London, 1863)

Merivale, Herman, *Introduction to a course of lectures on colonization and colonies begun in March, 1839* (London, 1839)

—*Lectures on colonization and colonies, delivered before the University of Oxford in 1839, 1840, & 1841* (London, 1841–1842)

—*Lectures on colonization and colonies, delivered before the University of Oxford in 1839, 1840, & 1841* (London, 2nd edn, 1861)

— 'Thirwall's History of Greece', *Edinburgh Review*, 62 (1835), 83–08
— 'Mexico and the Great Western Prairies', *Edinburgh Review*, 78 (1843), 157–192
—'The Colonial Question in 1870', *Fortnightly Review*, 7(38) (1870), 152–175
Mill, James, *The History of British India* (three volumes, London, 1817)
—*Essays on Government, Jurisprudence, Liberty of the Press and Law of Nations, written for the supplement to the Encyclopædia Britannica* (London, 1828?)
Mill, JS, *Memorandum of the Improvements in the Administration of India during the last Thirty Years, and the Petition of the East-India Company to Parliament* (London, 1858)
—*Utilitarianism, On Liberty and Considerations on Representative Government*, HB Acton (ed) (London, 1972)
Millar, John, *The Origin of the Distinction of Ranks; or, an inquiry into the circumstances which give rise to influence and authority, in the different members of society* (Edinburgh and London, 4th edn, 1806)
MLC [Trollope, Anthony], *The New-Zealander on London Bridge, or, Moral Ruins of the Modern Babylon* (London, 1878)
Molesworth, William, 'Parliamentary conduct of the radicals', *London and Westminster Review*, 5 and 27 (1837), 270–83
Morley, John, *The Life of William Ewart Gladstone* (three volumes, London, 1903)
Motte, Standish, *Outline of a System of Legislation, for securing the protection to the aboriginal inhabitants of all countries colonized by Great Britain, drawn up at the request of the committee of the Aborigines Protection Society* (London, 1840)
Munro, J (ed), *Acts of the Privy Council of England (colonial series); volume iv, 1745–1766* (London, 1911)
Napier, Charles, *Colonization, particularly in southern Australia* (London, 1835)
Napier, Macvey (ed), *The Encyclopædia Britannica* (twenty-one volumes, Edinburgh, 7th edn, 1842)
New Zealand Company, *The first report of the New Zealand Company, presented to the first general meeting of the shareholders, on the 14th May 1840* (London, 1840)
—*The fifth report of the directors of the New Zealand Company, presented to the annual court of proprietors, held on the 31st May 1842* (London, 1842)
—*The tenth report of the directors of the New Zealand Company, presented to a special court of proprietors, held on the 15th March 1844* (London, 1844)
—*The twelfth report of the directors of the New Zealand Company, presented to an adjourned special court of proprietors, held on the 26th April 1844* (London, 1844)
—*The thirteenth report of the directors of the New Zealand Company, presented to an adjourned annual court of proprietors, held on the 29th June 1844* (London, 1844)
—*The twentieth report of the court of directors of the New Zealand Company presented to the annual general court of proprietors: 29th May 1846* (London, 1846)
—*Supplementary Information relative to New-Zealand* (London, 1840)
Nicholas, John Liddiard, *A Narrative of a Voyage to New Zealand including a description of the country, and incidental remarks on the manners, customs and political economy of the natives* (two volumes, London, 1817)
Northbrook, Thomas George, Lord (ed), *Journals and Correspondence from 1808 to 1852 of Sir Francis Thornhill Baring* (Winchester, 1905)
O'Callaghan, EB (ed), *Documents Relative to the Colonial History of the State of New York: volume vii* (fifteen volumes, Albany, 1856)
Parliament, *A Corrected Report of the Debate in the House of Commons, on the 17th, 18th, and 19th of June on the state of New Zealand and the case of the New Zealand Company* (London, 1845)
—*Debate on the motion of T Fowell Buxton, esq, MP for protecting the civil rights and imparting civilization to the native inhabitants of the British colonies; in the House of Commons, on Tuesday, 1 July 1834* (London, 1834)
Peel, Sir Robert, *Sir Robert Peel from his private correspondence (papers)*, CS Parker (ed) (three volumes, London, 1891)

Petre, Henry, *An Account of the settlements of the New Zealand Company, from personal observation during a residence there* (London, 1841)
Polack, Joel S, *New Zealand: being a narrative of travels and adventures* (two volumes, London, 1838)
Polybius, *The Rise of the Roman Empire*, trans Ian Scott-Kilvert (London, 1979)
Pownall, Thomas, *The Administration of the Colonies* (London, 1764)
—*The Administration of the Colonies* (London, 2nd edn, 1765)
Prichard, James Cowles, 'On the Extinction of Human Races', *Edinburgh New Philosophical Journal*, 28 (1840), 166–70
—*Researches into the Physical History of Man*, George Stocking (ed) (London, 1813; Chicago, 1973)
—*Researches into the Physical History of Man* (five volumes, London, 3rd edn, 1836–1847)
—*The Eastern Origin of the Celtic Nations proved by a comparison of their dialects with the Sanskrit, Greek, Latin and Teutonic languages forming a supplement to 'Researches into the Physical History of Mankind')* (Oxford, 1831)
—*'On the Various Methods of Research which contribute to the advancement of ethnology, and of the relations of that science to other branches of knowledge', Report of the seventeenth meeting of the British Association for the Advancement of Science* (London, 1848)
Proprietor, *Facts versus Lord Durham Remarks upon that portion of the earl of Durham's report, relating to Prince Edward Island, shewing the fallacy of the statements contained therein* (London, 1839)
Robertson, William, *The History of America* (three volumes, London, 1777)
—*The Works of Wm Robertson, DD, in eight volumes* (Oxford, 1825)
Robson, John (ed), *Collected Works of John Stuart Mill* (33 volumes, London and Toronto, 1963–1991)
Roebuck, JA, *The Colonies of England* (London, 1849)
—(ed), *Democracy in America [Character and sufferings of the Irish clergy, by H S Chapman]* (London, 1835)
Rusden, GW, *Aureretanga: Groans of the Maoris* (London, 1888)
Russell, John (first Earl), *Essay on the History of the English government and constitution from the reign of Henry VII to the present time* (London, 1821)
Russell, Martin, *Polynesia: a history of the South Sea islands, including New Zealand: with narrative of the introduction of Christianity, &c* (London, 2nd edn, 1852)
Russell, Rollo (ed), *Early Correspondence of Lord John Russell, 1805–1840* (two volumes, London, 1913)
Savage, John, *Some Account of New Zealand* (London, 1807)
Scholefield, Guy (ed), *The Richmond-Atkinson Papers* (two volumes, Wellington, 1960)
Scriven, John, *A Treatise on Copyhold, Customary Freehold, and Ancient Desmesne Tenure, with the Jurisdiction of Courts Baron and Courts Leet* (two volumes, London, 3rd edn, 1833–1834)
Senior, Nassau, 'Law of nations', *Edinburgh Review*, 77 (1843), 303–73
Sewell, Henry, *The New Zealand Rebellion. A Letter from Henry Sewell, Esq, late Attorney-General of New Zealand to the Right Hon Lord Lyttelton* (London, 1864)
Shortland, Edward, *The Southern Districts of New Zealand; a journal, with passing notices of the customs of the aborigines* (London, 1851)
—*Traditions and Superstitions of the New Zealanders, with illustrations of their manners and customs* (London, 1854)
—*Maori Religion and Mythology* (London, 1882)
Smith, Adam, *Lectures on Jurisprudence*, Meek, Raphael, and PG Stein (eds) (Oxford, 1978)
—*An Inquiry into the Nature and Causes of the Wealth of Nations*, Andrew Skinner (ed) (two volumes, London, 1776)

Smith, Joshua Toulmin, *Local Self-Government and Centralization: the Characteristics of Each; and its practical tendencies as affecting Social, Moral and Political Welfare and Progress* (London, 1851)

Spedding, James, 'New theory of colonization', *Edinburgh Review*, 71 (1840), 517–44

—'A Second Visit to the United States of America', *Edinburgh Review*, 92 (1850), 339–71

Stewart, Dugald, *Elements of the Philosophy of the Human Mind* (three volumes, London, 1792)

—*'Account of the life and writings of Adam Smith, LL D', Essays on Philosophical Subjects* (Oxford, 1980)

Story, J, *Life and Letters of Joseph Story, Associate Justice of the Supreme Court of the United States, and Dane Professor of Law at Harvard University* (two volumes, Boston, 1851)

Sumner, John Bird, *A treatise on the records of creation, and on the moral attributes of the creator; with particular reference to the Jewish history in connexion with the moral prospects of society* (three volumes, London, 1816)

Swainson, William, *New Zealand. The Substance of Lectures on the Colonization of New Zealand, delivered at Lancaster, Plymouth, Bristol, Hereford, Kirkby Lonsdale, Richmond, and the Charter House, London* (London, 1856)

Tacitus, *The Agricola and The Germania*, trans H Mattingly (London, 1948)

Tamakihikurangi, Renata, *Ko Te Korero me te Pukapuka a Renata Tamakihikurangi, no te Pa Whakairo, ki a te Kaiwhakahaere tikanga o nga Pakeha ki Ahuriri* (Wellington, 1861)

Taylor, Henry, *Correspondence of Henry Taylor*, Edward Dowden (ed) (London, 1888)

—*Autobiography* (two volumes, London, 1885)

Thomson, Arthur, *The Story of New Zealand: past and present–savage and civilized* (two volumes, London, 1859)

Thucydides, *History of the Peloponnesian War*, trans R Warner (London, 1954)

Tocqueville, Alexis de, *Democracy in America (De La Démocratie en Amérique): Bilingual Edition*, Eduardo Nolla (ed) (four volumes, Indianapolis, 2010)

Tucker, HW (ed), *Memoir of the life and episcopate of George Augustus Selwyn, DD* (two volumes, London, 1879)

Turton, H (ed), *Epitome of official documents relative to the affairs and land purchases in the North island of New Zealand* (Wellington, 1883)

Twiss, Travers, *The Oregon Question examined, in respect to facts and the law of nations* (London, 1846)

—*On certain tests of a thriving population Four lectures delivered before the University of Oxford, in Lent term, 1845* (London, 1845)

— 'Austria and Germany', *Quarterly Review*, 84 (1848), 185–222

Vattel, Emerich de, *The Law of Nations or the Principles of the Law of Nature applied to the conduct and affairs of Nations and Sovereigns*, Joseph Chitty (ed) (Neuchatel, 1758; London, 1834)

Villier, Charles, *An Essay on the Spirit and Influence of the Reformation of Luther: The work which obtained the prize on the question proposed in 1802, by the National Institute of France*, trans James Mill (London, 1805)

Virgil, *The Aeneid*, trans Robert Fagles (London, 2006)

Wade, William, *A journey in the northern island of New Zealand: interspersed with various information relative to the country and people* (Hobart, 1842)

Wakefield, Edward Gibbon, *A letter from Sydney, the principal town of Australasia* (London, 1829)

—*The new British province of South Australia* (London, 1834)

—*A Statement of the Objects of the New Zealand Association* (London, 1837)

—*'Mr Dandeson Coates and the New Zealand Association; in a letter to Lord Glenelg'* (London, 12 December 1837)

—*A view on the art of colonization, with present reference to the British Empire, in letters between a statesman and a colonist* (London, 1849)

Wakefield, Edward Gibbon and John Ward, *The British Colonization of New Zealand* (London, 1837)

Wakefield, Edward Jerningham, *Adventure in New Zealand, from 1839 to 1844; with some account of the British colonization of the islands* (two volumes, London, 1845)

Wakefield, Felix, *Colonial surveying with a view to the disposal of waste land: in a report to the New Zealand Company* (London, 1849)

Ward, Henry George, *The debate upon Mr Ward's resolutions on colonization, in the House of Commons, 27 June 1839, containing the speeches of HG Ward, Esq, MP, Sir William Molesworth, Bart MP, Right Hon Henry Labouchere, MP, W Warburton, Esq MP, and Right Hon Viscount Howick, MP* (London, 1839)

Ward, John, *Information relative to New Zealand, compiled for the use of colonists* (London, 2nd edn, 1840)

—'The affairs of New Zealand', *Westminster Review*, 45 (1846), 133–222

—*New Zealand Nelson, the latest settlement of the New Zealand Company* (London, 1842)

Ward, Stephen H, *The Natural History of Mankind* (London, 1849)

Wells, Benjamin, *The History of Taranaki* (London, 1878)

Wesleyan Missionary Committee, *Correspondence between the Wesleyan Missionary Committee and the right honourable Earl grey, Her Majesty's principal secretary of state for the colonial department, on the apprehended infringement of the Treaty of Waitangi* (London, 1848)

Whately, Elizabeth Jane, *Life and Correspondence of Richard Whately* (two volumes, London, 1866)

Whately, Richard, *National blessings and judgements considered, in a discourse; with an appendix containing remarks on the present case* (London, 1831)

—*Substance of a speech on transportation, delivered in the House of Lords* (London, 1840)

—*Thoughts on secondary punishments, in a letter to Earl Grey (to which are appended, two articles on transportation to New South Wales, and on secondary punishments; and some observations on colonization* (London, 1832)

—*Remarks on transportation, in a second letter to Earl Grey* (London, 1834)

—*Introductory Lectures on political economy* (London, 1831)

—*Introductory Lectures on political economy* (London, 3rd edn, 1847)

—*Introductory Lectures on political economy* (London, 4th edn, 1855)

—*On the origin of civilisation* (London, 1855)

Wheaton, Henry, *History of the Northmen, or Dames and Normans, from the earliest times to the conquest* (London, 1831)

—*Elements of International Law: with a sketch of the history of the science* (two volumes, London, 1836)

—*Elements of International Law* (Philadelphia, 3rd edn, 1846)

White, W, *Colonization of New Zealand* (London, 1838)

Wilberforce, William, *A practical view of the prevailing religious system of professed Christians in the higher and middle classes contrasted with real Christianity* (London, 3rd edn, 1797)

—*A practical view of the prevailing religious system of professed Christians in the higher and middle classes contrasted with real Christianity* (London, 1835)

—*A practical view of the prevailing religious system of professed Christians in the higher and middle classes contrasted with real Christianity, with an introductory essay by Daniel Wilson, DD, lord bishop of Calcutta* (Glasgow, 1838)

Williams, Henry, *Plain facts relative to the late war in the northern district of New Zealand* (Auckland, 1847)

Willis, 'Notes on the acquisition of New Zealand as a Dependency of New South Wales with reference to lands obtained by British Subjects from the Aborigines', May 1840, Mitchell Library, Sydney, Pamphlets collected by Mr Justice Wise, ML A857, 11-68 (microfilm CY746)

Wilmot Horton, R, *The causes and remedies of pauperism in the United Kingdom considered [part I]: being a defence of the principles and conduct of the emigration committee, against the charges of Mr Sadler* (London, 1829)

Wyld, James, *The islands of New Zealand from the admiralty surveys of the English and French marine, from the observations of the affairs of the New Zealand Company and from private surveys & sketches* (London, 1851)
Yate, William, *An Account of New Zealand* (London, 2nd edn, 1835)

III Judicial decisions (reported)

Ahousaht v Attorney-General of Canada 2009 BCSC 1706
Attorney-General v Ngati Apa [2003] 3 NZLR 643
Cameron v Kyte (1835) 3 Knapp 332
The Case of Tanistry (1608) Dav 28, 80 ER 516
Cherokee Nation v state of Georgia 5 Pet 1, 8 L Ed 25 (1831)
Da Silva v Aotea Maori Committee and Hauraki Maori Trust Board [1999] 25 Tai Tokerau M[inute]B[ook] 216
Doe v Lock (1835) 2 Ad & El 705, 745, 111 ER 271, 287
Fletcher v Peck 6 Cranch 87 (1810)
Heathfield v Chilton (1767) 4 Burr 2015, 98 ER 50
Johnson v M'Intosh 8 Wheat 543 (1823)
Jones v Williams (1837) 2 M & W 326
Marshall v Clark 4 Call 268, 8 Va 268 (Va), 1791 WL 325 (Va) (1791)
Mitchel v United States 9 Pet 711, 9 L Ed 283 (1835)
Regina v Clarke [1840–1932] (1849–1851) NZPCC 516
Regina v Fitzherbert (1872) 2 NZCA 143
Regina v Marshall; Regina v Bernard 2005 SCC 43, [2005] 2 SCR 220
Regina v Niramoana (1880) *Olivier, Bell and Fitzgerald's New Zealand Law Reports* 78 (New Zealand Court of Appeal)
Regina [The Queen (on the prosecution of CH McIntosh)] v Symonds [1840–1932] (1847) NZPCC 387
Te Weehi v Regional Fisheries Officer [1986] 1 NZLR 680
Triquet v Bath (1764) 3 Burr 1478, 97 ER 936
Worcester v State of Georgia 6 Pet 515, 31 US 350 (1832)

IV Periodicals consulted

The Christian Observer, (1830–1847)
The Colonial Intelligencer; or Aborigines' Friend, (1840–1850)
The Dublin Review, volumes 1–29, (1836–1850)
Edinburgh Review, volumes 50–122 (1830–1865)
The Fortnightly Review, volume 1 (1865)
New Monthly Magazine, volumes 44–84, (1837–1848)
The New Zealand Journal, (1840–1844)
Quarterly Review, volumes 42–118, (1830–1865)
Sydney Herald, (1839–1842)
Westminster Review, volumes 12–45, (1830–1846)

SECONDARY SOURCES

I Articles, presentations and books

Adams, Peter, *Fatal Necessity: British Intervention in New Zealand, 1830–1847* (Auckland, 1977)
Ajzenstat, Janet, *The Political Thought of Lord Durham* (Montreal, 1988)
Alfred, Taiaiake, *Peace, Power, Righteousness: An Indigenous Manifesto* (Toronto, 1999)
Allison, JWF, *The English Historical Constitution: Continuity, Change and European Effects* (Cambridge, 2007)

Anstey, Roger, *The Atlantic Slave Trade and British Abolition 1760–1810* (London, 1975)
Appiah, Kwame Anthony, *The Ethics of Identity* (Princeton, 2005)
Armitage, David, *The Ideological Origins of the British Empire* (Cambridge, 2000)
—'Hobbes and the Foundations of Modern International Thought', in Annabel Brett, James Tully and Holly Hamilton-Bleakley (eds), *Rethinking the Foundations of Modern Political Thought* (Cambridge, 2006), 219–35
—and Michael J Braddick (eds), *The British Atlantic World, 1500–1800* (London, 2nd edn, 2009)
Arnold, David (ed), *Imperial Medicine and Indigenous Societies: Disease, Medicine and Empire in the Nineteenth and Twentieth centuries* (Manchester, 1978)
Atkinson, Neill, *Adventures in Democracy: a History of the Vote in New Zealand* (Dunedin, 2003)
Attwell, P, 'NZ Co land claims in the 1840s: the Spain Commission & the McCleverty awards' (Department of Internal Affairs, Historical Branch, Wellington, September 1992)
Attwood, Bain, '*The Law of the Land*' or the Law of the land? History, Law and Narrative in a Settler Society; *History Compass*, 2 (2004), 1–30
—*Possession: Batman's Treaty and the Matter of History* (Melbourne, 2009)
Attwood, Bain and Tom Griffiths (eds), *Frontier, Race, Nation: Henry Reynolds and Australian History* (Melbourne, 2009)
Baldwin, Peter, 'The Victorian State in Comparative Perspective', in Mandler, Peter (ed), *Liberty and Authority in Victorian Britain* (Oxford, 2006), 51–67
Ballantyne, Tony, 'The State, Politics and Power, 1769–1893', in Giselle Byrnes (ed), *The New Oxford History of New Zealand* (Melbourne, 2009), 99–124
—'Colonial Knowledge' in Sarah Stockwell (ed), *The British Empire: Themes and Perspectives* (Oxford, 2008), 177–97
—'On Place, Space and Mobility in Nineteenth-Century New Zealand', *NZJH*, 45 (2011), 50–70
Ballara, Angela, *Iwi: the Dynamics of Maori Tribal Organisation from c1769 to c1945* (Wellington, 1998)
—'The Pursuit of Mana? A Re-evaluation of the Process of Land Alienation by Maoris, 1840–1890', *JPS*, 91 (1982), 519–41
—*Taua: 'Musket Wars', 'Land Wars', or Tikanga? Warfare in Maori Society in the Early Nineteenth Century* (Auckland, 2003)
— *Te Kīngitanga: The People of the Māori King Movement—Essays from the Dictionary of New Zealand Biography* (Wellington, 1998)
Bank, Andrew, 'Losing Faith in the Civilizing Mission: The Premature Decline of Humanitarian Liberalism at the Cape, 1840–60', in Martin Daunton and Rick Halpern (eds), *Empire and Others: British Encounters with Indigenous Peoples 1600–1850* (London, 1999), 364–83
Barber, N, 'Against a Written Constitution', *Public Law* (2008), 11–18
Bayly, CA, *Imperial Meridian: the British Empire and the World, 1780–1830* (London, 1989)
—*Empire and Information: Intelligence Gathering and Social Communication in India, 1780–1870* (Cambridge, 1996)
—'The British and indigenous peoples, 1760–1860: power, perception and identity', in Daunton, Martin and Rick Halpern (eds), *Empire and Others: British Encounters with Indigenous Peoples 1600–1850* (London, 1999), 19–41
—*The Birth of the Modern World 1780–1914* (Oxford, 2004)
Beaglehole, J, *Captain Hobson and the New Zealand Company: a study in colonial administration* (Northampton, Mass, 1927)
Beales, D and G Best (eds), *History, Society and Churches: Essays in Honour of Owen Chadwick* (Cambridge, 1985)
Beasley, Edward, *Empire as the Triumph of Theory: Imperialism, Information, and the Colonial Society of 1868* (Abingdon, 2005)

Belgrave, Michael, 'Pre-emption, the Treaty of Waitangi and the Politics of Crown Purchase', *NZJH*, 31 (1997), 23–37

—*Historical Frictions: Maori Claims & Reinvented Histories* (Auckland, 2005)

Belich, James, *Making Peoples: a History of the New Zealanders from Polynesian Settlement to the end of the Nineteenth Century* (Auckland, 1996)

—'Hobson's choice (review article)', *NZJH*, 24 (1990), 200–7

—'The governors and the Maori (1840–1872)', in Keith Sinclair (ed), *The Oxford Illustrated History of New Zealand* (Auckland, 2nd edn, 1996), 75–98

—'Myth, race and identity in New Zealand', in Hiery, Hermann J, and John McKenzie (eds), *European impact and Pacific influence: British and German Colonial Policy in the Pacific islands and Indigenous Response* (London, 1997), 44–64

—'Neo-Britains: an overview/underview', *The British World: diaspora, culture and identity since c1880*, conference, 26 June 1998, Institute of Commonwealth Studies

—*The New Zealand Wars and the Victorian Interpretation of Racial Conflict* (Auckland, 1986)

—*Replenishing the Earth: The Settler Revolution and the Rise of the Anglo-World 1783–1939* (Oxford, 2009)

—'Riders of the Whirlwind: Tribal Peoples and European Settlement Booms, 1790s–1900', in Richard Boast and Richard Hill (eds), *Raupatu: The Confiscation of Maori Land* (Wellington, 2009), 33–47

—'How Much Did Institutions Matter? Cloning Britain in New Zealand' in J Greene (ed), *Exclusionary Empire: English Liberty Overseas, 1600–1900* (Cambridge, 2010), 248–68

Bell, Duncan, 'Empire and Imperialism', in Gareth Stedman Jones and Gregory Claeys (eds), *The Cambridge History of Nineteenth-Century Political Thought* (Cambridge, 2011), 862–892

Bellamy, Richard, *Political Constitutionalism: A Republican Defence of the Constitutionality of Democracy* (Cambridge, 2007)

Bennett, TW, 'Redistribution of Land and the Doctrine of Aboriginal Title in South Africa', *South African Journal of Human Rights*, 9 (1993), 443–76

Benton, Lauren, *A Search for Sovereignty: Law and Geography in European Empires, 1400–1900* (Cambridge, 2010)

Berlin, Isaiah, 'Two Concepts of Liberty', in Henry Hardy (ed), *Liberty* (Oxford, 2002), 166–217

Berman, Howard, 'The Concept of Aboriginal Rights in the Early Legal History of the United States', *Buffalo Law Review*, 27 (1978), 637–67

Best, G, 'The whigs and the church establishment in the age of Holland and Grey', *History*, 45 (1960), 103–18

Binney, Judith, 'Tuki's Universe', in Keith Sinclair (ed), *Tasman Relations: New Zealand and Australia 1788–1988* (Auckland, 1988), 15–33

—'The Maori and the signing of the Treaty of Waitangi', in *Towards 1990: Seven Leading Historians examine significant aspects of New Zealand History* (Wellington, 1990), 20–31

—'History and Memory: The Wood of the Whau Tree, 1766–2005', in Giselle Byrnes (ed), *The New Oxford History of New Zealand* (Melbourne, 2009), 73–98

—'Te Upokokohua: The Curse of Confiscation on Te Urewera', in Richard Hill and Richard Boast (eds), *Raupatu: The Confiscation of Māori Land* (Wellington, 2009), 222–32

—*Encircled Lands: Te Urewera 1820–1921* (Wellington, 2009)

Boast Richard, *Buying the Land, Selling the Land: Governments and Maori Land in the North Island, 1865–1921* (Wellington 2008)

—'Recognising Multitextualism: Rethinking New Zealand's Legal History', *VUWLR*, 37 (2007), 547–82

— 'Treaties and Agreements in Colonial New Zealand', paper for the New Zealand Historical Association Conference, 2007

Bogdanor, Vernon, *The New British Constitution* (Oxford, 2009)
Boldt, Menno and JA Long (eds), *The Quest for Justice: aboriginal peoples and aboriginal rights* (Toronto, 1985)
Boucher, David, *The Limits of Ethics in International Relations: Natural Law, Natural Rights, and Human Rights in Transition* (Oxford, 2009)
Bradley, Ian, *The Call to Seriousness: the evangelical impact on the Victorians* (London, 1976)
Brent, Richard, *Liberal Anglican Politics: Whiggery, Religion and Reform, 1830–1841* (Oxford, 1987)
Brett, Annabel, 'Scholastic Political Thought and the Modern Concept of the State' in Annabel Brett, James Tully, and Holly Hamilton-Bleakley (eds), *Rethinking the Foundations of Modern Political Thought* (Cambridge, 2006), 130–48
Brookfield, FM, *Waitangi and Indigenous Rights: Revolution, Law and Legitimation* (Auckland, 2006)
—'The Doctrine of Aboriginal Title in New Zealand: A Defence' (2010), draft paper on file with author
Brown, David, *Palmerston: A Biography* (New Haven, Connecticut, 2010)
Brown, Donald, 'Native Americans and the right of self-government in the United States', in Renwick, William (ed), *Sovereignty and Indigenous Rights: the Treaty of Waitangi in international contexts* (Wellington, 1991), 30–47
Brown, Stewart (ed), *William Robertson and the Expansion of Europe* (Cambridge, 1997)
Brownlie, I and FM Brookfield, *Treaties and Indigenous Peoples* (Oxford, 1992)
Buick, T Lindsay, *The Treaty of Waitangi, or how New Zealand became a British colony* (Wellington, 1914)
Burke, John, 'The wild man's pedigree: scientific method and racial anthropology', in Dudley, Edward, and M Novak (eds), *The Wild Man Within: an image in western thought from the Renaissance to Romanticism* (Pittsburgh, 1972)
Burns, Patricia, *Fatal Success: a history of the New Zealand Company* (Auckland, 1989)
Burroughs, Peter, *Britain and Australia 1831–1855: A Study in Imperial Relations and Crown Lands Administration* (Oxford, 1967)
—'Wakefield and the Ripon land regulations of 1831', *HSANZ*, 11 (1965), 452–66
Burrow, John, *Evolution and Society: a Study in Victorian Social Theory* (Cambridge, 1966)
—'The Uses of Philology in Victorian England', in Robson, Robert (ed), *Ideas and Institutions of Victorian Britain: Essays in Honour of George Kitson Clark* (London, 1967), 180–204
— 'The Village Community and the Uses of History' in Neil McKendrick (ed), *Historical Perspectives: Studies in English Thought and Society in Honour of J.H.Plumb* (London, 1974), 255–285
—*Whigs and Liberals: Continuity and Change in English Political Thought* (Oxford, 1988)
—*The Crisis of Reason: European Thought, 1848–1914* (New Haven, Connecticut, 2000)
—*A History of Histories: Epics, Chronicles, Romances and Inquiries from Herodotus and Thucydides to the Twentieth Century* (London, 2007)
—'Introduction', in Thomas Macaulay, *History of England* (London, 2009)
Byrnes, Giselle, 'Surveying—the Maori and the Land: an Essay in Historical Representation', *NZJH*, 31 (1997), 85–98
Calder, Alex, Jonathan Lamb, and Bridget Orr (eds), *Voyages and Beaches: Pacific encounters, 1769–1840* (Honolulu, 1999)
Canny, Nicholas, 'England's New World and Old, 1480a-1630s', in Nicholas Canny (ed), *The Oxford History of the British Empire: volume I, the origins of empire; British overseas enterprise to the close of the seventeenth century* (Oxford, 1998), 148–69
—(ed), *The Oxford History of the British Empire: volume I, the origins of empire; British overseas enterprise to the close of the seventeenth century* (Oxford, 1998)
Carter, Paul, *The Road to Botany Bay: an essay in spatial history* (London, 1987)

Cell, John, 'Imperial conscience', in Peter Marsh, *The Conscience of the Victorian State* (Syracuse, 1979), 173–213

—*British Colonial Administration in the mid-nineteenth century: the policy-making process* (New Haven, Connecticut, 1970)

Cheyne, Sonia, 'Act of Parliament or royal prerogative? James Stephen and the first New Zealand Constitution bill', *NZJH*, 24 (1990), 182–9

Childe-Pemberton, William, *Life of Lord Norton (Right Hon Sir Charles Adderley, KCMG, MP) 1814–1905—Statesman and Philanthropist* (London, 1909)

Cleave, Peter, 'Tribal and state-like political formations in New Zealand Maori society, 1750–1900', *JPS*, 92 (1983), 51–92

Cohen, Felix, 'Original Indian title', *Minnesota Law Review*, 32 (1947), 28–59

Collini, Stefan, *Public Moralists: Political Thought and Intellectual Life in Britain 1850–1930* (Oxford, 1991)

Collini, Stefan, D Winch, and J Burrow, *That Noble Science of Politics: A Study in Nineteenth-century Intellectual History* (Cambridge, 1983)

Condliffe, JB and Willis Airey, *Short History of New Zealand* (London, 5th edn, 1935)

Connolly, William, *The Terms of Political Discourse* (Oxford, 3rd edn, 1993)

Cooper, Frederick, *Colonialism in Question: Theory, Knowledge, History* (Los Angeles, 2005)

Cornish, William, Stuart Anderson, Raymond Cocks, Michael Lobban, Patrick Polden, and Keith Smith (eds), *The Oxford History of the Laws of England: Volume XI, 1820–1914: English Legal System* (Oxford, 2010)

Cowan, James, *The New Zealand Wars: a History of the Maori Campaigns and the Pioneering Period* (two volumes, Wellington, 1922)

Cox, Gary, *The Efficient Secret: The Cabinet and the Development of Political Parties in Victorian England* (Cambridge, 1987)

Crook, David, *American Democracy in English Politics 1815–1850* (Oxford, 1965)

Crosby, Alfred, *Ecological Imperialism: the Biological Expansion of Europe, 900–1900* (Cambridge, 1986)

Curnow, Jenifer, 'Wiremu Maihi Te Rangikaheke: His Life and Work', *JPS*, 94 (1985), 97–147

Dalton, B, *War and Politics in New Zealand 1855–1870* (Sydney, 1967)

Dalziel, Raewyn, 'Southern Islands: New Zealand and Polynesia', in Andrew Porter (ed), *The Oxford History of the British Empire: volume iii, the nineteenth century* (Oxford, 1999), 573–96

Daniels, Christine and Michael Kennedy (eds), *Negotiated Empires: Centers and Peripheries in the Americas, 1500–1820* (New York, 2002)

Darwin, John, 'Imperialism and the Victorians: the Dynamics of Territorial Expansion', *EHR*, 92 (1997), 614–42

—*The Empire Project: The Rise and Fall of the British World System, 1830–1970* (Cambridge, 2009)

Daunton, Martin, *Trusting Leviathan: The Politics of Taxation in Britain 1799–1914* (Cambridge, 2001)

Daunton, Martin and Rick Halpern (eds), *Empire and Others: British encounters with Indigenous Peoples 1600–1850* (London, 1999)

Davidson, Allan and Peter Lineham (eds), *Transplanted Christianity: documents illustrating aspects of New Zealand church history* (Palmerston North, 2nd edn, 1989)

Dening, Greg, *Mr Bligh's Bad Language: Power, Passion and Theatre on the Bounty* (Cambridge, 1994)

—'The Theatricality of Observing and Being Observed: Eighteenth-century Europe "Discovers" the? century "Pacific"', in Schwartz, Stuart (ed), *Implicit Understandings: Observing, Reporting, and Reflecting on the Encounters between Europeans and Other Peoples in the Early Modern Era* (Cambridge, 1994), 451–83

—*Performances* (Chicago and Melbourne, 1996)

—*Islands and Beaches: Discourse on a Silent Land, Marquesas 1774–1880* (Honolulu, 1980)
—*History's Anthropology: the death of William Gooch* (Latham, 1988)
Desmond, Adrian, *The Politics of Evolution: morphology, medicine, and reform in radical London* (Chicago, 1989)
Desmond, Adrian and James Moore, *Darwin* (London, 1992)
Donajgrodski, A, 'Sir James Graham at the Home Office', *HJ*, 20 (1977), 97–120
Dorsett, Shaunnagh, 'Sworn on the Dirt of Graves: Sovereignty, Jurisdiction and the Judicial Abrogation of "Barbarous" Customs in New Zealand in the 1840s', *JLH*, 30 (2009), 175–97
Dorsett, Shaunnagh and Shaun McVeigh, 'Questions of Jurisdiction', in Shaun McVeigh (ed), *Jurisprudence of Jurisdiction* (Abingdon, 2007), 3–18
Dorsett, Shaunnagh and Ian Hunter (eds), *Law and Politics in British Colonial Thought: Transpositions of Empire* (New York, 2010)
Drayton, Richard, 'Maritime Networks and the Making of Knowledge', in David Cannadine (ed), *Empire, the Sea and Global History: Britain's Maritime World, c.1763–c.1840* (Houndmills, 2007), 72–82
Drescher, Seymour, *Abolition: A History of Slavery and Antislavery* (New York, 2009)
Duly, Leslie, *British Land Policy at the Cape, 1795–1844: a study of administrative procedures in the empire* (Durham, NC, 1967)
Dumett, Raymond (ed), *Gentlemanly Capitalism and British imperialism: the new debate* (London, 1999)
Dworkin, Richard, *Justice for Hedgehogs* (Cambridge, Mass, 2011)
Eastwood, David, 'Men, Morals and the Machinery of Social Legislation, 1790–1840', *Parliamentary History*, 13, part 2 (1994), 190–205
—'The Age of Uncertainty: Britain in the Early Nineteenth Century', *TRHS*, sixth series, 8 (1998), 91–115
—'Making Public Policy in 19th Century Britain' (inaugural lecture, University of Wales Swansea, 24th November 1997)
—*Governing Rural England: Tradition and Transformation in Local Government, 1780–1840* (Oxford, 1994)
—'"Recasting our lot": Peel, the Nation, and the Politics of Interest', in David Eastwood and LW Brockliss (eds), *A Union of Multiple Identities: the British isles, c1750–c1850* (Manchester, 1997), 29–43
Eastwood, David and LW Brockliss (eds), *A Union of Multiple Identities: the British isles, c1750–c1850* (Manchester, 1997)
Edmond, R, *Representing the South Pacific: Colonial Discourse from Cook to Gauguin* (Cambridge, 1997)
Edwards, J, *The Law Officers of the Crown* (London, 1964)
Elias, Sian and Edwin Fletcher, '*Busby v White* (1859): A Collusive Suit to "Confound the Rights of Property through the Length and Breadth of the Colony"?', *VUWLR*, 41 (2010), 563–604
Elbourne, Elizabeth, 'Imperial Politics in the Family Way: Gender, Biography and the 1835–1836 Select Committee on Aborigines', in Bain Attwood and T Griffiths (eds), *Frontier, Race, Nation: Henry Reynolds and Australian History* (Melbourne, 2009), 111–35
Elphick, Richard and Hermann Giliomee (eds), *The Shaping of South African Society, 1652–1840* (Cape Town, 1989)
Evans, Eric, *The Forging of the Modern State: Early Industrial Britain, 1783–1870* (London, 2nd edn, 1996)
Evans, J, 'Change in the Doctrine of Precedent during the Nineteenth Century', in Laurence Goldstein (ed), *Precedent in Law* (Oxford, 1987), 35–72
Evison, H, *Te Wai Pounamu: the Greenstone Island—a history of the southern Maori during the European colonization of New Zealand* (Christchurch, 1993)
—*The Long Dispute: Maori land rights and European colonisation in southern New Zealand* (Christchurch, 1997)
Fabian, Johannes, *Time and the Other: How Anthropology makes its Object* (New York, 1983)

Fargher, Ray, *The Best Man Who Ever Served The Crown? A Life of Donald McLean* (Wellington, 2007)

Fish, Stanley, *Doing What Comes Naturally: Change, Rhetoric, and the Practice of Theory in Literary and Legal Studies* (Durham, NC, 1989)

Fisher, Robin, *Contact and Conflict: Indian-European relations in British Columbia, 1774–1890* (Vancouver, 1977)

—'With or Without Treaty: Indian Land Claims in Western Canada', in William Renwick (ed), *Sovereignty and Indigenous Rights: the Treaty of Waitangi in international contexts* (Wellington, 1991), 49–66

Fontana, Biancamaria, *Rethinking the Politics of Commercial Society: the Edinburgh Review 1802–1832* (Cambridge, 1985)

Forbes, Duncan, 'Sceptical Whiggism, Commerce and Liberty', in AS Skinner and T Wilson (eds), *Essays on Adam Smith* (Oxford, 1976), 179–201

—'Natural law and the Scottish enlightenment', in RH Campbell and AS Skinner (eds), *The Origins and Nature of the Scottish Enlightenment* (Edinburgh, 1982), 186–204

— *The Liberal Anglican Idea of History* (Cambridge, 1952)

Ford, Lisa, *Settler Sovereignty: Jurisdiction and Indigenous People in America and Australia 1788–1836* (Cambridge, Mass, 2010)

—'Before Settler Sovereignty and After Aboriginal Sovereignty', in Bain Attwood and T Griffiths (eds), *Frontier, Race, Nation: Henry Reynolds and Australian History* (Melbourne, 2009), 185–205

Foucault, Michel, *Discipline and Punish: the birth of the prison*, trans Allen Lane (London, 1977)

—'Two lectures', in Nicholas Dirks, G Eley, and S Ortner (eds), *Culture/Power/History: a reader in contemporary social theory* (Princeton, 1994), 200–21

Frame, Alexander, 'The *Kauwaeranga* judgment', *VUWLR*, 14 (1989), 227–45

—'Property and the Treaty of Waitangi: a tragedy of the commodities?', in J McLean (ed), *Property and the Constitution* (Oxford, 1999), 224–38

Francis, Mark, *Governors and Settlers: images of authority in the British colonies, 1820–60* (Christchurch, 1992)

—'The Contemplation of Colonial Constitutions as Political Philosophy', *Political Science*, 40 (1988), 142–59

Francis, Mark and John Morrow, *English Political Thought in the nineteenth century* (London, 1994)

Fraser, P, 'The growth of ministerial control in the nineteenth-century House of Commons', *EHR*, 75 (1960), 444–63

Friends of the Turnbull Library, *Edward Gibbon Wakefield and the colonial dream: a reconsideration* (Wellington, 1997)

Galbraith, JS, *Reluctant Empire: British policy on the South African frontier 1834–1854* (Berkeley and Los Angeles, 1963)

Gee, Graham, 'The Political Constitutionalism of JAG Griffith', *Legal Studies*, 28 (2008), 20–45

Gee, Graham and Grégoire Webber, 'What is a Political Constitution?', *OJLS*, 30 (2010), 273–99

Getzler, Joshua, 'Michael Taggart, *Private Property and Abuse of Rights in Victorian England: The Story of Edward Pickles and the Bradford Water Supply*', *Modern Law Review*, 66 (2003), 819–22

Geuss, Raymond, *Philosophy and Real Politics* (Princeton, 2008)

Ghosh, Peter, 'Gladstone and Peel', in Peter Ghosh and Lawrence Goldman (eds), *Politics and Culture in Victorian Britain: Essays in Memory of Colin Matthew* (Oxford, 2006) 45–73

Ghosh, Peter and Lawrence Goldman (eds), *Politics and Culture in Victorian Britain: Essays in Memory of Colin Matthew* (Oxford, 2006)

Gibbons, Peter, 'Non-fiction', in Terry Sturm (ed), *The Oxford History of New Zealand Literature in English* (Auckland, 1991), 27–104

Glacken, Clarence J, *Traces on the Rhodian shore: nature and culture in western thought from ancient times to the end of the eighteenth century* (Berkeley, 1973)

Goodall, Heather, *Invasion to Embassy: land in aboriginal politics in New South Wales, 1770–1972* (Sydney, 1996)

Goodin, RE, *Political Theory and Public Policy* (Chicago, 1982)

Gould, Eliga, 'Zones of Law, Zones of Violence: The Legal Geography of the British Atlantic, circa 1772', *William and Mary Quartely*, 3rd series, 60 (2003), 471–510

Gray, John, *Enlightenment's Wake: Politics and Culture at the Close of the Modern Age* (London, 1995)

Gray, Kevin and Susan Gray, *Elements of Land Law* (Oxford, 4th edn, 2005)

Griffith, JAG, 'The Political Constitution', *Modern Law Review*, 42 (1979), 1–21

Gross, Izhak, 'The Abolition of Negro Slavery and British Parliamentary Politics', *HJ*, 23 (1980), 63–85

Gunson, Niel, *Messengers of Grace: Missionaries in the South Seas 1797–1860* (Melbourne, 1978)

Haakonssen, Knud, *Natural Law and Moral Philosophy: from Grotius to the Scottish Enlightenment* (Cambridge, 1996)

— *The Science of the Legislator: The Natural Jurisprudence of David Hume and Adam Smith* (Cambridge, 1981)

Hackshaw, Frederika, 'Nineteenth century notions of aboriginal title and their influence on the interpretation of the Treaty of Waitangi', in Ian Kawharu (ed), *Waitangi: Maori and Pakeha perspectives of the Treaty of Waitangi* (Auckland, 1989), 92–120

Haines, Robin, *Emigration and the Labouring Poor: Australian recruitment in Britain and Ireland, 1831–60* (London, 1997)

Hall, Catherine, 'Imperial man: Edward Eyre in Australasia and the West Indies 1833–1866', in B Schwarz (ed), *The Expansion of England: race, ethnicity and cultural history* (London, 1996), 130–70

—*White, Male, and Middle Class: explorations in feminism and history* (New York, 1992)

—Keith McClelland and Jane Rendall, *Defining the Victorian Nation: Class, Race, Gender and the Reform Act of 1867* (Cambridge, 2000)

— *Civilising Subjects: Metropole and Colony in the English Imagination 1830–1867* (Oxford, 2002)

Hamer, David and Roberta Nicholls (eds), *The Making of Wellington 1800–1914* (Wellington, 1990)

Hamilton, Jonnette Watson and Nigel Bankes, 'Different Views of the Cathedral: The Literature on Property Law Theory', in Aileen McHarg, Barry Barton, Adrian Bradbrook, and Lee Godden (eds), *Property and the Law in Energy and Natural Resources* (Oxford, 2010), 19–59

Hardinge, Arthur, *The Life of Henry Howard Molyneux, Fourth Earl of Carnarvon 1831–1890* (three volumes, London, 1925)

Harling, Philip, *The Modern British State: An Historical Introduction* (Cambridge, 2001)

—'The Powers of the Victorian State', in Peter Mandler (ed), *Liberty and Authority in Victorian Britain* (Oxford, 2006), 25–50

Harris, Bruce, 'Judicial Review, Justiciability and the Prerogative of Mercy', *CLJ*, 62 (2003), 631–60

Harris, Jose (ed), *Civil Society in British History: Ideas, Identities, Institutions* (Oxford, 2003)

Harvie, C, 'Revolution and the rule of law', in Kenneth Morgan (ed), *The Oxford History of Britain* (Oxford, 1984), 470–517

Havemann, P, *Indigenous Peoples' Rights in Australia, Canada, & New Zealand* (Auckland, 1999)

Hawkins, Angus, *The Forgotten Prime Minister: The 14th Earl of Derby—Ascent, 1799–1851* (Oxford, 2007)

Head, Lyndsay, 'Wiremu Tamihana and the *Mana* of Christianity' in John Stenhouse and GA Wood (eds), *Christianity, Modernity and Culture* (Adelaide, 2005), 58–86

Held, Virginia, 'Justification: Legal and Political', *Ethics*, 36 (1975–1976), 1–16

Herron, DG, 'Provincialism and Centralism, 1853–1858' in Robert Chapman and Keith Sinclair (eds), *Studies of a Small Democracy: Essays in Honour of Willis Airey* (Auckland, 1963), 10–32

—'The Franchise and New Zealand Politics, 1853–8', *Political Science*, 12 (1960), 28–44

Hickford, Mark, '"Decidedly the Most Interesting Savages on the Globe": An Approach to the Intellectual History of Māori property rights, 1837–1853', *History of Political Thought*, 27 (2006), 122–67

—'John Salmond and Native Title in New Zealand: Developing a Crown theory on the Treaty of Waitangi, 1910–1920', *VUWLR*, 38 (2007), 853–924

—'"Settling Some Very Important Principles of Colonial Law": Three "Forgotten" Cases of the 1840s', *VUWLR*, 35 (2004), 1–71

—'"This Intricate Question"—Some Reflections on Māori Property Rights, Custom and Constitutionalism in the 1840s', *Transpositions of Empire Conference*, Presentation to Prato Symposium, 20-23 April 2009

—'Strands from the Afterlife of Confiscation: Property rights, constitutional histories and the political incorporation of Māori, 1920s', in Richard Hill and Richard Boast (eds), *Raupatu: The Confiscation of Māori Land* (Wellington, 2009), 169–204

—'"Vague Native Rights to Land": British Imperial Policy on Native Title and Custom in New Zealand, 1837–1853', *JICH*, 38 (2010), 175–206

—'Law and Politics in the Constitutional Delineation of Indigenous Property Rights in 1840s New Zealand', in Dorsett and Hunter (eds), *Law and Politics in British Colonial Thought: Transpositions of Empire* (New York, 2010), 249–68

—'Framing and Reframing the *Agōn*: Contesting Narratives and Counter-Narratives on Māori Property Rights and Political Constitutionalism, 1840–1861', in Saliha Belmessous (ed), *Native Claims: Indigenous Law against Empire, 1500–1920* (Oxford and New York, 2011), 152–181

Hiery, Hermann J and John McKenzie (eds), *European impact and Pacific influence: British and German colonial policy in the Pacific islands and indigenous response* (London, 1997)

Higgins, A Pearce, 'International law and the growth of the empire, 1783–1870', in *Cambridge History of the British Empire: II The growth of the new empire 1783–1870* (Cambridge, 1940)

Hill, Richard, *State Authority, Indigenous Autonomy: Crown-Maori Relations in New Zealand/Aotearoa 1900–1950* (Wellington, 2004)

—*Policing the Colonial Frontier: the Theory and Practice of Coercive Racial Control in New Zealand, 1767–1867* (two volumes, Wellington, 1986)

Hilton, Boyd, *The Age of Atonement: the Influence of Evangelicalism on Social and Economic Thought* (Oxford, 1988)

—'The Role of Providence in Evangelical Social Thought', in D Beales and G Best (eds), *History, Society and Churches: essays in honour of Owen Chadwick* (Cambridge, 1985), 215–33

—*A Mad, Bad, & Dangerous People? England 1783–1846* (Oxford, 2006)

Hogan, H, *Renata's Journey: Ko te Haerenga o Renata* (Christchurch, 1994)

Holland, Rose, A Newton, E Benions, and J Hight (eds), *The Cambridge History of the British Empire; volume vii, part ii: New Zealand* (Cambridge, 1933)

Holt, Thomas, *The Problem of Freedom: Race, Labor, and Politics in Jamaica and Britain, 1832–1938* (Baltimore, 1992)

Hont, Istvan and Michael Ignatieff (eds), *Wealth and Virtue: the shaping of political economy in the Scottish enlightenment* (Cambridge, 1983)

Hoppen, K Theodore, *The Mid-Victorian Generation 1846–1886* (Oxford, 1999)

Houlahan, Mark, 'The Canon on the Beach: H T Kemp translating *Robinson Crusoe* and *The Pilgrim's Progress*', in Alex Calder, Jonathan Lamb, and Bridget Orr (eds), *Voyages and Beaches: Pacific encounters, 1769–1840* (Honolulu, 1999), 304–16

Howe, DW, *What Hath God Wrought: The Transformation of America, 1815–1848* (New York, 2007)

Howe, KR, *Race Relations, Australia and New Zealand: a comparative survey, 1770s-1970s* (Auckland, 1977)

—'The Politics of Culture: A Personal History of History in New Zealand', in Roger Openshaw and Elizabeth Rata (eds), *The Politics of Conformity in New Zealand* (Auckland, 2009), 14–24

Hulsebosch, Daniel, *Constituting Empire: New York and the Transformation of Constitutionalism in the Atlantic World, 1664–1830* (Chapel Hill, North Carolina, 2005)

Hunter, Ian, 'Global Justice and Regional Metaphysics: On the Critical History of the Law of Nature and Nations', in Shaunnagh Dorsett and Ian Hunter (eds), *Law and Politics in British Colonial Thought: Transpositions of Empire* (New York, 2010), 11–29

—'Natural Law, Historiography, and Aboriginal Sovereignty', *Legal History*, 11 (2007), 137–67

—'Vattel's Law of Nations: Diplomatic Casuistry for the Protestant Nation', *Grotiana*, 31 (2010), 108–40

—*The Secularization of the Confessional State: The Political Thought of Christian Thomasius* (Cambridge, 2007)

Ilbert, Courtenay, *The Government of India: A Brief Historical Survey of Parliamentary Legislation relating to India* (Oxford, 1922)

Irwin, Geoffrey, 'Against, Across, and Down the Wind: a Case for the Systematic Exploration of the Remote Pacific Islands', *JPS*, 98 (1989), 167–206

Ivison, Duncan, *Postcolonial Liberalism* (Cambridge, 2002)

—'Consent, Contestation and the Subject of Rights' in Jeremy Webber and Colin McLeod (eds), *Between Consenting Peoples: Political Community and the Meaning of Consent* (Vancouver, 2010), 188–206

—'Pluralism and the Hobbesian Logic of Negative Constitutionalism', *Political Studies*, 47 (1999), 83–99

—'The Nature of Rights and the History of Empire', in David Armitage (ed), *British Political Thought in History, Literature and Theory, 1500–1800* (Cambridge, 2006), 191–211

Jackson, Moana, 'Tipuna Title as a Tikanga Construct re the Foreshore and Seabed', March 2010, <http://www.converge.org.nz/pma/mjtipuna.htm> (last accessed September 2010)

Jellicoe, Roland, *The New Zealand Company's Native Reserves* (Wellington, 1930)

Johansson, Jon, *The Politics of Possibility: Leadership in Changing Times* (Wellington, 2009)

Johnston, W Ross, *Sovereignty and Protection: a study of British jurisdictional imperialism in the late nineteenth century* (Durham, NC, 1973)

Joseph, Philip (ed), *Essays on the Constitution* (Wellington, 1995)

Juricek, John Thomas, 'English territorial claims in north America under Elizabeth and the early Stuarts', *Terræ Incognitæ*, 7 (1976), 7–22

Kades, Eric, 'History and Interpretation of the Great Case of *Johnson v McIntosh*', *Law and History Review*, 19 (2001), 67–116

Kahan, Alan, *Liberalism in Nineteenth Century Europe: The Political Culture of Limited Suffrage* (Basingstoke, 2003)

Kawharu, Ian H, *Maori Land Tenure: studies of a changing institution* (Oxford, 1977)

—(ed), *Waitangi: Maori and Pakeha perspectives of the Treaty of Waitangi* (Auckland, 1989)

Keegan, Timothy, *Colonial South Africa and the Origins of the Racial order* (London, 1996)

Kerr, Donald, *Amassing Treasures for All Times: Sir George Grey, Colonial Bookman and Collector* (New Castle, Delaware, and Dunedin, 2006)

Keynes, Richard, *Charles Darwin's Beagle Diary* (Cambridge, 1988)

Kidd, Colin, *Union and Unionsims: Political Thought in Scotland, 1500–2000* (Cambridge, 2008)

Kiernan, VJ, *The Lords of Human Kind: European attitudes towards the outside world in the imperial age* (London, 1969)

King, Robert, 'Terra Nullius and Terra Aboriginum', *Journal of the Royal Australian Historical Society*, lxxii (1986), 75–91

Knaplund, Paul, *James Stephen and the British colonial system, 1813–1847* (Madison, 1953)

Kociumbas, Jan, *The Oxford History of Australia: volume 2, 1770–1860 Possessions* (Melbourne, 1992)

Korman, Sharon, *The Right of Conquest: the Acquisition of Territory by Force in International Law and Practice* (Oxford, 1996)

Kriegel, AD, 'A Convergence of Ethics: Saints and Whigs in British Antislavery', *JBS*, 26 (1987), 423–50

Krisch, Nico, *Beyond Constitutionalism: The Pluralist Structure of Postnational Law* (Oxford, 2010)

Kymlicka, Will, *Multicultural Citizenship* (Oxford, 1995)

Kymlicka, Will and Bashir Bashir (eds), *The Politics of Reconciliation in Multicultural Societies* (Oxford, 2008)

LaCapra, Dominick, *Rethinking Intellectual History: texts, contexts, language* (Ithaca and London, 1983)

Laidlaw, Zoë, '"Aunt Anna's Report": The Buxton Women and the Aborigines Select Committee, 1835–37', *JICH*, 32 (2004), 1–28

—*Colonial Connections, 1815–45: Patronage, the Information Revolution and Colonial Government* (Manchester, 2005)

Langford, Paul, *A Polite and Commercial People, England 1727–1783* (Oxford, 1989)

Laski, Harold, *The Foundations of Sovereignty and Other Essays* (London, 1921)

Lenman, Bruce, 'Colonial wars and imperial instability, 1688–1793', in PJ Marshall (ed), *The Oxford History of the British Empire: volume ii, the eighteenth century* (Oxford, 1998), 151–68

Lennard, Guy, *Sir William Martin: The Life of the first Chief Justice of New Zealand* (Christchurch, 1961)

Lian, Kwen Fee, 'Interpreting Maori history: a case for historical sociology', *JPS*, 96 (1987), 445–71

Lieberman, David, 'The Mixed Constitution and the Common Law', in Mark Goldie and Robert Wokler (eds) *The Cambridge History of Eighteenth Century Political Thought* (Cambridge, 2006), 317–346

Lightman, Bernard (ed), *Victorian Science in Context* (Chicago, 1997)

Lindley, MF, *The Acquisition and Government of Backward Territory in International Law (being a treatise on the law and practice relating to colonial expansion)* (London, 1926)

Livingstone, David N, *The Geographical Tradition: episodes in the history of a contested enterprise* (Cambridge, MA, 1992)

Lobban, Michael, *The Common Law and English Jurisprudence* (Oxford, 1991)

Lorimer, Douglas, *Colour, Class and the Victorians: English attitudes to the Negro in the mid-nineteenth century* (Leicester, 1978)

—'Science and the Secularization of Victorian Images of Race', in Bernard Lightman (ed), *Victorian Science in Context* (Chicago, 1997), 212–35

Low, Peter, 'Pompallier and the Treaty: a new discussion', *NZJH*, 24 (1990), 190–9

MacDonagh, Oliver, *O'Connell: the life of Daniel O'Connell, 1775–1847* (London, 1991)

McHugh, Paul G, *The Maori Magna Carta: New Zealand law and the Treaty of Waitangi* (Auckland, 1991)

—*Aboriginal Societies and the Common Law* (Oxford, 2004)

—'The Legal Status of Maori Fishing Rights in Tidal Waters', *VUWLR*, 14 (1984), 247–73

—'The Historiography of New Zealand's Constitutional History', in Philip Joseph (ed), *Essays on the Constitution* (Wellington, 1995), 344–67

—'Aboriginal Title in the New Zealand Courts', *Canterbury Law Review*, 2 (1984), 235–65
—'Legal Reasoning and the Treaty of Waitangi: Orthodox and Radical Approaches', in Graham Oddie and RW Perrett (eds), *Justice, Ethics, and New Zealand Society* (Auckland, 1992), 91–108
—'The Common-law Status of Colonies and Aboriginal "Rights": How Lawyers and Historians treat the Past', *Saskatchewan Law Review*, 61 (1998), 393–429
—'A Tribal Encounter: the Presence and Properties of Common-law Language in the Discourse of Colonization in the Early Modern Period', in Alex Calder, Jonathan Lamb, and Bridget Orr (eds), *Voyages and Beaches: Pacific encounters, 1769–1840* (Honolulu, 1999), 114–31
—'A History of the Modern Jurisprudence of Aboriginal Rights—Some Observations on the Journey So Far', in David Dyzenhaus, Murray Hunt, and Grant Huscroft (eds), *A Simple Common Lawyer: Essays in Honour of Michael Taggart* (Oxford, 2009), 209–232
—'The Politics of Historiography and the Taxonomies of the Colonial Past: Law, History and the Tribes', in A Musson and C Stebbings (eds), *Making Legal History: Approaches and Methodology* (forthcoming, Cambridge)
McKenzie, DF, *Oral Culture, Literacy and Print in early New Zealand: the Treaty of Waitangi* (Wellington, 1985)
McLean, Janet, 'Property as Power and Resistance', in Janet McLean (ed), *Property and the Constitution* (Oxford 1999), 1–10
McLintock, AH, *Crown Colony Government in New Zealand* (Wellington, 1958)
—*The History of Otago* (Dunedin, 1949)
McMillen, Christian, *Making Indian Law: The Hualapai Land Case and the Birth of Ethnohistory* (New Haven, Connecticut, 2007)
McNeil, Kent, *Common Law Aboriginal Title* (Oxford, 1989)
McRae, Jane, 'Maori Literature: a Survey', in Terry Sturm (ed), *The Oxford History of New Zealand Literature in English* (Auckland, 1991), 1–24
Macmillan, William, *Bantu, Boer, and Briton: the making of the South African native problem* (Oxford, 1963)
—'The Frontier and the Kaffir Wars, 1792–1836', in EA Walker (ed), *The Cambridge History of the British Empire: volume xiii* (Cambridge, 2nd edn, 1963), 301–23
Madden, Frederick and David Fieldhouse, *Imperial Reconstruction, 1763–1840: the Evolution of Alternative Systems of Colonial Government* (Westport, Connecticut, 1987)
—*The Classical Period of the First British Empire, 1689–1783: the Foundations of a Colonial System of Government* (Westport, Connecticut, 1985)
Magee, Gary and Andrew Thompson, *Empire and Globalisation: Networks of People, Goods and Capital in the British World, c1850–1914* (Cambridge, 2010)
Mandler, Peter, *Aristocratic Government in the Age of Reform: Whigs and Liberals, 1830–1852* (Oxford, 1990)
—*The English National Character: The History of an Idea from Edmund Burke to Tony Blair* (New Haven, Connecticut, 2006)
—'"Race" and "Nation" in Mid-Victorian Thought', in Stefan Collini, Richard Whatmore, and Brian Young (eds), *History, Religion, and Culture: British Intellectual History 1750–1950* (Cambridge, 2000), 224–44
—'The Problem with Cultural History', *Cultural and Social History*, 1 (2004), 94–117
—(ed), *Liberty and Authority in Victorian Britain* (Oxford, 2006)
Manning, Helen Taft, 'Lord Durham and the New Zealand Company', *NZJH*, 6 (1972), 1–19
Mantena, Karuna, *Alibis of Empire: Henry Maine and the Ends of Liberal Imperialism* (Princeton, 2009)
Marais, JS, *The Colonisation of New Zealand* (Oxford, 1927)
March, JE and JP Olsen, *Ambiguity and Choice in Organizations* (Bergen 1976)
Margalit, Arvishai, *On Compromise and Rotten Compromises* (Princeton, 2009)

Marsh, Peter (ed), *The Conscience of the Victorian State* (Syracuse, 1979)
Marshall, PJ (ed), *The Oxford History of the British Empire: volume ii, the eighteenth century* (Oxford, 1998)
—'Parliament and Property Rights in the Late Eighteenth-century British Empire', in John Brewer and Susan Staves (eds), *Early Modern Conceptions of Property* (London, 1995), 530–44
—*The Making and Unmaking of Empires: Britain, India, and America c.1750–1783* (Oxford, 2005)
Martin, G, *Edward Gibbon Wakefield: Abductor and Mystagogue* (Edinburgh, 1997)
—*The Durham Report and British Policy* (Cambridge, 1972)
Martin, RH, *Evangelicals United: ecumenical stirrings in pre-Victorian Britain, 1795–1830* (Metuchen, NJ, and London, 1983)
Matthew, HCG, *Gladstone, 1809–1874* (Oxford, 1986)
—*Gladstone 1809–1898* (Oxford, 1999)
—(ed), *The Gladstone Diaries, Volume VI—1861–1868* (Oxford, 1978)
—Brian Howard Harrison and Lawrence Goldman (eds), *Oxford Dictionary of National Biography*, <http://www.oxforddnb.com>
Meek, Ronald, *Social Science and the Ignoble Savage* (Cambridge, 1976)
Mellor, George, *British Imperial Trusteeship, 1783–1850* (London, 1951)
Metge, Joan, *Talking Past Each Other: Problems of Cross-cultural Communication* (Wellington, 1984)
—*Tuamaka: The Challenge of Difference in Aotearoa New Zealand* (Auckland, 2010)
Ministerial Review of the Foreshore and Seabed Act 2004, *Pākia ki Uta, Pākia ki Tai: Report of the Ministerial Review Panel* (three volumes, Wellington, 2009)
Mitchell, Leslie, *Lord Melbourne, 1779–1848* (Oxford, 1997)
Mommsen, WJ and JA De Moor (eds), *European Expansion and Law: the Encounter of European and Indigenous Law in 19th- and 20th-century Africa and Asia* (Oxford, 1982)
Monin, Paul, *Hauraki Contested, 1769–1875* (Wellington, 2001)
—'Maori Economies and Colonial Capitalism', in Giselle Byrnes (ed), *The New Oxford History of New Zealand* (Melbourne, 2009), 125–46
Moore, James, 'Wallace's Malthusian Moment: the Common Context Revisited', in Bernard Lightman (ed), *Victorian Science in Context* (Chicago, 1997), 290–311
Moore, RJ, *Sir Charles Wood's Indian Policy 1853–66* (Manchester, 1966)
Morgan, Kenneth (ed), *The Oxford History of Britain* (Oxford, 1984)
Morrell, William P, *British Colonial Policy in the age of Peel and Russell* (Oxford, 1930)
—*British Colonial Policy in the Mid-Victorian Age* (Oxford, 1969)
Mouffe, Chantal, *On the Political* (London, 2005)
Muldoon, Paul '"The Very Basis of Civility": On Agonism, Consquest, and Reconciliation', in Will Kymlicka and Bashir Bashir (eds), *The Politics of Reconciliation in Multicultural Societies* (Oxford, 2008), 114–35
Mulgan, Alan, *The City of the Strait: Wellington and its Province, a Centennial History* (Wellington, 1939)
Mulholland, Malcolm and Veronica Tawhai (eds), *Weeping Waters: The Treaty of Waitangi and Constitutional Change* (Wellington, 2010)
Mutu, Margaret, '*Tuku whenua* and Land Sale in New Zealand in the Nineteenth Century', in Alex Calder, Jonathan Lamb, and Bridget Orr (eds), *Voyages and Beaches: Pacific encounters, 1769–1840* (Honolulu, 1999), 317–28
Neumann, Klaus, Nicholas Thomas, and Hilary Ericksen (eds), *Quicksands: Foundational Histories in Australia and Aotearoa New Zealand* (Canberra, 1999)
Newbould, Ian, *Whiggery and Reform, 1830–41: the Politics of Government* (London, 1990)
—'Lord Durham, the Whigs and Canada, 1838: the Background to Durham's Return', *Albion*, 8 (1976), 351–74

—'Sir Robert Peel and the Conservative Party, 1832–1841: A Study in Failure?', *EHR*, 98 (1983), 529–57
Nicolson, Malcolm, 'Medicine and Racial Politics: Changing Images of the New Zealand Maori in the Nineteenth Century', in David Arnold (ed), *Imperial Medicine and Indigenous Societies: Disease, Medicine and Empire in the Nineteenth and Twentieth Centuries* (Manchester, 1978), 66–104
Oakeshott, Michael, *Rationalism in Politics and Other Essays* (Indianapolis, 1991), 438–61
O'Brien, Karen, *Narratives of Enlightenment: Cosmopolitan History from Voltaire to Gibbon* (Cambridge, 1997)
Oddie, Graham and RW Perrett (eds), *Justice, Ethics, and New Zealand Society* (Auckland, 1992)
Oliver, William H, *The Story of New Zealand* (London, 1963)
—*Prophets and Millennialists: the Uses of Biblical Prophecy in England from the 1790s to the 1840s* (Auckland, 1978)
—(ed), *The New Zealand Dictionary of National Biography: volume I, 1769–1869* (Wellington, 1990)
—*The Oxford History of New Zealand* (Wellington, 1st edn, 1981)
—*Looking for the Phoenix: A Memoir* (Wellington, 2002)
Olssen, Erik, 'Mr Wakefield and New Zealand as an Experiment in Post-enlightenment Experimental Practice', *NZJH*, 31 (1997), 197–218
Orange, Claudia, *The Treaty of Waitangi* (Auckland, 1987)
—'The Maori People and the British Crown (1769–1840)', in Keith Sinclair (ed), *The Oxford Illustrated History of New Zealand* (Auckland, 2nd edn, 1996), 21–48
—*The People of Many Peaks: The Māori Biographies from The Dictionary of New Zealand Biography, volume 1: 1769–1869* (Wellington, 1991)
Owen, JMR, 'New Zealand before Annexation', in Geoffrey Rice (ed), *The Oxford History of New Zealand* (Auckland, 2nd edn, 1992), 28–53
Pagden, Anthony, *Lords of all the World: Ideologies of Empire in Spain, Britain and France, c1500–c1800* (New Haven, Connecticut, 1995)
—*The Fall of Natural Man: the American Indian and the Origins of Comparative Ethnology* (Cambridge, 1982)
—'The Struggle for Legitimacy and the Image of Empire in the Atlantic to c1700', in Nicholas Canny (ed), *The Oxford History of the British Empire: volume i, the origins of empire; British overseas enterprise to the close of the seventeenth century* (Oxford, 1998), 35–54
—(ed), *The Languages of Political Theory in Early-Modern Europe* (Cambridge, 1987)
—'Dispossessing the Barbarian: Rights and Property in Spanish America', *in Spanish Imperialism and the Political Imagination: Studies in European and Spanish-American Social and Political Theory 1513–1830* (New Haven, Connecticut, 1990), 13–36
Palmer, Matthew, *The Treaty of Waitangi in New Zealand's Law and Constitution* (Wellington, 2008)
Parkinson, P, '"Preserved in the Archives of the Colony": The English Drafts of the Treaty of Waitangi', *Revue Juridique Polynésienne*, 11 (2005)
—'"The Path of the Perfected Law": The Use of the Maori Language in the Government of New Zealand from 1840 to 1865', *The Māori Language and its Expression in New Zealand Law: Two Essays on the Use of Te Reo Māori in Government and in Parliament* (Wellington, 2001), 1–27
Parris, Henry, *Constitutional Bureaucracy: The development of British Central Administration since the Eighteenth Century* (London, 1969)
Parry, Jonathan, *The Rise and Fall of Liberal Government in Victorian Britain* (New Haven, Connecticut, 1993)
—*The Politics of Patriotism: English Liberalism, National Identity and Europe, 1830–1886* (Cambridge, 2006)

—'Liberalism and Liberty', in Peter Mandler (ed), *Liberty and Authority in Victorian Britain* (Oxford, 2006), 71–100

Parsonson, Ann, 'The Challenge to Mana Maori', in Geoffrey Rice (ed), *The Oxford History of New Zealand* (Auckland, 2nd edn, 1992), 167–98

—'The Pursuit of Mana', in WH Oliver (ed), *The Oxford History of New Zealand* (Wellington, 1st edn, 1981), 140–67

—'The Expansion of a Competitive Society: A Study in Nineteenth-century Maori Social History', *NZJH*, 14 (1980), 45–60

Paterson, Lachy, *Colonial Discourses: Niupepa Māori 1855–1863* (Dunedin, 2006)

Patterson, B, '"A queer cantankerous lot": the human factor in the conduct of the New Zealand Company's Wellington surveys', in David Hamer and Roberta Nicholls (eds), *The Making of Wellington 1800–1914* (Wellington, 1990), 61–87

Pearson, Noel, 'Land is Susceptible of Ownership' in Noel Pearson, *Up from the Mission: Selected Writings* (Melbourne, 2009), 100–125

Peires, J, *The Dead will Arise: Nongqawuse and the great Xhosa cattle-killing movement of 1856–7* (Johannesburg, 1989)

—*The House of Phalo: A History of the Xhosa People in the Days of their Independence* (Berkeley, 1982)

Petrie, Hazel, *Chiefs of Industry: Māori Tribal Enterprise in Early Colonial New Zealand* (Auckland, 2006)

Philipp, June, 'Wakefieldian influence and New South Wales 1830–1832', *HSANZ*, 9 (1960), 173–80

Phillipson, Nicholas, *Adam Smith: An Enlightened Life* (London, 2010)

Pike, Douglas, *Paradise of Dissent: South Australia 1829–1857* (London, 1957)

Pocock, JGA, *Virtue, Commerce and History: essays on political thought and history, chiefly in the eighteenth century* (Cambridge, 1985)

—'The Concept of Language and the *métier d'historien*: some considerations on practice', in Anthony Pagden (ed), *The Languages of Political Theory in Early-Modern Europe* (Cambridge, 1987), 19–38

—'Tangata Whenua and Enlightenment Anthropology', *NZJH*, 26 (1992), 28–53

—'Removal from the Wings', *London Review of Books*, 19 (1997), 12–13

—'Law, Sovereignty and History in a Divided Culture: the case of New Zealand and the Treaty of Waitangi', *McGill Law Journal*, 43 (1998), 481–506

—'Nature and history, self and other: European perceptions of world history in the age of encounter', in Alex Calder, Jonathan Lamb, and Bridget Orr (eds), *Voyages and Beaches: Pacific encounters, 1769–1840* (Honolulu, 1999), 25–44

—'The Treaty between Histories', in Andrew Sharp and Paul McHugh (eds), *Histories, Power and Loss: Uses of the Past—A New Zealand Commentary* (Wellington, 2001) 75–95

— *The Machiavellian Moment: Florentine Political Thought and the Atlantic Republican Tradition* (Princeton, rev edn, 2003)

—'Quentin Skinner: The History of Politics and the Politics of History', *Common Knowledge*, 10 (2004), 532–50

—*The Discovery of Islands: Essays in British History* (Cambridge, 2005)

—*Barbarism and Religion—Volume Four: Barbarians, Savages and Empires* (Cambridge, 2005)

—*Political Thought and History: Essays on Theory and Method* (Cambridge, 2009)

Pocock, JGA, G Schochet, and Lois Schwoerer (eds), *The Varieties of British Political Thought, 1500–1800* (Cambridge, 1993)

Polanyi, K, 'The Economy as Instituted Process', in Karl Polanyi, Conrad Arensberg, and H Pearson (eds), *Trade and Market in the Early Empires* (Glencoe, Ill, 1957), 243–70

Pole, JR, *Political Representation in England and the Origins of the American Republic* (London, 1966)

Porter, Andrew, '"Commerce and Christianity": the rise and fall of a nineteenth-century missionary slogan', *HJ*, 28 (1985), 597–621

—'North American experience and British missionary encounters in Africa and the Pacific, c1800–50', in Martin Daunton and Rick Halpern (eds), *Empire and Others: British encounters with indigenous peoples 1600–1850* (London, 1999), 345–63

—'Trusteeship, anti-slavery, and humanitarianism', in Andrew Porter (ed), *The Oxford History of the British Empire: volume iii, the nineteenth century* (Oxford, 1999)

—*Religion versus Empire? British Protestant Missionaries and Overseas Expansion, 1700–1914* (Manchester, 2004)

Porter, Bernard, 'Giant Vegetables (review of James Belich, *Replenishing the Earth: The Settler Revolution and the Rise of the Anglo-World*)', *Times Literary Supplement*, 25 September 2009, 8–9

Postema, Gerald, *Bentham and the Common Law Tradition* (Oxford, 1989)

Pratt, Mary, *Imperial Eyes: Travel Writing and Transculturation* (New York, 1992)

Pretorius, J, 'The British humanitarians and the Cape eastern frontier', in *Archives Yearbook for South African History* (Pretoria, 1988)

Price, Simon and Peter Thonemann, *The Birth of Classical Europe: A History from Troy to Augustine* (London, 2010)

Promislow, Janna, '"Thou Wilt Not Die of Hunger... For I Bring Thee Merchandise": Consent, Intersocietal Normativity, and the Exchange of Food at York Factory, 1682–1763', in Jeremy Webber and Colin McLeod (eds), *Between Consenting Peoples: Political Community and the Meaning of Consent* (Vancouver, 2010), 77–114

Rainger, R, 'Philanthropy and science in the 1830s: the British and Foreign Aborigines' Protection Society', *Man*, 15 (1980), 702–17

Rawlings, Richard, 'Distinction and Diversity; Law and the LSE', in Rawlings (ed), *Law, Society and Economy: Centenary Essays for the London School of Economics and Political Science* (Oxford, 1997), 1–22.

Redlich, Josef, *The procedure of the House of Commons: a study of its history and present form* (three volumes, London, 1968)

Renwick, William (ed), *Sovereignty and Indigenous Rights: the Treaty of Waitangi in International Contexts* (Wellington, 1991)

Reynolds, Henry, *The Law of the Land* (Melbourne, 1987)

—*Aboriginal Sovereignty: Reflections on Race, State and Nation* (Sydney, 1996)

—*Frontier: Aborigines, Settlers and Land* (Sydney, 1996)

Rice, GW (ed), *The Oxford History of New Zealand* (Auckland, 2nd edn, 1992)

Richards, Thomas, *The Imperial Archive: Knowledge and the Fantasy of Empire* (London, 1993)

Rigby, Nigel, 'The Politics and Pragmatics of Seaborne Plant Transplantation, 1769–1805', in Margarette Lincoln (ed), *Science and Exploration in the Pacific: European voyages to the southern ocean in the eighteenth century* (Woodbridge, 1998)

Robb, Peter, *Ancient Rights and Future Comfort: Bihar, the Bengal Tenancy Act of 1885, and British rule in India* (London, 1997)

Robertson, Lindsay, *Conquest by Law: How the discovery of America Dispossessed Indigenous Peoples of their Lands* (New York, 2005)

Robinson, Ronald and John Gallagher, *Africa and the Victorians: the Official Mind of Imperialism* (London, 1st edn, 1961)

—*Africa and the Victorians: the Official Mind of Imperialism* (London, 2nd edn, 1981)

Robson, Robert (ed), *Ideas and Institutions of Victorian Britain: Essays in Honour of George Kitson Clark* (London, 1967)

Rockwell, Stephen, *Indian Affairs and the Administrative State in the Nineteenth Century* (New York, 2010)

Rogan, Eugene, *The Arabs: A History* (London, 2009)

Rose, Michael, *Curator of the Dead: Thomas Hodgkin (1798–1866)* (London, 1981)
Rosman, Doreen, *Evangelicals and Culture* (London, 1984)
Ross, Adam, *John Philip (1775–1851): Missions, Race and Politics in South Africa* (Aberdeen, 1986)
Ross, John, 'Busby and the Declaration of Independence', *NZJH*, 14 (1980), 83–9
Ross, Ruth, 'Te Tiriti o Waitangi—Texts and Translations', *NZJH*, 6 (1972), 129–67
Rowse, T, 'The National Emergency and Indigenous Jurisdictions', in Jon Altman and Melinda Hinkson (eds), *Coercive Reconciliation: Stabilise, Normalise, Exit Aboriginal Australia* (Melbourne, 2007), 47–61
—'Britons, Settlers, and Aborigines: Civil Society and its Colonized "Other" in Colonial, Post-colonial, and Present-day Australia', in Jose Harris (ed), *Civil Society in British History: Ideas, Identities, Institutions* (Cambridge, 2003), 293–310
Runciman, David, *Political Hypocrisy: The Mask of Power, from Hobbes to Orwell and Beyond* (Princeton, 2008)
—*Pluralism and the Personality of the State* (Cambridge, 1997)
Rutherford, J, *Sir George Grey KCB, 1812–1898: A Study in Colonial Government* (London, 1961)
—*The Treaty of Waitangi and the Acquisition of British sovereignty in New Zealand* (Auckland, 1949)
Sahlins, Marshall, *How 'Natives' Think; about Captain Cook, for example* (Chicago, 1995)
Salesa, Damon, *Racial Crossings: Race, Intermarriage, and the Victorian British Empire* (Oxford, 2011)
Salmond, Anne, *Two Worlds: First Meetings between Maori and Europeans, 1642–1772* (Auckland, 1991)
—*Between Worlds: Early Exchanges between Maori and Europeans 1773–1815* (Auckland, 1997)
Samson, Jane, *Imperial Benevolence: Making British Authority in the Pacific Islands* (Honolulu, 1998)
—'British Voices and Indigenous Rights: Debating Aboriginal Legal Status in Nineteenth Century Australia and Canada', *Cultures of the Commonwealth: Essays and Studies*, 2 (1996–1997), 5–16
Sartori, Andrew, 'A Liberal Discourse of Custom in Colonial Bengal', *Past and Present*, 212 (2011), 163–97
Schwartz, Stuart (ed), *Implicit Understandings: Observing, Reporting, and Reflecting on the Encounters between Europeans and Other Peoples in the Early Modern Era* (Cambridge, 1994)
Scott, James C, *Seeing Like a State: How Certain Schemes to Improve the Human Condition Have Failed* (New Haven, Connecticut, 1998)
Scully, Pamela, *Liberating the Family? Gender and British Slave Emancipation in the Rural Western Cape, 1823–1853* (Oxford, 1997)
Shannon, Richard, 'Victorian *cahiers de doléance*' (review article), *HJ*, 32 (1989), 712–22
—*Gladstone, 1809–1865* (London, 1984)
Sharp, Andrew, *Justice and the Māori: The Philosophy and Practice of Māori Claims in New Zealand since the 1970s* (Auckland, 2nd edn, 1997)
—'History and Sovereignty: A Case of Judicial History in New Zealand/Aotearoa', in Michael Peters (ed), *Cultural Politics and the University in Aotearoa/New Zealand* (Palmerston North, 1997), 159–181
—'Recent Juridical and Constitutional Histories of Maori', in Andrew Sharp and Paul McHugh (eds), *Histories, Power and Loss: Uses of the Past—A New Zealand Commentary* (Wellington, 2001), 31–60
—'Justice, Self-government and Current Theories of Maori Organisation', 9 February 2004, unpublished paper presented to The Treasury, Wellington, New Zealand
—'The Treaty in the Real Life of the Constitution', in M Belgave, M Kawharu, and David Williams (eds), *Waitangi Revisited: Perspectives on the Treaty of Waitangi* (Melbourne, 2005), 308–29

—'Constitutionalism', in Raymond Miller (ed), *New Zealand Government and Politics* (Melbourne, 4th edn, 2006), 103–14
Shaw, Alan, 'James Stephen and colonial policy: the Australian experience', *JICH*, 20 (1992), 11–34
—'British Policy towards the Australian aborigines, 1830–1850', *AHS*, 25 (1992), 265–85
—*A History of the Port Phillip District: Victoria before separation* (Melbourne, 1996)
—(ed), *Great Britain and her Colonies 1815–1865* (London, 1970)
Sinclair, Keith, *The Origins of the Maori Wars* (Wellington, 1957)
—*A History of New Zealand* (Auckland, 4th edn, 1991)
—'Te Tikanga Pakeke: The Maori Anti-Land-Selling Movement in Taranki 1849–59', in P Munz (ed), *The Feel of Truth: Essays in New Zealand and Pacific History* (Wellington, 1969), 79–92
—'Why are Race Relations in New Zealand Better than in South Africa, South Australia or South Dakota?', *NZJH*, 2 (1971), 121–7
—(ed), *Tasman Relations: New Zealand and Australia 1788–1988* (Auckland, 1988)
—*The Oxford Illustrated History of New Zealand* (Auckland, 2nd edn, 1996)
Skinner, Quentin, *Visions of Politics: Volume I—Regarding Method* (Cambridge, 2002)
—*Visions of Politics: Volume II, Renaissance Virtues* (Cambridge, 2002)
—'Afterword', in David Armitage (ed), *British Political Thought in History, Literature and Theory, 1500–1800* (Cambridge, 2006), 278–85
Skinner, Quentin and James Tully (eds), *Meaning and Context: Quentin Skinner and his Critics* (Oxford, 1988)
Slattery, Brian, *Ancestral Lands, Alien Laws: Judicial Perspectives on Aboriginal Title* (Saskatoon, 1983)
— 'Making Sense of Aboriginal and Treaty Rights', *Canadian Bar Review*, 79 (2000), 194–224
— 'A Taxonomy of Aboriginal Rights', in Hamar Foster, Heather Raven, and Jeremy Webber (eds) *Let Right Be Done: Aboriginal Title, the Calder Case, and the Future of Indigenous Rights* (Vancouver, 2007), 111–128
Smith, Bernard, *European Vision and the South Pacific, 1768–1850* (Oxford, 1960)
Smith, Joseph H, *Appeals to the Privy Council from the American Plantations* (New York, 1950)
Sorrenson, Keith, 'Treaties and British Colonial Policy: Precedents for Waitangi', in William Renwick (ed), *Sovereignty and Indigenous Rights: the Treaty of Waitangi in International Contexts* (Wellington, 1991), 15–29
—'How to Civilize Savages: Some "Answers" from Nineteenth-century New Zealand', *NZJH*, 9 (1975), 97–110
—*Maori Origins and Migrations: the Genesis of Some Pakeha Myths and Legends* (Auckland, 1979)
—'Maori and Pakeha', in GW Rice (ed), *The Oxford History of New Zealand* (Auckland, 2nd edn, 1992), 141–66
—'The Maori King Movement, 1858–1885', in Robert Chapman and Keith Sinclair (eds), *Studies of a Small Democracy: Essays in Honour of Willis Airey* (Auckland, 1963), 33–55
—'The Politics of Land', in JGA Pocock (ed), *The Maori and New Zealand Politics* (Auckland, 1965), 21–45
—Appendix B, *Report of the Royal Commission on the Electoral System: 'Towards a Better Democracy'* (December 1986)
Stallybrass, Peter and A White, *The Politics and Poetics of Transgression* (Ithaca, 1986)
Stanley, Brian, *The Bible and the Flag: Protestant Missions and British Imperialism in the Nineteenth and Twentieth Centuries* (Leicester, 1990)
Stein, PG, *Legal Evolution: the Story of an Idea* (Cambridge, 1980)
—*Roman Law in European History* (Cambridge, 1999)
Stepan, Nancy, *The Idea of Race in Science: Great Britain 1800–1960* (London, 1982)
Stephen, CE, *The First Sir James Stephen* (London, 1906)

Stephen, Leslie and Sidney Lee (eds), *The Dictionary of National Biography* (66 volumes, Oxford, 1885–1901)
Stewart, MA (ed), *Studies in the Philosophy of the Scottish Enlightenment* (Oxford, 1990)
Stock, Eugene, *The History of the Church Missionary Society: Its Environment, its Men and its Work* (three volumes, London, 1899)
Stocking junior, George, *Victorian Anthropology* (New York, 1987)
—*Race, Culture and Evolution: Essays in the History of Anthropology* (New York, 1968)
—*Bones, Bodies, Behavior: Essays on Biological Anthropology* (Madison, 1988)
Stoler, Ann Laura, *Race and the Education of Desire: Foucault's History of Sexuality and the Colonial Order of Things* (Durham, NC, and London, 1995)
Stoler, Ann Laura and Frederick Cooper (eds), *Tensions of Empire: Colonial Cultures in a Bourgeois world* (Berkeley, 1997)
Sturm, Terry (ed), *The Oxford History of New Zealand Literature in English* (Auckland, 1991)
Sunstein, Cass, 'Incompletely Theorized Agreements', Harvard Law Review, 108 (1995), 1733–1772
— 'Leaving Things Undecided', Harvard Law Review, 110 (1996), 4–101
Swainson, Geoffrey (ed), *William Swainson FRS, FLS: naturalist and artist; family letters and diaries 1809–1855, final destiny New Zealand* (Palmerston North, 1992)
Sweetman, Edward, *The Unsigned New Zealand Treaty* (Melbourne, 1939)
Tapp, EJ, *Early New Zealand: a dependency of New South Wales, 1788–1841* (Melbourne, 1958)
Te Hurinui, Pei, *King Pōtatau: An Account of the Life of Pōtatau Te Wherowhero the First Māori King* (Wellington, 2010)
Thomas, Nicholas, *Out of Time: History and Evolution in Anthropological Discourse* (Ann Arbor, 2nd edn, 1997)
—*Entangled Objects: Exchange, Material Culture, and Colonialism in the Pacific* (Cambridge, 1991)
—*In Oceania: Visions, Artifacts, Histories* (Durham, NC, 1997)
—*Colonialism's Culture, Anthropology, Travel and Government* (Cambridge, 1994)
—'"On the Varieties of the Human Species": Forster's Comparative Ethnology', in Nicholas Thomas, Harriet Guest, and Michael Dettelbach (eds), *Observations made during a voyage round the world, on physical geography, natural history, and ethnic philosophy* (Honolulu, 1996), xxiii–xl
Thomas, Nicholas, Harriet Guest, and Michael Dettelbach (eds), [Forster], *Observations made during a voyage round the world, on physical geography, natural history, and ethic philosophy* (Honolulu, 1996)
Thomas, Peter DG, *The House of Commons in the Eighteenth Century* (Oxford, 1971)
Thomas, William, *The Philosophic Radicals: nine studies in theory and practice, 1817–1841* (Oxford, 1979)
Thompson, EP, *The Making of the English Working Class* (London, 1963)
—'Custom, Law and Common Right', in *Customs in Common* (Pontypool, 1991), 97–184
Tonk, R, '"A difficult and complicated question": the New Zealand Company's Wellington, Port Nicholson, claim', in David Hamer and Roberta Nicholls (eds), *The Making of Wellington 1800–1914* (Wellington, 1990), 35–59
Travers, Robert, *Ideology and Empire in Eighteenth Century India: The British in Bengal* (Cambridge, 2007)
Tuck, Richard, *The Rights of War and Peace: Political Thought and the International Order from Grotius to Kant* (Oxford, 1999)
Tully, James, 'Placing the *Two Treatises*', in Nicholas Phillipson and Quentin Skinner (eds), *Political Discourse in Early Modern Britain* (Cambridge, 1993), 253–80
—*An Approach to Political Philosophy: Locke in contexts* (Cambridge, 1993)
—*Strange Multiplicity: constitutionalism in an age of diversity* (Cambridge, 1995)

—'Aboriginal property and western theory: recovering a middle ground', in Ellen Frankel Paul, FD Miller, junior, and Jeffrey Paul (eds), *Property Rights* (Cambridge, 1994), 153–80
—'Introduction', in Alain-G Gagnon and Tully (eds), *Multicultural Democracies* (Cambridge, 2001), 1–33
—*Public Philosophy in a New Key—Volume I: Democracy and Civic Freedom* (Cambridge, 2008)
—*Public Philosophy in a New Key—Volume II: Imperialism and Civic Freedom* (Cambridge, 2008)
—'Consent, Hegemony, and Dissent in Treaty Negotiations', in Jeremy Webber and Colin Macleod (eds), *Between Consenting Peoples: Political Community and the Meaning of Consent* (Vancouver, 2010), 233–56
Turnbull, Michael, *The New Zealand Bubble* (Wellington, 1959)
Van Meijl, Toon, 'Maori socio-political organization in pre- and proto-history', *Oceania*, 65 (1995), 304–22
—'The reemergence of Maori chiefs: devolution as a strategy to maintain tribal authority', in Geoffrey White and Lamont Linckstrom (eds), *Chiefs Today: traditional Pacific leadership and the postcolonial state* (Stanford, 1997), 84–107
Waddams, SM, *Law, Politics and the Church of England: the career of Stephen Lushington 1782–1873* (Cambridge, 1992)
Waitangi Tribunal, *The Taranaki Report; Kaupapa Tuatahi—Wai-143* (Wellington, 1996)
—*The Muriwhenua Land Report—Wai-45* (Wellington, 1997)
—*Turanga Tangata, Turanga Whenua—The Report on the Turanganui a Kiwa Claims—Wai 814* (two volumes, Wellington, 2004)
Wake, CH, 'George Clarke and the government of the Maoris, 1840–45', *HSANZ*, 10 (1962), 339–56
Waldron, Jeremy, *Law and Disagreement* (Oxford, 1999)
Walker, EA (ed), *The Cambridge History of the British Empire: volume xiii* (Cambridge, 2nd edn, 1963)
Walker, Ranginui, *Ka Whawhai Tonu Motou, Struggle without end* (Auckland, 1990)
Walters, Mark, '*Mohegan* v *Connecticut* (1705–1773) and the legal status of aboriginal customary laws and government in British North America', *Osgoode Hall Law Journal*, 33 (1995), 786–829
—'Histories of Colonialism, Legality, and Aboriginality', *University of Toronto Law Journal*, 57 (2007), 819–32
—'The Jurisprudence of Reconciliation: Aboriginal Rights in Canada', in Will Kymlicka and Bashir Bashir (eds) *The Politics of Reconciliation in Multicultural Societies* (Oxford, 2008), 165–91
Ward, Alan, 'The Treaty and the purchase of Maori land', *NZJH*, 22 (1988), 169–74
—*A Show of Justice: racial 'amalgamation' in nineteenth century New Zealand* (Auckland, 1995)
—*An Unsettled History: Treaty claims in New Zealand today* (Wellington, 1999)
— *National Overview: Waitangi Tribunal Rangihaua Whanui Series* (two volumes, Waitangi Tribunal Wellington, 1997)
Ward, Damen, 'Civil Jurisdiction, Settler Politics, and the Colonial Constitution, circa 1840–1858', *VUWLR*, 39 (2008), 497–532
—'A Means and Measure of Civilisation: Colonial Authorities and Indigenous Law in Australasia', *History Compass*, 1 (2003), AU 049, 001-023
—'Constructing British Authority in Australasia: Charles Cooper and the Legal Status of Aborigines in the South Australian Supreme Court, c1840–60', *JICH*, 34 (2006), 483–504
—'Imperial Policy, Colonial Government and Indigenous Testimony in South Australia and New Zealand in the 1840s', in Dorsett and Hunter (eds), *Law and Politics in British Colonial Thought: Transpositions of Empire* (New York, 2010), 229–47

—'Legislation, Repugnancy and the Disallowance of Colonial Laws: The Legal Structure of Empire and *Lloyd's Case* (1844)', *VUWLR*, 41 (2010), 381–402
Ward, John M, *British Policy in the South Pacific, 1786–1893* (Sydney, 1948)
—*Empire in the Antipodes: the British in Australasia 1840–1860* (London, 1966)
Wards, Ian, *The Shadow of the Land: a study of British policy and racial conflict in New Zealand, 1832–1852* (Wellington, 1968)
Weaver, John, 'Beyond the fatal shore: pastoral squatting and the occupation of Australia', *American Historical Review*, 101 (1996), 980–1007
— *The Great Land Rush and the Making of the Modern World, 1650–1900* (Montreal, 2003)
Webber, Jeremy, 'Relations of Force and Relations of Justice: The Emergence of Normative Community between Colonists and Aboriginal Peoples', *Osgoode Hall Law Journal*, 33 (1995), 623–60
—'Beyond Regret: *Mabo's* Implications for Australian Constitutionalism', in Duncan Ivison, Paul Patton, and Will Sanders (eds), *Political Theory and the Rights of Indigenous Peoples* (Cambridge, 2000), 60–88
Wells, Kentwood, 'The Historical Context of Natural Selection: the Case of Patrick Matthew', *Journal of the History of Biology*, 6 (1973), 225–58
White, Richard, *The Middle Ground: Indians, Empires, and Republics in the Great Lakes Region, 1650–1815* (Cambridge, 1991; twentieth anniversary edition, 2011)
Wickham, C, *Framing the Early Middle Ages: Europe and the Mediterranean, 400–800* (Oxford, 2005)
Wilberg, Hanna, 'Judicial Remedies for the Original Breach?', *New Zealand Law Review*, (2007), 713–48
Wilentz, Sean, *The Rise of American Democracy: Jefferson to Lincoln* (New York, 2005)
Williams, Bernard, *In the Beginning was the Deed: Realism and Moralism in Political Argument* (Princeton, 2005)
Williams, David, '*The Queen v Symonds* reconsidered', *VUWLR*, 19 (1989) 385–402
—'The foundation of colonial rule in New Zealand', *NZULR*, 13 (1988), 54–67
—'*Te Kooti tango whenua*': *The Native Land Court 1864–1909* (Wellington, 1999)
—*A Simple Nullity? The* Wi Parata *Case in New Zealand Law and History* (Auckland, 2011)
Williams, Glyndwr, 'The Pacific', in PJ Marshall (ed), *The Oxford History of the British Empire: volume ii, the eighteenth century* (Oxford, 1998), 552–75
Williams, Glyndwr, and Peter Marshall, *The Great Map of Mankind: British Perceptions of the World in the Age of Enlightenment* (London, 1982)
Williams junior, Robert A, *The American Indian in Western Legal Thought: the Discourse of Conquest* (Oxford, 1991)
Williams, Trevor, 'James Stephen and the British intervention in New Zealand, 1838–1840', *JMH*, 13 (1941), 19–35
Wilson, E, *Land Problems of the New Zealand Settlers of the forties* (Dunedin, 1935)
Wilson, Jon, *The Domination of Strangers: Modern Governance in Eastern India, 1780–1835* (London, 2008)
—'"A Thousand Countries to Go To": Peasants and Rulers in Late Eighteenth-Century Bengal', *Past and Present*, 189 (2005), 81–109
Winch, Donald, *Riches and Poverty: an intellectual history of political economy in Britain 1750–1834* (Cambridge, 1996)
—*Classical Political Economy and Colonies* (London, 1965)
—*Wealth and Life: Essays on the Intellectual History of Political Economy in Britain, 1848–1914* (Cambridge, 2009)
Wittgenstein, Ludwig, *Philosophical Investigations* (Oxford, 1996)
Wood, Gordon, *Empire of Liberty: A History of the Early Republic, 1789–1815* (New York, 2009)

Woodward, EL, *The Age of Reform, 1815–1870* (Oxford, 1938)
Woolrych, Austin, *Britain in Revolution 1625–1660* (Oxford, 2002)
Wormald, Patrick, *The Making of English Law: King Alfred to The Twelfth Century–Volume I: Legislation and its Limits* (Oxford, 1999)
Wright, Harrison M, *New Zealand, 1769–1840: early years of western contact* (Cambridge, Mass, 1959)
Yates, Timothy, 'Images of "heathen" and Christian in the early CMS mission to New Zealand', *North Atlantic Missiology Project* (position paper number 15, Cambridge University, 1996)
Yirush, Craig, *Settlers, Liberty, and Empire: The Roots of Early American Political Theory*, 1675–1775 (Cambridge, 2011)
Young, Robert JC, *White Mythologies: writing history and the west* (London, 1990)
—*Colonial Desire: hybridity in theory, culture and race* (London, 1995)
Ziegler, Paul, *Palmerston* (Houndmills, 2003)

II Theses

Adams, Peter, 'British intervention in New Zealand, 1830–1846', DPhil thesis, Oxford University, 1974
Brent, Richard, 'The emergence of liberal Anglican politics: the Whigs and the Church, 1830–41', DPhil thesis, Oxford University, 1984
Cadogan, Bernard, 'Constituting the Settler Colony and Reconstituting the Indigene: The Native Administration and Constitutionalism of Sir George Grey KCB during his two New Zealand Governorships until the Outbreak of the Waikato War 1863', DPhil thesis, Oxford University, 2010
Dorsett, Shaunnagh, 'Thinking Jurisdictionally: A Genealogy of Native Title', PhD thesis, University of New South Wales, 2005
Elbourne, Elizabeth, '"To colonize the mind": evangelical missionaries and the eastern Cape', DPhil thesis, Oxford University, 1991
Fletcher, Edwin Thomas, 'A rational experiment: the bringing of English law to New Zealand', MA thesis, University of Auckland, 1998
Gambles, Anna, 'The boundaries of political economy: tory economic argument, 1809–1847', DPhil thesis, Oxford University, 1996
Goode, Penelope, 'The Kaingatara Letters: the correspondence of Tamati Te Ito Ngamoke in the A.S Atkinson Papers, 1875–1865', MA thesis, Canterbury University, 2001
Gross Izhak, 'Commons and empire 1833–1841: a study of the treatment of colonial questions in the House of Commons with special reference to domestic politics and pressure groups and to the role of the House in the policy-making process', DPhil thesis, Oxford University, 1975
Head, Lyndsay, 'Land, Authority and the Forgetting of Being in Early Colonial Maori History', PhD thesis, Canterbury University, 2006
Hickford, Mark, 'Making "Territorial Rights of the Natives": British and New Zealand, 1830–1847', DPhil thesis, Oxford University, 1999
Hutton, John, '"Troublesome Specimens": A Study of the Relationship between the Crown and the Tangata Whenua of Hauraki 1863–1869', MA thesis, University of Auckland, 1995
MacDonald, Lindsey, 'The Political Philosophy of Property Rights', PhD Thesis, Canterbury University, 2009
McHugh, Paul, 'The aboriginal rights of the New Zealand Maori at common law', PhD thesis, Cambridge University, 1987
McLay, Geoffrey, 'Crown Liability in the Time of Constitutional Foxes', SJD thesis, University of Michigan, 2008
Madden, AF, 'Towards trusteeship, a study in the influence of the evangelicals on native policy in New Zealand, 1814–1854', BLitt thesis, Oxford University, 1939

—'The attitudes of the Evangelicals to the empire and imperial problems', DPhil thesis, Oxford University, 1950
Orchard, SC, 'English Evangelical Eschatology 1790–1850', PhD thesis, Cambridge University, 1969)
Pagden, Anthony, 'The American Indian as Barbarian: A Reassessment of Some Sixteenth Century Views on the Nature of Amerindian Man and His Society', DPhil thesis, Oxford University, 1980
Parsonson, Ann, 'He Whenua te Utu ("the payment will be land")', PhD thesis, Canterbury University, 1978
Renwick, William, 'Self-Government and Protection: A Study of Stephen's Two Cardinal Points of Policy in their bearing upon Constitutional Development in New Zealand in the years 1838–1867', M.A. thesis, Victoria University of Wellington, 1962
Salesa, Damon, 'Race Mixing: A Victorian Problem in Britain and New Zealand 1830–1870', DPhil thesis, Oxford University, 2000
Sinclair, Keith, 'The Aborigines Protection Society and New Zealand: a study in nineteenth century opinion', MA thesis, University of Auckland, 1946
Slattery, Brian, 'The Land Rights of Indigenous Canadian peoples, as affected by the Crown's acquisition of sovereignty of their territories', DPhil thesis, Oxford University, 1979
Sorrenson, MPK, 'The Purchase of Maori Land', MA thesis, University of Auckland, 1955
Soutar, Monty, 'Ngāti Porou Leadership—Rāpata Wahawaha and the Politics of Conflict', PhD thesis, Massey University, 2000
Tonk, Rosemarie, 'The First New Zealand Land Commissions, 1840–1845', MA thesis, Canterbury University, 1986
Walters, Mark, 'The Continuity of Aboriginal Customs and Government under British Imperial Constitutional Law as applied in Colonial Canada, 1760–1860', DPhil thesis, Oxford University, 1995
Ward, Damen, 'The Politics of Jurisdiction: "British" Law, Indigenous Peoples and Colonial Government in Southern Australia and New Zealand, c.1834–60', D.Phil thesis, Oxford University, 2003
Wilson, Jon E, 'Governing Property, Making Law Land, Local Society and Colonial Discourse in Agrarian Bengal, c1785–1830', DPhil thesis, Oxford University, 2000

III Research Reports

Daamen, Rose, 'The Crown's Right of Pre-emption and FitzRoy's Waiver Purchases', *Rangahaua Whanui series* (Wellington, August 1998)
Head, Lyndsay, 'Maori Land Tenure and Chiefly Authority in Whanganui, 1840–1865: A Study based in Contemporary Maori Writing' (a report for the Crown Law Office; Wai 903; #A113)
Loveridge, Donald, 'The New Zealand Land Claims Act of 1840', *Muriwhenua land claim evidence—Wai-45 I2* (18 June 1993)
—'Origins of the Native Land Acts and Native Land Court in New Zealand' (report for the Crown Law Office, 3 November 2000; Wai 686)
—'Development of Crown Policy on the Purchase of Maori Land: A Preliminary Survey' (research report, 2001; Wai 1200; A77)
—'The Development and Introduction of Institutions for the Governance of Maori, 1852–1865' (report for the Crown Law Office, September 2007; Wai 903)
Phillipson, GA, *Rangahaua Whanui District 13: The Northern South Island* (Waitangi Tribunal, Wellington, June 1995)

Index

The manufacturer's authorised representative in the EU for product
safety is Oxford University Press España S.A. of El Parque Empresarial
San Fernando de Henares, Avenida de Castilla, 2 - 28830 Madrid
(www.oup.es/en or product.safety@oup.com). OUP España S.A. also acts
as importer into Spain of products made by the manufacturer.
Printed and bound by CPI Group (UK) Ltd, Croydon, CR0 4YY
14/09/2026
02216306-0015